Applied Social Psychology

Edited by

Marilynn B. Brewer

and

Miles Hewstone

Blackwell
Publishing

Editorial material and organization © 2004 by Blackwell Publishing Ltd

350 Main Street, Malden, MA 02148-5020, USA
108 Cowley Road, Oxford OX4 1JF, UK
550 Swanston Street, Carlton, Victoria 3053, Australia

The right of Marilynn B. Brewer and Miles Hewstone to be identified as the Authors of the
Editorial Material in this Work has been asserted in accordance with the UK Copyright,
Designs, and Patents Act 1988.

First published 2004 by Blackwell Publishing Ltd

Library of Congress Cataloging-in-Publication Data

Applied social psychology / edited by Marilynn B. Brewer and Miles Hewstone.
p.   cm. – (Perspectives on social psychology)
Includes bibliographical references and index.
ISBN 1-4051-1067-8 (pbk. : alk. paper)
1. Social psychology.   I. Brewer, Marilynn B., 1942–
II. Hewstone, Miles.   III. Series.
HM1033.A64 2004
302–dc21
2003011034

A catalogue record for this title is available from the British Library.

Set in 10/12¹/₂pt Adobe Garamond
by Graphicraft Limited, Hong Kong
Printed and bound in the United Kingdom
by MPG Books, Bodmin, Cornwall

For further information on
Blackwell Publishing, visit our website:
http://www.blackwellpublishing.com

Contents

Preface

When the *Blackwell Handbooks of Social Psychology* project was conceived, we sought to go beyond a simple topical structure for the content of the volumes in order to reflect more closely the complex pattern of cross-cutting theoretical perspectives and research agendas that comprise social psychology as a dynamic enterprise. The idea we developed was to represent the discipline in a kind of matrix structure, crossing levels of analysis with topics, processes, and functions that recur at all of these levels in social psychological theory and research. Taking inspiration from Willem Doise's 1986 book (*Levels of Explanation in Social Psychology*) four levels of analysis – intrapersonal, interpersonal, intragroup, and intergroup – provided the basis for organizing the Handbook series into four volumes. The two co-editors responsible for developing each of these volumes selected content chapters on the basis of cross-cutting themes represented by basic social psychological processes of social cognition, attribution, social motivation, affect and emotion, social influence, social comparison, and self and identity.

The four-volume *Handbook* that resulted from this organizational framework represents the collective efforts of two series editors, eight volume editors, and 191 contributing authors. The *Intraindividual Processes* volume, edited by Abraham Tesser and Norbert Schwarz, provides a comprehensive selection of work on social cognition, affect, and motivation, which focuses on the individual as the unit of analysis. The *Interpersonal Processes* volume, edited by Garth Fletcher and Margaret Clark, also covers the cognition, affect, and motivation themes as they are played out in the context of close interpersonal relationships and dyadic exchanges. Again in the volume on *Group Processes*, edited by Michael Hogg and Scott Tindale, the themes of cognition, affect, and motivation are well represented in work on collective behavior in small groups and social organizations. Finally, the volume on *Intergroup Processes*, edited by Rupert Brown and Samuel Gaertner, covers work that links cognitive, affective, and motivational processes to relationships between social groups and large collectives.

In all four volumes of the *Handbook*, a specific section was devoted to applications of social psychological theory and research in various domains of personal, institutional, and societal well being. The readings selected for this volume illustrate how social psychological analyses of individual, interpersonal, and group level processes have contributed to three important areas of applied psychology.

Marilynn Brewer and Miles Hewstone

Acknowledgments

The editor and publishers gratefully acknowledge the following for permission to reproduce copyright material:

Brown, Rupert and Gaertner, Sam (Eds.) (2001). *Blackwell Handbook of Social Psychology: Intergroup Processes*. Oxford: Blackwell Publishing. Reprinted with permission.
Fletcher, Garth J. O. and Clark, Margaret S. (Eds.) (2001). *Blackwell Handbook of Social Psychology: Interpersonal Processes*. Oxford: Blackwell Publishing. Reprinted with permission.
Hogg, Michael A. and Tindale, Scott (Eds.) (2001). *Blackwell Handbook of Social Psychology: Group Processes*. Oxford: Blackwell Publishing. Reprinted with permission.
Tesser, Abraham and Schwarz, Norbert (Eds.) (2001). *Blackwell Handbook of Social Psychology: Intraindividual Processes*. Oxford: Blackwell Publishing. Reprinted with permission.

The publishers apologize for any errors or omissions in the above list and would be grateful to be notified of any corrections that should be incorporated in the next edition or reprint of this book.

Introduction

The readings in this volume cross three broad domains of application of social psychological theory and research. The chapters in Part I review the role of social psychological factors in physical and mental health with implications for clinical practice. Social psychological research on stress and coping has contributed significantly to our understanding of how individuals adapt to adversity and negative life events (Aspinwall; Mikulincer and Florian). In addition to the role of social cognition and self-regulatory processes, social processes such as social comparison, interpersonal attachment, and social support prove to be significant factors in coping with life stresses and psychological well-being. Social psychological research has had a significant influence in other domains of mental health and clinical practice as well. Research on close relationships and attachment theory has had both direct and indirect application to marital therapy (Beach and Fincham), and basic research on group dynamics, leadership, and group development has contributed to the understanding and effectiveness of therapeutic groups (Forsyth). Thus, the social psychology of mental health clearly illustrates the importance of research that cuts across the individual, interpersonal, and group levels of analysis.

In Part II, we move to the level of social institutions to examine the role of social psychology in law, politics, and social policy. In the first chapter, Köhnken, Fiedler, and Mohlenbeck review the many interfaces between psychology and legal practice, including police psychology, enhancing the accuracy of eyewitness testimony, the psychology of witness credibility, jury selection and decision making, and the field of "therapeutic jurisprudence." In the following chapter, Tindale et al. focus more specifically on the application of social psychological research on group decision making to judicial procedures such as jury selection, presentation of evidence and instructions to the jury, and specification of jury size. Going beyond the field of law, social psychological research on attitudes and social perception finds application in various domains of political judgment and decision making, including evaluation of political candidates and formation of opinions on social issues (Ottati). And social psychological research on prejudice, discrimination, and intergroup relations has had significant influence in public policy domains such as desegregation (Schofield and Eurich-Fulcer), affirmative action (Crosby et al.), and international relations (Pettigrew).

Part III represents yet another area of interface between social psychological processes and social institutions in the world of business and commerce. At the individual level, research on social cognition and attitude formation and change is well represented in applied research on consumer behavior, product evaluation, and marketing (Shavitt and Wänke). At the interpersonal level, social psychological research has been valuable in understanding the effects of social relationships, attributions, and emotions in the process and outcomes of bargaining and negotiation (Bazerman et al.). And group research has found direct application in the utilization of communication technology (Hollingshead) and organizational behavior (McGrath and Argote).

Across these different domains of application and practice, social psychological research and theory has played a role that is both descriptive (explanation and understanding) and prescriptive (guides to good practice and social change). The readings in this volume also illustrate that the relationship between basic and applied research is a two-way street. Just as basic research and theory can inform good practice, application inevitably also informs and enriches theory.

Mental and Physical Health

CHAPTER ONE

Dealing with Adversity: Self-regulation, Coping, Adaptation, and Health

Lisa G. Aspinwall

How do people cope with chronic or life-threatening illness and other negative life events, such as bereavement, disability, and long-term unemployment? The study of adversity – of serious, protracted, and often uncontrollable negative experiences – has provided a great deal of information about how personal, social, and other resources are related to psychological well-being and physical health as people manage negative events and information.

In this chapter, I will review what is known about how people cope with adversity and how such efforts are related to psychological adaptation and physical health.[1] In doing so, I will draw on two large research literatures that have yet to be integrated: coping and self-regulation. *Coping* consists of activities undertaken to master, reduce, or tolerate environmental or intrapsychic demands perceived as representing potential threat, existing harm, or loss (Lazarus & Folkman, 1984). *Self-regulation* is defined as the process through which people control, direct, and correct their own actions as they move toward or away from various goals (Carver, 2001; Carver & Scheier, 1998). Although these literatures have developed largely in isolation, they share a fundamental concern with the relation of personal, social, and situational factors to people's emotions, thoughts, and behaviors as they anticipate or encounter adversity (Aspinwall & Taylor, 1997; Carver & Scheier, 1999; Skinner, in press).

One task of this review is to examine the unique contributions of each literature to understanding how people deal with adversity. I will examine potential contributions in five areas: (1) the conceptualization and measurement of stress and coping; (2) individual differences in coping and outcomes; (3) adaptational processes and outcomes; (4) social processes, such as social comparison and social support; and (5) emotions. In each area, I will highlight a few examples to illustrate the potential for integration across these two active research areas.

I am grateful to Chuck Carver, Ron Duran, Doug Hill, JongHan Kim, Carolyn Morf, Len Pearlin, J. T. Ptacek, Shelley Taylor, and Camille Wortman for helpful comments on an earlier version of this chapter. Preparation of this chapter was facilitated by NSF grant SBR-9709677 awarded to Lisa G. Aspinwall.

What the Study of Self-regulation Has to Offer the Study of Coping

The first goal of this review is to consider several issues at the forefront of research in self-regulation that might profitably be exported to the study of stress and coping. I will first review some common problems in the conceptualization and measurement of stress, coping, and outcomes, and then suggest two ways in which concepts from self-regulation might afford greater precision in understanding what stressors are, what people are doing to manage them, and how specific ways of coping are related to psychosocial and health outcomes over time.

Problems in the conceptualization and measurement of stress, coping, and outcomes

In general, in its focus on identifying different ways of coping and relating them to psychosocial and health outcomes, the coping literature has spent relatively little time characterizing the stressor. As early as 1984, this lack of attention lead Susan Folkman to plead for greater conceptual clarity by asking researchers studying personal control and coping to specify, "Control over what?" Even today, "Coping with what?" would be a reasonable question to ask of most studies, including my own, with no easy answer.

Much of this problem stems from the nearly exclusive use of checklists to assess coping (for detailed critiques, see Coyne & Gottlieb, 1996; Stone, Greenberg, Kennedy-Moore, & Newman, 1991). Respondents are asked to select the most stressful aspect of their situation (e.g. entering college, cancer surgery, relocation) within a given time period (e.g. the past six months), and to rate their use of 50–60 different coping strategies ("made a plan of action and followed it," "tried to forget the whole thing," "let my feelings out somehow"; Folkman & Lazarus, 1980). This method can create substantial variation in what people are responding to when they complete inventories, because there may be many different stressors for each "stressful situation," and it is not known exactly what people are responding to as they complete the inventory. To make matters worse, these checklists also provide limited and inconsistent information about what people are doing to manage the stressor. For example, there is enormous variation, both within and between respondents, in what people are reporting on when they rate their use of various strategies (e.g. their frequency or their effectiveness; Stone, Greenberg, Kennedy-Moore, & Newman, 1991). There are also substantial biases in retrospective recall for coping strategies compared to same-day ratings, especially among people reporting high levels of stress (Smith, Leffingwell, & Ptacek, 1999). Finally, reports of coping may be at least somewhat confounded with psychological distress and/or physical symptoms. Frustration with these limitations has sparked the development of careful process-oriented approaches to *daily coping*, in which daily diary records – for example, of pain, social interaction, and coping – are collected, often in conjunction with physiological measures and objective assessments of demand (e.g. see Affleck & Tennen, 1996; Repetti, 1989; Stone & Neale, 1984).

In addition to these measurement problems, most approaches to coping fail to capture the complexity of the process. The predominant conceptual model in the study of stress and coping – Lazarus & Folkman's (1984) transactional model – is based on the idea that coping is a complex, ongoing process in which relations among appraisals of the event and one's resources to manage it, coping efforts, and outcomes are recursive (Lazarus, 1990). Current approaches simply do not capture these aspects of the transactional model. For example, coping checklists provide little information about the social or environmental context of a stressful event (Aldwin & Stokols, 1988; Coyne & Gottlieb, 1996; Revenson, 1990) or its meaning to the person. They also neglect the temporal ordering and functional interrelation among different coping strategies as people manage ongoing stressors and acquire information about them (Aspinwall & Taylor, 1997). For these reasons, it is difficult to determine what made the event stressful, what people did to manage it and why, and how specific ways of coping were related to psychosocial and health outcomes months later. In the following sections, I will examine two ways of conceptualizing stress and coping that may elucidate these issues.

The potential value of goals in understanding stress and coping

One useful starting point in understanding what the stressor is, what it means to people, and how they think about it would be to identify how negative events and information affect people's pursuit of their goals. That is, what specific goals are affected by the experience of adversity? A large literature on self-regulation and goal-striving has identified several properties of goals and the way we represent them that may be useful in clarifying the nature of stress and people's efforts to manage it (for reviews, see Austin & Vancouver, 1996; Gollwitzer & Bargh, 1996). In this section, I will present a few of these approaches and discuss their potential value in understanding responses to adversity.

Idiographic approaches to goal-striving

Idiographic approaches, whether they are called personal projects (Little, 1983), personal strivings (Emmons & King, 1988), life tasks (Cantor, 1990), or possible selves (Markus & Nurius, 1986), examine self-regulation with respect to important personally defined goals. Respondents are asked to list their goals (both hoped for and feared), rate such aspects as importance or centrality to the self-concept, indicate whether they are in conflict, and so forth, in ways that provide a rich picture of people managing multiple goals and self-conceptions.

These approaches offer several advantages over current methods. First, allowing respondents to identify and describe their goals makes it clear what people are responding to when they describe their coping efforts. As King (1996) has noted, behavior that appears counterproductive with respect to one goal may actually have been undertaken in the service of a completely different goal. For example, the student adjusting to college who reports drinking may be doing so to make new friends, not to avoid thinking about his chemistry course.

Second, this approach allows people to list multiple goals and to describe how they are related. People rarely work toward one goal or experience a stressor in isolation. Instead, the experience of a setback in one area is likely to create changes, for better or for worse, in efforts to meet other goals. Some researchers have hypothesized that individual differences in coping outcomes may actually be due to the differential impact of a focal stressor on other areas of life (Pearlin, Aneshensel, & LeBlanc, 1997). That is, the experience of adversity in one life domain, such as adopting a caregiving role, may have most of its impact on outcomes like depression by creating problems in other domains, such as work and social activities.

Third, these approaches provide one way to incorporate the study of the self into the study of stress and coping. Many studies have used constructs such as self-esteem or self-confidence to predict coping and outcomes, but relatively few studies have assessed the effects of adversity and ways of coping with it on the self-concept (see Kling, Ryff, & Essex, 1997, for an exception). The experience of serious illness and other life events is sure to create a multitude of changes in goals, the self-concept, and their interrelation that are just beginning to be examined (Emmons, Colby, & Kaiser, 1998). Further embedding the study of stress in the context of developmental tasks and larger life goals may provide additional insight into how people understand and respond to particular kinds of adversity.

Beliefs about the threatened goal

Beliefs about the nature and future course of a threatened goal are highly important influences on self-regulation. Consider a college freshman who receives a "D" on her first chemistry exam. The meaning of this event may critically depend on her beliefs about whether students typically mature and "hit their stride" as sophomores, or whether initial difficulties are a signal that one will encounter future difficulties (Aspinwall, 1997). Additionally, her beliefs about whether academic performance is a stable entity (you have it or you don't) or an incremental one that can be developed through effort will play a large role in how she prepares for the next exam (Dweck, 1996). Such beliefs may stem from many sources, for example, from a more general attributional style (Peterson & Seligman, 1984), from socially prescribed beliefs about the time course of adjustment to particular kinds of adversity (e.g. bereavement; Wortman & Silver, 1987), or from expectations about developmental phenomena, such as maturation and aging (Aspinwall, 1997).

Ways of framing goals

A third area that has yet to be fully mined for its value in understanding stress, coping, adaptation, and health is a rich literature on how people represent goals (approach vs. avoidance goals: Elliott, Sheldon, & Church, 1996; promotion vs. prevention regulatory focus: Higgins, 1996). These properties of goal-pursuit – whether one is coping to attain something or to avoid something – have profound implications for the strategies and criteria that people use to see if they have met their goal. For example, a person striving for an approach goal (being independent) will look for confirming instances of independence, whereas a person with an avoidance goal in the same domain (not being dependent) will monitor his behavior for instances of dependence. The former gets to experience moments of success, while the latter attends mostly to instances of failure (Coats, Janoff-Bulman, & Alpert, 1996). Such differences are likely to have profound implications for emotional experience, persistence, and self-confidence in the threatened domain and for psychological well-being over time (Coats, Janoff-Bulman, & Alpert, 1996; Elliot, Sheldon, & Church, 1996).

Summary

People's beliefs about how adversity affects multiple, personally defined goals, their beliefs about themselves, and their likely future outcomes are essential to understanding how people respond to negative events and information. Some of these concepts are just beginning to be incorporated in the study of stress and coping with good success. A broader and more systematic integration of these goal constructs with the study of stress and coping has even greater promise.

Understanding How Individual Differences are Related to Psychosocial and Health Outcomes

A second major way in which theories and concepts from self-regulation could advance the coping literature is in elucidating the processes through which individual differences are reciprocally related to psychosocial and health outcomes. A reliable cast of "heroes" and "villains" has emerged from two decades of studies of individual differences in coping. The heroes – optimism, control beliefs (e.g. self-mastery, self-efficacy), hardiness, and perhaps high self-esteem – are prospectively linked to constructive ways of coping, good psychosocial outcomes, and good health. In contrast, the villains – neuroticism, depression, anxiety, and pessimistic explanatory style – have been prospectively linked to ineffective and often destructive ways of coping, poor psychosocial outcomes, and an alarming array of poor health outcomes, including earlier mortality (see Taylor & Aspinwall, 1996, for a review).

Despite the consistency of these findings, relatively little is known about how these individual differences "work"; that is, how do the "good guys" help people achieve or maintain psychological well-being and physical health during times of stress, and how do the "bad guys" compromise such outcomes?

There are many potential mediators of such effects, including the effects of mood and chronic stress on immune function, stress reactivity, and health behaviors (Cohen & Rodriguez, 1995); however, the most-studied link between individual differences and adaptational outcomes is reported ways of coping with stress. In the following section, I present a model that may elucidate how specific individual differences are related to coping and outcomes as people respond to negative events and information.

A process-oriented framework for understanding how psychological resources and vulnerabilities may "work" as people anticipate or encounter adversity

Figure 1.1 presents a five-part model of the process of detecting and responding to negative events and information (Aspinwall & Taylor, 1997). The first stage of the model is *resource*

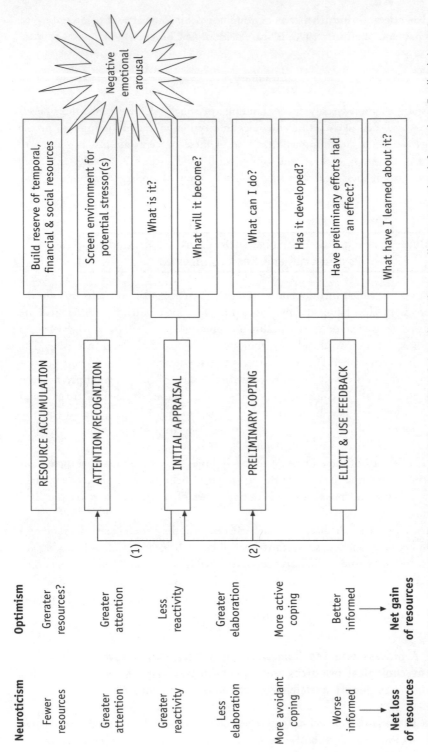

Figure 1.1 Aspinwall & Taylor's (1997) five-step model of the process of detecting and responding to negative information. Feedback Loop 1 represents the reciprocal relation among attention/recognition, initial appraisals, and the regulation of negative emotional arousal. Feedback Loop 2 represents the reciprocal relation among appraisals, coping efforts, and information gained from one's efforts to manage an actual or potential stressor. The chart at the left of the figure illustrates how neuroticism and optimism may work at each stage of the model as people anticipate or encounter negative events and information. Figure adapted with permission, copyright American Psychological Association and L. G. Aspinwall and S. E. Taylor (1997).

accumulation. Resources are the first step of our model for three reasons. According to Hobfoll's (1989) conservation of resources theory, people are motivated to retain, protect, and build resources. Hobfoll defines stress as the loss of resources, the potential loss of resources, or the failure to gain resources in proportion to one's investment in a task. These resources can be objects, personal characteristics (mastery, self-esteem), conditions (employment, marriage), or energies (time, money, knowledge) that have either symbolic or instrumental value to the individual. The presence of resources, therefore, plays a large role in determining the kinds of events and information that may be stressful to a given person. Second, most of the critical tasks of coping and self-regulation, such as attention to negative information, coping, and the use of feedback, require personal, social, and other kinds of resources. Third, increasing evidence suggests that such resources may be depleted over time as a function of the ways people deal with adversity (Bolger, Foster, Vinokur, & Ng, 1996; Smith & Wallston, 1992).

The next step of the model is *attention/recognition*. In this step, one screens the environment for potential stressors. If one is detected, a process of *initial appraisal* begins. In this step, people are trying to figure out what a potential or actual stressor is and what it is likely to mean for them. An important part of the model is that the detection of stressors often creates *negative emotional arousal* that may not only prompt efforts to regulate these emotions, but may also interfere with subsequent processing of information. Initial appraisals give rise to *preliminary coping efforts*, such as efforts to solve the problem, to gain more information about it, or to enlist the aid of others. A final and critical part of the model is the *elicitation and use of feedback* about the success of one's coping efforts and the information such efforts have yielded about the stressor and one's resources to manage it.

The model is recursive in three important ways that will be illustrated in greater detail in subsequent sections. First, as illustrated by Feedback Loop 1, attention, appraisal, and the regulation of emotion are interrelated as people maintain attention to actual or potential stressors. Second, as illustrated by Feedback Loop 2, appraisals may be revised in light of information obtained in the course of trying to manage the stressor. Finally, the entire sequence of events is recursive, as the component activities of the model – attention, appraisal, coping, and use of feedback – are related over time to the conservation, development, or depletion of resources. Such a process may account for intriguing patterns of resource depletion and gain that have been identified in a number of stressed populations.

In the following sections, I use this model to examine the role that psychological resources, like optimism, and psychological vulnerabilities, like neuroticism, may play at each stage in the model, starting with baseline resources and finishing with resource gain or depletion as a result of exposure to adversity. It is important to note that similar findings have been obtained for other potential resources (such as self-mastery, hardiness, and other control-related constructs) and vulnerabilities (such as anxiety, depression, and pessimism; see Aspinwall & Taylor, 1997, and Taylor & Aspinwall, 1996, for reviews). I have chosen optimism and neuroticism to highlight the possibility that psychological resources and vulnerabilities may have distinct effects. That is, the presence of positive beliefs or emotions may have unique effects on coping, adaptation, and health that cannot be explained by simply the absence of negative beliefs or emotions, and vice versa. A full discussion of the conceptual status of these two constructs, however, is beyond the scope of this chapter.

Understanding neuroticism as a psychological vulnerability

Neuroticism or negative affectivity is the propensity to experience negative emotions, such as anxiety, depression, and hostility (Watson & Clark, 1984). Often overlooked in the study of stress and coping is the possibility that certain individual differences are associated with greater exposure to stressful events in the first place and with differences in the baseline availability of social support. From the outset, people high in N have more stress to manage, and at every stage in the coping process, this individual difference appears to compromise effective appraisal and action. As I will describe, the net result may be cumulative loss of resources with each successive exposure to adversity.

Stress-generation and baseline resources   Large-scale panel studies of exposure to stressful life events find that people high in N experience more negative life events (Headey & Wearing, 1989), possibly through a process of interpersonal stress-generation. People high in N also report greater reactivity to negative events (Bolger & Schilling, 1991). Both greater exposure and greater reactivity to negative events increase cumulative load and deplete resources. Therefore, the person high in N who encounters a new negative event starts with fewer resources.

Attentional processes   Neuroticism has been found not only to increase attention to negative information, but also to make it difficult to turn away from it (Derryberry & Reed, 1994). Such amplifications in attention to threatening information are likely to affect coping in several ways. First, one might see potential threat or danger in most situations. Second, hypervigilance to negative information may deplete resources, because it takes energy to stay on the lookout for and respond to several different potential sources of stress. Third, the ability to regulate one's attention flexibly and appropriately is essential. A person devoting resources to monitoring several potential threats simultaneously may be unable to discriminate those that require immediate attention from those that do not.

Appraisal processes   Neuroticism is linked to greater appraisals of threat or loss, especially in ongoing situations, and to less favorable appraisals of problem-solving ability. This combination of high appraisals of threat and low appraisals of resources to manage it is, by definition, what creates stress in Lazarus & Folkman's (1984) model. It is also the pattern of appraisals that predicts physiological threat responses and poor performance on demanding mental tasks (Blascovich & Tomaka, 1996). As a result, as shown in Feedback Loop 1, even though people high in N may be devoting a great deal of attention to negative information, their appraisals of it may not correspond well to the nature of the stressor because of their greater reactivity to it.

Preliminary coping efforts   The perception of low problem-solving resources may lead to the failure to engage in active coping. N has been linked to many forms of avoidant coping, such as wishing the problem would go away, avoiding thinking about the problem, and substance use, that are themselves linked to poor outcomes over time (Bolger, 1990; Holahan

& Moos, 1986; McCrae & Costa, 1986; Watson & Hubbard, 1996). When people high in *N* do try coping actively, the poor quality of their appraisals may lead to coping efforts that do not match the problem.

Elicitation and use of feedback In addition to creating new problems, avoidant strategies carry another serious liability: they are less likely than active ones to elicit information about the problem. Avoidance coping is unlikely to elicit useful information about the particular problem or about coping in general and thus does not contribute to the acquisition and refinement of procedural knowledge about coping. Further, as distress increases, people's ability to generate alternatives and to use multiple criteria in their decisions has been shown to decrease, further compromising appraisals and coping efforts, especially if the problem is ongoing and changing (Aspinwall & Taylor, 1997). The increasing divergence between the coping strategies used and the nature of the problem illustrated in Feedback Loop 2 may further exacerbate the problem, because resources are being wasted while the problem is going unchecked.

Depletion of social resources Finally, although it is not shown as a separate step in the model, neuroticism and avoidant coping have both been prospectively linked to the depletion of social resources in ways that have implications for coping efforts and subsequent well-being. First, the use of social withdrawal as a coping strategy prospectively predicts declines in social support (Evans & Lepore, 1993; Smith & Wallston, 1992). Avoiding others during times of stress also prevents one from receiving appraisal support that might be useful in understanding the problem, from receiving informational and instrumental support that might aid in its solution, and from receiving emotional or esteem support that might offset feelings of failure and decreasing confidence.

A second pathway through which social resources are depleted begins when people make frequent, exaggerated efforts to obtain social support, often through excessive reassurance seeking (Coates & Wortman, 1980; Joiner, Metalsky, Katz, & Beach, in press). Intense displays of negative affect and poor coping have been shown to cut short social interaction, to create increasing distance between the sufferer and those who might help (Silver, Wortman, & Crofton, 1990), and to erode social support over time (Bolger, Foster, Vinokur, & Ng, 1996). Finally, these two patterns may be interrelated if people first make exaggerated attempts to obtain support, then withdraw when they find it lacking. The net result of either pathway is the depletion of valuable social resources for coping.

Summary: a downward spiral of ineffective coping and resource loss In sum, people high in *N* and related characteristics, such as depression and anxiety, appear to generate more stress and to respond to negative events and information in ways that deplete resources through hypervigilance, reactivity, ineffective coping efforts, social isolation or alienation, and diminished opportunities for learning about different ways of coping with problems. Additionally, once people are distressed, they may simply be less likely to perceive their resources favorably even when they do exist (Evans & Lepore, 1993). Working in concert, these factors may create a downward spiral of resource loss with exposure to adversity that increases one's vulnerability to psychological distress, social isolation, and poor health.

Understanding optimism as a psychological resource

A vastly different sequence of events characterizes the psychological resources in our list. I will use research on dispositional optimism, the generalized expectation of good future outcomes (Scheier, Carver, & Bridges, 1994), to illustrate how each step of the model may contribute to a net resource gain or to lower levels of resource loss following adversity among people with such resources.

Attention, appraisal, and the regulation of arousal   Increasing evidence suggests that optimism is related to the ability to attend to negative information that is self-relevant or otherwise useful. Aspinwall & Brunhart (1996) demonstrated that optimists differentially attend to and recall information about the risks of their own health behaviors, compared to benefit or neutral information, and compared to risk information about behaviors they do not practice. The exact mechanism underlying such effects has yet to be fully understood, but related experimental work supports the idea that induced positive states increase people's interest in and veridical processing of negative information about themselves (see Aspinwall, 1998, for review).

The ability to maintain attention to self-relevant negative information is likely to confer many advantages in appraising potential stressors. Additionally, optimism and related constructs, such as constructive thinking, have been linked to more favorable appraisals of problem-solving resources and to lower levels of threat-related physiological responding to demanding mental tasks (Katz & Epstein, 1991). As a result, as illustrated in Feedback Loop 1, optimists may be more likely to sustain attention to negative information and may therefore make more accurate and well-elaborated appraisals of it than pessimists.

Preliminary coping efforts   Optimism has been linked to greater reports of active coping in several studies. For example, in a prospective study of entering freshmen, Aspinwall & Taylor (1992) found that optimists were more likely to report active ways of coping (such as problem solving) and less likely to report avoidant ways of coping (such as avoiding thoughts about the problem). More active coping and less avoidant coping, in turn, predicted better adjustment to college three months later. These results provide a clear account of how resources like optimism may "work:" because optimists expect good outcomes, they actively work toward them when they encounter adversity.

There is, however, an interesting exception to these findings that may prove to be at least equally important in understanding optimists' responses to adversity. In some studies, optimism is not linked to greater active coping, but instead to greater acceptance of situations beyond one's control. For example, Carver and his colleagues (1993) found that optimistic women with breast cancer were more likely than pessimists to indicate that they had accepted the reality of the fact that they had surgery for breast cancer. This acceptance was related to lower psychological distress at various points in the year following the surgery. It may seem paradoxical that the same psychological "resource" can be linked to both active coping and to acceptance. That is, if the active ingredient in optimism is continued persistence in goal-directed behavior, why do optimists report greater acceptance of problems beyond their control? In the following section, I examine how the final step of the model may account for some of these effects.

Elicitation and use of feedback   As illustrated by Feedback Loop 2, active coping is more likely than avoidant coping to elicit information about a problem. Optimists not only tend to cope more actively, but seem also, as discussed earlier, to be better able to attend to negative information. As a result, they may be better able to benefit from feedback about the success or failure of their coping efforts. In this way, optimists may become well-informed about how and when to cope actively, even when their initial attempts are unsuccessful (Aspinwall & Taylor, 1997; see also Armor & Taylor, 1998; Aspinwall, Richter, & Hoffman, in press; Skinner, in press). Such knowledge may be useful in determining whether a problem is amenable to one's efforts or must simply be accepted.

Summary: an upward spiral of efficient coping and resource gain   Through the mechanisms outlined in this section, optimists may conserve resources by detecting and managing problems early in their course. Through their active preliminary coping efforts, they may also acquire procedural knowledge about different kinds of problems and ways of coping with them. Such knowledge may be useful in identifying which efforts are most likely to work for certain kinds of problems, leading to more efficient use of coping resources. In sum, optimism seems to lead people to act in ways that may preserve and even build resources, even under conditions of adversity.

This analysis is consistent with others suggesting that positive emotions and experiences serve to build personal and social resources and to broaden action repertoires (Ashby, Isen, & Turken, 1999; Fredrickson, 1998; Isen, 1993). Extending coping research to examine how optimism and other psychological resources are related to the mobilization and preservation of social resources may also provide additional information about how different ways of managing stress are related to subsequent social resources and well-being. Working in concert, such processes may create an upward spiral of increasing resources, skills, and knowledge that may increase people's ability to anticipate and prevent stress and to cope more effectively when it does occur.

Summary

In the preceding sections, I examined two ways in which concepts and methods from the study of self-regulation might provide insight into the coping process. Reconceptualizing stressors in terms of their effects on goals and examining how personal resources and vulnerabilities may influence people's responses to negative events and information may provide insight into what is stressful to people, how people cope with adversity, and how such efforts are related to subsequent outcomes and resources.

What the Study of Coping Has to Offer the Study of Self-regulation

The second major goal of this review is to examine the ways in which studying the beliefs, behaviors, and emotions of people dealing with adversity provides a window on crucial self-regulatory processes that the study of ordinary activities and tasks cannot. In many ways, the study of coping with adversity is the study of personality under stress (Bolger, 1990; Bolger & Zuckerman, 1995). Serious illness and other negative life events threaten cherished goals, challenge long-held beliefs about the self and the world, and deplete personal and social resources over time. In addition, such events create the conditions of high distress and uncertainty that make the experiences, assistance, and reactions of others especially important in understanding what we are facing and how to manage it. As a result, the coping literature may be uniquely informative in three areas: (1) how people adapt to such challenges, (2) how social processes, such as social comparison and social support, affect coping, adaptation, and health, and (3) how negative and positive emotions affect ways of dealing with adversity. I will provide a brief review of each of these areas.

Adaptation to serious illness and other negative life events

People who have experienced some kinds of negative life events not only manage to survive, but also report profound changes in their lives, often to the point of rating their current situation as superior to their life before the event (Affleck & Tennen, 1996; Updegraff & Taylor, in press; see Davis, Lehman, & Wortman, 1999, for important exceptions). People often report having learned valuable information – both positive and negative – from their experience. The following section examines some of these changes and discusses their implications for understanding self-regulatory processes.

Cognitive adaptation to negative life events

How is it that people who have encountered severe adversity experience positive changes in their lives and maintain hope for the future? In her seminal paper on cognitive adaptation, Taylor (1983) suggested that these changes arise in response to three tasks that people undertake following a negative life event: *searching for meaning* (why did the event happen?, what is its impact?), *regaining mastery* (how can I keep the event from happening again?, how can I manage it now?), and *enhancing self-esteem*. Consider the following comments from Taylor's (ibid., p. 1,163) interviews of women with breast cancer:

> I have much more enjoyment of each day, each moment. I am not so worried about what is and what isn't or what I wish I had. All those things you get entangled with don't seem to be part of my life right now.

> I was very happy to find out I am a very strong person. I have no time for game-playing any more. I want to get on with life. And I have become more introspective and also let others fend for their own responsibilities. And now almost five years later, I have become a very different person.

These comments illustrate a number of key elements of psychological adaptation to serious illness: the increased enjoyment of everyday activities, changes in control efforts, and changes in views of the self as stronger and more focused. I will consider each of these elements in more detail.

Finding meaning   Finding meaning in a negative event turns out to be a common (but by no means universal) response to serious illness (for reviews, see Davis, Lehman, & Wortman, 1999; Emmons, Colby, & Kaiser, 1998; Updegraff & Taylor, in press). In Taylor's (1983) interviews with women with breast cancer, 95 percent of the patients had generated some explanation for why their cancer occurred. No specific causal explanation was linked to better psychological adjustment, but the large number of patients who found some sort of explanation suggests that the process of finding some meaning is important.

Although there are many ways to find meaning, one frequently reported way involves finding benefit in adversity. In Affleck & Tennen's (1996) extensive program of research on adjustment to chronic illness, the vast majority of patients reported gains in the strength of their relationships with family and friends, perceptions of positive personality changes, such as greater patience, tolerance, empathy, and courage, and valued changes in life priorities and personal goals (see also Tedeschi & Calhoun, 1996). Interestingly, the perception of benefits from adversity and active attempts to remind oneself of such benefits are linked to other outcomes, such as lower mood disturbance and better health outcomes. For example, people who found meaning in their first heart attack were less likely to suffer a second one (Affleck & Tennen, 1996). Finding meaning in adversity has also been prospectively linked to improved immune function and decreased mortality among HIV-seropositive gay men dealing with the death of their partner (Bower, Kemeny, Taylor, & Fahey, 1998).

Restoring mastery   The coping literature provides many striking examples of people's attempts to restore feelings of control and mastery following adversity. Control may take many forms, such as seeing oneself as responsible for the event (Janoff-Bulman, 1989), or it may involve finding new outlets for achieving mastery. For example, people with serious illnesses seem to transfer their control efforts away from the stressor itself (the illness or their prognosis) and toward more manageable aspects of it (the management of symptoms and daily experience). Such selective control attempts – exercising control where one reasonably can and relinquishing control where it is not possible – are linked to superior psychological adjustment, especially as one's condition progresses (Heckhausen, 1997; Thompson, Sobolew-Shubin, Galbraith, Schwankovsky, & Cruzen, 1993).

Patterns of benefit-finding also seem to show this selective pattern. In a study of life changes following a diagnosis of cancer, Collins, Taylor, & Skokan (1990) found that respondents reported both positive and negative changes in five major domains (views of themselves, relations with others, priorities and daily activities, views of the future, and views of the world). Of particular interest, the two life domains that had the greatest ratio of positive to negative changes were those that were most directly controllable by the patients themselves – personal relationships and priorities and daily activities.

Restoring self-esteem   In Taylor's (1983) interviews, almost all of the respondents thought they were better off than other women with breast cancer. Self-enhancement through *downward comparisons* to others who are worse off has been found to be a common response to adversity (Buunk & Gibbons, 1997; Wills, 1981). Taylor, Wood, & Lichtman (1983) coined the term *selective evaluation* to describe not only the process of making downward comparisons, but of selecting dimensions that would allow one to achieve such favorable comparisons. The following excerpts illustrate this process (Taylor, 1983, p. 1,166):

> An older woman: "The people I really feel sorry for are these young gals. To lose a breast when you're so young must be awful. I'm 73; what do I need a breast for?"

> A younger woman: "If I hadn't been married, I think this thing would have really gotten to me. I can't imagine dating or whatever knowing you have this thing and not knowing how to tell the man about it."

By viewing their situations in ways that emphasized their relative advantage, the vast majority of respondents thought they were adjusting better than other women with breast cancer.

Downward comparisons are not the only way in which social comparison information is used by those coping with adversity. *Upward comparisons* to people doing better than the self play an important role in sustaining hope among people with serious illness (Taylor & Lobel, 1989). Interestingly, as was the case with the selective exercise of control efforts, people seem to be highly skilled in managing their exposure to comparison information to ensure that upward comparisons are encouraging, rather than discouraging. For example, people may avoid upward comparisons on dimensions they cannot change (such as the severity of the illness), but seek them on dimensions they can change (such as ways of coping with the illness; see Aspinwall, 1997, for review).

Learning from adversity: Taking the good and the bad

A second, related area of research on adjustment to adversity examines what people learn from negative life events. Most research on this topic has been conducted from the perspective of Janoff-Bulman's work on *assumptive worlds*. Janoff-Bulman (1989; Janoff-Bulman & Frieze, 1983) argued that we hold favorable beliefs about ourselves, about other people, and about the fairness and meaningfulness of events in the world that remain unquestioned until something negative happens to us. Negative life events challenge and may even shatter such beliefs. In a study of college students, those who had experienced negative life events, such as death of a parent or sibling, incest, rape, a fire that destroyed their home, or a disabling accident, scored lower on beliefs about the benevolence of the world and saw themselves as lower in self-worth than those who had not experienced such events (Janoff-Bulman, 1989).

These findings suggest that adversity has effects that go beyond the event itself to affect core beliefs about the self and the world. How do people cope with such challenges? Janoff-Bulman (1989) argued that one can (1) change one's beliefs, or (2) reinterpret the negative experience to fit one's existing beliefs. There is some evidence that people act in order to restore their worldview. For example, in order to avoid seeing the world as a random place in which bad things happen to good people, people may see themselves as having caused the negative event. To believe that one controlled one's fate means that one can do better next time or take additional precautions. This strategy to restore mastery seems to work, as long as people don't blame less mutable aspects of themselves, such as their character, for the negative event. In cases in which the event cannot be reinterpreted to match one's beliefs, people may experience persisting distress (Davis, Lehman, & Wortman, 1999).

As suggested earlier, people frequently report both positive and negative changes in response to adversity. However, many authors have questioned the nature and adaptiveness of self-reports of finding benefits in adversity. Do such reports, for example, reflect denial of negative experience or social pressure to report benefit in adversity? These are difficult questions to answer. With respect to the first question, perceptions of benefits seem to be largely uncorrelated with perceptions of the negative impacts of illness (Affleck & Tennen, 1996), a finding that suggests that finding benefit in adversity is not accomplished through denial of its negative aspects. Similarly, in the Collins, Taylor, & Skokan (1990) study, positive and negative changes were reported with nearly equal frequency in three major life domains. A recent experiment by King & Miner (in press) suggests that there are some relatively objective gains from finding benefit in adversity. In a variation of the Pennebaker (1993) disclosure paradigm, college students randomly assigned to write about the benefits they perceived from their experience of traumatic events experienced the same reduction in health center visits relative to controls over the next three months as those assigned to write about negative aspects of such events.

Individual differences and adaptation following adversity

Thus far, I have considered multiple aspects of psychological adaptation and suggested that the process of dealing with adversity involves learning both good and bad things about the self, the world, and other people, and learning that some things are more amenable to control than others. There is increasing interest in the implications of these aspects of adaptation for personality change and growth (Affleck & Tennen, 1996; Carver, 1998; Ickovics & Park, 1998; Tedeschi, Park, & Calhoun, 1998). Interestingly, there seem to be several reciprocal relations between individual differences and the adaptational processes reviewed here. First, certain individual differences, such as optimism, extroversion, and openness to experience, have been linked to finding positive changes in adversity (Affleck & Tennen, 1996; Tedeschi & Calhoun, 1996). In turn, self-reported personal growth from negative events has been linked to subsequent increases in optimism and positive affectivity (Park, Cohen, & Murch, 1996). Second, optimism and self-mastery have been linked to selective control attempts whereby people disengage from active attempts to control uncontrollable problems and report greater acceptance of such problems. It is likely that these two strategies – finding benefits and applying control efforts selectively – serve to preserve the favorable beliefs and expectations that promote them by helping people profit from adversity and by protecting people from repeated failures to exercise control (Aspinwall, Richter, & Hoffman, in press).

Implications of research on adaptation for the study of self-regulation

There are several implications of these findings for understanding self-regulation. The first is that people not only withstand, but may also learn from adversity. They may also make profound changes in their daily activities, personal priorities, and comparison standards. Thus, the experience of a major negative life event can create changes in the values and priorities that may fundamentally affect the goals people strive to obtain, as well as the standards people use to evaluate their progress (see Biernat, & Billings, 2001).

Understanding the causes and consequences of people's efforts to find meaning, restore mastery, and bolster self-esteem may lead to new insights into ways that people learn from adversity and into the kinds of events that make such efforts more difficult. Research to date suggests that the process of adaptation is considerably more complex than seeing all aspects of one's situation favorably or unfavorably following adversity. Additionally, accumulating evidence about the domains in which people with serious illness report finding benefit and meaning suggests a number of promising domains in which to study self-regulation with respect to important goals. Specifically, expanding the study of self-regulation beyond achievement-oriented tasks to consider such goals as positive relations with others, environmental mastery, meaning in life, and personal growth may give us new information about self-regulation with respect to larger life goals and developmental tasks (Emmons, Colby, & Kaiser, 1998; Ryff, 1989).

The role of social processes in coping, adaptation, and health

If coping is the study of personality under stress, it is just as surely the study of social processes under stress. Research on stress and coping has identified several ways in which the experience of adversity and different ways of coping with it not only alter people's social environments, but also change the ways they use information and assistance from other people. In this section, I will provide a brief overview of research relating social processes to coping, adaptation, and health and discuss the implications of this research for self-regulation more generally.

Social comparison and coping with adversity

Starting with Schachter's (1959) classic studies of fear and affiliation and continuing with present-day research on people facing highly threatening and uncertain situations, social comparisons have been found to play a central role in our attempts to understand what we are facing, how we should feel about it, and what we should do about it (Buunk & Gibbons, 1997). This information is so important to how we understand and manage adversity that simple exposure to someone who has undergone what we are about to face has dramatic health effects. In several field experiments, Kulik & Mahler (1997) found that male cardiac patients awaiting surgery who were randomly assigned to a postsurgical roommate (even one who had had surgery for a different condition) were less anxious and were released sooner from the hospital than patients assigned to a presurgical roommate. In this situation, social comparisons seem to aid people in two critical coping tasks: problem solving and the regulation of emotion. Seeing someone who has experienced surgery may benefit patients by providing information about the sensations and procedures they might experience after surgery (information useful in problem solving) and by providing living evidence that people do weather surgery (information useful in regulating emotions, such as anxiety).

Such findings have several implications for the study of self-regulation. With few exceptions, the study of self-regulation has been conceptualized as an individual process. In most approaches to goal-directed behavior, social comparisons enter the picture only or primarily when they affect the standards used to judge progress toward a goal. However, it is increasingly clear that social comparison information affects goal-directed behavior far earlier in the chain, starting with decisions about whether to adopt a specific goal (Ruble & Frey, 1991), and continuing with appraisals of tasks and their demands (Aspinwall, Frazier, & Cooper, 1999), perceptions of self-efficacy during the course of task engagement (Bandura & Jourden, 1991), the selection of specific coping methods, and decisions about disengagement (see Aspinwall, 1997, for a review).

Social support and coping with adversity

Social support has been linked through multiple pathways to more active coping efforts, better psychological outcomes, and better health outcomes among people confronting adversity (Cohen & Wills, 1985; Cohen, 1988; Holahan, Moos, Holahan, & Brennan, 1997; Taylor & Aspinwall, 1996). In her classic paper, Peggy Thoits (1986) defined social support as the participation of other people in an individual's coping efforts, including both problem-focused and emotion-focused coping. She outlined four functions of social support: *instrumental* (help with problem-solving efforts, such as rides to the doctor, loans, or other tangible assistance); *information* (also useful in problem solving); *appraisal* (help figuring out what the stressful event is and what it means); and *esteem support* (helping the person feel loved and valued, despite the adverse event). It may be worth noting that these well-documented functions of social support map nicely on to the three major tasks of cognitive adaptation identified by Taylor (1983), namely regaining mastery, finding meaning, and restoring self-esteem.

An important part of this large literature has examined how social support can go awry; that is, how the experience of adversity can lead members of one's social network to avoid the affected person or to interact in awkward and unhelpful ways (e.g. see Dunkel-Schetter & Wortman, 1982; Lehman, Ellard, & Wortman, 1986). As I reviewed earlier, how people cope with adversity, especially how they manage emotional distress and their needs for information and reassurance, also affects the amount and kind of social support they receive (Colby & Emmons, 1997). Such findings highlight the fact that social support is not a static resource, but one that is influenced by coping and also by potential helpers' own fears and beliefs about what would be helpful (Wortman & Silver, 1987). In turn, people who perceive that others are not meeting their needs often react in ways that further the divide between them and their social networks. A final level of complexity is added by emerging evidence that social support may not be a purely external resource. That is, the temperament and personality of the person seeking support seem to be related to both perceived and actual availability and use of social support (Taylor & Aspinwall, 1996). In sum, social support can play an important role in coping with adversity, but people dealing with adversity do not always receive or perceive the support they desire.

Summary

In this brief review of the role of social processes in coping with adversity, I have tried to highlight ways in which social comparisons and social support influence coping, adaptation, and health. In addition to their use as standards for self-evaluation, people use information and assistance from others to inform their coping efforts and to understand and regulate their emotions. Such information is also used to establish goals and priorities among them. In turn, the ways in which people cope with adversity seem to have reliable effects on the availability of social resources. Considering these social aspects of self-regulation may yield a more comprehensive portrait of social influences on goal-directed behavior.

The role of emotions in coping and self-regulation

A final area that is ripe for greater attention in both literatures is the effects of emotions on efforts to deal with adversity. In the coping literature, emotions are typically conceptualized as things that must be managed (as in emotion-focused coping), rather than as major influences on other parts of the coping process. In theories of self-regulation, affect is thought to arise from (Carver & Scheier, 1990) or to inform one's perceived rate of progress toward goals (Martin & Tesser, 1996). However, the effects of positive and negative affect, once elicited, on other aspects of self-regulation are not generally considered.

In the case of chronic illness and other stressors, it will be critical to understand how negative states such as fatigue, depression, uncertainty, anxiety, and pain influence self-regulatory processes. These states may have profound (and likely detrimental) influences on attention to and appraisals of potential problems, selection of coping strategies, and evaluation and integration of new information about problems and the success of one's efforts to manage them. However, there may be ways of expressing and managing negative emotions that have beneficial effects on mental and physical health (Pennebaker, 1993; Stanton, Danoff-Burg, Cameron, & Ellis, 1994). Understanding and cultivating these more adaptive ways may lead to the development of interventions to help people cope with adversity and to prevent the deterioration in social resources that may accompany the display of negative emotions.

Finally, the role of positive emotions in sustaining attention to negative information, fueling goal-pursuit, and generating multiple, creative solutions to one's problems remains understudied. These emotions may be linked to processes such as benefit-finding and reminding, the selective exercise of control, and different kinds of social support in ways that are just beginning to be explored.

Summary and Conclusion

Chronic illness, negative life events, and other stressors represent an important set of circumstances in which to study personal and social factors in self-regulation, as resources are taxed over long periods of time; as valued goals, self-beliefs, and worldviews may be disconfirmed, reaffirmed, or changed; as social ties may be strengthened or weakened; and as negative and positive emotions may influence appraisals, coping efforts, and social behavior. Importantly, all of these things are going on at once, most often in life domains that are highly important to people.

What can be gained by considering potential interrelations between the stress and coping and self-regulation literatures? Some of the suggestions I've made here might broaden scope of inquiry of both literatures, but at the same time provide increased precision. First, reconceptualizing coping as goal-directed behavior might provide insight into the nature of stress, the kinds of coping strategies employed, and their effects on both the problem and the person. Second, a focus on how psychological and social resources "work" may extend the study of individual differences beyond the question of *which* factors are linked to psychosocial and health outcomes to ask *how* such relations are obtained. Greater attention to conceptual models of self-regulation, including research on psychological resources, attention to negative information, emotional regulation, problem solving, and procedural knowledge, would likely elucidate why certain individual differences are so reliably related to good or poor outcomes over time. Such models may also provide insight into the processes through which personality is maintained over the lifespan.

Third, research on self-regulation might profit from greater attention to both the processes and outcomes of psychological adaptation to stressful life events. People who experience adversity change their comparison standards, value different life domains than before, and often gain valuable knowledge about themselves, others, and the world as a result of the illness. They may change their goals, change the meaning or importance they accord to different goals, or make more nuanced distinctions between controllable and uncontrollable aspects of goals. These creative, adaptive changes to find meaning, exercise mastery, and restore self worth have documented links to psychological well-being and, increasingly, to physical health that merit increased research attention. Importantly, these changes do not take place in a social vacuum, nor are they independent of the nature of the stressor. It will continue to be important to examine different kinds of life events and social responses to them that make it more or less difficult to find meaning, to exercise mastery, or to restore self-worth.

Fourth, greater attention to social processes, such as social comparison and social support, may provide insight not only into how people manage adversity, but also how people select, pursue, and disengage from different goals. Increased attention to the social interactions of people managing adversity may shed light on the processes that maintain, build, or deplete social resources, as well as those that generate conflictual interactions that are themselves potent sources of stress. Finally, greater attention to the role of both positive and negative emotions in the process of detecting and managing negative events and information may increase our understanding of emotions in such critical areas as problem solving, goal pursuit, and the maintenance or depletion of personal and social resources.

In conclusion, integrating the study of coping with adversity with the study of self-regulation may increase our understanding of what people are trying to do in their lives, what is stressful to people, why particular coping strategies are enacted, and how ways of dealing with adversity affect all areas of life.

NOTE

1　This review will necessarily be selective, rather than comprehensive. For reviews of major topics in stress, coping, adaptation and health, see Aspinwall & Taylor (1997); Basic Behavioral Science Task Force (1996); Buunk & Gibbons (1997); Cohen (1988); Friedman (1990); Kaplan (1996); Lazarus (1990); Pennebaker (1993); Revenson (1994); Suls & Harvey (1996); Taylor & Aspinwall (1990, 1996); Taylor, Repetti, & Seeman (1997); Tedeschi, Park, & Calhoun (1998); and Wortman & Silver (1987).

REFERENCES

Affleck, G., & Tennen, H. (1996). Construing benefits from adversity: Adaptational significance and dispositional underpinnings. *Journal of Personality*, *64*, 899–922.

Aldwin, C., & Stokols, D. (1988). The effects of environmental change on individuals and groups: Some neglected issues in stress research. *Journal of Environmental Psychology*, *8*, 57–75.

Armor, D. A., & Taylor, S. E. (1998). Situated optimism: Specific outcome expectancies and self-regulation. In M. P. Zanna (Ed.), *Advances in experimental social psychology*, Vol. 30 (pp. 309–379). New York: Academic Press.

Ashby, F. G., Isen, A. M., & Turken, A. U. (1999). A neurological theory of positive affect and its influence on cognition. *Psychological Review*, *106*, 529–550.

Aspinwall, L. G. (1997). Future-oriented aspects of social comparisons: A framework for studying health-related comparison activity. In B. P. Buunk & F. X. Gibbons (Eds.), *Health, coping, and well-being: Perspectives from social comparison theory* (pp. 125–165). Mahwah, NJ: Erlbaum.

Aspinwall, L. G. (1998). Rethinking the role of positive affect in self-regulation. *Motivation and Emotion*, *22*, 1–32.

Aspinwall, L. G., & Brunhart, S. M. (1996). Distinguishing optimism from denial: Optimistic beliefs predict attention to health threats. *Personality and Social Psychology Bulletin*, *22*, 993–1003.

Aspinwall, L. G., & Taylor, S. E. (1992). Modeling cognitive adaptation: A longitudinal investigation of the impact of individual differences and coping on college adjustment and performance. *Journal of Personality and Social Psychology*, *63*, 989–1003.

Aspinwall, L. G., & Taylor, S. E. (1997). A stitch in time: Self-regulation and proactive coping. *Psychological Bulletin*, *121*, 417–436.

Aspinwall, L. G., Frazier, L. E., & Cooper, D. A. (1999). Being shown up vs. being shown how: When upward comparisons foster superior performance. Manuscript in preparation.

Aspinwall, L. G., Richter, L., & Hoffman, R. R. (in press). Understanding how optimism "works:" Mediators and moderators. In E. C. Chang (Ed.), *Optimism and pessimism: Theory, research, and practice*.Washington: American Psychological Association.

Austin, J. T., & Vancouver, J. B. (1996). Goal constructs in psychology: Structure, process, and content. *Psychological Bulletin*, *120*, 338–375.

Bandura, A., & Jourden, F. J. (1991). Self-regulatory mechanisms governing the impact of social comparison on complex decision-making. *Journal of Personality and Social Psychology*, *60*, 941–951.

Basic Behavioral Science Task Force of the National Advisory Mental Health Council (1996). Vulnerability and resilience. *American Psychologist*, *51*, 22–28.

Biernat, M., & Billings, L. S. (2001). Standards, expectancies, and social comparison. In A. Tesser & N. Schwarz (Eds.), *Blackwell handbook of social psychology: Intraindividual processes* (pp. 257–283). Oxford: Blackwell Publishing.

Blascovich, J., & Tomaka, J. (1996). The biopsychosocial model of arousal regulation. In M. Zanna (Ed.), *Advances in experimental social psychology*, Vol. 28 (pp. 1–51). New York: Academic Press.

Bolger, N. (1990). Coping as a personality process: A prospective study. *Journal of Personality and Social Psychology, 59*, 525–537.

Bolger, N., & Schilling, E. A. (1991). Personality and the problems of everyday life: The role of neuroticism in exposure and reactivity to daily stressors. *Journal of Personality and Social Psychology, 59*, 355–386.

Bolger, N., & Zuckerman, A. (1995). A framework for studying personality in the stress process. *Journal of Personality and Social Psychology, 69*, 890–902.

Bolger, N., Foster, M., Vinokur, A. D., & Ng, R. (1996). Close relationships and adjustment to a life crisis: The case of breast cancer. *Journal of Personality and Social Psychology, 70*, 283–294.

Bower, J. E., Kemeny, M. E., Taylor, S. E., & Fahey, J. L. (1998). Cognitive processing, discovery of meaning, CD4 decline, and AIDS-related mortality among bereaved HIV-seropositive men. *Journal of Consulting and Clinical Psychology, 66*, 979–986.

Buunk, B. P., & Gibbons, F. X. (Eds.) (1997). *Health, coping, and well-being: Perspectives from social comparison theory.* Mahwah, NJ: Erlbaum.

Cantor, N. (1990). From thought to behavior: "Having" and "doing" in the study of personality and cognition. *American Psychologist, 45*, 735–750.

Carver, C. S. (1998). Resilience and thriving: Issues, models, and linkages. *Journal of Social Issues, 54* (2), 245–266.

Carver, C. S. (2001). Self regulation. In A. Tesser & N. Schwarz (Eds.), *Blackwell handbook of social psychology: Intraindividual processes* (pp. 307–328). Oxford: Blackwell Publishing.

Carver, C. S., & Scheier, M. F. (1990). Principles of self-regulation: Action and emotion. In E. T. Higgins & R. M. Sorrentino (Eds.), *Handbook of motivation and cognition*, Vol. 2 (pp. 3–52). New York: Guilford Press.

Carver, C. S., & Scheier, M. F. (1998). *On the self-regulation of behavior.* New York: Cambridge University Press.

Carver, C. S., & Scheier, M. F. (1999c). Stress, coping, and self-regulatory processes. In L. A. Pervin & O. P. John (Eds.), *Handbook of Personality.* 2nd. edn. (pp. 553–575). New York: Guilford Press.

Carver, C. S., Scheier, M. F., & Weintraub, J. K. (1989). Assessing coping strategies: A theoretically based approach. *Journal of Personality and Social Psychology, 56*, 267–283.

Carver, C. S., Pozo, C., Harris, S. D., Noriega, V., Scheier, M. F., Robinson, D. S., Ketcham, A. S., Moffat, F. I., Jr., & Clark, K. C. (1993). How coping mediates the effect of optimism on distress: A study of women with early stage breast cancer. *Journal of Personality and Social Psychology, 65*, 375–390.

Coates, D., & Wortman, C. B. (1980). Depression maintenance and interpersonal control. In A. E. Baum & J. E. Singer (Eds.), *Advances in environmental psychology: Applications of personal control,* Vol. 2 (pp. 149–182). Hillsdale, NJ: Erlbaum.

Coats, E. J., Janoff-Bulman, R., & Alpert, N. (1996). Approach versus avoidance goals: Differences in self-evaluation and well-being. *Personality and Social Psychology Bulletin, 22*, 1057–1067.

Cohen, S. (1988). Psychosocial models of the role of social support in the etiology of physical disease. *Health Psychology, 7*, 269–297.

Cohen, S., & Rodriguez, M. S. (1995). Pathways linking affective disturbances and physical disorders. *Health Psychology, 14*, 374–380.

Cohen, S., & Wills, T. A. (1985). Stress, social support, and the buffering hypothesis. *Psychological Bulletin, 98*, 310–357.

Colby, P. M., & Emmons, R. A. (1997). Openness to emotion as predictor of perceived, requested, and observer reports of social support. In G. R. Pierce, B. Lakey, I. G. Sarason, & B. R. Sarason (Eds.), *Sourcebook of social support and personality* (pp. 445–472). New York: Plenum Press.

Collins, R. L., Taylor, S. E., & Skokan, L. A. (1990). A better world or a shattered vision? Changes in perspective following victimization. *Social Cognition, 8*, 263–285.

Coyne, J. C., & Gottlieb, B. H. (1996). The mismeasure of coping by checklist. *Journal of Personality, 64,* 959–991.

Davis, C., Lehman, D. R., & Wortman, C. B. (1999). Searching for meaning following a life crisis: Making sense of the literature. Manuscript submitted for publication.

Derryberry, D., & Reed, M. A. (1994). Temperament and attention: Orienting toward and away from positive and negative signals. *Journal of Personality and Social Psychology, 66,* 1128–1139.

Dunkel-Schetter, C., & Wortman, C. B. (1982). The interpersonal dynamics of cancer: Problems in social relationships and their impact on the patient. In H. S. Friedman & M. R. DiMatteo (Eds.), *Interpersonal issues in health care* (pp. 69–100). New York: Academic Press.

Dweck, C. S. (1996). Implicit theories as organizers of goals and behavior. In P. M. Gollwitzer & J. A. Bargh (Eds.), *The psychology of action: Linking cognition and motivation to behavior* (pp. 69–90). New York: Guilford Press.

Elliot, A. J., Sheldon, K. M., & Church, M. A. (1996). Avoidance, personal goals and subjective well-being. *Personality and Social Psychology Bulletin, 23,* 915–927.

Emmons, R. A., & King, L. A. (1988). Conflict among personal strivings: Immediate and long-term implications for psychological and physical well-being. *Journal of Personality and Social Psychology, 54,* 1040–1048.

Emmons, R. A., Colby, P. M., & Kaiser, H. A. (1998). When losses lead to gains: Personal goals and the recovery of meaning. In P. T. P. Wong & P. S. Fry (Eds.), *The human quest for meaning: A handbook of psychological research and clinical applications* (pp. 163–178). Mahwah, NJ: Lawrence Erlbaum Associates.

Evans, G. W., & Lepore, S. J. (1993). Household crowding and social support: A quasiexperimental analysis. *Journal of Personality and Social Psychology, 65,* 308–316.

Folkman, S. (1984). Personal control and stress and coping processes: A theoretical analysis. *Journal of Personality and Social Psychology, 46,* 839–852.

Folkman, S., & Lazarus, R. L. (1980). An analysis of coping in a middle-aged community sample. *Journal of Health and Social Behavior, 21,* 219–239.

Fredrickson, B. L. (1998). What good are positive emotions? *Review of General Psychology, 2,* 300–319.

Friedman, H. S. (1990). (Ed.) *Personality and disease.* New York: John Wiley & Sons.

Gollwitzer, P. M., & Bargh, J. A. (Eds.) (1996). *The psychology of action: Linking cognition and motivation to behavior.* New York: Guilford Press.

Headey, B., & Wearing, A. (1989). Personality, life events, and subjective well-being: Toward a dynamic equilibrium model. *Journal of Personality and Social Psychology, 57,* 731–739.

Heckhausen, J. (1997). Developmental regulation across adulthood: Primary and secondary control of age-related challenges. *Developmental Psychology, 33,* 176–187.

Higgins, E. T. (1996). Ideals, oughts, and regulatory focus: Affect and motivation from distinct pains and pleasures. In P. M. Gollwitzer & J. A. Bargh (Eds.), *The psychology of action: Linking cognition and motivation to behavior* (pp. 91–114). New York: Guilford Press.

Hobfoll, S. E. (1989). Conservation of resources: A new attempt at conceptualizing stress. *American Psychologist, 44,* 513–524.

Holahan, C. J., & Moos, R. H. (1986). Personality, coping, and family resources in stress resistance: A longitudinal analysis. *Journal of Personality and Social Psychology, 51,* 389–395.

Holahan, C. J., Moos, R. H., Holahan, C. K., & Brennan, P. L. (1997). Social context, coping strategies, and depressive symptoms: An expanded model with cardiac patients. *Journal of Personality and Social Psychology, 72,* 918–928.

Ickovics, J. R., & Park, C. L. (1998). Paradigm shift: Why a focus on health is important. *Journal of Social Issues, 54* (2), 237–244.

Isen, A. M. (1993). Positive affect and decision making. In M. Lewis & J. M. Haviland (Eds.), *Handbook of emotions* (pp. 261–277). New York: Guilford Press.

Janoff-Bulman, R. (1989). Assumptive worlds and the stress of traumatic events: Applications of the schema construct. *Social Cognition, 7,* 113–136.

Janoff-Bulman, R., & Frieze, I. H. (1983). A theoretical perspective for understanding reactions to victimization. *Journal of Social Issues, 39* (2), 1–17.

Joiner, T. E., Metalsky, G. I., Katz, J., & Beach, S. R. H. (in press). Depression and excessive reassurance-seeking. *Psychological Inquiry.*

Kaplan, H. B. (Ed.) (1996). *Psychosocial stress: Perspectives on structure, theory, life-course, and methods.* San Diego, CA: Academic Press.

Katz, L., & Epstein, E. (1991). Constructive thinking and coping with laboratory-induced stress. *Journal of Personality and Social Psychology, 61,* 789–800.

King, L. (1996). Who is regulating what and why? The motivational context of self-regulation. *Psychological Inquiry, 7,* 57–60.

King, L. A., & Miner, K. N. (in press). Writing about the perceived benefits of traumatic events: Implications for physical health. *Personality and Social Psychology Bulletin.*

Kling, K. C., Ryff, C. D., & Essex, M. J. (1997). Adaptive changes in self-concept during a life transition. *Personality and Social Psychology Bulletin, 23,* 981–990.

Kulik, J. A., & Mahler, H. I. M. (1997). Social comparison, affiliation, and coping with acute medical threats. In B. P. Buunk & F. X. Gibbons (Eds.), *Health, coping, and well-being: Perspectives from social comparison theory* (pp. 227–261). Mahwah, NJ: Erlbaum.

Lazarus, R. L. (1990). Theory-based stress measurement. *Psychological Inquiry, 1,* 3–13.

Lazarus, R. L., & Folkman, S. (1984). *Stress, appraisal, and coping.* New York: Springer.

Lehman, D. R., Ellard, J. H., & Wortman, C. B. (1986). Social support for the bereaved: Recipients' and providers' perspectives on what is helpful. *Journal of Consulting and Clinical Psychology, 54,* 438–446.

Little, B. R. (1983). Personal projects: A rationale and method for investigation. *Environment and Behavior, 15,* 273–309.

McCrae, R. R., & Costa, P. T., Jr. (1986). Personality, coping, and coping effectiveness in an adult sample. *Journal of Personality and Social Psychology, 54,* 385–405.

Markus, H., & Nurius, P. (1986). Possible selves. *American Psychologist, 41,* 954–969.

Martin, L. L., & Tesser, A. (1996). *Striving and feeling: Interactions between goals, affect, and self-regulation.* Hillsdale, NJ: Erlbaum.

Park, C. L., Cohen, L. H., & Murch, R. L. (1996). Assessment and prediction of stress-related growth. *Journal of Personality, 64,* 71–105.

Pearlin, L. I., Aneshensel, C. S., & LeBlanc, A. J. (1997). The forms and mechanisms of stress proliferation: The case of AIDS caregivers. *Journal of Health and Social Behavior, 38,* 223–236.

Pennebaker, J. W. (1993). Putting stress into words: Health, linguistic, and therapeutic implications. *Behaviour Research and Therapy, 31,* 539–548.

Peterson, C., & Seligman, M. E. P. (1984). Causal explanations as a risk factor for depression: Theory and evidence. *Psychological Review, 91,* 347–374.

Repetti, R. L. (1989). Effects of daily workload on subsequent behavior during marital interaction: The roles of social withdrawal and spouse support. *Journal of Personality and Social Psychology, 57,* 651–659.

Revenson, T. A. (1990). All other things are not equal: An ecological approach to personality and disease. In H. S. Friedman (Ed.), *Personality and disease* (pp. 65–94). New York: John Wiley & Sons.

Revenson, T. A. (1994). Social support and marital coping with chronic illness. *Annals of Behavioral Medicine, 16,* 122–130.

Ruble, D. N., & Frey, K. S. (1991). Changing patterns of comparative behavior as skills are acquired: A functional model of self-evaluation. In J. Suls & T. A. Wills (Eds.), *Social comparison: Contemporary theory and research* (pp. 79–113). Hillsdale, NJ: Erlbaum.

Ryff, C. D. (1989). Happiness is everything, or is it? Explorations on the meaning of psychological well-being. *Journal of Personality and Social Psychology, 57,* 1069–1081.

Schachter, S. (1959). *The psychology of affiliation.* Stanford, CA: Stanford University Press.

Scheier, M. F., Carver, C. S., & Bridges, M. W. (1994). Distinguishing optimism from neuroticism (and trait anxiety, self-mastery, and self-esteem): A re-evaluation of the Life Orientation Test. *Journal of Personality and Social Psychology, 67,* 1063–1078.

Silver, R. C., Wortman, C. B., & Crofton, C. (1990). The role of coping in support provision: The self-presentational dilemma of victims of life crises. In B. R. Sarason & I. G. Sarason (Eds.), *Social support: An interactional view* (pp. 397–426). New York: John Wiley & Sons.

Skinner, E. A. (in press). Action regulation, coping, and development. In J. Brandtstädter & R. M. Lerner (Eds.), *Action and self-development: Theory and research through the life-span.* Thousand Oaks, CA: Sage.

Smith, C. A., & Wallston, K. A. (1992). Adaptation in patients with chronic rheumatoid arthritis: Application of a general model. *Health Psychology, 11,* 151–162.

Smith, R. E., Leffingwell, T. R., & Ptacek, J. T. (1999). Can people remember how they coped?: Factors associated with discordance between same-day and retrospective reports. *Journal of Personality and Social Psychology, 76,* 1050–1061.

Stanton, A. L., Danoff-Burg, S., Cameron, C. L., & Ellis, A. P. (1994). Coping through emotional approach: Problems of conceptualization and confounding. *Journal of Personality and Social Psychology, 66,* 350–362.

Stone, A. A., & Neale, J. M. (1984). Effects of severe daily events on mood. *Journal of Personality and Social Psychology, 46,* 137–144.

Stone, A. A., Greenberg, M. A., Kennedy-Moore, E., & Newman, M. G. (1991). Self-report, situation-specific coping questionnaires: What are they measuring? *Journal of Personality and Social Psychology, 61,* 648–658.

Suls, J., & Harvey, J. H. (Eds.) (1996). Personality and coping: Special issue. *Journal of Personality, 64.*

Taylor, S. E. (1983). Adjustment to threatening events: A theory of cognitive adaptation. *American Psychologist, 38,* 1163–1173.

Taylor, S. E., & Aspinwall, L. G. (1990). Psychosocial aspects of chronic illness. In P. T. Costa, Jr., & G. R. VandenBos (Eds.), *Psychological aspects of serious illness: Chronic conditions, fatal disease, and clinical care* (pp. 3–60). Washington, DC: American Psychological Association.

Taylor, S. E., & Aspinwall, L. G. (1996). Mediating and moderating processes in psychosocial stress: Appraisal, coping, resistance and vulnerability. In H. B. Kaplan (Ed.), *Psychosocial stress: Perspectives on structure, theory, life-course, and methods* (pp. 71–110). San Diego, CA: Academic Press.

Taylor, S. E., & Lobel, M. (1989). Social comparison activity under threat: Downward evaluation and upward contacts. *Psychological Review, 96,* 569–575.

Taylor, S. E., Repetti, R. L., & Seeman, T. (1997). Health psychology: What is an unhealthy environment and how does it get under the skin? *Annual Review of Psychology, 48,* 411–447.

Taylor, S. E., Wood, J. V., & Lichtman, R. R. (1983). It could be worse: Selective evaluation as a response to victimization. *Journal of Social Issues, 39* (2), 19–40.

Tedeschi, R. G., & Calhoun, L. G. (1996). The Posttraumatic Growth Inventory: Measuring the positive legacy of trauma. *Journal of Traumatic Stress, 9,* 455–471.

Tedeschi, R. G., Park, C. L., & Calhoun, L. G. (Eds.) (1998). *Posttraumatic growth: Positive changes in the aftermath of crisis.* Mahwah, NJ: Erlbaum.

Thoits, P. A. (1986). Social support as coping assistance. *Journal of Consulting and Clinical Psychology,* *54,* 416–423.

Thompson, S. C., Sobolew-Shubin, A., Galbraith, M. E., Schwankovsky, L., & Cruzen, D. (1993). Maintaining perceptions of control: Finding perceived control in low-control circumstances. *Journal of Personality and Social Psychology, 64,* 293–304.

Updegraff, J. A., & Taylor, S. E. (in press). From vulnerability to growth: The positive and negative effects of stressful life events. In J. Harvey & E. Miller (Eds.), *Handbook of loss and trauma.* Philadelphia, PA: Taylor & Francis.

Watson, D., & Clark, L. A. (1984). Negative affectivity: The disposition to experience aversive emotional states. *Psychological Bulletin, 96,* 465–490.

Watson, D., & Hubbard, B. (1996). Adaptational style and dispositional structure: Coping in the context of the five-factor model. *Journal of Personality, 64,* 737–774.

Wills, T. A. (1981). Downward comparison principles in social psychology. *Psychological Bulletin, 90,* 245–271.

Wortman, C. B., & Silver, R. L. (1987). Coping with irrevocable loss. In G. R. VandenBos & B. K. Bryant (Eds.), *Cataclysms, crises, and catastrophes: Psychology in action* (pp. 189–235). Washington, DC: American Psychological Association.

CHAPTER TWO

Attachment Style and Affect Regulation: Implications for Coping with Stress and Mental Health

Mario Mikulincer and Victor Florian

In contemporary social psychology, a wealth of theoretical and empirical work has been carried out in understanding the ways in which people regulate emotional distress, cope with stressful events, and maintain an adequate level of mental health. In this context, Bowlby's (1969, 1973, 1980) attachment theory appears to provide one of the best frameworks for examining individual differences and psychological processes related to the broad issue of affect regulation. In this chapter, we present our conceptualization of the attachment system as a psychoevolutionary affect regulation device and our view of adult attachment style as a basic source of individual differences in the use of specific regulatory strategies. Then we review the existing body of empirical knowledge, examining (1) the contribution of adult attachment style to the process of coping with stressful events and the management of negative emotions, and (2) the implications of attachment-style differences in affect regulation for mental health and psychopathology.

A Brief Introduction to Attachment Theory and Research

Bowlby's theory (1969, 1973) is based on three tenets. First, human infants are born with a repertoire of behaviors aimed at maintaining proximity to other persons, who help them to survive and provide a "secure base" for exploring the environment. Second, proximity maintenance also depends on the availability and responsivity of other persons to one's attachment needs. Third, experiences with significant others are internalized into mental working models of the world and the self and generalized to new relationships. Bowlby (1988) suggested that these models are the building blocks of a person's attachment style – stable patterns of relational cognitions, emotions, and behaviors.

Following Bowlby's premises, Ainsworth, Blehar, Waters, and Wall (1978) delineated three prototypical attachment styles in infancy (secure, avoidant, and anxious-ambivalent), and Hazan and Shaver (1987) constructed a self-report scale tapping these styles in adulthood. Hazan and Shaver defined the secure style by comfort with closeness and confidence in others' responses; the avoidant style by insecurity in others' intentions and preference for distance; and the anxious-ambivalent style by insecurity in others' responses and a strong desire for intimacy. While secure people perceive others as a "secure base," avoidant and anxious-ambivalent people have serious doubts about others' responses in times of need.

Using self-reports of adult attachment style, extensive research has shown theoretically congruent attachment-style differences in the experience of love (e.g., Feeney & Noller, 1990; Kirkpatrick & Davis, 1994), marital relationships (e.g., Kobak & Hazan, 1991), self disclosure (Mikulincer & Nachshon, 1991), self-image (Mikulincer, 1995), and social perception (Collins, 1996). In this context, there is also evidence on the links between attachment style, affect regulation, and mental health. This is the main focus of the current chapter.

Attachment as an Affect Regulation System

Although Bowlby's theory mainly deals with developmental and interpersonal issues, the association between the attachment system, affect regulation, and mental health is one of the basic pillars of this theoretical framework. According to Bowlby (1969), attachment-related behaviors are organized around a psychoevolutionary affect regulation system. Attachment figures function as a haven of safety to which people can retreat for comfort and reassurance in times of stress. These figures also act as an "auxiliary ego" in managing distress and as a "secure base" from which people can develop their personality in an approving atmosphere. On this basis, proximity to significant others can be seen as an inborn affect regulation device, which allows people to manage distress with the assistance of others.

The affect regulation function of the attachment system is also highlighted by the fact that attachment theory was formulated in order to understand animal and human reactions to two major life stressors, loss and separation (Bowlby, 1969, 1973, 1980). Overall, Bowlby (1973) proposed that the attachment system functions as a protective mechanism, which is activated when the individual experiences distress. In his view, the goal of attachment responses is to maintain proximity to a significant other, who may assist the person in the process of managing distress and may promote a sense of well-being and security.

The link between the activation of the attachment system and distress arousal led Bowlby to suggest that basic emotions are constructed around attachment experiences. In his terms, the activation of the attachment system usually goes together with anxiety and anger, which are adaptive signals that something is going wrong and some coping action should be taken (Bowlby, 1973). Moreover, the deactivation of this system following distress management may elicit relief, positive feelings, and gratitude toward significant others. If, however, the significant others fail to manage distress, anxiety and anger may become chronic and may lead to a sense of helplessness and detachment. Furthermore, attachment relationships may become by themselves an additional source of distress (Bowlby, 1973, 1988).

On this basis, one can claim that attachment experiences play a major role in determining the habitual affective tone of a person's inner world. On the one hand, interactions with significant others who are available and responsive to one's attachment needs may lead to the experience of more and longer episodes of positive affect, the development of positive feelings toward the world and the self, and the appraisal of anxiety and anger as valued signals for restoring well being. On the other hand, interactions with unavailable and rejecting others may elicit chronic distress, dysfunctional experiences of anxiety and anger, and may create problems around attachment themes.

Bowlby's premises also imply that attachment experiences may be viewed as a major source of individual differences in the way people regulate distress and cope with life adversities. Interactions with available and responsive others may signal that the inborn attachment system is an effective method of affect regulation and may lead people to continue to rely on this system when facing distress and other life problems. In contrast, when people perceive significant others as unavailable and unresponsive, they may learn that inborn attachment behaviors fail to bring the expected relief and that other defensive strategies should be developed and employed. According to Bowlby (1988), these strategies replace the original attachment system. However, they lack the backing of a secure base and the hope that one can rely on the support of significant others.

On this basis, we claim that a basic component of a person's attachment style is the habitual regulatory strategies he or she employs in coping with different sources of distress. The basic hypothesis here is that people differing in attachment style would differ in the strategies of affect regulation they employ while facing stress. These strategies would shape the management of negative emotions and coping with life stressors, and would have meaningful repercussions on the individual's mental health.

The positive attachment experiences of secure persons may create the basis for the formation of a salutatory pattern of reality appraisal. These persons may find out that distress is manageable and external obstacles can be overcome. Moreover, they may learn about the good intentions of others in times of need and about the control they can exert over the course and outcomes of external events. In this way, secure persons could develop optimistic beliefs regarding distress management, a sense of trust in others' responses, and a sense of self-efficacy in dealing with distress (Shaver & Hazan, 1993).

The experience of significant others as a "secure base" also may set the basis for the construction of effective distress management strategies (Mikulincer & Florian, 1998). First, secure persons may find out that acknowledgment and display of distress elicit positive responses from significant others. Second, they learn that their own active responses are instrumental means for bringing relief and managing distress. Third, they may become aware that seeking for the support of others is an effective way of coping. In this way, secure persons would be prone to regulate affect through the basic guidelines of the attachment system: acknowledgment and display of distress, engagement in instrumental actions, and support seeking (Kobak, Cole, Ferenz, & Fleming, 1993; Kobak & Sceery, 1988; Mikulincer & Florian, 1998; Rholes, Simpson, & Grich-Stevens, 1998).

Another important aspect of secure attachment is the construction of reality-tuned affect regulation strategies. Secure people's belief in their skills for dealing with stress may lead them to open themselves to new, even threatening, information (Mikulincer, 1997), and then to develop suitable strategies for dealing with environmental demands. Moreover, their experience of attachment figures as approving may allow them to revise erroneous beliefs without fear of criticism or rejection (Mikulincer, 1997). In this way, secure people could avoid cognitive entrapments derived from the inability to revise these beliefs.

In the case of insecure attachment, the negative and painful experiences with significant others may hinder the normal activation of the attachment system and lead to the adoption of less effective ways of affect regulation (Bowlby, 1988). However, although both insecure types may hold a negative appraisal of reality (Collins, 1996; Collins & Read, 1990), they seem to differ in the ways they manage distress (Kobak et al., 1993; Mikulincer & Florian, 1998; Shaver & Hazan, 1993). In fact, Ainsworth's attachment typology already implies the existence of two antagonistic coping responses. On the one hand, people characterized by the avoidant style appear to adopt a "flight" response in dealing with the unavailability of significant others. On the another hand, people characterized by the anxious-ambivalent style seem to "fight" to elicit others' love, compassion, and support.

The "flight" response of avoidant persons seems to have two facets (Kobak et al., 1993; Mikulincer, 1998; Mikulincer, Orbach, & Iavnieli, 1998). One includes defensive attempts to "deactivate" the attachment system in order to avoid confrontation with attachment related distress (Fraley & Shaver, 1997). These attempts include cognitive and behavioral distancing from others' lack of involvement and interdependence in close relationships, and denial of attachment needs. The second facet consists of compulsive attempts to attain self-reliance (Bowlby, 1973, 1988). Due to the deactivation of the attachment system, avoidant persons may remain without a "secure base." As a result, they may search for comfort within their selves and may believe that they can rely only on themselves in times of need. This facet also involves pursuit of autonomy, control, and individuality as well as avoidance of situations in which they would need others' help.

In our terms, the way avoidant persons deal with attachment insecurity would be generalized to the management of other sources of distress. Their tendency to detach from negative attachment figures would, in general, result in behavioral and cognitive distancing from distress-related cues (Kobak et al., 1993; Mikulincer & Florian, 1998). Moreover, their pursuit of self-reliance may lead them to suppress personal imperfections and weaknesses as a way of preventing the recognition that their own self is a source of distress (Mikulincer, 1998a). As a result, avoidant people would restrict awareness of self-aspects that they do not want to possess, suppress bad thoughts and emotions, inhibit displays of distress, repress painful memories, and attempt to escape from any confrontation with life problems (Mikulincer & Florian, 1998; Shaver & Hazan, 1993).

The way anxious-ambivalent people deal with insecurity implies an "hyperactivation" of the attachment system (Kobak et al., 1993). They attempt to minimize distance from distressing attachment figures and to maximize the "secure base" they can obtain (Mikulincer et al., 1998). This is a "fight" strategy aimed at eliciting others' positive affect and responses via clinging, controlling, and hypervigilant responses. The problem with this strategy is that it may create excessive anxious focus on attachment-related distress and may lead to preoccupation with relationships, anxious demands for proximity, conflictual feelings toward others, fear of rejection, and inability to leave frustrating partners (Brennan & Shaver, 1995; Hazan & Shaver, 1987; Shaver & Hazan, 1993).

In our terms, anxious-ambivalent persons' excessive focus on attachment-related distress would result, in general, in a hyperactivation of distress-related cues. This hyperactivation

may lead people to direct attention to distress in a hypervigilant manner, to mentally ruminate on its causes and meanings, and to deliberate on related negative thoughts, memories,
and emotions. As a result, anxious-ambivalent persons would have free access to negative
emotions and thoughts, would be unable or unwilling to suppress these negative inner
experiences, and therefore might become overwhelmed with negative feelings about the self
and the world (Mikulincer, 1998).

According to the above reasoning, secure attachment can be viewed as an inner psychological resource and a resilience factor, which may foster a constructive attitude toward life
and buffer the psychological distress resulting from the encounter with stressful events. In
contrast, insecure attachment can be viewed as a risk factor, which may increase a person's
vulnerability while facing stress and may obstruct the development of the inner resources
necessary for coping with life stressors and maintaining psychological well-being.

With regard to anxious-ambivalent persons, their regulatory strategies may lead to an
exaggeration of the appraisal of adversities as irreversible and uncontrollable and may impair
the ability to control the arousal and spreading of distress throughout the cognitive system.
As a result, anxious-ambivalent persons may experience an endless and uncontrollable flow of
negative affect, which, in turn, may lead to cognitive disorganization and fragmentation and
may, in certain cases, culminate in psychopathology (Shaver & Hazan, 1993). In the case of
avoidant persons, their regulatory strategies may emphasize the need to rely exclusively on
oneself and the maintenance of distance from attachment and distress cues. Although these
strategies may reduce overt expressions of distress, they may be unable in the long run to
mitigate internalized sources of insecurity and may be shattered upon confrontation with
severe and persistent problems.

In the rest of this chapter, we review data on (1) the way attachment-related regulatory
strategies are manifested in the process of coping with life stressors as well as in the management of emotions, and (2) the repercussions of these strategies on mental health. Most
of the reviewed studies have assessed attachment style via self-report scales (e.g., Hazan &
Shaver's Adult Attachment Scale), which have been developed within a personality and social
psychology context and tap current attachment to significant others. However, there are
some studies that have used the Adult Attachment Interview (Main, Kaplan, & Cassidy,
1985), which is derived from a developmental perspective and taps a person's state of mind
regarding attachment to parents. Importantly, despite these conceptual and methodological differences, similar and coherent patterns of associations between attachment style,
coping, and mental health were found in studies using either self-report scales or the Adult
Attachment Interview.

Adult Attachment Style and Coping with Life Stressors

In this section, we present empirical data on attachment-style differences in the process
of coping with life stressors. Although this process has been analyzed from a wide variety
of theoretical and empirical perspectives, Lazarus and Folkman's (1984) theoretical framework has become during the last decade the most prominent model for conceptualizing coping and stress. In this model, coping responses are sorted into the following

four categories: problem-focused coping, emotion-focused coping, distancing coping, and support seeking.

(1)   Problem-focused coping attempts to channel resources to solve the stress-inducing problem. It consists of a vast array of cognitive and behavioral maneuvers aimed at making changes in the environment and eliminating the external sources of stress. For example, Carver, Scheier, and Weintraub (1989) mentioned four basic problem-focused coping strategies: (1) active coping – procedures to remove obstacles from one's goals; (2) planning – thinking about action strategies and about how to solve the problem; (3) suppression of competing activities – disengagement from other goals and activities that may divert resources away from problem solving; and (4) restraint – holding back actions and avoiding premature decisions. There is extensive evidence that problem-focused coping has beneficial adaptive outcomes (e.g., Epstein & Meier, 1989; McCrae & Costa, 1986).

(2)   Emotion-focused coping attempts to ease inner tension without trying to solve the distress-eliciting problem. It consists of cognitive strategies aimed at understanding and alleviating distress, such as self-preoccupation, self-criticism, mental rumination on distress-related feelings and thoughts, affect amplification, overt displays of distress, and wishful thinking. There is extensive evidence documenting the negative adaptive outcomes of emotion-focused coping, mainly when the stressful situation can be ended by problem-focused responses (e.g., McCrae & Costa, 1984; Mikulincer, 1994). Although emotion-focused coping may help in maintaining emotional balance, an adaptive response still requires active attempts to solve the problem.

(3)   Distancing coping seems to encompass two types of strategies. First, cognitive maneuvers aimed at preventing the intrusion of threatening thoughts into consciousness, such as suppression of painful emotions and thoughts and repression of painful memories (e.g., Carver et al., 1989; Lazarus & Folkman, 1984). Second, behavioral disengagement from the stressful situation by either withdrawing problem-focused efforts or consuming drugs and alcohol (e.g., Carver et al., 1989; Stone & Neale, 1984). Although distancing coping strategies may initially have beneficial adaptive outcomes, in the long run they may have detrimental adaptive effects (Lazarus, 1983; Roth & Cohen, 1986).

(4)   Support seeking consists of responses aimed at maintaining or restoring proximity to a significant other who can help us in coping with stress. According to Lazarus and Folkman (1984), this coping category includes the seeking of love, reassurance, and affection; the search for information, advice, and/or feedback; and the seeking of material aid and services. There is extensive evidence on the positive adaptive outcomes of support seeking (Lazarus & Folkman, 1984).

In examining the above four categories of coping responses, Folkman and Lazarus (1985) developed a self-report scale – the Ways of Coping Checklist, which has been used in hundred of studies around the world. This scale includes items assessing problem-focused coping (e.g., "I try to analyze the problem in order to understand it better"), emotion-focused coping (e.g., "I wish I could change how I feel," "I criticize myself"), distancing coping (e.g., "I try to forget the whole thing"), and support seeking (e.g., "I talk to someone to find out more about the situation"), which can be tailored to specific stressful events. In all the studies we review below, a person's coping responses were assessed through the Ways of Coping Checklist.

In integrating Lazarus and Folkman's (1984) ways of coping with our analysis of attachment-related regulatory strategies, one can easily predict how these strategies would be manifested in the way people cope with life adversities. Secure persons' constructive and optimistic attitude toward life problems would lead them to try to remove the source of stress by employing problem-focused coping strategies and/or by seeking the support of relevant others. Whereas avoidant persons' deactivating strategy would lead them to rely on cognitive and behavioral distancing ways of coping, anxious-ambivalent persons' hyperactivating strategy would lead them to ruminate on their emotional state and then to adopt emotion-focused ways of coping. Moreover, one can predict that the two insecure styles would be reluctant to seek support due to their basic mistrust of others' intentions and responses (Collins, 1996; Shaver & Hazan, 1993). In examining these predictions, we would review studies which have been conducted on three major life areas: coping with military and war-related stressors, coping with pregnancy and motherhood, and coping with separation and loss.

Ways of coping with military and war-related stress

Three major studies have examined the role of attachment style in explaining coping responses to military and war-related stressful events. One study dealt with the reactions of young adults to the stressful experience of Iraqi Scud missile attacks on Israeli cities during the Gulf War (Mikulincer, Florian, & Weller, 1993). Some 140 Israeli university students who lived in cities that either were or were not attacked by missiles were approached two weeks after the end of the Gulf War. They completed the adult attachment style scale (Hazan & Shaver, 1987) and the Ways of Coping Checklist (Folkman & Lazarus, 1985), which was adapted to ways of coping with the missile attacks.

The findings supported the hypothesis that attachment style is a useful construct for explaining individual differences in coping with the missile attack. Secure persons reported having sought more support from relevant others during the missile attacks than insecure persons. Anxious-ambivalent persons were found to report heightened reliance on emotion-focused coping (e.g., ruminating on their own distress, wondering why this happened to them), whereas avoidant persons were found to report heightened reliance on distancing coping (e.g., dismissing the immediate threat, avoiding thinking about their own distress or about the implications of the missile attack).

In another relevant study, Mikulincer and Florian (1995) examined the reactions of young Israeli recruits undergoing a four-month combat training. One should be aware that soldiers who undergo combat training are exposed to stressful experiences, such as long periods of physical exercise and short periods of sleep. Ninety-two young Israeli recruits completed the adult attachment style scale (Hazan & Shaver, 1987) at the beginning of the training. Four months later (one week before ending this training), they completed Folkman and Lazarus's (1985) appraisal and coping measures regarding their current experiences.

The findings partially replicated Mikulincer et al.'s (1993) findings. As expected, anxious-ambivalent soldiers reported more emotion-focused strategies than secure soldiers, and avoidant soldiers reported more distancing coping. However, both secure andanxious-ambivalent persons reported seeking more support than avoidant persons. It may be that anxious-ambivalent persons seek support mainly when they are in intensive interactions with peers who experience the same stress, like combat training. In this case, the sharing of stress with their peers may allow anxious-ambivalent soldiers to talk freely about their worries without feeling any fear of being misunderstood, criticized, or rejected, and, then, to seek social support. In fact, one of the reasons that inhibits anxious-ambivalent persons from support seeking is the fear that others would discover and criticize their helplessness.

The findings also revealed attachment-style differences in the cognitive appraisal of combat training. In line with their basic optimistic attitude, secure soldiers appraised the training in more challenging terms, and appraised themselves as capable of coping with it. In contrast, anxious-ambivalent soldiers appraised the training in more threatening terms and reported a sense of personal inadequacy in dealing with it. This pessimistic pattern may reflect the hyperactivation of the distress cues that anxious-ambivalent soldiers encounter during the combat training. Quite interestingly, avoidant soldiers also appraised the training in threatening terms, but revealed a sense of personal adequacy in dealing with it. This pattern of appraisal may reflect two conflictual facets of avoidant persons' way of affect regulation: their basic insecurity and the compensatory belief in their own self-reliance and personal strength.

In a more recent study, Solomon, Ginzburg, Mikulincer, Neria, and Ohry (1998) examined the association between attachment style of ex-prisoners of war (POWs) and their retrospective accounts of the experience of captivity. Some 164 Israeli ex-POWs of the Yom Kippur War were interviewed 18 years after the war about their personal recollection of the captivity period and completed the adult attachment style scale (Hazan & Shaver, 1987). A content analysis of the ex-POWs' retrospective accounts revealed interesting differences among attachment styles. Compared to insecure ex-POWs, secure ex-POWs reported lower levels of suffering, less helplessness, they felt less abandoned and less hostile toward the army, and relied on more active coping strategies. It is important to note that secure ex-POWs reported having dealt with the helpless nature of captivity by recruiting positive memories or imaginary encounters with others, which may have created a sense of security and served as positive coping models.

The negative experience of insecure ex-POWs seemed to reflect their habitual regulatory strategies. The suffering of anxious-ambivalent ex-POWs was mainly characterized by feelings of abandonment and loss of control, which may reflect their preoccupation with rejection. The negative experience of avoidant ex-POWs was characterized by hostile feelings and reactions toward the army, which can be viewed as a manifestation of their basic mistrust toward non-supportive others.

Ways of coping with pregnancy and motherhood

In the process of becoming a mother, women are exposed to pleasant and challenging experiences together with episodes of worries, anxieties, and uncertainties. In this subsection, we review a series of recent studies dealing with the possible impact of women's attachment style on the ways of coping with several aspects of their motherhood.

A study conducted by Mikulincer and Florian (in press) focused on the process of coping with pregnancy-related stress. In this study, a sample of first-time pregnant Israeli women (N = 30), previously classified according to their attachment style, were followed up during the first, second, and third trimesters of pregnancy. In each one of the trimesters, women answered a self-report scale on their attachment to the fetus (Cranley, 1981) and completed the Ways of Coping Checklist (Folkman & Lazarus, 1985), which was adapted to pregnancy-related problems. The findings indicated that anxious-ambivalent women reported having relied on more emotion-focused coping in dealing with pregnancy-related stress than avoidant and secure women. In addition, avoidant women were found to rely on more distancing coping than secure women, whereas secure women were found to seek more support than other women. It is worth noting that these differences were replicated in the three stages of pregnancy. This finding emphasizes the stable nature of the ways by which each attachment style coped with the demands of pregnancy.

The psychological literature has documented the demands and pressures that the delivery of a newborn may impose on the mother's well-being (e.g., Power & Parke, 1984; Terry, 1991). In a recent chapter, Mikulincer and Florian (1998) cited a study of 80 healthy young women who delivered their first child 2–3 months before the study. All the women completed the adult attachment style scale (Hazan & Shaver, 1987) and Lazarus and Folkman's (1984) appraisal scale, tapping the way they appraised motherhood, and the Ways of Coping Checklist (Folkman & Lazarus, 1985), tapping the strategies they used to deal with motherhood-related tasks. Again, results were in line with the hypothesized strategies of affect regulation that characterize each attachment style. Specifically, secure women appraised the task of being a mother in less threatening terms than anxious-ambivalent women, and reported having used more problem-focused strategies in coping with motherhood tasks. However, the findings did not support the hypothesis that secure persons are more likely to seek support than insecure persons. Interestingly, this is one of the few studies that failed to find the expected attachment-style differences in support seeking. One can only speculate that secure women in Mikulincer and Florian's (1998) study were so engaged in problem-focused activities that they did not feel any urge to seek support and help.

At this point, one may wonder how mothers differing in attachment style react to the birth of an infant who suffers from a physical, life-threatening illness. In an attempt to provide some initial empirical answers to this question, Berant (1998) designed a field study examining the association between the attachment style of mothers of infants with congenital heart disease (CHD) and the pattern of cognitive appraisal and coping with the task of motherhood. In this study, three groups were approached around three months after the birth of an infant: (1) a group of 46 mothers of healthy infants, (2) a group of 53 mothers of infants who had been diagnosed by physicians two weeks previously as suffering from mild CHD, and (3) a group of 47 mothers of infants who had been diagnosed two weeks before as suffering from severe, life-threatening CHD. All the mothers completed the adult attachment style scale (Hazan & Shaver, 1987) and Folkman & Lazarus's (1985) scales tapping appraisal of and coping with motherhood-related tasks.

Whereas the findings regarding cognitive appraisal in the control group were similar to those reported by Mikulincer and Florian (1998), attachment-style differences in appraisal were somewhat different in the two other groups. Among mothers of infants with mild CHD, secure and avoidant mothers appraised motherhood tasks in less threatening terms and themselves as having more control over these tasks than anxious-ambivalent mothers. However, among mothers of infants with severe CHD, only those with secure attachment still viewed their condition as manageable and themselves as capable of coping with it. Both avoidant and anxious-ambivalent mothers appraised their plight as more threatening and viewed themselves as less able to deal with it.

It seems that secure mothers could maintain a positive appraisal even after encountering a severe stressful situation, maintaining a sense of mastery in dealing with the special demands imposed by motherhood. In contrast, anxious-ambivalent mothers showed a basic negative appraisal of their motherhood even when the infant's health condition was not severe. Interestingly, avoidant mothers seem to be the most affected by the infant's medical condition: while they showed a positive appraisal of their motherhood when their infant suffered from mild CHD, they revealed a more pessimistic appraisal when their infant was diagnosed as having a severe, life-threatening problem.

The findings also showed that the three attachment groups differed in the ways in which they coped with motherhood tasks and that these differences depended on the infant's health condition. Secure mothers of both healthy infants and infants having mild CHD tended to rely on support-seeking strategies in coping with motherhood tasks. However, when their infant had severe CHD, secure mothers tended to cope with these tasks by relying on both support-seeking and distancing strategies (e.g., mental suppression of painful thoughts and feelings about the infant's CHD, engagement in distracting thoughts unrelated to the infant's health). The findings are in line with the hypothesis that support seeking is the basic regulatory strategy of secure attachment. They also imply that secure mothers can flexibly employ distancing coping whenever thoughts about the stressful condition can impair functioning and well-being, as in the case of a real threat to the infant's life.

It may be that the suppression of painful thoughts and feelings about the infant's CHD, which was found to be positively associated with the mother's mental health (Berant, 1998), might have provided a moratorium until mothers could grasp the meaning of their predicament. Moreover, this coping strategy may prevent secure mothers from being occupied or preoccupied with pessimistic and distressing thoughts, and, then, may allow them to maintain a positive appraisal of motherhood. As a result, the overwhelming demands of the infant's illness may not discourage secure mothers. Rather, they may be able to mobilize internal and external resources for caring for the baby without feeling any interfering intrusion of negative thoughts.

With regard to anxious-ambivalent mothers, their ways of coping directly reflected their hyperactivating regulatory strategies. In all the three research groups, these mothers reported heightened reliance on emotion-focused strategies and tended to mentally ruminate on their condition regardless of the objective health status of their infants. With regard to avoidant mothers, their habitual deactivating regulatory strategies were only manifested when infants were healthy or had mild CHD. In these cases, they reported heightened reliance on distancing strategies. However, the reported frequency of these strategies was reduced when avoidant mothers had to face an infant's severe health condition. Here, these mothers, like anxious-ambivalent mothers, reported heightened reliance on emotion-focused coping strategies.

The above findings may reflect the fragile nature of the "pseudo-safe" world of avoidant persons. Their habitual confident appraisal of coping abilities and their reliance on distancing coping seems to be sufficient when dealing with daily hassles or minor stressors. However, when facing uncontrollable and persisting stressors, this facade may fade out and the basic insecurity of avoidant persons may become overtly manifested, leading to pessimistic appraisals and the adoption of more ineffective ways of coping.

Ways of coping with interpersonal loss

In the third volume of his classic trilogy, Bowlby (1980) suggested that when people feel that their attachment figures are lost, they may experience an upsurge of attachment needs and their regulatory strategies may be activated in order to adjust to the painful condition. The above ideas were recently examined by Unger (1998), who interviewed 93 middle-aged women who had lost their husband two to five years before. These women filled out the adult attachment style scale (Hazan & Shaver, 1987) and Folkman and Lazarus's (1985) scales tapping cognitive appraisal and coping with widowhood. Findings indicated that secure attachment was significantly related to higher appraisal of one's ability to deal with widowhood and more frequent reliance on problem-focused coping and distancing strategies. Anxious-ambivalent attachment was significantly related to higher appraisal of widowhood in threatening terms, lower appraisal of one's ability to deal with it, and more frequent reliance on emotion-focused coping strategies. The avoidant style was significantly related only to a more frequent reliance on emotion-focused strategies.

It is worth noting that the above pattern of findings is quite similar to that found by Berant (1998). It may be that when facing a severe real-life crisis related to the potential or actual loss of a loved person (e.g., child, spouse), both problem-solving and distancing strategies serve as protective mechanisms, which allow the securely attached person to maintain an adequate level of functioning despite the traumatic circumstances. In contrast, it seems that when encountering a potential or actual loss, avoidant persons' habitual use of repression and suppression is impaired, and they may be driven to focus on their own negative emotions like anxious-ambivalent persons.

The above attachment-style differences also have been found in the emotional and cognitive reactions to another life crisis related to separation and loss – divorce (Birnbaum, Orr, Mikulincer, & Florian, 1997). A sample of 123 Israeli individuals who were involved in a long process of divorce were interviewed in the waiting rooms of the rabbinic divorce court. They filled out the adult attachment style scale (Hazan & Shaver, 1987) and reported on how they appraised and coped with the stressful experience of the divorce. As expected, secure persons appraised themselves as more capable of coping with the divorce and appraised this crisis in less threatening terms than anxious-ambivalent persons. Moreover, anxious-ambivalent persons reported more social withdrawal and more self-defeating thoughts in coping with divorce than secure persons. However, unexpectedly, avoidant persons tended to resemble anxious-ambivalent persons in the way they appraised and coped with the divorce crisis. Specifically, they appraised divorce in more threatening terms and reported more self-defeating thoughts and social withdrawal in coping with it than secure persons.

Secure persons, who handle separations constructively and learn that separation is a solvable episode, seem to react to the reconstruction of this experience as it reappears in the process of divorce with their habitual optimistic and constructive attitudes. In contrast, anxious ambivalent persons tended to appraise divorce as a threat and themselves as being unable to deal with the crisis, and tended to rely on their habitual hyperactivating strategies. Interestingly, the observed reactions of avoidant persons imply that their habitual deactivating strategies prove to be again ineffective in dealing with separation and loss. Divorce may reactivate early unresolved separations from attachment figures and lead to a flood of overwhelming negative feelings, which avoidant persons fail to repress.

Summary

The reviewed data clearly indicate that people varying in attachment style differ in the way they habitually cope with acute and chronic life stressors. Moreover, findings show that these differences seem to be a direct manifestation of the hypothesized regulatory strategies that characterize each attachment style. Findings also indicate that whereas secure and anxious-ambivalent persons' strategies seem to be stable across different levels of stress intensity, avoidant persons' strategies seem to fade under severe stressful circumstances. In these conditions, avoidant persons resemble anxious-ambivalent persons in their reliance on emotion-focused coping. Findings also provide initial evidence about the flexibility and richness of secure persons' ways of coping under severe and persistent stressful events.

Adult Attachment Style and the Management of Negative Emotions

Another hypothesis derived from our conceptualization of attachment-related regulatory strategies is that attachment style would be related to the way people process emotions. On the one hand, secure people would acknowledge negative emotions without being overwhelmed by them and show easy accessibility and well-elaborated processing of them. On the another hand, avoidant people would repress negative emotions and show low accessibility and poor processing of them. For anxious-ambivalent persons, their tendency to ruminate mentally on negative emotional states may prevent the use of repression and increase the chronic accessibility of emotional states as well as the likelihood of experiencing different emotions together. This coping strategy may facilitate the creation of associative links between distinct emotions in the semantic memory network, so that the arousal of one emotion could easily activate other associated emotions. As a result, anxious-ambivalent persons' experience of one particular emotion would be automatically followed by the activation of other emotional states.

In examining the above ideas, Mikulincer and Orbach (1995) conducted a study on the processing of negative emotional memories. Participants completed the adult attachment style scale (Hazan & Shaver, 1987), the Crowne-Marlowe social desirability scale tapping defensiveness and the Taylor Anxiety Scale. People also were asked to recall early experiences in which they felt anger, sadness, anxiety, and happiness, and the time for retrieving a memory was taken as a measure of cognitive accessibility. Then people rated the intensity of dominant and nondominant emotions in each recalled event.

The findings fit the above hypothesis. Avoidant and secure persons scored higher in defensiveness than anxious-ambivalent persons, and the two insecure groups scored higher in anxiety than secure people. That is, while anxious-ambivalent people hyperactivated anxiety and failed to defend themselves against it, avoidant people repress negative thoughts but failed to reduce anxiety, and secure persons were able to defend themselves with minimal anxiety. In the memory task, avoidant people showed the lowest accessibility (highest reaction time) to sadness and anxiety memories, anxious-ambivalent people showed the highest, and secure people were in between them. In addition, anxious-ambivalent people were rated as having experienced stronger emotions in sadness and anxiety memories than avoidant persons. As expected, avoidant persons had difficulties in accessing negative memories and those recalled were characterized by emotional shallowness. In contrast, due to the hyperactivation of distress cues, anxious-ambivalent people had easy accessibility to negative memories and to their related emotions.

The emotional architecture of secure persons' memories indicated a highly differentiated pattern: they rated dominant emotions (sadness in a sad memory) as highly intense and nondominant emotions (anger in a sad memory) as far less intense. These persons may acknowledge distress while controlling for its spreading to other emotions. Anxious-ambivalent people revealed a non-differentiated emotional architecture: They rated both dominant and non-dominant emotions as highly intense. These persons seem to be unable or unwilling to limit the spreading of distress to other emotions. In contrast, avoidant people rated both dominant and nondominant emotions as far less intense than secure persons. As expected, avoidant people inhibited the processing of negative memories and the spreading of the dominant emotional tone.

Following the same line of research, Mikulincer (1998b) conducted two studies dealing with the experience of anger. In Study 1, participants completed the adult attachment style scale (Hazan & Shaver, 1987) and the Multidimensional Anger Inventory (Siegel, 1986) tapping anger-proneness, hostility, mental rumination over anger feelings (anger-in), and overt expression of anger (anger-out). They also completed the Experience of Anger Scale (Averill, 1982). People recalled an anger event and reported the control they exerted over anger as well as goals (constructive, malevolent), responses (adaptive, escapist, aggressive), and emotions they felt in that episode (positive, negative).

Findings indicated that anxious-ambivalent persons scored higher in anger proneness, anger-in, and displaced aggression than other persons; avoidant persons reported higher hostility and more escapist responses; and secure persons scored higher in anger-out, constructive goals, adaptive responses, and positive affect. Moreover, secure and avoidant people reported more anger control than anxious-ambivalent persons.

In Study 2, participants were exposed to hypothetical anger-eliciting scenarios differing in the intentions of a romantic partner: hostile, ambiguous, non-hostile. Then they rated their anger feelings and the extent to which partners were hostile. In addition, data were collected on changes in heart rate (a sign of physiological arousal).

Overall, anxious-ambivalent persons reported more anger than other persons, and anxious-ambivalent and avoidant people showed higher heart rate changes and higher hostility attributions than secure people. However, while avoidant persons showed relatively high hostility attributions and low anger in the three scenarios, secure persons reacted with more hostility attribution and anger to the hostile scene than to the other scenes. Anxious-ambivalent persons reacted with more hostility attribution and anger to hostile and ambiguous scenes.

Taken as a whole, secure persons' experience of anger fits the guidelines of the attachment system: they acknowledged physiological signs of anger, adopted constructive goals aimed at repairing the relationship with the anger instigator, engaged in adaptive problem-solving actions, expressed anger outward in a controlled and non-hostile way, and experienced positive affect. In addition, they tended to attribute hostility to another person only when there were clear contextual cues. That is, for these persons, anger arousal seems to depend on a rational analysis of the situation and it seems to be a trigger for adaptive and constructive actions.

The anger experience of anxious-ambivalent people may result from their hyperactivating strategy: they tended to report high levels of anger-proneness and to react with strong anger feelings. This strategy also was manifested in the tendency of anxious-ambivalent persons to ruminate on anger feelings, to allow uncontrollable access to anger and negative affect, and to appraise ambiguous stimuli as hostile. As a result, anger may become an interfering emotion, which may overwhelm the cognitive system and draw resources away from adaptive actions.

Avoidant persons' deactivating strategy seems to produce dissociated anger. While avoidant persons did not report intense anger, they still revealed intense physiological signs of anger, intense hostility, and an undifferentiated tendency to attribute hostility to other persons. A dissociated attitude was also manifested in avoidant persons' tendency to enact escapist responses, which diffuse the conscious experience of anger feelings without solving the problem that elicited the anger. These attempts may leave avoidant persons unaware of their own anger, full of paranoid suspicions and hostile feelings, and unable to reduce tension.

Adult Attachment Style, Mental Health, and Psychopathology

Bowlby (1973, 1988) has emphasized the important role of the attachment system for the normal and abnormal development of personality and social behavior. Fitting these ideas, several studies have reported consistent associations between adult attachment style and mental health (e.g., Brennan, Shaver, & Tobey, 1991, Brennan & Shaver, 1995; Mickelson, Kessler, & Shaver, 1997). In all these studies, secure attachment seems to be a crucial inner resource that facilitates adjustment and well-being, whereas insecure attachment seems to act as a risk factor for the development of distress and maladjustment. In this section, we review empirical data that examine the various facets of the attachment–mental health association.

Adult attachment style and psychological well-being

In a series of studies conducted in our laboratory, we have assessed the association between attachment style and mental health in different populations (Berant, 1998; Birnbaum et al., 1997; Mikulincer & Florian, 1998, in press; Unger, 1998). In all these studies, we have employed a well-validated measure of mental health: the Mental Health Inventory (MHI, Veit & Ware, 1983). This scale taps two separate, but related, facets of mental health (psychological well-being and psychological distress), and possesses a robust psychometric basis (Veit & Ware, 1983). Specifically, it includes 14 items tapping psychological well-being (e.g., life satisfaction, engagement in enjoyable activities) and 24 which tap psychological distress (e.g., sadness, nervousness).

Without exception, all the above studies have shown that secure attachment is positively associated with well-being and negatively related to distress. In contrast, anxious-ambivalent attachment reveals an inverse relationship with well-being and a positive association with distress. These associations have been found both in so-called "normal" community samples and in samples of people who were under stressful conditions that demanded immediate readjustment (e.g., divorce, the birth of an infant suffering from CHD, widowhood). They have been also found in both cross-sectional and longitudinal prospective designs.

Avoidant attachment seemed to have differential associations with mental health, depending on the presence of stressful circumstances. Most of the above studies have found no significant association between avoidant attachment and mental health in community samples. However, under stressful circumstances, avoidant attachment has been found to be inversely related to well-being and positively associated with distress. In one longitudinal study assessing the mental health of mothers whose babies were born with severe CHD (Berant, 1998), avoidant attachment (measured immediately following the diagnosis of the dysfunction) was more strongly related to high psychological distress (measured one year later) than anxious-ambivalent attachment.

The above pattern of findings seems to be in line with previously reviewed findings on avoidant persons' ways of coping with stressful events. In normal circumstances, the deactivation strategy of these people seems to help them to maintain adequate levels of well-being. However, under persistent stressful conditions, this strategy seems to collapse and avoidant persons tend to reveal similar patterns of coping and distress to anxious-ambivalent persons.

Two studies also provide initial support for the hypothesis that attachment-style differences in mental health may result from the activation of habitual regulatory strategies (Berant, 1998; Birnbaum et al., 1997). In these studies, structural analyses have shown that the association between attachment styles and mental health under stressful circumstances was mediated by cognitive appraisal and ways of coping. Specifically, security in attachment was associated with less distress and more well-being via the high appraisal of one's ability to cope with the stressor and a tendency to rely on support seeking. Avoidant attachment was associated with more distress via the appraisal of the stressful circumstance in threatening terms and reliance on more emotion-focused coping. Anxious-ambivalent attachment was related to more distress via the low appraisal of one's abilities to cope with the stressor and reliance on more emotion-focused coping.

Adult attachment style and affective disorders

Several studies have documented a consistent pattern of relationship between attachment style and depressive symptomatology. In a series of studies, Kobak and his colleagues (Cole-Detke & Kobak, 1996; Kobak & Ferenz-Gillies, 1995; Kobak, Sudler, & Gamble, 1991) assessed attachment styles and regulatory strategies, using the Adult Attachment Interview (Main et al., 1985), and measured depressive symptoms in adolescents. Findings indicated that anxious-ambivalent attachment was positively associated with the report of depressive symptoms. This was replicated in cross-sectional and prospective analyses. Accordingly, the more the adolescent relied on hyperactivation strategies of affect regulation, the more depressive symptoms they tended to report. Findings also indicated that depressive symptoms in adolescence were positively related to cognitive and behavioral aspects of the anxious-ambivalent style, such as appraisal of mothers as unavailable, expressions of anger toward parents, exaggerated processing of attachment-related worries, and lack of autonomy in communication patterns with mothers (Cole-Detke & Kobak, 1996; Kobak & Ferenz-Gillies, 1995).

Another group of studies conceptually replicated the association described above between anxious-ambivalent attachment and depression in adult samples and using self-report scales of attachment styles (Brennan & Shaver, 1995; Carnelley, Pietromonaco, & Jaffe, 1994; Roberts, Gotlib, & Kassel, 1996; Kennedy, Malowney, & McIntosh, 1996; Mikulincer et al., 1993; Pearson, Cohn, Cowan, & Cowan, 1994). Moreover, some of these studies have provided evidence about the mediating factors that may underlie this association. For example, Roberts et al. (1996) found that dysfunctional attitudes (negative conceptions of the self, world, and future) and low self-esteem seem to mediate between insecure attachment and depressive symptomatology. Accordingly, Kennedy et al. (1996) found that the association between anxious-ambivalent attachment style and depression also appears to be mediated by mental rumination on negative thoughts and memories.

It is worth noting that most of the studies have not found significant association between avoidant attachment and depressive symptomatology. However, one study, which differentiated between two kinds of depression, made some interesting findings about such an association (Zuroff & Fitzpatrick, 1995). Specifically, whereas anxious-ambivalent attachment was positively related to anaclitic depression (overdependence, lack of autonomy), avoidant attachment was positively related to self-critical depression (perfectionism, self-punishment, self-criticism). That is, avoidant attachment appears to be related to depressive symptoms of perfectionism and unachievable standards. This conclusion is in line with Mikulincer's (1995) finding that avoidant persons showed high levels of discrepancies between the way they perceive themselves and their self-standards.

Adult attachment style and severe psychopathology

Insecure styles also seem to be related to severe types of psychopathology, such as personality disorders – rigid and maladaptive patterns of relating to other people, situations, and events (Halgin & Whitbourne, 1994). In a recent study, Tweed and Dutton (1996) found positive correlations between self-reports of anxious-ambivalent attachment style and high scores in scales tapping the following personality disorders:

1 borderline personality disorder (extreme fluctuations in mood, unstable interpersonal relationships, and negative self-image);
2 paranoid personality disorder (suspiciousness about others' intentions and fear of being persecuted or harassed);
3 passive-aggressive personality disorder (angry feelings that are expressed indirectly rather than openly);
4 avoidant personality disorder (fear of being involved in close relationships and terror of being publicly embarrassed);
5 antisocial personality disorder (lack of regard for social norms and rules); and
6 schizotypical personality disorder (indifference to social relationships and a very limited range of emotional expression).

Following the same line of research, Williams and Schill (1993, 1994) found a positive relationship between self-reports of anxious-ambivalent attachment and cognitive and behavioral signs of self-defeating personality disorder (a tendency to avoid gratification, to undermine one's interests, and to choose suffering). Lamentably, these studies did not provide any data on the psychological mechanisms that underlie the associations between anxious-ambivalent attachment style and personality disorders. However, one can see that basic facets of this style (mood fluctuations, negative self-image, worries about rejection and abandonment, mistrust of others' intentions) are also the definitional components of the above personality disorders.

Additional studies have found that avoidant attachment style was positively related to both dissociative disorders (Ogawa, Sroufe, Weinfield, Carlson, & Egeland, 1997) and eating disorders (Cole-Detke & Kobak, 1996). These findings may reflect avoidant persons' deactivation strategy, which may lead to fragmentation of the self (Mikulincer, 1995) and the expression of overwhelming distress through more somatic symptomatology (Mikulincer et al., 1993).

It is important to note that studies that were conducted on clinical hospitalized samples have found a very similar pattern of findings. In these cases, the two types of insecure attachment have been found to be positively related to the severity of borderline and schizophrenic symptoms (Fonagy et al., 1996; Patrick, Hobson, Castle, & Howard, 1994; Wilson & Constanzo, 1996). In addition, Fonagy et al. (1996) found a high frequency of random fluctuations between anxious-ambivalent and avoidant styles, unresolved conflicts around attachment themes, and memories of childhood abuse. All these cognitive responses have been conceptualized by Main et al. (1985) as signs of a disorganized attachment style and severe psychopathology.

Concluding Remarks

An overall look at the reviewed studies indicates the importance of adult attachment style as a key factor in coping with life stressors, managing negative emotions, and maintaining an adequate level of mental health. Specifically, secure persons seem to be characterized by optimistic and constructive regulatory strategies, which have been manifested in reliance on problem solving and support seeking as well as in the maintenance of an adequate level of mental health even in stressful circumstances. Avoidant persons seem to be characterized by deactivating strategies, which have been manifested in reliance on distancing coping, repression, and dissociation as well as in the failure to maintain well-being in times of stress. Anxious-ambivalent persons seem to be characterized by hyperactivating strategies, which have been found to be manifested in reliance on emotion-focused coping and ruminative thinking, inability to control the flow of negative emotions, and failure to maintain psychological well-being even in the absence of any recognizable stressful event.

The findings reviewed above clearly indicate that secure attachment seems to serve as a resilience factor that, even in times of stress, prevents the development of psychopathology and maintains high levels of well-being. In our terms, this adaptational advantage seems to result from three major sources. The first is secure people's optimistic attitude toward life, their basic trust of the world, and their tendency to seek support from others in times of need (Collins & Read, 1990). The second source may be the positive view secure persons have of themselves, their ability to organize experiences into differentiated self-schemata, and the coherence of their self-structure (Mikulincer, 1995). The third possible source of resilience might be secure persons' open, flexible, and positive attitude toward information processing – high tolerance for unpredictability, disorder, and ambiguity, reluctance to endorse rigid beliefs, and a tendency to integrate new evidence within cognitive structures when making social judgments (Mikulincer, 1997).

In contrast, the two insecure attachment styles seem to be a risk factor for poor mental health and sometimes for the development of psychopathology. For anxious-ambivalent persons, there is a danger that their hyperactivating strategies could culminate in chronic emotional overwhelming and mental disorganization and lead to poor mental health even during regular life circumstances. For avoidant persons, their deactivating strategies may put them at risk mainly when they encounter severe and persistent life stressors. In fact, avoidant persons may have the required abilities to endure minor hassles and stressors and to maintain a certain level of mental health in everyday life.

The studies reviewed above are only a first step in delineating attachment-related strategies of affect regulation. Research should examine how these strategies affect non-attachment behaviors and processes of attention, memory, reasoning, and language. In fact, an affect regulation approach expands attachment research beyond dyadic relationships and highlights the central role the attachment system may play in explaining individual differences in broad areas of adult life.

Research should also deal with questions that an affect regulation approach arises. First, why do negative attachment experiences evolve into deactivating strategies in some cases and into hyperactivating strategies in others? In this context, studies should adopt a multifactorial approach and examine the contribution of temperamental factors, family dynamic dimensions, parental personality, and other relationships within and out of the family of origin to adult attachment style. Second, research should examine the effectiveness of attachment-related strategies, to reveal those conditions in which deactivating or hyperactivating strategies are effective in maintaining mental health, and to explore the mechanisms that underlie secure persons' strategies (e.g., cognitive flexibility, emotional intelligence). Third, research should attempt to deal with other typologies of adult attachment, such as Bartholomew and Horowitz's (1991) distinction of dismissing and fearful avoidance. In our terms, the dismissing type may reflect the habitual way by which avoidant people regulate affect, whereas the fearful type may reflect the failure of this defensive armour due to extreme negative attachment history or current stressful events.

Finally, our conceptualization of attachment-related strategies of affect regulation has important implications for attachment-centered psychotherapy. In our terms, psychotherapy has two main tasks: (1) to work through negative attachment history and ineffective strategies of affect regulation, and (2) to provide patients with a "secure base" that may allow them to rediscover the basic guidelines of the attachment system and to heighten confidence in their biological potential for adaptation. In this context, patients should recover the sense of hope and faith implicit in the attachment system. In fact, infants' automatic activation of attachment behavior upon signals of distress implies the existence of a basic hope that there will be someone who will respond to our cry for help. Maybe this hope is the basic human potential that, after being fulfilled through positive experiences with responsive caregivers and consolidated in secure attachment, allows us to confront life's adversities and develop our unique personality.

REFERENCES

Ainsworth, M. D. S., Blehar, M. C., Waters, E., & Wall, S. (1978). *Patterns of attachment: A psychological study of the strange situation*. Hillsdale, NJ: Erlbaum.

Averill, J. R. (1982). *Anger and aggression: An essay on emotion*. New York: Springer-Verlag.

Bartholomew, K., & Horowitz, L. M. (1991). Attachment styles among young adults: A test of a four category model. *Journal of Personality and Social Psychology, 61*, 226–244.

Berant, E. (1998). *The contribution of adult attachment style to women's coping and adjustment with the birth of a child with cardiac problems*. Unpublished PhD dissertation. Bar-Ilan University.

Birnbaum, G., Orr, I., Mikulincer, M., & Florian, V. (1997). When marriage breaks up: Does attachment style contribute to coping and mental health? *Journal of Social and Personal Relationships, 14*, 643–654.

Bowlby, J. (1969). *Attachment and loss: Attachment*. New York: Basic Books.

Bowlby, J. (1973). *Attachment and loss: Separation, anxiety and anger*. New York: Basic Books.

Bowlby, J. (1980). *Attachment and loss: Sadness and depression*. New York: Basic Books.

Bowlby, J. (1988). *A secure base: Clinical applications of attachment theory*. London: Routledge.

Brennan, K. A., & Shaver, P. R. (1995). Dimensions of adult attachment, affect regulation, and romantic relationship functioning. *Personality and Social Psychology Bulletin, 21*, 267–283.

Brennan, K. A., Shaver, P. R., & Tobey, A. E. (1991). Attachment styles, gender, and parental problem drinking. *Journal of Social and Personal Relationships, 8*, 451–466.

Carnelley, K. B., Pietromonaco, P. R., & Jaffe, K. (1994). Depression, working models of others, and relationship functioning. *Journal of Personality and Social Psychology, 66*, 127–140.

Carver, C. S., Scheier, M. F., & Weintraub, J. K. (1989). Assessing coping strategies: A theoretically-based approach. *Journal of Personality and Social Psychology, 56*, 267–283.

Cole-Detke, H., & Kobak, R. (1996). Attachment processes in eating disorder and depression. *Journal of Consulting and Clinical Psychology, 64*, 282–290.

Collins, N. L. (1996). Working models of attachment: Implications for explanation, emotion, and behavior. *Journal of Personality and Social Psychology, 71*, 810–832.

Collins, N. L., & Read, S. J. (1990). Adult attachment, working models, and relationship quality in dating couples. *Journal of Personality and Social Psychology, 58,* 644–663.

Cranley, M. S. (1981). Development of a tool for the measurement of maternal attachment during pregnancy. *Nursing Research, 30,* 281–284.

Epstein, S., & Meier, P. (1989). Constructive thinking: A broad coping variable with specific components. *Journal of Personality and Social Psychology, 57,* 332–350.

Feeney, J. A., & Noller, P. (1990). Attachment style as a predictor of adult romantic relationships. *Journal of Personality and Social Psychology, 58,* 281–291.

Folkman, S., & Lazarus, R. S. (1985). If it changes it must be a process: Study of emotion and coping during three stages of a college examination. *Journal of Personality and Social Psychology, 48,* 150–170.

Fonagy, P., Leigh, T., Steele, M., Steele, H., Kennedy, R., Mattoon, G., Target, M., & Gerber, A. (1996). The relationship of attachment status, psychiatric classification, and response to psychotherapy. *Journal of Consulting and Clinical Psychology, 64,* 22–31.

Fraley, R. C., & Shaver, P. R. (1997). Adult attachment and the suppression of unwanted thoughts. *Journal of Personality and Social Psychology, 73,* 1080–1091.

Halgin, R. P., & Whitbourne, S. K. (1994). *Abnormal psychology.* Fort Worth, TX: Harcourt Brace.

Hazan, C., & Shaver, P. (1987). Romantic love conceptualized as an attachment process. *Journal of Personality and Social Psychology, 52,* 511–524.

Kennedy, J. H., Malowney, C. L., & McIntosh, W. D. (1996). *Relationships among attachment style, rumination, self-esteem, and depressive affect.* Poster presented at the annual meeting of the American Psychological Association, Toronto, Canada.

Kirkpatrick, L. A., & Davis, K. E. (1994). Attachment style, gender, and relationship stability: A longitudinal analysis. *Journal of Personality and Social Psychology, 66,* 502–512.

Kobak, R. R., Cole, H. E., Ferenz, G. R., & Fleming, W. S. (1993). Attachment and emotion regulation during mother teen problem solving: A control theory analysis. *Child Development 64,* 231–245.

Kobak, R., & Ferenz-Gillies, R. (1995). Emotion regulation and depressive symptoms during adolescence: A functionalist perspective. *Development and Psychopathology, 7,* 183–192.

Kobak, R. R., & Hazan, C. (1991). Attachment in marriage: Effects of security and accuracy of working models. *Journal of Personality and Social Psychology, 60,* 861–869.

Kobak, R. R., & Sceery, A. (1988). Attachment in late adolescence: Working models, affect regulation, and representations of self and others. *Child Development, 59,* 135–146.

Kobak, R. R., Sudler, N., & Gamble, W. (1991). Attachment and depressive symptoms during adolescence: A developmental pathways analysis. *Development and Psychopathology, 3,* 461–474.

Lazarus, R. S. (1983). The costs and benefits of denial. In Breznitz, S. (Ed.), *The denial of stress* (pp. 1–30). New York: International Universities Press.

Lazarus, R. S., & Folkman, S. (1984). *Stress, appraisal, and coping.* New York: Springer.

Main, M., Kaplan, N., & Cassidy, J. (1985). Security in infancy, childhood, and adulthood: A move to level of representation. *Monographs of the Society for Research in Child Development, 50,* 66–104.

McCrae, R. R., & Costa, R. T. (1986). Personality, coping, and coping-effectiveness in an adult sample. *Journal of Personality, 54,* 385–405.

Mickelson, K. D., Kessler, R. C., & Shaver, P. R. (1997). Adult attachment in a nationally representative sample. *Journal of Personality and Social Psychology, 73,* 1092–1106.

Mikulincer, M. (1994). *Human learned helplessness: A coping paradigm.* New York: Plenum.

Mikulincer, M. (1995). Attachment style and the mental representation of the self. *Journal of Personality and Social Psychology, 69,* 1203–1215.

Mikulincer, M. (1997). Adult attachment style and information processing: Individual differences in curiosity and cognitive closure. *Journal of Personality and Social Psychology, 72,* 1217–1230.

Mikulincer, M. (1998a). Adult attachment style and affect regulation: Strategic variations in self-appraisals. *Journal of Personality and Social Psychology, 75*, 420–435.

Mikulincer, M. (1998b). Adult attachment style and individual differences in functional versus dysfunctional experiences of anger. *Journal of Personality and Social Psychology, 74*, 513–524.

Mikulincer, M., & Florian, V. (1995). Appraisal of and coping with a real life stressful situation: The contribution of attachment styles. *Personality and Social Psychology Bulletin, 21*, 406–414.

Mikulincer, M., & Florian, V. (1998). The relationship between adult attachment styles and emotional and cognitive reactions to stressful events. In J. A. Simpson & W. S. Rholes (Eds.), *Attachment theory and close relationships* (pp. 143–165). New York: Guilford Press.

Mikulincer, M., & Florian, V. (in press). Maternal–fetal bonding, coping strategies, and mental health during pregnancy: The contribution of attachment style. *Journal of Social and Clinical Psychology.*

Mikulincer, M., Florian, V., & Weller, A. (1993). Attachment styles, coping strategies, and posttraumatic psychological distress: The impact of the Gulf War in Israel. *Journal of Personality and Social Psychology, 64*, 817–826.

Mikulincer, M., & Nachshon, O. (1991). Attachment styles and patterns of self disclosure. *Journal of Personality and Social Psychology, 61*, 321–331.

Mikulincer, M., & Orbach, I. (1995). Attachment styles and repressive defensiveness: The accessibility and architecture of affective memories. *Journal of Personality and Social Psychology, 68*, 917–925.

Mikulincer, M., Orbach, I., & Iavnieli, D. (1998). Adult attachment style and affect regulation: Strategic variations in subjective self-other similarity. *Journal of Personality and Social Psychology, 75*, 436–448.

Ogawa, J. R., Sroufe, A., Weinfield, N. S., Carlson, E. A., & Egeland, B. (1997). Development and the fragmented self: Longitudinal study of dissociative symptomatology in a nonclinical sample. *Development and Psychopathology, 9*, 855–879.

Patrick, M., Hobson, R. P., Castle, D., & Howard, R. (1994). Personality disorder and the mental representation of early social experience. *Development and Psychopathology, 6*, 375–388.

Pearson, J. L., Cohn, D. A., Cowan, P. A., & Cowan, C. P. (1994). Earned and continuous security in adult attachment: Relation to depressive symptomatology and parenting style. *Development and Psychopathology, 6*, 359–373.

Power, T. G., & Parke, R. D. (1984). Social network factors and the transition to parenthood. *Sex Roles, 10*, 949–972.

Rholes, W. S., Simpson, J. A., & Grich-Stevens, J. (1998). Attachment orientations, social support, and conflict resolution in close relationships. In J. A. Simpson & W. S. Rholes (Eds.), *Attachment theory and close relationships* (pp. 166–188). New York: Guilford Press.

Roberts, J. E., Gotlib, I. H., & Kassel, J. D. (1996). Adult attachment security and symptoms of depression: The mediating roles of dysfunctional attitudes and low self-esteem. *Journal of Personality and Social Psychology, 70*, 310–320.

Roth, S., & Cohen, L. J. (1986). Approach, avoidance, and coping with stress. *American Psychologist, 41*, 813–819.

Shaver, P. R., & Hazan, C. (1993). Adult romantic attachment: Theory and evidence. In D. Perlman & W. Jones (Eds.), *Advances in personal relationships* (Vol. 4, pp. 29–70). London: Jessica Kingsley.

Siegel, J. M. (1986). The multidimensional anger inventory. *Journal of Personality and Social Psychology, 51*, 191–200.

Solomon, Z., Ginzburg, K., Mikulincer, M., Neria, Y., & Ohry, U. (1998). Attachment style and long-term adjustment to captivity in war. *European Journal of Personality, 12*, 271–285.

Stone, A. A., & Neale, J. M. (1984). New measure of daily coping: Development and preliminary results. *Journal of Personality and Social Psychology, 46*, 892–906.

Terry, D. J. (1991). Stress, coping, and adaptation to new parenthood. *Journal of Social and Personal Relationships, 8,* 527–547.

Tweed, R. G., & Dutton, D. G. (1996). *The relationship of attachment style to the axis II Personality Disorders.* Poster presented at the annual meeting of the American Psychological Association, Toronto, Canada.

Unger, L. (1998). *Personality and adjustment to widowhood.* Unpublished PhD dissertation. Bar-Ilan University

Veit, C. T., & Ware, J. E. (1983). The structure of psychological stress and well-being in general populations. *Journal of Consulting and Clinical Psychology, 51,* 730–742.

Williams, D., & Schill, T. (1993). Attachment histories for people with characteristics of self defeating personality. *Psychological Reports, 73,* 1232–1234.

Williams, D., & Schill, T. (1994). Adult attachment, love styles, and self defeating personality characteristics. *Psychological Reports, 75,* 31–34.

Wilson, J. S., & Constanzo, P. R. (1996). A preliminary study of attachment, attention, and schizotypy in early adulthood. *Journal of Personality and Social Psychology, 15,* 231–260.

Zuroff, D. C., & Fitzpatrick, D. K. (1995). Depressive personality styles: Implications for adult attachment. *Personality and Individual Differences, 18,* 253–265.

CHAPTER THREE

Marital Therapy and Social Psychology: Will We Choose Explicit Partnership or Cryptomnesia?

Steven R. H. Beach and Frank D. Fincham

How can social psychological research contribute to the development of increasingly powerful marital therapies? This question is of interest to both social psychologists and clinical researchers. The natural partnership between social and clinical psychology has a long history (cf. Morton Prince and Floyd Allport's establishment of *Journal of Abnormal and Social Psychology* in 1921) and has been remarked on many times (e.g., Brehm, 1976; Kanfer & Schefft, 1988; Snyder & Forsyth, 1991 among many others). However, in the marital area it is a partnership that has been strained for several years by the view of many marital therapy researchers that theory may be irrelevant to the advancement of treatment efficacy. At the same time, the partnership may be strained to the extent that social psychological researchers have not kept up with recent changes in the marital area, leading their commentary to miss the mark in some cases. Because the partnership between social psychology and marital therapy research is one that neither side can afford to abandon, it is prudent to examine carefully the view that theory is irrelevant to clinical progress, and to provide updated information about current developments in the field of marital therapy.

Agenda and Rationale

The chapter begins by situating our discussion in a broader literature on the interface between social and clinical psychology. We then consider the role of social psychology in the

We would like to express our appreciation to Richard Marsh and Benjamin Karney for helpful suggestions regarding this chapter. Work on the chapter was supported, in part, by a grant from the National Science Foundation award to Steven R. H. Beach and by a grant from the Templeton Foundation awarded to Frank Fincham and Steven R. H. Beach.

origins and development of Behavioral Marital Therapy (BMT). In doing so, we identify developments that led to some of its more prominent offspring (e.g., Integrative Couple Therapy (ICT), Jacobson & Christensen, 1996; Cognitive-Behavioral Marital Therapy (CBMT), Baucom & Epstein, 1990; Prevention and Relationship Enhancement Program (PREP), Markman, Stanley, & Blumberg, 1994). However, because Integrative Couple Therapy is the most recent development, and because it may be of particular interest to social psychologists, we emphasize ICT in our historical discussion. Next, we turn to the phenomenon of cryptomnesia or unconscious plagiarism (Marsh, Landau, & Hicks, 1996) to explain the phenomenology of clinical innovation and the perplexingly common view that basic research and theory do not help applied researchers and clinicians. Finally, in looking towards the future, we examine how two different perspectives, attachment theory and goal theory, might facilitate interplay between social psychology and marital therapy.

We utilize the literature on marital therapy to inform our discussion of the interplay between clinical practice and social psychology because marital relationships provide a proto-type of close relationships for which therapies are available and relatively well developed. Accordingly, a focus on marital therapy allows for full exploration of the social–clinical interface in an arena well studied by both subdisciplines.

Before turning to our task, we need to address the question of whether focusing on BMT and its offspring is overly restrictive given the basic equivalence in outcome of several approaches to marital therapy (see Baucom, Shoham, Mueser, Daiuto, & Stickle, 1998). However, limiting our focus to BMT and recent developments has several advantages. First, BMT's relatively clear boundaries allow more precise discussion of historical events. Second, because BMT has grown up in an academic environment, the citation trail within the field, while far from perfect, provides a foundation for speculation about the origin of ideas and the timeline for advances. Finally, a careful case study of BMT is ideal for our purposes because the debate over the role of theory has been raised explicitly by several BMT leaders (e.g., Jacobson's preface to Jacobson & Christensen, 1996, p. viii; Markman, Notarius, Stephen, & Smith, 1981).

Accordingly, we can use the special case of BMT and its offspring to provide for social psychologists a window on the historical and psychological processes that lead clinical psy-chologists to engage in rhetorical practices that have baffled social psychologists over the years. To the extent that this "anthropological" examination is successful, it should accom-plish two important goals. First, it should demonstrate to social psychologists that they have an important role to play in the continuing development of marital therapy and alert them to particular areas of potential interest. Second, it should demonstrate the need to be skeptical in evaluating the self-reports of marital therapy researchers when they claim independence from social psychology. At the same time, we hope this examination may help marital therapy researchers reclaim a theoretical foundation for their research. Parenthetically, we believe there is considerable opportunity for positive bi-directional influence between social psychological research and research on marital therapy. We focus on one direction of influence, that from social psychology to marital therapy, because this aspect of the rela-tionship has not been well documented in the past. As a result, the literature on marital therapy is awash with mythological accounts that may be destructive of future progress in the marital area.

The Broader Social–Clinical Interface

Even among clinical researchers who view basic research as a source of creative inspiration, there may be limited enthusiasm for a continuing interface between basic and applied research once a set of techniques has been generated. As a consequence, there are many possible positions regarding the appropriate relationship between basic research on personal relationships and the development of increasingly powerful marital therapies. For example, one common position in the broader clinical literature is that good theory may lead to innovation, but that the subsequent process of refining and developing the intervention for purposes of dissemination is better viewed as a-theoretical (see the Agras & Berkowitz, 1980, model).

The shedding of theoretical underpinnings can be viewed as necessary and important in that a transition from "theory-laden" to "theory-independent" intervention allows for the emergence of a technically "eclectic" approach to psychotherapy (see Beutler & Consoli, 1992). This position therefore implies a split between basic and applied research as a therapeutic intervention matures. It further suggests that this split should not be alarming. Indeed, recent writings on the relationship between outcome research and clinical practice (e.g., Nathan & Gorman, 1998; see also Barlow & Hofmann, 1997), show that variants of this view have become normative within the field of behavior therapy and are closely tied to the movement to disseminate empirically supported treatment (see Chambless & Hollon, 1998).

Some variants of the Agras and Berkowitz (1980) model even suggest a destructive role for theory should it be retained too long. For example, it has been argued that theory may sometimes be problematic in that it blocks openness to the results of outcome research and so may interfere with the dissemination of effective therapies (Goldfried, 1980). In particular, rigid adherence to theory has been viewed as being responsible for the resistance of therapists to new and better forms of therapy. This view suggests that after an intervention is well specified, one should rapidly eschew theory.

Perry London (1972), the first to propose technical eclecticism, argued that the first issue for applied researchers was not theoretical but rather factual, "do they [the interventions] work? On whom? When? The how and why come later." From this perspective, theory development is always secondary to the identification of effective therapies, and the identification of effective therapy can be done a-theoretically. Indeed, the recently adopted standards for "Empirically Supported Therapy" (Chambless & Hollon, 1998) make no mention of the viability of the theoretical underpinnings of an approach. Accordingly, the current standard for empirically supported intervention appears to assume a clean break between the context of discovery and the context of application. There is no emphasis on the need to examine or support the theoretical underpinnings of a particular intervention approach as part of the empirical validation process.

The Agras and Berkowitz (1980) model also posits that careful "clinical observation" may represent an alternative to basic research and theory development. This has typically been viewed as an innocuous recognition of the important role of active clinician-researchers in generating new techniques (e.g., Beck and Ellis in the development of cognitive therapy; or Stuart, Weiss, Greenberg, Wile in the marital area). However, an emphasis on the role of clinical observation in generating clinical advances becomes anti-theoretical if it is taken to imply that such clinical observations are "a-theoretical." That is, if most, or even many of the innovations we now view as clinical advances resulted when persons, isolated from developments in basic research, reacted to the clinical processes they saw in front of them, this could suggest that basic research in social psychology is irrelevant to clinical advancement.

Comment

No doubt many social psychologists view with some bemusement the assertion that a technique can be divorced from its theoretical underpinnings, or the claim that clinicians can open themselves to "reality" uninfluenced by theoretical preconceptions. However, such assertions, at least in their milder forms, are not at all uncommon among clinical researchers and are entertained as well by many in the marital area. Accordingly, it is important to examine closely such claims and correct them to the extent that correction is warranted. To do so, in the next section we examine sources of change in technique in behavioral marital therapy over the last three decades of the twentieth century.

The Role of Social Psychology in the Origins and Development of BMT

Behavioral Marital Therapy, like other forms of behavior therapy, has its roots in the psychology laboratory. However, in the case of BMT, it was not simply the rat lab of Skinner or the dog kennel of Pavlov that have been cited as the inspiration.

Social psychological roots

Among other influences (e.g., Blau, 1964; Homans, 1961), BMT therapists also credited a small volume published in 1959 by Thibaut and Kelley, *The social psychology of groups*. Awareness of Thibaut and Kelley's theoretical framework was ubiquitous, and all early behavioral marital texts cite Thibaut and Kelley's (1959) and/or Kelley's (1979) work (e.g., Gottman, et al., 1976a; Jacobson & Margolin, 1979; Stuart, 1980). Clearly, most early BMT researchers were familiar with some variant of interdependence and social exchange theory and viewed it, along with social learning principles more generally, as providing a framework within which to understand marital satisfaction and commitment.

Reading Thibaut and Kelley (1959) today remains both interesting and instructive. Most concepts used by BMT researchers and therapists can be found in this volume. In particular, enhancing satisfaction by increasing rewards minus costs relative to some comparison level is discussed (pp. 21–24). The concept of the behavioral repertoire as skills to be taught is explicated (p. 20, pp. 38–39). The potential importance of communication and communication training (p. 73) and the value of brainstorming in problem solving discussions (pp. 263–270) are dealt with. Even developments commonly attributed to later sources are presaged by Thibaut and Kelley. For example, the potential importance of idiographic analysis of dyadic interaction and the need to examine sequences of observed interaction are discussed (p. 10, pp. 18–19). The likely impact of inferences about partner behavior and factors that could influence perception of partner behavior (later called filters by Gottman et al., 1976a, and then elaborated by attribution researchers and incorporated into cognitive marital therapy) were discussed (pp. 73–77). Anticipating the structure of the Prevention and Relationship Enhancement Program (PREP), it was suggested that a general discussion, emphasizing participation by all parties, might be an important preliminary step to effective problem-solving discussion (pp. 261–263). Anticipating a goal-theoretic analysis of marital conflict (Fincham & Beach, 1999), a goal framework was alluded to as a way of understanding the organization of individual and dyadic behavior.

Notwithstanding the above observations, over a decade passed between the publication of Thibaut and Kelley (1959) and the emergence of BMT in its mature form. By the mid-1970s BMT emphasized the instigation of positive behavior between spouses (e.g., Gottman et al.'s, 1976a, "up deck"; Weiss Patterson, and Hops's, 1973, Love days). Communication training had been formalized (e.g., Gottman et al., 1976a), and it was commonly held that the behavioral repertoire of distressed couples might be lacking important "skills" that could be taught as a way of interrupting coercive cycles (e.g., Weiss, Patterson, & Hops, 1973). Thus, it appears that on the basis of theory (including social psychological theory), and in interaction with clinical creativity but well before randomized clinical outcome trials of BMT began in earnest (e.g., Crowe, 1978; Turkewitz & O'Leary, 1976; Jacobson, 1977, etc.), BMT had reached a mature form. Outcome research served, primarily, as a check on the generalizability of various techniques (e.g., O'Leary & Turkewitz, 1978), and not as a stimulus to innovation. Indeed, positive outcome results were typically characterized as supporting the broad strategies of change proposed as important by behavioral marital therapists rather than the specific procedures used in a given investigation. In sum, BMT owes much of its current form to the theory and basic science of the 1950s and 1960s, and particularly to the social psychology of that period.

The importance of a unifying framework

A key factor in the remarkable progress made during the early 1970s was the presence of a shared framework or paradigm. A unifying theoretical framework was important both in allowing couple interactions to be described and in allowing possible points of therapeutic intervention to be identified. A strong shared theoretical framework also allowed topographically dissimilar interventions based on the use of token exchange (e.g., Stuart, 1969) or quid pro quo contracts between spouses (e.g., Azrin, Naster, & Jones, 1973) to be viewed as having conceptual continuity with later BMT outcome research that used neither technique. Thus, the shared framework influenced even the perceived strength of the cumulative support for BMT. But, most importantly, it was the existence of this conceptual framework that stimulated a group of creative, applied researchers to think along similar lines, see similar processes, discuss the implications of these processes, and view as reasonable a certain set of possible interventions. Accordingly, social psychological theory appears to have been important in enabling the emergence of BMT as a recognizable form of therapy.

Comment. It should not be surprising that traditional BMT, and by extension CBMT, ICT, and PREP, owe their existence to a basic science foundation. BMT arose in the context of the behavioral movement in clinical psychology. At its best, this movement represented a pragmatically motivated attempt to tie applied clinical intervention to basic experimental psychology. To ensure the ongoing transfer of basic research into clinical applications, those establishing early behavioral training programs decided to house them within psychology departments. They believed that a close connection was necessary in order to facilitate the incorporation of the evolving scientific base into ongoing clinical applications (see Davison, 1998). We explore this theme in more detail as we discuss the importance of cryptomnesia for clinical advances. In the present context, it suffices to note that the founders of behavior therapy self-consciously encouraged the ongoing transfer of ideas, values, and developments from the experimental lab to clinical application. In brief, BMT grew up looking to experimental psychology for inspiration at many levels and so it was quite natural, within that context, to extrapolate from the social psychology lab to the marital therapy hour.

The development of an intellectual crisis

Given its initial development, BMT seemed destined to become the poster child for the social–clinical interface. Yet, by the mid-1970s there was a growing sentiment that innovation in the marital area would be largely driven by the efforts of marital researchers and that it was unlikely that further clinical advancement would result from attention to basic research. How then did BMT lose its theoretical grounding? We turn to consider several factors that might provide an answer to this question.

Outcome studies? Early BMT outcome studies were often portrayed as rather striking in their demonstration of effectiveness (e.g., Hahlweg & Markman, 1988). In addition, early studies using techniques that were more closely tied to the interdependence framework produced slightly better outcomes than did later outcome studies that utilized more "sophisticated" versions of BMT (Jacobson et al., 1984; Christensen & Heavey, 1999). If anything, the outcome research available in the early 1980s seemed to argue against innovation. Indeed, the strong showing of outcome studies maintained considerable stability in the field, and was often used as a persuasive tool in favor of adopting BMT as an approach for dealing with marital problems (Jacobson & Margolin, 1979; Stuart, 1980). Accordingly, it is hard to find evidence that outcome results brought into question the theoretical underpinnings of the field.

Intellectual rigidity? Was it, then, their strong adherence to interdependence and social learning theory that led behavioral marital therapists to turn away from social psychology as the field of social psychology further emphasized cognitive accounts of behavior with the emergence of social cognition? Stated differently, did clinicians cling to the past and allow new developments to pass them by? This is also not supported by the data. The BMT field was clearly open to the idea of cognitive interventions and cognitive processes relatively early in its development (cf. Gottman et al., 1976a; O'Leary & Turkewitz, 1978). While early cognitive theorizing in the marital area was simplistic, this feature simply reflected the social psychology of the 1950s and 1960s. In addition, these early theorists and researchers made no claim to have all the answers, often suggested the potential for continuing advances in the enhancement of outcome, and explicitly called for more data.

Inability to tolerate ambiguity?   So, what was responsible for the emergence of an increasingly a-theoretical stance in the marital area? One influence must be the broader clinical psychology context we discussed earlier. This broader context readily supported a shift toward a-theoretical, technical eclecticism. At the same time, the desire among clinical psychologists to find some a-theoretical foundation for claims of therapeutic efficacy may be fueled, in part, by the needs of clinicians and marital therapy researchers to feel confident about the applied aspects of their work. Because therapists are attempting to influence the lives of others, it may be more comfortable to base their prescriptions and suggestions on something perceived as more "solid" and "factual" than the shifting sands of theory. That particular outcome results cannot really be considered "more solid" or "factual" than well-tested theoretical propositions need not diminish the allure of this position. Certainly, marital therapists are as vulnerable to the allure of "facts" as clinical psychologists (and psychiatrists) in general.

Critical tests of theory.   In our view, however, the more important source of the intellectual shift was a series of studies that were conducted by marital researchers to test the theoretical underpinnings of their treatment approach. In particular, in research designed to test key aspects of interdependence theory it was found that "skill level" or "the behavioral repertoire" as measured with strangers did not differentiate satisfied and dissatisfied couples (Vincent, Weiss, & Birchler, 1975). Similarly, performance on prisoner's dilemma games failed to discriminate distressed and non-distressed couples (e.g., Speer, 1972), but observed interaction did (e.g., Birchler, Weiss, & Vincent, 1975). These studies falsified claims that BMT was useful to the extent that it expanded the "behavioral repertoire" of couples, thereby opening them to the "natural contingencies" that would then maintain their more positive behavior with each other. Because the skills were typically already established in the behavioral repertoire of distressed couples, something else was keeping the natural contingencies from working with these couples. In addition, these investigations seemed to call into question the utility of methods drawn from social psychology and to highlight the need for new methods of studying patterns of interaction.

   Around the same time, it was also shown that greater reciprocity of positive behavior did not predict greater satisfaction as was predicted by interdependence theory (Gottman, Notarius, Markman, et al., 1976). That is, direct, immediate application of reinforcing contingencies in response to the spouse's positive behavior did not reliably predict a better marriage. In their 1976 book, *A couple's guide to communication*, Gottman, Notarius, Gonso, and Marman noted that "Although non-distressed couples may seem to be reciprocating positive codes more often than distressed couples, that may only be an artifact of the higher probability of positive codes in non-distressed couples." As numerous replications have shown, these early findings were correctly interpreted as disconfirming key elements of the Thibaut and Kelley framework. Indeed, they fed back into the social psychology literature and led to significant conceptual advances (e.g., Kelley et al., 1983a; Clark & Mills, 1979). But these developments were yet to come. In the mid 1970s what seemed clear to behavioral marital researchers was that key theoretical assumptions and predictions of the Thibaut and Kelley (1959) model were not true. Further, some of the basic research methods of the time appeared inadequate for investigating "real world" marital behavior.

Thus, by the mid- to late 1970s the theoretical underpinnings of BMT were under siege by prominent behavioral marital researchers (for a similar account of the details but a different interpretation, see Baucom, Epstein, Rankin, & Burnett, 1996). Studies had been conducted with the expectation that they would support the theoretical underpinnings of BMT, but the results were opposite to expectations and were stunningly conclusive. In effect, BMT researchers found themselves without a unifying theoretical framework. Rather than repair or extend the framework that inspired BMT, leaders in the area called for careful description and an inductive approach to science. Dust bowl empiricism therefore triumphed over a theory-driven approach to scientific advancement. However, it was not a rejection of theory per se. Theory was simply put on long-term hold (see Gottman, 1998, for a recent call for integrative theory in the marital area). As we shall see below, inevitably theory will be reintroduced. The only question is whether it will be reintroduced knowingly and explicitly, or implicitly in the form of cryptomnesia.

Comment

It is worth digressing at this point to note the potential for mutual enrichment between marital therapy research on the one hand and social psychological research on the other. It took clinical marital researchers, interested in applied issues, to frame pivotal tests of interdependence theory. Without the applied focus of behavioral marital researchers, it is hard to know how long we might have waited before game-theoretic tests with undergraduate subjects would have led to similar conclusions. This example demonstrates well the need for social psychologists to move beyond the examination of convenient undergraduate samples in the laboratory to adequately test social psychological theories, a need that received extensive discussion by social psychologists in the 1980s (e.g., Sommer, 1982).

Without such research it was all too easy for marital researchers to attribute the problems encountered with interdependence theory (Thibaut & Kelley, 1959) to social psychologists' preoccupation with theories of convenience samples and with prisoner's dilemma games (see Gottman et al., 1976a). Because this preoccupation was viewed as stable and as precluding further fruitful exchange, BMT researchers determined that they would need to create their own basic, observational literature pertaining to marital interaction (again, see Gottman et al., 1976a). They therefore began documenting observed differences between distressed and non-distressed couples. Because they believed that starting with theory had misled the field, they determined to engage the work a-theoretically. This time theory would be formed only after careful observation. The strength of this new agenda is exemplified by Markman's comment several years later that "a solid data base is a prerequisite to theory development [and] can best be accomplished by descriptive studies which focus on observable behavior" (Markman et al., 1981, p. 236). Indeed, this a-theoretical, descriptive agenda remains strong today. On the positive side, the commitment to careful observation has led to many of the methodological advances in the marital area over the past 20 years, and much of the data linking marital behavior to longitudinal outcomes (see Bradbury, 1998; but see Glenn, 1998, for a cautionary note).

The emergence of a-theoretical BMT

At the same time that a literature on marital interaction was being created through inductive procedures, BMT researchers found themselves saddled with an unanticipated paradox. They had a technology that worked, and that has continued to work over many replications for the past 20 years (Baucom et al., 1998; Christensen & Heavey, 1999), but whose theoretical underpinnings had been called into question. A broadly shared enthusiasm in the field for the great inductive enterprise was sufficient to maintain some intellectual momentum. However, by its very nature such a process could not be expected to yield dramatic results overnight and it led to a shift in the focus of BMT research away from theory development and toward methodological and measurement issues. Indeed, the most creative thinkers in the area devoted themselves to untangling the nuances of observational methodology.

At the same time, the limitations of an a-theoretical approach to intervention became apparent as marital researchers noticed the difficulty they had in describing goals for therapy and conveying overall strategies of therapy without making reference to theoretical constructs. To compound the problem, there were no new theoretical constructs being offered to account for the efficacy of BMT techniques. In the face of a relative theoretical vacuum left by the demise of the Thibaut and Kelley (1959) framework, clinicians and clinical researchers continued to describe BMT in terms that had already been discredited on theoretical grounds (see for example the descriptions of BMT provided in Jacobson & Margolin, 1979; Stuart, 1980, or more recently in Christensen & Heavey, 1999). Widespread discomfort with framing interventions in terms of a discredited theory, rather than discomfort with the outcome results obtained, is the more plausible explanation for the round of innovation in BMT that began in the late 1970s and early 1980s. For some sense of this discomfort one may examine Jacobson and Margolin (1979, pp. 14–17) or, more recently, Gottman (1998, p. 190).

The collapse of a-theoretical BMT

Oddly, and perhaps perversely from the perspective of doctrinaire behaviorists, in the late 1970s and early 1980s, behavioral marital therapists began borrowing widely from non-behavioral approaches. Often they borrowed from approaches with no outcome data supporting the efficacy of the approach. During this period one can discern efforts to find a new integrative theory, albeit not theory drawn from the empirical, social psychological literature. Instead BMT researchers turned to other therapeutic traditions for possible inspiration. Systems theory concepts were an early favorite of those looking for a more inclusive theoretical framework (e.g., Weiss, 1978). Cognitive therapy also emerged as providing a possible inclusive framework (e.g., Baucom & Epstein, 1990). However, neither of these potential organizing frameworks proved sufficiently unifying or powerful to galvanize the field as a whole. Instead, BMT researchers adopted a technique-oriented approach to innovation, borrowing techniques or "modules" of therapy from distinct forms of marital therapy in the hopes of enhancing therapeutic outcomes (e.g., Baucom, Sayers, & Sher, 1990). This approach also fostered the view that BMT was a collection of techniques applied in a modular format (see Jacobson & Christensen, 1996, for a similar characterization). Of course, in the absence of theory, the pull of a modular, technique-driven approach to marital therapy is nearly irresistible. In line with the modular view of marital therapy, a series of outcome investigations were conducted in which topography rather than function guided the differentiation of component interventions (see Baucom et al., 1998).

During this period outcome research began to play an increasingly important, albeit negative, intellectual role. Precisely because there was no theoretical standard by which to evaluate the potential value of innovations, BMT researchers increasingly turned to outcome research for vindication of their new composite therapies. Accordingly, when none of the new approaches was able to demonstrate significantly enhanced impact on marital satisfaction (Baucom et al., 1998), this was interpreted as failure and stagnation. As it became clear that the various clinical innovations were not translating into more powerful treatments, researchers in the field became increasingly dissatisfied both with traditional BMT and with its alternatives (see also Gottman, 1998). Arguably, however, outcome research is an overly blunt instrument with which to determine the "potential" of a particular technique or approach. Rather, due to overlap in goals and strategies of intervention across approaches, outcome research in the marital area may be biased toward "null" results for comparisons between active treatments. In addition, two interventions could appear equally effective in an outcome study despite one approach having greater potential to become more powerful with relatively minor modifications. Accordingly, outcome research alone may be a particularly problematic foundation for the identification of "promising" technical innovations.

Notwithstanding the increasing dissatisfaction with the BMT framework, there were significant achievements during the 1980s and early 1990s in the application of traditional BMT to various problems. For example, this period saw the successful application of BMT to the treatment of alcoholism (Epstein & McCrady, 1998; O'Farrell, Choquette, Cutter, Brown, & McCourt, 1993), depression (Beach, Fincham, & Katz, 1998), divorce prevention (Sayers, Kohn, & Heavey, 1998), and violence (O'Leary, Heyman, & Neidig, in press). However, there were modest achievements, at best, in the generation of a more powerful theoretical framework to guide marital intervention. In addition, because no theoretical structure guided BMT outcome research, there was little opportunity for theory-driven outcome research of the sort that could potentially guide clinical innovation (see Beach, 1991; Borkovec & Castonguay, 1998; Whisman & Snyder, 1997). In brief, in the absence of a robust theoretical framework, openness to innovation proved insufficient to avoid stagnation.

Comment.   While the field of behavioral marital therapy was *Waiting for Godot* in the form of an ultimate, inductively derived answer about the nature of marital interaction, the once-thriving applied tradition of BMT was approaching intellectual collapse. In retrospect, more rapid applied progress might have been prompted by theory-focused efforts to amend or replace the social psychological theory that had initially informed BMT.

The ascendance of the field of personal relationships

A development with the potential to enhance the rocky relationship between (social psychological) theory and marital application began in the early 1980s. Concurrent with resurgent interest in the general social–clinical psychology interface (e.g., Harvey, 1983), a new dialogue began, broad enough to include BMT researchers, social psychologists, developmental psychologists, and persons in the closely related fields of communication, cognitive science, and sociology. An important intellectual product of this emerging dialogue was the volume, *Close Relationships* (Kelley et al., 1983a). In the 1980s and early 1990s the dialogue expanded exponentially and the field of personal relationship research was progressing. The dialogue spawned a number of important developments and new developments continue to emerge. Among these continuing developments are the integration of the attachment and social cognition literatures (Shaver, Collins, & Clark, 1996; Baldwin et al., 1996), and the introduction of goal theory into characterization of marital conflict (Fincham & Beach, 1999), two areas to which we return later in the chapter.

Movement toward a new integrative framework

A further important development was the emergence of social cognition as an area of interest within social psychology. Although a burgeoning social cognition literature failed to transform clinical technique in marital therapy during the 1980s (but see Baucom & Epstein, 1990, and Fincham, Fernandes, & Humphreys, 1993, for evidence of some impact), it was incorporated wholeheartedly into the new "personal relationships" movement. As a result, this movement occasioned the emergence of a broader and more flexible framework for understanding and describing interaction. To be attractive to the field of marital therapy, social psychological theory needed to be wedded to a wide-ranging framework that could describe a variety of dyadic behaviors and could allow for the possibility of multiple influences. Even if it was not really a theory, and even if it did not directly incorporate all the available and potentially useful mid-level theories, such a framework might provide a springboard for a new round of creative clinical innovation.

In their 1983 book, Kelley et al. provided such a preliminary framework, but by the early 1980s relatively few applied marital researchers were looking at developments in social psychology. Among applied researchers, most of the attention devoted to basic processes focused rather narrowly either on understanding the role of attributional processes in marriage (see Bradbury & Fincham, 1990; Fletcher & Fincham, 1991), or on the description of marital interaction (see Gottman, 1998; Fincham & Beach, 1999). Kelley et al. however, presented a new framework for understanding and examining personal relationships. This new framework dealt with many of the problems left unanswered in the earlier Thibaut and Kelley (1959) volume. In addition, the framework highlighted the importance of "patterning" in dyadic relationships (p. 47), causal connectedness between partners leading to positive (and negative) feedback loops (p. 58), and the resulting emergence of stable interaction patterns. As was the case for Thibaut and Kelley, the framework provided is not so much a particular theory as it is an organizing scheme capable of accommodating many different mid-level theories and perhaps allowing for their integration.

One behavioral marital therapy researcher who was listening to the discussion of the new framework (and indeed participating in the dialogue) was Andy Christensen. Interestingly, around this same time, his clinical work began to shift profoundly. These shifts led eventually to Christensen's co-creation of Integrative Couple Therapy (ICT) with Jacobson. From the standpoint of the current discussion, it is particular interesting to examine ICT and the Kelley et al. (1983a) framework to see if there are any points of connection. Indeed, there are several. For example, Kelley et al.'s discussion of positive feedback loops appears to be a direct conceptual precursor of the "polarization process" discussed in ICT. "Polarization" is described in ICT as the process by which a focus on change may lead to an increase in the perceived discrepancy between the partners' positions. Hence, through polarization a relatively small area of disagreement may grow to be an area of perceived incompatibility. Likewise, Kelley et al.'s discussion of the way in which stable interaction patterns develop and are maintained appears to be the direct intellectual precursor of the ICT discussion of the "mutual trap." The "mutual trap" is described in ICT as the feeling of entrapment experienced by both partners in distressed couples that results from their perceiving that they must continue doing exactly what they are already doing despite the realization that it does not appear to help. Finally, Kelley et al.'s analysis of patterning in relationships appears to be a precursor of the identification of the couple "theme" in ICT. The "theme" is described in ICT as the underlying structure of the couple's interaction that ties together what may appear to be disparate areas of conflict. Thus, although the techniques of ICT are not directly given by theory, they appear to be built upon and constrained by the framework provided in the Kelley et al. (1983a) book. Parenthetically, it may be that placing ICT back into the Kelley et al. framework could prove useful in generating interesting marital therapy process questions.

Implications for the interrelationship of BMT, ICT and social psychological research

There is a relationship between the techniques ultimately generated by applied researchers and the framework that guided their thinking. In addition, we would argue that techniques are typically more useful when wedded to a theoretical context and that innovation is likely to be more sustained when the links between theory and technique are explicitly recognized. Thus, we do not mean to detract from the creativity displayed in the clinical innovation process by highlighting links to underlying theory. Rather, we hope that this exercise will help sustain clinical innovation and prevent a return to the doldrums of BMT in the 1980s. It may also highlight for social psychologists potential areas in which their research may have direct implications for understanding marital therapy, or for the identification of boundary conditions on the effectiveness of marital intervention.

As may be apparent already, while applauding much about ICT, the assertion that it owes little to basic psychological science, and to social psychology in particular, seems to us jarringly incorrect. In addition, the assertion (Jacobson & Christensen, 1996, p. viii) that one might be better off by eschewing theory, and opening up instead to the "natural contingencies" operating in the therapy session, seems potentially misleading. We would suggest that this type of assertion come with a warning label: "Try this only if you have strong implicit theories at work." In particular, we would argue that BMT and ICT are healthier with explicit theory than without, and that modern social psychology and the emerging field of personal relationships is an excellent place to look for relevant theoretical advances.

What are the consequences of failing to acknowledge the theoretical foundation of BMT and its various offshoots, including ICT? First, failure to acknowledge the theoretical ground upon which a set of techniques rests undermines the important activity of process research. If we have not acknowledged the basic processes that inform the techniques being proposed, we are in a poorer position to capture these processes in process research. Hence, we are likely to conduct sub-optimal variants of outcome research, condemning outcome research to be used as a mere persuasive device rather than as a truly informative experiment (for extended discussion, see Beach, 1991; Borkovec & Castonguay, 1998).

Second, recent developments in BMT and in the field of close relationships give rise to the hope that BMT may once again be able to claim a coherent and explicit theoretical foundation. This was the situation during the early 1970s, arguably the time of fastest growth and development for BMT. After the apparent collapse of that theoretical foundation in the early 1980s BMT moved increasingly toward the modular and technique-oriented approach rightly criticized by Jacobson and Christensen (1996). Technique-oriented approaches are vulnerable to decreasing fidelity as they are copied and variants proliferate. Without a coherent nomological network to steer development and to provide a context within which to detect and correct errors, a technique-oriented system is doomed to accumulate fatal errors during the replication process. Much like an organism with no autoimmune system to identify defective cells, an approach without a theoretical foundation has no way to catch and correct problematic drift in technique. Indeed, as Snyder and Forsyth (1991) point out, without theoretical grounding it is impossible even to gauge the range of applicability of one's techniques.

Finally, in addition to the problem of limiting the clinical potential of BMT and ICT, failure to acknowledge the theoretical grounding of ICT has the additional unfortunate side effect of inappropriately devaluing the generative heuristic power of new work coming from social, developmental, and personal relationship perspectives. Indeed, there is considerable new basic research that suggests the potential for further development of the power of BMT or ICT (cf. Fincham & Beach, in press). It would be unfortunate, and probably wrong, to think that BMT and ICT have reached their zenith in terms of their power (efficacy) or their accessibility (effectiveness) for distressed couples (see Gottman, 1998, for a similar view). To the extent that we recognize basic research and theory as the engine of innovation, we will be more likely to tap this resource appropriately.

In view of such observations, one is left to wonder why the contributions of social psychologists are underestimated in the BMT literature. When the facts do not support the importance of "outcome research" in stimulating clinical innovation and appear to point to a critical role for "theory," why do so many bright and creative individuals appear to think otherwise?

Understanding the Problem of Cryptomnesia

In this section we discuss several factors that bear upon the underestimation of social psychology's contribution to the development of marital therapy. We grapple with the question of how marital therapy researchers come to view their intervention packages as "new" and uninfluenced by basic research. We use the term "cryptomnesia," or literally "theft of ideas," to refer to this phenomenon, not to suggest that marital therapy researchers are blameworthy, but rather to highlight the continuity of their behavior with that of other persons who are asked to be creative. The term "cryptomnesia" has appeared in the basic cognitive psychology literature recently and seems to capture many of the processes of interest rather well.

Figure versus ground

The simple distinction between figure and ground is useful for understanding cryptomnesia in its simplest form: the under-citation of work that is known to be logically prior to one's own. To illustrate in a neutral context, we first discuss the way in which therapists in private practice may under-credit marital therapy researchers and highlight the similarity of this behavior to that of academic psychologists who under-credit basic research. In this context we also discuss whether an increased focus on process research, by itself, would reverse the tendency toward under-citation.

Marital therapists in practice.   It is relatively common for behaviorally trained marital therapists in private practice settings to indicate that they are "eclectic" in their practice and that they do not follow any particular treatment package, or to suggest that they have created their own treatment approach over the years. However, if asked to describe what they do in therapy these same individuals may describe the use of techniques that have a strong resemblance to those described in various treatment manuals. Marital therapists in clinical practice appear to emphasize the differences and overlook the similarities between their favorite techniques and those appearing in various marital therapy manuals, leading perhaps to an underestimate of the extent to which manualized approaches have influenced their work. Perhaps marital therapists overlook the influence of treatment manuals on their practice for the same reason that marital researchers overlook the influence of basic research on their innovations. In each case the problem may be one of figure versus ground.

For the marital therapist, the goal that structures their attention and activity is what to do with a particular couple presenting for therapy. What to do "on average," or what works "in general," is not the pivotal issue and may not even seem to be a very compelling issue to therapists working with couples. Rather, the compelling issue for clinicians in practice remains "what treatment, by whom, is most effective for this individual with that specific problem, under which set of circumstances" (Paul, 1969). The goal of deciding what to do with this particular couple makes the tailoring of treatment the "figure" for clinicians and makes the broad set of techniques and guidelines for couples in general the "background." That is, clinicians are likely to think of themselves as having creatively combined techniques from across sources and as having developed a novel intervention that fits "this particular couple" even if their overall strategy is consistent with a treatment manual. In this view, clinicians are led to underestimate the extent to which the existence of treatment manuals has influenced their work because the techniques from treatment manuals provide only the "background" for their choices. In just the same way, marital therapy researchers may be led to underestimate the extent to which theory or findings from basic research have influenced them.

Marital researchers designing new treatment packages.   Academic marital researchers may have as their goal the development of new treatment packages that influence positive couple outcomes on average. This goal focuses attention on whether a particular approach works, on average, and for whom, but draws attention away from how distressed couples change, or why therapy produces its benefits. It also leads to attempts to standardize treatments, increase fidelity to manuals, and provide comparisons to alternative treatments. Alternatively stated, the context of treatment design and outcome evaluation focuses attention on accounting for the most variance possible, not on cleanly explicating the various processes that may be contributing to the power of the intervention. Indeed, hypothesized mechanisms of change may be viewed as important only insofar as they are conveyed to clients as part of the rationale for treatment, i.e., to the extent that they become embedded in the intervention itself. Because the truth value of assertions about mechanisms seems relatively unimportant in this context, marital therapy researchers may feel little pressure to cite the relevant basic literature. A focus on "what works" to the exclusion of "how things work" may therefore obscure the relationship between basic research and therapeutic innovation.

Marital therapy process researchers.   One way to increase attention on mechanisms of change by behavioral marital therapy researchers is greater encouragement of technique-oriented and processes-oriented research (cf. Goldfried & Wolfe, 1996; Whisman & Snyder, 1997). Such an approach focuses attention on understanding the way important aspects of therapeutic intervention work to produce change. Measures designed to capture the process of change in marital therapy might be more likely to have a theoretical component and to reflect the content of the basic literature on personal relationships. However, it would not be surprising if there continued to be a focus on variance accounted for, rather than clean tests of theoretical propositions. In turn, the potential for under-citing the basic literature, and perhaps underestimating its heuristic importance, might remain high even if marital therapy researchers became more attentive to therapy processes issues.

Consider the hypothetical example of a researcher examining the effect of BMT on the occurrence of benign attributions among distressed spouses. Assume that BMT is found to render attributions for partner behavior more benign, and it is found that the occurrence of benign attributions at the end of therapy is associated with greater positive change in satisfaction. This would be of great interest to marital therapists, and is a prediction that comes directly from the literature on responsibility attributions in close relationships. However, in the clinical literature the investigation would most probably not be discussed as a test of an attributional model of change in marital therapy, but rather as an attempt to determine the relative importance of attending to dysfunctional attributions or changing negative behavior in producing positive marital outcomes. This presentation of the study would prompt attention to variance accounted for in the dependent variable, and pit topographically distinct aspects of marital change against each other to see which one better accounted for variance in change. At best, this type of presentation would tend to obscure any discussion of mediation. At worst it would preempt any discussion of theoretically specified mechanisms. Thus, while process investigations have the potential to help tie applied results to a more basic set of results, in practice "mediational" issues are unlikely to be addressed (as has been the case for the example relating to attributions, see Fincham; Beach, & Bradbury, 1990), and applied researchers may still be prone to underestimate the relevance and importance of basic research.

In sum, practicing clinicians and clinical researchers share at least one reason to under-credit the influence of others doing more basic work. It is common to view as figure those things that are the focus of one's own creative efforts. Those aspects that are shared or logically prior to one's own creative efforts recede into the background, while those aspects that are different or are novel are emphasized and become figure. Thus, the work of others working in the same area on the same problem at the same level of abstraction is likely to be well cited. However, the work of others doing pertinent work that is more basic may be under-cited.

Cryptomnesia proper

A second, less conscious reason, for under-citation of basic research may be the common tendency to overlook ways in which one's work has borrowed from a template or used the work of others as an outline (Marsh et al., 1996). As highlighted in a series of interesting studies, there is a pervasive tendency to steal the ideas of others and not realize the theft. This practice of cryptomnesia or unconscious plagiarism is extremely common. In one study, when people were asked to draw "novel" alien creatures and were given examples that others had drawn "just to get the creative process going," there was an overwhelming tendency to incorporate those aspects of the examples that were consistent. So, for example, if all the sample aliens had four legs, the newly generated aliens were far more likely to have four legs. The plagiarism occurred despite warnings and admonitions. In addition, the plagiarism did not appear to result from laziness. Even though the examples constrained the shape of the creatures, they did not decrease the volume of new alien creatures that were generated (Marsh et al., 1996).

Apparently, there is a strong tendency to pick up ideas that are "in the air" and run with them. The new creations that result are viewed as purely novel and not in need of attribution to anyone else. Thus, it may be relatively easy for psychologists in the marital area to come in contact with many ideas about interpersonal, cognitive, and developmental processes, and abstract from this intellectual milieu a template about processes that may be important in guiding and structuring couple interactions. However, as is highlighted by the Marsh et al. (1996) data, marital researchers may never conclude that they have an intellectual debt to those who informed their work in important ways.

Contextual embeddedness

Under-citation of influences from the social psychology literature relative to influences from other marital therapy literature may also result from differences in the way information from these two sources are represented in memory. Given a focus on differentiating one's work from that of other applied researchers, as well as the direct relevance of the comments of such individuals for one's own work, one might expect that suggestions made by other marital therapy researchers would be embedded in a rich network of relevant information. In contrast, information from social or developmental psychology might be encoded in a less rich semantic network. If so, there could be considerably greater difficulty in generating cues for accurate source monitoring in the latter case than in the former case, leading to the expectation of more errors of source monitoring in relation to social and developmental literatures (cf. Johnson & Raye, 1981), and so greater under-citation.

From partnership to cryptomnesia and back again

As a result of these three factors – figure-ground, cryptomnesia, and contextual embeddedness – there is the potential to profoundly underestimate the impact of social and developmental psychology on the marital therapy literature. Even if the basic literature had a considerable number of direct and indirect effects on the generation of new techniques, there might still be few direct citations.

Ironically, cryptomnesia and an exaggerated sense of one's own unique contribution may tend to degrade the quality of the creative process over time for both clinicians and researchers. In particular, as the theoretical "ground" for the creative process recedes and so is less chronically accessible, it may exert less influence on creative decision making. In place of explicit theory, other less reliable influences will come to carry more weight. Thus, over time, the failure to remember and consider the foundation of one's creative activity should lead to poorer quality innovations. Equally as problematic, the shared framework offered by theory and basic research that allows clinicians, clinical researchers, and basic researchers to share observations and see the relevance of one domain for the other is eroded by the process of cryptomnesia. It therefore seems important for the long-term health of marital therapy that the tendency to under-recognize the impact of theory be reversed. Accordingly, although we suspect that the three processes outlined above can never be eradicated, it is important to mitigate their worst effects. One way to do this is to return to the initial, explicit partnership that existed between social psychology and BMT. Such a partnership would explicitly acknowledge the contributions and the need for communication between social psychologists, marital therapy researchers, and marital therapists.

In the 1960s such a three-way connection was forged by the presence of common framework that facilitated communication and interchange. Indeed, we suspect a common intellectual framework is essential for the partnership in that it makes sensible the exchanges between social psychologists and those working at different levels of abstraction and application. The identification of a robust framework that can support such a three-way interchange is therefore key to stimulating a new period of creativity and development in marital therapy. While we do not suggest that such a framework is already available, there are signs that such a framework is possible. We therefore identify two areas that exemplify the potential for renewed synergy between social psychology and behavioral marital therapy in the future.

A Look Toward the Future

If a comprehensive framework can be advanced that builds on the Kelley et al. (1983b) framework and incorporates recent developments in the study of personal relationships, it may generate the level of sustained enthusiasm within the marital therapy area necessary to re-ignite a period of rapid applied progress. Past success suggests that such a framework need not be a fully fledged theory or provide a complete integration of relevant mid-level theories in order to stimulate applied creativity and progress. As happened in the late 1960s and early 1970s, a shared paradigm can allow strong collaboration and implicit coordination of effort across labs and geographic regions.

Toward a broader framework for understanding "close relationships"

Below we provide a very brief sketch of attachment and goal theory as potential components of a broader framework for the study of dyadic conflict and marital distress, and articulate some of their current and potential connections to marital therapy. Before doing so, we need to make a brief observation about the central construct of marital/relationship quality and the utility of a "vulnerability-stress-adaptation" model (Karney & Bradbury, 1995).

In our view, it is important to conceptualize the construct of marital satisfaction in terms that are consistent with recent developments in research on the structure of attitudes and emotions (Cacioppo, Gardner & Berntson, 1997; Russell & Carroll, in press). Specifically, conceptualizing marital/relationship quality in terms of evaluative judgments (see Fincham & Bradbury, 1987) that vary along positive and negative dimensions (Fincham & Linfield, 1997) helps ensure conceptual clarity as well as reclaim the close connection with social psychology sought in this section (see also Fincham, Beach, & Kemp-Fincham, 1997).

We also find it useful to have a "meta-framework" for thinking about change processes in marital satisfaction. Karney and Bradbury (1995) offer such a "meta-framework" that identifies the potential importance of enduring vulnerabilities, life events, the various coping responses couples make or fail to make, and the impact of both the context and the dyadic response on changes in marital quality and marital stability. The suggestions that follow are meant to identify processes that may explicate particular pathways within such a broad framework.

Attachment

Because attachment theory appears to have been particularly influential in the development of ICT, and because it provides an important link to social psychology, we elaborate several aspects of its utility for marital therapy. It should be noted, however, that extensive and well-crafted discussions of the relevance of attachment theory for marital therapy, albeit with a different focus, can be found elsewhere (e.g., Kobak, Ruckdeschel, & Hazan, 1994; Whiffen & Johnson, 1998). In addition, excellent discussions of the integration of attachment theory with the broader social cognition and adaptation literatures are also available (e.g., Shaver et al., 1996).

Attachment theory has made its way into behavioral marital therapy both through the influence of attachment-inspired approaches to marital therapy (e.g., Kobak et al., 1994; Greenberg & Johnson, 1988) and indirectly through the influence of ego-analytic writers (e.g., Wile, 1981, 1995). Its contribution to behavioral marital therapy has been directly acknowledged by some BMT researchers (e.g., Notarius, Lashley, & Sullivan, 1997) and indirectly acknowledged through the citation of those who themselves cite attachment theory (e.g., Jacobson & Christensen, 1996). Nonetheless, its contribution tends to be underestimated.

In our view, the contribution of the attachment literature to the evolution of BMT has been both dramatic and profound. The attachment literature suggests that behavioral marital therapists should look for a universal mechanism, activated by the perception that the partner is psychologically or physically unavailable or unresponsive, that has as its goal the reinstatement of a sense of "felt security" (Sroufe & Waters, 1977). At the same time, it suggests that this universal mechanism could take different forms for different individuals (Rholes, Simpson, & Stevens, 1998). It also introduces into behavioral marital therapy the notion that attachment-related emotions may be masked, or entirely deactivated, or hyper-activated, leading to interesting marital dilemmas and sources of confusion and misunderstanding within marital dyads. For example, the attachment perspective suggests that anger may sometimes be prompted by feelings of hurt and vulnerability. But rather than clearly signaling a need for nurturance, the angry response may be misunderstood by the partner and lead to further unavailability and defensiveness. Thus attachment models have introduced the idea that couple problems are not the result of "skill deficits," but rather may be understood as resulting from a positive feedback loop triggered by unacknowledged or masked feelings of neediness.

In addition, by emphasizing working models, the attachment literature also focuses attention on the human capacity for future-oriented simulation and so the potential for strong affective reactions to events that "might" happen, or implications for possible future selves. Thus, attachment accounts lend themselves to elaboration in social-cognitive terms. Attachment-like accounts have been incorporated into marital therapy as a vehicle for "formulating the couples problem" (Jacobson & Christensen, 1996, p. 46), and for helping couples understand their problems in a non-blaming manner (Notarius et al., 1997). Attachment explanations are particularly good in this regard in that they suggest a way of construing marital difficulties that renders them understandable to partners while indicating that symptoms of marital distress may be adaptive and constructive at base (see also *Emotion Focused Therapy for Couples*, Greenberg & Johnson, 1988).

Likewise, the implications for therapists are clear. If concerns about partner availability result in masked signals that are interpreted by the partner as signs of unavailability, this may be the source of a vicious cycle maintaining marital discord. Later forms of BMT such as ICT (Jacobson & Christensen, 1996) and PREP (Markman et al., 1994), highlight the central importance of perceiving the partner to be available and interested. Indeed, Markman et al. label lack of acceptance "the mother of all hidden agendas." Thus, the notion that perceived lack of availability or acceptance may result in misunderstanding and extreme forms of dysfunctional interaction is explicitly included in both these newer versions of BMT. Further, this attachment-like idea entirely supplants the previous notion that miscommunication is the result of not knowing how to implement certain communication skills. Accordingly, in recent BMT writings, one might conclude that attachment theory has become the de facto theoretical foundation for communication training as well as for the instigation of positive behavior. It has become a favorite vehicle for reattribution training with distressed couples as well, supplanting to some degree the cognitive-behavioral movement in BMT (e.g., Notarius et al., 1997).

The mere presence of attachment ideas, and the discussion of those ideas, appears to have led to changes in the way BMT researchers think about the process of therapy. In turn, this changed conceptualization seems to have led to changes in the types of techniques proposed in innovative treatment packages. Thus, exposure to ideas from attachment theory has led to changes in the way BMT researchers apply the interventions retained from previous variants of BMT. In particular, rather than focusing on problem-solving communication per se, behavioral marital therapists now focus on the "theme" of the conflict, hidden agendas are likely to be viewed in attachment terms, the critical importance of expressed commitment to the relationship receives greater attention, and the power of the simple act of attentive listening (Markman et al., 1994) has received a new emphasis. In turn this has led behavioral marital therapy researchers to take a new and closer look at the role of supportive interactions between partners (e.g., Carels & Baucom, 1999; Pasch & Bradbury, 1998). We believe that greater recognition of the impact of attachment research on marital therapy and its incorporation into a broader framework for close relationships will have further salutary effects. In particular, making explicit the ongoing incorporation of attachment theory into BMT should allow assumptions that are currently implicit to be explicated clearly and so be better tested. In addition, making attachment influences explicit should highlight possible additional innovations, and should allow BMT (or BCT) researchers to take advantage of ongoing developments in research on adult attachment (e.g., Simpson & Rholes, 1998).

Goals

As important as attachment theory has been for recent changes in BMT, it may be viewed as only a specific instance of goal theory. In attachment theory, many behaviors are made sensible by reference to the goal of maintaining felt security and a comfortable level of proximity/distance. However, even a cursory examination of the social psychological literature suggests that a variety of goals impinge directly or indirectly on couple interaction and have the potential to affect satisfaction or distress. For example, self-evaluation maintenance goals (e.g., Beach et al., 1996; 1998a), belongingness goals (Baumeister & Leary, 1995), self-verification and self-enhancement goals (e.g., Katz & Beach, 1997; Murray & Holmes, 1996; Murray, Holmes, & Griffin, 1996; Snyder & Stukas, 1999), communal relationship goals (Clark & Mills, 1979), and identity and personal growth goals (Aron & Aron, 1996; Ryan, Sheldon, Kasser, & Deci, 1996), among others, may influence behavior in relationships. Adopting a framework that allows for the interaction of multiple goal systems could therefore be particularly useful for guiding the study of marital interaction and stimulating innovative marital interventions. However, developing a framework that can readily incorporate a range of goals will probably need to go beyond a reliance on attachment theory.

Recent work on goal-directed behavior provides insights into the nature and organization of goals, important characteristics of goals, and the impact of goal orientation on behavior (see Austin & Vancouver, 1996; Gollwitzer & Bargh, 1996). We have argued elsewhere (Fincham & Beach, 1999) that a goal-theoretic perspective has the potential to provide an overarching framework for understanding marriage. Dunning (1999) similarly points to the importance of studying goals to "break open the black box implicit in social cognitive work" and "in exploring how people manage their relations with loved ones" (p. 8). We begin by considering whether such a perspective adds anything new to the marital literature.

A potentially serious obstacle to adopting a broad, goal framework in the marital area is that use of the goal construct remains largely unacknowledged both in work on marriage and in work on personal relationships (see Berscheid, 1994, for a similar lament). Thus, despite frequent, indirect references to goals, there is relatively little in the way of direct guidance on the effect of goals on marital interaction. Also, there is little guidance on how to understand the interplay of multiple goals. This is unfortunate, as a number of heuristic and conceptual advantages follow from making explicit our implicit reliance on the goal construct.

Five premises capture much of the promise of a goal framework for marital therapy. First, all behavior is goal-directed (discrepancies between current and desired states drive behavior to reduce the difference through such processes as test-operate-test-exit cycles; Miller, Galanter, & Pribram, 1960). In marital therapy, this premise highlights the importance of identifying the goal that problem behavior serves. This allows alternative, non-problematic ways of meeting the goal to be generated.

Second, spouses don't always know what the goal is even for their own behavior (goals can be latent or implicit as well as consciously experienced). For marital therapy, this premise highlights the potentially limited value of self-report. In the same vein, it should be noted that some goals may emerge in a situation rather than being well formed in advance. In such circumstances, it may not be possible for spouses to self-report all goals that will ultimately influence their interaction because some of the goals will not be elicited until after the interaction is under way.

Third, goals vary widely (from internal set points to complex, cognitively represented outcomes) and cannot be understood in isolation from each other or the dynamics of the larger goal system in which they are embedded (establishing, planning, striving towards, and revising goals; see Austin & Vancouver, 1996). In the marital context, this underscores the importance of allowing for multiple goal influences on behavior. In addition, goal theory provides a theoretically informed way of understanding the potential interaction of contextual effects and enduring vulnerabilities on coping and adaptation in marriage, as well as the way in which such effects could result in shifts in marital satisfaction and stability (cf. Karney & Bradbury, 1995).

Fourth, affect results from moving toward or away from goals, with avoidance goals generating negative affect as discrepancies are reduced, and approach goals generating positive affect as discrepancies are reduced (Carver & Scheier, in press). In the marital context, this premise suggests different emotional experiences for defensive versus collaborative goals and suggests that affect will be directed toward the partner primarily when the partner is perceived as facilitative or obstructive with regard to active goals. Accordingly, this premise suggests the hypothesis that satisfaction with the partner may vary somewhat as a function of the dimension primed prior to asking for satisfaction ratings and the role of the partner vis-à-vis that dimension (see Fincham & Beach, 1999). Perhaps more importantly, this premise also suggests that careful attention to affective reactions may illuminate unspoken goals or unstated evaluations of partner behavior as facilitative or obstructive.

Therapeutic implications. As noted above, goal theory lends itself to the generation of novel hypotheses about therapeutic processes. Carver and Scheier (in press), for example, point out that it is not merely the degree to which individuals meet their goals that influences affective reactions. Instead, the direction, velocity, and acceleration of movement toward goals is related to magnitude of positive feelings. As a result, goal theory suggests that structuring therapy so that it provides frequent, and concrete feedback about improvement on various goals may help increase positive feelings about therapy and about the partner, even if initial goals have not been met. In a similar vein, it is likely that a focus on concrete goals may be associated with more positive affect in marital therapy (Emmons & Kaiser, 1996).

Importantly, if the partner is viewed as thwarting valued goals, this could lead to ruminative thought regarding the blocked goal (Tesser, Martin, & Cornell, 1996). This should lead to more thinking about the partner and about the thwarted goal. Internal rehearsal of one's own arguments and one's own view of the problem will commonly prove polarizing (Tesser, 1976), and lead to feelings of powerlessness to change (Vanzetti, Notarius & NeeSmith, 1992). Such a pattern may be among the most undesirable consequences of traditional behavioral marital therapy with its strong focus on change and its implicit tendency to encourage partners to locate needed changes in the spouse rather than in the self (see Jacobson & Christensen, 1996), and suggests additional possible changes in therapeutic format.

New marital therapies. A marital therapy approach tied to a self-regulatory, goal-setting, framework has been suggested by Halford (1998). Reasoning that couples are likely to experience the greatest sense of control over changes in their own behavior, Halford, Sanders, and Behrens (1994) proposed an emphasis on individual, self-directed change by partners entering marital therapy. This approach emphasizes helping each partner identify ways in which they can begin to address relationship problems without any requirement or expectation that the partner change (see also Coyne & Benazon, in press, for a similar suggestion about marital therapy in the context of depression). Halford et al. (1994) highlight five different types of goals that may follow from adopting this approach. First, partners may be encouraged to think of new ways to communicate their concerns. Second, the partners may be encouraged to consider ways of making their spouse's behavior less stressful to them even if their partner continues engaging in the behavior. Third, the partners may be encouraged to generate ways of meeting needs that do not require the spouse. Fourth, the partners may consider ways to dissolve their current relationship. And fifth, the partners may decide to uphold the status quo in their relationship. In all cases, the goal of Self-Regulation Couples Therapy (SRCT) is to assist both partners to identify their problems in a way that leads to the formulation of individual goals to address the problem area (Weiss & Halford, 1996).

The self-regulatory approach to marital therapy has the advantages of potentially shortening the course of marital therapy (e.g., Halford, Osgarby, & Kelly, 1996) and of being considerably more flexible in format than traditional BMT. At the same time, this innovative approach illustrates the potential for social psychological theory to guide the elaboration and development of an emerging form of marital therapy.

In sum, the assumptions of goal theory outlined earlier provide a vehicle for integrating attachment and self-regulation perspectives within a single framework. In addition, goal theory would appear to be compatible with an emphasis on understanding key contextual and developmental issues in marriage such as the effect of stressors and enduring vulnerabilities (Karney & Bradbury, 1995). Wedded to other considerations highlighted in the Kelley et al. (1983a) framework, the result might be a framework sufficiently flexible to accommodate ongoing developments in broad areas of social psychology such as the psychology of self and the rapidly developing area of social cognition. At the same time, such a framework has the potential to be sufficiently specific to speak to practical issues that are central in such applications as ICT and SRCT. Because work on the goal framework is already quite advanced (e.g., Austin & Vancouver, 1996), and because the Kelley et al. framework has already inspired clinical innovation, it seems possible that a new clinically informative framework may be close to becoming a reality. In combination with a new willingness by marital therapy researchers to be explicit about their theoretical commitments, such a framework seems promising indeed.

Conclusion

Behavioral Marital Therapy (BMT) has changed dramatically over the 1980s and 1990s. It changed from a vibrant, theory-driven enterprise to a stagnant, outcome-study driven enterprise characterized by a focus on the topography rather than the function of marital interventions. Happily, it now appears to be moving back toward recognition of the importance of a unifying framework. At the same time, the most recent innovations (Integrative Couples Therapy [ICT] and Self-Regulation Couples Therapy, [SRCT]) appear to have clear links to thriving areas of investigation of interest to social psychologists. We propose that with appropriate input from social psychologists, ICT and SRCT could help stimulate a return to explicit partnership between social psychologists and marital therapy researchers. ICT appears to take a number of technical developments and use the Kelley et al. (1983a) framework to integrate them into a cohesive pattern. At the same time, changes introduced in both PREP and ICT are understandable as responses to developments in the basic attachment literature, even if these influences are somewhat under-cited. Conversely, SRCT is explicitly tied to the self-regulatory framework of Karoly (1993), and this provides a direct route to the consideration of the broader literature on goals. In both cases, the dialogue between marital therapy researchers and social psychologists seems full of promise.

Epilogue

The absence of theoretical development during the 1980s, and the concomitant stagnation of BMT, appears to have resulted from a considered decision to avoid theory, rather being the result of some inevitable split between behavioral marital therapy and its social psychological roots. Because behavioral marital therapy researchers believed that the documentation of couple behavior was necessary before clinically useful theory building could occur, they quit looking to developments in social psychology as a source of creative inspiration. However, there is now an opportunity for a renewed dialogue between behavioral marital therapy researchers and social psychologists.

A new integrative framework that may incorporate many potentially useful mid-level theories appears within reach. To realize this potential it is important for marital therapy researchers to acknowledge more fully the role of basic research in inspiring creative leaps in technique. Likewise, it will be important for social psychologists to look past the shroud of cryptomnesia and see the opportunity to comment on the many interesting processes that unfold in the context of marital therapy. Such commentary, if it is to be credible, may require social psychologists to do research with samples other than undergraduate students, to learn more about clinical phenomena, and to be receptive to input from sources other than the social psychological literature. Likewise, such a dialogue requires greater willingness on the part of marital therapy researchers and marital therapists to examine the social psychological literature and not require that every theoretical proposition be tested on married couples before it is considered potentially relevant to understanding marital dynamics. If social psychologists and clinical psychologists interested in marital therapy each carry out even a small part of this prescription, the first decade of the new century is likely to be an exceptionally exciting period for marital research.

REFERENCES

Agras, W. S., and Berkowitz, R. (1980). Clinical research and behavior therapy: Halfway there? *Behavior Therapy, 11*, 472–487.

Aron, A., and Aron, E. N. (1996). Self and self-expansion in relationships. In G. J. O. Fletcher and J. Fitness (Eds.), *Knowledge structures in close relationships* (pp. 324–344). Mahwah, NJ: Erlbaum.

Austin, J. T., & Vancouver, J. B. (1996). Goal constructs in psychology: Structure, process, and content. *Psychological Bulletin, 120*, 338–375.

Azrin, N., Naster, B., & Jones, R. (1973). Reciprocity counseling: A rapid learning-based procedure for marital counseling. *Behavior Research and Therapy, 11*, 365–382.

Baldwin, M. W., Keelan, J., Patrick, R., Fehr, B., Enns, V., & Koh-Rangarajoo, E. (1996). Social-cognitive conceptualization of attachment working models: Availability and accessibility effects. *Journal of Personality and Social Psychology, 71*, 94–109.

Barlow, D. H., & Hofmann, S. G. (1997). Efficacy and the dissemination of psychological treatments. In D. M. Clark & C. G. Fairburn (Eds.), *Science and practice of cognitive behaviour therapy* (pp. 95–117). Oxford: Oxford University Press.

Baucom, D. H., & Epstein, N. (1990). *Cognitive behavioral marital therapy*. New York: Brunner/Mazel.

Baucom, D. H., Epstein, N., Rankin, L. A., & Burnett, C. K. (1996). Understanding and treating marital distress from a cognitive-behavioral orientation. In K. S. Dobson & K. D. Craig (Eds.), *Advances in cognitive-behavioral therapy* (pp. 210–236). Thousand Oaks, CA: Sage.

Baucom, D. H., Sayers, S., & Sher, T. G. (1990). Supplementing behavioral marital therapy with cognitive restructuring and emotional expressiveness training: An outcome investigation. *Journal of Consulting and Clinical Psychology, 58*, 636–645.

Baucom, D. H., Shoham, V., Mueser, K. T., Daiuto, A. D., & Stickle, T. R. (1998). Empirically supported couple and family interventions for marital distress and adult mental health problems. *Journal of Consulting and Clinical Psychology, 66*, 53–88.

Baumeister, R. F., & Leary, M. R. (1995). The need to belong: Desire for interpersonal attachments as a fundamental human motivation. *Psychological Bulletin, 117*, 497–529.

Beach, S. R. H. (1991). Social cognition and the relationship repair process: Toward better outcome in marital therapy. In G. J. O. Flecher & F. D. Fincham (Eds.), *Cognition in close relationships* (pp. 307–328). Hillsdale, NJ: Erlbaum.

Beach, S. R. H., Fincham, F. D., & Katz, J. (1998). Marital therapy in the treatment of depression: Toward a third generation of therapy and research. *Clinical Psychology Review, 18*, 635–661.

Beach, S. R. H., Tesser, A., Fincham, F. D., Jones, D. J., Johnson, D., & Whitaker, D. J. (1998a). Pleasure and pain in doing well, together: An investigation of performance related affect in close relationships. *Journal of Personality and Social Psychology, 74*, 923–938.

Beach, S. R. H., Tesser, A., Mendolia, M., Anderson, P., Crelia, R., Whitaker, D. G., & Fincham, F. D. (1996). Self-evaluation maintenance in marriage: Toward a perfomance ecology of the marital relationship. *Journal of Family Psychology, 10*, 379–396.

Berscheid, E. (1994). Interpersonal relationships. *Annual Review of Psychology, 45*, 79–129.

Beutler, L. E., & Consoli, A. J. (1992). Systemic Eclectic Psychotherapy. In J. C. Norcross and M. R. Goldfried (Eds.), *Handbook of psychotherapy integration* (pp. 264–299). New York: Basic Books.

Birchler, G. R., Weiss, R. L., & Vincent, J. P. (1975). A multimethod analysis of social reinforcement exchange between maritally distressed and nondistressed spouse and stranger dyads. *Journal of Personality and Social Psychology, 31*, 349–360.

Blau, P. M. (1964). *Exchange and power in social life*. New York: Wiley.

Borkovec, T. D., & Castonguay, L. G. (1998). What is the scientific meaning of empirically supported therapy? *Journal of Consulting and Clinical Psychology, 66*, 136–142.

Bradbury, T. N. (1998). *The developmental course of marital dysfunction*. Cambridge, UK: Cambridge University Press.

Bradbury, T. N., & Fincham, F. D. (1990). Attributions in marriage: Review and critique. *Psychological Bulletin, 107*, 3–33.

Brehm, S. S. (1976). *The application of social psychology to clinical practice*. Washington, DC: Hemisphere.

Cacioppo, J. T., Gardner, W. L., & Berntson, G. G. (1997). Beyond bipolar conceptualizations and measures: The case of attitudes and evaluative space. *Personality and Social Psychology Review, 1*, 3–25.

Carels, R. A., & Baucom, D. H. (1999). Support in marriage: Factors associated with on-line perceptions of support helpfulness. *Journal of Family Psychology, 13*, 131–144.

Carver, C. S., & Scheier, M. F. (in press). Themes and issues in the self-regulation of behavior. In R. Wyer (Ed.), *Advances in social cognition*, Vol. 12.

Chambless, D. L., & Hollon, S. D. (1998). Defining empirically supported therapies. *Journal of Consulting and Clinical Psychology, 66*, 7–18.

Christensen, A., & Heavey, C. L. (1999). Interventions for couples. *Annual Review of Psychology, 50*, 165–190.

Clark, M. S., & Mills, J. (1979). Interpersonal attraction in exchange and communal relationships. *Journal of Personality and Social Psychology, 37*, 12–24.

Coyne, J. C., & Benazon, N. (in press). Coming to terms with the nature of depression in marital research and treatment. In S. R. H. Beach (Ed.), *Marital and family processes in depression: Providing a scientific foundation for marital therapy for depression*. Washington, DC: American Psychological Association.

Crowe, M. J. (1978). Conjoint marital therapy: A controlled outcome study. *Psychological Medicine, 8,* 623–636.

Davison, G. (1998). Being bolder with the boulder model: The challenge of education and training in empirically supported treatments. *Journal of Consulting and Clinical Psychology, 66,* 163–167.

Dunning, D. (1999). Postcards from the edge: Notes on social psychology, the story so far. *Contemporary Psychology, 44,* 6–8.

Emmons, R. A., & Kaiser, H. A. (1996). Goal orientation and emotional well-being: Linking goals and affect through the self. In L. Martin & A. Tesser (Eds.), *Striving and feeling: Interactions among goals, affect, and self-regulation* (pp. 79–98). Mahwah, NJ: Erlbaum.

Epstein, E. E., & McCrady, B. S. (1998). Behavioral couples treatment and drug use disorders: Current status and innovations. *Clinical Psychology Review, 18,* 689–711.

Fincham, F. D., & Beach, S. R. H. (1999). Conflict in marriage: Implications for working with couples. *Annual Review of Psychology, 50,* 47–77.

Fincham, F. D., & Beach, S. R. H. (1999). Marriage in the new Millennium: Is there a place for social cognition in marital research? *Journal of Social and Personal Relationships, 16,* 685–704.

Fincham, F. D., Beach, S. R. H., & Bradbury, T. N. (1990). Purging concepts from the study of marriage and marital therapy. *Journal of Family Psychology, 4,* 195–201.

Fincham, F. D., Beach, S. R. H., & Kemp-Fincham, S. I. (1997). Marital quality: A new theoretical perspective. In R. J. Sternberg & M. Hojjat (Eds.), *Satisfaction in close relationships* (pp. 275–304). New York: Guilford Press.

Fincham, F. D., & Bradbury, T. N. (1987). The assessment of marital quality: A reevaluation. *Journal of Marriage and the Family, 49,* 797–809.

Fincham, F. D., Fernandes, L. O. L., & Humphreys, K. (1993). *Communicating in relationships.* Champaign, Il: Research Press.

Fincham, F. D., & Linfield, K. J. (1997). A new look at marital quality: Can spouses feel positive and negative about their marriage? *Journal of Family Psychology, 11,* 489–502.

Fletcher, G. J. O. & Fincham, F. D. (Eds.) (1991). *Cognition in close relationships.* Hillsdale, NJ: Erlbaum.

Glenn, N. D. (1998). Problems and prospects in longitudinal research on marriage: A sociologist's perspective. In T. N. Bradbury (Ed.), *The developmental course of marital dysfunction* (pp. 427–440). Cambridge, UK: Cambridge University Press.

Goldfried, M. R. (1980). Toward the delineation of therapeutic change principles. *American Psychologist, 35,* 991–999.

Goldfried, M. R., and Wolfe, B. E. (1996). Psychotherapy practice and research: Repairing a strained alliance. *American Psychologist, 51,* 1007–1015.

Gollwitzer, P. M., & Bargh, J. A. (Eds.) (1996). *The psychology of action.* New York: Guilford Press.

Gottman, J. M. (1998). Psychology and the study of marital processes. *Annual Review of Psychology, 49,* 169–197.

Gottman, J. M., Notarius, C., Gonso, J., & Marman, H. (1976a). *A couple's guide to communication.* Champaign, Il: Research Press.

Gottman, J. M., Notarius, C., Markman, H., Yoppi, B., & Rubin, M. R. (1976b). Behavior exchange theory and marital decision making. *Journal of Personality and Social Psychology, 34,* 14–23.

Greenberg, L. S., & Johnson, S. M. (1988). *Emotionally focused therapy for couples.* New York: Guilford Press.

Hahlweg, K., & Markman, H. J. (1988). Effectiveness of behavioral marital therapy: Empirical status of behavioral techniques in preventing and alleviating marital distress. *Journal of Consulting and Clinical Psychology, 56,* 440–447.

Halford, W. K. (1998). The ongoing evolution of behavioral couples therapy: Retrospect and prospect. *Clinical Psychology Review, 18,* 613–634.

Halford, W. K., Sanders, M. R., & Behrens, B. C. (1994). Self-regulation in behavioral couples therapy. *Behavior Therapy, 25,* 431–452.

Halford, W. K., Osgarby, S., & Kelly, A. (1996). Brief behavioral couples therapy: A preliminary evaluation. *Behavioural and Cognitive Psychotherapy, 24,* 263–273.

Harvey, J. (1983). The founding of the *Journal of Social and Clinical Psychology. Journal of Social and Clinical Psychology, 1,* 1–3.

Homans, G. C. (1961). *Social behavior: Its elementary forms.* New York: Harcourt, Brace, & World.

Jacobson, N. S. (1977). Problem solving and contingency contracting in the treatment of marital discord. *Journal of Consulting and Clinical Psychology, 46,* 442–452.

Jacobson, N. S., & Christensen, A. (1996). *Integrative couple therapy: Promoting acceptance and change.* New York: Norton.

Jacobson, N. S., Follette, W. C., Revenstorf, D., Baucom, D. H., Hahlweg, K., & Margolin, G. (1984). Variability in outcome and clinical significance of behavioral marital therapy: A reanalysis of outcome data. *Journal of Consulting and Clinical Psychology, 52,* 497–504.

Jacobson, N. S., & Margolin, G. (1979). *Marital therapy.* New York: Brunner/Mazel.

Johnson, M. K., & Raye, C. L. (1981). Reality monitoring. *Psychological Review, 88,* 67–85.

Kanfer, F. H., & Schefft, B. K. (1988). *Guiding the process of therapeutic change.* Champaign IL: Research Press.

Karney, B. R., & Bradbury, T. N. (1995). The longitudinal course of marital quality and stability: A review of theory, method, and research. *Psychological Bulletin, 118,* 3–34.

Karoly, P. (1993). Mechanisms of self-regulation: A systems view. *Annual Review of Psychology, 44,* 175–184.

Katz, J., & Beach, S. R. H. (1997). Self-verification and depressive symptoms in marriage and courtship: A multiple pathway model. *Journal of Marriage and the Family, 59,* 903–914.

Kelley, H. H. (1979). *Personal relationships.* Hillsdale, NJ: Erlbaum.

Kelley, H. H., Berscheid, E., Christensen, A., Harvey, J. H., Huston, T. L., Levinger, G., McClintock, E., Peplau, L. A., & Peterson, D. R. (1983a). *Close relationships.* New York: Freeman.

Kelley, H. H., Berscheid, E., Christensen, A., Harvey, J. H., Huston, T. L., Levinger, G., McClintock, E., Peplau, L. A., & Peterson, D. R. (1983b). Analyzing close relationships. In Kelley, H. H., Berscheid, E., Christensen, A., Harvey, J. H., Huston, T. L., Levinger, G., McClintock, E., Peplau, L. A., & Peterson, D. R. (Eds.), *Close relationships* (pp. 20–67). New York: Freeman.

Kelley, H. H., & Thibaut, J. W. (1978). *Interpersonal relations: A theory of interdependence.* New York: Wiley.

Kobak, R., Ruckdeschel, K., & Hazan, C. (1994). From symptom to signal: An attachment view of emotion in marital therapy. In S. M. Johnson & L. S. Greenberg (Eds.), *The heart of the matter* (pp. 46–71). New York: Brunner/Mazel.

London, P. (1972). The end of ideology in behavior modification. *American Psychologist, 27,* 913–920.

Markman, H. J., Notarius, C. I., Stephen, T., & Smith, T. (1981). Behavioral observation systems for couples: The current status. In E. Filsinger & R. Lewis (Eds.), *Assessing marriage: New behavioral approaches* (pp. 234–262). Beverly Hills, CA: Sage.

Markman, H. J., Stanley, S., & Blumberg, S. L. (1994). *Fighting for your marriage.* San Fancisco: Jossey-Bass.

Marsh, R. L., Landau, J. D., & Hicks, J. L. (1996). How examples may (and may not) constrain creativity. *Memory and Cognition, 24,* 669–680.

Miller, G. E., Galanter, E., & Pribram, K. H. (1960). *Plans and the structure of behavior.* New York: Holt.

Murray, S. L., & Holmes, J. G. (1996). The construction of relationship realities. In G. J. O. Fletcher & J. Fitness (Eds.), *Knowledge structures in close relationships* (pp 91–120). Mahwah, NJ: Erlbaum.

Murray, S. L., Holmes, J. G., & Griffin, D. W. (1996). The benefits of positive illusions: Idealization and the construction of satisfaction in close relationships. *Journal of Personality and Social Psychology, 71*, 1155–1180.

Nathan, P. E., & Gorman, J. M. (1998). *A guide to treatments that work.* Oxford: Oxford University Press.

Notarius, C. I., Lashley, S. L., & Sullivan, D. J. (1997). Angry at your partner? Think again. In R. J. Sternberg & M. Hojjat (Eds.), *Satisfaction in close relationships* (pp. 219–248). New York: Guilford Press.

O'Farrell, T. J., Choquette, K. A., Cutter, H. S. G., Brown, E. D., & McCourt, W. F. (1993). Behavioral marital therapy with and without additional couples relapse prevention sessions for alcoholics and their wives. *Journal of Studies on Alcohol, 54*, 652–666.

O'Leary, K. D. & Turkewitz, H. (1978). Marital therapy from a behavioral perspective. In T. J. Paolino & B. S. McCrady (Eds.), *Marriage and marital therapy* (pp. 240–297). New York: Brunner/Mazel.

O'Leary, K. D., Heyman, R. E., & Neidig, P. (in press). Treatment of wife abuse: A comparison of gender specific and conjoint approaches. *Behavior Therapy.*

Pasch, L. A., & Bradbury, T. N. (1998). Social support, conflict, and the development of marital dysfunction. *Journal of Consulting and Clinical Psychology, 66*, 219–230.

Paul, G. L. (1969). Behavior modification research: Design and tactics. In C. M. Franks (Ed.), *Behavior therapy: Appraisal and status.* New York: McGraw-Hill.

Rholes, W. S., Simpson, J. A., & Stevens, J. G. (1998). Attachment orientations, social support, and conflict resolution in close relationships. In J. A. Simpson, & W. S. Rholes (Eds.), *Attachment theory and close relationships* (pp. 166–188). New York: Guilford Press.

Russell, J. A., & Carroll, J. M. (in press). On the bipolarity of positive and negative affect. *Psychological Bulletin.*

Ryan, R. M., Sheldon, K. M., Kasser, T., & Deci, E. (1996). All goals are not created equal: An organismic perspective on the nature of goals and their regulation. In P. M. Gollwitzer & J. A. Bargh (Eds.), *Psychology of action: Linking cognition and motivation to behavior* (pp. 7–26). New York: Guilford Press.

Sayers, S. L., Kohn, C. S., & Heavey, C. (1998). Prevention of Marital Dysfunction: Behavioral approaches and beyond. *Clinical Psychology Review, 18*, 713–745.

Shaver, P. R., Collins, N., & Clark, C. L. (1996). Attachment styles and internal working models of self and relationship patterns. In G. J. O. Fletcher and J. Fitness (Eds.), *Knowledge structures in close relationships* (pp. 25–62). Mahwah, NJ: Erlbaum.

Simpson, J. A., & Rholes, W. S. (1998). *Attachment theory and close relationships.* New York: Guilford Press.

Snyder, C. R., & Forsyth, D. R. (1991). *Social and clinical psychology united.* In C. R. Snyder & D. R. Forsyth (Eds.), *Handbook of social and clinical psychology* (pp. 3–17). New York: Pergamon.

Snyder, M., & Stukas, A. A. (1999). Interpersonal processes: The interplay of cognitive, motivational, and behavioral activities in social interaction. *Annual Review of Psychology, 50*, 273–304.

Sommer, R. (1982). The district attorney's dilemma: Experimental games and the real world of plea bargaining. *American Psychologist, 37*, 526–532.

Speer, D. C. (1972). Marital dysfunctionality and two person non-zero-sum game behavior. *Journal of Personality and Social Psychology, 21*, 18–24.

Sroufe, L. A., & Waters, E. (1977). Attachment as an organizational construct. *Child Development, 48*, 1184–1199.

Stuart, R. B. (1969). Operant interpersonal treatment for marital discord. *Journal of Consulting and Clinical Psychology, 33*, 675–682.

Stuart, R. B. (1980). *Helping couples change: A social learning approach to marital therapy*. New York: Guilford Press.

Tesser, A. (1976). Thought and reality constraints as determinants of attitude polarization. *Journal of Research in Personality, 10*, 183–194.

Tesser, A., Martin, L. L., & Cornell, D. P. (1996). On the substitutability of self-protective mechanisms. In P. M. Gollwitzer & J. A. Bargh (Eds.), *The psychology of action: Linking cognition and motivation to behavior*. New York: Guilford Press.

Thibaut, J., & Kelley, H. H. (1959). *The social psychology of groups*. New York: Wiley.

Turkewitz, H., & O'Leary, K. D. (1976, December). *Communication and behavioral marital therapy: An outcome study*. Paper presented at the Annual Meeting of the Association for the Advancement of Behavior Therapy. New York.

Vanzetti, N. A., Notarius, C. I., & NeeSmith, D. (1992). Specific and generalized expectancies in marital interaction. *Journal of Family Psychology, 6*, 171–183.

Vincent, J. P., Weiss, R. L., & Birchler, G. R. (1975). Dyadic problem solving as a function of marital distress and spousal vs. stranger interactions. *Behavior Therapy, 6*, 475–487.

Weiss, R. L. (1978). The conceptualization of marriage from a behavioral perspective. In T. J. Paolino, Jr. and B. S. McCrady (Eds.), *Marriage and marital therapy: Psychoanalytic, behavioral and systems theory perspectives* (pp. 165–239). New York: Brunner/Mazel.

Weiss, R. L., & Halford, W. K. (1996). Managing marital therapy: Helping partners change. In V. Van Hasselt & M. Hersen (Eds.), *Sourcebook of psychological treatment manuals for adult disorders* (pp. 312–341). New York: Plenum.

Weiss, R. L., Patterson, G. R., & Hops, H. (1973). A framework for conceptualizing marital conflict: A technology for altering it, some data for evaluating it. In L. D. Handy & E. L. Mash (Eds.), *Behavior change: Methodology, concepts and practice* (pp. 309–342). Champaign, IL: Research Press.

Whiffen, V. E., & Johnson, S. M. (1998). An attachment framework for the treatment of childbearing depression. *Clinical Psychology: Science and Practice, 5*, 478–493.

Whisman, M. A., & Snyder, D. K. (1997). Evaluating and improving the efficacy of conjoint marital therapy. In W. K. Halford & H. J. Markman (Eds.), *Clinical handbook of marriage and couples intervention* (pp. 679–693). New York: Wiley.

Wile, D. B. (1981). *Couples therapy: A nontraditional approach*. New York: Wiley.

Wile, D. B. (1995). The ego-analytic approach to couple therapy. In N. S. Jacobson & A. S. Gurman (Eds.), *Clinical handbook of couple therapy* (pp. 91–120). New York: Guilford Press.

CHAPTER FOUR

Therapeutic Groups

Donelson R. Forsyth

Throughout history people have used groups, and the powerful interpersonal dynamics that occur in them, to promote adjustment and beneficial change. Small tribal groups have, for eons, been a source of social and material support for members. The spiritual rites of most religions were conducted in small groups, as were most educational activities. So the progression from individualistic forms of psychological treatments to group-centered approaches is a natural one. As practitioners developed their methods of psychotherapeutic methods in the early part of the 20th century, some preferred to meet with their patients in groups where members discussed their illnesses. In time, these early group treatments stimulated a concerted and more systematic application of groups to help people improve their well-being.

This chapter examines the nature of psychotherapeutic groups as groups. Although treatment groups have many unique features, they are groups none the less. Even though members may display behavioral perturbations that severely disrupt routine group processes and their psychological disturbances may prevent the kinds of interpersonal exchanges characteristic of nontherapeutic groups, these groups form, develop, work, and disband much like groups in other settings. This review, after offering a three-part classification scheme for differentiating the major types of therapeutic groups, selectively examines topics that dominated researchers' efforts to understand therapeutic groups: Group development, leadership, motives, and therapeutic factors.

Types of Therapeutic Groups

The three most typical types of therapeutic groups in use today – the therapy group, the interpersonal learning group, and the self-help group – gained acceptance as therapeutic procedures between 1920 and 1950. Psychotherapy itself emerged as a means of helping people deal with mental and emotional problems during this period and, in some cases, physicians, psychiatrists, psychologists, and other mental health practitioners conducted their therapeutic sessions in group settings. Many practitioners preferred individualized approaches and turned to groups only when forced to by limited time and resources, but this view gave way as groups emerged as appropriate treatments for a variety of problems, including addiction, thought disorders, depression, eating disorders, and personality disorders (Kaplan & Sadock, 1993; Long, 1988).

Psychotherapy groups

Most people trace group therapy back to 1905 and a physician named Pratt who arranged for patients to gather in groups so that he could give them instruction on personal hygiene. He originally used groups to save time, but he quickly recognized that group-level processes were contributing to the success of his treatments. The method, however, did not gain widespread acceptance until the mid-1940s as publications with such titles as "Group psychotherapy: A study of its application" (Wender, 1940), "The psychoanalysis of groups" (Wolf, 1949), "Results and problems of group psychotherapy in severe neurosis" (Schilder, 1939), and "Group activities in a children's ward as methods of psychotherapy' (Bender, 1937) appeared in the literature. Therapists who traditionally used only dyadic, one-on-one methods added group sessions, either supplementing or completely replacing their individual sessions.

Group psychotherapists are usually credentialed mental health professionals and their patients tend to be suffering from diagnosed clinical conditions. The methods used by group psychotherapists are as varied as individual approaches to therapy, for therapists draw on psychoanalysis, psychodrama, systems-theory, object relations, existentialism, Gestalt, humanistic, cognitive-behavioral techniques, and other methods in designing their interventions (Brabender & Fallon, 1993; Dies, 1992; Kaplan & Sadock, 1993; Spira, 1997). Psychoanalytically oriented therapists, for example, exploit transference mechanisms to promote change in members. The therapist becomes the central authority in such groups, and usually relies on the traditional tools of the analyst as he or she directs the session and summarizes the group's efforts (Day, 1981; Rutan & Stone, 1993). Whereas some psychoanalytically oriented therapists stress the importance of the individual in the group, rather than the group itself (e.g., Kutash & Wolf, 1993), others integrate the treatment of the individual with the analysis of the group itself. These so-called group-as-a-whole approaches capitalize on group tensions to promote growth and development (Bion, 1961; Foulkes, 1964).

Cognitive-behavioral and behavioral approaches, in contrast, focus more on explicit, observable cognitions and behaviors, such as social or relationship skills (Flowers, 1979; Hollander & Kazaoka, 1988; Rose, 1993). Behavioral therapists are more directive, the group's goals are more clearly identified, and the interaction among members may be structured through role-playing activities and specific exercises.

Yalom's (1995) widely used interpersonal group psychotherapy, more than psychoanalytic or cognitive-behavioral methods, exploits the group's interpersonal processes to achieve change. Yalom assumes that most problems, such as depression, anxiety, and personality disorders, can be traced back to social sources, so he uses the group as a "social microcosm" where members respond to one another in ways that are characteristic of their interpersonal tendencies outside of the group. Members do not discuss problems they are facing at home or work, but instead focus on interpersonal experiences within the group: The *here and now* rather than the *then and there*. Yalom's interpersonal model is unique in its emphasis on identifying, and exploiting, curative factors in groups.

Interpersonal learning groups

Most people who join interpersonal learning groups do so voluntarily to gain insight into themselves, to improve their interpersonal skills, or to enhance the quality of their emotional experiences. The training group, or T group, assembled in 1946 by Lewin, Benne, and their colleagues, is the prototype of such groups. Lewin and his colleagues used unstructured group discussions to help trainees improve their interpersonal skills, but when the trainees were given permission to join in the post-training review sessions Lewin recognized the value of interpersonal feedback and sharing perceptions of the group situation (Bradford, Gibb, & Benne, 1964). Lewin shifted the sessions to include more process analysis and feedback, and participants reported gains in self-insight. These T groups became the basis of the curriculum of the National Training Laboratory (NTL), which has trained thousands of educators, executives, and leaders through group exercises that stress communication and interpersonal skills (Bednar & Kaul, 1979; Kaplan, 1979). As Marrow (1964, p. 25) explains, T groups are a "special environment in which they [participants] learn new things about themselves. . . . It is a kind of emotional re-education."

This early innovation formed the basis for at least three types of small-group learning experiences. During the 1950s and 1960s a version of the T group emerged that focused explicitly on enhancing positive emotions and the quality of one's relations. As the purpose of the training shifted from learning about group processes to enhancing spontaneity, personal growth, and sensitivity to others, a new label developed for such groups: Sensitivity-training, or encounters (Johnson, 1988; Lieberman, 1994). These groups lost much of their popularity in the 1980s, but in recent years they have changed into a second form: Large group awareness training (LGAT). EST, FORUM, and Lifespring are all examples of LGATs, for members seek to improve their overall level of satisfaction and interpersonal relations by carrying out such experiential exercises as role-playing, group singing and chanting, and guided group interaction. Lieberman (1994) suggests that at least 1.3 million Americans have taken part in LGAT sessions.

Workshops, or structured training groups, are also based on the T-group concept of interpersonal learning, but they regulate the learning experience by using didactic presentations, guided group discussion, and exercises that help trainees practice certain skills. Although these interventions often focus on management and professional skills, as telegraphed by such titles as How to Manage People Effectively, Stress-Management Seminar, or Negotiate Your Way to Success, workshops are also frequently used to promote adjustment. Sherill, Frank, Geary, and Stack (1997), for example, used psychoeducational workshops to provide information and support to families of elderly patients who were suffering from depression. The workshops were primarily informational rather than supportive, but attendance was associated with reduced recidivism in an ongoing treatment program. Similarly, Beem, Eurelings-Bontekoe, Cleiren, and Garssen (1998) recommend using workshops with individual and group counseling to help individuals suffering from an interpersonal loss. Their workshops provided information about the bereavement process and sources of support and other community resources. Gray, Verdieck, Smith, and Freed (1997) developed and evaluated the effectiveness of court-mandated workshops for divorcing families, and concluded that attendance was associated with reduced parental conflict, both legal and interpersonal, and improved adjustment for children.

Self-help groups

Self-help groups (SHGs) are voluntary associations of individuals who share a common problem (see Hollingshead, 2001, for discussion of virtual self-help groups). SHGs exist for nearly every major medical, psychological, or stress-related problem. Groups exist for people who are suffering from such physical illnesses as asthma, heart disease, cancer, and AIDS. SHGs also exist for people who provide care for chose suffering from chronic diseases and disabilities, and for individuals striving to overcome addictions to alcohol and other substances. Other groups focus on weight loss, domestic problems, time and money management, and personality disorders. Such groups are growing in terms of numbers and members, with perhaps as many as 8 million people in the United States alone belonging to such groups (Christensen & Jacobson, 1994; Goodman & Jacobs, 1994; Jacobs & Goodman, 1989). Alcoholics Anonymous, for example, is one of the most widely used methods for treating addictions (Miller, 1995). Jacobs and Goodman explain the rise of SHGs in terms of the erosion of the family, increase in the number of people living with significant diseases, consumers' skepticism of care-providers and mental health services, and increased recognition in the value of interpersonal remedies.

Self-help groups are usually self-governing, with members rather than experts or mental health professionals determining activities. They are also egalitarian groups, with norms that insist that all members be treated fairly. The members, although often very different in terms of backgrounds, ages, and educational level, all face a common predicament, problem, or concern. Hence, as Jacobs and Goodman (1989, p. 537) note, the members are "psychologically bonded by the compelling similarity of member concerns." These groups all stress the importance of reciprocal helping, for members are supposed to both give help to others as well as receive it from others. SHGs usually charge little in the way of fees, and they form because the members' needs are not being met by existing educational, social, or health agencies.

Group Development

Therapeutic groups, like all groups, change over time (see also Levine, Moreland, & Choi, 2001; Worchel & Coutant, 2001). When the group is first convened members are reluctant to disclose personal information, and the leader is generally regarded as the sole source of therapeutic information and expertise. Over time the group interaction becomes more structured, as regularities or response patterning in the interactions of members become more predictable. In many cases this regularity is disrupted by conflict in the group, but in successful groups this conflict is resolved as the members develop a working alliance among themselves.

Bennis and Shepard's model

Bennis and Shepard (1956) were among the first theorists to describe the stage-like nature of this development. They based their theory on observations of groups at the NTL in the 1950s. These groups included a leader, but that individual did not actively structure the group interaction. Bennis and Shepard noted that initially the groups were concerned with structure, order, and authority relations (dependence), but over time the focus shifted to questions of interpersonal relations (interdependence). They also noted subphases within these two general stages. When the group first forms members look to the leader for guidance, and during this dependence–submission subphase discussion focuses on personal concerns of group members rather than the group's goals. When the leader does not provide structure, a counterdependence phase begins marked by conflict between the group and the leader. This phase ends when the group members take responsibility for the group's activities, redefine the role of the leader, and begin to work in earnest on the goals the group identifies in the resolution subphase. Those groups that move through this subphase then shift their attention to interpersonal relations and the next phase begins with its three subphases: Enchantment-flight, disenchantment-fight, and consensual validation. The enchantment-flight subphase is marked by extreme group cohesion, and discussions are characterized by laughter, joking, humor, and having fun. This cohesion dissolves during the disenchantment-fight stage, when individual members begin to express their unwillingness to go along with the group's inter-pretations, coalitions form, and the members disparage the group through "absenteeism, tardiness, balkiness in initiating total group interaction, frequent statements concerning worthlessness of group, denial of importance of the group" (Bennis, 1964, p. 267). Groups that make their way to the final subphase establish a balance between the emotional demands of the group, and the value of using the group to reach personal and group goals. Winter (1976), Mabry (1975), and Davies and Kuypers (1985) offer evidence that lends general support to the model, with Burnand (1990) suggesting that the subphases correspond to six basic human goals: Certainty, freedom, reward, other's good state, unity, and fairness.

Tuckman's five-stage model

Tuckman (1965), after reviewing both theory and data collected in studies of therapeutic and nontherapeutic groups, offered a model of group development that stresses four basic stages: Forming, storming, norming, and performing. During the forming stage the group members must become oriented toward one another. Next, members experience conflict (storming), often because members challenge the authority of the leader. In the norming phase norms and roles develop that regulate behavior, and the group achieves greater unity. In the performing phase the group reaches a point at which it can perform as a unit to achieve desired goals. Tuckman later added a fifth stage, the adjourning stage, when the group deals with issues of independence and closure (Tuckman & Jensen, 1977).

Research evidence is generally consistent with the Tuckman (1965) model. Hill and Gruner (1973), for example, observed and coded the behaviors displayed by adolescents in a program of behavioral change. These groups did not immediately start to work on self-development issues, nor did the group members try to help one another. Rather, the groups first moved through orientation, conflict, and cohesion-building stages before they began to make therapeutic progress (Hill & Gruner, 1973). Stiles, Tupler, and Carpenter (1982) asked members of a sensitivity-training group to rate each session on a series of adjective pairs such as good/bad, labored/easy, and uncertain/definite. These ratings, when examined by the researchers, followed the general pattern suggested by Tuckman's stage theory: A period of mild tension followed by increased conflict that was resolved by the ninth session. Group members rated the next four sessions as smooth and comfortable, but as the group entered the work phase (sessions 13–15) the positive ratings dropped slightly, whereas ratings of the potency of the meetings increased (Stiles, Tupler, & Carpenter, 1982). Maples (1988) coded the journals of 230 members of psychoeducational groups. The forming stage was characterized by courtesy, confusion, caution, and commonality, the group was rife with controversy and confrontation during the storming stage, whereas cooperation, collaboration, cohesion, and commitment characterized the norming stage. During the performing phase members reported feeling challenged to work hard by the group, whereas communication and increased consensus marked the group's final stage.

Studies of process structuring that occur later in the group's development also support the Tuckman model (Kivlighan, McGovern, & Corazzini, 1984; Warren & Rice, 1972). Kivlighan and his colleagues, for example, tested the hypothesis that interventions that are timed to match the developmental needs of the group will lead to more positive outcomes than interventions that are not appropriate given the "maturity" of the group. They gave group members written handouts pertaining to either anger or intimacy in group therapy prior to either the fourth group session or the ninth group session. The information dealing with anger clarified the value of anger in therapy by providing a justification for anger as a natural part of group participation and suggestions for communicating anger. In contrast, the information dealing with intimacy clarified the value of intimacy in groups, and provided suggestions for the appropriate expression of intimacy toward others. As anticipated, when the interventions were matched to the most appropriate developmental stage – for example, group members received the anger information during the storming phase (session four) or the intimacy information during the norming phase (session nine) – rather than mismatched, subjects displayed more comfort in dealing with intimacy, more appropriate expressions of intimacy and anger, fewer inappropriate expressions of intimacy, and more congruence between self-ratings and other ratings of interpersonal style.

The Tuckman (1965) model is also generally consistent with the Group Development Questionnaire (GDQ) developed by Wheelan (1994; Wheelan, Buzaglo, & Tsumura, 1998; Wheelan & Hochberger, 1996). Her instrument, which is available in English, Spanish, and Japanese, includes items that pertain to dependency/inclusion (forming), counterdependency/fight (storming), trust/structure (norming), and work and productivity (performing). Example items for each stage are, respectively, "Members tend to go along with whatever the leader suggests," People seem to have very different views about how things should be done in this group," "The group is spending its time planning how it will get its work done," and

"The group gets, gives, and uses feedback about its effectiveness and productivity" (Wheelan, Murphy, Tsumura, & Kline, 1998, p. 379).

MacKenzie's four-stage model

MacKenzie (1994, 1997) collapses the norming and performing stages identified by Tuckman (1965). Therapeutic groups – with their focus on interpersonal processes, growth, adjustment, and self-exploration – rarely concentrate wholly on therapeutic topics to the exclusion of process-related topics, therefore the period of normative development and focus on individual adjustment blend together. MacKenzie's stage 1, engagement, occurs gradually as participation in "the developing group system is accompanied by an early sense of well-being at finding that one is accepted and understood, which has the effect of encouraging greater self-disclosure" (p. 279). Stage 2, differentiation, corresponds to Tuckman's (1965) storming phase. Members must develop "patterns for conflict resolution and tolerance of a negative emotional atmosphere" (p. 279). Most outpatient groups meeting weekly need four to eight sessions to move through these two stages to the interpersonal work stage. During this stage the group is "able to address individual problematic matters in a more vigorous manner. The focus tends to shift to greater introspection and personal challenge" (p. 279). Most groups become more cohesive during this period, and the theme of individual autonomy and group dependence tends to occupy many members' minds. In time, the group reaches stage 4, termination.

MacKenzie's model has stimulated more research than other approaches, in part because of MacKenzie's development of the Group Climate Questionnaire, which assesses three aspects of groups that vary with group development: engaged (a positive working alliance in the group), conflict (interpersonal tensions), and avoiding (denial of personal responsibility for the group's outcomes). MacKenzie (1997) finds that scores on the engaged scale increase initially, but then drop during the differentiation phase. They then rise again until the termination phase, although drops occur when the group works through difficult material. The avoiding scale scores decrease over the life of the group, whereas conflict scores peak during the differentiation stage. Kivlighan and Lilly (1997) confirmed these trends, in part, but found that in the groups they studied – where members were relatively well adjusted – the engaged scores did not build during the early group meetings, but instead started out high and remained elevated until the differentiation stage.

Issues and implications

Group development can, of course, sometimes take a course that differs from that suggested by Bennis and Shepard (1956), Tuckman (1964), and MacKenzie (1997). Interpersonal exploration is often a prerequisite for other therapeutic outcomes, and cohesion and conflict often precede effective performance, but this pattern is not universal. Some groups manage to avoid particular stages, others move through the stages but in a unique order, and still others seem to develop in ways that can't be described by the stage models (Seeger, 1983). Lichtenberg and Knox (1991), for example, carefully coded transcriptions of therapy sessions, searching for evidence of increasing regularity in communication patterns. Unexpectedly they found little change in the groups' communication patterns over time, and they also found that people who spoke frequently in the group tended to have lower, rather than higher, status. Also, the demarcation between stages is not clear-cut. When group conflict is waning, for example, feelings of cohesion may be increasing, but these time-dependent changes do not occur in a discontinuous, step-like sequence. Many theorists also prefer cyclical models to the stage theory proposed by Tuckman (Hill & Gruner, 1973; Shambaugh, 1978).

Evidence also suggests that the developmental processes of therapy groups are similar to stages seen in other groups, with two exceptions. First, much of the group's development is related to issues of conflict and authority. Many nontherapeutic groups bypass entirely the conflict period, or this phase occurs much later in the life of the group. But because therapeutic groups are often relatively unstructured and participants are uncomfortable with this flexibility, conflict often emerges early in the group and they center around the relationship between the leader and the rest of the group. In the orientation stage members are reticent, but as the group matures leader–member conflicts disrupt the group's functioning. Members may oscillate between "fight and flight": some may openly challenge the leader's policies and decisions (fight) whereas others may respond by minimizing contact with the leader (flight; Wheelan & McKeage, 1993). Most therapy experts note that, despite the temporary disruptions created by the conflict, this period is an essential one for the group to experience (Bales & Cohen, with Williamson, 1979; Bennis & Shepard, 1956; Fisher, 1980). Conflicts also help groups clarify their goals by forcing members to make choices that reflect the group's negotiated preferences. Conflict even provides a means of venting personal hostilities, but members can reduce this stress by confronting the problem and communicating dissatisfactions honestly and openly. If hostilities are never expressed in the group, they may build up to a point at which the group can no longer continue as a unit.

The dissolution stage also appears to be more problematic for members of therapeutic groups than nontherapeutic groups. Clients, in both group and individual therapies, often experience the end of therapy as a significant relationship loss, and unless their termination is properly managed the gains achieved during treatment can vanish (Quintana, 1993). This sense of loss can be magnified in group treatment, for if group members have become psychologically connected to the group, they may be reluctant to sever this source of psychological and social support. Therapists must help members cope with the emotional consequences of the group's dissolution by clarifying deadlines, teaching members to identify new groups that can provide the resources formerly provided by their therapeutic group, by recognizing through group rituals the group's end, and by offering continued support to members (Brabender & Fallon, 1996; Fieldsteel, 1996; Paternel, 1991; Schermer & Klein, 1996).

Leadership in Therapeutic Groups

Just as studies of groups in business, organizational, and military settings stress the impact of the leaders on the group (see also Chemers, 2001; Lord, Brown, & Harvey, 2001), so studies of therapeutic groups suggest that the group's processes and outcomes are shaped, to a great extent, by the characteristics, skills, and methods used by the therapist-leader.

Personal characteristics of leaders

On the trait side, some theorists, researchers, and practitioners believe that effective group therapists possess certain specific personality traits. For example, Slavson (1962, 1964) suggested that group therapists should be characterized by poise, maturity, ego-strength, perceptiveness, empathy, intuition, creativity, interest in others, a desire to help people, and a high tolerance for frustration. Parker (1972) emphasized a different set of traits: broad personal experience, self-awareness, open acceptance of others, expressiveness, and personal security. Kellerman's (1979) list is particularly lengthy and includes: simplicity, honesty, straight-forwardness, an ability to succeed, commitment to diversity, tolerance, authenticity, trust, ability to empathize, warmth, acceptance, understanding, spontaneity, capability of maintaining distance, experimentation, sense of humor, and flexibility. Bowers, Gauron, and Mines (1984) even offer a procedure that identifies good group psychotherapists by assessing such personality traits as need for closure, individualism, extroversion, and "regression in the service of the ego." These conclusions are primarily speculative, however, as researchers have not yet conducted any systematic investigations of the identifying personal characteristics of group therapists.

Other analyses of the qualities desired in a group therapist stress outlook and attitude rather than personality traits. MacLennan (1975), for example, suggests that leaders should be skilled at expressing their feelings, and that they should be both perceptive and warm. Ideally the leaders should also be trained in the management of group situations, and be capable of responding empathically to others (Day, 1993). Carkhuff (1969a, 1969b) pinpoints specific behaviors that facilitate positive therapeutic outcomes: empathy, positive regard, concreteness, genuineness, confrontation, and immediacy. Anderson and Robertson (1985) expand Carkhuff's list by adding such specific skills as attending, communicating clearly, modeling, linking, interpreting, regulating, and facilitating closure.

Leaders should also be capable of developing sophisticated and accurate appraisals of group processes, which is a skill that develops through time and experience (Kivlighan & Quigley, 1991). Interpersonal learning also occurs as members become recipients, willing or not, of the advice and guidance of the leader and the other group members. When researchers analyzed recordings of therapy sessions, they discovered that therapists respond to clients at several levels. They provide information and guidance, ask a variety of questions, repeat and paraphrase the client's statements, confront the client's interpretations of problems, offer their own interpretation of the causes of client's problems, and express their approval of and support for the client (Hill, Helms, Tichenor, Spiegel, O'Grady, & Perry, 1988).

Leadership style

The classic distinction between task and relationship leader that permeates virtually all studies of leadership emerges robustly in therapeutic groups. As early as 1948 Benne and

Sheats suggested that an effective leader must fill such task roles as "initiator contributor," "information seeker," "opinion seeker," and "elaborator," as well as such socioemotional roles as "encourager," "harmonizer," and "group commentator." Lieberman, Yalom, and Miles (1973), in their study of therapeutic groups, noted that whereas some therapists stress the task at hand, others are supportive and warm. They describe one taskoriented leader they studied as follows (1973, p. 59):

> He seemed to have a preplanned script of exercises he had decided to use in a particular meeting. . . . He did relatively little challenging or confrontation, but he frequently questioned individuals or invited them to participate in the group. In the observers' view, he was a highly managerial, highly structuring leader who made little use of his own person.

In contrast, the relationship-oriented leader focuses on the feelings, attitudes, and satisfactions of the group members. These group-oriented approaches, which are typified by encounters or T groups, encourage the analysis of the group's processes, with the therapist-leader sometimes facilitating process, but sometimes providing no direction whatsoever. Such leaders strive to make certain the group atmosphere is positive by boosting morale, increasing cohesiveness, and monitoring any interpersonal conflict. From Lieberman et al. (1973, p. 29):

> He often invited questions and confronted members in an effort to "open them up." However, he gave a great deal of support. . . . He offered friendship, as well as protection, to group members. [He] expressed considerable warmth, acceptance, genuineness, and caring for other human beings.

Tinsley, Roth, and Lease (1989) surveyed therapists to assess self-reported variations in leadership style. They developed a large set of items measuring a variety of qualities including modeling ("I reveal my own feelings and personal attitudes to the group"), cogniz-ing ("I help the group understand the meaning of nonverbal cues as they come up"), command stimulation ("I directly request members to respond"), managing/limit setting ("I intervene and stop the interaction if I feel it is necessary)", and personal ("I express con-siderable warmth, acceptance, and genuineness to individuals in the group," p. 50). Factor analysis of these self-ratings revealed eight factors that accounted for nearly 70% of the variance in ratings. The first factor was concerned primarily with task-focused leadership. This factor, labeled "cognitive direction" by the researchers, stressed management, mirroring, command, and charisma. The second factor, labeled "affective direction," stressed leadership behaviors that helped the group members express their emotions. The third factor concerned socioemotional support for members, with such items as affective support, personal, and member liking loading significantly on this factor. The remaining factors pertained to group functioning, verbal stimulation, charismatic expertise, individual functioning, and reliance on nonverbal exercises.

Are task-oriented leaders more effective than socioemotional ones? Yalom (1995) suggests that the most effective leaders are ones that provide clear structure and direction, but at the same time make sure certain members' socioemotional needs are met. Bolman (1971), however, reports that leaders who were more relationship-oriented were better liked by group members, and the members of their groups reported more positive therapeutic gains. Other evidence suggests that, just as effective leaders in organizational settings sometimes vary their interventions to fit the situation, so effective leaders in therapeutic settings shift their methods as the group matures. Kivlighan (1997) arranged for all the members of psychoeducational groups to rate their leaders on their task-orientation (conditionality) and relationship-orientation (congruence/empathy) early and late in their groups' 26-session duration. He found that group members' stress reduction was positively correlated with task ratings taken early in treatment and with relationship ratings taken late in treatment. Kivlighan concludes that his findings are consistent with Hersey and Blanchard's (1977) model of leadership, which suggests that different types of leadership are most effective at different times in the group's developmental cycle.

Leaders' theoretical orientation

Group practitioners also vary greatly in their orientations and techniques. Some focus on emotions with Gestalt exercises, others concentrate on the here-and-now of the group's inter-personal process, and others train members to perform certain behaviors through videotaped feedback, behavioral rehearsal, and systematic reinforcement. Some are strict Freudians who seek deep interpretations of their patients' thoughts, whereas others only direct their comments at the group as a whole, refusing to even address specific members.

Lieberman, Yalom, and Miles studied the relationship between therapy leaders' orientation and their effectiveness as change agents in their classic 1973 study of experiential learning groups (Yalom, 1985; Lieberman, Yalom, & Miles, 1973). They randomly assigned 206 Stanford University students to groups representing 10 theoretical orientations: Gestalt, transactional analysis, T groups, Synanon, Esalen, psychoanalytic, marathon, psychodrama, encounter tape, and encounter. Trained observers coded the group's interactions, with particular attention to the leader's style. Before, during, immediately after, and six months following the participation they administered a battery of items assessing group members' self-esteem, attitudes, self-satisfactions, values, satisfaction with friendships, and so on. Measures also were completed by the co-members, the leaders, and by group members' acquaintances.

Somewhat unexpectedly, the project discovered that no one theoretical approach had a monopoly on effectiveness: For example, two separate Gestalt groups with different leaders were included in the design, but the members of these two groups evidenced widely discrepant gains. One of the Gestalt groups ranked among the most successful in stimulating participant growth, but the other group yielded fewer benefits than all of the groups. These findings may have resulted from the lack of experience of the group leaders, as Russell (1978) suggests, but more recent studies provide general confirmation for the equivalency among treatments reported by Lieberman, Yalom, and Miles (Berah, 1981; Coche, Cooper, & Petermann, 1984; Falloon, 1981; Gonzalez-Menendez, 1985; Hajek, Belcher, & Stapleton, 1985; Knauss, Jeffrey, Knauss, & Harowski, 1983; Markham, 1985; Rosenberg & Brian, 1986; Sanchez, Lewinsohn, & Larson, 1980; Weinstein & Rossini, 1998; cf., Graff, Whitehead, & LeCompte, 1986; Kaplan, 1982).

Leadership and structure

The leader's directiveness is a key component of leadership style. Whereas task-oriented leaders tend to provide more structure than relationship-oriented leaders, the leader's tendency to structure the group's work can vary from high to low across both types of leaders (Eagly, Karau, & Makhijani, 1995). Some therapy-group leaders provide considerable structure for the group, particularly those who base their treatment on psychoanalytic, Gestalt, or behavioral methods. Leaders of such groups guide the course of the interaction, assign various tasks to the group members, and they occupy the center of the centralized communication network. In some instances, the group members may not even communicate with one another but only with the group leader. In contrast, other therapists advocate a nondirective style of leadership in which all group members communicate with one another. These group-oriented approaches, which are typified by encounters or T groups, encourage the analysis of the group's processes, with the therapist/leader sometimes facilitating the process, but at other times providing no direction whatsoever.

Studies of groups indicate that both directive and nondirective leaders are effective agents of change so long as they are caring, they help members interpret the cause of their problems, they keep the group on course, and they meet the members' socioemotional needs (Lieberman et al., 1973). Some evidence, though, suggests that moderate levels of structure and centralization are best for individuals with severe psychological problems. As Strong and Claiborn (1982) suggest, individuals who are highly aggressive, pathological, or resistant may be quite unresponsive to the social influences within groups. In consequence, greater structure is needed to produce beneficial change. Similarly, Grotjahn, Kline, and Friedmann (1983) argue that the structure a leader-centered approach provides is needed with severe behavior problems typical of inpatient and crisis groups. Friedmann (1983, p. 75), when working with crisis groups, argues that "passivity on the part of the therapist will be seen by the patient as a sign of disinterest." In consequence, the leader must be both directive and active, to the point of facilitating group processes, prompting self-disclosure, pointing out commonalties among members, and providing interpretation. The length of the treatment must be considered as well when evaluating the value of structure. Waltman and Zimpfer (1988), in a meta-analysis of studies of structure and group composition, found that highly structured groups suppress the relationship between the group's composition and its outcome. Hence, even if the group's members are compatible or incompatible in terms of their presenting problem or the personal qualities, these compatibilities will not influence the outcome of their therapy if the group is highly structured and meets for only a limited number of sessions.

Co-leadership

Many therapists work in teams of two when leading groups. Dies (1994), in his comprehensive review of 230 studies of leadership of therapeutic groups, found that 45% of the groups examined were co-led. Roller and Nelson (1993) identify a number of advantages of co-therapy for both group members and practitioners. Members of groups with two therapists can observe the therapist's "model [of] how to behave in a relationship" (p. 307), and the therapists can "help each other stay centered, probe their feelings, and analyze counter-transference issues" (p. 307). Dies (1994, p. 141), however, is skeptical of the value of co-leadership, and concludes, "there is no evidence that the presence of two therapists enhances the quality or efficacy of therapeutic outcome." Indeed, Dies notes that co-leadership tends to complicate groups' processes, for the therapists must deal with power issues, negotiate over interpretation of group events, and sustain their trust in one another. Dugo and Beck (1997) also urge caution; they outline a detailed nine-stage model of co-therapy in groups that identifies a number of problems that therapists working together must confront. They note that in some cases the co-leaders of therapy groups must themselves seek counseling to deal with their relationship difficulties.

Gender and leadership

The tendency for group members to respond to men and women leaders differently has been documented in therapeutic groups (Greene, Morrison, & Tischler, 1981; Thune, Manderscheid, & Silbergeld, 1981; cf. Chemers, 2001). Greene and his colleagues, for example, examined group members' perceptions of male and female therapists in co-led groups. Although the therapists differed little in terms of skills and qualifications, male co-leaders were perceived as significantly more potent, active, instrumental and insightful than female co-leaders. Similarly, Thune and her colleagues, after examining co-leaders in several psychotherapy groups, discovered that gender was a more important determinant of status than either professional experience or professional affiliation (social worker vs. psychiatric nurse). These findings, which support sociological studies of status-formation processes, suggest that gender stereotypes may cause status problems for women (Lazerson & Zilbach, 1993). Many women overcome these problems, at least initially, by working with a male co-leader (Paulson, Burroughs, & Gelb, 1976; Rutan & Alonso, 1982).

Motives and Goals in Therapeutic Groups

Therapeutic groups, despite their emphasis on process and individual adjustment, none the less are working groups with procedures, agendas, and goals. In consequence, many of the conclusions drawn from studies of production units that pertain to agenda-setting, goal-clarification, and increasing member motivation apply equally well to therapeutic groups (Higgenbotham, West, & Forsyth, 1988). For example, just as decision-making groups that spend time deliberately structuring their approach to their tasks generally outperform those who begin without first planning their activities, therapeutic groups that spend time planning their procedures yield greater gains than those that do not include any preplanning of strategy (Bednar & Battersby, 1976; Bednar & Kaul, 1978; Kaul & Bednar, 1994). This planning need not be elaborate to be effective. Martin and Shewmaker (1962) found that simply giving patients written instructions concerning group processes led to more positive outcomes. Similarly, when Truax and Carkhuff (1965) and Truax, Shapiro, and Wargo

(1968) presented clients with tapes of several segments of actual group therapy sessions, they found that this exposure to group processes led to a reduction of schizophrenic symptoms (Truax & Carkhuff, 1965), and positive changes in MMPI scores (Truax et al., 1968). Strupp and Bloxom (1973) pretrained some group members by exposing them to a film describing the basis for psychotherapy, group members' roles, and the activities to be undertaken during therapy. The film also emphasized a number of specific points, including expression of personal feelings, the value of emotional expression, the responsibilities of the group member, the difference between adaptive and maladaptive behavior, and the potential gains that could be reasonably expected. On measures of improvement, satisfaction with treatment, symptom discomfort, and motivation, clients who saw the film responded more positively than clients who saw an irrelevant film.

These and other studies suggest that attempts to clarify the processes used to achieve change in groups by providing either pregroup training or information during the therapy lead to more positive therapeutic outcomes. As Bednar and Kaul (1978) conclude, "Ambiguity and lack of clarity tend to be associated with increased anxiety and diminished productivity and learning in a variety of settings" (p. 793), whereas interventions designed to decrease ambiguity "have been associated with significant and constructive effects" (p. 794; see Hardin, Subich, & Holvey, 1988). More recently they have put it more simply: "practice would be improved with the judicious application of pregroup training" (Kaul & Bednar, 1994, p. 183).

Therapeutic Factors in Groups

How does therapy work? Experts such as Strupp (1986; Butler & Strupp, 1986) and Frank (1982) suggest that individualistic, one-on-one therapies, despite their differences, share some common properties, and these commonalties may be responsible for their effectiveness. Most therapies increase clients' confidence in themselves, and provide them with a new way of viewing themselves and their problems. Therapists, too, tend to deal with their clients in positive, empathic ways, and this relationship may prove to be more helpful than the lessons learned through the relationship.

The nonspecific factors hypothesis applies equally well to group approaches to treatment. Lakin (1972), for example, argued that the successful group must facilitate emotional expression and feelings of belongingness, but it also must stimulate interpersonal comparisons and provide members with an interaction forum. Bednar and Kaul (1978) identified the "developing social microcosm," "interpersonal feedback and consensual validation," and "reciprocal opportunities to be both helpers and helpees in group settings" as key ingredients (p. 781). Yalom (1995) similarly identifies a number of curative factors operating in therapeutic groups, including the installation of hope, universality, the imparting of information, altruism, the corrective recapitulation of the primary family group, the development of socializing techniques, imitative behavior, interpersonal learning, group cohesiveness, catharsis, and existential factors.

Yalom based his model of curative factors on his clinical experience and his own empirical research, but the list is generally consistent with theoretical analyses of groups in general and

Table 4.1 Factors that Promote Change in Groups

Factor	Definition	Meaning to member
Universality	Recognition of shared problems, reduced sense of uniqueness	We all have problems
Hope	Increased sense of optimism from seeing others improve	If other members can change, so can I
Vicarious learning	Developing social skills by watching others	Seeing others talk about their problems inspired me to talk, too
Interpersonal learning	Developing social skills by interacting with others	I'm learning to get along better with other people
Guidance	Accepting advice and suggestions from the group members	People in the group give me good suggestions
Cohesion	Feeling accepted by others	The group accepts me and understands me
Self-disclosure	Revealing personal information to others	I feel better for sharing things I've kept secret for too long
Catharsis	Releasing pent-up emotions	It feels good to get things off my chest
Altruism	Increase sense of efficacy from helping others	Helping other people has given me more self-respect
Insight	Gaining a deeper understanding of oneself	I've learned a lot about myself

Source: Forsyth (1999).

therapeutic groups in particular (e.g., Butler & Fuhriman, 1983a, 1983b; Crouch, Bloch, & Wanlass, 1994; Forsyth, 1991, 1999; Markovitz & Smith, 1983; Maxmen, 1973, 1978; Rohrbaugh & Bartels, 1975; Rugel & Myer, 1984; Sherry & Hurley, 1976; Yalom, 1995; Yalom & Vinogradov, 1993). These change-promoting factors are summarized in Table 4.1 and discussed below.

Universality and hope

All groups, but therapeutic groups in particular, reduce members' feelings of anxiety, stress, and discomfort. When lone individuals find themselves in dangerous or anxietyprovoking situations, they prefer the company of other people rather than remain alone. This gregariousness is based, in part, on the instinctive recognition of safety in numbers, but it also serves psychological and information purposes. Baumeister and Leary (1995), for example, argue that human beings need to belong to intimate groups characterized by reliable interrelationships among members. As Schachter (1959) suggests, when individuals cannot evaluate the accuracy of their understanding of a situation, they seek out others to acquire information through social comparison. Affiliating with others also reduces the stress and anxiety, provided the other group members supply reassuring, fearallaying information about the situation. Whereas individuals facing unpleasant circumstances alone may feel discouraged and pessimistic, as group members they gain a sense of universality and hope.

Many groups – and self-help groups in particular – encourage social comparisons through rituals and traditions. Everyone at an AA meeting, for example, publicly states "I am an alcoholic," and this ritual reassures participants that their problems are shared by others. Evidence confirms this practice, for Frable, Platt, and Hoey (1998) found that individuals responded more positively to a stressful situation when they were with people who faced problems that were similar to their own. Because of these benefits, some therapists avoid diversity in their groups, particularly with regard to dysfunction and diagnostic category (Piper, 1994).

Groups also provide members with targets for both downward social comparison and upward social comparison. When individuals compare themselves with someone who is experiencing even more severe hardships or someone who is not coping with their problems effectively – downward social comparison – their sense of victimization decreases and their overall sense of self-esteem increases (Gibbons & Gerrard, 1989; Wood, Taylor, & Lichtman, 1985). And when they compare themselves to people who are coping effectively with their problems, members identify ways to improve their own situation (Buunk, 1995; Taylor & Lobel, 1989). Exposure to extraordinarily successful people – a group member who, despite many personal problems, seems to be adjusting marvelously – can threaten group members, but can also remind members that their problems are solvable. Contact with such people tends to be reassuring, but direct comparison with them is not (Taylor & Lobel, 1989).

Snyder and his colleagues suggest that joining with others sustains and enhances hope. Hope, in Snyder's model, is not then just a sense of confidence, but an enhanced motivational state that is sustained by clearly identified goals, pathway thoughts, and a sense of agency (Klausner, Snyder, & Cheavens, in press; Snyder, 1994; Snyder, Cheavens, & Sympson, 1997). Snyder's model of hope explains why Kolb and Boyatizis (1970) found that positive changes in personality were most pronounced among T-group members who developed personal plans for evaluating their performance in relationship to clearly established goals. The hope model also explains why pretraining clients, which was discussed earlier in the chapter, improves therapeutic outcome. Pretraining, by clarifying pathway thinking directly, raises hope indirectly.

Klausner et al. (in press) confirmed the value of a hope-based group intervention in a study of geriatric outpatients suffering from depression. The investigators developed a group intervention that stressed individualized goal formation and training in both pathway and agency thinking. At the end of 11 weeks of treatment group members were less depressed than they were at the start of treatment, and their depression levels were also lower than those shown by control-group subjects. Worthington, Hight, Ripley, Perrone, Kurusu, and Jones (1997) also developed a successful marital-enrichment intervention based on Snyder's model of hope. They reduced the pessimism felt by many married people about their chances of avoiding divorce in a hope-enrichment therapy that stressed the components of Snyder's model. Training involved structured exercises designed to help participants identify their relationship goals and the steps that they should take to reach these goals. Trained couples had higher relationship satisfaction and better interaction skills than couples in a control condition.

Social learning

Most therapists, when contrasting individual and group therapies, stress the interpersonal resources of group approaches. The patient learns from the therapist in one-on-one therapy, but in group therapy the patient can learn from the therapist, from other group members, and by watching the interactions between the therapist and other group members (Lieberman, 1980; Yalom, 1975, 1995). When a group member appropriately expresses pent-up hostility, observing group members learn how they can express emotions that they have been suppressing. When the group leader skillfully draws a reticent group member into the discussion by disclosing some personal information, the other group members learn about the relationship between self-disclosure and intimacy. Group leaders also model desirable behaviors by treating the group members in positive ways and avoiding behaviors that are undesirable (Dies, 1994). Vicarious learning (modeling), interpersonal learning, and guidance (direct instruction) all occur in therapeutic groups (see Table 4.1).

Modeling.   Researchers confirmed the importance of modeling in a study of phobias. People seeking help for their disabling fear of spiders were randomly assigned to small (3 or 4 members) or large (7 or 8 members) groups. The groups then spent three hours observing a model who showed no fear when handling a spider. Members of both groups showed sharp reductions in their fear of spiders, although improvement rate was slightly higher in the small group rather than the large group (Lars-Goeran, 1996). Groups that use explicit modeling methods show greater improvement than groups that only discuss the problematic behaviors (Falloon, Lindley, McDonald, & Marks, 1977).

Interpersonal learning.   All groups provide members with direct feedback about personal qualities ("You are a warm, sensitive person," "You seem lonely,"), but also indirect feedback in the form of nonverbal signals and reactions. Group members themselves tend to appreciate the feedback they get from their groups, for when rating the most valuable aspect of the group experience they give high scores to interpersonal processes: "the group's teaching me about the type of impression I make on others," "learning how I come across to others," and "other members honestly telling me what they think of me" (Yalom, 1975, p. 79). Extended contact with others in a group setting may provide individuals with corrective information about their skills and abilities.

Some therapeutic groups exchange so much evaluative information that members withdraw from the group rather than face the barrage of negative feedback (Scheuble, Dixon, Levy, & Kagan-Moore, 1987). Group leaders must intervene to regulate the flow of information between members so that individuals learn the information they need to change in positive ways. Group members also tend to deny the validity of information that is too discrepant from their own self-views. Jacobs and his colleagues, for example, arranged for subjects to participate in a short-term, highly structured "sensitivity" group (Jacobs, 1974). When subjects rated one another on a series of adjectives, Jacobs found that they consistently accepted positive feedback, but consistently rejected negative feedback. This "credibility gap" occurred despite attempts to vary the source of the information (Jacobs, 1974), the sequencing of the information (Jacobs, Jacobs, Gatz, & Schaible, 1973; Schaible & Jacobs, 1975), the behavioral and affective focus of the feedback (Jacobs, Jacobs, Cavior, & Feldman, 1973), and the anonymity of the appraisals (Jacobs, Jacobs, Cavior, & Burke, 1974). These findings attest to the potential value of group interventions as self-esteem-enhancing mechanisms, for the tendency to accept only positive feedback screens the group members from negative, but therapeutic, social information.

Guidance.   Groups also influence members by guiding, directly and indirectly, their opinions, attitudes, and values. As Newcomb (1943) verified in his study of college students, when individuals move from one group to another they more often than not abandon their old group's outlook and adopt the view of their new group. An individual having problems regulating his use of alcohol may, for example, believe that he can learn to drink in moderation. If he joins an AA group, however, he will be repeatedly exposed to a different set of values and beliefs: ones that maintain that alcoholism is a disease that can only be controlled by abstinence. Over time the individual's beliefs will likely change to match the group's opinion (e.g., Crandall, 1988; Fisher, 1988; Miller & Prentice, 1996). Fisher (1988), for example, developed an extensive educational program designed to change people's perceptions of norms related to sexual conduct. His AIDS Risk Reduction Project changed participants' attitudes toward condoms and anti-condom norms by exposing them to videotaped testimonials of medical experts and fellow students (Fisher & Fisher, 1993). Participants also watched videotapes of couples discussing safe sexual practices, negotiating the use of condoms, and exiting threatening situations, and they practiced these behavioral skills with other members of the group, who provided them with encouragement and social support (Fisher & Fisher, 1992).

Cohesion

Yalom (1985) suggests that therapeutic groups are most effective when they are cohesive; that unity within the group, although not a sufficient condition for change, is a necessary one. Yalom's suggestion is consistent with Cartwright's 1951 analysis of groups as change agents, for he argued that members must be committed to the group before they will change in reaction to its influence. Others, too, have noted that the "cotherapeutic influence of peers" in the therapy group requires group cohesion (Bach, 1954, p. 348; Frank, 1957; Goldstein, Heller, & Sechrest, 1966).

Cohesion likely influences the curative impact of a group by increasing the psychological intensity of the therapeutic experience (Marziali, Munroe-Blum, & McCleary, 1997). People in cohesive groups more readily accept the group's goals, decisions, and norms. Furthermore, pressures to conform are greater in cohesive groups, and individuals' resistance to these pressures is weaker (Back, 1951). Once a norm emerges in a cohesive group, members take harsher measures to bring dissenters into line than do the members of noncohesive groups (Schachter, 1951). Cohesive groups, more than noncohesive ones, probably provide members with more emotional support, advice and guidance, tangible assistance, and positive feedback (Posluszny, Hyman, & Baum, 1998). People also cope more effectively with stress when they are in cohesive groups (Bowers, Weaver, & Morgan, 1996; Zaccaro, Gualtieri, & Minionis, 1995).

Cohesive groups are not, however, without drawbacks. Cohesion has also been linked to social pressures of such intensity that individual members are overwhelmed and prey to illusions, misperceptions, and faulty communication. Furthermore, given the right (or wrong) combination of circumstances, cohesiveness encourages hostility and interpersonal rejection and promotes disabling overdependence in long-term members. If group members reject the therapist's attempts to establish change-producing norms cohesiveness will only intensify their resistance (Forsyth & Elliott, 1999).

Disclosure and catharsis

In many cases members of therapeutic groups hope to learn better ways to communicate with other people. They may, for example, be unable to reveal personal, intimate information to others (Corey & Corey, 1992; Leichtentritt & Shechtman, 1998). They may also fail to express their emotions. Individuals experiencing personality and psychological disturbances, for example, often disclose the wrong sorts of information at the wrong time (McGuire & Leak, 1980) and males, in particular, tend to be reserved in their rate of self-disclosure (Brooks, 1996; Kilmartin, 1994; Shechtman, 1994).

Group treatments provide a venue for self-expression. Groups generally insist on open disclosure by members, with such disclosure protected by the promise of confidentiality (Kaul & Bednar, 1986; Roark & Sharah, 1989; Tschuschke & Dies, 1994). By sharing information about themselves, members are expressing their trust in the group and signaling their commitment to the therapeutic process (Rempel, Holmes, & Zanna, 1985). Moreover, as Pennebaker's (1990) studies of confession suggest, the disclosure of troubling, worrisome thoughts can reduce the discloser's level of tension and stress. Individuals who keep their problems secret, but continually ruminate about them, display signs of physiological and psychological distress.

Members also can vent strong emotions in groups. The group offers members the opportunity to express strong emotions that they cannot express in any other circumstances, and this catharsis might ease their level of anxiety. Emotional release has been identified by some as a great benefit of groups, but others suggest that "blowing off steam" may actually heighten members' psychological distress and upset (see Ormont, 1984).

Altruism

Group approaches to treatment, unlike individualistic methods, capitalize and exploit people's natural tendency to seek help from peers and friends first, and professional therapists second. When individuals experience problems, they usually turn to friends and families for help (Wills & DePaulo, 1991). Individuals experiencing work-related stress cope by joining with coworkers rather than human resource specialists (Caplan, Vinokur, Price, & van Ryn, 1989; Cooper, 1981). Psychotherapy groups include an expert leader, but they also include peers who offer insights and advice to one another. This mutual assistance provides benefits for both parties, for the helper "feels a sense of being needed and helpful; can forget self in favor of another group member; and recognizes the desire to do something for another group member" (Crouch et al., 1994, p. 285).

Self-help groups place mutual assistance among members at center-stage. Such groups usually resist the leadership of a professional, and instead insist that members help themselves and one another. A support group that deals with psychological consequences of open-heart surgery, for example, tells members that "you are not completely mended until you help mend others" (Lieberman, 1993, p. 297). AA groups formalize and structure helping by pairing newcomers with sponsors who meet regularly with the new member outside of the regular group meetings.

Insight

Many individuals feel that mental health and self-knowledge are highly correlated; that only people who know themselves well are truly normal and well-adjusted. Although this assumption appears to be groundless (Sedikides & Strube, 1997), group members tend to rate therapeutic experiences positively when they feel they have promoted self-understanding. When participants in therapeutic groups were asked to identify events that took place in their groups that helped them the most, they stressed universality, interpersonal learning, cohesion (belonging), and insight (Kivlighan & Mullison, 1988; Kivlighan, Multon, & Brossart, 1996). Other studies that asked group members to rank or rate the importance of various curative factors generally find that group members emphasize self-understanding, interpersonal learning, and catharsis (Butler & Fuhriman, 1983a; Markovitz & Smith, 1983; Maxmen, 1973, 1978; Rohrbaugh & Bartels, 1975; Rugel & Meyer, 1984). In general, individuals who stress the value of self-understanding tend to benefit the most from participation in a therapeutic group (Butler & Fuhriman, 1983b).

The Effectiveness of Groups

Therapeutic groups have one basic goal: To enhance the psychological adjustment of their members. So, just as a production line is evaluated by reviewing its efficiency or the caliber of a sports team is determined by its record in competitive contests, the value of a therapeutic group is determined by its success in reaching its goal: Do members leave the group better adjusted than when they entered?

Unfortunately, the available data are insufficient to draw clear conclusions about the effectiveness of group approaches to treatment. Groups are difficult to study, and so studies of their effectiveness often suffer from fatal flaws in design and execution. The use of varied and undocumented therapeutic methods, with different types of clients, by therapists who differ in skills and experience, in studies that too frequently lack valid measures and inadequate controls, make it difficult to draw firm conclusions (Bednar & Kaul, 1978, 1979, 1994; Burlingame, Kircher, & Taylor, 1994; Fuhriman & Burlingame, 1994; Kaul & Bednar, 1986). Meltzoff and Kornreich (1970), for example, were guardedly optimistic about the utility of group therapies because 80% of the methodologically sound studies reported either major or minor benefits for clients, whereas nearly all of the studies that reported no benefit were methodologically flawed. Bednar and Kaul's comprehensive and long-term monitoring of group methods are guardedly positive, although they continue to lament the lack of rigor in research (Bednar & Kaul, 1978, 1979, 1994; Kaul & Bednar, 1986).

Meta-analytic reviews, including those that code studies for methodological rigor, generally suggest that group approaches are as effective as individual methods (Davis, Olmsted, Rockert, Marques, & Dolhanty, 1997; Fuhriman & Burlingame, 1994; Hoag & Burlingame, 1997; Robinson, Berman, & Neimeyer, 1990; Shapiro & Shapiro, 1982; Smith, Glass, & Miller, 1980; Tillitski, 1990). Smith et al. (1980) and Miller and Berman (1983) found that individual and group treatments were roughly equivalent in terms of effectiveness. Fuhriman and Burlingame (1994), in their massive review of 700 group therapy studies and seven meta-analytic reviews of prior research, concluded that group methods are effective treatments for a wide variety of psychological problems. Similarly, Faith, Wong, and Carpenter (1995), in a meta-analytic review of 63 studies of sensitivity-training, concluded that these groups generally led to increases in self-actualization and self-esteem, and improved interpersonal relations. They noted that these effects increased in larger groups, when the groups met for longer periods of time, and when the measures focused on behavioral outcomes rather than self-reported ones. Burke and Day's (1986) analysis of the long-term effectiveness of T groups in organization-development interventions reached similar conclusions.

Burlingame and his colleagues (McRoberts, Burlingame, & Hoag, 1998) also concluded that groups are as effective as individual treatments when they meta-analyzed studies that compared both individual and group approaches. They also tracked a number of other treatment and procedural variables that past researchers identified as key determinants of therapeutic success, but the only factors that covaried significantly with outcome were client diagnosis, number of treatment sessions, and the year in which the study was conducted. Group therapies were more effective with clients: (a) who were not diagnosed clinically; (b) who were suffering from substance abuse problems and/or chemical dependencies; (c) who attended 10 or fewer sessions. Older studies – those conducted prior to 1980 – were more likely to favor group over individual approaches.

Bednar and Kaul, in summarizing the literature on group therapy, conclude the "accumulated evidence indicates that group treatments have been more effective than no treatment, than placebo or nonspecific treatments, or than other recognized psychological treatments, at least under some circumstances" (Bednar & Kaul, 1994, p. 632). This positive conclusion, however, requires some qualification. First the empirical evidence is not definitive. Whereas a number of reviews are positive, others conclude that group therapy is not as potent as individual therapy (e.g., Abramowitz, 1977; Dush, Hirt, & Schroeder, 1983; Engels & Vermey, 1997; Kilmann & Sotile, 1976; Nietzel, Russel, Hemmings, & Gretter, 1987; Parloff & Dies, 1977; Solomon, 1982; Stanton & Shadish, 1997). Second, the changes brought about by group experiences *may* be more perceptual than behavioral. Bednar and Kaul (1979), after culling the studies of change in groups that were methodologically flawed, concluded that most studies had reported changes only on self-report data, rather than behavioral data. Reviews of experiential groups also generally find stronger evidence of perceptual changes than of behavioral changes (Bates & Goodman, 1986; Berman & Zimpfer,

1980; Budman, Demby, Feldstein, & Gold, 1984; Ware, Barr, & Boone, 1982). Faith et al. (1995), however, did not confirm this tendency in their review. Third, in some cases, groups can do more harm than good for participants. As Bednar and Kaul note, a participant may decide to leave the group before he or she has benefited in any way, and in rare cases an individual may be significantly harmed by the group experience.

Therapeutic Groups as Groups

Therapeutic groups, despite their focus on the psychological health of their members, none the less share many of the properties common to all groups. They develop over time. They have goals to accomplish. They have leaders that guide them, and members who strive to reject the authority of those leaders. Therapeutic groups possess features that set them apart from other groups, but their development, their structures, and their outcomes are shaped by processes that are common to all groups. Therapeutic groups are groups first, and therapeutic groups second.

Many issues related to therapeutic groups – their development, structure, leadership, and effectiveness – remain only dimly understood. Curiously, when psychology emerged as a mental health field after World War II, many of its central practitioners were academicians who specialized in the study of group processes: Lewin (1951) being the prime example of an individual who prospered in the science and in the practice of groups. Over time, however, the professional identity of researchers and therapists diverged until now their shared roots are nearly unrecognizable. Even though group researchers and group therapists are likely to agree on foundational assumptions, those who study groups and those who use them to promote change rarely travel the same path (Forsyth, 1997). In consequence, practitioners have not yet fully exploited the power of groups, and researchers have only begun to explain the dynamic interrelationships between a group and its members. Given the importance of groups, this rift between the scientific study of groups and use of groups to achieve therapeutic goals must be closed by developing more elaborate conceptualizations of groups that take into account both their change-producing properties and their properties as groups per se.

REFERENCES

Abramowitz, C. V. (1977). The effectiveness of group psychotherapy with children. *Annual Progress in Child Psychiatry and Child Development*, 393–408.

Anderson, L. E., & Robertson, S. E. (1985). Group facilitation: Functions and skills. *Small Group Behavior, 16*, 139–156.

Bach, G. (1954). *Intensive group psychotherapy.* New York: Ronald Press.

Back, K. W. (1951). Influence through social communication. *Journal of Abnormal and Social Psychology, 46*, 9–23.

Bales, R. F., & Cohen, S. P. with Williamson, S. A. (1979). *SYMLOG: A system for the multiple level observation of groups.* New York: Free Press.

Bates, B., & Goodman, A. (1986). The effectiveness of encounter groups: Implications of research for counselling practice. *British Journal of Guidance and Counselling, 14*, 240–251.

Baumeister, R. F., & Leary, M. R. (1995). The need to belong: Desire for interpersonal attachments as a fundamental human motivation. *Psychological Bulletin, 117*, 497–529.

Bednar, R. L., & Battersby, C. P. (1976). The effects of specific cognitive structure on early group development. *Journal of Applied Behavioral Science, 12*, 513–522.

Bednar, R. L., & Kaul, T. (1978). Experiential group research: Current perspectives. In S. L. Garfield & A. E. Bergin (Eds.), *Handbook of psychotherapy and behavior change* (2nd Ed., pp. 769–815). New York: Wiley.

Bednar, R. L., & Kaul, T. (1979). Experiential group research: What never happened. *Journal of Applied Behavioral Science, 15*, 311–319.

Bednar, R. L., & Kaul, T. (1994). Experiential group research: Can the canon fire? In S. L. Garfield & A. E. Bergin (Eds.), *Handbook of psychotherapy and behavior change* (4th Ed., pp. 631–663). New York: Wiley.

Beem, E. E., Eurelings-Bontekoe, E. H. M., Cleiren, M. P. H. D., & Garssen, B. (1998). Workshops to support the bereavement process. *Patient Education and Counseling, 34*, 53–62.

Bender, L. (1937). Group activities in a children's ward as methods of psychotherapy. *American Journal of Psychiatry, 93*, 1151–1173.

Benne, K. D., & Sheats, P. (1948). Functional roles of group members. Journal of Social Issues, 4(2), 41–49.

Bennis, W. G. (1964). Patterns and vicissitudes in T-group development. In L. P. Bradford, J. R. Gibb, & K. D. Benne (Eds.), *T-group theory and laboratory method* (pp. 248–278). New York: Wiley.

Bennis, W. G., & Shepard, H. A. (1956). A theory of group development. *Human Relations, 9*, 415–437.

Berah, E. F. (1981). Influence of scheduling variations on the effectiveness of a group assertion-training program for women. *Journal of Counseling Psychology, 28*, 265–268.

Berman, J. J., & Zimpfer, D. G. (1980). Growth groups: Do the outcomes really last? *Review of Educational Research, 50*, 505–524.

Bion, W. (1961). *Experiences in groups.* New York: Basic Books.

Bolman, L. (1971). Some effects of trainers on their groups: A partial replication. *Journal of Applied Behavioral Science, 9*, 534–539.

Bowers, C. A., Weaver, J. L., & Morgan, B. B., Jr. (1996). Moderating the performance effects of stressors. In J. E. Driskell & E. Salas (Eds.), *Stress and human performance* (pp. 163–192). Mahwah, NJ: Erlbaum.

Bowers, W. A., Gauron, E. F., & Mines, R. A. (1984). Training of group psychotherapists: An evaluation procedure. *Small Group Behavior, 15*, 125–137.

Brabender, V., & Fallon, A. (1993). *Models of inpatient group psychotherapy.* Washington, DC: American Psychological Association.

Brabender, V., & Fallon, A. (1996). Termination in inpatient groups. *International Journal of Group Psychotherapy, 46*, 81–98.

Bradford, L. P., Gibb, J. R., & Benne, K. D. (1964). Two educational innovations. In L. P. Bradford, J. R. Gibb, & K. D. Benne (Eds.), *T-group theory and laboratory method: Innovation in re-education* (pp. 1–14). New York: Wiley.

Brooks, G. R. (1996). Treatment for therapy-resistant men. In M. P. Andronico (Ed.), *Men in groups: Insights, interventions, and psychoeducational work* (pp. 7–19). Washington, DC: American Psychological Association.

Budman, S. H., Demby, A., Feldstein, M., & Gold, M. (1984). The effects of time-limited group psychotherapy: A controlled study. *International Journal of Group Psychotherapy, 34*, 587–603.

Burke, M. J., & Day, R. R. (1986). A cumulative study of the effectiveness of managerial training. *Journal of Applied Psychology, 71*, 232–245.

Burlingame, G. M., Kircher, J. C., & Taylor, S. (1994). Methodological considerations in group psychotherapy research: Past, present, and future practices. In A. Fuhriman & G. M. Burlingame (Eds.), *Handbook of group psychotherapy: An empirical and clinical synthesis* (pp. 41–82). New York: Wiley.

Burnand, G. (1990). Group development phases as working through six fundamental human problems. *Small Group Research, 21*, 255–273.

Butler, S. F., & Strupp, H. H. (1986). Specific and nonspecific factors in psychotherapy: A problematic paradigm for psychotherapy research. *Psychotherapy, 23*, 30–40.

Butler, T., & Fuhriman, A. (1983a). Curative factors in group therapy: A review of the recent literature. *Small Group Behavior, 14*, 131–142.

Butler, T., & Fuhriman, A. (1983b). Level of functioning and length of time in treatment variables influencing patients' therapeutic experience in group psychotherapy. *International Journal of Group Psychotherapy, 33*, 489–505.

Buunk, B. P. (1995). Comparison direction and comparison dimension among disabled individuals: Toward a refined conceptualization of social comparison under stress. *Personality and Social Psychology Bulletin, 21*, 316–330.

Caplan, R. D., Vinokur, A. D., Prince, R. H., & van Ryn, M. (1989). Job seeking, reemployment, and mental health: A randomized field experiment in coping with job loss. *Journal of Applied Psychology, 74*, 759–769.

Carkhuff, R. R. (1969a). *Helping and human relations: Selection and training* (Vol. 1). New York: Holt, Rinehart, & Winston.

Carkhuff, R. R. (1969b). *Helping and human relations: Research and practice* (Vol. 2). New York: Holt, Rinehart, & Winston.

Cartwright, D. (1951). Achieving change in people: Some applications of group dynamics theory. *Human Relations, 4*, 381–392.

Chemers, M. M. (2001). Leadership effectiveness – an integrative review. In M. A. Hogg & S. Tindale (Eds.), *Blackwell handbook of social psychology: Group processes* (pp. 376–399). Oxford: Blackwell Publishing.

Christensen, A., & Jacobson, N. S. (1994). Who (or what) can do psychotherapy: The status and challenge of nonprofessional therapies. *Psychological Science, 5*, 8–12.

Coche, E., Cooper, J. B., & Petermann, K. J. (1984). Differential outcomes of cognitive and interactional group therapies. *Small Group Behavior, 15*, 497–509.

Cooper, C. L. (1981). Social support at work and stress management. *Small Group Behavior, 12*, 285–297.

Corey, M., & Corey, G. (1992). *Groups: Process and practice* (4th Ed.). Pacific Grove, CA: Brooks/Cole.

Crandall, C. S. (1988). Social contagion of binge eating. *Journal of Personality and Social Psychology, 55*, 588–598.

Crouch, E. C., Bloch, S., & Wanlass, J. (1994). Therapeutic factors: Interpersonal and intrapersonal mechanisms. In A. Fuhriman & G. M. Burlingame (Eds.), *Handbook of group psychotherapy: An empirical and clinical synthesis* (pp. 269–315). New York: Wiley.

Davies, D., & Kuypers, B. C. (1985). Group development and interpersonal feedback. *Group and Organizational Studies, 10*, 184–208.

Davis, R., Olmsted, M., Rockert, W., Marques, T., & Dolhanty, J. (1997). Group psychoeducation for bulimia nervosa with and without additional psychotherapy process sessions. *International Journal of Eating Disorders, 22*, 25–34.

Day, M. (1981). Psychoanalytic group therapy in clinic and private practice. *American Journal of Psychiatry, 138*, 64–69.

Day, M. (1993). Training and supervision in group psychotherapy. In H. I. Kaplan & M. J. Sadock (Eds.), *Comprehensive group psychotherapy* (3rd Ed., pp. 656–673). Baltimore, MD: Williams & Wilkins.

Dies, R. (1992). The future of group therapy. *Psychotherapy, 29*, 58–61.

Dies, R. (1994). Therapist variables in group psychotherapy research. In A. Fuhriman & G. M. Burlingame (Eds.), *Handbook of group psychotherapy: An empirical and clinical synthesis* (pp. 114–154). New York: Wiley.

Dugo, J. M., & Beck, A. P. (1997). Significance and complexity of early phases in the development of the co-therapy relationship. *Group Dynamics, 1*, 294–305.

Dush, D. M., Hirt, M. L., & Schroeder, H. (1983). Self-statement modification with adults: A meta-analysis. *Psychological Bulletin, 94*, 408–422.

Eagly, A. H., Karau, S. J., & Makhijani, M. (1995). Gender and the effectiveness of leaders: A meta-analysis. *Journal of Personality and Social Psychology, 117*, 125–145.

Engels, G. I., & Vermey, M. (1997). Efficacy of nonmedical treatments of depression in elders: A quantitative analysis. *Journal of Clinical Geropsychology, 3*, 17–35.

Faith, M. S., Wong, F. Y., and Carpenter, K. M. (1995). Group sensitivity training: Update, meta-analysis, and recommendations. *Journal of Counseling Psychology, 42*, 390–399.

Falloon, I. R. (1981). Interpersonal variables in behavioural group therapy. *British Journal of Medical Psychology, 54*, 133–141.

Falloon, I. R., Lindley, P., McDonald, R., & Marks, I. M. (1977). Social skills training of outpatient groups: A controlled study of rehearsal and homework. *British Journal of Psychiatry, 131*, 599–609.

Fieldsteel, N. D. (1996). The process of termination in long-term psychoanalytic group therapy. *International Journal of Group Psychotherapy, 46*, 25–39.

Fisher, B. A. (1980). *Small group decision making* (2nd Ed.). New York: McGraw-Hill.

Fisher, J. D. (1998). Possible effects of reference group-based social influence on AIDS-risk behavior and AIDS-prevention. *American Psychologist, 43*, 914–920.

Fisher, J. D., & Fisher, W. A. (1992). Changing AIDS risk behavior. *Psychological Bulletin, 111*, 454–474.

Fisher, W. A., & Fisher, J. D. (1993). A general social psychological model for changing AIDS risk behavior. In J. B. Pryor & Glenn D. Reeder (Eds.), *The social psychology of HIV infection* (pp. 127–153). Hillsdale, NJ: Erlbaum.

Flowers, J. (1979). Behavioral analysis of group therapy and a model for behavioral group therapy. In D. Upper & S. Ross (Eds.), *Behavioral group therapy, 1979: An annual review*. Champaign, IL: Research Press.

Forsyth, D. R. (1991). Change in therapeutic groups. In C. R. Snyder & D. R. Forsyth (Eds.), *Handbook of social and clinical psychology: The health perspective* (pp. 664–680). New York: Pergamon.

Forsyth, D. R. (1997). The scientific study of groups. *Group Dynamics: Theory, Research, and Practice, 1*, 3–6.

Forsyth, D. R. (1999). *Group dynamics* (3rd Ed.). Pacific Grove, CA: Brooks/Cole.

Forsyth, D. R., & Elliott, T. R. (1999). Group dynamics and psychological well-being: The impact of groups on adjustment and dysfunction. In R. Kowalski & M. R. Leary (Eds.), *The social psychology of emotional and behavioral problems: Interfaces of social and clinical psychology* (pp. 339–361). Washington, DC: American Psychological Association.

Foulkes, S. (1964). *Therapeutic group analysis*. New York: International Universities Press.

Frable, D. E. S., Platt, L., & Hoey, S. (1998). Concealable stigmas and positive self-perceptions: Feeling better around similar others. *Journal of Personality and Social Psychology, 74*, 909–922.

Frank, J. D. (1957). Some determinants, manifestations, and effects of cohesiveness in therapy groups. *International Journal of Group Psychotherapy, 7*, 53–63.

Frank, J. D. (1982). Therapeutic components shared by all psychotherapies. In J. H. Harvey & M. M. Parks (Eds.), *The master lecture series, Vol. 1: Psychotherapy research and behavior change* (pp. 540, 560, 562). Washington, DC: American Psychological Association.

Friedmann, C. T. H. (1983). Crisis groups. In M. Grotjahn, F. M. Kline, & C. T. H. Friedmann (Eds.), *Handbook of group therapy*. New York: Van Nostrand Reinhold.

Fuhriman, A., & Burlingame, G. M. (1994). Group psychotherapy: Research and practice. In A. Fuhriman & G. M. Burlingame (Eds.), *Handbook of group psychotherapy: An empirical and clinical synthesis* (pp. 3–40). New York: Wiley.

Gibbons, F. X., & Gerrard, M. (1989). Effects of upward and downward social comparison on mood states. *Journal of Social and Clinical Psychology, 8*, 14–31.

Goldstein, A. P., Heller, K., & Sechrest, L. B. (1966). *Psychotherapy and the psychology of behavior change*. New York: Wiley.

Gonzalez-Menendez, R. (1985). La psicoterapia de grupo didactica en psicoticos hospitalizados: Estudio comparativo de tres variantes. (Didactic group psychotherapy in hospitalized psychotic patients: Comparative study of 3 variations.) *Revista del Hospital Psiquiatrico de La Habana, 26*(4, Suppl.), 212–228.

Goodman, G., & Jacobs, M. K. (1994). The self-help, mutual-support group. In A. Fuhriman & G. M. Burlingame (Eds.), *Handbook of group psychotherapy: An empirical and clinical synthesis* (pp. 489–526). New York: Wiley.

Graff, R. W., Whitehead, G. I., LeCompte, M. (1986). Group treatment with divorced women using cognitive-behavioral and supportive-insight methods. *Journal of Counseling Psychology, 33*, 276–281.

Gray, C., Verdieck, M. J., Smith, E. D., & Freed, K. (1997). Making it work: An evaluation of court-mandated parenting workshops for divorcing families. *Family and Conciliation Courts Review, 35*, 280–292.

Greene, L. R., Morrison, T. L., & Tischler, N. G. (1981). Gender and authority: Effects on perceptions of small group co-leaders. *Small Group Behavior, 12*, 401–413.

Grotjahn, M., Kline, F. M., & Friedmann, C. T. H. (Eds.). (1983). *Handbook of group therapy*. New York: Van Nostrand Reinhold.

Hajek, P., Belcher, M., & Stapleton, J. (1985). Enhancing the impact of groups: An evaluation of two group formats for smokers. *British Journal of Clinical Psychology, 24*, 289–294.

Hardin, S. I., Subich, L. M., & Holvey, J. M. (1988). Expectancies for counseling in relation to premature termination. *Journal of Counseling Psychology, 35*, 37–40.

Hersey, P., & Blanchard, K. H. (1977). *Management of organizational behavior: Utilizing human resources* (3rd Ed.). Englewood Cliffs, NJ: Prentice Hall.

Higginbotham, H. N., West, S. G., & Forsyth, D. R. (1988). *Psychotherapy and behavior change: Social, cultural, and methodological perspectives*. New York: Pergamon.

Hill, C. E., Helms, J. E., Tichenor, V., Spiegel, S. B., O'Grady, K. E., & Perry, E. S. (1988). Effects of therapist response modes in brief psychotherapy. *Journal of Counseling Psychology, 35*, 222–233.

Hill, W. F., & Gruner, L. (1973). A study of development in open and closed groups. *Small Group Behavior, 4*, 355–381.

Hoag, M. J., & Burlingame, G. M. (1997). Evaluating the effectiveness of child and adolescent group treatment: A meta-analytic review. *Journal of Clinical Child Psychology, 26*, 234–246.

Hollander, M., & Kazaoka, K. (1988). Behavior therapy groups. In S. Long (Ed.), *Six group therapies* (pp. 257–326). New York: Plenum.

Hollingshead, A. B. (2001). Communication technologies, the internet, and group research. In M. A. Hogg & S. Tindale (Eds.), *Blackwell handbook of social psychology: Group processes* (pp. 557–573). Oxford: Blackwell Publishing.

Jacobs, A. (1974). The use of feedback in groups. In A. Jacobs & W. W. Spradlin (Eds.), *Group as an agent of change.* New York: Behavioral Publications.

Jacobs, M. K., & Goodman, G. (1989). Psychology and self-help groups: Predictions on a partnership. *American Psychologist, 44,* 536–545.

Jacobs, A., Jacobs, M., Cavior, N., & Burke, J. (1974). Anonymous feedback: Credibility and desirability of structured emotional and behavioral feedback delivered in groups. *Journal of Counseling Psychology, 21,* 106–111.

Jacobs, M., Jacobs, A., Cavior, N., & Feldman, A. (1973). Feedback II: The "credibility gap": Delivery of positive and negative emotional and behavior feedback in groups. *Journal of Consulting and Clinical Psychology, 41,* 215–223.

Jacobs, M., Jacobs, A., Gatz, M., & Schaible, T. (1973). Credibility and desirability of positive and negative structured feedback in groups. *Journal of Consulting and Clinical Psychology, 40,* 244–252.

Johnson, F. (1988). Encounter group therapy. In S. Long (Ed.), *Six group therapies* (pp. 115–158). New York: Plenum.

Kaplan, D. A. (1982). Behavioral, cognitive, and behavioral-cognitive approaches to group assertion training therapy. *Cognitive Therapy and Research, 6,* 301–314.

Kaplan, H. I., & Sadock, B. J. (Eds.). (1993). *Comprehensive group psychotherapy* (3rd Ed.). Baltimore, MD: Williams & Wilkins.

Kaplan, R. E. (1979). The conspicuous absence of evidence that process consultation enhances task performance. *Journal of Applied Behavioral Science, 15,* 346–360.

Kaul, T. J., & Bednar, R. L. (1986). Experiential group research: Results, questions, and suggestions. In S. L. Garfield & A. E. Bergin (Eds.), *Handbook of psychotherapy and behavior change* (3rd Ed., pp. 671–714). New York: Wiley.

Kaul, T. J., & Bednar, R. L. (1994). Pretraining and structure: Parallel lines yet to meet. In A. Fuhriman & G. M. Burlingame (Eds.), *Handbook of group psychotherapy: An empirical and clinical synthesis* (pp. 155–188). New York: Wiley.

Kellerman, H. (1979). *Group psychotherapy and personality: Intersecting structures.* New York: Grune & Stratton.

Kilmann, P. R., & Sotile, W. M. (1976). The marathon encounter group: A review of the outcome literature. *Psychological Bulletin, 83,* 827–850.

Kilmartin, C. T. (1994). *The masculine self.* New York: Macmillan.

Kivlighan, D. M., Jr. (1997). Leader behavior and therapeutic gain: An application of situational leadership theory. *Group Dynamics: Theory, Research, and Practice, 1,* 32–38.

Kivlighan, D. M., Jr., & Lilly, R. L. (1997). Developmental changes in group climate as they relate to therapeutic gain. *Group Dynamics, 1,* 208–221.

Kivlighan, D. M., Jr., McGovern, T. V., & Corazzini, J. G. (1984). Effects of content and timing of structuring interventions on group therapy process and outcome. *Journal of Counseling Psychology, 31,* 363–370.

Kivlighan, D. M., Jr., Multon, K. D., & Brossart, D. F. (1996). Helpful impacts in group counseling: Development of a multidimensional rating system. *Journal of Counseling Psychology, 43,* 347–355.

Kivlighan, D. M., Jr., & Mullison, D. (1988). Participants' perception of therapeutic factors in group counseling: The role of interpersonal style and stage of group development. *Small Group Behavior, 19,* 452–468.

Kivlighan, D. M., Jr., & Quigley, S. T. (1991). Dimensions used by experienced and novice group therapists to conceptualize group process. *Journal of Counseling Psychology, 38,* 415–423.

Klausner, E. J., Snyder, C. R., & Cheavens, J. (in press). A hope-based group treatment for depressed older adult outpatients. In G. M. Williamson, P. A. Parmelee, & D. R. Shaffer (Eds.), *Physical illness and depression in older adults: A handbook of theory, research, and practice.* New York: Plenum.

Knauss, M. R., Jeffrey, D. B., Knauss, C. S., & Harowski, K. (1983). Therapeutic contact and individual differences in a comprehensive weight loss program. *Behavior Therapist, 6*, 124–128.

Kolb, D. A., & Boyatizis, R. E. (1970). Goal-setting and self-directed behavior change. *Human Relations, 23*, 439–457.

Kutash, I. L., & Wolf, A. (1993). Psychoanalysis in groups. In H. I. Kaplan & M. J. Sadock (Eds.), *Comprehensive group psychotherapy* (3rd ed., pp. 126–138). Baltimore, MD: Williams & Wilkins.

Lakin, M. (1972). *Experiential groups: The uses of interpersonal encounter, psychotherapy groups, and sensitivity training.* Morristown, NJ: General Learning Press.

Lars-Goeran, O. (1996). One-session group treatment of spider phobia. *Behaviour Research and Therapy, 34*, 707–715.

Lazerson, J. S., & Zilbach, J. J. (1993). Gender issues in group psychology. In H. I. Kaplan & M. J. Sadock (Eds.), *Comprehensive group psychotherapy* (3rd Ed., pp. 682–693). Baltimore, MD: Williams & Wilkins.

Leichtentritt, J., & Shechtman, Z. (1998). Therapist, trainee, and child verbal response modes in child group therapy. *Group Dynamics: Theory, Research, and Practice, 2*, 36–47.

Levine, J. M., Moreland, R. L., & Choi, H.-S. (2001). Group socialization and newcomer innovation. In M. A. Hogg & S. Tindale (Eds.), *Blackwell handbook of social psychology: Group processes* (pp. 86–106). Oxford: Blackwell Publishing.

Lewin, K. (1951). *Field theory in social science.* New York: Harper.

Lichtenberg, J. W., & Knox, P. L. (1991). Order out of chaos: A structural analysis of group therapy. *Journal of Counseling Psychology, 38*, 279–288.

Lieberman, M. A. (1980). Group methods. In F. H. Kanfer & A. P. Goldstein (Eds.), *Helping people change.* New York: Pergamon.

Lieberman, M. A. (1993). Self-help groups. In H. I. Kaplan & M. J. Sadock (Eds.), *Comprehensive group psychotherapy* (3rd Ed., pp. 292–304). Baltimore, MD: Williams & Wilkins.

Lieberman, M. A. (1994). Growth groups in the 1980s: Mental health implications. In A. Fuhriman & G. M. Burlingame (Eds.), *Handbook of group psychotherapy: An empirical and clinical synthesis* (pp. 527–558). New York: Wiley.

Lieberman, M. A., Yalom, I., & Miles, M. (1973). *Encounter groups: First facts.* New York: Basic Books.

Long, S. (Ed.). (1988). *Six group therapies.* New York: Plenum.

Lord, R. G., Brown, D. J., & Harvey, J. L. (2001). System constraints on leadership perceptions, behavior, and influence – an example of connectionist-level processes. In M. A. Hogg & S. Tindale (Eds.), *Blackwell handbook of social psychology: Group processes* (pp. 283–310). Oxford: Blackwell Publishing.

Mabry, E. A. (1975). Exploratory analysis of a developmental model for task-oriented small groups. *Human Communication Research, 2*, 66–74.

MacKenzie, K. R. (1994). Group development. In A. Fuhriman & G. M. Burlingame (Eds.), *Handbook of group psychotherapy: An empirical and clinical synthesis* (pp. 223–268). New York: Wiley.

MacKenzie, K. R. (1997). Clinical application of group development ideas. *Group Dynamics: Theory, Research, and Practice, 1*, 275–287.

MacLennan, B. W. (1975). The personalities of group leaders: Implications for selection and training. *International Journal of Group Psychotherapy, 25*, 177–183.

Maples, M. F. (1988). Group development: Extending Tuckman's theory. *Journal for Specialists in Group Work, 13*, 17–23.

Markham, D. J. (1985). Behavioral rehearsals vs. group systematic desensitization in assertiveness training with women. Special Issue: Gender roles. *Academic Psychology Bulletin, 7*, 157–174.

Markovitz, R. J., & Smith, J. E. (1983). Patients' perceptions of curative factors in short-term group psychotherapy. *International Journal of Group Psychotherapy, 33*, 21–39.

Marrow, A. J. (1964). *Behind the executive mask.* New York: American Management Association.

Martin, H., & Shewmaker, K. (1962). Written instructions in group psychotherapy. *Group Psychotherapy, 15,* 24–29.

Marziali, E., Munroe-Blum, H., & McCleary, L. (1997). The contribution of group cohesion and group alliance to the outcome of group psychotherapy. *International Journal of Group Psychotherapy, 47,* 475–497.

Maxmen, J. (1973). Group therapy as viewed by hospitalized patients. *Archives of General Psychiatry, 28,* 404–408.

Maxmen, J. (1978). An educative model for in-patient group therapy. *International Journal of Group Psychotherapy, 28,* 321–338.

McGuire, J. P., Leak, G. K. (1980). Prediction of self-disclosure from objective personality assessment techniques. *Journal of Clinical Psychology, 36,* 201–204.

McRoberts, C., Burlingame, G. M., & Hoag, M. J. (1998). Comparative efficacy of individual and group psychotherapy: A meta-analytic perspective. *Group Dynamics: Theory, Research, and Practice, 2,* 101–117.

Meltzoff, J., & Kornreich, M. (1970). *Research in psychotherapy.* New York: Atherton Press.

Miller, D. T., & Prentice, D. A. (1996). The construction of social norms and standards. In E. T. Higgins & A. Kruglanski (Eds.), *Social psychology: Handbook of basic principles* (pp. 799–829). New York: Guilford Press.

Miller, N. S. (1995). *Treatment of addictions: Applications of outcome research for clinical management.* New York: The Haworth Press.

Miller, R. C., & Berman, J. S. (1983). The efficacy of cognitive behavior therapies: A quantitative review of the research evidence. *Psychological Bulletin, 94,* 39–53.

Newcomb, T. M. (1943). *Personality and social change.* New York: Dryden.

Nietzel, M. T., Russell, R. L., Hemmings, K. A., & Gretter, M. L. (1987). Clinical significance of psychotherapy for unipolar depression: A meta-analytic approach to social comparison. *Journal of Consulting and Clinical Psychology, 55,* 156–161.

Ormont, L. R. (1984). The leader's role in dealing with aggression in groups. *International Journal of Group Psychotherapy, 34,* 553–572.

Parker, R. S. (1972). Some personal qualities enhancing group therapist effectiveness. *Journal of Clinical Issues in Psychology, 4,* 26–28.

Parloff, M. B., & Dies, R. R. (1977). Group psychotherapy outcome research 1966–1975. *International Journal of Group Psychotherapy, 27,* 281–319.

Paternel, F. (1991). The ending of a psychotherapy group. *Group Analysis, 24,* 159–169.

Paulson, I., Burroughs, J. C., & Gelb, C. B. (1976). Cotherapy: What is the crux of the relationship? *International Journal of Group Psychotherapy, 26,* 213–224.

Pennebaker, J. W. (1990). *Opening up: The healing power of confiding in others.* New York: Morrow.

Piper, W. E. (1994). Client variables. In A. Fuhriman & G. M. Burlingame (Eds.), *Handbook of group psychotherapy: An empirical and clinical synthesis* (pp. 83–113). New York: Wiley.

Posluszny, D. M., Hyman, K. B., & Baum, A. (1998). Group interventions in cancer: The benefits of social support and education on patient adjustment. In R. S. Tindale, L. Heath, J. Edwards, E. J. Posavac, F. B. Bryant, Y. Suarez-Balcazar, E. Henderson-King, & J. Myers (Eds.), *Theory and research on small groups* (pp. 87–105). New York: Plenum.

Pratt, J. H. (1922). The principles of class treatment and their application to various chronic diseases. *Hospital Social Services, 6,* 401–417.

Quintana, S. M. (1993). Toward an expanded and updated conceptualization of termination: Implications for short-term, individual psychotherapy. *Professional Psychology: Research and Practice, 24,* 426–432.

Rempel, J. K., Holmes, J. G., & Zanna, M. P. (1985). Trust in close relationships. *Journal of Personality and Social Psychology, 49,* 95–112.

Roark, A. E., & Sharah, H. S. (1989). Factors related to group cohesiveness. *Small Group Behavior, 20,* 62–69.

Robinson, L. A., Berman, J. S., & Neimeyer, R. A. (1990). Psychotherapy for the treatment of depression: A comprehensive review of controlled outcome research. *Psychological Bulletin, 108,* 30–49.

Rohrbaugh, M., & Bartels, B. D. (1975). Participants' perceptions of curative factors in therapy and growth groups. *Small Group Behavior, 6,* 430–456.

Roller, B., & Nelson, V. (1993). Co-therapy. In H. I. Kaplan & M. J. Sadock (Eds.), *Comprehensive group psychotherapy* (3rd Ed., pp. 304–312). Baltimore, MD: Williams & Wilkins.

Rose, S. D. (1993). Cognitive-behavioral group psychotherapy. In H. I. Kaplan & M. J. Sadock (Eds.), *Comprehensive group psychotherapy* (3rd Ed., pp. 205–214). Baltimore, MD: Williams & Wilkins.

Rosenberg, H., & Brian, T. (1986). Group therapy with alcoholic clients: A review. *Alcoholism Treatment Quarterly, 3,* 47–65.

Rugel, R. P., & Meyer, D. J. (1984). The Tavistock group: Empirical findings and implications for group therapy. *Small Group Behavior, 15,* 361–374.

Russell, E. W. (1978). The facts about Encounter groups: First facts. *Journal of Clinical Psychology, 34,* 130–137.

Rutan, J. S., & Alonso, A. (1982). Group therapy, individual therapy, or both? *International Journal of Group Psychotherapy, 32,* 267–282.

Rutan, J. S., & Stone, W. (1993). *Psychodynamic group psychotherapy* (2nd Ed.). New York: Guilford Press.

Sanchez, V. C., Lewinsohn, P. M., & Larson, D. W. (1980). Assertion training: Effectiveness in the treatment of depression. *Journal of Clinical Psychology, 36,* 526–529.

Schachter, S. (1951). Deviation, rejection, and communication. *Journal of Abnormal and Social Psychology, 46,* 190–207.

Schachter, S. (1959). *The psychology of affiliation.* Stanford, CA: Stanford University Press.

Schaible, T., & Jacobs, A. (1975). Feedback III: Sequence effects: Enhancement of feedback acceptance and group attractiveness by manipulation of the sequence and valence of feedback. *Small Group Behavior, 6,* 151–173.

Schermer, V. L., & Klein, R. H. (1996). Termination in group psychotherapy from the perspectives of contemporary object relations theory and self psychology. *International Journal of Group Psychotherapy, 46,* 99–115.

Scheuble, K. J., Dixon, K. N., Levy, A. B., & Kagan-Moore, L. (1987). Premature termination: A risk in eating disorder groups. *Group, 11,* 85–93.

Schilder, P. (1939). Results and problems of group psychotherapy in severe neurosis. *Mental Hygiene, 23,* 87–98.

Sedikides, C., & Strube, M. J. (1997). Self-evaluation: To thine own self be good, to thine own self be sure, to thine own self be true, and to thine own self be better. *Advances in Experimental Social Psychology, 29,* 209–269.

Seeger, J. A. (1983). No innate phases in group problem solving. *Academy of Management Review, 8,* 683–689.

Shambaugh, P. W. (1978). The development of the small group. *Human Relations, 31,* 283–295.

Shapiro, D. A., & Shapiro, D. (1982). Meta-analysis of comparative therapy outcome studies: A replication and refinement. *Psychological Bulletin, 92,* 581–604.

Shechtman, Z. (1994). The effect of group psychotherapy on close same-gender friendships among boys and girls. *Sex Roles, 30,* 829–834.

Sherrill, J. T., Frank, E., Geary, M., & Stack, J. A. (1997). Psychoeducational workshops for elderly patients with recurrent major depression and their families. *Psychiatric Services, 48,* 76–81.

Sherry, P., & Hurley, J. R. (1976). Curative factors in psychotherapeutic and growth groups. *Journal of Clinical Psychology, 32,* 835–837.

Slavson, S. R. (1962). Personal qualifications of a group psychotherapist. *International Journal of Group Psychotherapy, 12,* 411–420.

Slavson, S. R. (1964). *A textbook in analytic group psychotherapy.* New York: International Universities Press.

Smith, M. L., Glass, G. V., & Miller, T. I. (1980). *The benefits of psychotherapy.* Baltimore, MD: Johns Hopkins University Press.

Snyder, C. R. (1994). *The psychology of hope: You can get there from here.* New York: Free Press.

Snyder, C. R., Cheavens, J., & Sympson, S. C. (1997). Hope: An individual motive for social commerce. *Group Dynamics: Theory, Research, and Practice, 1,* 107–118.

Solomon, S. D. (1982). Individual versus group therapy: Current status in the treatment of alcoholism. *Advances in Alcohol and Substance Abuse, 2,* 69–86.

Spira, J. L. (1997). Understanding and developing psychotherapy groups for medically ill patients. In J. L. Spira (Ed.), *Group therapy for medically ill patients* (pp. 3–52). New York: Guilford Press.

Stanton, M. D., & Shadish, W. R. (1997). Outcome, attrition, and family-couples treatment for drug abuse: A meta-analysis and review of the controlled, comparative studies. *Psychological Bulletin, 122,* 170–191.

Stiles, W. B., Tupler, L. A., & Carpenter, J. C. (1982). Participants' perceptions of self-analytic group sessions. *Small Group Behavior, 13,* 237–254.

Strong, S. R., & Claiborn, C. D. (1982). *Change through interaction: Social psychological processes of counseling and psychotherapy.* New York: Wiley.

Strupp, H. H. (1986). The nonspecific hypothesis of therapeutic effectiveness: A current assessment. *American Journal of Orthopsychiatry, 56,* 513–520.

Strupp, H. H., & Bloxum, A. L. (1973). Preparing lower-class patients for group psychotherapy: Development and evaluation of a role-induction film. *Journal of Consulting and Clinical Psychology, 41,* 373–384.

Taylor, S. E., & Lobel, M. (1989). Social comparison activity under threat: Downward evaluation and upward contacts. *Psychological Review, 96,* 569–575.

Thune, E. S., Manderscheid, R. W., & Silbergeld, S. (1981). Sex, status, and cotherapy. *Small Group Behavior, 12,* 415–442.

Tillitski, L. (1990). A meta-analysis of estimated effect sizes for group versus individual versus control treatments. *International Journal of Group Psychotherapy, 40,* 215–224.

Tinsley, H. E., Roth, J. A., & Lease, S. H. (1989). Dimensions of leadership and leadership style among group intervention specialists. *Journal of Counseling Psychology, 36,* 48–53.

Truax, C. B., & Carkhuff, R. R. (1965). Personality change in hospitalized mental patients during group psychotherapy as a function of alternate session and vicarious therapy pretraining. *Journal of Clinical Psychology, 21,* 190–201.

Truax, C. B., Shapiro, J. G., & Wargo, D. G. (1968). The effects of alternative sessions and vicarious therapy pre-training on group psychotherapy. *International Journal of Group Psychotherapy, 18,* 186–198.

Tschuschke, V., & Dies, R. R. (1994). Intensive analysis of therapeutic factors and outcome in long-term inpatient groups. *International Journal of Group Psychotherapy, 44,* 185–208.

Tuckman, B. W. (1965). Developmental sequences in small groups. *Psychological Bulletin, 63,* 384–399.

Tuckman, B. W., & Jensen, M. A. C. (1977). Stages of small group development revisited. *Group and Organizational Studies, 2,* 419–427.

Waltman, D. E., & Zimpfer, D. G. (1988). Composition, structure, and duration of treatment: Interacting variables in counseling groups. *Small Group Behavior, 19,* 171–184.

Ware, R., Barr, J. E., & Boone, M. (1982). Subjective changes in small group processes: An experimental investigation. *Small Group Behavior, 13,* 395–401.

Warren, N. C., & Rice, L. N. (1972). Structuring and stabilizing of psychotherapy for low-prognosis clients. *Journal of Consulting and Clinical Psychology, 39,* 173–181.

Weinstein, M., & Rossini, E. D. (1998). Academic training in group psychotherapy in clinical psychology doctoral programs. *Psychological Reports, 82,* 955–959.

Wender, L. (1940). Group psychotherapy: A study of its application. *Psychiatric Quarterly, 14,* 708–718.

Wheelan, S. A. (1994). *Group process: A developmental perspective.* Boston, MA: Allyn & Bacon.

Wheelan, S. A., Buzaglo, G., & Tsumura, E. (1998). Developing assessment tools for cross-cultural group research. *Small Group Research, 29,* 359–370.

Wheelan, S. A., & Hochberger, J. M. (1996). Validation studies of the group development questionnaire. *Small Group Research, 27,* 143–170.

Wheelan, S. A., & McKeage, R. L. (1993). Developmental patterns in small and large groups. *Small Group Research, 24,* 60–83.

Wheelan, S. A., Murphy, D., Tsumura, E., & Kline, S. F. (1998). Member perceptions of internal group dynamics and productivity. *Small Group Research, 29,* 371–393.

Wills, T. A., & De Paulo, B. M. (1991). Interpersonal analysis of the help-seeking process. In C. R. Snyder & D. R. Forsyth (Eds.), *Handbook of social and clinical psychology: The health perspective* (pp. 350–375). New York: Pergamon.

Winter, S. K. (1976). Developmental stages in the roles and concerns of group co-leaders. *Small Group Behavior, 7,* 349–362.

Wolf, A. (1949). The psychoanalysis of groups. I. *American Journal of Psychotherapy, 3,* 525–558.

Wood, J. V., Taylor, S. E., & Lichtman, R. R. (1985). Social comparison in adjustment to breast cancer. *Journal of Personality and Social Psychology, 49,* 1169–1183.

Worchel, S. & Coutant, D. (2001). It takes two to tango – relating group identity to individual identity within the framework of group development. In M. A. Hogg & S. Tindale (Eds.), *Blackwell Handbook of social psychology: Group processes* (pp. 461–481). Oxford: Blackwell Publishing.

Worthington, E. L., Jr., Hight, T. L., Ripley, J. S., Perrone, K. M., Kurusu, T. A., & Jones, D. R. (1997). Strategic hope-focused relationship-enrichment counseling with individual couples. *Journal of Counseling Psychology, 44,* 381–389.

Yalom, I. D. (1975). *The theory and practice of group psychotherapy* (2nd Ed.). New York: Basic Books.

Yalom, I. D. (1985). *The theory and practice of group psychotherapy* (3rd Ed.). New York: Basic Books.

Yalom, I. D. (1995). *The theory and practice of group psychotherapy* (4th Ed.). New York: Basic Books.

Yalom, V. J., & Vinogradov, S. (1993). Interpersonal group psychotherapy. In H. I. Kaplan & M. J. Sadock (Eds.), *Comprehensive group psychotherapy* (3rd Ed., pp. 185–195). Baltimore, MD: Williams & Wilkins.

Zaccaro, S. J., Gualtieri, J., & Minionis, D. (1995). Task cohesion as a facilitator of team decision making under temporal urgency. *Military Psychology, 7,* 77–93.

PART II

Law and Politics

CHAPTER FIVE

Psychology and Law

Günter Köhnken, Maria Fiedler, and Charlotte Möhlenbeck

Psychological research in legal contexts involves applying psychology's methodologies and knowledge to studying jurisprudence, substantive law, legal processes, and law breaking (Farrington, Hawkins, & Lloyd-Bostock, 1979). It is an area of applied research which refers to various fields of basic psychological research such as cognitive, developmental, personality, and social psychology. Furthermore, considerable overlaps exist to psychological assessment, clinical and organizational psychology.

The application of psychology to law has been differentiated into three areas (Kapardis, 1997): (1) psychology *in* law, (2) psychology *and* law, and (3) psychology *of* law. According to Blackburn (1996), "psychology in law" refers to specific applications of psychology within law (e.g. police psychology, psychology of eyewitness testimony). "Psychology and law" refers to psycholegal research into offenders, lawyers, judges, and jurors (e.g. jury decision making, offender treatment). "Psychology of law" covers areas of research like, for example, why people obey/disobey laws, the effects of laws, and the application of laws on people's behavior (e.g. therapeutic jurisprudence). The traditional term "forensic psychology" denotes the application of psychology in the courts.

Psycholegal research has a long tradition with an initial flourishing period at the beginning of the twentieth century (see, for example, Marbe, 1913; Münsterberg, 1908; Stern, 1903). Following a less active period, psycholegal research has grown enormously during the last three decades. Evidence for this revival is found in the publication of more and more books on various aspects of psychology and law (e.g. Bull & Carson, 1995; Kapardis, 1997; Kaplan, 1986; Ross, Read, & Toglia, 1994; Sporer, Malpass, & Köhnken, 1996), the establishment of journals (e.g. *Law and Human Behavior*; *Behavioral Sciences and the Law*; *Law and Psychology Review*; *Legal and Criminological Psychology, Public Policy, Psychology, and Law*), the constitution of national and international professional organizations, the growing number of national and international conferences and symposia, and the strong increase in empirical publications during the past twenty years.

The results of psychological research are applied to legal practice in various ways and at a number of levels within the criminal and civil justice system. For example, in the investigation of crime the police may use techniques of offender profiling to draw conclusions about the life style, criminal history, and residential location of a person who has committed a number of crimes (e.g. Canter, 1994; Jackson & Bekerian, 1997). Witnesses are interviewed using interview techniques which are based on research on memory and communication (Fisher & Geiselman, 1992). Lineup identifications are constructed according to guidelines which are derived from psychological research (e.g. Sporer, et al., 1995). At trial, attorneys may rely on advice and empirical analysis of social scientists when selecting juries (Ellsworth & Reifman, in press; Hans & Vidmar, 1982). Courts employ psychologists as expert witnesses to assist in evaluating witness statements. Finally, if a defendant is convicted he or she may be subject to correctional treatment that is derived from research on behavior modification and psychotherapy (McGuire, 1995).

It would be impossible to cover all areas of psycholegal research in this chapter. The discussion will therefore focus on psychological research in the area of criminal law. The vast majority of research has focused on various levels of the criminal justice system, whereas civil proceedings have received considerably less attention. This chapter will address topics from each of the three areas of psycholegal research as mentioned above: police psychology, including eyewitness identification and interviewing witnesses as an example of "psychology in law," jury decision making as an example of "psychology and law," and therapeutic jurisprudence as an example of "psychology of law."

Psychology and Policing

Psychology and policing has become a remarkably diverse field of applied psychology and covers almost all major areas of psychology (e.g. organizational psychology, personnel selection, clinical psychology and counseling, psychological assessment, social and personality psychology). Most of these topics are discussed in other chapters of this handbook and are therefore not covered here.

Direct operational assistance

Apart from an indirect impact of psychology on the police mission by optimizing personal skills and situational variables, psychology can directly support criminal investigations by providing empirically based guidelines for such things as conducting interviews or preparing eyewitness identification procedures.

Interviewing witnesses   Kebbell & Milne (1998) report that police officers are of the opinion that witnesses usually provide the central leads in criminal investigations. A report by the Rand Corporation (1975) also noted that a major factor that determines whether or not a crime is solved is the completeness and accuracy of the witness account. Indeed law enforcement personnel were found to spend as much as 85 percent of their total working time talking to people. Thus, a critical component of effective law enforcement is the ability of police officers to obtain accurate and detailed information from witnesses. However, police officers have also reported that witnesses rarely provided as much information as the officers required for an investigation (Kebbell & Milne, 1998).

One approach to increase the information a witness provides is forensic hypnosis. However, the empirical evidence for the memory enhancing potential of hypnosis is equivocal. Whereas some anecdotal reports claim that hypnosis may enhance memory in criminal cases (Reiser, 1980), controlled laboratory studies have produced mixed results (Smith, 1983; Wagstaff, 1984).

A less controversial technique for improving memory retrieval is the Cognitive Interview which was developed by Geiselman and Fisher (Geiselman, Fisher, Firstenberg, Hutton, Avetissian, & Prosk, 1984). In its original form it comprises four basic retrieval aids or mnemonic strategies together with some ways of helping witnesses to recall specific bits of information. First, interviewees are instructed to mentally reconstruct the context of the witnessed event, to form an image or an impression of the environmental aspects of the scene, and to remember their emotional feelings and thoughts. The second strategy is to encourage witnesses to report everything they remember, even if they think the details are not important. The third component is to ask witnesses to recall the event in a variety of temporal orders or to make retrieval attempts from different starting points, for example, from the most memorable element. Finally, witnesses are encouraged to recall the event from different physical locations, just as if they were viewing it with another person's eyes.

Fisher and Geiselman later refined the technique considerably, particularly by addressing the social dynamics and communication between the interviewer and the eyewitness (e.g. interview structure, rapport building, using non-verbal responses, witness-compatible questioning), and called this refined version the Enhanced Cognitive Interview (Fisher, Geiselman, Raymond, Jurkevich, & Warhaftig, 1987; for recent overviews see Fisher & Geiselman, 1992; Fisher, McCauley, & Geiselman, 1994).

During recent years the effectiveness of the Cognitive Interview has been evaluated in more than fifty experiments. In a series of experiments conducted by Geiselman and Fisher, the original version of the cognitive interview generated about 25–30 percent more correct information without increasing the number of false details. The cognitive interview enhanced memory in written reports as well as in oral interviews. Furthermore, the effect has been demonstrated with a variety of interviewees, including, for example, adults, children, and people with learning disabilities. It has also been shown that the cognitive interview may decrease the effect of misleading post-event information (Milne, Bull, Köhnken, & Memon, 1995).

A recent meta-analysis (Köhnken, Milne, Memon, & Bull, 1999) including 55 experiments with nearly 2,500 participants obtained a significant overall effect size $d = 0.87$ for the difference in correct information between cognitive and conventional or standard interviews. The overall difference for the amount of incorrect information, although considerably smaller, was also significant ($d = 0.28$). However, the average accuracy rate (i.e. the proportion of correct details relative to the total number of recalled details) was similar in both types of interview (85 percent for the cognitive interview compared to 82 percent for the standard interview). Thus, the Cognitive Interview generates more information than a standard police interview and this larger amount of information is no less accurate.

Eyewitness identification   Whereas courts and juries often view the identification of a defendant by an eyewitness as a particularly convincing piece of evidence, analyses of proven wrongful
convictions have consistently shown that mistaken eyewitness identification is responsible for
more miscarriages of justice than all other potential causes combined (Rattner, 1988). In a
survey of 205 cases of wrongful convictions mistaken identification was found to be involved
in 52 percent (Rattner, 1988). The most disturbing evidence for wrongful identifications
as a major cause of miscarriages of justice comes from the use of DNA analysis. The re-
evaluation of cases where people had been convicted and where DNA material had been
preserved revealed 40 cases of wrongful convictions. Of these 40 cases, 36 (or 90 percent)
involved eyewitness identification evidence in which one or more witnesses falsely identified
the defendant (Wells, Small, Penrod, Malpass, Fulero, & Brimacombe, 1998).

   Why do false identifications occur? On the one hand, witnesses may have had a poor view
of the criminal; a long delay between the encounter and the recognition test may have
weakened the memory representation of the culprit, or post-event information (e.g. a photo
of an innocent suspect) may have contaminated the witnesses' memory. These and similar
factors have in common that their likely effects on identification accuracy in a given case can
only be post-dicted or estimated. Wells (1978) has labeled these variables *estimator variables*.
On the other hand, the police may conduct the recognition test in a way that is biased
towards the suspect (e.g. because he is the only blond person among a group of dark
haired foils) or the witness may have observed the suspect being escorted by police officers.
These factors are called *system variables* because they are under the control of the criminal
justice system.

Estimator variables   Shapiro & Penrod (1986) conducted a meta-analysis in order to assess
the effects of various estimator variables on identification accuracy. This meta-analysis included
128 experiments with 960 experimental conditions, almost 17,000 subjects, and more than
700,000 separate recognition judgments.

   The results of the meta-analysis suggest that stable characteristics of eyewitnesses such as
intelligence, gender, and personality traits (e.g. self-monitoring) are only weakly, if at all,
related to identification accuracy. In particular, self-reported facial recognition skill is not
reliably associated with actual performance. In a series of studies, Malpass, Parada, Corey,
Chavez, Bowles, & McQuiston (1999) found very little consistency across two recognition
tests. Shapiro & Penrod (1986) report that children and the elderly tend to perform more
poorly in face recognition tasks than other adults. However, a more recent meta-analysis
conducted by Pozzulo & Lindsay (1999) found that correct identification rates for children
over the age of five were comparable to the performance level of adults. Four-year-old
preschoolers, however, were less likely than adults and older children to make a correct
identification when presented with a target-present lineup. In contrast, the adult rate of
correct rejections in target-absent lineups was not reached by even the eldest children
included in the analysis (aged 12–13 years).

   The most important variable of the stable target characteristics seems to be facial distinct-
iveness. Faces that are highly attractive or highly unattractive are substantially better recognized than nondistinct faces. Whereas neither the race of the perpetrator nor the race of the
witness alone are strongly associated with recognition performance these variables interact

such that cross-race identifications are less accurate than own-race identifications (Chance & Goldstein, 1996). Malleable target characteristics are important predictors of identification accuracy. In particular, if the perpetrator wore a disguise or changed facial appearance between initial exposure and recognition test the identification accuracy is significantly reduced.

The majority of experiments on estimator variables has looked at the effects of environmental conditions at the time of the crime. In general, these situational factors were found to be important predictors of identification accuracy. For example, recognition performance is reduced for less salient targets, if the exposure duration is short, if the crime is less serious, if a weapon was present during the crime, and if the witness was intoxicated. The effects of stress and arousal are less clear due to ethical restrictions in the manipulation of high levels of arousal. However, there appears to be a tendency for extreme stress to reduce identification accuracy.

With regard to post-event factors Shapiro & Penrod (1986) found that face recognition accuracy shows a linear decline with retention interval. Interestingly, time delay has a smaller impact on the number of false identifications than it has on the proportion of correct recognitions.

System variables   Factors that are under the control of the criminal justice system are called system variables (Wells, 1978). With regard to recognition tests (lineups or photo arrays) false identifications can have two causes. First, random error can occur. In this case, the witness chooses the suspect purely by chance. Any other member of the lineup was just as likely to be selected as the alleged offender. Second, a false identification may result from systematic error. A systematic error occurs when certain properties of the lineup procedure or the composition of the lineup leads the witness to choose the suspect even if he or she is not the criminal.

Random errors   Witnesses may want to present themselves as "good" and constructive persons who can help the police catch the offender and thereby solve the crime. Further, witnesses tend to see the whole lineup procedure as a technique to convict an already sufficiently well-known criminal (e.g. Malpass & Devine, 1984). In the erroneous belief that the police are best served by a positive identification of one of the individuals in the lineup, they may choose the individual who most resembles the fuzzy picture of the offender in their memory. As long as no systematic errors are made that would direct the witnesses' choice to a specific individual the selection is likely to be more or less random. Under these circumstances the likelihood that an innocent suspect is selected is inversely related to the number of foils in the lineup or the photo array (Köhnken, Malpass, & Wogalter, 1996; Wells & Turtle, 1986). Consequently, the larger the pool of foils from which the suspect is chosen the more informative is the identification.

Systematic errors   A lineup is conducted in order to test the hypotheses that (a) the suspect is the guilty party, and (b) the suspect is not the criminal (null hypothesis). The lineup recognition test thus resembles an experiment and the general methodological principles for experimental research and hypothesis testing apply (Wells & Luus, 1990). From this point of view two types of systematic errors can be distinguished (Köhnken, Malpass, & Wogalter,

1996; Malpass & Devine, 1983): (1) The composition of the lineup or the arrangement of the photographs can lead to the suspect standing out from the other individuals. Malpass & Devine (1983) referred to this as a *structural error*. (2) Errors can occur during the procedure of the recognition test that would lead the witness to select the suspect. This type of error is referred to as a *procedural error*.

Structural errors   Several experiments have demonstrated that unfair lineups where the suspects stands out from the foils can dramatically increase the risk of false identifications. For example, Lindsay & Wells (1980) found that an uninvolved person who was noticeably different from the other foils in a photo array was incorrectly identified by 70 percent of the subjects. It is therefore essential to select foils who are sufficiently similar to the suspect. This can be achieved by using a combination of "objective" and "subjective" selection procedures (Köhnken, Malpass, & Wogalter, 1996). In the objective selection procedure, selection of alternatives is determined by the presence of a few objectively important personal character-istics (e.g. size, weight, age, facial hair, race). However, the selection of alternatives on the basis of objective physical characteristics does not always ensure the formation of a fair group for the lineup. Often, when comparing his or her memory of the culprit to the individuals in the lineup, the witness is guided by highly subjective impressions. These non-objective impressions noted by the witness should also be taken into account in selecting the foils (Luus & Wells, 1991).

Procedural errors   Procedural errors are present when peculiarities during the preparation and execution of a lineup cause the witnesses to draw their attention to the police suspect. Such errors may, for example, result from repeated recognition tests. Sometimes the police request a witness to do a mug shot search. If a person is recognized on one of the mug shots he or she is arrested and a lineup identification may be staged by the police. However, several experiments have shown that witnesses tend to repeat their first decision in later lineups even if they are false (Brigham & Cairns, 1988).

Whereas these and some other potential sources of procedural errors are fairly obvious, false identifications may also result from more subtle, maybe even unintended manipulations like systematic changes in the nonverbal behavior of a police officer (e.g. Smith, Pleban, & Shaffer, 1982). In order to avoid such biases it has been suggested that a recognition test be conducted by a police officer who was not involved in the investigation and who has no knowledge as to who the suspect is (Köhnken, Malpass, & Wogalter, 1996; Wells, et al., 1998).

Evaluating Witness Statements: Assessment and Attribution of Credibility

---

Witness statements, whether they be descriptions of events or person identifications, can rarely be taken at face value. Numerous factors have been found to be able to cause discrep-ancies between statements and the actual facts. These factors can be separated into two different classes. On the one hand, witnesses, although trying to give a correct and complete report of an event or an accurate description of a person, may be subject to unintended errors and distortions, caused for example by forgetting, suboptimal perception conditions, misleading post-event information, etc. The term *accuracy* describes the extent to which statements are free from this kind of unintended error. On the other hand, a statement may deviate from reality because the witness deliberately tries to deceive the police or the court. Intentional deceptions or lies affect the truthfulness or credibility of a statement. Thus, in forensic psychology the term *credibility* describes the witness's motivation to give a truthful account of his or her experiences.

Deception is a communication phenomenon that involves at least two individuals: a communicator (or witness in the present context) and a recipient (e.g. a detective, a judge, or a juror). Consequently, research can focus on each of the two participants of an interaction. With regard to the communicator (or witness) it can be examined whether or not there are any behaviors that are systematically associated with the deceptiveness of a statement. Such behaviors have been called *correlates of deception* (Zuckerman, DePaulo, & Rosenthal, 1981), *authentic cues of deception* (Fiedler & Walka, 1993), or *objective indicators of deception* (Vrij, 1998). From a different point of view, a set of content characteristics has been proposed as being indicative for the truthfulness of a statement. These are called *reality criteria* (Steller & Köhnken, 1989).

Assessment of credibility

Objective indicators of truth and deception have been examined in four behavioral areas: (1) the content of the statement (e.g. amount and type of detail, logical consistency; see Steller & Köhnken, 1989); (2) the way the statement is verbally presented, i.e. speech behavior (e.g. speech rate, speech disturbances) and stylostatistic characteristics (e.g. word frequency statistics; see Morton & Farrindgon, 1992; Köhnken, 1985); (3) the accompanying nonverbal behavior of the witness (e.g. arm movements, facial expression; see Zuckerman, DePaulo, & Rosenthal, 1981); and (4) psychophysiological phenomena (e.g. electrodermal responses, heart rate, blood pressure; see Raskin, 1989).

Research on nonverbal and speech behavior suggests that some observable behaviors are indeed associated with deception. Several meta-analyses (Zuckerman, DePaulo, & Rosenthal, 1981; DePaulo, Stone, & Lassiter, 1985) have shown that of 24 different verbal, nonverbal, and speech behaviors, 14 are significantly related to deception. There appears to be a tendency for highly motivated compared to less motivated liars to decrease the frequency of a number of nonverbal behaviors (Vrij, 1998). In the area of speech behavior liars engage in more and/or longer speech hesitations, produce more speech errors (e.g. stutter, repetition) and grammatical errors, and show longer response latencies. However, the association of these behaviors with deception, although statistically significant, is rather weak.

Burgoon & Buller (1994) have proposed an "Interpersonal Deception Theory." They are critical of most investigations of deception for having used a unidirectional view, such that a liar actively transmits signals which a receiver passively absorbs. However, this paradigm lacks the process of interpersonal communication that involves feedback and mutual influence. In an ongoing conversation the character of deceit may change when deceivers continually monitor their own performance while adapting to the receiver's feedback. As a consequence, behavioral patterns evidenced at the outset of an exchange may differ radically from those manifested later (Buller & Aune, 1987). According to this position, averaging behavior frequencies across a lengthy interaction may produce weak effects, although clues to deception may indeed exist.

A very different approach to the assessment of the credibility of a statement has been developed in literature research and in psycholinguistics. In order to assign pieces of literature of unknown authorship to a certain author, the style of the disputed document was analyzed according to various statistical parameters (hence the term "stylostatistics") which are then compared with the respective data derived from an undisputed text. Such parameters are, for example, the number of words per sentence, the number of different words relative to the total number of words in a text body, the average word length, the proportion of verbs to adjectives, and the proportion of grammar (like prepositions, articles, etc.) as an indicator of the grammatical complexity of a sentence. Köhnken (1985) found that some of these stylostatistic parameters did reliably discriminate between truthful and fabricated statements.

An alternative way to assess the truthfulness of a statement was developed in German forensic psychology by Undeutsch (1967) and Arntzen (1983). Based on their work, Steller & Köhnken (1989) have compiled a list of criteria and described a procedure for evaluating the veracity of a statement which led to the development of Statement Validity Assessment (SVA) as a comprehensive method for evaluating witness statements. In contrast to research on nonverbal detection of deception, this approach focuses on the content of a statement rather than on the witness's nonverbal and speech behavior. Furthermore, SVA is not a "verbal lie detector." Instead of searching for "lie symptoms" it focuses on specific content characteristics which, if present in a statement, support the hypothesis that the account is based on genuine personal experience.

SVA consists of three major components. The first component is an open-ended investigative interview. The second component of SVA is a criteria-based content analysis (CBCA). In this phase the transcript of the statement is analyzed with regard to certain content characteristics (the reality criteria) like, for example, quantity of detail or the description of unexpected complications during the incident (Steller & Köhnken, 1989). Third, all obtained case information including the witness's cognitive and verbal abilities and information about the origin of the statement is integrated into a final judgment as to whether or not the statement is likely to be an account of what actually happened.

CBCA is based on the hypothesis – originally stated by Undeutsch (1967) – that truthful and fabricated statements differ in content and quality. This basic hypothesis comprises two components, one cognitive and the other motivational. The latter can be related to impression management theory (Tedeschi & Norman, 1985). The cognitive part of the hypothesis states that, given a certain level of cognitive and verbal abilities, only a person who has actually experienced an event will be able to produce a statement with the characteristics that are described in the CBCA criteria. The impression management component relates to motivation and social behavior. It is assumed that lying is a goal directed behavior and that a person who deliberately invents a story wants to be perceived as honest in order to achieve his or her goals. Therefore, the person is likely to avoid behaviors which, in his or her view, may be interpreted as clues to deception. For instance, if a liar believes that admitting lack of memory will undermine his or her perceived credibility, he or she will try to avoid such behavior. This impression management approach assumes that people have a common stereotype about the typical behavior accompanying a lie. Provided that a particular behavior can be sufficiently controlled it is expected that a liar, in order to conceal his or her lie, attempts to avoid such behavior.

Several studies have demonstrated that SVA can be a useful tool in distinguishing truthful from fabricated accounts. Using children of various age groups or adolescents, Esplin, Boychuk, & Raskin (1988), Joffe & Yuille (1992), Köhnken & Wegener (1982), Steller, Wellershaus, & Wolf (1992), and Yuille (1988) found significant differences either in at least some of the CBCA criteria or hit rates that were significantly better than chance level if the decisions had been based on CBCA. Other studies have also demonstrated that CBCA may reliably discriminate between truthful and fabricated adults' accounts (Köhnken, Schimossek, Aschermann, & Höfer, 1995; Porter & Yuille, 1996).

Alonso-Quecuty (1992), Höfer, Akehurst, & Metzger (1996), Sporer (1996), and Porter & Yuille (1995) have suggested supplementing the CBCA criteria with reality monitoring criteria (Johnson & Raye, 1981). Two studies that have combined these approaches have produced mixed results. Whereas Sporer (1996) reports beneficial effects of the additional reality monitoring criteria, Höfer, Akehurst, & Metzger (1996) found no differences.

Surprisingly little controlled research has been published regarding the inter-rater agreement in coding of the CBCA criteria, although reliability of coding is an essential requirement. Some studies report rather low agreement among raters (Anson, Golding, & Gully, 1993; Ruby & Brigham, 1997). However, a recently reported series of experiments (Köhnken & Höfer, 1998) suggests that these results may be due to insufficient training of the coders. These studies show that after a three week training program inter-rater agreement as well as re-test reliabilities are in a range which is deemed sufficient for personality questionnaires.

Attribution of credibility

Research on the attribution of credibility has examined how successful people are in discriminating truthful and deceptive statements, which behavioral cues they utilize for their judgments, and how access to different communication channels influences their attributions.

The results of several meta-analyses of more than fifty experimental studies provide a rather disillusioning picture. In these experiments the hit rates (i.e. the proportion of correct judgments) generally falls into a range between 45 percent and 60 percent, where 50 percent correct decisions can be expected by chance alone. The mean detection accuracy across all studies is only slightly (although significantly) better than the 50 percent chance level (DePaulo, Stone, & Lassiter, 1985; Zuckerman, DePaulo, & Rosenthal, 1981).

Interestingly, people with experience in credibility judgments (e.g. police and customs officers) achieve no better results than inexperienced subjects (DePaulo & Pfeifer, 1986; Vrij & Winkel, 1994). Experienced subjects are, however, more confident in the cor-rectness of their judgments than lay people. Apparently the mere frequency of credibility judgments does not help to improve judgment accuracy because subjects don't receive any detailed feedback (DePaulo & Pfeifer, 1986; Fiedler & Walka, 1993; Vrij, 1994).

Legal Decision Making

Psychological research on courtroom proceedings differs from the other areas of research outlined in this chapter in one important respect. Whereas, for example, psychological aspects of eyewitness testimony or correctional treatment are relevant regardless of the specifics of national law, courtroom proceedings differ in various countries. Within the *adversarial system* of justice, which is by and large characteristic of English-speaking countries, the proceedings are structured as a dispute between two sides (Damaska, 1973). The role of the judge is kept to a minimum and can best be described as that of a referee. The evidence is presented by the prosecution and the defense. Although the jury trial is not an essential element of adversarial procedure, it is found most regularly within Anglo-Saxon countries (McEwan, 1995). An adversary process is marked by a clear distinction between matters of fact and matters of law. Matters of fact are for the lay-persons (the jury), whereas matters of law are for the judge (Sealy, 1989). In contrast, in *inquisitorial systems,* which are roughly descriptive for continental Europe, judges have a considerably more active role. They play a major part in the preparation of evidence before the trial and in the questioning of the defendant and the witnesses. Witnesses (including expert witnesses) are called by the court rather than testifying for one of the opposing sides. Most important, the judge or the panel of judges decides on guilt or innocence of the defendant, whereas in the adversarial system this decision is for the jury.

The first substantial contribution by psychologists to an understanding of jury functioning was presented by Kalven & Zeisel (1966), a survey of trial judges' opinions concerning jury verdicts, the determinants of jury verdicts, and the judges' evaluations of the quality of those verdicts. Another major landmark was the research program conducted by Thibaut and his associates (e.g. Thibaut & Walker, 1975), which had a significant impact on social psychology and its application to law. The jury has now become, beside the witness, the most popular research object in the entire area of psychology and law, especially in the criminal trial (Davis, 1989). Psychologists have, for example, examined the impact of jury size, decision rules, jury composition, instructions to the jury from the trial judge, and the evaluation of evidence by juries.

Jury size

Most countries with the adversarial system have opted for twelve-member juries, although proposals have been made in the USA to reduce the jury to a minimum of six members. It has been argued that larger juries have a better chance to be representative of the various social groups in a community and that the margin of error would diminish, compared to a small jury. Different twelve-member juries would therefore be more likely to reach the same decision than different six-member juries (Hans & Vidmar, 1982). Numerous experiments have been carried out to examine the effects of jury size on decisions (usually verdicts). As Vollrath & Davies (1980) conclude in their review, the surprising outcome from this now rather large body of data is that no significant size-attributable differences in verdicts have been found.

Jury selection

Since the seminal work of Kalven & Zeisel (1966) the possibility that jurors could be subject to judgment biases has received much attention in the literature. In search of factors that could cause such biases, the impact of personality variables, gender, demographic factors, and experimental influences on group performance in general has been examined in a number of studies. The basic idea underlying these efforts was that identification of variables that could cause biases would enable scientifically based procedures for the selection of jurors and thus reduce decision biases. However, the results of this line of research are mixed. For example, some studies found that men's verdicts differed in some cases from those of women (Efran, 1974), other studies did not find any differences related to gender (Griffitt & Jackson, 1973). Research on the effects of race has been equally inconsistent and the same is true for various personality variables. Thus, efforts for "scientific jury selection" (Kairys, Schulman, & Harring, 1975) seem to lack conclusive empirical support (Hans & Vidmar, 1982).

Moreover, the question is whether or not jury selection procedures, however sophisticated they may be, can indeed offer a solution to the problems. As Ellsworth & Reifman (in press) have emphasized, the characteristics of the person are far less important in determining who conforms, who obeys, and who turns away from a call for help than are the characteristics of the situation. Consequently, social psychologists have focused on situational factors as potential causes for deficiencies in jury performance (e.g. the disorganized presentation of evidence, the prohibition against asking for clarification or even taking notes, the oral recitation of lengthy instructions in an unfamiliar language; see Ellsworth & Reifman, in press). Reforms of the jury system that have been proposed by social scientists, therefore, focus on aspects of the jurors' tasks rather than on the jurors' qualifications. From this point of view it has been suggested, for example, that jurors be given an orientation session before trial (Heuer & Penrod, 1994), that the judge instruct jurors on law, both at the beginning and at the end of a trial (Liebermann & Sales, 1997), that the judge explain the reasons behind particular rules (Kassin & Sommers, 1997), and that jurors be provided with notebooks containing a list of witnesses and a glossary of technical terms (Munstermann, Hannaford, & Whitehead, 1997). Most of these reform proposals are based on theory and research from cognitive and social psychology.

Evaluation of evidence and decision making

How individual jurors and juries as groups evaluate the evidence and finally reach a decision has been investigated from two different perspectives. Psychologists have examined the cognitive processes in individual juror decision making. The other major research interest concerns the social dynamics of group decision making.

With regard to individual jurors' decision processes, up until the early 1980s research was dominated by the application of algebraic or stochastic models, mostly derived from Bayesian probability models (reviewed by Pennington & Hastie, 1981). The typical research paradigm was a laboratory experiment using undergraduate psychology students as mock jurors who read brief 10- to 20-sentence summaries of imaginary evidence. Usually, little attempt was made to mimic the conditions, procedures, and instructions of a typical jury trial (Pennington & Hastie, 1990). Furthermore, it has been argued that these models are too mechanical and much too elemental to provide a satisfactory account for what people actually do when making difficult decisions about complex events (Ellsworth & Mauro, 1998). A shift in perspective was initiated by Pennington & Hastie (1993), who criticized the artificiality of laboratory research on juror decision making. In contrast to previous research methods, these authors attempted to create conditions and stimulus events that were comparable to those at an actual trial. The participants were sampled from courthouse jury pools rather than from undergraduate psychology students and the analyses of evaluation and decision processes were based on think-aloud protocols.

From this research Pennington and Hastie concluded that the traditional mathematical models were inadequate and proposed an alternative model to explain evidence evaluation and decisions that is embedded in cognitive psychology (e.g. Kintsch & Van Dijk, 1978; Schank & Abelson, 1977): the *story* or *explanation model*. This model is supposed to provide a framework for explaining how jurors comprehend, recall, and use the evidence in criminal trials in terms of verdict categories. The idea is that jurors attempt to make sense of the entirety of evidence by imposing a summary structure on it that they feel captures what was true about the events referred to in the testimony. Furthermore, it is assumed that jurors engage in a deliberate effort to match the explanatory story that they had constructed with the verdict categories, seeking a "best fit" between one of the verdict categories and their story (Pennington & Hastie, 1990). In other words, it is hypothesized that the "story" mediates between the evidence presented and the final judgment or decision.

The story approach introduces some clarification regarding the mixed results on the effects of psychosocial variables on verdicts by suggesting that these variables are not related to verdicts directly. Instead, they are linked to stories, which in turn are related to verdicts. For example, Pennington & Hastie (1990) report that in some of their studies the social class of the juror was related to the harshness of verdicts. They found that jurors from poorer neighborhoods did not find the possession of a weapon particularly surprising, whereas jurors from a wealthier suburb did find this fact remarkable. As a consequence, these jurors inferred that the defendant had a special purpose in mind for the knife: namely to injure or kill the victim. This example shows that social class is related to particular life experiences which influence the way the jury members construct a story for this particular case but perhaps not for different cases.

Jury deliberation and group decision making

Two of the central assumptions underlying trial by jury are that (1) the deliberation will act as a counter-measure against individual biases and (2) that group decisions are superior to individual decisions. In particular, information seeking and processing is assumed to be more efficient in groups as compared to individuals. However, in contrast to these assumptions research by Janis (1972, 1982) has shown that under certain conditions (especially homogeneity, isolation, structural faults, lack of decision procedures) groups may be affected by the phenomenon of "groupthink." Under these circumstances groups tend to develop an illusion of invulnerability, a belief in a shared morality, closed-mindedness, and exhibit pressure on individual group members to conform with the majority opinion (e.g. Park, 1990; Tetlock, Peterson, McGuire, Chang, & Feld, 1992). One important consequence of these processes for the evaluation of evidence and the construction of a "story" is the tendency towards a biased search for and evaluation of information. This would then result in a strong confirmation bias (Snyder, 1984).

A series of studies by Schulz-Hardt and colleagues (Schulz-Hardt, Frey, Lüthgens, & Moscovici, 1999) has demonstrated that groups do indeed show a greater confirmation bias than individuals: they were more confident about the correctness of their decision as well as more selective when seeking information. This was particularly the case in homogeneous groups (i.e. when group members share the same initial opinion). Furthermore, the more certain the group members are, and the more they deem themselves to be unanimous, the more they look for consistent information (Frey, 1995).

Acre, Sobral, & Fariña (1992) have examined the impact of group homogeneity on jury decision making by forming ideologically homogeneous juries (only conservatives or progressives) and attributionally homogeneous juries (subjects preferring either internal or external attribution). They found that in some criminal cases these juries differed in post but not in pre-deliberation verdicts, indicating that the bias derived from the deliberation of homogeneous groups. Pennington & Hastie (1986) found that evidence that is incongruent with the verdict is not equally considered. Acre (1995) concludes from these data that the appreciation of evidence during the deliberation is selective, that homogeneous juries either avoid using certain information that is not congruent with their bias or that they interpret it according to their bias. Hence, contrary to the assumptions underlying the trial by jury idea, individual bias may be magnified rather than reduced in the deliberation under homogeneous conditions.

Criminal Behavior: Explanation and Prediction

How criminal behavior is explained and predicted has enormous influence on all levels of the criminal justice system. Theoretical models of criminal behavior will more or less determine how a society deals with the phenomenon of crime. Such models can, for example, be used to assist the investigation of crime; crime prevention programs are influenced by theories of criminal behavior and this is even more so with regard to the treatment of offenders.

There appears to be some consistency about criminal behavior which calls for psychological explanation. Cross-sectional as well as longitudinal epidemiological research on criminal behavior has repeatedly shown that the prevalence of offending (officially recorded as well as self-reported) increases with age to reach a peak in the teenage years and from then on decreases through the twenties and thirties (e.g. Farrington, 1990; Gottfredson & Hirschi, 1988; Stephenson, 1992). There is also a remarkable continuity of offending over time. In other words, the best predictor of offending at one age is offending at a preceding age. In a prospective longitudinal study, Farrington & West (1990) found that of those convicted as juveniles (age 10–16) almost 75 percent were reconvicted between the ages of 17 and 24, and nearly half of the juvenile offenders were reconvicted between ages 25 and 32. Furthermore, those convicted early tend to become the most persistent offenders, in committing large numbers of offences at high rates over long time periods.

From a psychological point of view, offending is a certain type of behavior, similar in many respects to other types of antisocial or deviant behaviors. Offending has indeed been found to be part of a more general anti-social behavior syndrome that arises in childhood and persists into adulthood (Robins, 1979). Farrington & West (1990) report that the most serious offenders at each age were deviant in a number of other aspects. Among other things, at age 18 offenders drank, smoked, and gambled more, used more drugs, admitted to drinking and driving, and fought more than did their non-convicted peers. Of 110 18-year-old males diagnosed as anti-social on non-criminal criteria, 70 percent were convicted up to the age of 20 and this anti-social tendency persists into adulthood.

Offending and anti-social behavior in general seem to be linked to a configuration of personality factors variously termed "hyperactivity–impulsivity–attention deficit." For example, Farrington, Loeber, & Van Kammen (1990) found that diagnosis of this syndrome at age 8–10 predicted juvenile convictions independently of conduct disorders at that age. Delinquency has also been related to certain patterns of thinking. In particular, criminal activities are associated with a strong tendency to justify and excuse criminal behavior. For example, Farrington, Biron, & LeBlanc (1982) have reported that offenders tend to blame the world for their problems and believe that they had a lot of bad luck. Mitchell & Dodder (1983) found that delinquents attempt to neutralize their guilt feelings by finding excuses and justifications for their behavior. They deny their responsibility as well as the injury of the victim. Over time, the justification employed to explain past delinquency may subsequently be used in an anticipatory way to justify future, intended deviation (Stephenson, 1992).

There also seems to be a considerable familial similarity in criminal behavior. In the Cambridge Study of Delinquent Development (West & Farrington, 1975), the percentage of boys convicted up to age 20 rose linearly from no convicted parents (18 percent) to one convicted parent (42 percent) and two convicted parents (61 percent). Of the boys with criminal brothers, 50 percent were convicted versus 19 percent of the boys with non-criminal brothers. Crime concentrates in families: 11 percent of families accounted for half of all convicted persons (Rowe & Farrington, 1997).

Does this pattern of results indicate that offending is a stable personality characteristic, a trait, or that the possession of certain personality characteristics facilitates criminality? Eysenck (1977) and Eysenck & Eysenck (1978) have put forward a theory that suggests just that. These authors hypothesize that extroverts are less well conditioned than introverts and therefore more difficult to socialize. They are said to be more sensation seeking and less likely to feel anxious when contemplating or performing a criminal act. This theory links criminal behavior to genetics in that extroversion–introversion is assumed to have a biological basis and that this is to a considerable degree rooted in genetics. Eysenck's theory on criminal behavior has been strongly criticized (e.g. Sarbin, 1979). Moreover, the empirical data do not seem to support this position. For example, Hollin (1989) concluded from a literature review that studies on the relation of extroversion and offending have had inconsistent results. Some did find the predicted relationship, others found no difference, while still others reported lower extroversion scores in offender groups. Furthermore, Raine & Venables (1981) failed to confirm the notion that poorly socialized people are less conditionable than better socialized individuals. West & Farrington (1973) reported that convicted juveniles did not differ in extroversion and neuroticism from their non-convicted peers.

Based on prospective longitudinal study and on literature reviews, Farrington (1992; Farrington & West, 1990) has suggested that a combination of factors eventually leads to delinquency. West & Farrington (1973) and Loeber & Stouthamer-Loeber (1986) reported that poor parental supervision and monitoring, erratic or harsh parental discipline, cruel, passive, or negligent parental attitude, and parental conflicts and separation were all important predictors of offending. Criminal, anti-social, and alcoholic parents tend to have criminal sons (Robins, 1979). These results suggest that offending occurs when the normal social learning process is disrupted by erratic discipline, poor supervision, and unsuitable parental models. These children tend to have a below-average intelligence (Wilson & Herrnstein, 1985; West & Farrington, 1973). Farrington (1992) hypothesizes that, because of their poor ability to manipulate abstract concepts, they have problems foreseeing the consequences of their offending and appreciating the feelings of victims. He further assumes that children with low intelligence are likely to fail in school and later to have erratic employment careers. As a consequence, they are less able to satisfy their desires for material goods, excitement, and social status by legal or socially approved methods and so tend to choose illegal or socially disapproved methods (Farrington, 1986).

Apparently, no definitive answer can be given yet as to the ultimate causes of criminal behavior. Empirical research in this area is extremely difficult due to the impossibility of experimental control. As a consequence, the available data are sometimes vague and inconclusive and subject to highly controversial debates.

Therapeutic Jurisprudence

The concept of therapeutic jurisprudence is a rather recent development in the field of psychology and law which has become increasingly popular during the last decade. The idea behind the concept of therapeutic jurisprudence is that legal rules and procedures and the roles of legal practitioners are social forces which produce therapeutic and anti-therapeutic consequences with regard to psychological well-being and behavior modification. It holds that scholars and practitioners must recognize this and modify behavior and systems to account for it, without violating legal norms (Hora & Schma, 1998).

Therapeutic jurisprudence was originally offered as a new perspective on mental health law. During the past ten years, however, it has developed into a therapeutic perspective on the law in general (Wexler, 1997). Scholars and practitioners have recognized that therapeutic jurisprudence has many applications, including in the areas of sentencing and correctional law, criminal law and procedure, family and juvenile law, disability law, workers' compensation law, personal injury and tort law, labor arbitration law, and contract law. Within the conceptual framework of therapeutic jurisprudence, for example, it has been discussed how the criminal justice system might traumatize victims of sexual battery, how workers' compensation laws might create the moral hazard of prolonging work-related injury, how a fault based (rather than a no-fault) tort compensation scheme might enhance recovery from personal injury, and how the current law of contracts might operate to reinforce the low self-esteem of disadvantaged contracting parties (see Wexler, 1999).

It has been emphasized that therapeutic jurisprudence does not intend to touch basic constitutional, moral, and normative values. Rather, it concentrates on how existing law, whatever its nature, can be therapeutically applied (Hora, Schma, & Rosenthal, 1999), although law reform still is an option. This approach requires an analysis of the effects of existing legal rules, and the way they are applied, on the psychological well-being and behavior of a particular sector of the population. If this analysis shows that the law or the way it is applied has negative (side-) effects, the first step within a therapeutic jurisprudence approach would be to look for procedures that could help to reduce these negative effects without altering the law itself or the way it is applied. If these procedures are insufficient the focus is shifted to the modification of the application of the law. If this, too, does not effectively reduce the observed negative effects, a reform of the law itself may be required.

An illustrative example of this approach is the treatment of those child witnesses who are presumed to be victims of sexual abuse. A number of studies have consistently shown that the criminal investigation as well as the trial process may have severe negative effects on the children (e.g. Goodman, Taub, Jones, England, Port, Rudy, & Prado, 1992; Spencer & Flin, 1990; Wolf, 1997; Dannenberg, Mantwill, Stahlmann-Liebelt, & Köhnken, 1997). These negative effects are by no means restricted to a potential traumatization of child witnesses. Emotional stress usually impairs information processing and, as a consequence, the evidence given by the child may be incomplete and/or incorrect (e.g. Yuille & Daylen, 1998). Furthermore, parents who anticipate severe negative effects for their children may be reluctant to report sexual abuse to the authorities in order to protect their children from additional stress.

In an attempt to reduce stress and potential traumatization of child witnesses without changing the law, court preparation programs have been introduced in various countries (e.g. Dezwirek-Sas, 1992; Keeney, Amacher, & Kastanakis, 1992; Köhnken, 1999). In addition to a court preparation program the British government has published a Memorandum of Good Practice for Interviewing Child Witnesses which has become the de facto standard for interviewing child witnesses by the police. The introduction of the Memorandum of Good Practice did not change the law but the way the existing procedural law is applied. Furthermore, several states of the US as well as the UK and Germany have introduced modifications of procedural law which allow child witnesses to give evidence without having to appear in a courtroom by using closed-circuit TV and the use of earlier video recorded interviews as evidence.

The explicit therapeutic perspective seems to have raised some interesting questions and generated some interesting research and writing that might otherwise not have occurred, and it brings together under a single conceptual umbrella a number of areas that otherwise might not seem to be particularly related.

REFERENCES

Acre, R. (1995). Evidence evaluation in jury decision-making. In R. Bull & D. Carson (Eds.), *Handbook of psychology in legal contexts* (pp. 565–580). Chichester, UK: Wiley.

Acre, R., Sobral, J., & Fariña, F. (1992). Verdicts of psychosocially biased juries. In F. Lösel, D. Bender, & T. Bliesener (Eds.), *Psychology and law: International perspectives* (435–439). Berlin: De Gruyter.

Alonso-Quecuty, M. L. (1992). Deception detection and reality monitoring: A new answer to an old question? In F. Lösel, D. Bender, & T. Bliesener (Eds.), *Psychology and law: International perspectives* (pp. 328–332). Berlin: De Gruyter.

Anson, D. A., Golding, S. L., & Gully, K. J. (1993). Child sexual abuse allegations: Reliability of criteria-based content analysis. *Law and Human Behavior, 17*, 331–341.

Arntzen, F. (1983). *Psychologie der Zeugenaussage*. Munich: Beck.

Blackburn, R. (1996). What is forensic psychology? *Legal and Criminological Psychology, 1*, 3–16.

Brigham, J. C., & Cairns, D. L. (1988). The effect of mugshot inspections on eyewitness identification accuracy. *Journal of Applied Social Psychology, 18*, 1394–1410.

Bull, R. & Carson, D. (Eds.) (1995). *Handbook of psychology in legal contexts*. Chichester: Wiley.

Buller, D. B., & Aune, R. K. (1987). Nonverbal cues to deception among intimates, friends, and strangers. *Journal of Nonverbal Behavior, 11*, 269–290.

Burgoon, J. K., & Buller, D. B. (1994). Interpersonal deception III: Effects of deceit on perceived communication and nonverbal behavior dynamics. *Journal of Nonverbal Behavior, 18*, 155–185.

Canter, D. (1994). *Criminal shadows*. London: HarperCollins.

Chance, J. E., & Goldstein, A. G. (1996). The other-race effect and eyewitness identification. In S. L. Sporer, R. M. Malpass, & G. Köhnken (Eds.), *Psychological issues in eyewitness identification* (pp. 153–176). Mahwah, NJ: Erlbaum.

Damaska, M. (1973). Evidentiary barriers to conviction and two models of criminal procedure: A comparative study. *University of Pennsylvania Law Review, 506*.

Dannenberg, U., Mantwill, M., Stahlmann-Liebelt, U., & Köhnken, G. (1997). Reduzierung von Informationsdefiziten und Ängsten kindlicher Zeugen. In L. Greuel, T. Fabian, & M. Stadler (Eds.), *Psychologie der Zeugenaussage* (pp. 237–245). Weinheim: Beltz.

Davies, A. (1997). Specific profile analysis: A data-based approach to offender profiling. In J. L. Jackson & D. A. Bekerian (Eds.), *Offender profiling: Theory, research, and practice* (pp. 191–207). New York: Wiley.

Davis, J. H. (1989). Psychology and law: The last 15 years. *Journal of Applied Social Psychology, 19*, 199–230.

DePaulo, B. M., & Pfeifer, R. L. (1986). On-the-job experience and skill at detecting deception. *Journal of Applied Social Psychology, 16*, 249–267.

DePaulo, B. M., Stone, J. L., & Lassiter, G. D. (1985). Deceiving and detecting deceit. In B. R. Schenker (Ed.), *The self and social life* (pp. 323–370). New York: McGraw-Hill.

Dezwirek-Sas, L. (1992). Empowering child witnesses for sexual abuse prosecution. In H. Dent & R. Flin (Eds.), *Children as witnesses* (pp. 181–199). Chichester, UK: Wiley.

Efran, M. G. (1974). The effect of physical appearance on the judgment of guilt, interpersonal attraction and severity of recommended punishment on a simulated jury task. *Journal of Research in Personality, 85*, 395–461.

Ellsworth, P. C., & Mauro, R. (1998). Psychology and law. In D. T. Gilbert, S. T. Fiske, & G. Lindzey (Eds.), *The handbook of social psychology*, Vol. 2 (pp. 684–732). Boston: McGraw-Hill.

Ellsworth, P. C., & Reifman, A. (in press). Juror comprehension and public policy: Perceived problems and proposed solutions. *Psychology, Public Policy, and Law*.

Esplin, P., Boychuk, T., and Raskin, D. (1988). Application of statement validity analysis. Paper presented at the NATO Advanced Study Institute on Credibility Assessment, Maratea, Italy.

Eysenck, H. J. (1977). *Crime and personality*, 2nd. edn. London: Routledge & Kegan Paul.

Eysenck, H. J., & Eysenck, S. B. G. (1978). Psychopathy, personality and genetics. In R. D. Hare & D. Schalling (Eds.), *Psychopathic behaviour* (pp. 197–223). Chichester, UK: Wiley.

Farrington, D. P. (1986). Stepping stones to adult criminal careers. In D. Olweus, J. Block, & M. R. Yarrow (Eds.), *Development of anti-social and pro-social behavior: Research, theories and issues.* New York: Academic Press.

Farrington, D. P. (1990). Age, period, cohort, and offending. In D. M. Gottfredson & R. V. Clarke (Eds.), *Policy and theory in criminal justice: Contributions in honor of Leslie T. Wilkins.* Aldershot, UK: Gower.

Farrington, D. P. (1992). Psychological contributions to the explanation, prevention and treatment of offending. In F. Lösel, D. Bender, & T. Bliesener (Eds.), *Psychology and law: International perspectives* (pp. 35–51). Berlin: De Gruyter.

Farrington, D. P., & West, D. J. (1990). The Cambridge study in delinquent development: A long-term follow-up of 411 London males. In H. J. Kerner & G. Kaiser (Eds.), *Criminality: Personality, behavior, and life history* (pp. 115–138). Berlin: Springer.

Farrington, D. P., Biron, L., & LeBlanc, M. (1982). Personality and delinquency in London and Montreal. In J. Gunn & D. P. Farrington (Eds.), *Abnormal offenders, delinquency and the criminal justice system* (pp. 153–201). Chichester, UK: Wiley.

Farrington, D. P., Hawkins, K., & Lloyd-Bostock, S. M. (1979). Introduction: Doing psycholegal research. In D. P. Farrington, K. Hawkins, & S. M. Lloyd-Bostock (Eds.), *Psychology, law and legal processes.* London: Macmillan.

Farrington, D. P., Loeber, R., & Van Kammen, W. B. (1990). Long-term criminal outcomes of hyperactivity–impulsivity–attention deficit and conduct problems in childhood. In L. N. Robins & M. Rutter (Eds.), *Straight and devious pathways from childhood to adulthood* (pp. 62–81). Cambridge, UK: Cambridge University Press.

Fiedler, K., & Walka, I. (1993). Training lie detectors to use nonverbal cues instead of global heuristics. *Human Communication Research, 20,* 199–223.

Fisher, R. P., and Geiselman, R. E. (1992). *Memory-enhancing techniques for investigative interviewing.* Springfield, IL: Charles C. Thomas.

Fisher, R. P, McCauley, M. R., and Geiselman, R. E. (1994). Improving eyewitness testimony with the cognitive interview. In D. Ross, J. D. Read, & M. Toglia (Eds.), *Adult eyewitness testimony: Current trends and developments.* Cambridge, UK: Cambridge University Press.

Fisher, R. P., Geiselman, R. E., Raymond, D. S., Jurkevich, L. M., and Warhaftig, M. L. (1987). Enhancing enhanced eyewitness memory: Refining the Cognitive Interview. *Journal of Police Science and Administration, 15,* 291–297.

Frey, D. (1995). Information seeking among individuals and groups and possible consequences for decision-making in business and politics. In E. Witte & J. Davis (Eds.). *Understanding group behavior, Vol. II: Small group processes and interpersonal relations.* Hillsdale, NJ: Lawrence Erlbaum.

Geiselman, R. E., Fisher, R. P., Firstenberg, I., Hutton, L. A., Avetissian, I., & Prosk, A. (1984). Enhancement of eyewitness memory: An empirical evaluation of the cognitive interview. *Journal of Police Science and Administration, 12,* 74–80.

Goodman, G., Taub, E. P., Jones, D., England, P., Port, L., Rudy, L., & Prado, L. (1992). Testifying in criminal court: Emotional effects on child sexual assault victims. *Monographs of the Society for Research in Child Development, 57* (5), Serial No. 229.

Gottfredson, M., & Hirschi, T. (1988). Science, public policy and the career paradigm. *Criminology, 26,* 37–56.

Gottschalk, R., Davidson II, W. S., Gensheimer, L. K., & Mayer, J. P. (1987). Community-based interventions. In H. C. Quay (Ed.), *Handbook of juvenile delinquency* (pp. 266–289). New York: Wiley.

Griffitt, W., & Jackson, T. (1973). Simulated jury decisions: The influence of jury defendant attitude similarity–dissimilarity. *Social Behavior and Personality, 1,* 73–93.

Hans, V. P., & Vidmar, N. (1982). Jury selection. In N. L. Kerr & R. M. Bray (Eds.), *The psychology of the courtroom* (pp. 39–82). London: Academic Press.

Herdan, G. (1964). *Quantitative linguistics*. London: Butterworths.

Heuer, L., & Penrod, S. D. (1994). Trial complexity: A field investigation of its meaning and its effects. *Law and Human Behavior, 18,* 29–51.

Höfer, E., Akehurst, L., & Metzger, G. (1996). *Reality monitoring: A chance for further development of CBCA?* Paper presented at the Conference of the European Association on Psychology and Law, Siena, Italy.

Hollin, C. R. (1989). *Psychology and crime*. London: Routledge.

Hora, P. F., & Schma, W. G. (1998). Therapeutic jurisprudence. *Judicature, 82,* 8–12.

Hora, P. F., Schma, W. G., & Rosenthal, J. T. A. (1999). Therapeutic jurisprudence and the drug treatment court movement: Revolutionizing the criminal justice system's response to drug abuse and crime in America. *Notre Dame Law Review, 74,* 439–537.

Jackson, J. L., & Bekerian, D. A. (Eds.). *Offender profiling: Theory. research, and practice*. New York: John Wiley & Sons.

Janis, I. L. (1972). Victims of groupthink. Boston: Houghton Mifflin.

Janis, I. L. (1982). *Groupthink*. 2nd. revd. edn. Boston: Houghton Mifflin.

Joffe, R., and Yuille, J. (1992). Criteria-based content analysis: An experimental investigation. Paper presented at the meeting of the American Psychology–Law Society, San Diego.

Johnson, M. K., & Raye, C. L. (1981). Reality monitoring. *Psychological Reviews, 88,* 67–85.

Kalven, H., Jr., & Zeisel, H. (1966). *The American jury*. Boston: Little, Brown.

Kapardis, A. (1997). *Psychology and law*. Cambridge, UK: Cambridge University Press.

Kaplan, M. F. (Ed.) (1986). *The impact of social psychology on procedural justice*. Springfield, IL: Charles C. Thomas.

Kassin, S. M., & Sommers, S. R. (1997). Inadmissible testimony, instructions to disregard, and the jury: Substantive versus procedural considerations. *Personality and Social Psychology Bulletin, 23,* 1046–1054.

Kebbell, M., & Milne, R. (1998). Police officers' perceptions of eyewitness performance in forensic investigations. *Journal of Social Psychology, 138,* 323–330.

Keeney, K. S., Amacher, E., & Kastanakis, J. A. (1992). The court prep group: A vital part of the court process. In H. Dent & R. Flin (Eds.), *Children as witnesses* (pp. 201–209). Chichester, UK: Wiley.

Kintsch, W., & Van Dijk, T. A. (1978). Toward a model of text comprehension and production. *Psychological Review, 85,* 363–394.

Köhnken, G. (1985). Speech and deception of eyewitnesses: An information processing approach. In F. L. Denmark (Ed.), *Social/ecological psychology and the psychology of women* (pp. 141–163). Amsterdam: North-Holland.

Köhnken, G. (1999). Der Schutz kindlicher Zeugen vor Gericht. In G. Schütze, R. Lempp, & G. Köhnken (Eds.), *Forensische kinder- und jugendpsychiatrie und-psychologie*.

Köhnken, G., & Höfer, E. (1998). Assessing statement credibility. Paper presented at the International Congress of Applied Psychology, San Francisco.

Köhnken, G., & Wegener, H. (1982). Zur Glaubwürdigkeit von Zeugenaussagen. Experimentelle Überprüfung ausgewählter Glaubwürdigkeitskriterien [Credibility of witness statements: experimental examination of selected reality criteria]. *Zeitschrift für Experimentelle und Angewandte Psychologie, 29,* 92–111.

Köhnken, G., Malpass, R. S., & Wogalter, M. S. (1996). Forensic applications of lineup research. In S. L. Sporer, R. M. Malpass, & G. Köhnken (Eds.), *Psychological issues in eyewitness identification* (pp. 205–231). Hillsdale, NJ: Erlbaum.

Köhnken, G., Milne, R., Memon, A., & Bull, R. (1999). The cognitive interview: A meta-analysis. *Psychology, Crime and Law, 5,* 3–27.

Köhnken, G., Schimossek, E., Aschermann, E., & Höfer, E. (1995). The cognitive interview and the assessment of the credibility of adults' statements. *Journal of Applied Psychology, 80,* 671–684.

Liebermann, J. D., & Sales, B. D. (1997). What social science teaches us about the jury instruction process. *Psychology, Public Policy, and Law, 3,* 589–644.

Lindsay, R. C. L., & Wells, G. L. (1980). What price justice? Exploring the relationship of lineup fairness to identification accuracy. *Law and Human Behavior, 4,* 303–313.

Luus, C. A. E., & Wells, G. L. (1991). Eyewitness identification and the selection of distractors for lineups. *Law and Human Behavior, 14,* 43–57.

McCauley, M. R., & Fisher, R. P. (1995). Facilitating children's eyewitness recall with the revised cognitive interview. *Journal of Applied Psychology, 80,* 510–516.

McEwan, J. (1995). Adversarial and inquisitorial proceedings. In R. Bull & D. Carson (Eds.), *Handbook of psychology in legal contexts* (495–508). Chichester, UK: Wiley.

McGuire, J. (1995). *What works? Reducing reoffending.* Chichester, UK: Wiley.

Malpass, R. S., & Devine, P. G. (1983). Measuring the fairness of eyewitness identification lineups. In S. M. A. Lloyd-Bostock & R. B. Clifford (Eds.), *Evaluating witness evidence* (pp. 81–102). Chichester, UK: Wiley.

Malpass, R. S., & Devine, P. G. (1984). Research on suggestion in lineups and photospreads. In G. L. Wells & E. F. Loftus (Eds.), *Eyewitness testimony: Psychological perspectives* (pp. 64–91). New York: Cambridge University Press.

Malpass, R. S., Parada, M., Corey, D., Chavez, J., Bowles, S., & McQuiston, D. (1999). Reliability of face recognition. Manuscript submitted for publication.

Marbe, K. (1913). *Grundzüge der Forensischen Psychologie* [Elements of forensic psychology]. Munich: Beck.

Milne, R., Bull, R., Köhnken, G., & Memon, A. (1995). The cognitive interview and suggestibility. In G. M. Stephenson & N. K. Clark (Eds.), *Criminal behaviour: Perceptions, attributions and rationality* (pp. 21–27). Division of criminological and legal psychology occasional papers, 22. Leicester, UK: British Psychological Society.

Mitchell, J., & Dodder, R. A. (1983). Types of neutralization and types of delinquency. *Journal of Youth and Adolescence, 12,* 307–318.

Morton, A. Q., & Farringdon, M. G. (1992). Identifying utterance. *Expert Evidence, 1,* 84–92.

Münsterberg, H. (1908). *On the witness stand: Essays on psychology and crime.* New York: Clark, Boardman, Doubleday.

Munstermann, G. T., Hannaford, P. L., & Whitehead, G. M. (Eds.) (1997). *Jury trial innovations.* Williamsburg, VA: National Center for State Courts.

Park, W. W. (1990). A review of research on groupthink. *Journal of Behavioral Decision Making, 3,* 229–245.

Pennington, N., & Hastie, R. (1981). Juror decision making models: The generalization gap. *Psychological Bulletin, 89,* 246–287.

Pennington, N., & Hastie, R. (1986). Evidence evaluation in complex decision making. *Journal of Personality and Social Psychology, 51,* 242–258.

Pennington, N., & Hastie, R. (1990). Practical implications of psychological research on juror and jury decision making. *Personality and Social Psychology Bulletin, 16,* 90–105.

Pennington, N., & Hastie, R. (1993). The story model for juror decision making. In R. Hastie (Ed.), *Inside the juror: The psychology of juror decision making* (pp. 192–221). New York: Cambridge University Press.

Porter, S., & Yuille, J. C. (1996). The language of deceit: An investigation of the verbal clues to deception in an interrogation context. *Law and Human Behavior, 20,* 443–459.

Pozzulo, J. D., & Lindsay, R. C. L. (1999). Identification accuracy of children versus adults. Manuscript submitted for publication.

Raine, A., & Venables, P. H. (1981). Classical conditioning and socialization – a biosocial interaction. *Personality and Individual Differences, 2,* 273–283.

Rand Corporation (1975). The criminal investigation process, Vols. 1–3. Rand Corporation Technical Report R-1777-DOJ. Santa Monica.

Raskin, D. C. (1989). Polygraph techniques for the detection of deception. In D. C. Raskin (Ed.), *Psychological methods in criminal investigation and evidence* (247–296). New York: Springer.

Rattner, A. (1988). Convicted but innocent: Wrongful conviction and the criminal justice system. *Law and Human Behavior, 12,* 283–293.

Reiser, M. (1980). *Handbook of investigative hypnosis.* Los Angeles: Lehi.

Robins, L. N. (1979). Sturdy childhood predictors of adult outcomes: Replications from longitudinal studies. In J. E. Barrett, R. M. Rose, & G. L. Klerman (Eds.), *Stress and mental disorder.* New York: Raven Press.

Ross, D., Read, J. D., & Toglia, M. (Eds.) (1994). *Adult eyewitness testimony: Current trends and developments.* Cambridge, UK: Cambridge University Press.

Rowe, D. C., & Farrington, D. P. (1997). The familial transmission of criminal convictions. *Criminology, 35,* 177–201.

Ruby, C. L., & Brigham, J. C. (1997). The usefulness of the criteria-based content analysis technique in distinguishing between truthful and fabricated allegations: A critical review. *Psychology, Public Policy, and Law, 3/4,* 705–734.

Sarbin, T. R. (1979). The myth of the criminal type. In T. R. Sarbin (Ed.), *Challenges to the criminal justice system: The perspectives of community psychology.* New York: Human Science.

Saywitz, K. J., Geiselman, R. E., & Bornstein, G. K. (1992). Effects of cognitive interviewing and practice on children's recall performance. *Journal of Applied Psychology, 77,* 744–756.

Schank, R. C., & Abelson, R. P. (1977). *Scripts, plans, goals, and understanding.* Hillsdale, NJ: Lawrence Erlbaum Associates.

Schulz-Hardt, S., Frey, D., Lüthgens, C., & Moscovici, S. (1999). Biased information search in group decision making. Manuscript submitted for publication.

Sealy, A. P. (1989). Decision processes in the jury room. In H. Wegener, F. Lösel, & J. Haisch (Eds.), *Criminal behavior and the justice system: Psychological perspectives* (pp. 163–180). New York: Springer.

Shapiro, P., & Penrod, S. D. (1986). A meta-analysis of facial identification studies. *Psychological Bulletin, 100,* 139–156.

Smith, J. E., Pleban, R. J., & Shaffer, D. (1982). Effects of interrogator bias and a police trait questionnaire on the accuracy of eyewitness identification. *Journal of Social Psychology, 116,* 19–26.

Smith, M. (1983). Hypnotic memory enhancement of witnesses: Does it work? *Psychological Bulletin, 94,* 387–407.

Snyder, M. (1984). When belief creates reality. In L. Berkowitz (Ed.), *Advances in experimental social psychology,* Vol. 18 (pp. 247–305). New York: Academic Press.

Spencer, J. R., & Flin, R. (1990). *The evidence of children: The law and the psychology.* London: Sage.

Sporer, S. L. (1996). The less traveled road to truth: Verbal cues in deception detection in accounts of fabricated and self-experienced events. Paper presented at the meeting of the American Psychology–Law Society, Hilton Head.

Sporer, S. L., Malpass, R. M., & Köhnken, G. (Eds.) (1996). *The psychology of eyewitness identification: New evidence and practical guidelines.* Hillsdale, NJ: Erlbaum.

Sporer, S. J., Penrod, S. D., Read, J. D., & Cutler, B. L. (1995). Gaining confidence in confidence: A new meta-analysis on the confidence-accuracy relationship in eyewitness identification. *Psychological Bulletin*.

Steller, M., & Köhnken, G. (1989). Statement analysis: Credibility assessment of children's testimonies in sexual abuse cases. In D. C. Raskin (Ed.), *Psychological methods in criminal investigation and evidence* (pp. 217–245). New York: Springer.

Steller, M., Wellershaus, P., & Wolf, T. (1992). Realkennzeichen in Kinderaussagen: Empirische Grundlagen der Kriterienorientierten Aussageanalyse [Reality criteria in child witness statements: Empirical foundations of the criteria-based content analysis]. *Zeitschrift für Experimentelle und Angewandte Psychologie, 39*, 151–170.

Stephenson, G. M. (1992). *The psychology of criminal justice.* Oxford, UK: Blackwell Publishers.

Stern, W. (1903). *Beiträge zur Psychologie der Aussage, 1. Heft.* Leipzig: Barth.

Tedeschi, J. T., & Norman, N. (1985). Social power, self-presentation, and the self. In B. R. Schlenker (Ed.), *The self and social life* (pp. 293–322). New York: McGraw-Hill.

Tetlock, P. E., Peterson, R. S., McGuire, C., Chang, S., & Feld, P. (1992). Assessing political group dynamics: A test of the groupthink model. *Journal of Personality and Social Psychology, 63*, 403–425.

Thibaut, J., & Walker, L. (1975). *Procedural justice: A psychological analysis.* New York: Spectrum.

Undeutsch, U. (1967). Beurteilung der Glaubhaftigkeit von Aussagen [Evaluation of statement credibility]. In U. Undeutsch (Ed.), *Handbuch der Psychologie, Vol. 11: Forensische Psychologie* (pp. 26–181). Göttingen: Hogrefe.

Vollrath, D. A., & Davis, J. H. (1980). Jury size and decision rule. In R. J. Simon (Ed.), *The jury: Its role in American society.* Lexington: Lexington Books.

Vrij, A. (1994). The impact of information and setting on detection of deception by police detectives. *Journal of Nonverbal Behavior, 18*, 117–136.

Vrij, A. (1998). Nonverbal communication and credibility. In A. Memon, A. Vrij, & R. Bull (Eds.), *Psychology and Law: Truthfulness, accuracy and credibility* (pp. 32–58). Maidenhead, UK: McGraw-Hill.

Vrij, A., & Winkel, F. W. (1994). Objective and subjective indicators of deception. *Issues in Criminological and Legal Psychology, 20*, 51–57.

Wagstaff, G. F. (1984). The enhancement of witness testimony by "hypnosis:" A review and methodological critique of the experimental literature. *British Journal of Experimental and Clinical Hypnosis, 22*, 3–12.

Wells, G. L. (1978). Applied eyewitness research: System variables and estimator variables. *Journal of Personality and Social Psychology, 36*, 1546–1557.

Wells, G. L., & Luus, C. A. E. (1990). Police lineups as experiments: Social methodology as a framework for properly conducted lineups. *Personality and Social Psychology Bulletin, 16*, 106–117.

Wells, G. L., & Turtle, J. W. (1986). Eyewitness identification: The importance of lineup models. *Psychological Bulletin, 99*, 320–329.

Wells, G. L., Small, M., Penrod, S. D., Malpass, R. S., Fulero, S. M., & Brimacombe, C. A. E. (1998). Eyewitness identification procedures: Recommendations for lineups and photospreads. *Law and Human Behavior, 22*, 603–647.

West, D. J., & Farrington, D. P. (1973). *Who becomes delinquent?* London: Heinemann.

Wexler, D. B. (1997). The development of therapeutic jurisprudence: From theory to practice. Paper presented at the University of Virginia's Institute of Law, Psychiatry and Public Policy Practice conference.

Wexler, D. B. (1999). The Development of Therapeutic Jurisprudence: From Theory to Practice. 68 Revista Juridica, UPR 691 (1999).

Wilson, J. Q., & Herrnstein, R. J. (1985). *Crime and human nature.* New York: Simon & Schuster.

Wolf, P. (1997). *Was wissen Kinder und Jugendliche über Gerichtsverhandlungen?* Regensburg: Roederer.

Yuille, J. (1988). The systematic assessment of children's testimony. *Canadian Psychologist, 29,* 247–262.

Yuille, J. C., & Daylen, J. (1998). The impact of traumatic events on eyewitness memory. In C. P. Thompson, D. J. Herrmann, J. D. Read, D. Bruce, D. G. Payne, & M. P. Toglia (Eds.), *Eyewitness memory: Theoretical and applied perspectives* (pp. 155–178). Mahwah, NJ: Lawrence Erlbaum Associates.

Zuckerman, M., DePaulo, B. M., & Rosenthal, R. (1981). Verbal and nonverbal communication of deception. In L. Berkowitz (Ed.), *Advances in experimental social psychology,* Vol. 14 (pp. 1–57). New York: Academic Press.

Zuckerman, M., Koestner, R., & Colella, M. J. (1985). Learning to detect deception from three communication channels. *Journal of Nonverbal Behavior, 9,* 188–194.

Zuckerman, M., Koestner, R., & Driver, R. E. (1981). Beliefs about cues associated with deception. *Journal of Nonverbal Behavior, 6,* 105–114.

CHAPTER SIX

Procedural Mechanisms and Jury Behavior

R. Scott Tindale, Janice Nadler, Andrea Krebel, and James H. Davis

The citizen's jury has a long and distinguished history as a way of administering justice in Western civilizations (see Hastie, Penrod, & Pennington, 1983; Kalvin & Zeisel, 1966). Stemming from early British common law, the right to a trial by a jury of one's peers has been present in many cultures throughout history, and serves as a cornerstone of the U.S. legal system to this day. However, many of the laws and procedures governing how juries are used, chosen, instructed, and so forth, have been formalized through reliance on tradition and intuition. In more recent times, many of these procedures have been questioned, for reasons of both fairness and practicality. Thus, numerous controversies have arisen about how, when, and in some cases whether, juries should be used. In the United States, many of these controversies have been addressed by appeals to the U.S. Supreme Court (e.g., *Ballew* v. *Georgia*, 1978; *Lockhart* v. *Mcree*, 1986; *Williams* v. *Florida*, 1972; *Witherspoon* v. *Illinois*, 1968). Unfortunately, in many cases, empirical evidence addressing these questions was either sparse or non-existent.

Partly in response to the controversies mentioned above, the study of juries (or more typically and unfortunately, jurors) has been a common practice in social psychology, particularly in the United States. Juries provide a natural context for many of the basic social psychological processes deemed central to the field: impression formation, attribution, social influence, social comparison, attitude change, etc. all come into play in the typical courtroom. Juries are asked to make important decisions about people and their behavior. They are presented with different types of information from different sources. They must evaluate the validity of the information presented, the truthfulness of the information sources, and the viability of the arguments presented by both sides. They must make judgments about motives and intentions of the relevant actors associated with the specific behaviors of interest. And at the

Preparation of this chapter was supported by National Science Foundation grants SBR 9730822 (R. Scott Tindale, Co-Principal Investigator), and SBR 9507955 (James H. Davis, Co-Principal Investigator), and a Doctoral Fellowship from the American Bar Foundation (Janice Nadler, recipient).

end of the trial, they must, as a group, reach a consensus concerning the implications of the evidence for the questions at hand.

This last phase, the group consensus process, has served as a major focus for small-group research in social psychology (Davis, 1980; Stasser, Kerr, & Bray, 1982; Tindale & Davis, 1983). Juries must deliberate and reach a single group decision, placing the focus squarely on the group level of analysis. Juries are also fairly easily simulated in laboratory settings, where some number of heretofore strangers come together for a brief period of time with a common purpose. In this way, laboratory groups and juries share a number of similar features. In addition, experimental participants find it relatively straightforward to role-play a jury situation, and often find the experience enjoyable. Thus, it is not surprising that mock jury research has been, and still is, one of the dominant paradigms in small group research in social psychology. It has fostered both theoretical knowledge about how groups process information and reach consensus on complex tasks, and practical knowledge on the conditions under which juries are best capable at carrying out their mandate – rendering justice in a fair and unbiased manner.

Other chapters in *the Blackwell Handbook of Social Psychology: Group Processes* focus on various aspects of the basic knowledge obtained, in part, from research using a mock jury paradigm (particularly Stasser & Dietz-Uhler, 2001). Our focus is oriented toward how aspects of courtroom and legal procedures can and do influence jury decision making. Our emphasis on procedural mechanisms stems from both their importance and their often under-appreciated role in jury behavior. All task-performing groups follow some type of procedure while attempting to reach their goal. Some of these procedures are informal, implicit, and governed by shared norms. However, procedures can also be formal, explicit, and governed by stature. Many of the controversies surrounding juries involve formal procedures, such as mandated jury size, consensus rule, empanelling procedures, and rules for appropriate juror behavior during deliberation. As such, much of the research discussed here concerns attempts to address these issues. But other procedures are more informal and often not recognized as programmatic or normatively governed interpersonal patterns of behavior at all. For example, juries are not usually directed to discuss "joined" charges in any particular order, or provided instructions on when and how often to poll verdict preferences. Yet such informal procedures can and do influence both the processes and outcomes of decision-making groups – including juries (Davis, 1984; Kameda, 1996). From a practical standpoint, if certain informal procedures typically lead to better jury performance, they can be formalized and included in standard rules or instructions. Thus, justice can be better served by understanding how both formal and informal procedures influence jury behavior.

In an attempt to impose some structure on the rather large body of research on courtroom procedures and juries, we have divided the chapter into three sections: (a) procedures that occur prior to the actual courtroom proceedings (e.g., jury selection); (b) trial/courtroom procedures (e.g., presentation of evidence, judges instructions, etc.); and (c) procedures guiding jury deliberations. However, these are not clearly identifiable categories, since procedures at one stage often impact both the procedures and their implications at other stages. In addition, we have attempted to focus mainly on research using actual or mock juries, in contrast to jurors, the more common research target. However, due to the difficulty of doing group-level research, some rather important issues have only been addressed at the individual juror level. In some cases, simulations or "thought experiments," based on empirically tested models of jury behavior, have been used to help bridge the gap in knowledge. However, there are still many areas where our conclusions must remain tentative due to a lack of group-level rescarch. This remains a weakness in social psychological research on juries since there is plenty of evidence to show that group-level phenomena are not always commensurate with individual-level reactions. Thus, we start (and finish) this chapter by pointing out the need for more research on juries as opposed to jurors, because it is on the former that the burden of rendering justice rests. In addition, much of the research discussed here is based solely on the U.S. jury system – an issue to be addressed later. Some of the research discussed in later portions of the chapter relies on some standard models of jury decision making. Thus, a brief discussion of such models precedes the review of the literature. (For a more formal and complete discussion of these models, see Stasser, Kerr, & Davis, 1989, and Stasser & Dietz-Uhler, 2001.)

Formal Models of Jury Decision Making

Actual jury behavior is difficult to observe directly. Jury deliberations are conducted in private to encourage jurors to deliberate freely and without the concerns that would naturally arise in the presence of an outside observer. Moreover, each jury considers a unique case with unique characteristics. It would be difficult to generalize about jury behavior on the basis of a single case, or on the basis of many cases, each with its own unique evidence, cause of action, legal basis, etc. Thus, a substantial portion of the research on juries has involved formulating and testing formal models of jury behavior. These models have then been used to help address procedural questions that would be difficult to address empirically. A full review of jury models is beyond the scope of the present chapter (see Stasser & Dietz-Uhler, 2001, for more detailed descriptions of these models). However, they are similar in a number of respects. Thus, we will simply describe some of the main features, using social decision scheme (SDS) theory (Davis, 1973) as a focal point.

SDS theory posits that group decision making in general can be conceptualized as a combinatorial process. In order to reach consensus, group members must combine their varying preferences in such a way as to reach a final group response. For criminal juries (on which most of the modeling work has been focused), the individual member preferences are for verdicts (typically guilty vs. not guilty, but some charges have multiple verdict categories, e.g., 1st degree vs. 2nd degree murder, etc.). In a 12-person jury deciding between guilty and not guilty, there are 13 ways in which the members can array themselves over the response alternatives: 12 for guilty and 0 for not guilty, 11 for guilty and 1 for not guilty, . . . , 0 for guilty and 12 for not guilty. SDS theory then posits that the ways in which the different member preference arrays lead to specific jury verdicts can be described by an SDS matrix. The matrix contains the conditional probabilities associated with each possible jury outcome (guilty, not guilty, or hung), given a specific member array (e.g., 7 members for guilty vs. 5 for not guilty). Based on extensive empirical work, the SDS matrix described as "two-thirds majority wins, defendant protection otherwise" tends to provide a relatively good description of the combinatorial process for juries. This model is described in Table 6.1. As shown in the

Table 6.1 Two-thirds Majority Wins, Defendant Protection Otherwise Social Decision Scheme Model

Juror preference distribution		Jury verdict distribution		
Guilty	Not guilty	Guilty	Not guilty	Hung
12	0	1.00	0.00	0.00
11	1	1.00	0.00	0.00
10	2	1.00	0.00	0.00
9	3	1.00	0.00	0.00
8	4	1.00	0.00	0.00
7	5	0.00	0.75	0.25
6	6	0.00	0.75	0.25
5	7	0.00	0.75	0.25
4	8	0.00	1.00	0.00
3	9	0.00	1.00	0.00
2	10	0.00	1.00	0.00
1	11	0.00	1.00	0.00
0	12	0.00	1.00	0.00

table, for a 12-person jury, factions containing 8 or more members are quite powerful and will lead the jury to their preferred verdict with probabilities near 1.0. (Note that, for convenience, probabilities of 1.0 and 0 are used in the models, but are meant to convey probabilities near those values.) When no faction contains two-thirds of the members, the model predicts that juries will either hang (about 25% of the time) or coalesce around the not guilty alternative (about 75% of the time). This asymmetry toward protecting the defendant appears to be a function of the reasonable doubt criterion used in most criminal trials (MacCoun & Kerr, 1988).

A number of jury models similar to the one described above exist. Some are extensions of the general SDS approach, while others are formalized in other ways (i.e., computer models like JUS, Hastie, Penrod, & Pennington, 1983). For example, Kerr's (1981) social transition scheme model looks at the changes from one member preference array (e.g., 7 for guilty, 5 for not guilty) to a different array (e.g., 8 vs. 4) over time. Similarly, Stasser and Davis' (1981) social interaction sequence model focuses on member changes in both confidence and verdict over time. Probably the most sophisticated model of jury behavior is JUS (Hastie et al., 1983). The basis of the model is an influence function which specifies whether, where, and when a juror in a given verdict faction will move to another verdict faction. The model also takes into account individual differences in resistance to influence, aspects of jury selection, and other procedural factors (jury size, decision rule, etc.). Although each of these models differs in some important ways, they all predict that factions containing at least two-thirds of the jury members will probably win out in the end.

The aforementioned models all focus on criminal trials where the decision alternatives are discrete verdict categories. However, civil juries often are asked to reach consensus on dollar amounts or percentages of liability. In order to encompass continuous response domains, Davis (1996) formulated the social judgment scheme (SJS) model. Since faction size is often not a viable concept for continuous response formats, the SJS model focuses on relative distances between members along the continuum. It then weights each member in terms of influence in the groups using an exponential function based on the sum of the relative distances. In general, the model gives little weight to members whose preferences are discrepant from most other members, and greater weight to members who are similar (in terms of distance) to most other members. Thus, the model argues that shared preferences (shared here meaning similar rather than identical) are more likely to end up being chosen by the group/jury (Tindale & Kameda, in press). Although formulated only recently, it has provided adequate fits to data from a number of mock civil jury experiments (Davis, Au, Hulbert, Chen, & Zarnoth, 1997: Davis, Stasson, Parks, Hulbert, Kameda, Zimmerman, & Ono, 1993).

Procedures Prior to Trial: Jury Selection

The Sixth Amendment to the U.S. Constitution guarantees the right to a trial by an impartial jury of one's peers in the jurisdiction where the crime was committed (Way, 1980). Although this may appear clear and straightforward, the actual procedures used to provide such a jury have often been questioned. For example, crimes that receive a lot of publicity in the area where they were committed often make finding an impartial jury in the jurisdiction where the crime was committed difficult (McConahay, Mullin, & Frederick, 1977). Additionally, if the defendant in a trial is a member of an under-represented group, what does a "jury of one's peers" really mean? Thus, the Courts have had to rule on a number of cases concerning the procedures used to empanel juries (e.g., *Duren* v. *Missouri*, 1979; *Thiel* v. *Southern Pacific Company*, 1946; *Witherspoon* v. *Illinois*, 1968).

There are three main factors that determine the composition of a specific jury (Hans & Vidmar, 1982). First, is the venue or location of the trial where the jury will be chosen. This depends, in part, on the type of trial (e.g., criminal vs. civil, state vs. federal, etc.), but mainly on the location of the crime/cause of action, and the parties. The second aspect concerns the panel of eligible jurors from which the specific jury will be drawn. Each particular court district has a list containing the eligible jurors for that district. In theory, such lists should contain all the eligible jurors in a given area, but in practice, the lists are often incomplete, especially in areas of high population density. Courts have defined an impartial jury panel as one that represents a fair cross-section of the community, and have held that officials cannot systematically or intentionally exclude any particular group (*Thiel* v. *Southern Pacific Company*, 1946). More recently (*Duren* v. *Missouri*, 1979), courts have set forth specific criteria that must be satisfied to demonstrate that the fair cross-section requirement has been violated.

(T)he defendant must show (1) that the group alleged to be excluded is a "distinctive" group in the community; (2) that the representation of this group in the venires from which juries are selected is not fair and reasonable in relation to the number of such persons in the community; and (3) that this under-representation is due to systematic exclusion of this group in the jury selection process. (Finch & Ferraro, 1986, p. 30)

The third aspect of jury selection involves the "voir dire" – an initial questioning of jurors in order to insure that they are acceptable to both sides in the trial. Voir dire procedures vary widely across cases and jurisdictions, with judges usually given a fair amount of leeway in defining the relevant parameters. Jurors can be "struck" or removed from a jury panel in two ways. First, jurors can be struck for "cause" if the judge finds that they could not be fair and impartial jurors. Examples of removals for cause include jurors who are relatives of witnesses or one of the parties, or jurors who express a biased attitude toward the case that would prejudice their judgment in some way. Second, each party is given a fixed number of peremptory challenges that can be used at their discretion for removing particular jurors from the panel. These are limited in number and vary in terms of the type of case.

Folk wisdom dictates (and many attorneys agree) that jury selection is one of the most important aspects of a trial (Penrod, 1980). Thus, it is somewhat surprising that there has been so little research on jury selection in general. Probably the main reason for the lack of empirical effort in this area stems from the practical difficulties involved. In actual trials, 40 or 50 (or more) potential jurors may be questioned in order to find the 12 (14 with alternates) to actually serve. To recreate such procedures in a more controlled environment would be very costly in terms of time and participants. Thus, much of the research that has been done has either restricted itself to the individual (juror) level of analysis, or used mathematical or computer simulations. Most research on jury selection has revolved around two recent controversies. The first involves the use of social science methods to aid one side or the other in jury selection (Kairys, Schulman, & Harris, 1975; Shulman, 1973). The technique referred to as "Scientific Jury Selection" began as an attempt to aid defendants in political trials in the late 1960s and early 1970s. It was controversial on two dimensions – whether it was ethical (Etzioni, 1974; Moskitis, 1976) and whether it actually worked (Saks, 1976; Saks & Hastie, 1978). The research focus was mainly on the latter issue.

Proponents of the method (Shulman, 1973; McConahay, Mullin, & Frederick, 1977) argue that using social science methods can be useful in all three aspects of jury selection. Survey techniques and interviews can be used to demonstrate that a particular venue contains mostly jurors who have been biased by pretrial publicity or have attitudes that would make them inappropriate for jury service in a particular trial (McConahay et al., 1977). They can also be used to challenge the "representative cross-section" assumption of a particular jury roll (Shulman, 1973). However, most of the controversy has surrounded the use of social science to help select the actual jury during the voir dire process.

For the actual selection phase, the social science method involves conducting, prior to voir dire, a sample survey of the community addressing demographic, personality, and attitudinal characteristics of the potential jurors. The data are then used to create profiles of "good versus bad" jurors for the party for which the survey was administered.

Typically, multiple regression and profile analysis techniques are used to assess which demographic/attitudinal variables are most useful. Then, during the voir dire, the questions posed are designed to reveal the juror characteristics necessary to categorize them, in terms of the profile (see Kairys et al., 1975 for a more thorough description of the techniques involved).

Proponents of the technique argue for its validity based on the outcomes of trials where it has been used – usually acquittals or hung juries (Christie, 1976; McConahay et al., 1977). However, it is difficult to ascertain the effectiveness of a technique based on only case studies.

In addition, Saks (1976) has argued that most of the aforementioned cases were weak in terms of incriminating evidence, many of them involving charges of conspiracy, which is a difficult charge to prove.

Attempts to assess the efficacy of scientific jury selection with more valid techniques have provided somewhat mixed but, at best, weak evidence for its usefulness. Saks (1976) reported the results of a survey study where large numbers of valid attitudinal and demographic measures could account for only 13% of the variance in juror verdict, while evidence accounted for 33%. Hastie et al. (1983) took a number of demographic measures of jurors in a large-scale jury simulation experiment using a murder trial and found little if any evidence for their ability to predict juror verdict preferences. However, Horowitz (1980) ran an experiment attempting to directly test whether scientific methods were better able to pick favorable jurors than were law students. His results suggested that for trials where political attitudes were directly relevant, the scientific methods were somewhat more effective in that they led to fewer guilty verdicts. However, for the murder trial, the scientific selection method was no better at influencing jury verdicts than were the law student selections.

In an attempt to address the potential efficacy of scientific selection techniques across all three aspects of the selection process (venue, panel, and actual jury), Tindale and Nagao (1986) performed a series of computer simulations. The simulations assumed that only the defense was using scientific techniques and that jury decision making could be represented by a 2/3 majority decision model (see Table 6.1). Tindale and Nagao assessed the expected jury verdicts under a variety of different assumptions concerning biases in the jury panel and the ability of the techniques to identify more or less defense-favorable jurors. The simulations showed that quite powerful effects on jury verdicts could be found if one could exchange a biased jury panel (80% or 60% favoring guilt prior to deliberation) for an unbiased one (50% favoring guilt). The effects for targeting particular jurors for challenges in the selection process showed weaker albeit meaningful effects. Increases in not guilty jury verdicts ranged from non-existent for very weak or very strong cases to about 12% for moderately strong cases (where the 2/3 majority model shows its steepest slope across strength of case). However, these later simulations assumed at least some ability to predict juror's verdicts from their answers to voir dire questions.

A more recent controversy surrounding jury selection procedures involves the notion of "death qualified" juries (Thompson, 1989). For capital cases (those that might lead to the death penalty), prior to 1968, judges would allow jurors to be challenged for cause if they had any negative feelings toward the death penalty. Because many capital juries also decided whether the death penalty is warranted, this practice seemed appropriate. However, early research looking at the relationship between death penalty attitudes and verdicts showed that people in favor of the death penalty were also more conviction prone (e.g., Zeisel, 1968). Based in part on this early evidence, death qualification procedures were questioned in Witherspoon v. Illinois (1968). Although the court continued to allow the procedure, it provided a set of criteria to be used in the death qualification procedures and also opened the door to eliminating the procedure if more and better research could demonstrate that it produced juries biased against the defendant in terms of verdict.

Since 1968, a number of studies have shown that jurors who are death qualified according to the Witherspoon criteria are more likely to vote guilty than are jurors who would be removed from the jury (e.g., Cowan, Thompson, & Ellsworth, 1984; Ellsworth, Bukaty, Cowan, & Thompson, 1984; Thompson, Cowan, Ellsworth, & Harrington, 1984). Although the findings are not totally consistent, two recent meta-analyses have both shown that the effect at the juror level is reliable if not large (Allen, Mabry, & McKelton, 1998; Filkins, Smith, & Tindale, 1998). In addition, Haney (1984) showed that simply sitting through a death qualification voir dire can predispose jurors toward conviction. However, the Supreme Court chose to ignore the research evidence in their *Lockhart* v. *McCree* (1986) decision. One of the reasons the Court gave for paying little heed to the social psychological research was that the bias had not been demonstrated at the jury level.

Interestingly enough, recent computer simulations have shown that the effect of death qualification at the jury level is actually quite small (Filkins et al., 1998). Since only about 17% of the population in general would be ineligible for jury service based on death qualification procedures, and the effect size is fairly small, the maximum impact at the jury level was less than one more guilty verdict in 100 trials using the average effect size. Using the largest effect size in the sample, it rose to slightly more than three additional guilty jury verdicts in 100 trials. Obviously more research is needed on both this issue and the effects of jury selection in general. But the current evidence does not seem to support the widespread belief among lawyers and laypersons alike that jury selection plays a major role in determining final jury verdicts.

Procedures During Trial: Evidence Presentation and Judges' Instructions

Order of evidence presentation

One of the key issues in any set of procedures concerns the order in which things are carried out. Since courtroom procedures are enacted over time, some aspects must occur prior to others. Concerning evidence presentation, the current system in the United States provides that the party with the burden of proof (the prosecution in criminal trials or the plaintiff in civil trials) presents its case first. Thus, a number of researchers have attempted to ascertain how this order influences juror verdict preferences. Overall, the findings on this issue are quite consistent; jurors' verdict preferences are more strongly influenced by later than earlier information (i.e., a recency effect – Furnham, 1990; Kassin, Reddy, & Tulloch, 1990; Thibaut & Walker, 1975).

Unfortunately, very little research has looked at presentation order and jury verdicts. However, what evidence there is at the jury level implies that juries also show recency effects. Horowitz and Bordens (1990) had juries make either one or several judgments (e.g., causality, liability, punitive damages, etc.) in a civil trial context. Some of the juries were only given information concerning a specific judgment (and were asked only about that judgment) while others were presented with all the relevant information, and asked to make all of the judgments after receiving all of the information. Although complicated by other factors, their findings indicated that, for juries making all of the judgments, in comparison to juries that made only one judgment, information relevant for later judgments in the sequence tended to influence the earlier judgments. The reverse was not found. Thus, juries seem to place more weight on later evidence as well. Given that many procedures are in place to protect the rights of the accused, the recency effects would seem to be consistent with such goals.

Inadmissible evidence

A key question concerning a jury's ability to carry out its mandate is whether it can focus only on the information that is legally relevant. Thus, by legal standards, juries should be immune to factors such as the race, gender, etc. of the defendant and/or witnesses, pretrial publicity, and evidence ruled inadmissible during the trial. The research evidence is not completely consistent on these issues, but in general, it seems that jurors (and potentially juries) are not proficient at ignoring information that is legally irrelevant. For example, Bodenhausen and Lichtenstein (1987) found that in cases where the crime and racial stereotypes converged, the defendant's race affected juror verdicts. Such effects may be difficult to protect against because racial stereotypes are often automatically accessed (Bargh, 1997; Wegner & Bargh, 1998).

The same pattern seems to hold for other extralegal influences. Information obtained through a third party (hearsay), from illegal wiretaps, and through inappropriate questions by lawyers all have been found to impact juror verdicts (Kassin & Studebaker, 1998; Rind, Jaeger, & Strohmetz, 1995; Schuller, 1995). Unfortunately, instructions by judges to ignore such information tend to have little if any effect (Kassin & Studebaker, 1998; Thompson & Fuqua, 1998). However, a number of variables appear to moderate the influence of inadmissible evidence. The effect of inadmissible evidence is reduced for more serious charges (Rind et al., 1995). In addition, information that leads jurors to question the credibility of the inadmissible evidence (e.g., an unreliable source, poor quality wiretap, etc.) tends to reduce or ameliorate its effects (Fine, McClosky, & Tomlinson, 1997; Miene, Borgida, & Park, 1993; Schuller, 1995). A recent study by Kassin and Sommers (1997) showed that inadmissible evidence that was made to appear unreliable had no effect on verdicts, while the same evidence declared inadmissible for due process reasons increased guilty verdicts.

Although extralegal information tends to influence individual juror verdict preferences, there is some evidence that its impact on jury verdicts is considerably less. For example, Kerwin and Shaffer (1994) compared jurors and juries in a case where incriminating evidence was presented as either admissible or inadmissible. The manipulation of admissibility had no impact on juror verdict preferences, but juries were less likely to convict if the incriminating evidence was presented as inadmissible. Kaplan and Miller (1987) found that jury deliberation tended to ameliorate the effects of an attorney's behavioral style on verdicts, whereas individual jurors were influenced by this extralegal factor. However, why jury deliberation reduces such biases is unclear. There is some evidence (Hastie et al., 1983) that errors made by an individual juror, if voiced during deliberation, can be corrected by other jurors. Thus, if inadmissible evidence is brought up during deliberation, one of the other jury members may point out that it is inadmissible and thus not relevant for the verdict decision.

Recent work on group decision biases in general (Kerr, MacCoun, & Kramer, 1996), however, points to a different explanation. Kerr et al. showed that a majority group decision process can reduce biases present in the individual juror verdict distribution without any assumptions concerning the content of deliberation. They also demonstrated that the Kaplan and Miller (1987) results could be explained in this way (see also Kerr, Niedermeier, & Kaplan, 1999). In addition, Kerr et al. (1996) showed that majority processes can both increase and decrease the impact of extralegal information on jury as opposed to juror verdicts depending on the initial individual verdict preference distribution. Thus, further investigations of the effects of deliberation on different types of biases using different trials with different initial verdict distributions (i.e., stronger vs. weaker cases) are necessary before any definitive claims concerning this issue can be made.

Trial complexity and procedural remedies

Over the past 20 to 30 years, a recurring criticism of the jury system has revolved around a jury's ability to deal with the complexities of modern trials and legal technicalities. As the legal system has become more complex, and as new methods of investigation and evidence gathering have become common, the information-processing demands placed on jurors has increased drastically. These issues have been readily apparent in cases involving medical malpractice and antitrust issues, but have also surfaced in criminal trials due to issues surrounding DNA testing and other types of probabilistic evidence. Thus, much research, has focused on whether juries are competent to make judgments in complex trials. In addition, a number of researchers have assessed the efficacy of various different procedural mechanisms for aiding juries in understanding and using the complex information available.

Heuer and Penrod (1994) discuss three different types of complexity: complexity of evidence, quantity of evidence, and complexity of law. All three can create problems for juror comprehension. Evidence complexity has been most often looked at either in terms of technical jargon (Bourgeois, Horowitz, & FosterLee, 1993; Scott & Tindale, 1989) or the use of probabilistic information (Smith, Penrod, Otto, & Park, 1996; Tindale, Filkins, Smith, Sheffer, & Thomas, 1992; Wells, 1992), although amount of evidence has also received some attention (Heuer & Penrod, 1994; Horowitz, FosterLee, & Brolly, 1996). In general, evidence complexity can cause problems for juror comprehension, but the problems do not seem overly severe. Horowitz et al. (1996) found that jurors were less able to distinguish between plaintiffs in a multi-plaintiff civil trial when cognitive load was high. In addition, they were less likely to realize the pro-plaintiff nature of the trial evidence. Bourgeois et al. (1993) found similar results for a jargon-filled trial, but the effects were attenuated when jurors were allowed to look at the trial transcript.

Although much of this research has only looked at the effects of complexity at the juror level, there is reason to believe that juries will have fewer problems with complexity – at least when defined in terms of quantity. In general, memory performance by juries is superior to that of individual jurors (Hinsz, 1990; Vollrath, Sheppard, Hinsz, & Davis, 1989). In addition, there is some evidence that misstatements by individual jurors can be corrected by other jurors during deliberation (Hastie et al., 1983). However, complexity not related to quantity may be just as problematic for juries as it is for jurors. Complexity of information in general has been found to lead to less systematic information processing and a reliance on heuristics to make sense of the information (e.g., Eagly & Chaiken, 1993; Kahneman, Slovic, & Tversky, 1982). Although not tested in a jury context, evidence tends to show that groups exacerbate such heuristic tendencies (Argote, Devadas, & Melone, 1990; Tindale, 1993). Thus, it is unlikely that jury deliberation attenuates difficulties in understanding found at the juror level.

The use of probabilistic information remains controversial in both civil and criminal trials (Smith et al., 1996). One of the main fears presented by legal scholars was that probabilistic information, due to its quantitative and scientific nature, would dominate other types of evidence (Tribe, 1971). However, the research results show the opposite; probabilistic information is underutilized, if it is used at all (Smith et al., 1996; Tindale et al., 1992; Wells, 1992). Smith et al. found that jurors were not prone to misusing probabilities, though on average, they used them less than normative models would warrant. Wells (1992) showed that probabilities (e.g., base rates) typically were not used by jurors unless they could relate them specifically to issues of fact in the trial at hand. Similar results were found by Tindale et al. (1992) in a civil trial context. Probabilistic information concerning the relationship between toxic exposure and cancer rates was only used by both jurors and juries if a strategy for mapping the probabilities onto compensation amounts was provided. Interestingly, attempts to instruct jurors as to the appropriate way to use probabilistic information (i.e., discussions of Bayes Theorem) have had no influence on whether and/or how jurors actually use the information (Faigman & Baglioni, 1988; Smith et al., 1996).

Probably the aspect of complexity that has received the greatest amount of research attention is complexity in law – specifically, the judge's final instructions to the jury. Here, the research evidence is not so favorable. In general, jurors (and in some cases juries) misunderstand many aspects of judges' instructions (Elwork & Sales, 1985). Part of the problem involves the "incomprehensible language" associated with legal definitions of crimes (Elwork & Sales, 1985, p. 283). For example, a recent study by Hastie, Schkade, and Payne (1998) found that scores on a memory for instructions test ranged from 0% to 67% after jury deliberations. This is particularly problematic given that the mock jurors in this study had copies of the judge's instructions during the deliberations. In addition, they found that jury deliberation did not improve jurors' understanding of the instructions. A number of researchers have also found that the instructions concerning aggravating and mitigating circumstances in death penalty cases are not well understood by jurors (Blankenship, Luginbuhl, Cullen, & Redick, 1997; Diamond, 1993; Haney & Lynch, 1994). Haney, Sontag, and Costanzo (1994) provided evidence that these misinterpretations can lead jurors to be more likely to choose death as the appropriate penalty. Again, there was very little evidence that jury deliberation worked to reduce misconceptions.

One of the key instructions provided by judges to juries is the criterion to use for the decision to convict. In criminal trials, this is typically referred to as the "reasonable doubt" criterion. However, different jurisdictions provide very different definitions of what constitutes a "reasonable doubt" (Horowitz & Kirkpatrick, 1996; Kerr, Atkin, Stasser, Meek, Holt, & Davis, 1976; Koch & Devine, 1999). These differences have been found to drastically influence juror and jury decisions, in that more stringent definitions (restricting what is to be considered a reasonable doubt) lead to more guilty verdicts. Horowitz and Kirkpatrick (1996) found that some definitions actually led jurors to vilify the defendant. Kagehiro

(1990) found that most jurors were very uncertain as to what different criteria were meant to imply (e.g., preponderance of the evidence vs. reasonable doubt) unless they were associated with quantitative (percent certainty) ranges.

Obviously, trial and instruction complexity poses a serious threat to the viability of a justice system based on jury decision making. Thus, a number of procedural remedies have been suggested, many of which have received at least some empirical support. One procedure that is now frequently used allows expert witnesses to testify on complex issues (Greene, Schooler, & Loftus, 1985). The evidence concerning how effective expert witnesses are at improving jurors' comprehension and sensitivity is mixed at best (Maas, Brigham, & West, 1985; Penrod, Fulero, & Cutler, 1995), and it is often the expert testimony that is most difficult for the jury to follow (Bourgeois et al., 1993). However, as Bourgeois et al. showed, allowing juries access to trial transcripts may help to alleviate some of the problems due to complexity.

Probably the major procedural changes concerning legal complexity involve the timing of, and language used in, judges' instructions to the jury (Elwork & Sales, 1985). The problems with instructions (besides rather vast differences across different jurisdictions – that is, reasonable doubt definitions – see Horowitz & Kirkpatrick, 1996) basically stem from competing purposes; instructions must be both comprehensible and legally accurate (Severance, Greene, & Loftus, 1984). Most of the emphasis has been placed on legal accuracy, but as laws become more complex, the more accurate the language, the more difficult it is to understand. However, with work, both goals can be accomplished. Avoiding legal jargon and uncommon words can lead to better comprehension (Severance et al., 1984). However, Wiener, Pritchard, and Weston (1995) found that revised death penalty instructions were somewhat more comprehensible, but jurors still made a number of reasoning errors with the "simplified" instructions. Thus, there may be limits to how effective rewritten instructions can be for legal non-experts – like jurors.

There is now considerable evidence that giving jurors the judge's instructions prior to hearing the evidence can be beneficial (Kassin & Wrightsman, 1987; Smith, 1990, 1991). Much social cognition research has shown that a clear processing goal can aid information retention and retrieval (Wyer & Srull, 1989). Providing jurors with the appropriate standards of proof and legal definitions of crimes prior to hearing testimony provides such processing goals. Thus, it is not surprising that pre-trial instructions (typically followed by post-trial reiteration) help jurors to encode relevant evidence and use the instructions effectively (Kassin & Wrightsman, 1987). However, there is less evidence to support the prediction that jurors recall relevant facts better (Heuer & Penrod, 1989; Smith, 1991). Except for one study which found a tendency for a confirmatory hypothesis testing strategy for a complex case (Bourgeois, Horowitz, FosterLee, & Grahe, 1995), none of the research on this issue has supported any of the potential negative impacts of pre-trial instructions (narrowing juror viewpoints, disrupting the trial, etc., see Heuer & Penrod, 1989; Smith, 1991).

Two other techniques for helping jurors/juries handle complex cases that have received recent attention are note taking and question asking by jurors (Penrod & Heuer, 1998). As with many of the aforementioned procedural issues, legal scholars have hypothesized both advantages and disadvantages associated with these juror behaviors. The empirical results have provided moderate evidence in their favor. There is some evidence that note taking can improve juror recall, mainly due to better encoding of information (FosterLee, Horowitz, & Bourgeois, 1994), though the benefits of both of these procedures seem modest at best (Penrod & Heuer, 1998). However, virtually none of the potential disadvantages emerged. Jurors did not ask inappropriate questions, the questions were not disruptive, and note taking did not lead to biased recall or more literate jurors gaining influence (Penrod & Heuer, 1998). Given that trials will continue to become more complex and that current forms of judges' instructions do not prevent juror/jury errors due to confusion (Haney et al., 1994; Hastie et al., 1998), any procedure that aids jurors' understanding of the evidence and/or instructions should be used. In addition, further innovations and evaluative research concerning these issues is definitely necessary.

Procedural Effects During Deliberation

Jury size

Interest in the effects of jury size on the decision process became focused in the 1970s when the U.S. Supreme Court decided several cases regarding how many jurors constitute a permissible jury size. Traditionally, 12 was the standard jury size, but considerations of economic efficiency prompted the use of smaller juries. In a series of decisions, the Court ruled that juries composed of fewer than 12 members are permissible, but in criminal trials the jury must be composed of at least 6 people (*Williams* v. *Florida* (1970); *Colgrove* v. *Battin* (1973); *Ballew* v. *Georgia* (1978)). In its decisions, the Court explicitly relied on psychological research. Subsequent empirical research therefore sought to investigate whether juries of different sizes are indeed functionally equivalent (Beiser & Varrin, 1975; Bermant & Coppock, 1973; Buckhout, Weg, Reilly, & Frohboese, 1977; Davis et al., 1975; Kerr & MacCoun, 1985; Kessler, 1973; Mills, 1973; Padawer-Singer, Singer, & Singer, 1977; Roper, 1980; Saks, 1977; Valenti & Downing, 1975). Taken as a whole, these studies do not point to any clear-cut conclusion regarding the effects of jury size on verdict outcome. The preponderance of negative findings suggests that jury size effects are subtle phenomena, if they exist at all.

However, there are theoretical grounds to believe that variations in jury size have a small but reliable effect on verdict outcome. For example, Davis, Bray, and Holt (1977) estimated that under certain conditions, verdict differences between 6- and 12-member juries amount to a maximum of 8%. Using assumptions consistent with empirical evidence concerning initial verdict preferences of individual jurors and the social decision scheme aggregating those preferences, the expected effects of jury size on verdict were assessed in the context of a criminal trial. As a thought experiment, Davis et al. (1977) considered the probability with which a juror favors a guilty or not guilty verdict under a simple majority, otherwise equiprobability social decision scheme. A similar thought experiment is presented here in Figure 6.1, using the 2/3 majority model presented in Table 6.1. As shown in the figure, the difference in conviction probability due to juries of different sizes is nowhere very large (largest difference is .15 in the present figure). As the probability of individual juror preference for a guilty verdict nears .00, 1.00 or 0.73, the differences due to jury size almost disappear. Above individual probabilities of .73, the largest different between 6- and 12-person juries is

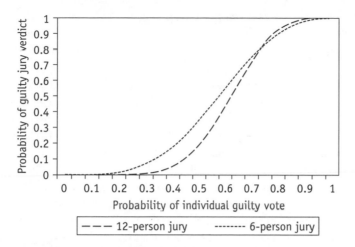

Figure 6.1 The probability of a guilty jury verdict as a function of jury size (6 vs. 12) and the probability of an individual juror voting guilty.

predicted to be .027. Null differences in verdict due to jury size where the probability of an individual vote of guilty is .00 or is 1.0 are to be expected in "slanted cases" (Diamond, 1974). However, the more surprising prediction is very small differences when the probability of an individual guilty vote is near .70. An interesting feature of Figure 6.1 is that the difference between the two curves reverses direction when the probability of an individual voting for guilty is .73. The model predicts that smaller juries are more likely than larger juries to convict when individual jurors are leaning toward not guilty, but are less likely to convict when jurors are leaning toward guilty.

With the small, predicted differences between different jury sizes, we might ask how many subjects would be required to detect an actual difference as small as .08 (the maximum difference found by Davis, Bray, and Holt using a simple majority model). Assuming standard levels of statistical significance (.05) it turns out that samples of 62 juries of each size would be needed. Thus, in a study comparing 6- and 12-person juries, 6(62) + 12(62) = 1116 subjects would be required to detect such an effect. The failure of early studies to find verdict differences due to differences in jury size is therefore not surprising.

Saks and Marti (1997) performed a meta-analysis of the effects of jury size on a number of different dependent measures. They found that compared to 6-person juries, 12-person juries are more likely to contain more members of racial minority groups, deliberate slightly longer, hang more often, and appear to recall trial testimony better. In addition, there is some evidence in the three studies reviewed in the meta-analysis that 6-person juries award larger damages awards than 12-person juries. Subsequent work confirms that 12-person juries tend to give smaller money damages awards than 6-person juries (Davis et al., 1997). This could be a sign of the times in that public statements against overly large awards have been prevalent in the 1990s. Assuming that group interaction fosters pro-normative behavior, and larger groups do so more than smaller groups, one would expect smaller awards by larger juries given current societal norms.

Jury decision rule

Soon after permitting juries of fewer than 12 persons, the U.S. Supreme Court ruled that non-unanimous juries were constitutional in state criminal and civil trials. (*Apodaca* v. *Oregon*, 1972; *Johnson* v. *Louisiana*, 1972). Following these decisions, there has been considerable empirical investigation regarding the effect of decision rule on outcome. In criminal cases, Kerr et al. (1976) observed that unanimous juries hung more frequently than those using a two-thirds majority rule. Nemeth (1977) obtained a similar result when mock juries were composed of members who were divided 4 to 2 in opinion. However, a small sample of randomly composed juries showed no significant differences in outcome due to decision rule. In civil cases, the earliest empirical investigation of decision rule (Broeder, 1958) found that unanimous and three-fourths majority juries did not differ significantly in damages awarded. Similarly, Bray and Struckman-Johnson (1977) observed no significant differences in verdicts between unanimous and five-sixths majority mock civil juries. In an extensive jury simulation study, Hastie, Penrod, and Pennington (1983) also found no verdict differences due to different decision rules, but they did find that unanimous juries deliberated more thoroughly and spent more time discussing the legal definitions of the verdict categories. However, Kaplan and Miller (1987) observed that mock civil juries deciding punitive damages awarded more to the plaintiff under a unanimity rule than under a majority decision rule. Interestingly, under the unanimity decision rule, jury members made more use of normative arguments, compared to jurors in the majority decision rule condition. Because unanimous agreement is more difficult to attain than majority agreement, jurors recognizing this make more use of normative argument. Using normative arguments (e.g., "the defendant was wrong not to repair the furnace") focuses more attention on extreme awards in the context of punitive damages, and thus the plaintiff has an advantage when the jury uses a unanimity rule to deliberate punitive damages.

Like jury size, the relationship of decision rule and verdict can also be assessed via thought experiments (i.e., computer simulations). To do so we regard group size as fixed and vary the social decision scheme. We assume a jury of 12 operating according to one of the following social decision schemes: proportionality; two-thirds majority, defendant protection otherwise (see Table 6.1); and simple majority, defendant protection otherwise. The probability of conviction as a function of the probability of a guilty vote by jurors is given in Figure 6.2. The proportionality social decision scheme functions as a baseline of sorts; the other two curves are especially notable. The magnitude of the difference in conviction probabilities to be expected from decision scheme alone is small, except for cases where the probability of an individual juror voting for guilty is near .5 – the maximum level of individual uncertainty. Here, juries functioning under a simple majority model are considerably more likely to convict than juries functioning under a two-thirds majority model.

Straw polls – Method and timing

Procedures for jury deliberations are most often informal, with few explicit mechanisms mandated by the court for managing actual deliberations. Conventional procedural mechanisms

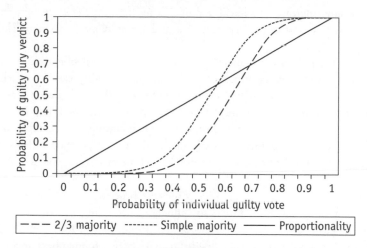

Figure 6.2 The probability of a guilty jury verdict as a function of decision rule and the probability of an individual juror voting guilty.

tend to arise in the informal context of jury deliberation, stemming from shared social norms. Some of these informal procedural mechanisms have been shown to play a causal role in the structure and outcome of the jury's decision. One such procedural mechanism that arises informally is the informal ballot, or straw poll. It is often the case that the jury will take one or more straw polls during the course of its deliberation. The straw poll can serve to manage the jury deliberation process; the act of publicizing member preferences can facilitate consensus.

The straw poll can be used as a predictor of final verdict. In their study of actual juries, Kalven and Zeisel (1966) found that the first poll taken by a jury predicts that jury's verdict via a simple-majority social decision scheme. Sandys and Dillchay (1995) replicated this result, finding that the final verdict is consistent with the initial majority in 93% of the cases sampled. But Kalven and Zeisel (1966) explicitly assumed that first-ballot preferences are equivalent to predeliberation opinions, concluding that verdicts are predetermined by the preference of individual jurors when they first enter the jury room. This assumption is probably unwarranted in most cases. Sandys and Dillehay (1995) found that only 11% of the actual juries they sampled had taken a vote prior to any discussion. Thus, in 89% of the juries sampled, the first ballot poll was taken after deliberation began, often well into the deliberation. In fact, juries spent an average of 44 minutes deliberating before taking the first ballot poll. While the connection between first poll and verdict is an interesting one, the predeliberation preferences of individual jurors are subject to the influence processes occurring prior to the first poll.

In addition to being a predictor of verdict, experiments using mock juries have shown that the polling process can itself play a causal role in the final decision. For example, Kerr and MacCoun (1985) found that public voting resulted in a higher likelihood of a hung jury, compared with secret voting. Davis et al. (1993) found that mandated polling, in contrast to deliberation only, increases the likelihood of a hung jury. At the same time, mock juries that do reach a decision after polling tend to award larger damages than mock juries that do not poll.

The timing of the poll can also affect the jury's decision and deliberation process. In the Davis et al. (1993) study, mock juries decided a product liability case in which a teenage farm-worker was injured; those juries that took a poll late in the deliberation tended to make larger damage awards than mock juries that polled early in the deliberation. In addition, the timing of the poll can affect the length of time spent deliberating. For example, in one study groups prompted to take a public poll early in the discussion reached a decision twice as quickly as groups prompted to take a public poll late in the discussion (Nadler, Au, Zarnoth, Irwin, & Davis, 1999).

Polling sequence can also affect the jury consensus process. For example, the particular sequence of straw votes has been found to influence succeeding individual voter opinion about defendant guilt. Davis, Stasson, Ono, and Zimmerman (1988) composed 6-person mock juries so that they were evenly divided (3, 3) between members inclined to vote guilty (G) or not guilty (NG). When polls were taken within factions (e.g., 3 mock jurors in a row saying, "Guilty"), it was found that the fourth juror was influenced by the preceding faction's votes. Moreover, the fourth juror polled was more likely to be influenced by a sequence of 3 not guilty roll-call votes than a sequence of 3 guilty roll-call votes. This asymmetry in interpersonal influence is perhaps a manifestation of the leniency bias (MacCoun & Kerr, 1988) reflecting defendant protection norm (Tindale & Davis, 1983); not guilty majorities have greater power than guilty majorities in establishing group-level consensus. Indeed, subsequent research (Davis, Kameda, Parks, Stasson, & Zimmerman, 1989) uncovered that the third juror polled in a 6-person jury can be significantly influenced to change preference if he/she is polled immediately after 2 jurors publicly stating their preference for not guilty. This change occurred after only 2 preceding votes, and is normatively consistent.

However, this directional bias observed in individual opinion change, although consistent with widely shared cultural norms that value the two types of errors differently (e.g. "better that the guilty be acquitted than the innocent be convicted"), was sensitive to vote timing (i.e., whether a poll was taken early or late in the discussion period) (Davis et al., 1988). Counter-normative preference change (not guilty to guilty) was fairly likely at an early poll in response to a contrary preceding sequence, but was not observed to occur later, suggesting perhaps that discussion had increased norm salience and an awareness of contrary opinions. However, norm-consistent change (guilty to not guilty) was more likely later than earlier, again suggesting the importance of normative factors that may have been emphasized in discussion.

Despite the significant influence of polling sequence and timing on individual member preferences, the final verdict of the jury remains robust against social influence pressures observed at the individual level (Davis et al., 1989). That individual polling sequence effects fail to have influence at the group level demonstrates that the individual–group relationship is not straightforward. The expressed preferences of individual jurors, in the form of straw votes, may be: (a) insincere (a strategic calculation that is itself designed to influence events); (b) sincere but highly unstable (based on little or inaccurate information, confused reasoning, etc.); (c) sincere and highly stable (a consequence of a well-developed cognitive structure, powerful motive, etc.); or (d) an accident, due to misunderstood instructions, apathy, or the like (Davis et al., 1989). The instability of expressed preferences may be especially high in a straw poll, where the vote was explicitly made for the purpose of collecting information and not binding. Regardless of the explanation, there is a clear demonstration that Kalven and Zeisel's (1966) conclusions about the easy predictability of jury verdict must be approached with caution: individual-level juror preferences may not accurately forecast group outcomes.

Context-dependence of decisions involving multiple charges

The jury's task often involves making more than one decision. For example, a jury deciding a homicide case might be instructed to consider several different charges: the principal charge upon which the defendant is accused (e.g., first-degree murder) and one or more lesser-included charges (e.g., second-degree murder, manslaughter). In such a case, the verdict form (filled out by the foreperson to indicate the jury's verdict) would request the jury first to indicate its verdict on the charge of first-degree murder. If the verdict on that charge is not guilty, the jury would next render a verdict on the charge of second-degree murder, and so on. If at any point the jury finds the defendant guilty on one of the charges, the decision procedure stops, and the jury does not consider any of the remaining lesser-included charges. This procedure requires the jury to make a series of decisions on several charges that arise from the same conduct.

In other situations, the defendant could be charged with separate crimes arising from separate conduct. For example, a defendant might be charged with possession of a controlled substance and also with resisting arrest. In a typical criminal case, these charges would be joined so that evidence on each charge would be presented within a single trial, and a verdict on each charge would be rendered by a single jury. Similarly, it is common for a plaintiff in a civil case to include more than one claim or cause of action against one or more defendants. For example, a plaintiff suing her employer for discrimination might allege two claims in her complaint: violation of civil rights laws and breach of contract.

The primary justification for a single jury to decide on multiple charges or causes of action is efficiency. If a separate jury were required to decide each cause of action or charge in every case, the resources consumed by such a procedure would be staggering. But implicit in this policy is an assumption that juries will decide charges in a context-independent manner. That is, it is assumed that the presence of other charges, or the order in which charges are decided, will not affect the jury's decision process. To take an example outside the legal context, rational choice theory predicts that if I prefer strawberry ice cream to vanilla, the presence on the menu of mint chip ice cream should not alter my preference for strawberry to vanilla. And the order that flavors are listed on the menu should not affect which ice cream I most prefer. Similarly, we expect that a jury's verdict on a particular charge (e.g., possession of a controlled substance) will not be altered by the presence or absence of some other charge on the verdict form (e.g., resisting arrest). And we expect that a jury's decision on any given charge will not be influenced by the order in which the charges are decided.

Yet, there is ample evidence demonstrating that, in certain situations, jurors' and juries' judgments are in fact context-dependent.

Joined versus severed charges.   The question of how jurors' judgments are influenced by the joining of charges has been addressed in the context of the mock criminal trial. Generally it has been demonstrated that mock jurors are more likely to favor conviction on a charge when it is joined with others. For example, Tanford and Penrod (1982) asked mock jurors to make a judgment on rape and trespass charges presented alone or joined with other charges. There was a higher proportion of guilty votes on the rape and trespass charges when they were joined with other charges, compared to when they were presented without other charges. In another study, Greene and Loftus (1981) asked mock jurors to judge the guilt of the defendant on two charges – murder and rape. The conviction rate was higher on both charges when both were joined compared to when they each were presented alone. Thus, guilt decisions on multiple charges in mock trial contexts are not independent, and there is an increase in conviction preferences when charges are presented together, compared to when charges are presented separately. It should be noted that an important limitation on both of these studies is the use of mock *jurors*, as opposed to mock *juries* which deliberate – it is unclear whether the biasing effects of joined charges would be enhanced or even mitigated by jury deliberation.

Order of consideration of joined charges.   While there appears to be a bias in favor of conviction when charges are joined, the joining of charges is a practice that is unlikely to disappear, given the pressures for judicial efficiency and the problem of overcrowded court dockets in many jurisdictions. Given the apparent inevitability of joined charges in criminal cases (and joined causes of action in civil cases), a further point of exploration is the implication of the jury's consideration of charges in one order or another, given that the charges are joined in a single trial. This question was investigated in the context of a simulated criminal trial by Davis, Tindale, Nagao, Hinsz, and Robertson (1984). In this study, three logically independent charges arose out of events contiguous in time: the defendant had an argument in a bar in which a glass table was broken (criminal damage to property). The argument turned into a fistfight (battery). After leaving the bar the defendant was alleged to have hit and killed a pedestrian while driving recklessly (manslaughter). The charges were presented in either ascending or descending order of seriousness, with the battery charge being presented second in both orders. The results for both mock jurors and mock juries showed a higher proportion of guilty verdicts on the battery charge in the descending, compared to the ascending, order. Ascending order resulted in a lower proportion of convictions than no assigned order. It appeared that deliberation neither exaggerated nor mitigated individual juror preferences. Subjects therefore did not consider the three charges independently from one another.

The results also showed a statistically significant association between guilt judgment on first and second charges. Thus, saying guilty on the first charge makes it more likely that a juror (or jury) will say guilty on the second charge. It appears that participants viewed the trial process as a whole, and were unable or unwilling to consider the charges independently. It may be that participants inferred a criminal disposition – that is, the kind of person who would recklessly kill someone is the same kind of person who would commit battery. In addition, participants may also develop complex causal links between charges regardless of lack of logical connections.

Lesser included charges and sentencing options.   Charges arising from one person's separate criminal acts are often joined together in a single trial. In other situations, the jury in a criminal trial is charged with deciding on a principal charge as well as lesser-included charges for a single criminal act. For example, a jury deciding about a single homicide might be asked to decide whether the defendant is guilty of first-degree murder, second-degree murder, or manslaughter. As with decisions about charges that are joined, decisions among one principal and one or more lesser-included charges are also context-dependent. In a study of decision making of mock jurors, Kelman, Rottenstrech, and Tversky (1996) demonstrated two types of context-dependent decisions to which jurors are vulnerable. The first type, compromise effects, occur when the same option is evaluated more favorably when it is seen as falling in the middle of the set of options, rather than when it is viewed as more extreme. Kelman et al. presented mock jurors with a simulated trial scenario and asked them to determine which charge the defendant was guilty of. Mock jurors in one group chose among the following charges: capital murder, murder, and voluntary manslaughter. Mock jurors in a second group chose among: murder, voluntary manslaughter, and involuntary manslaughter. Focusing on the charge of murder reveals an interesting context-dependence: 57% of mock jurors in the first group indicated murder as their verdict preference; but only 38% of mock jurors in the second group indicated murder as their verdict preference. Thus, when murder is presented as the intermediate of three choices, it is more attractive (as in the first group) compared to when it is presented as an extreme choice (as in the second group).

Another consequence of context-dependent decision making examined by Kelman et al. (1996) is the contrast effect – this occurs when the same option is evaluated more favorably in the presence of a similar but clearly inferior option. To test for contrast effects, mock jurors in one group were given two sentencing options: jail or community service. Mock jurors in the second group chose among three sentencing options: jail, community service, or "self-esteem counseling." While 74% of mock jurors in the first group chose community service, 88% of mock jurors in the second group chose the same community service option. Mock jurors in the second group were faced with contrasting a favorable option (community service) with a similar but clearly inferior option (self-esteem counseling). In the face of this contrast, the favorable option of community service became even more favorable.

In several respects, the decisions made in these studies by mock jurors and mock juries depended heavily on the context in which the choices were presented. First, order of consideration influenced mock juries' (and mock jurors') judgment of the defendant's guilt on the middle charge. Second, the mere presence of joined charges increased the likelihood that mock jurors would find the defendant guilty on the target charge. Third, the framing of a charge as compromise, or middle ground, increased the likelihood that it would be selected as the verdict choice. Finally, the presentation of a sentencing option together with an inferior option enhanced the perceived attractiveness of that option. Given that juries must often make multiple decisions, or decide among multiple options, it is worthwhile to consider in advance the likely effect of such multiple decisions or options.

Special verdicts and elements of the claim.   In most civil cases, the jury returns a general verdict, which identifies the prevailing party (plaintiff or defendant) and amount of damages awarded (if any). However, in some civil cases, especially where the issues are numerous or complex, the jury is required to return a special verdict. Under the special verdict system, the jury fills out a questionnaire addressing key facts in dispute. The court then enters a judgment in favor of the plaintiff or the defendant based on the jury's answers on the special verdict form. Does the procedural mechanism of type of verdict (special or general) affect the jury's decision process? Lombardero (1996) argues that there are several ways in which type of verdict form can impact the verdict. We focus here on the conjunction problem, that is, the failure to distinguish between the probability of a single fact being true and the probability of several facts being true simultaneously.

Any claim brought by a plaintiff in a civil case is composed of elements, each of which must be proved in order to prove the claim as a whole. For example, the elements comprising the claim of fraud might consist of the following: (1) A false representation of fact; (2) made intentionally by the defendant; (3) which the plaintiff relied upon; (4) which caused damage to the plaintiff. For a plaintiff to meet its burden of proof on the claim of fraud, it must prove each element of its claim by a preponderance of the evidence (i.e., with a probability greater than 0.5).

When a general verdict form is used, juries are routinely instructed that if the plaintiff has proven each element of the claim by a preponderance of the evidence, then the jury must return a verdict in favor of the plaintiff. Lombardero (1996) points out that even when the probability of each element of the claim is greater than 0.5, the probability that all elements are true simultaneously might still be less than 0.5. Therefore, the use of a general verdict form in conjunction with an instruction to find for the plaintiff if each element is proven can result in a bias in favor of the plaintiff.

However, the effects of the conjunction bias probably are not severe. First, the elements of any given claim are rarely independent from one another. Rather, the same evidence that proves one element also might prove other elements. For example, the evidence might show that the defendant, a used car salesman, said, "This car is as good as new. It's never been in an accident." This evidence might tend to prove two elements of the claim (a false statement of fact, and made intentionally by defendant), and so the first two elements of the claim are not independent. In this situation, the probability that all the elements are simultaneously true cannot be determined simply by multiplying together the probabilities of each individual element.

A second reason that the conjunction effect is not severe is that empirical research on jury decision making suggests that juries often do not analyze the evidence in an element-by-element fashion (see, e.g., Pennington & Hastie, 1986). Instead, each juror constructs a story that best explains the juror's understanding of the evidence. After understanding each verdict choice, the juror chooses a verdict preference based on the best match between the story and the verdict choice. Because jurors often do not weigh each piece of evidence in sequence, the conjunction bias might not be as severe as it first appears. But the use of the special verdict exacerbates any bias resulting from the conjunction rule. The special verdict form simply requires the jury to answer specific questions. If the jury's answers on the special verdict form indicate that each element has been proved, the court enters a verdict in favor of the plaintiff.

Thus, the jury is forced to evaluate each individual element, rather than try to construct a plausible story upon which a verdict can be based. Thus, the special verdict form exaggerates the conjunction bias. In this sense the special verdict can favor the plaintiff.

Concluding Comments

Although procedural variables are often overlooked or considered to be uninteresting from a social psychological perspective (not nearly as intuitively appealing to the conventional as "cognitive dissonance" or "psychological reactance," for example), they none-the-less play an important role in much social behavior – particularly in formal and quasi-formal task-oriented groups. Probably the reason procedural mechanisms have received somewhat more attention in research on juries is that the context within which juries perform (the legal system) is heavily governed by such operational specifics. Although there is much more to be learned even concerning juries, research to date has pointed out a number of consistent procedural influences. Some of these (e.g., the leniency bias and recency effects) tend to conform nicely to the values of the legal system in the United States (i.e., protecting the innocent is more important than punishing the guilty). However, others (e.g., incomprehensibility of judges' instructions, reductions in jury size, etc.) seem inconsistent with such values and should receive more attention from researchers and policy makers alike. More work is also needed on how aspects of jury decision making that are not governed by formal procedures operate – what procedures are used and what are their implications (e.g., order of deliberating on joined charges). And as we stated early on in this chapter, more of this work should focus on interacting *juries* rather than individual juror behavior. Although more difficult, the theoretical and practical importance of focusing on the entity (jury) that actually performs the judiciary function seems well worth the cost in time, effort, and resources.

One other limitation concerning the work on procedures and juries is that almost all of the research reviewed focused on juries (or more typically jurors) in the United States. This is not surprising given the central role that juries play in the U.S. legal system. However, as pointed out by Hackman and Morris (1978) in their discussion of group performance in general, studying what groups currently do may tell you much about how they perform, but it will not necessarily tell you much about how they could perform better. Thus, a potentially fruitful future research endeavor may be to study how citizen juries compare to legal decision-making procedures in other cultures. A recent study by Kaplan and Martin (1999) has moved in just such a direction. Juries in Spain are made up of citizens and legal experts, and Kaplan and Martin focused on the different types of influence strategies used by expert versus lay factions within the juries. It seems it would also be useful to compare all citizen juries to mixed (expert and citizen) juries, or to panels comprised completely of experts. By studying and comparing procedures from a variety of different cultures, we may be able to locate procedures, or combinations thereof, that administer justice in more optimal ways. Such comparative research should also provide a better understanding of the effects of procedural mechanisms on group decision making in general. Thus, we close with a call for more comparative and cross-cultural research on legal decision making in an attempt to learn both more about juries and potentially how to make them better.

REFERENCES

Allen, M., Mabry, E., & McKelton, D. (1998). Impact of juror attitudes about the death penalty on juror evaluations of guilt and punishment. *Law and Human Behavior, 23*, 715–732.

Argote, L., Devadas, R., & Melone, N. (1990). The base-rate fallacy: Contrasting processes and outcomes of group and individual judgment. *Organizational Behavior and Human Decision Processes, 46*, 296–310.

Ballew v. Georgia (1978). United States Law Week, 46, 4217–4224.

Bargh, J. A. (1997). The automaticity of everyday life. In R. S. Wyer, Jr. (Ed.), *Advances in social cognition* (Vol. 10, pp. 1–62). Mahwah, NJ: Erlbaum.

Beiser, E., & Varrin, R. (1975). Six-member juries in the federal courts. *Judicature, 58*, 423–433.

Bermant, G., & Coppock, R. (1973). Outcomes of six- and twelve-member jury trials: An analysis of 128 civil cases in the State of Washington. *Washington Law Review, 48*, 593–596.

Blankenship, M. B., Luginbuhl, J., Cullen, F. T., & Redick, W. (1997). Jurors' comprehension of sentencing instructions: A test of the death penalty process in Tennessee. *Justice Quarterly, 14*, 325–351.

Bodenhausen, G. V., & Lichtenstein, M. (1987). Social stereotypes and information processing strategies: The impact of task complexity. *Journal of Personality and Social Psychology, 52*, 871–880.

Bourgeois, M. J., Horowitz, I. A., & FosterLee, L. (1993). Effects of technicality and access to trial transcripts on verdicts and information processing in a civil trial. *Personality and Social Psychology Bulletin, 19*, 220–227.

Bourgeois, M. J., Horowitz, I. A., FosterLee, L., & Grahe, J. (1995). Nominal and interactive groups: Effects of preinstruction and deliberations on decision and evidence recall in complex trials. *Journal of Applied Psychology, 80*, 58–67.

Bray, R. M., & Struckman-Johnson, C. (1977, August). *Effects of juror population, assigned decision rule and insurance option on decisions of simulated juries.* Paper presented at the meeting of the American Psychological Association, San Francisco, CA.

Broeder, D. (1958). The University of Chicago jury project. *Nebraska Law Review, 38*, 744–761.

Buckhout, R., Weg, S., Reilly, V., & Frohboese, R. (1977). Jury verdicts: Comparison of 6- and 12-person juries and unanimous vs. majority decision rule in a murder trial. *Bulletin of the Psychonomic Society, 10*, 175–178.

Christie, R. (1976). Probability vs. precedence: The social psychology of jury selection. In G. Bermont, C. Nemeth, & N. Vidmar (Eds.), *Psychology and the law* (pp. 265–281). New York: Lexington Books.

Cowan, C. L., Thompson, W. C., & Ellsworth, P. C. (1984). The effects of death qualification on jurors' predisposition to convict and on the quality of deliberation. *Law and Human Behavior, 8*, 53–80.

Davis, J. H. (1973). Group decision and social interaction: A theory of social decision schemes. *Psychological Review, 80*, 97–125.

Davis, J. H. (1980). Group decision and procedural justice. In M. Fishbein (Ed.), *Progress in social psychology* (Vol. 1, pp. 157–229). Hillsdale, NJ: Erlbaum.

Davis, J. H. (1984). Order in the courtroom. In D. J. Muller, D. E. Blackman, & A. J. Chapman (Eds.), *Psychology and law.* New York: Wiley.

Davis, J. H. (1996). Group decision making and quantitative judgments: A consensus model. In E. Witte & J. H. Davis (Eds.), *Understanding group behavior: Consensual action by small groups* (Vol. 1, pp. 35–59). Mahwah, NJ: Erlbaum.

Davis, J. H., Au, W. T., Hulbert, L., Chen, X. P., & Zarnoth, P. (1997). Effects of group size and procedural influence on consensual judgments of quantity: The example of damage awards and mock civil juries. *Journal of Personality and Social Psychology, 73*, 703–718.

Davis, J. H., Bray, R. M., & Holt, R. W. (1977). The empirical study of decision processes in juries: A critical review. In J. Tapp & F. Levine (Eds.), *Law, justice and the individual in society: Psychological and legal issues.* New York: Holt, Rinehart, & Winston.

Davis, J. H., Kameda, T., Parks, C., Stasson, M., & Zimmerman, S. (1989). Some social mechanics of group decision making: The distribution of opinion, polling sequence, and implications for consensus. *Journal of Personality and Social Psychology, 57,* 1000–1012.

Davis, J. H., Kerr, N. L., Atkin, R. S., Holt, R., & Meek, D. (1975). The decision processes of 6- and 12-person juries assigned unanimous and two-thirds majority rules. *Journal of Personality and Social Psychology, 32,* 1–14.

Davis, J. H., Stasson, M. F., Ono, K., & Zimmerman, S. K. (1988). The effects of straw polls on group decision making: Sequential voting pattern, timing, and local majorities. *Journal of Personality and Social Psychology, 50,* 918–926.

Davis, J. H., Stasson, M. F., Parks, C. D., Hulbert, L., Kameda, T., Zimmerman, S. K., & Ono, K. (1993). Quantitative decisions by groups and individuals: Voting procedures and monetary awards by mock civil juries. *Journal of Experimental Social Psychology, 29,* 326–346.

Davis, J. H., Tindale, R. S., Nagao, D. H., Hinsz, V. B., & Robertson, B. A. (1984). Order effects in multiple decisions by groups: A demonstration with mock juries and trial procedures. *Journal of Personality and Social Psychology, 47,* 1003–1012.

Diamond, S. S. (1974). A jury experiment reanalyzed. *University of Michigan Journal of Law Reform, 7,* 520–532.

Diamond, S. S. (1993). Instructing on death: Psychologists, juries, and judges. *American Psychologist, 48,* 423–434.

Duren v. *Missouri,* 439 U.S. 357 (1979).

Eagly, A. H., & Chaiken, S. (1993). *The psychology of attitudes.* Fort Worth, TX: Harcourt Brace Jovanovich.

Elwork, A., & Sales, B. D. (1985). Jury instructions. In S. M. Kassin & L. S. Wrightsman (Eds.), *The psychology of evidence and trial procedure* (pp. 280–297). Beverly Hills, CA: Sage.

Ellsworth, P. C., Bukaty, R. M., Cowan, C. L., & Thompson, W. C. (1984). The death qualified jury and the defense of insanity. *Law and Human Behavior, 8,* 81–93.

Etzioni, A. (1974). Creating an imbalance. *Trial, 10,* 28–30.

Faigman, D. L., & Baglioni, A. J. (1988). Bayes' theorem in the trial process: Instructing jurors on the value of statistical evidence. *Law and Human Behavior, 12,* 1–17.

Filkins, J., Smith, C. M., & Tindale, R. S. (1998). The fairness of death qualified juries: A meta-analytic/simulation approach. In R. S. Tindale, J. E. Edwards, L. Heath, E. J. Posavac, F. B. Bryant, E. Henderson-King, Y. Suarez-Balcazar, & J. Myers (Eds.), *Social psychological applications to social issues: Theory and research on small groups* (Vol. 4, pp. 153–176). New York: Plenum Press.

Finch, F., & Ferraro, M. (1986). The empirical challenge to death qualified juries: On further examination. *Nebraska Law Review, 65,* 21–74.

Fine, S., McCloskey, A. L., & Tomlinson, T. M. (1997). Can the jury disregard that information? The use of suspicion to reduce the prejudicial effects of pretrial publicity and inadmissible evidence. *Personality and Social Psychology Bulletin, 23,* 1215–1226.

FosterLee, L., Horowitz, I. A., & Bourgeois, M. J. (1994). Effects of note taking on verdicts and evidence processing in a civil trial. *Law and Human Behavior, 18,* 567–578.

Furnham, A. (1986). The robustness of the recency effect: Studies using legal evidence. *Journal of General Psychology, 113,* 351–357.

Greene, E., & Loftus, E. F. (1985). When crimes are joined at trial. *Law and Human Behavior, 9,* 193.

Greene, E., Schooler, J. W., & Loftus, E. F. (1985). Expert psychological testimony. In S. M. Kassin & L. S. Wrightsman (Eds.), *The psychology of evidence and trial procedure* (pp. 201–229). Beverly Hills, CA: Sage.

Hackman, J. R., & Morris, C. G. (1978). Group tasks, group interaction process, and group performance effectiveness: A review and proposed integration. In L. Berkowitz (Ed.), *Group processes* (pp. 1–66). New York: Academic Press.

Haney, C. (1984). On the selection of capital juries: The biasing effects of the death qualification process. *Law and Human Behavior, 8,* 121–132.

Haney, C., & Lynch, M. (1994). Comprehending life and death matters: A preliminary study of California's capital penalty instructions. *Law and Human Behavior, 18,* 411–436.

Haney, C., Sontag, L., & Costanzo, S. (1994). Deciding to take a life: Capital juries, sentencing instructions, and the jurisprudence of death. *Journal of Social Issues, 50,* 149–176.

Hans, V. P., & Vidmar, N. (1982). Jury selection. In N. Kerr & R. Bray (Eds.), *The psychology of the courtroom* (pp. 39–81). New York: Academic Press.

Hastie, R., Penrod, S. D., & Pennington, N. (1983). *Inside the jury.* Cambridge, MA: Harvard University Press.

Hastie, R., Schkade, D. A., & Payne, J. W. (1998). A study of juror and jury judgments in civil cases: Deciding liability for punitive damages. *Law and Human Behavior, 22,* 287–314.

Heuer, L., & Penrod, S. (1989). Instructing jurors: A field experiment with written and preliminary instructions. *Law and Human Behavior, 13,* 409–430.

Heuer, L., & Penrod, S. (1994). Trial complexity: A field investigation of its meaning and its effect. *Law and Human Behavior, 18,* 29–51.

Hinsz, V. B. (1990). Cognitive and consensus processes in group recognition memory performance. *Journal of Personality and Social Psychology, 59,* 709–718.

Horowitz, I. A. (1980). Juror selection: A comparison of two methods in several criminal cases. *Journal of Applied Social Psychology, 10,* 86–99.

Horowitz, I. A., & Bordens, K. S. (1990). An experimental investigation of procedural issues in complex tort trials. *Law and Human Behavior, 14,* 269–285.

Horowitz, I. A., FosterLee, L., & Brolly, I. (1996). Effects of trial complexity on decision making. *Journal of Applied Psychology, 81,* 757–768.

Horowitz, I. A., & Kirkpatrick, L. C. (1996). A concept in search of a definition: The effects of reasonable doubt instructions on certainty of guilt standards and jury verdicts. *Law and Human Behavior, 20,* 655–670.

Kagehiro, D. K. (1990). Defining the standard of proof in jury instructions. *Psychological Science, 1,* 194–200.

Kahneman, D., Slovic, P., & Tversky, A. (Eds.) (1982). *Judgment under uncertainty: Heuristics and biases.* New York: Cambridge University Press.

Kairys, D., Shulman, J., & Harring, S. (Eds.) (1975). *The jury system: New methods for reducing prejudice.* Cambridge, MA: National Jury Project and National Lawyers Guild.

Kalven, H., & Zeisel, H. (1966). *The American jury.* Boston, MA: Little, Brown.

Kameda, T. (1996). Procedural influence in consensus formation: Evaluating group decision making from a social choice perspective. In E. Witte & J. H. Davis (Eds.), *Understanding group behavior: Consensual action by small groups* (Vol. 1, pp. 137–161), Mahwah, NJ: Erlbaum.

Kaplan, M. F., & Martin, A. (1999). Effects of differential status of group members on process and outcome of deliberation. *Group Processes and Intergroup Relations, 2,* 347–364.

Kaplan, M. F., & Miller, C. E. (1987). Group decision making and normative versus informational influence: Effects of type of issue and assigned decision rule. *Journal of Personality and Social Psychology, 53,* 306–313.

Kassin, S. M., Reddy, M. E., & Tulloch, W. F. (1990). Juror interpretations of ambiguous evidence. The need for cognition, presentation order, and persuasion. *Law and Human Behavior, 14*, 43–55.

Kassin, S. M., & Sommers, S. R. (1997). Inadmissible testimony, instructions to disregard, and the jury: Substantive versus procedural considerations. *Personality and Social Psychology Bulletin, 23*, 1046–1054.

Kassin, S. M., & Studebaker, C. A. (1998). Instructions to disregard and the jury: Curative and paradoxical effects. In J. M. Golding & C. M. MacLeod (Eds.), *Intentional forgetting: Interdisciplinary approaches* (pp. 155–171). Mahwah, NJ: Erlbaum.

Kassin, S. M., & Wrightsman, L. S. (1987). On the requirements of proof: The timing of judicial instruction and mock juror verdicts. In L. S. Wrightsman & S. M. Kassin (Eds.), *The jury box: Controversies in the courtroom* (pp. 143–160). Newbury Park, CA: Sage.

Kelman, M., Rottenstreich, Y., & Tversky, A. (1996). Context-dependence in legal decision making. *Journal of Legal Studies, 25*, 287–318.

Kerr, N. L. (1981). Social transition schemes: Charting the group's road to agreement. *Journal of Personality and Social Psychology, 41*, 684–702.

Kerr, N. L. (1983). *Studies of the group decision making process.* Paper presented at the Third International Conference on Group Processes, Nags Head, NC.

Kerr, N. L., Atkin, R. S., Stasser, G., Meek, D., Holt, R. W., & Davis, J. H. (1976). Guilty beyond a reasonable doubt: Effects of concept definition and assigned decision rule on the judgments of mock jurors. *Journal of Personality and Social Psychology, 34*, 282–294.

Kerr, N. L., & MacCoun, R. J. (1985). The effects of jury size and polling method on the process and product of jury deliberation. *Journal of Personality and Social Psychology, 48*, 349–363.

Kerr, N. L., MacCoun, R. J., & Kramer, G. P. (1996). Bias in judgment: Comparing individuals and groups. *Psychological Review, 103*, 687–719.

Kerr, N. L., Niedermeier, K. E., & Kaplan, M. F. (1999). Bias in jurors vs. bias in juries: New evidence from the SDS perspective. *Organizational Behavior and Human Decision Processes, 80*, 70–86.

Kerwin, J., & Shaffer, D. R. (1994). Mock jurors versus mock juries: The role of deliberations in reactions to inadmissible testimony. *Personality and Social Psychology Bulletin, 20*, 153–162.

Kessler, J. B. (1973). An empirical study of six- and twelve-member jury decision-making processes. *University of Michigan Journal of Law Reform, 6*, 712–734.

Koch, C. M., & Devine, D. J. (1999). Effects of reasonable doubt definitions and inclusion of a lesser charge on jury verdicts. *Law and Human Behavior, 23*, 653–674.

Lockhart v. *McCree*, 106 S. Ct. 1758 (1986).

Lombardero, D. A. (1996). Do special verdicts improve the structure of jury decision-making? *Jurimetrics Journal, 36*, 275–324.

Maass, A., Brigham, J. C., & West, S. G. (1985). Testifying on eyewitness reliability: Expert advice is not always persuasive. *Journal of Applied Social Psychology, 15*, 207–229.

MacCoun, R. J., & Kerr, N. L. (1988). Asymmetric influence in mock jury deliberations: Jurors' bias for leniency. *Journal of Personality and Social Psychology, 54*, 21–33.

McConahay, J., Mullin, C., & Frederick, J. (1977). The use of social science in trials with political and racial overtones: The trial of Joan Little. *Law and Contemporary Problems, 41*, 205–229.

Miene, P., Borgida, E., & Park, R. (1993). The evaluation of hearsay evidence: A social psychological approach. In N. Castellan, Jr. (Ed.), *Individual and group decision making: Current issues* (pp. 137–166). Hillsdale, NJ: Erlbaum.

Mills, L. R. (1973). Six-member and twelve-member juries: An empirical study of trial results. *University of Michigan Journal of Law Reform, 6*, 671–711.

Moskitis, R. L. (1976). The constitutional need for discovery of pre-voir dire juror studies. *Southern California Law Review, 49*, 597–633.

Nadler, J., Au, W. T., Zarnoth, P., Irwin, J., & Davis, J. H. (1999). *Quantitative decisions by mock citizen panels: The effects of dread risk, accountability, and voting mechanisms.* Unpublished manuscript, University of Illinois.

Nemeth, C. (1977). Interaction between jurors as a function of majority vs. unanimity decision rules. *Journal of Applied Social Psychology, 7*, 38–56.

Padawer-Singer, A. M., Singer, A. N., & Singer, R. L. (1977). An experimental study of twelve vs. six member juries under unanimous v. nonunanimous decisions. In B. D. Sales (Ed.), *Psychology in the legal process.* New York: Spectrum.

Pennington, N., & Hastie, R. (1986). Evidence evaluation in complex decision making. *Journal of Personality and Social Psychology, 51*, 242–258.

Penrod, S. (1980). *Practice attorney's jury selection strategies.* Paper presented at the American Psychological Association Annual Convention, Montreal.

Penrod, S. D., Fulero, S. M., & Cutler, B. L. (1995). Expert psychological testimony on eyewitness reliability before and after *Daubert*: The state of the law and the science. *Behavioral Sciences and the Law, 13*, 229–259.

Penrod, S., & Hastie, R. (1980). A computer simulation of jury decision making. *Psychological Review, 87*, 133–159.

Penrod, S., & Heuer, L. (1998). Improving group performance: The case of the jury. In R. S. Tindale, J. E. Edwards, L. Heath, E. J. Posavac, F. B. Bryant, E. Henderson-King, Y. Suarez-Balcazar, & J. Myers (Eds.), *Social psychological applications to social issues: Theory and research on small groups* (Vol. 4, pp. 127–152). New York: Plenum Press.

Rind, B., Jaeger, M., & Strohmetz, D. B. (1995). Effects of crime seriousness on simulated jurors' use of inadmissible evidence. *Journal of Social Psychology, 135*, 417–424.

Roper, R. T. (1980). Jury size and verdict consistency: "A line has to be drawn somewhere?" *Law & Society Review, 14*, 977–999.

Saks, M. J. (1976). The limits of scientific jury selection: Ethical and empirical. *Jurimetrics Journal, 17*, 3–22,

Saks, M. J. (1977). *Jury verdicts: The role of group size and social decision rule.* Lexington, MA: Lexington Books.

Saks, M. J., & Hastie, R. (1978). *Social psychology in court.* Princeton, NJ: Van Nostrand-Reinhold.

Saks, M. J., & Marti, M. W. (1997). A meta-analysis of the effects of jury size. *Law and Human Behavior, 21*, 451–467.

Sandys, M., & Dillehay, R. C. (1995). First-ballot votes, predeliberation dispositions, and final verdicts in jury trials. *Law and Human Behavior, 19*, 175–195.

Schuller, R. A. (1995). Expert evidence and hearsay: The influence of "Secondhand" information on jurors' decisions. *Law and Human Behavior, 19*, 345–362.

Scott, L. A., & Tindale, R. S. (1989). *An application of the Elaboration-Likelihood model to jurors' decision making in a complex lawsuit.* Paper presented at the Midwestern Psychological Association Annual Convention, Chicago, IL.

Severance, L. J., Greene, E., & Loftus, E. F. (1984). Criminology: Toward criminal jury instructions that jurors can understand. *Journal of Criminal Law and Criminology, 75*, 198–233.

Shulman, J. (1973). A systematic approach to successful jury selection. *Guild Notes*, November.

Smith, B. C., Penrod, S. D., Otto, A. L., & Park, R. C. (1996). Jurors' use of probabilistic information. *Law and Human Behavior, 20*, 49–82.

Smith, V. L. (1990). The feasibility and utility of pretrial instruction in the substantive law: A survey of judges. *Law and Human Behavior, 14*, 235–248.

Smith, V. L. (1991). Impact of pretrial instruction on jurors' information processing and decision making. *Journal of Applied Psychology, 76*, 220–228.

Stasser, G., & Davis, J. H. (1981). Group decision making and social influence: A social interactions sequence model. *Psychological Review, 88*, 523–551.

Stasser, G., & Dietz-Uhler, B. (2001). Collective choice, judgment and problem solving. In M. A. Hogg & S. Tindale (Eds.), *Blackwell handbook of social psychology: Group processes* (pp. 31–55). Oxford: Blackwell Publishing.

Stasser, G., Kerr, N. L., & Bray, R. (1982). The social psychology of jury deliberations: Structure, process, and product. In N. Kerr & R. Bray (Eds.), *The psychology of the courtroom* (pp. 186–219). New York: Academic Press.

Stasser, G., Kerr, N. L., & Davis, J. H. (1989). Influence processes and consensus models in decision-making groups. In P. B. Paulus (Ed.), *Psychology of Group Influence* (2nd Ed., pp. 279–326). Hillsdale, NJ: Erlbaum.

Tanford, S., & Penrod, S. (1983). Computer modeling of influence in the jury: The role of the consistent juror. *Social Psychology Quarterly, 46*, 200–212.

Thiel v. *Southern Pacific Co.* 328 U.S. 217 (1946).

Thibaut, J., & Walker, L. (1975). *Procedural justice*. Hillsdale, NJ: Erlbaum.

Thompson, W. C. (1989). Death qualification after Wainwright v. Witt and Lockhart v. McCree. *Law and Human Behavior, 13*, 185–216.

Thompson, W. C., Cowan, C. L., Ellsworth, P. C., & Harrington, J. C. (1984). Death penalty attitudes and conviction proneness: The translation of attitudes into verdicts. *Law and Human Behavior, 8*, 95–113.

Thompson, W. C., & Fuqua, J. (1998). "The jury will disregard . . .": A brief guide to inadmissible evidence. In J. M. Golding & C. M. MacLeod (Eds.), *Intentional forgetting: Interdisciplinary approaches* (pp. 133–154). Mahwah, NJ: Erlbaum.

Tindale, R. S. (1993). Decision errors made by individuals and groups. In N. Castellan, Jr. (Ed.), *Individual and group decision making: Current issues* (pp. 109–124). Hillsdale, NJ: Erlbaum.

Tindale, R. S., & Davis, J. H. (1983). Group decision making and jury verdicts. In H. H. Blumberg, A. P. Hare, V. Kent, & M. F. Davies (Eds.), *Small groups and social interaction* (Vol. 2, pp. 9–38). Chichester, UK: Wiley.

Tindale, R. S., Filkins, J., Smith, C., Sheffey, S., & Thomas, L. S. (1992). *Use of "proportional liability" information by mock juries in tort litigation*. Paper presented at the Midwestern Psychological Association Annual Convention, Chicago, IL.

Tindale, R. S., & Kameda, T. (in press). "Social sharedness" as a unifying theme for information processing in groups. *Group Processes and Intergroup Relations*.

Tindale, R. S., & Nagao, D. H. (1986). An assessment of the potential utility of "Scientific Jury Selection": A "thought experiment" approach. *Organizational Behavior and Human Decision Processes, 37*, 409–425.

Tribe, L. H. (1971). Trial by mathematics: Precision and ritual in the legal process. *Harvard Law Review, 84*, 1329–1393.

Valenti, A. C., & Downing, L. L. (1975). Differential effects of jury size on verdicts following deliberations as a function of the apparent guilt of a defendant. *Journal of Personality and Social Psychology, 32*, 655–663.

Vollrath, D. A., Sheppard, B. H., Hinsz, V. B., & Davis, J. H. (1989). Memory performance by decision-making groups and individuals. *Organizational Behavior and Human Decision Processes, 43*, 289–300.

Way, H. F. (1980). *Criminal justice and the American Constitution*. North Scituate, MA: Duxbury Press.

Wegner, D. M., & Bargh, J. A. (1998). Control and automaticity in everyday life. In D. T. Gilbert, S. T. Fiske, & G. Lindzey (Eds.), *Handbook of social psychology* (4th Ed., pp. 446–496). Boston, MA: McGraw Hill.

Wells, G. L. (1992). Naked statistical evidence of liability: Is subjective probability enough? *Journal of Personality and Social Psychology, 62,* 739–752.

Wiener, R. L., Pritchard, C. C., & Weston, M. (1995). Comprehensibility of approved jury instructions in capital murder cases. *Journal of Applied Psychology, 80,* 455–467.

Williams v. *Florida,* 90 S. Ct. 1893 (1970).

Witherspoon v. *Illinois,* 391 U.S. 550 (1968).

Wyer, Jr., R. S., & Srull, T. K. (1989). *Memory and cognition in its social context.* Hillsdale, NJ: Erlbaum.

Zeisel, H. (1968). *Some data on juror attitudes toward capital punishment.* Monograph, Center for Studies in Criminal Justice, University of Chicago Law School, Chicago, IL.

CHAPTER SEVEN

The Psychological Determinants of Political Judgment

Victor C. Ottati

One might view political psychology simply as an application of psychological theory and research to the study of political behavior. Yet this characterization is misleading in at least two respects. First, it suggests that political psychology merely consists of conceptual replications of basic psychological research. In fact, examination of psychological functioning in a political context often requires that researchers develop new and more realistic models of psychological processing. Second, this conceptualization inaccurately portrays psychology as the source discipline and political science as the receptor discipline. To the contrary, political psychology involves a balanced dialogue between these two parent disciplines characterized by reciprocal intellectual exchange (Iyengar & Ottati, 1994).

This chapter focuses on recent research regarding the psychological determinants of two types of political judgment. The first is referred to as a "candidate evaluation judgment," here defined as an individual's summary evaluation of a political candidate along a bipolar, like-versus-dislike dimension. Because candidate evaluation figures prominently in determining the vote decision, it occupies a central role in the study of political behavior. The second category of judgment reflects the voter's specific position on a political issue (e.g. welfare). Because issue positions constitute the fundamental elements of public opinion, and because issue positions influence a variety of political decisions, an examination of this second type of judgment is equally fundamental to an understanding of political behavior.

The Psychological Determinants of Candidate Evaluation

Traditional models of candidate evaluation and voter decision making emphasized the sociological, attitudinal, and rational determinants of the voting choice (see Iyengar & Ottati, 1994, for a review). Yet none of these approaches provided a realistic or precise description of the cognitive process mechanisms that underlie candidate evaluation and the voting decision. The present section reviews more recent advances in candidate evaluation research that have been inspired by developments in the social cognition and attitude literature. These approaches place greater emphasis upon mediating psychological process mechanisms.

In reviewing this work, a variety of factors that determine candidate evaluation are considered. The first two factors are of long-standing interest to political researchers. These are the candidate's specific issue positions and party affiliation. This is followed by a discussion of factors that occupy a central position in the social cognition and attitude literature, and more recent emphasis in the candidate evaluation literature. These are trait assessments of a political candidate, visual cues of a political candidate (physical attractiveness, facial expression), and the affective state of the voter. Lastly, because the voting choice involves a comparison between competing alternatives, research regarding the impact of comparative standards is discussed. Before discussing these determinants, however, it is important to distinguish different "procedural styles" that characterize the process whereby voters arrive at candidate evaluation judgments.

Processing style en route to candidate evaluation

Process models of candidate evaluation can be distinguished along two dimensions: (a) systematic versus heuristic processing (see Chaiken, Liberman, & Eagly, 1989), and (b) on-line versus memory based processing (see Hastie & Park, 1986). Systematic processing occurs when voters deliberatively consider a candidate's specific, individuating attributes to arrive at an overall candidate evaluation. This mode of processing requires that the voter possess adequate cognitive resources and motivation to carefully scrutinize information pertaining to the candidate. It is most commonly manifested as voter preference for a candidate who possesses specific issue positions that are shared by the voter (Ottati, 1990). Heuristic processing requires less capacity and effort. In this case, the voter relies on a simple heuristic cue (e.g. physical attractiveness, party membership) to evaluate the candidate (Ottati, 1990).

The distinction between on-line and memory based processing is of critical importance in the candidate evaluation literature. Survey researchers have implicitly embraced a memory based model by assuming candidate judgments are based on specific pieces of information retrieved from memory. If this is true, the net valence of recalled information should correlate strongly with global evaluation of the candidate. In contrast, the on-line model posits that the individual evaluates each piece of candidate information as it is encountered, and immediately integrates these valences into a running tally as each piece of information is acquired. This summary tally is stored in long-term memory. When a judgment is later required, this on-line tally is retrieved from memory rather than the specific pieces of information that contributed to it (Lodge, Steenbergen, & Brau, 1995; McGraw, Lodge, & Stroh, 1990). This on-line model predicts that the correlation between summary evaluation and the net valence of specific information recalled can be very low. Research confirms that this is often the case (e.g. Lodge, Steenbergen, & Brau, 1995). Lodge, Steenbergen, & Brau (1995) recently examined the candidate evaluation process over a sizable time frame. Consistent with the on-line model, they found that memory for specific candidate information fades quickly, whereas memory for the summary evaluation remains relatively stable across time. Their findings also suggest that specific information recalled serves primarily to justify (not determine) the summary evaluation (see Krosnick, 1988; Ottati, Fishbein, & Middlestadt, 1988, for related evidence).

It is important to note, however, that on-line processing is not necessarily universal. Although on-line processing is prevalent among political experts, memory based processing often occurs among political novices (McGraw, Lodge, & Stroh, 1990). Political novices are especially likely to engage in memory based processing when candidate information is presented in a complex format (Rahn, Aldrich, & Borgida, 1994). Also, some people may compute a new judgment of a candidate based upon specific information recalled, even when they already possess a summary evaluation stored in memory.

Issues and candidate evaluation

According to classic democratic theory, voters should evaluate a candidate on the basis of the issues. Yet many researchers argue that citizens rarely possess the motivation or ability to systematically evaluate candidates in terms of such issue calculations. This characterization of the voter may be overly pessimistic, however. For one thing, the on-line model posits that candidate evaluation can be responsive to a candidate's specific issue positions even if voters are unable to recall these issue stances (Lodge, Steenbergen, & Brau, 1995). Second, if one abandons the assumption that issues are equally weighted when determining candidate evaluation, calculations of issue agreement often figure prominently in determining these judgments (Krosnick, Berent, & Boninger, 1994).

A variety of factors can affect the weight ascribed to a given issue. These include the subjective importance of the issue, personal relevance of the issue, the voter's subjective certainty that the candidate holds the issue position, the serial position in which the issue was originally encountered, the valence of the issue position, and media priming of the issue. Three of these determinants of issue weighting have been given the most extensive coverage in the candidate evaluation literature. These are subjective importance, valence (i.e. negativity effects), and media priming.

Subjective importance   Krosnick and his associates (e.g. Krosnick, Berent, & Boninger, 1994) have provided a comprehensive account of issue importance effects. They define issue importance as a subjective perception of importance that is specific to a given issue and that is relatively stable across time. Issues that are relevant to self-interest, ingroup interests, or core values are often high in subjective importance. Moreover, subjectively important issues are cognitively represented in a more organized fashion than unimportant issues (Berent & Krosnick, 1993). Subjectively important issues are given greater weight than unimportant issues when individuals evaluate a candidate. This effect is probably mediated by a variety of factors. These include increased accessibility of important issues and greater awareness of candidate differences on important issues (Krosnick, Berent, & Boninger, 1994).

Negativity effects   Negativity effects are present when individuals give greater weight to negative information relative to equally extreme and equally likely positive information (Lau,

1985). This effect is not limited to issue information. Negativity effects can occur for a candidate's trait characteristics, with negative traits carrying more weight than positive traits when predicting candidate evaluation (Klein, 1991).

Lau (1985) offers two explanations for negativity effects in political behavior. According to the "figure–ground hypothesis," individuals generally expect that others will possess positive characteristics. Negative information, due to its infrequency or novelty, stands out against this positive background and is given greater weight in determining judgments. From this perspective, negativity effects should be moderated by individual differences in the degree to which "background" expectations are indeed positive. Namely, individuals who generally trust politicians should be more likely to exhibit negativity effects than those who generally distrust politicians. Lau's second hypothesis, labeled the "cost orientation hypothesis," begins with the assumption that people are more motivated to avoid costs than approach gains. From this perspective, negativity effects should be most prevalent when individuals believe the election outcome will produce notable costs and benefits. Lau's (1985) findings support both predictions, suggesting both mechanisms elicit negativity effects.

Recent work on negativity effects raises questions about these interpretations. According to Skowronski & Carlston (1989), negative information is given considerable weight when it serves as a diagnostic cue that discriminates between a given trait inference (e.g. honest) and its alternative (e.g. dishonest). Factors such as novelty or infrequency may contribute to diagnosticity. However, this need not always be the case. For example, infrequent negative behaviors are often highly diagnostic when making honesty judgments, but not when making ability judgments (Skowronski & Carlston, 1989). Lau's (1989) finding that negativity effects are moderated by general expectations regarding the honesty of politicians is consistent with this formulation.

One might predict that negative political campaigning is an especially potent determinant of candidate evaluation due to negativity effects. In fact, the effects of negative campaigning (i.e. attacking the opponent) are quite complex. Effects of negative campaigning differ depending on whether the attack centers on the opponent's issue stances, character, or both, and also depending on whether the source of the attack falls within the voter's ideological ingroup or outgroup (Budesheim, Houston, & DePaolo, 1996). For example, candidates can energize their supporters by making strong character attacks that are justified with issue attacks (which the supporters will agree with). Yet this effect does not emerge for voters ideologically opposed to the source (Budesheim, Houston, & DePaolo, 1996). As this example illustrates, negative campaigning not only influences evaluations of the attack target, but also the source (see Houston, Doan, & Roskos-Ewoldson, 1998, for further evidence).

Media induced priming effects   Issues accessible in the voter's mind carry considerable weight when voters evaluate a candidate. Prominent and frequent media coverage of an issue serves to prime that issue, thereby increasing the accessibility and weight ascribed to that issue when voters evaluate a candidate. Effects of this nature have been demonstrated in both experimental (e.g. Iyengar & Kinder, 1987) and survey (e.g. Krosnick & Kinder, 1990) studies. This effect is magnified when coverage of an issue suggests that political officials are responsible for national conditions related to the issue (Iyengar & Kinder, 1987). Other moderators of this effect include relevance and political involvement. Not surprisingly, priming effects are more prominent when predicting judgments about the candidate that are relevant to the primed issue than when predicting judgments that are less directly relevant to the primed issue (Iyengar & Kinder, 1987). Evidence regarding the moderating role of political involvement (exposure, interest, knowledge) is somewhat mixed. Some studies indicate that media induced priming effects are more likely to emerge among political novices than experts. However, Krosnick & Brannon (1993) note that this research has failed to disentangle the effects of exposure, interest, and knowledge. When examining the unique contribution of these factors, Krosnick and Brannon find that political interest reduces priming effects whereas political expertise increases priming effects. Further research is needed to identify the psychological mechanism responsible for this effect.

Partisanship and candidate evaluation

Political researchers have long noted that partisanship is an important determinant of candidate evaluation. Partisanship plays a critical role in many traditional models of voting behavior, including the "Michigan School" model of voting preference (Campbell, Converse, Miller, & Stokes, 1960). In addition, many models of media influence suggest that, when campaigns do influence voter preferences, voters move in the direction of their prior partisan predispositions (Iyengar & Petrocik, 1998).

While early research concerning partisanship failed to focus on mediating process mechanisms, recent research has more directly assessed this question. This work suggests that the effect of party on candidate evaluation is mediated by a variety of process mechanisms that occur at distinct stages of information processing (see Iyengar & Ottati, 1994; Ottati & Wyer, 1992). These include selective exposure to information consistent with the voter's party orientation, biased encoding or interpretation of a candidate's policy positions, inferring that the candidate's specific policy positions coincide with the party stereotype, biased retrieval of a candidate's issue positions, and biased weighting of a candidate's issue positions (Iyengar & Ottati, 1994; Wyer & Ottati, 1993). Lodge & Hamill (1986) have explicitly considered the psychological mediators of the effect of party on candidate evaluation. They found that, relative to "party aschematics," "party schematics" were more likely to accurately categorize policy statements in terms of party. In addition, "party schematics" were more likely to exhibit a party consistency bias when using recognition measures of memory for a candidate's issue positions.

While the research described above suggests that the effect of party on candidate evaluation is mediated by biased processing of specific issue information, other work indicates party labels can function as heuristic cues that elicit category based evaluation of a political candidate (e.g. Fiske, 1986; Ottati, 1990). From this perspective, voters categorize the candidate in terms of party and simply evaluate the candidate on the basis of their evaluation of their party stereotype. This heuristic mode of party based candidate evaluation occurs when voters possess little or no individuating information pertaining to a candidate, or alternatively, when voters lack the ability or motivation to engage in more systematic, issue based processing (e.g. Fiske, 1986; Ottati, 1990). Consistent with this view, Ottati (1990) obtained party based evaluation effects in a comparative judgment task, but not in a singular judgment task (which presumably requires less cognitive capacity or ability). Individual differences in ability to process political information (i.e. political expertise) also moderate reliance upon the party stereotype. Rahn & Cramer (1996) report that political experts are less likely than novices to "apply" (i.e. give weight to) the party stereotype when evaluating a political candidate.

Factors that moderate party based candidate evaluation serve an analogous role as moderators of other heuristic cues. Ottati, Terkildsen, & Hubbard (1997) demonstrate that a candidate's ideology can function as a heuristic cue that determines candidate preference under conditions of low motivation. Miller & Krosnick (1998) demonstrate that the order in which names appear on the ballot determines voting preference when voters possess little information regarding the competing candidates.

Trait based candidate evaluation

Recent research emphasizes that candidate evaluation is not solely determined by political criteria (e.g. issues, partisanship). Many factors that influence evaluations of non-political actors also influence candidate evaluation. These include trait characteristics, the candidate's visual image, and the affective state of the voter. The role of trait perceptions is emphasized by models that describe the representation of candidate information. McGraw, Pinney, & Neumann (1991) argue that representations of a candidate contain two information clusters. One contains the candidate's issues positions, whereas the other contains traits. Other research questions this conclusion, arguing that trait inferences are partially based on reactions to a candidate's issue stands (Forgas, Kagan, & Frey, 1977; Miller, Wattenberg, & Malanchuk, 1986; Rahn, Aldrich, Borgida, & Sullivan, 1990). Many researchers propose that voters organize trait information in terms of a limited number of broad trait categories that remain relatively constant across elections (Kinder, 1986; Miller, Wattenberg, & Malanchuk, 1986). Examples of these trait categories include leadership/competence and integrity/empathy (Kinder, 1986), as well as task oriented and socio-emotional traits (Rahn, Aldrich, Borgida, & Sullivan, 1990).

Do traits and issues function as independent determinants of candidate evaluation? Kinder (1986) emphasizes that trait ratings exert an effect on candidate evaluation that is independent of issue considerations. However, Rahn, Aldrich, Borgida, & Sullivan (1990) suggest that the effect of political criteria (e.g. issues, ideology, partisanship) on voting preference is mediated by trait assessments of the candidate – suggesting considerable redundancy among these two classes of predictors.

If traits play a role in determining candidate evaluation, what is the relative weight ascribed to the various dimensions? Funk (1997) argues that, based on normative considerations, task oriented traits (i.e. competence) should be given greater weight than socio-emotional traits (i.e. warmth). Consistent with this assumption, political experts were more likely than novices to give greater weight to the competence dimension (Funk, 1977). Because experts possess an extensive and complex knowledge base, they are presumably better able to discriminate important traits from traits of lesser importance.

Effects of visual cues on candidate evaluation

Research regarding the effects of visual cues on candidate evaluation has focused primarily on the effects of candidate physical attractiveness and facial expression.

Physical attractiveness Consistent with social psychological research on the physical attractiveness stereotype, several studies indicate that people evaluate physically attractive candidates more positively than physically unattractive candidates (e.g. Budesheim & DePaola, 1994; Ottati, 1990). This effect is clearly present when individuals possess no other relevant information pertaining to the candidate (Ottati, 1990). Yet physical attractiveness also influences candidate evaluation when accompanied by more substantive candidate information (e.g. issue stances, party). In this latter case, effects associated with physical attractiveness are more complex (Ottati, 1990; Riggle, Ottati, Wyer, Kuklinski, & Schwarz, 1992). Ottati (1990) finds that physical attractiveness is more likely to influence candidate evaluation in a comparative judgment task than in a more simple, singular judgment task. Even within the comparative judgment task, Ottati (1990) reports that physical attractiveness influences candidate evaluation only when the voter perceives that the candidate's party and issue stances are of opposite valence. However, Budesheim & DePaola (1994) failed to replicate this later finding and report that physical attractiveness influences candidate evaluation regardless of the valence ascribed to party and issue information.

Facial expression A number of studies demonstrate that a candidate's nonverbal cues (e.g. facial display) influence voters' evaluations of a candidate (e.g. Masters, Sullivan, Lanzetta, McHugo, & Englis, 1986; Ottati, Terkildsen, & Hubbard, 1997). An interesting question concerns how voters combine nonverbal with verbal candidate information to arrive at a summary evaluation. Many political researchers regard a candidate's facial expression as a stimulus cue that elicits positive or negative reactions to a candidate, with this effect being unique and distinct from the impact of a candidate's verbal remarks (e.g. Masters, Sullivan, Lanzetta, McHugo, & Englis, 1986). This account of facial display effects accounts for a variety of candidate image effects occurring throughout history. For example, in the Kennedy–Nixon debate, Nixon's facial expressions conveyed a sense of insecurity whereas Kennedy's facial expressions projected an image of confidence. Most political analysts believe that televised presentation of this debate negatively influenced evaluations of Nixon and positively influenced evaluations of Kennedy.

A second category of research focuses on facial displays that convey information that is discrepant from the implication of verbally acquired information. In this case, facial expressions might constitute a form of "nonverbal leakage" that betrays a person's true emotional state when that person's verbal statements are designed to deny or disguise an underlying emotion. Under such conditions, perceivers may give greater weight to the nonverbal channel (Mehrabian & Ferris, 1967). In the political arena, nonverbal leakage might undermine a candidate's denial of suspicious, inappropriate, or illegal behavior. Alternatively, nonverbal leakage might convey anger or irritation when a candidate's verbal remarks attempt to project a veneer of civility. Facial expressions that contradict a person's verbal remarks may also convey sarcasm or humor (Bugental, Kaswan, & Love, 1979). For example, if a disgusted expression accompanies the remark "Clinton's health care proposal is obviously completely flawless," it is clear that the speaker's intended meaning is precisely opposite to the literal meaning of the verbal utterance.

A third perspective emphasizes that a candidate's nonverbal cues moderate the voter's tendency to engage in systematic versus heuristic processing of verbally acquired information (Ottati, Terkildsen, & Hubbard, 1997; see also Wyer et al., 1991). Ottati, Terkildsen, & Hubbard (1997) argue that neutral or more somber facial expressions signal that a candidate's verbal remarks address serious concerns that require systematic scrutiny. In contrast, happy displays signal that a candidate's verbal remarks address benign or "light" issues that do not require systematic scrutiny. Consistent with these assumptions, perceivers were more likely to engage in systematic, issue based candidate evaluation when the candidate's verbal remarks were accompanied by a neutral facial expression than when these remarks were accompanied by a happy facial expression. Conversely, the tendency to rely on candidate ideology as a heuristic basis for candidate evaluation was more pronounced in the happy display condition than in the neutral display condition (Ottati, Terkildsen, & Hubbard, 1997).

Episodic affect and candidate evaluation

Social psychological research concerning the effect of affect on social judgment is quite extensive. Under appropriate conditions, positive affective states elicit more positive social judgments than negative affective states. This effect may be mediated by mood congruent encoding, interpretation, or elaboration of information pertaining to the object judged (e.g. Forgas, 1995). Alternatively, this effect may occur when individuals (correctly or incorrectly) attribute their episodic affective state to the object judged (Schwarz & Clore, 1983). Episodic affect may also influence processing style en route to judgment (e.g. chapter 18, this volume; Schwarz, 1990; Martin, Ward, Achee, & Wyer, 1993).

In the candidate evaluation literature, many researchers report that beliefs about a candidate and emotional reactions to a candidate function as unique predictors of global candidate evaluation (Abelson, Kinder, Peters, & Fiske, 1982; Ottati, Steenbergen, & Riggle, 1992). However, this finding does not generalize across all conditions or methods of measurement. For example, beliefs fully account for the predictive role of emotions when using an open-ended measure of "emotionally relevant" beliefs (Ottati, 1997). Moreover, affective–cognitive ambivalence moderates these effects. The unique role of affect is prominent among individuals possessing oppositely valenced affective and cognitive reactions to a candidate. However, this unique effect is less pronounced among individuals possessing similarly valenced affective and cognitive reactions to a candidate (Lavine, Thomsen, Zanna, & Borgida, 1998).

Campaign strategists employ a variety of tactics designed to place voters in a good mood when they are exposed to a political candidate. The use of this strategy rests upon the assumption that positive reactions to contextual stimuli (e.g. the flag, music, hoopla) will translate into positive reactions to a political leader. Experimental attempts to investigate this phenomenon have often used non-political contextual cues (e.g. movie footage, success or failure at an irrelevant task) to place individuals in a positive or negative mood. Immediately following this "mood induction procedure," participants perform an ostensibly unrelated task in which they read about a political candidate. After some period of delay (e.g. two weeks), they report their evaluation of the candidate.

Using this procedure, Ottati & Isbell (1996) have demonstrated that the effect of mood on candidate evaluation is moderated by political expertise of the voter. Among political novices, mood produced an assimilation effect with positive mood eliciting more positive evaluations than negative mood. However, among political experts mood produced a contrast effect with positive mood eliciting more negative evaluations than negative mood. Thus, mood produced an assimilation effect among perceivers who processed the candidate information in an inefficient manner (novices), whereas mood produced a contrast effect among perceivers who processed this information in an efficient manner (experts). Supplementary analyses suggested that these effects were not mediated by biased recall of candidate information.

Ottati & Isbell (1996) postulate that mood during exposure to the candidate information is misattributed to the candidate, influencing on-line evaluation of the candidate. This summary evaluation is stored in memory and later retrieved to report a judgment – producing a mood assimilation effect among low efficiency perceivers (novices). Perceivers who process the candidate information in an efficient manner (experts) are assumed to possess the capacity or ability to correct for this judgmental bias. However, because they overestimate the initial biasing influence of mood, they over-correct for this influence. Among experts, this produces a contrast effect in which positive mood elicits a more negative candidate evaluation than negative mood.

Using a nearly identical procedure, Isbell & Wyer (1998) report that motivation to evaluate a political candidate moderates the impact of mood on candidate evaluation. Namely, mood produced an assimilation effect when participants possessed low motivation, whereas mood produced a contrast effect when participants possessed high motivation. Taken together, these studies suggest that individuals will attempt to correct for the biasing influence of mood when they possess the ability or motivation to do so (see also Petty & Wegener, 1993). As such, campaign tactics designed to elicit a positive mood in the voter may not always produce their intended effect.

Inspired by basic research on mood effects (Schwarz, Bless, & Bohner, 1991), a third line of research emphasizes that affective states influence motivation to carefully attend to a political communication. For example, Marcus & Mackuen (1993) demonstrate that anxiety stimulates attention toward political issues and discourages reliance upon habitual (e.g. heuristic) cues for voting. Nadeau, Niemi, & Amato (1995) argue that this effect is mediated by issue importance, and that this effect only occurs when voters expect that careful attention to an issue stands a realistic chance of influencing tangible outcomes. Clore & Isbell (in press) propose that, in addition to anxiety, sadness might produce more deliberative and systematic processing of political information (see Schwarz, Bless, & Bohner, 1991, for evidence in a non-political context).

In sum, the effect of affect on candidate evaluation is a multifaceted and complex phenomenon. Attempts to provide a comprehensive description of these effects must therefore include a variety of psychological mechanisms that operate under varying conditions (Glaser & Salovey, 1998; Ottati & Wyer, 1992).

Comparative standards and candidate evaluation

Politicians are often evaluated relative to some internally generated standard or relative to other political actors. Sullivan, Aldrich, Borgida, & Rahn (1990) hypothesize that voters might rely on either of two internally generated standards. The "superman model" predicts that voters will evince the greatest support for politicians who approach perfection – politicians who possess the highest possible altruism, willpower, and trustworthiness. The "everyman model" predicts that voters will show the greatest support for politicians who best typify the average person. From this second perspective, candidates who present themselves as too superior may be perceived as self-righteous, pretentious, or out of touch with the common person. Sullivan, Aldrich, Borgida, & Rahn (1990) obtain strong support for the "superman model," but also a modicum of support for the "everyman model." It is conceivable that voters value ideal qualities along certain dimensions while preferring that candidates remain average along other dimensions.

Other research focuses on the effects of externally presented standards. One such line of research emphasizes that voters are often presented with two competing candidates who serve as standards of comparison for each other in the general election. This approach is best exemplified by Houston & Roskos-Ewoldsen's (in press) "cancellation and focus" model (see also Tversky, 1977). According to this model, comparison involves starting from one candidate (the "subject") and mapping this candidate's features on to the opposing candidate (the "referent"). Shared features are canceled and thereby fail to influence preference judgments. Because individuals use the subject as a starting point, unique features of the subject carry considerable weight, whereas unique features of the referent are ignored when evaluating the candidates. Predictions generated by this model are strongly supported. If two competing candidates share positive features but possess unique negative features, voters prefer the referent over the subject. A reverse preference ordering occurs when the two candidates share negative features but possess unique positive features.

Other research considers the effects of externally presented standards contained within a public opinion survey. For example, Staper & Schwarz (1998) demonstrate that an item which makes respondents think about Colin Powell reduces their subsequent evaluation of Bob Dole. In this particular case, Powell serves as a positive standard against which Dole is contrasted. Contrast effects of this nature are discussed in more detail in Schwarz & Bohner (2001).

Summary of the candidate evaluation literature

The past two decades of political psychology research are marked by a tremendous interest in the psychological mediators of candidate evaluation judgments. This has led political psychologists to reconsider the influence of issues and partisanship by examining their effects within the context of more precise and realistic models of information processing. In addition, this has led political researchers to consider a variety of factors that have traditionally fallen within the purview of social cognition and attitude research (e.g. trait assessments, visual cues, episodic affect). Moreover, work regarding the psychological underpinnings of comparative judgment has been fruitfully applied to examine the process whereby comparative standards influence candidate evaluation judgments. Omitted from this section is a discussion of the effects of race, gender, economic performance, and other determinants of candidate evaluation. To gain a more comprehensive understanding of the candidate evaluation process, the reader is encouraged to explore additional sources (e.g. Lodge & McGraw, 1995).

The Psychological Determinants of Issue Opinion

What are the psychological determinants of an individual's position on a specific issue? For example, what psychological factors lead an individual to favor or oppose affirmative action? In addressing this question, this section considers several determinants of political issue judgments. The first factor, liberal versus conservative ideological orientation, has been explored since the very beginning of public opinion research. Research on a second set of factors, abstract values such as individualism and isolationism, can be viewed as outgrowth and reaction to this earlier, exclusive emphasis upon ideology. Third, this section reviews research that suggests specific issue positions are derived from underlying racist attitudes and motivations. The last portion of this section shifts attention toward more transient and situational determinants of public opinion by exploring the effects of context on political issue judgments. Before addressing these concerns, however, it is useful to highlight some important aspects of information processing that occur en route to political issue judgment.

Information processing en route to political issue judgment

Between the moment an individual is exposed to issue-relevant information and the moment an individual reports an issue judgment, many stages of information processing unfold. These include comprehension, encoding and interpretation, representation, retrieval, integration, and the report of an overt judgment. A comprehensive discussion of these stages as they apply to issue judgment is presented elsewhere (Iyengar & Ottati, 1994; Wyer & Ottati, 1993). For present purposes, it is useful to briefly highlight some important findings regarding the representation, retrieval, and use of political information when individuals formulate a specific issue judgment.

When representing issue information in memory, the individual may try to construct a temporally or causally related scenario of the policy event that includes its antecedents and consequences. Evidence suggests that positive and negative consequences associated with an issue are represented in separate clusters, and that this tendency is most pronounced among political experts (McGraw & Pinney, 1990). The particular set of consequences included in this representation may reflect the set of consequences primed by a communication, consequences that are chronically accessible in the message recipient, or both (Lau, Smith, & Fiske, 1991). Chronically accessible consequences associated with various issues interpretations often reflect the individual's priorities with regard to more abstract values. Thus, specific policy positions may be organized around superordinate core values that are chronically accessible in the voter (e.g. free market conservatism, the Protestant work ethic).

When asked to report an issue judgment, individuals often engage in a limited search for issue-relevant information. In such cases, individuals might rely on heuristics or a previously computed judgment when reporting their issue opinion (Burnstein, Abboushi, & Kitayama, 1993). When more motivated, individuals will perform a more exhaustive or systematic search for case information relevant to the issue judgment. In this case, the individual must combine the implications of numerous criteria to arrive at an issue judgment. Evidence suggests that a limited search produces retrieval of unqualified and unidirectional information, resulting in more extreme issue judgments. Conversely, an exhaustive search often yields more qualified and mixed considerations, resulting in more moderate judgments (Burnstein, Abboushi, & Kitayama, 1993).

Having highlighted important aspects of information processing that occur en route to issue judgment, I now focus on the substantive content of information that determines these judgments. These include ideology, abstract values, and racism.

Ideology and political issue judgment

The central role ascribed to ideology in political thinking seems incontrovertible. Self-reported ideology (liberal versus conservative) is associated with a variety of individual difference dimensions. These include authoritarianism (Adorno, et al., 1950), resistance to stereotype disconfirmation (Karasawa, 1998), and integrative complexity (Tetlock, 1986). Yet despite the assumed centrality of ideology, early work suggested ideology plays only a weak role in determining specific issue positions. Converse (1964) noted that individuals lack "issue constraint." That is, knowing an individual holds a conservative position on one issue (e.g. defense) does not necessarily imply that the individual will adopt a conservative position on another issue (e.g. affirmative action). This finding contradicts the notion that specific issue positions are derived from a single, liberal versus conservative orientation. More recent work suggests that a liberal versus conservative ideological dimension may indeed underlie specific issue beliefs (e.g. Jacoby, 1995). However, ideology appears to determine specific issue positions only under certain conditions (Skitka & Tetlock, 1992, 1993).

Skitka & Tetlock (1992, 1993) consider the impact of ideology on issue positions related to the allocation of public assistance. Their "contingency model of distributive justice" emphasizes that endorsement of public assistance programs is contingent upon both scarcity and attribution. Scarcity exists when available resources are insufficient to help all individuals in need. Attribution involves the degree to which social problems (e.g. poverty) are attributed to internal-controllable causes (e.g. laziness) versus other factors (e.g. unfair social conditions). When need for public assistance is urgent and public assistance is likely to be effective, Skitka and Tetlock obtain the following results. Under scarcity conditions, both liberals and conservatives deny assistance to personally responsible (internal-controllable) claimants. In the absence of scarcity, liberals allocate assistance to all claimants (regardless of personal responsibility), whereas conservatives continue to deny assistance to personally responsible claimants. These results suggest ideology is indeed associated with opinions regarding public assistance. However, this effect is moderated by scarcity, attribution, need for assistance, and the perceived effectiveness of assistance. Analyses that ignore these contingencies may fail to uncover the relation between ideology and specific issue positions.

Values and political issue judgment

Many researchers question the assumption that individuals organize specific issue opinions along a single, bipolar liberal versus conservative ideological dimension (e.g. Conover & Feldman, 1984; Hurwitz & Peffley, 1987). From this perspective, specific issue beliefs may be derived from multiple crowning postures or values. While Converse's (1964) operationalization of issue constraint focused on the absence of horizontal inter-issue linkages, this more recent work focuses on vertical linkages that exist between more abstract values and specific issue beliefs. For example, Hurwitz & Peffley found considerable evidence of vertical linkages between "core values" (e.g. ethnocentrism), "general postures" (e.g. isolationism), and "specific issue positions" (e.g. Soviet policy, international trade). Individuals also differ in the degree to which they are "schematic" for a given value (Conover & Feldman, 1984). Schwartz, Bardi, & Bianchi (1998) have recently argued that political values reflect adaptation to objective political conditions. For example, their evidence suggests communist rule engenders a hierarchical perspective that emphasizes power distance as a means to ensure socially responsible behavior. More generally, they propose that objective political conditions afford or magnify the importance of certain values, which in turn form the basis of specific issue beliefs.

Tetlock's (Tetlock, Bernzweig, & Gallant, 1985; Tetlock, 1986) value pluralism model of ideological reasoning suggests that liberal and conservative ideologies are embedded in and related to a variety of value orientations that influence specific issue opinions. In addition, this model proposes that thinking about specific issues is often characterized by fundamental conflicts of value. For example, efforts to control crime may conflict with constitutional guarantees regarding the right to privacy. Integrative complexity with regard to a given issue is characterized by the conjunction of conceptual differentiation and integration. Conceptual differentiation is high when an individual recognizes that a policy possesses many facets or consequences that are relevant to multiple values. Because these values are often in conflict, a policy position will commonly be perceived as possessing both positive and negative consequences. Integration involves developing conceptual connections among differentiated components of a policy position, recognition of inherent tradeoffs, and resolution toward a reasonable opinion (Tetlock, 1986; Tetlock, Bernzweig, & Gallant, 1985). Low integrative complexity reflects reliance on a rigid and simplistic interpretation of a policy event that is based on either a single or minimal number of value dimensions.

Tetlock has demonstrated that integrative complexity is associated with ideology among members of the electorate (Tetlock, 1986) and among members of the Supreme Court (Tetlock, Bernzweig, & Gallant, 1985). His findings generally indicate that liberals possess higher integrative complexity than conservatives, and that integrative complexity reaches its peak among moderate liberals. Low integrative complexity among conservatives is assumed to arise from a rigid, dichotomous style of interpretation that develops as a means of restoring order to a chaotic and threatening world (Adorno, et al., 1950).

Gruenfeld (1995) has challenged Tetlock's conclusion, arguing that ideology is confounded with majority versus minority status in many of Tetlock's studies. Gruenfeld independently varied ideology and majority versus minority status in a content analysis of Supreme Court opinions. Her results support a "status contingency model" which predicts higher levels of complexity among majority members than minority members (Gruenfeld, 1995). Further questions are raised by Judd & Krosnick's (1989) model of representation. They argue that political expertise engenders greater consistency among political values and specific issue positions. This appears to contradict the notion that sophisticated thinkers are more likely to recognize conflict and inconsistency between multiple values related to a single issue position.

Racism and political issue judgment

It has long been suggested that racism plays a role in determining specific issue opinions. For example, opposition to affirmative action might reflect simple prejudice against blacks or other minorities. White racism toward blacks has been defined and measured in many ways. "Old-fashioned racism" is typically assessed in terms of agreement with survey items that explicitly ascribe negative trait characteristics to blacks. These derogatory items about blacks often focus on purported deficiencies in their innate ability or intelligence (Sidanius, Pratto, & Bobo, 1996; Virtanen & Huddy, 1998). Old-fashioned racism has declined since the 1950s (Sniderman & Piazza, 1993). However, many claim that racism continues to exist, albeit in a more subtle form. Survey measures of this more subtle, new form of racism often emphasize deficiencies in black motivation (Virtanen & Huddy, 1998). Kinder & Sears (1981) define "symbolic racism" as "resistance to change in the racial status quo based on moral feelings that blacks violate traditional American values of individualism, self-reliance, the work ethic, obedience, and discipline" (ibid., p. 416). Items composing this scale often emphasize that blacks are "lazy" and should "try" harder (see also Sidanius, Pratto, & Bobo, 1996).

Another modern approach views racism as an initial (perhaps even unconscious) negative reaction to blacks that is subsequently "adjusted" or "corrected for" on the basis of more conscious or deliberative thought processes (e.g. Fazio, Jackson, Dunton, & Williams, 1995; Devine, 1989). For example, Fazio, et al. (1995) presented subjects with a black versus white relevant prime immediately followed by a positive (e.g. ocean) or negative (e.g. poison) target word. Categorization of the target word as "good" or "bad" was facilitated when black primes were followed by negative words or white primes were followed by positive words. Interference occurred when black primes were followed by positive words or white primes were followed by negative words. The degree to which responses conform to this pattern serves as an implicit, unobtrusive measure of racism prior to "adjustment" or "correction."

A variety of studies suggest prejudice and racism can figure prominently in determining policy positions. Whites are more opposed to racially targeted policies than similar policies targeted toward poor people in general (Bobo & Kluegel, 1993). Indeed, individual differences in racism are associated with a number of issue positions. These include busing, affirmative action, and welfare. These effects occur even when controlling for a myriad of non-racial factors (Sears, Van Laar, Carillo, & Kosterman, 1997), including the effects of ideology, authoritarianism, and realistic self/group interest (Sears, 1997; Huddy & Sears, 1995). Moreover, the effect of new racism (e.g. symbolic racism) on these issue stances is distinct from the effect of old-fashioned racism. Sears, et al. (1997) report that symbolic racism predicts specific policy preferences even when controlling for old-fashioned racism. Virtanen & Huddy (1988) demonstrate that, while old-fashioned racism is associated with opposition to virtually all minority assistance programs, symbolic racism is associated with opinions regarding a more circumscribed set of assistance programs that reward individual initiative and effort.

Effects of context on reported issue position

Many theorists question the assumption that individuals possess stable, enduring political opinions. From this perspective, individuals "construct" a political opinion when they are asked to report a judgment. As a consequence, the immediate context of judgment can have a powerful impact on expressed opinions (Ottati, et al., 1989). According to the "inclusion/exclusion model" (Schwarz & Bless, 1992), an individual will retrieve a representation of the issue stimulus and a representation of some standard of comparison when asked to report an issue opinion. The information used to construct these two representations is influenced by both chronic accessibility (context independent factors) and temporary accessibility (context dependent factors). In survey research, the context of a particular issue judgment is defined by the survey items that precede that judgment. These contextual items temporarily prime information that is used to construct the representation of either the target issue or standard of comparison.

Assimilation effects emerge when information primed by a preceding item is included in the target issue representation. For example, Ottati, Fishbein, & Middlestadt (1988) asked respondents to judge whether "Citizens should have the right to speak freely in public." In one condition, this general item was preceded by a specific item pertaining to a favorable group (e.g. "The Parent–Teacher Association should have the right . . ."). In another condition, this general item was preceded by a specific item pertaining to a negative group (e.g. "The Ku Klux Klan should have the right . . ."). As expected, respondents expressed a more favorable attitude toward the general statement in the first condition than in the second condition. This assimilation effect emerged, however, only when the items were separated by eight filler items.

Contrast effects emerge when information primed by a preceding item is excluded from the target representation. This might occur if the primed item serves as an accessible standard of comparison, respondents consciously attempt to correct for the biasing influence of the priming episode, or conversational norms lead respondents to exclude the primed material (e.g. "KKK") from the target representation (e.g. "Citizens") to avoid redundancy of communication. These later two possibilities are most likely to occur when respondents are consciously aware that the former item bears upon their response to the subsequent item. Consistent with this conceptualization, Ottati, Fishbein, & Middlestadt (1988) obtained contrast effects when the two items were presented immediately adjacent to one another.

Summary of issue opinion literature

Research regarding the psychological determinants of political issue opinions has abandoned its original, exclusive focus on the role of ideology. By exploring the role that multiple values play in determining specific issue opinions, political psychologists have gained a more differentiated and realistic view of the determinants of public opinion. Moreover, research regarding the role of racism demonstrates that abstract ideology and value offer only a partial understanding of the etiology of public opinion. Lastly, research on context effects demonstrates that what was previously regarded as "measurement error" often reflects the systematic effect of situational context on political issue judgments. Omitted in the present section is a discussion of many other determinants of political issue opinions. These include the role of media, emotion, and cultural background. The reader is encouraged to explore related coverage of these issues (e.g. Delli-Carpini, Huddy, & Shapiro, 1997).

Conclusion

The field of political psychology has now grown into an extensive and detailed literature. This chapter has focused primarily on the most recent era of political psychology research, an era characterized by increased attention to the psychological mediators of political judgment and decision making. Two major conclusions can be derived from the research summarized in this chapter. One is theoretical while the other is methodological. First, political psychologists have become increasingly aware that political judgment is a highly complex and subtle phenomenon. Awareness of mediating process mechanisms has produced heightened sensitivity to the conditions that moderate the influence of a given factor on political judgment. Thus, for example, the question is no longer "Does the episodic affective state of the voter determine candidate evaluation?" This question has been replaced by two more sophisticated questions: (1) "What psychological process mediates the effect of episodic affect on candidate evaluation?" (2) "Under what conditions does the affective state of the voter determine candidate evaluation?" These theoretically driven questions give rise to related methodological issues. Namely, to obtain a clear understanding of moderating conditions, it is often useful to experimentally manipulate these moderating conditions. Thus, political psychologists are increasingly embracing an eclectic methodological approach that includes both survey and experimental methods of investigation. Disciplinary and methodological provincialism can only serve to impede progress within the field of political psychology. The most exciting developments in this field occur when psychologists and political scientists engage in a bona fide, reciprocal intellectual exchange.

REFERENCES

Abelson, R. P., Kinder, D. R., Peters, M. D., & Fiske, S. T. (1982). Affective and semantic components in political person perception. *Journal of Personality and Social Psychology, 42,* 619–630.

Adorno, T., Frenkel-Brunswick, E., Levinson, D., & Sanford (1950). *The authoritarian personality.* New York: Harper & Row.

Berent, M. K., & Krosnick, J. A. (1993). Attitude importance and the organization of attitude-relevant knowledge in memory. Unpublished manuscript.

Bobo, L., & Kluegel, J. R. (1993). Opposition to race-targeting: Self-interest, stratification, ideology, or racial attitudes? *American Sociological Review, 58,* 443–464.

Budesheim, T. L., & DePaola, S. J. (1994). Beauty or the beast? The effects of appearance, personality, and issue information on evaluations of political candidates. *Personality and Social Psychology Bulletin, 20,* 339–348.

Budesheim, T. L., Houston, D., & DePaolo, S. J. (1996). Persuasiveness of in-group and out-group political messages: The case of negative political campaigning. *Journal of Personality and Social Psychology, 70,* 523–534.

Bugental, D. E., Kaswan, J. W., & Love, L. R. (1970). Perception of contradictory meanings conveyed by verbal and nonverbal channels. *Journal of Personality and Social Psychology, 16,* 647–655.

Burnstein, E., Abboushi, M., & Kitayama, S. (1993). How the mind preserves the image of the enemy: The mnemonics of Soviet–American relations. In W. Zimmerman & H. Jacobson (Eds.), *Behavior, culture, and conflict in world politics.* Ann Arbor: University of Michigan Press.

Chaiken, S., Liberman, A., & Eagly, A. (1998). Heuristic and systematic information processing within and beyond the persuasion context. In J. S. Uleman & J. A. Bargh (Eds.), *Unintended thought* (pp. 212–252). New York: Guilford Press.

Clore, G. L., & Isbell, L. M. (in press). Emotion as virtue and vice. In J. Kuklinski (Ed.), *Political psychology in practice.*

Conover, P., & Feldman, S. (1984). How people organize the political world: A schematic model. *American Journal of Political Science, 28,* 95–126.

Converse, P. E. (1964). The nature of belief systems in mass publics. In D. Apter (Ed.), *Ideology and discontent* (pp. 206–261). New York: Free Press.

Delli-Carpini, M. X., Huddy, L., & Shapiro, R. Y. (1997). *Research in micropolitics: Rethinking rationality,* Vol. 5. Greenwich, CT: JAI Press.

Devine, P. G. (1989). Stereotypes and prejudice: Their automatic and controlled components. *Journal of Personality and Social Psychology, 56,* 5–18.

Fazio, R. H., Jackson, J. R., Dunton, B. C., & Williams, C. J. (1995). Variability in automatic activation as an unobtrusive measure of racial attitudes. A bona fide pipeline? *Journal of Personality and Social Psychology, 69,* 1013–1027.

Fiske, S. T. (1986). Schema based versus piecemeal politics: A patchwork quilt, but not a blanket of evidence. In R. R. Lau & D. O. Sears (Eds.), *Political cognition: The 19th annual Carnegie symposium on cognition.* Hillsdale, NJ: Erlbaum.

Forgas, J. P. (1995). Mood and judgment: The affect infusion model (AIM). *Psychological Review, 117,* 39–66.

Forgas, J. P., Kagan, C., & Frey, D. (1977). The cognitive representation of political personalities. A cross-cultural comparison. *International Journal of Psychology, 12,* 19–30.

Funk, C. L. (1997). Implications of political expertise in candidate trait evaluations. *Political Research Quarterly, 50,* 675–697.

Glaser, J., & Salovey, P. (in press). Affect in electoral politics. *Personality and Social Psychology Review.*

Gruenfeld, D. H. (1995). Status, ideology, and integrative complexity on the US Supreme Court: Rethinking the politics of political decision making. *Journal of Personality and Social Psychology, 68,* 5–20.

Hastie, R., & Park, B. (1986). The relationship between memory and judgments depends on whether the task is memory based or on-line. *Psychological Review, 93,* 258–268.

Houston, D. A., & Roskos-Ewoldsen, D. (in press). The cancellation-and-focus model of choice and preferences for political candidates. *Basic and Applied Social Psychology.*

Houston, D. A., Doan, K., & Roskos-Ewoldsen, D. (in press). Negative political advertising and choice conflict. *Journal of Experimental Psychology: Applied.*

Huddy, L., & Sears, D. O. (1995). Opposition to bilingual education: Prejudice or the defense of realistic interests? *Social Psychology Quarterly, 58,* 133–143.

Hurwitz, J., & Peffley, M. A. (1987). How are foreign policy attitudes structured? A hierarchical model. *American Political Science Review, 81,* 1099–1120.

Isbell, L. M., & Wyer, R. S. (in press). Correcting for mood-induced bias in the evaluation of political candidates: The roles of intrinsic and extrinsic motivation. *Personality and Social Psychology Bulletin.*

Iyengar, S., & Kinder, D. R. (1987). *News that matters: Television and American opinion.* Chicago: University of Chicago Press.

Iyengar, S., & Ottati, V. (1994). Cognitive perspective in political psychology. In R. S. Wyer & T. K. Srull (Eds.), *Handbook of social cognition, Vol. 2: Applications* (pp. 143–187). Hillsdale, NJ: Erlbaum.

Iyengar, S., & Petrocik, J. R. (1998). "Basic rule" voting: The impact of campaigns on party and approval based voting. Paper presented at the Conference on Political Advertising in Election Campaigns, American University, Washington, DC.

Jacoby, W. G. (1995). The structure of ideological thinking in the American electorate. *American Journal of Political Science, 39,* 314–335.

Judd, C. M., & Krosnick, J. A. (1989). The structural bases of consistency among political attitudes: Effects of political expertise and attitude importance. In A. R. Pratkanis, S. J. Breckler, & A. G. Greenwald (Eds.), *Attitude structure and function* (pp. 99–128). Hillsdale, NJ: Erlbaum.

Karasawa, M. (1998). Eliminating national stereotypes: Direct versus indirect disconfirmation of beliefs in covariation. *Japanese Psychological Review, 40,* 61–73.

Kinder, D. R. (1986). Presidential character revisited. In R. R. Lau & D. O. Sears (Eds.), *Political cognition: The 19th annual Carnegie symposium on cognition* (pp. 233–255). Hillsdale, NJ: Erlbaum.

Kinder, D. R., & Sears, D. O. (1981). Prejudice and politics: Symbolic racism versus racial threats to the good life. *Journal of Personality and Social Psychology, 40,* 414–431.

Klein, J. G. (1991). Negativity effects in impression formation: A test in the political arena. *Personality and Social Psychology Bulletin, 17,* 412–418.

Krosnick, J. (1988). Psychological perspectives on political candidate perception: A review of the projection hypothesis. Paper presented at the 1988 annual meeting of the Midwest Political Science Association.

Krosnick, J. A., & Brannon, L. A. (1993). The media and the foundations of presidential support: George Bush and the Persian Gulf conflict. *Journal of Social Issues, 49,* 167–182.

Krosnick, J. A., & Kinder, D. R. (1990). Altering the foundations of popular support for the president through priming. *American Political Science Review, 84,* 497–512.

Krosnick, J. A., Berent, M. K., & Boninger, D. S. (1994). Pockets of responsibility in the American electorate: Findings of a research program on attitude importance. *Political Communication, 11,* 391–411.

Kuklinski, J. H., Riggle, E., Ottati, V., Schwarz, N., & Wyer, R. S. (1991). The cognitive and affective bases of political tolerance judgments. *American Journal of Political Science, 35,* 1–27.

Lau, R. R. (1985). Two explanations for negativity effects in political behavior. *American Journal of Political Science, 29,* 119–138.

Lau, R. R., Smith, R. A., & Fiske, S. T. (1991). Political beliefs, policy interpretations, and political persuasion. *Journal of Politics, 58,* 644–675.

Lavine, H., Thomsen, C. J., Zanna, M. P., & Borgida, E. (1998). On the primacy of affect in the determination of attitudes and behavior: The moderating role of affective–cognitive ambivalence. Unpublished manuscript.

Lodge, M., & Hamill, R. (1986). A partisan schema for political information processing. *American Political Science Review, 80*, 505–519.

Lodge, M., & McGraw, K. (1995). *Political judgment: Structure and process.* Ann Arbor: University of Michigan Press.

Lodge, M., Steenbergen, M. R., & Brau, S. (1995). The responsive voter: Campaign information and the dynamics of candidate evaluation. *American Political Science Review, 89*, 309–326.

McGraw, K., & Pinney, N. (1990). The effects of general and domain-specific expertise on political memory and judgment. *Social Cognition, 8*, 9–30.

McGraw, K., Lodge, M., & Stroh, P. (1990). Order effects in the evaluation of political candidates. *Political Behavior, 12*, 41–58.

McGraw, K., Pinney, N., & Neumann, D. (1991). Memory for political actors: Contrasting the use of semantic and evaluative organizational strategies. *Political Behavior, 13*, 165–189.

Marcus, G. E., & Mackuen, M. B. (1993). Anxiety, enthusiasm, and the vote: The emotional under-pinnings of learning and involvement during presidential campaigns. *American Political Science Review, 87*, 672–685.

Martin, L. L., Ward, D. W., Achee, J. W., & Wyer, R. S. (1993). Mood as input: People have to interpret the motivational implications of their moods. *Journal of Personality and Social Psychology, 64*, 317–326.

Masters, R. D., Sullivan, D. G., Lanzetta, J. T., McHugo, G. J., & Englis, B. G. (1986). *Journal of Social Biological Structure, 9*, 319–343.

Mehrabian, A., & Ferris, S. R. (1967). Inference of attitudes from nonverbal communication. *Journal of Consulting Psychology, 31*, 248–252.

Miller, A. H., Wattenberg, M. P., & Malanchuk, O. (1986). Schematic assessments of presidential candidates. *American Political Science Review, 80*, 521–540.

Miller, J. M., & Krosnick, J. A. (in press). The impact of candidate name order on election outcomes. *Political Opinion Quarterly.*

Nadeau, R., Niemi, R. G., & Amato, T. (1995). Emotions, issue importance, and political learning. *American Journal of Political Science, 39*, 558–574.

Ottati, V. (1990). Determinants of political judgments: The joint influence of normative and heuristic rules of inference. *Political Behavior, 12*, 159–179.

Ottati, V. (1997). When the survey question directs retrieval: Implications for assessing the cognitive and affective predictors of global evaluation. *European Journal of Social Psychology, 26*, 1–21.

Ottati, V., & Isbell, L. M. (1996). Effects of mood during exposure to target information on subsequently reported judgments: An on-line model of misattribution and correction. *Journal of Personality and Social Psychology, 71*, 39–53.

Ottati, V., & Wyer, R. S. (1992). Affect and political judgment. In S. Iyengar & W. J. McGuire (Eds.), *Explorations in political psychology* (pp. 296–320). Durham, NC: Duke University Press.

Ottati, V., Fishbein, M., & Middlestadt, S. (1988). Determinants of voters' beliefs about the candidates' stands on the issues: The role of evaluative bias heuristics and the candidates' expressed message. *Journal of Personality and Social Psychology, 55*, 517–529.

Ottati, V., Steenbergen, M., & Riggle, E. (1992). The cognitive and affective components of political attitudes: Measuring the determinants of candidate evaluation. *Political Behavior, 14*, 423–442.

Ottati, V., Terkildsen, N., & Hubbard, C. (1997). Happy faces elicit heuristic processing in a televised impression formation task: A cognitive tuning account. *Personality and Social Psychology Bulletin, 23*, 1144–1157.

Ottati, V., Riggle, E. J., Wyer, R. S., Schwarz, N., & Kuklinski, J. (1989). The cognitive and affective bases of opinion survey responses. *Journal of Personality and Social Psychology, 57*, 405–415.

Petty, R. E., & Wegener, D. T. (1993). Flexible correction processes in social judgment: Correcting for context-induced contrast. *Journal of Experimental Social Psychology, 29*, 137–165.

Rahn, W. M., & Cramer, K. J. (1996). Activation and application of political party stereotypes: The role of television. *Political Communication, 13*, 195–212.

Rahn, W. M., Aldrich, J. H., & Borgida, E. (1994). Individual and contextual variations in political candidate appraisal. *American Political Science Review, 88*, 193–199.

Rahn, W. M., Aldrich, J. H., Borgida, E., & Sullivan, J. L. (1990). A social–cognitive model of candidate appraisal. In J. Ferejohn & J. Kuklinski (Eds.), *Information and democratic process* (pp. 136–159). Urbana: University of Illinois Press.

Riggle, E., Ottati, V., Wyer, R. S., Kuklinski, J., & Schwarz, N. (1992). Bases of political judgments: The role of stereotypic and nonstereotypic information. *Political Behavior, 14*, 67–87.

Schwartz, S. H., Bardi, A., & Bianchi, G. (1998). Value adaptation to the imposition and collapse of Communist regimes in Eastern Europe. Unpublished manuscript.

Schwarz, N. (1990). Happy but mindless: Mood effects on problem-solving and persuasion. In R. M. Sorrentino & E. T. Higgins (Eds.), *Handbook of motivation and cognition*, Vol. 2 (pp. 527–561). New York: Guilford Press.

Schwarz, N., & Bless, H. (1992). Constructing reality and its alternatives: An inclusion/exclusion model of assimilation and contrast effects in social judgment. In L. Martin & A. Tesser (Ed.), *The construction of social judgment* (pp. 217–245). Hillsdale, NJ: Erlbaum.

Schwarz, N., & Bohner, G. (2001). The construction of attitudes. In A. Tesser & N. Schwarz (Eds.), *Blackwell Handbook of social psychology: Intraindividual processes* (pp. 436–457). Oxford: Blackwell Publishing.

Schwarz, N., & Clore, G. L. (1983). Mood, misattribution, and judgments of well-being: Informative functions of affective states. *Journal of Personality and Social Psychology, 45*, 513–523.

Schwarz, N., Bless, H., & Bohner, G. (1991). Mood and persuasion: Affective states influence the processing of persuasive communications. In M. Zanna (Ed.), *Advances in experimental social psychology*, Vol. 24 (pp. 161–199). San Diego, CA: Academic Press.

Sears, D. O. (1997). The impact of self-interest on attitudes: A symbolic politics perspective on differences between survey and experimental findings: Comment of Crano (1997). *Journal of Personality and Social Psychology, 72*, 492–496.

Sears, D. O., Van Laar, C., Carillo, M., & Kosterman, R. (1997). Is it really racism? The origins of white Americans' opposition to race targeted policies. *Public Opinion Quarterly, 61*, 16–53.

Sidanius, J., Pratto, F., & Bobo, L. (1996). Racism, conservatism, affirmative action, and intellectual sophistication: A matter of principled conservatism or group dominance? *Journal of Personality and Social Psychology, 70*, 476–490.

Skitka, L. J., & Tetlock, P. E. (1992). Allocating scarce resources: A contingency model of distributive justice. *Journal of Experimental Social Psychology, 28*, 491–522.

Skitka, L. J., & Tetlock, P. E. (1993). Of ants and grasshoppers: The political psychology of allocating public assistance. In B. Mellers & J. Baron (Eds.), *Psychological perspectives on justice*. Cambridge, UK: Cambridge University Press.

Skowronski, J. J., & Carlston, D. E. (1989). Negativity and extremity biases in impression formation: A review of explanations. *Psychological Bulletin, 105*, 131–142.

Sniderman, P. M., & Piazza, T. (1993). *The scar of race.* Cambridge, MA: Harvard University Press.

Stapel, D. A., & Schwarz, N. (1998). The republican who did not want to become president: Colin Powell's impact on evaluations of the Republican Party and Bob Dole. Unpublished manuscript.

Sullivan, J. L., Aldrich, J. H., Borgida, E., & Rahn, W. (1990). Candidate appraisal and human nature: Man and Superman in the 1984 election. *Political Psychology, 11*, 459–484.

Tetlock, P. E. (1986). A value pluralism model of ideological reasoning. *Journal of Personality and Social Psychology, 50,* 819–827.

Tetlock, P. E., Bernzweig, J., & Gallant, J. L. (1985). Supreme Court decision making: Cognitive style as a predictor of ideological consistency of voting. *Journal of Personality and Social Psychology, 48,* 1127–1239.

Tversky, A. (1977). Features of similarity. *Psychological Review, 84,* 327–352.

Virtanen, S., & Huddy, L. (1998). Old-fashioned racism and new forms of racial prejudice. *Journal of Politics, 60.*

Wyer, R. S., & Ottati, V. (1993). Political information processing. In S. Iyengar & J. McGuire (Eds.), *Explorations in political psychology* (pp. 264–295). Durham, NC: Duke University Press.

Wyer, R. S., Budesheim, T. L., Shavitt, S., Riggle, E. D., Melton, R. J., & Kuklinski, J. H. (1991). Image, issues, and ideology: The processing of information about political candidates. *Journal of Personality and Social Psychology, 61,* 533–545.

CHAPTER EIGHT

When and How School Desegregation Improves Intergroup Relations

Janet W. Schofield and Rebecca Eurich-Fulcer

For centuries humankind has struggled with conflicts among racial and ethnic groups. This conflict shows no sign of abating. Indeed, in recent years animosity between groups has sparked problems ranging from genocidal wars in Bosnia and Rwanda to individual hate crimes around the globe (Levin & McDevitt, 1993; Mays, Bullock, Rosenweig, & Wessells, 1998). Thus, the issue of how to improve intergroup relations is still of vital importance.

In the United States, school desegregation has been viewed as a possible route for improving intergroup relations, as indicated in the famous social science brief filed in the *Brown* v. *The Board of Education* case that laid the basis for school desegregation there. Thus, a substantial amount of research has focused on this outcome. A smaller amount of similar research has been conducted in other countries, most especially Israel. Although pertinent research from other countries is included in this chapter, the vast majority of the works cited here are from the United States because so much of the research on school desegregation has been produced there. In this chapter we explore the conditions under which school desegregation is likely to positively impact intergroup relations. However, before turning to that we first briefly examine some of the complexities arising in determining whether, generally speaking, school desegregation can be viewed as a social policy successful in improving intergroup relations.

Assessing the Success of Desegregation as a Social Policy for Improving Intergroup Relations

---

Research suggests that school desegregation often, but far from always, has positive effects on intergroup relations (Schofield, 1995b). Specifically, there is a modest-sized body of work suggesting that desegregation tends to have long-term positive effects on relations between individuals from different backgrounds (Stephan & Stephan, 1996). For example, students who attend desegregated schools are more likely to work and live in desegregated environments as adults than their peers from segregated schools (e.g., Astin, 1982; Braddock & McPartland,

1989; Braddock, McPartland, & Trent, 1984). Similarly, having attended a desegregated school is associated with more positive responses to White co-workers among adult African Americans (Braddock & McPartland, 1989).

However, research on the short-term effects of desegregation on intergroup relations suggests a more mixed picture (Schofield, 1991; St. John, 1975). Indeed, Stephan and Stephan (1996) conclude that desegregation more often reduces than increases prejudice among African American students but that the opposite is true for White students. Similarly, work in Israel suggests that contact between students can lead to either improved or worsened relations (Ben-Ari & Amir, 1986).

Other factors in addition to these somewhat inconsistent results contribute to the difficulty of coming to a definitive conclusion about whether, generally speaking, desegregation is a successful mechanism for improving intergroup relations. First, there are numerous ways to define success. Conceptualizing success as the creation of schools in which students from diverse backgrounds function without significant amounts of overt conflict might well lead to a different conclusion than conceptualizing it as creating schools which positively change the attitudes that students carry with them to other settings since these two changes do not necessarily go hand in hand. In fact, in one desegregated school the first author and her colleagues found generally neutral to positive peer-oriented classroom behavior (Schofield & Francis, 1982), improvements in intergroup behavior over time (Schofield & Sagar, 1977), and increased racial prejudice on the part of White students over time (Schofield, 1989). Patchen's (1982) large-scale study of 12 desegregated high schools in a Midwestern city in the United States similarly found varying results, with attitudes toward outgroup members as a group, the amount of friendly interaction with outgroup members, and the amount of unfriendly interaction with outgroup members being influenced by different aspects of the school situation.

A number of methodological problems also limit our ability to draw unambiguous conclusions about desegregation's impact on intergroup relations. Researchers working on this topic face serious measurement challenges. For example, some human subjects committees object to measures inquiring about negative relations between students from different racial and ethnic backgrounds, fearing that completing such instruments might spark conflict. Furthermore, there are often practical constraints on the length of measurement instruments related to concerns over lost class time. Finally, evaluation apprehension and social desirability are especially serious challenges here since evaluation of students by adults is the norm in schools and intergroup relations is such an emotion-laden topic.

Studies in this area have also been criticized for flaws related to the uncritical borrowing of instruments from earlier work that make it difficult to interpret their meaning. For example, the dependent measures in almost two-thirds of the studies considered for a meta-analysis on school desegregation (Schofield & Sagar, 1983) were structured so that improvement in minority/majority relations could occur only if students began to choose outgroup members *rather than* ingroup members, thus embodying the questionable assumption that intergroup relations can improve only at the expense of intragroup relations. In addition, many studies have used sociometric techniques that capture information on children's best friends (Asher, 1993; Schofield & Whitely, 1983). Although friendship is important in fostering improved intergroup attitudes (Pettigrew, 1997), using a stringent criterion such as best friendship as a measure of change in desegregated schools seems likely to lead to the conclusion that there has been little or no change in situations where change in less stringent outcomes, such as willingness to associate with outgroup members, may have occurred. Finally, measures developed using one population, often Whites, have been too readily used with other populations without adequate attention to whether the phenomena studied are parallel enough in the different populations to justify this (Schofield, 1995b).

There are also several issues of study design that undercut the conclusiveness of findings in this area. First, desegregation studies are often plagued by self-selection problems at both the institutional and individual levels (Schofield, 1995b). Second, much of this research is correlational in nature, leaving open the question of the causal direction of any links found between school policies and student outcomes (Schofield, 1991, 1995a). Third, the majority of research dealing with the impact of desegregation is cross-sectional (i.e., comparing different groups of students with varying degrees of exposure to desegregation) rather than longitudinal (i.e., measuring the same students at various points in time, usually before and after desegregation) (Schofield, 1995b).

Unfortunately, even longitudinal studies in this area frequently have serious problems. Few span more than one year, often the first year of desegregation, which limits generalization from their findings since all involved are in the midst of adjusting to the desegregated situation during that year (Schofield, 1995b). Although occasional studies do span two to five or more years (e.g., Gerard & Miller, 1975; Savage, 1971; Schofield, 1979, 1989; Smith, 1971), they often have marked attrition problems. For example, Gerard and Miller lost approximately one-third of their sample during three years of data collection. Finally, many longitudinal studies employ no control group because of difficulties associated with locating appropriate ones (Schofield, 1995b). Given that there are both age trends (see Aboud & Amato, 2001) and historical trends in many of the variables studied as outcomes of desegregation, this is an especially serious problem.

Moreover, the production of research on desegregation slowed dramatically after the mid-1970s for a variety of reasons (Schofield, 1991). The mere fact that much of this research is 20 or more years old does not necessarily invalidate it (Schofield, 1998). It does, however, limit its usefulness for drawing conclusions about the present given that substantial changes in racial attitudes have taken place over that time period (Schuman, Steeh, Bobo, & Krysan, 1997). Furthermore, demographic changes mean that schools increasingly serve multiple groups of children from diverse backgrounds rather than virtually exclusively White and African American children which was often the case in the United States in the desegregated schools studied in earlier years (Orfield & Yun, 1999). This clearly changes the nature of many of the intergroup relations issues that arise (Peshkin, 1991).

Another factor that makes it difficult to reach a definitive conclusion about the success of desegregation is that researchers have often ignored the fact that desegregation can be implemented in very different ways, and that these differences may well affect their outcomes (Cook, 1979). For example, school desegregation can occur as a result of a court order or voluntarily. Either of these kinds of desegregation can be achieved through a wide variety of mechanisms such as pairing previously segregated schools, closing segregated schools, or redistricting. Additionally, studies of schools with diverse student populations are often seen as part of this literature even though no formal desegregation plan was involved because many of the intergroup relations issues that can be addressed in such milieus are similar to those addressed in studies of schools under formal desegregation orders. Further, researchers sometimes do not provide clear descriptions of the situation and implementation process, making it difficult to decide if a study involves formal desegregation or not, in addition to inhibiting comparisons across studies that might illuminate the factors accounting for their varied results.

Despite these important limitations, which make it difficult to assess the overall success of desegregation as a social policy designed to improve intergroup relations, the literature does offer substantial insight into when and how school desegregation may improve intergroup relations among students. Thus we now turn to an exploration of this topic.

Conditions that Promote Positive Intergroup Contact within Desegregated Schools

The social psychological perspective that has most importantly influenced work on school desegregation is known as the contact hypothesis. Allport's (1954) classic statement of this approach emphasized that the nature of the contact between groups would influence its effect and highlighted the importance of several specific factors including (a) the existence of opportunities to engage in close personalized contact with members of the other group; (b) an emphasis on cooperative rather than competitive activities; (c) the existence of equal status within the situation for members of all groups; and (d) the explicit support of relevant authority figures for positive intergroup relations. Since then researchers from around the world have suggested additional situational factors conducive to improving intergroup relations (e.g., Ben-Ari & Amir, 1986). Although this approach has been widely criticized as being little more than a "laundry list" whose increasing length has limited its utility (Pettigrew, 1986, 1998), the contact hypothesis has generated and helped organize a large body of research on school desegregation (Pettigrew, 1986). We now turn to a discussion of findings from school desegregation research organized by the set of conditions most commonly associated with the contact hypothesis.

Opportunities for close personalized contact with outgroup members: Contact as a necessary but not sufficient condition

From the perspective of the contact hypothesis, contact is a necessary but not sufficient condition for improving intergroup relations, since the structure of the contact situation is a moot point if there is no contact. Ironically, experience demonstrates that resegregation within desegregated schools is common (Eyler, Cook, & Ward, 1983; Schofield, 1995b), suggesting that even mere contact may be much less frequent there than one would expect. Indeed, in one racially mixed school a student remarked, "All the segregation in this city was put in this school," reflecting the fact that although students from different backgrounds attended that school they had little contact with each other there (Collins & Noblit, 1978, p. 195).

A number of common educational practices foster resegregation within desegregated schools. The most obvious and widespread of these are tracking and ability grouping. Schools that categorize students on the basis of standardized tests, grades, or related criteria tend to have resegregated classrooms (Epstein, 1985). Furthermore, it is difficult to provide an education for children for whom English is not a first language without a certain amount of resegregation, although constructive approaches to this situation have been suggested (California State Department of Education, 1983; Carter & Chatfield, 1986; Cazabon, Lambert, & Hall, 1993; Fernandez & Guskin, 1978; Garcia, 1976; Gonzalez, 1979; Heleen, 1987; Lindholm, 1992; Morrison, 1990; Ovando, 1990a, 1990b; Roos, 1978; Wright & Tropp, 1998).

Although being in classes together is a start, sitting in the same classroom may well not be enough to bring about substantial change over time as both Klein and Eshel's (1980) study of desegregated schools in Israel and Gerard, Jackson, and Conolley's work (1975) in the United States suggest. Anxiety about dealing with outgroup members is often prevalent and can lead to avoidance of the very opportunities for contact that might help to improve intergroup relations (Stephan & Stephan, 1985). Indeed, students often voluntarily resegregate themselves due to anxiety and other causes (Cusick & Ayling, 1973; Friedlaender, Lazarin, Soukamneuth, & Yu, 1998; Gerard, Jackson, & Conolley, 1975; Pinderhughes, 1998; Rogers, Hennigan, Bowman, & Miller, 1984; Schofield, 1989). For example, one set of studies of seating patterns in the cafeteria of a school whose student body was roughly half African American and half White reported that only about 5% of the students sat next to someone of the other race on a typical day (Schofield, 1979; Schofield & Sagar, 1977) in spite of the fact that there was little overt racial friction there.

Unfortunately, this resegregation is often especially marked during free time and extracurricular activities in school – situations quite likely to allow the kind of sustained and close personalized contact that contact theorists suggest is crucial to improving relations between students from diverse backgrounds (Amir, 1969, 1976). Although certain kinds of partial resegregation can serve useful purposes, such as helping minority adolescents cope with the personal impact of racial stereotypes (Davidson, 1996; Tatum, 1995, 1997), it is undeniably true that extensive resegregation undermines opportunities for the kind of close personalized contact which Allport (1954) and his intellectual heirs such as Cook (1978) and Pettigrew (1998) propose as an important first step toward improved intergroup relations.

Cooperation in the pursuit of common goals

One way in which opportunities for personalized interaction among members of diverse groups occur is through cooperative interaction in the pursuit of common goals. Consistent with this, Allport (1954) argues that it is important that the contact situation foster cooperation rather than competition. The type of cooperation most likely to lead to improved intergroup relations is cooperation toward achieving a shared goal that cannot be accomplished without the contribution of members of both groups (Bossert, 1988/89; Johnson & Johnson, 1992). Cooperation that is based solely on the receipt of shared rewards (i.e., reward interdependence) does not appear to reduce intergroup hostility (Brewer & Miller, 1984).

Schools in numerous countries have historically stressed competition which research suggests can lead to stereotyping, unwarranted devaluation of the other group's accomplishments, and marked hostility, even when the groups initially have no history that might predispose them to negative reactions to each other (Worchel, 1979). Thus, schools are not typically milieus particularly conducive to promoting cooperation.

However, during the past 30 years seven distinct approaches to cooperative learning suitable for use in schools have been developed and tested over substantial periods in field settings (Slavin, 1995). This research has been carried out in the United States with groups of African American, Hispanic, Asian, and White students; in Canada with recent European immigrants, West Indian immigrants, and Anglos (Ziegler, 1981); and in Israel with various groups as well.

All of these approaches pay careful attention to the way cooperation is structured. For example, in the jigsaw method each student in a heterogeneous six-person group is given information on a subtopic related to the unit on which their group is working. After reading and discussing this segment of the unit in another group composed of individuals from other teams in the class who are also responsible for this particular information, students return to their original group to share this information with its members so they can achieve their common goal of learning the entire unit. Thus students on a team have a common goal, all students play an essential part in their groups, and the impact of possible pre-existing status differentials relating to academic achievement or other factors is mitigated by all students having the opportunity to become an "expert" on their particular topic (Aronson, Blaney, Stephan, Sikes, & Snapp, 1978). Another of these approaches, group investigation, which has been developed and tested extensively in Israel, emphasizes mechanisms that produce participation and joint decision making regarding joint products by small heterogeneous groups of students (Sharan & Sharan, 1992).

A host of researchers have found positive results in experiments on the impact of these cooperative team approaches with children from diverse backgrounds (Aronson et al., 1978; Aronson & Gonzales, 1988; Bossert, 1988/89; Cook, 1985; DeVries and Edwards, 1974; Hertz-Lazarowitz & Miller, 1992; Johnson & Johnson, 1982; Johnson, Johnson, & Maruyama, 1983, 1984; Sharan, 1980; Sharan & Sharan, 1992; Slavin, 1997). Such cooperative groups appear not only to foster improved intergroup relations but also to have positive academic consequences (Johnson, Maruyama, Johnson, Nelson, & Skon, 1981; Slavin, 1995).

Although research on cooperation in extracurricular activities is much more limited than research on cooperative learning teams, extracurricular activities, especially those that foster cooperation, can also play a constructive role in desegregated schools (Hawley et al., 1983). For example, Patchen (1982) found that participation in extracurricular activities had a stronger relation to interracial friendship than almost any of the numerous other variables in his study. Consistent with this, one of the few variables correlated with a variety of positive intergroup attitudes and behaviors in Slavin and Madden's (1979) study was participation in integrated athletics. Similarly, Clement and Harding (1978) found that participation in a group designed to help teachers maintain order in a desegregated school created a sense of cohesiveness among the sixth grade students that fostered positive relations among them. Unfortunately, given the preceding, extracurricular activities are often segregated, becoming the "turf" of one group or another in a school (Schofield & Sagar, 1983).

Although cooperation holds great potential for improving intergroup relations, it must be carefully structured (Hertz-Lazarowitz, Kirkus, & Miller, 1992; Miller & Harrington, 1992; Slavin, 1992). For example, inter-team competition has been found to reduce the benefits of cooperative interdependence among team members (Johnson, Johnson, & Maruyama, 1983; Sharan, 1980). Furthermore, it is important that the students involved contribute to group efforts in ways that do not reinforce traditional modes of interaction between majority and minority group members. For example, Cohen (1972) has found that when White and African American children interact with each other, the White children tend to be more active and influential even when the children have been matched on a wide variety of factors likely to influence their performance. Only after a carefully planned program that included having the Black children teach their White peers new skills did this tendency abate (Cohen & Lotan, 1997). Moreover, it has been suggested that in order for cooperation to positively impact intergroup relations students should be assigned to groups in a manner that makes their race or ethnicity low in salience (Miller & Harrington, 1992), although more recent studies found that positive change does not generalize well under such circumstances (Brown, Vivian, & Hewstone, 1999; Van Oudenhoven, Groenewoud, & Hewstone, 1996). Thus, although conditions conducive to improving intergroup relationships are found in many cooperative situations, they are neither inevitable aspects of all cooperative situations nor are they strictly limited to them.

Reducing the salience of racial/ethnic identities.   One approach to reducing the salience of any one social category is to create what are called crosscutting categories (Schofield & McGivern, 1979; Vanbeselaere, 1991). It appears that creating additional, orthogonal bases of social categorization reduces the importance of any one categorization, such as race or ethnicity. Thus, for example, having African American and White students on each of two different cooperative learning teams means that racial background and team membership are crosscut. That is, students from different racial backgrounds now share something (i.e., team membership) with some members of the racial outgroup and simultaneously differ on that dimension from some members of their racial ingroup. If the social category that crosscuts racial or ethnic background is valued, meaningful, and salient, it may well undermine the tendency to discriminate based on the former (Brewer & Miller, 1984). Crosscutting role assignments with social categorizations during cooperative activities can also decrease intergroup bias (Bettencourt & Dorr, 1998) although it may not always be beneficial (Pepels, 1998).

Another constructive strategy is to create or emphasize shared social-category memberships for youths of different backgrounds, such as membership in a particular school or community (which rather than being crosscut with these memberships may be inclusive of them). Gaertner, Rust, Dovidio, Bachman, and Anastasio (1994) argue that the conditions espoused by contact theorists work because they induce individuals to alter their cognitive representations from that of separate ingroups and outgroups to a super-ordinate ingroup which encompasses previous outgroups. Based on this assumption, they conducted a study in a high school with a heterogeneous student body which measured students' perceptions of the extent to which the student body was one group or different groups. Students who held stronger perceptions that the student body was a unified group tended to show lower levels of bias than others. Thus, the creation of meaningful signs and symbols of shared identity (ranging from school T-shirts and traditions to special songs or the like) whether crosscutting racial identities or inclusive of them should be helpful in improving relations among diverse groups of students.

Creating affectively positive environments.   Research on cooperation suggests that its impact on intergroup relations may be influenced by the outcome of the cooperative effort. Specifically, cooperation appears to be beneficial when individuals experience success on the task, whereas failure has been found to be detrimental to intergroup relations since it can lead to scapegoating of the outgroup (Worchel, Andreoli, & Folger, 1977). Such findings are consistent with research demonstrating that positive emotions caused by a wide variety of events (including presumably those stemming from success in cooperative efforts) increase self-disclosure and interaction with previously unknown others (e.g., Cunningham, 1988).

Serow and Solomon's (1979) findings that the teacher's warmth and acceptance of children, which presumably create a positive atmosphere, were correlated with positive interracial peer behavior suggest that positive emotions may also operate to improve intergroup relations in desegregated settings. However, the relationship between positive emotions and positive intergroup relations is not necessarily a simple one since there is also research demonstrating that positive affect can lead to greater stereotyping and increased perceptions of outgroup homogeneity (Wilder & Simon, 2001).

Equal status

According to Allport (1954) the contact situation must also be structured in a way that gives equal status to the groups involved. Although some have concluded that equal status is not absolutely essential for improving intergroup relations (e.g., Patchen, 1982), others emphasize its importance (e.g., Amir, 1976; Brown, 1995; Schofield, 1979). Researchers working in the area of school desegregation have tended to distinguish between equal status among groups *within* the contact situation and equal status among the groups *outside* the contact situation (i.e., on the basis of pre-existing factors such as socio-economic status).

The relative status of racial or ethnic groups within a school may be influenced by the composition of the student body (Longshore & Prager, 1985). For example, if only a small number of students of a given background are present, they are unlikely to enjoy equal status since they form such a small group they will be unlikely to exert much influence in the institution. Consistent with the contact hypothesis, when minorities are a very small proportion of the total student body self-segregation seems to be heightened (Crain, Mahard, & Narot, 1982; Schofield & Sagar, 1983). For this and other reasons, experts suggest that minorities should represent at least 20% of the student body (Hawley et al., 1983) although some studies conducted in Israel have found no link between school composition and attitudinal change (Bizman & Amir, 1984).

The composition of the faculty and the administration is also important in the achievement of equal status within schools since, as in most organizations, the various occupational roles there are ordered in a status hierarchy. Unfortunately, there is a marked decline and shortage in the number of African American and other minority individuals who hold relatively high-status positions as teachers and administrators in schools in the United States (Boyer & Baptiste, 1996; Irvine & Irvine, 1983; King, 1993). Indeed, King (1993) notes that a large number of African Americans lost their jobs as teachers and administrators as a result of desegregation. Consequently, the way desegregation was implemented contributed to the under-representation of such individuals in high-status positions in the schools, which works against the improvement of intergroup relations.

Tracking and ability grouping, practices that clearly influence students' formal status within a school, are often instituted or emphasized in schools with heterogeneous student bodies. Unfortunately, given the substantial relationship between social class and academic achievement, unequal social status outside the school is likely to translate into unequal distribution of students from different backgrounds into the high- and low-status groups. Research suggests that tracking can undermine the achievement and motivation of students in lower tracks and has a negative effect on intergroup relations (Collins & Noblit, 1978; Epstein, 1985; National Opinion Research Center, 1973; Oakes, 1992). For example, Schofield (1979) reported that middle school students who had shown an increasing propensity to sit with other-race peers during lunchtime when they were seventh graders in heterogeneous classrooms moved toward more racially isolated seating patterns as eighth graders attending heavily tracked classes in the same school.

It is also important to realize that the extent to which the contact situation affords equal status to different groups may be a matter of interpretation (Robinson & Preston, 1976). Take something as apparently straightforward as the racial composition of the student body, which can be linked to status within the school as indicated earlier. Groups may misinterpret objective reality in a way that makes them feel disadvantaged. For example, Schofield (1989) reports that White students in a school that was roughly 50% African American were prone to overestimate the proportion of the student body that was Black, with one student even asserting it was "Wall to wall Blacks" (p. 167). Furthermore, groups may have quite different views of whether a given procedure indicates that they have equal status in a situation. For example, in this same public school White parents generally believed admissions polices were fair. However, their Black counterparts pointed out that all White children applying there were accepted whereas hundreds of Black children were turned away out of concern for racially balancing the school, a situation which they argued suggested that Black students were treated as less desirable than White ones.

Even if schools avoid practices and policies that foster unequal status within their walls by reflecting status differences outside of the school, differences in group status outside the contact situation can influence the evolution of intergroup relations within it. For example, Bizman and Amir's (1984) work suggests that the intergroup attitudes of Israeli minority group members may change more positively when their group has higher status than their majority peers, whereas an equal status situation produces the most positive change for majority group members. Furthermore, as previously mentioned, research stimulated by status expectations theory suggests that external status differentials may replicate themselves in specific contact situations by influencing individuals' expectancies. Thus, characteristics such as age, sex, race, or ethnicity may generate expectations that shape interactions by influencing the power and prestige order that emerges (Cohen & Lotan, 1997).

Finding ways to prevent the unequal status of students in the larger society from creating unequal status within the school is a difficult problem that has not yet been satisfactorily solved. However, efforts to achieve equal status within the contact situation do seem to make some difference. For example, textbooks often ignore or demean the experiences and contributions of minority group members (Boateng, 1990; McAdoo & McAdoo, 1985; National Alliance of Black School Educators, 1984; Oakes, 1985) which is not conducive to creating equal status for all students within the schools. However, efforts to remedy this can have positive results. For example, Stephan and Stephan (1984) conclude that multiethnic curricula have a positive effect on intergroup relations when the program elements are of some reasonable complexity and duration. A more recent review by Banks (1995) comes to the same conclusion. In addition, status intervention treatments developed by Cohen (Cohen & Lotan, 1997) also show encouraging results. Finally, Epstein (1985) found a clear positive link between equal status programs (e.g., emphasis on the equality and importance of all students and avoidance of inflexible, academically based grouping) and African American students' attitudes toward desegregated schooling.

Support of authorities for positive relations

Finally, Allport (1954) contends that the support of authority, law, and custom for positive equal status relationships is vital to producing positive change through intergroup contact. Indeed, Pettigrew (1961) found that when authorities sanctioned desegregation the events surrounding it transpired less violently than otherwise. Moreover, research which examines individual cases of school desegregation within the United States suggests that both community and leadership support are key variables associated with the successful implementation of desegregation plans (Beck, 1980; Stave, 1995).

Support from authorities is likely to lead to beneficial effects partly because it fosters the formation of values supporting positive intergroup contact. Consistent with this, Brewer and Brown (1998) argue that decisions such as the 1954 Brown ruling and the British Race and Sex Discrimination Acts of 1965 and 1975 created a social climate in which it became unacceptable to openly degrade or discriminate against minorities. However, such rulings are not likely to be translated directly into changes in students' intergroup attitudes and behavior although they are important symbolically.

For schoolchildren the most relevant authorities are probably their school's principal, their teachers, and their parents. In addition, as children move into adolescence peers become increasingly important arbiters of opinion and behavior. Although there is little research that empirically links principals' attitudes and behaviors to students' intergroup outcomes, those familiar with the functioning of desegregated schools generally agree that principals play an important role in shaping intergroup relations (Hawley et al., 1993). Principals can influence the course that desegregation takes through their actions toward teachers, students, and parents. First, they play an enabling function; that is, they make choices that facilitate or impede practices that promote positive intergroup relations, such as the adoption of cooperative learning teams. Second, they can model positive intergroup attitudes and behavior. Although there is no guarantee that others will follow the principal's example, it is likely to be helpful. Third, they can play a sensitizing function by putting the issue of intergroup relations on the school's agenda. Finally, the principal has the power to reward positive behavior and to discourage negative behavior through sanctions. Preventing negative intergroup behaviors is crucial because they can stimulate other negative behaviors in an escalating spiral. Indeed, one of the strongest predictors of unfriendly intergroup contact for both White and African American students is the students' general aggressiveness (Patchen, 1982). This highlights the importance of the principal's role in constructing an environment in which aggressive behavior is minimized.

Teachers are also important authority figures whose behavior affects relations between students. For example, Epstein (1985) found that teachers with positive attitudes toward desegregation use equal status instructional programs more than others and that students in such classrooms have more positive attitudes toward desegregation than peers in other classrooms. Patchen (1982) found a clear link between teachers' negative intergroup attitudes and White students' tendency to avoid their African American classmates. Gerard et al. (1975) found a relationship between teachers' prejudice and White children's acceptance of minority group students as friends that appeared to be mediated by the teachers' willingness to assign students to heterogeneous small groups for some of their classwork. Finally, Wellisch, Marcus, MacQueen, and Duck (1976) found more interracial mixing in informal settings among elementary school children whose teachers used classroom seating assignment policies that resulted in a lot of cross-race proximity than among children whose teachers tended to group children by race in their classrooms.

Awareness on the part of school authorities of the fact that individuals in a desegregated school may misunderstand each other's motives or intentions can be helpful. Also important is care in handling situations likely to result in intergroup conflict. For example, Greenfield's (1998) qualitative study of multiethnic sports teams in California high schools suggests that the coach's leadership style is crucial. The coach of the team that ended up having the fewest ethnic and racial tensions made it clear that intergroup hostility would not be accepted by meting out immediate public punishment to the team members when one member, a Euro-American boy, spoke in a disrespectful way to his African American teammate. In contrast, the coach of a team that ended up rife with such conflict typically avoided dealing with it or dealt with it as a private and individual manner, thus failing to set clear public norms against such behavior.

Although, as Aboud and Amato (2001) point out, children's racial attitudes are not simply a mirror of their parents' attitudes, parents are also important authority figures whose attitudes and behaviors can make a difference (Flanagan, Gill, & Gallay, 1998). For example, the active and violent resistance of parents in Boston to school desegregation, which included stoning buses and keeping their children out of school, clearly exacerbated the problems that occurred in implementing the desegregation plan there as did the actions of parents in many cities in the southern United States as well (Lukas, 1985). Furthermore, Patchen's (1982) work demonstrates that students who perceived negative parental attitudes toward the racial outgroup were likely to avoid intergroup encounters and to have more unfriendly intergroup encounters than their peers who perceived more positive parental attitudes. It is possible that participants in this study misperceived their parents' attitudes, so that this connection is a function of their own attitudes rather than those of their parents.

However, this and similar studies provide at least suggestive evidence of the importance of parental attitudes.

Thus, finding ways to encourage parents to support positive intergroup contact is likely to be important. Involving parents early in the planning process for desegregation, creating school and community-wide multiethnic committees involving parents, and providing information and opportunities for parental contact with the school all appear to be helpful (Hawley et al., 1983). Indeed, a study by Doherty, Cadwell, Russo, Mandel, and Longshore (1981) suggests that parent involvement in school activities can create more positive attitudes toward majority group members on the part of minority group students.

Peers may also be conceptualized as serving as authorities whose attitudes and behaviors regarding intergroup relations matter. Especially during adolescence, most students are members of peer groups and these tend to be important in influencing behavior, especially in times of anxiety or uncertainty when individuals tend to look to others for cues about their behavior (Fine, Weis, & Powell, 1997). Indeed, Blanchard, Lilly, and Vaughn's (1991) work shows that peers influence each other's expression of racist opinions. In addition, Patchen (1982) found that individuals' avoidance of outgroup members was clearly related to negative racial attitudes among their same race peers, which suggests that concerns about peer disapproval of intergroup contact can contribute to resegregation. Similarly, recent studies of multiracial schools by Carlson and Lein (1998), Friedlaender et al. (1998), and Pinderhughes (1998) suggest that peers play a strong role in influencing intergroup relations. Indeed, it seems likely that peer attitudes can inhibit or facilitate the development of intergroup friendships which is important in light of the accumulating evidence that such friendships positively influence intergroup attitudes (Pettigrew, 1997; Wright, Ropp, & Tropp, 1998).

Since pre-existing peer groups are likely to be racially homogeneous prior to desegregation, and contact may increase the salience of racial group membership, students are likely to look to their same-race peers for cues that influence them in important ways. Indeed, recently Wright, Aron, McLaughlin-Volpe, and Ropp (1997) concluded that there is considerable support for the idea that knowing that an ingroup peer has a close relationship with an outgroup member leads to more positive intergroup attitudes. This idea was tested in a recent quasi-experiment (Liebkind & McAlister, 1999). In this study, conducted with almost 1500 Finnish students aged 13–15 in schools with varying densities of foreign pupils, students in the experimental schools were presented with printed stories of ingroup members engaged in close friendships with members of the outgroup that were said to result in positive change in their attitudes toward the outgroup. They also participated in a discussion of these stories structured to elicit positive responses. Attitudes toward foreigners improved or remained stable in the experimental schools but declined or remained stable in the control schools in which students neither read the stories nor participated in the related discussion.

Although a well-structured contact situation is likely to be very important in influencing intergroup behavior, it must also be recognized that students often encounter each other outside of school in contexts that may be less well structured and that tensions from those encounters can spill over into the school day. Thus, peer tensions generated outside the contact situation may well affect what happens inside that situation. Furthermore, and more positively, work like that of Aboud and Doyle (1996), Tatum and Brown (1998), and Barroso, McAlister, Ama, Peters, and Kelder (1998) demonstrates that creative approaches can be developed to fostering peer processes to support positive intergroup relations.

Conclusions

In sum, there is no simple answer to the question of whether school desegregation has been successful in improving intergroup relations. A number of studies suggest that desegregation does have a positive long-term impact on intergroup realtions, but short-term outcomes appear to be more mixed. However, a substantial body of research has accumulated which provides useful guidance about the conditions that are likely to promote positive relations among students from diverse backgrounds, providing us with insights with the potential to enhance the known benefits of desegregation and to minimize possible negative outcomes.

Ironically, just as this body of research has accumulated, alongside a body of research that suggests that desegregation has modest positive effects on academic achievement and adult earnings for African Americans (Schofield, 1995b; Stephan & Stephan, 1996), commitment to desegregation as a social policy in the United States has virtually disappeared. A series of Supreme Court decisions in the 1990s changed the legal landscape significantly. Mandatory desegregation plans are being dissolved, voluntary ones are being challenged, and major districts in all regions of the country are phasing out their desegregation plans (Orfield & Yun, 1999). Furthermore, there appears to be a widespread public perception that desegregation has failed (Orfield, 1996), including an inaccurate perception that it has led to the massive exodus of Whites from the school districts involved. It is undeniable that desegregation has not eradicated the stubborn achievement gap between students of different backgrounds, that it has not automatically produced respectful positive relations between all students, and that some Whites leave desegregated districts (Rossell, 1990). Yet, in light of its documented accomplishments, the knowledge that has accumulated about how to enhance these outcomes, and the paucity of viable alternatives being considered to achieve the goals it serves, it seems shortsighted to abandon this policy because its benefits are less consistent and smaller in magnitude than many originally hoped they would be.

REFERENCES

Aboud, F. E., & Amato, M. (2001). Developmental and socialization influences on intergroup bias. In R. Brown & S. Gaertner (Eds.), *Blackwell handbook of social psychology: Intergroup processes* (pp. 65–85). Oxford: Blackwell Publishing.

Aboud, F. E., & Doyle, A. B. (1996). Parental and peer influences on children's racial attitudes. *International Journal of Intercultural Relations, 20*, 371–383.

Allport, G. W. (1954). *The nature of prejudice.* Cambridge, MA: Addison-Wesley.

Amir, Y. (1969). Contact hypothesis in ethnic relations. *Psychological Bulletin, 71*, 319–342.

Amir, Y. (1976). The role of intergroup contact in change of prejudice and ethnic relations. In P. A. Katz (Ed.), *Towards the elimination of racism.* New York: Pergamon Press.

Aronson, E., Blaney, N., Stephan, C., Sikes, J., & Snapp, M. (1978). *The jigsaw classroom.* Beverly Hills, CA: Sage.

Aronson, E., & Gonzalez, A. (1988). Desegregation, jigsaw, and the Mexican-American experience. In P. A. Katz & D. A. Taylor (Eds.), *Eliminating racism: Profiles in controversy* (pp. 301–314). New York: Plenum Press.

Asher, S. R. (1993, May). *Assessing peer relationship processes and outcomes in interracial and interethnic contexts.* Paper presented at the Carnegie Corporation Consultation on Racial and Ethnic Relations in American Schools, New York.

Astin, A. (1982). *Minorities in American education.* San Francisco, CA: Jossey-Bass.

Banks, J. A. (1995). Multicultural education and the modification of students' racial attitudes. In W. D. Hawley & A. W. Jackson (Eds.), *Toward a common destiny* (pp. 315–339). San Francisco, CA: Jossey-Bass.

Barroso, C., McAlister, A., Ama, E., Peters, R. J., & Kelder, S. (1998, November). *Reducing prejudice and promoting tolerance among Hispanic high school students: Preliminary results from a quasi-experimental pilot study in Houston, Texas.* Paper presented at the Workshop on Research to Improve Intergroup Relations Among Youth, National Research Council, Washington, DC.

Beck, W. W. (1980). Identifying school desegregation leadership styles. *Journal of Negro Education, 49,* 115–133.

Ben-Ari, R., & Amir, Y. (1986). Contact between Arab and Jewish youth in Israel: Reality and potential. In M. Hewstone & R. Brown (Eds.), *Contact and conflict in intergroup encounters* (pp. 45–58). Oxford, UK: Blackwell.

Bettencourt, B. A., & Dorr, N. (1998). Cooperative interaction and intergroup bias: Effects of numerical representation and cross-cut role assignment. *Personality and Social Psychology Bulletin, 24,* 1276–1293.

Bizman, A., & Amir, Y. (1984) Integration and attitudes. In Y. Amir & S. Sharan (Eds.), *School desegregation: Cross-cultural perspectives.* Hillsdale, NJ: Erlbaum.

Blanchard, F. A., Lilly, T., & Vaughn, L. A. (1991). Reducing the expression of racial prejudice. *Psychological Science, 2,* 101–105.

Boateng, F. (1990). Combating deculturalization of the African-American child in the public school system: A multi-cultural approach. In K. Lomotey (Ed.), *Going to school: The African-American experience* (pp. 73–84). Albany, NY: State University of New York Press.

Bossert, S. T. (1988/89). Cooperative activities in the classroom. In E. Z. Rothkopf (Ed.), *Review of research in education* (Vol. 15, pp. 225–250). Washington, DC: American Educational Research Association.

Boyer, J. B., & Baptiste, H. P., Jr. (1996). The crisis in teacher education in America: Issues of recruitment and retention of culturally different (minority) teachers. In J. Sikula, T. J. Buttery, & E. Guyton (Eds.), *Handbook of research on teacher education* (2nd ed., pp. 779–794). New York: Simon & Schuster Macmillan.

Braddock, J. H., & McPartland, J. M. (1989). Social-psychological processes that perpetuate racial segregation: The relationship between school and employment desegregation. *Journal of Black Studies, 19,* 267–289.

Braddock, J., McPartland, J., & Trent, W. (1984). *Desegregated schools and desegregated work environments.* Paper presented at the annual meeting of the American Educational Research Association, New Orleans, LA.

Brewer, M. B., & Brown, R. J. (1998). Intergroup relations. In D. T. Gilbert, S. T. Fiske, & G. Lindzey (Eds.), *Handbook of social psychology* (Vol. 2, 4th ed., pp. 554–594). Boston, MA: McGraw Hill.

Brewer, M. B., & Miller, N. (1984). Beyond the contact hypothesis: Theoretical perspectives on desegregation. In N. Miller & M. B. Brewer (Eds.), *Groups in contact: The psychology of desegregation* (pp. 281–302). Orlando, FL: Academic Press.

Brown, R. (1995). *Prejudice. Its social psychology*. Oxford, UK: Blackwell.

California State Department of Education. (1983). *Desegregation and bilingual education – partners in quality education*. Sacramento, CA: California State Department of Education.

Brown, R., Vivian, J., & Hewstone, M. (1999). Changing attitudes through intergroup contact: The effects of group membership salience. *European Journal of Social Psychology, 29*, 741–764.

Carlson, C., & Lein, L. (1998). *Intergroup relations among middle school youth*. Paper presented at the Workshop on Research to Improve Intergroup Relations Among Youth, National Research Council, Washington, DC.

Carter, T., & Chatfield, M. L. (1986). Effective bilingual schools: Implications for policy and practice. *American Journal of Education, 95*, 200–232.

Cazabon, M., Lambert, W. E., & Hall, G. (1993). *Two-way bilingual education: A progress report on the Amigos Program*. Santa Cruz, CA: National Center for Research on Cultural Diversity.

Clement, D. C., & Harding, J. R. (1978). Social distinctions and emergent student groups in a desegregated school. *Anthropology and Education Quarterly, 8–9*, 272–282.

Cohen, E. (1972). Interracial interaction disability. *Human Relations, 25*, 9–24.

Cohen, E. G., & Lotan, R. A. (Eds.) (1997). *Working for equity in heterogeneous classrooms: Sociological theory in practice*. New York: Teachers College Press.

Collins, T. W., & Noblit, G. W. (1978). *Stratification and resegregation: The case of Crossover High School, Memphis, Tennessee* (Final report). Washington, DC: National Institute of Education.

Cook, S. W. (1978). Interpersonal and attitudinal outcomes in cooperating interracial groups. *Journal of Research and Development in Education, 12*, 97–113.

Cook, S. W. (1979). Social science and school desegregation: Did we mislead the Supreme Court? *Personality and Social Psychology Bulletin, 5*, 420–437.

Cook, S. W. (1985). Experimenting on social issues: The case of school desegregation. *American Psychologist, 40*, 452–460.

Crain, R. L., Mahard, R., & Narot, R. (1982). *Making desegregation work*. Cambridge, MA: Ballinger.

Cunningham, M. R. (1988). Does happiness mean friendliness? Induced mood and heterosexual self-disclosure. *Personality and Social Psychology Bulletin, 14*, 283–297.

Cusick, P., & Ayling, R. (1973, February). *Racial interaction in an urban secondary school*. Paper presented at the meeting of the American Educational Research Association, New Orleans, LA.

Davidson, A. (1996). *Making and molding of identity in schools: Students' narratives on race, gender, and academic engagement*. Albany, NY: State University of New York Press.

DeVries, D. L., & Edwards, K. (1974). Student teams and learning games: Their effects on cross-race and cross-sex interaction. *Journal of Educational Psychology, 66*, 741–749.

Doherty, W. J., Cadwell, J., Russo, N. A., Mandel, V., & Longshore, D. (1981). *Human relations study: Investigations of effective human relations strategies* (Vol. 2). Santa Monica, CA: System Development Corporation.

Epstein, J. L. (1985). After the bus arrives: Resegregation in desegregated schools. *Journal of Social Issues, 41*(3), 23–43.

Eyler, J., Cook, V., & Ward, L. (1983). Resegregation: Segregation within desegregated schools. In C. H. Rossell & W. D. Hawley (Eds.), *The consequences of school desegregation* (pp. 126–162). Philadelphia: Temple University Press.

Fernandez, R. R., & Guskin, J. T. (1978). Bilingual education and desegregation: A new dimension in legal and educational decision-making. In H. LaFontaine, B. Persky, & L. H. Glubshick (Eds.), *Bilingual education* (pp. 58–66). Wayne, NJ: Avery Publishing.

Fine, M., Weis, L., & Powell, L. C. (1997). Communities of difference: A critical look at desegregated spaces created for and by youth. *Harvard Educational Review, 67*, 247–284.

Flanagan, C., Gill, S., & Gallay, L. (1998, November). *Intergroup understanding, social justice, and the "social contract" in diverse communities of youth: Foundations for civic understanding*. Paper presented at the Workshop on Research to Improve Intergroup Relations Among Youth, National Research Council, Washington, DC.

Friedlaender, D., Lazarin, M., Soukamneuth, S., & Yu, H. C. (1998, November). *From intolerance to understanding: A study of intergroup relations among youth*. Paper presented at the Workshop on Research to Improve Intergroup Relations Among Youth, National Research Council, Washington, DC.

Garcia, G. F. (1976). The Latino and desegregation. *Integrated Education, 14*, 21–22.

Gaertner, S. L., Rust, M. C., Dovidio, J. F., Bachman, B. A., & Anastasio, P. A. (1994). The contact hypothesis: The role of a common ingroup identity on reducing intergroup bias. *Small Group Research, 25*, 224–249.

Gerard, H. B., Jackson, D., & Conolley, E. (1975). Social context in the desegregated classroom. In H. B. Gerard & N. Miller (Eds.), *School desegregation: A long-range study* (pp. 211–241). New York: Plenum Press.

Gerard, H. B., & Miller, N. (Eds.) (1975). *School desegregation: A long-range study*. New York: Plenum Press.

Gonzalez, J. M. (1979). *Bilingual education in the integrated school*. Arlington, VA: National Clearinghouse for Bilingual Education.

Greenfield, P. (1998). *How can sports teams promote racial tolerance and positive intergroup relations? Key lessons from recent research*. Paper presented at the Workshop on Research to Improve Intergroup Relations Among Youth. Washington, DC.

Hawley, W., Crain, R. L., Rossell, C. H., Smylie, M., Fernandez, R., Schofield, J., Tompkins, R., Trent, W. P., & Zlornik, M. (1983). *Strategies for effective desegregation: Lessons from research*. Boston, MA: Lexington Books, D. C. Heath.

Heleen, O. (Ed.). (1987). Two-way bilingual education: A strategy for equity [Special issue]. *Equity and Choice, 3*(3).

Hertz-Lazarowitz, R., Kirkus, V. B., & Miller, N. (1992). Implications of current research on cooperative interaction for classroom application. In R. Hertz-Lazarowitz & N. Miller (Eds.), *Interaction in cooperative groups* (pp. 253–280). New York: Cambridge University Press.

Hertz-Lazarowitz, R., & Miller, N. (Eds.) (1992). *Interaction in cooperative groups*. New York: Cambridge University Press.

Irvine, I. W., & Irvine, J. J. (1983). The impact of the desegregation process on the education of Black students: Key variables. *The Journal of Negro Education*, 410–422.

Johnson, D. W., & Johnson, R. T. (1982). The study of cooperative, competitive, and individualistic situations: State of the area and two recent contributions. *Contemporary Education, 1*(1), 7–13.

Johnson, D. W., & Johnson, R. T. (1992). Positive interdependence: Key to effective cooperation. In R. Hertz-Lazarowitz & N. Miller (Eds.), *Interaction in cooperative groups* (pp. 174–199). New York: Cambridge University Press.

Johnson, D. W., Johnson, R., & Maruyama, G. (1983). Interdependence and interpersonal attraction among heterogeneous and homogeneous individuals: A theoretical formulation and meta-analysis of the research. *Review of Educational Research, 53*(1), 5–54.

Johnson, D. W., Johnson, R. T., & Maruyama, G. (1984). Goal interdependence and interpersonal attraction in heterogeneous classrooms: A meta-analysis. In N. Miller & B. Brewer (Eds.), *Groups in contact: The psychology of desegregation* (pp. 187–212). Orlando, FL: Academic Press.

Johnson, D. W., Maruyama, G., Johnson, R., Nelson, D., & Skon, L. (1981). Effects of cooperative, competitive, and individualistic goal structures on achievement: A meta-analysis. *Psychological Bulletin, 89*, 47–62.

King, S. H. (1993). The limited presence of African-American teachers. *Review of Educational Research,* *63*(2), 115–149.

Klein, Z., & Eshel, Y. (1980). *Integrating Jerusalem schools.* New York: Academic Press.

Levin, J., & McDevitt, J. (1993). *Hate crimes: The rising tide of bigotry and bloodshed.* New York: Plenum Press.

Liebkind, K., & McAlister, A. L. (1999). Extended contact through peer modelling to promote tolerance in Finland. *European Journal of Social Psychology, 29,* 765–780.

Lindholm, K. J. (1992). Two-way bilingual/immersion education: Theory, conceptual issues, and pedagogical implications. In R. V. Padilla & A. H. Benavides (Eds.), *Critcal perspectives on bilingual education research* (pp. 195–220). Tempe, AZ: Bilingual Press/Editorial Bilingue.

Longshore, D., & Prager, J. (1985). The impact of school desegregation: A situational analysis. *Annual Review of Sociology, 11,* 75–91.

Lukas, J. A. (1985). *Common ground.* New York: Knopf.

Mays, V. M., Bullock, M., Rosenweig, M. R., & Wessells, M. (1998). Ethnic conflict: Global challenges and psychological perspectives. *American Psychologist, 53,* 737–742.

McAdoo, H. P., & McAdoo, J. W. (Eds.) (1985). *Black children: Social educational and parental environments.* Beverly Hills, CA: Sage.

Miller, N., & Harrington, H. J. (1992). Social categorization and intergroup acceptance: Principles for the design and development of cooperative learning teams. In R. Hertz-Lazarowitz & N. Miller, (Eds.), *Interactions in cooperative groups* (pp. 203–222). New York: Cambridge University Press.

Morrison, S. H. (1990). A Spanish–English dual-language program in New York City. In C. B. Cazden & C. E. Snow (Eds.), *English plus issues in bilingual education* (pp. 160–169). Newbury Park, CA: Sage.

National Alliance of Black School Educators (1984). *Saving the African-American child.* Washington, DC.

National Opinion Research Center (1973). *Southern schools: An evaluation of the effects of the Emergency School Assistance Program and of school desegregation* (Vols. 1 & 2). Chicago, IL.

Oakes, J. (1985). *Keeping track: How schools structure inequality.* New Haven, CT: Yale University Press.

Oakes, J. (1992). Can tracking research inform practice? Technical, normative, and political consideration. *Educational Researcher, 21*(4), 12–21.

Orfield, G. (1996). Plessy parallels: Back to traditional assumptions. In G. Orfield & S. E. Eaton, and the Harvard Project on School Desegregation (Eds.) *Dismantling desegregation: The quiet reversal of Brown v. Board of Education.* New York: New Press.

Orfield, G., & Yun, J. T. (1999). *Resegregation in American schools.* Cambridge, MA: The Civil Rights Project, Harvard University.

Ovando, C. J. (1990a). Intermediate and secondary school curricula: A multicultural and multilingual framework. *The Clearing House, 63*(7), 294–298.

Ovando, C. J. (1990b). Politics and pedagogy: The case of bilingual education. *Harvard Educational Review, 60*(3), 341–356.

Patchen, M. (1982). *Black-White contact in schools: Its social and academic effects.* West Lafayette, IN: Purdue University Press.

Pepels, J. (1998). *The myth of the positive crossed categorization effect.* The Netherlands: Thela Thesis.

Peshkin, A. (1991). *The color of strangers, the color of friends.* Chicago, IL: University of Chicago Press.

Pettigrew, T. F. (1961). Social psychology and desegregation research. *American Psychologist, 15,* 61–71.

Pettigrew, T. F. (1986). The intergroup contact hypothesis reconsidered. In M. Hewstone & R. Brown (Eds.), *Contact and conflict in intergroup encounters* (pp. 169–195). Oxford, UK: Blackwell.

Pettigrew, T. F. (1997). The affective component of prejudice: Empirical support for the new view. In S. A. Tuck & J. K. Martin (Eds.), *Racial attitudes in the 1990s: Continuity and change*. Westport, CT: Praeger.

Pettigrew, T. F. (1998). Intergroup contact theory. *Annual Review of Psychology, 49*, 65–85.

Pinderhughes, H. (1998, November). *Forging a multicultural school environment: An examination of intergroup relations at an innercity high school – The P.R. O.P.S. program*. Paper presented at the Workshop on Research to Improve Intergroup Relations Among Youth, National Research Council, Washington, DC.

Robinson, J. W., & Preston, J. D. (1976). Equal-status contact and modification of racial prejudice: A reexamination of the contact hypothesis. *Social Forces, 54*, 911–924.

Rogers, M., Hennigan, K., Bowman, C., & Miller, N. (1984). Intergroup acceptance in classrooms and playground settings. In N. Miller & M. B. Brewer (Eds.). *Groups in contact: The psychology of desegregation* (pp. 213–227). New York: Academic Press.

Roos, P. D. (1978). Bilingual education: The Hispanic response to unequal educational opportunity. *Law and Contemporary Problems, 42*, 111–140.

Rossell, C. H. (1990). *The carrot or the stick for school desegregation policy*. Philadelphia: Temple University Press.

St. John, N. H. (1975). *School desegregation: Outcomes for children*. New York: Wiley.

Savage, L. W. (1971). *Academic achievement of Black students transferring from a segregated junior high school to an integrated high school*. Unpublished master's thesis, Virginia State College, Petersberg, VA.

Schofield, J. W. (1979). The impact of positively structured contact on intergroup behaviors: Does it last under adverse conditions? *Social Psychology Quarterly, 42*, 280–284.

Schofield, J. W. (1989). *Black and White in school: Trust, tension or tolerance?* New York: Teachers College Press.

Schofield, J. W. (1991). School desegregation and intergroup relations: A review of the literature. In G. Grant (Ed.), *Review of research in education* (Vol. 17, pp. 335–409). Washington, DC: American Educational Research Association.

Schofield, J. W. (1995a). Improving intergroup relations among students. In J. A. Banks & C. A. McGee Banks (Eds.), *Handbook of research on multicultural education* (pp. 635–646). New York: Macmillan.

Schofield, J. W. (1995b). Review of research on school desegregation's impact on elementary and secondary school students. In J. A. Banks & C. A. McGee Banks (Eds.), *Handbook of research on multicultural education* (pp. 597–616). New York: Macmillan.

Schofield, J. W. (1998). *Research on intergroup relations: The state of the field*. Paper presented at the meeting of the Forum on Adolescence, National Research Council, National Academy of Sciences, Washington, DC.

Schofield, J. W., & Francis, W. D. (1982). An observational study of peer interaction in racially mixed "accelerated" classrooms. *The Journal of Educational Psychology, 74*, 722–732.

Schofield, J. W., & McGivern, E. P. (1979). Creating interracial bonds in a desegregated school. In R. G. Blumberg & W. J. Roye (Eds.), *Interracial bonds* (pp. 106–119). Bayside, NY: General Hall.

Schofield, J. W., & Sager, H. A. (1977). Peer interaction patterns in an integrated middle school. *Sociometry, 40*, 130–138.

Schofield, J. W., & Sagar, H. A. (1983). Desegregation, school practices, and student race relations. In C. H. Rossell & W. D. Hawley (Eds.), *The consequences of school desegregation* (pp. 58–102). Philadelphia: Temple University Press.

Schofield, J. W., & Whitley, B. E. (1983). Peer nominations vs. rating scale measurement of children's peer preference. *Social Psychology Quarterly, 46*, 242–251.

Schuman, H., Steeh, C., Bobo, L., & Kryson, M. (1997). *Racial attitudes in America: Trends and interpretation, revised edition*. Cambridge, MA: Harvard University Press.

Serow, R. C., & Solomon, D. (1979). Classroom climates and students' intergroup behavior. *Journal of Educational Psychology, 71*, 669–676.

Sharan, S. (1980). Cooperative learning in teams: Recent methods and effects on achievement, attitudes, and ethnic relations. *Review of Educational Research, 50*, 241–272.

Sharan, Y., & Sharan, S. (1992). *Expanding cooperative learning through group investigation*. New York: Teachers College Press.

Slavin, R. E. (1992). When and why does cooperative learning increase achievement? Theoretical and empirical perspectives. In R. Hertz-Lazarowitz & N. Miller (Eds.), *Interaction in cooperative groups* (pp. 145–173). New York: Cambridge University Press.

Slavin, R. E. (1995). Cooperative learning and intergroup relations. In J. A. Banks & C. A. McGee Banks (Eds.), *Handbook of research on multicultural education* (pp. 628–634), New York: Macmillan.

Slavin, R. E. (1997). Cooperative learning and student diversity. In Y. Amir, R. Ben-Ari, & Y. Rich (Eds.), *Enhancing education in heterogeneous schools: Theory and application* (pp. 215–247), Ramat-Gan: Bar-Ilan University Press.

Slavin, R. E., & Madden, N. A. (1979). School practices that improve race relations. *American Educational Research Journal, 16*, 169–180.

Smith, L. R. (1971). *A comparative study of the achievement of Negro students attending segregated junior high schools and Negro students attending desegregated junior high schools in the City of Tulsa*. Unpublished doctoral dissertation, University of Tulsa.

Stave, S. A. (1995). *Achieving racial balance: Case studies of contemporary school desegregation*. Westport, CN: Greenwood Press.

Stephan, W. G., & Stephan, C. W. (1984). The role of ignorance in intergroup relations. In N. Miller & M. B. Brewer (Eds.), *Groups in contact: The psychology of desegregation* (pp. 229–255), Orlando, FL: Academic Press.

Stephan, W. G., & Stephan, C. W. (1985). Intergroup anxiety. *Journal of Social Issues, 41*(3), 157–175.

Stephan, W. G., & Stephan, C. W. (1996). *Intergroup relations*. Boulder, CO: Westview Press.

Tatum, B. D. (1995). Talking about race, learning about racism: The application of racial identity development theory in the classroom. *Harvard Educational Review, 62*, 1–24.

Tatum, B. D. (1997). Identity development in adolescence: "Why are all the Black kids sitting together in the cafeteria?" In B. D. Tatum, *"Why are all the Black kids sitting together in the cafeteria?" And other conversations about race* (pp. 52–74). New York: Basic Books.

Tatum, B. D., & Brown, P. C. (1998, November). *Improving interethnic relations among youth: A school-based project involving teachers, parents, and children*. Paper presented at the Workshop on Research to Improve Intergroup Relations Among Youth, National Research Council, Washington, DC.

Van Oudenhoven, J. P., Groenewoud, J. T., & Hewstone, M. (1996). Cooperation, ethnic salience, and generalization of interethnic attitudes. *European Journal of Social Psychology, 26*, 649–661.

Vanbeselaere, N. (1991). The different effects of simple and crossed social categorizations: A result of the category differentiation process or of differential category salience? In W. Stroebe & M. Hewstone (Eds.), *European review of social psychology* (Vol. 2, pp. 247–278). Chichester, UK: Wiley.

Wilder, D. & Simon, A. F. (2001). Affect as a cause of intergroup bias. In R. Brown & S. Gaertner (Eds.), *Blackwell handbook of social psychology: Intergroup processes* (pp. 153–172). Oxford: Blackwell Publishing.

Wellisch, J. B., Marcus, A., MacQueen, A., & Duck, G. (1976). *An in-depth study of Emergency School Aid Act (ESAA) schools: 1974–1975*. Report to the Department of Health, Education and Welfare, Office of Education. Washington, DC: System Development Corporation.

Worchel, S. (1979). Cooperation and the reduction of intergroup conflict: Some determining factors. In W. G. Austin & S. Worchel (Eds.), *The social psychology of intergroup relations* (pp. 262–273). Monterey, CA: Brooks/Cole.

Worchel, S., Andreoli, V., & Folger, R. (1977). Intergroup cooperation and intergroup attraction: The effect of previous interaction and outcome of combined efforts. *Journal of Experimental Social Psychology, 13,* 131–140.

Wright, S. C., Aron, A., McLaughlin-Volpe, T., & Ropp, S. A. (1997). The extended contact effect: Knowledge of cross-group friendships and prejudice. *Journal of Personality and Social Psychology, 73*(1), 73–90.

Wright, S. C., Ropp, S. A., & Tropp, L. R. (1998, August). *Intergroup contact and the reduction of prejudice: Findings in support of the friendship hypothesis.* Paper presented at the meeting of the American Psychological Association, San Francisco, CA.

Wright, S. C., & Tropp, L. R. (1998). Language of instruction and contact effects: Bilingual education and intergroup attitudes. Submitted to the *Journal of Educational Psychology.*

Ziegler, S. (1981). The effectiveness of cooperative learning teams for increasing cross-ethnic friendship: Additional evidence. *Human Organization, 40,* 264–268.

CHAPTER NINE

Addressing and Redressing Discrimination: Affirmative Action in Social Psychological Perspective

Faye J. Crosby, Bernardo M. Ferdman, and Blanche R. Wingate

Social justice has been a recurring theme in social psychology. Theorists and researchers in our field have long been interested in understanding how interactions among groups and individuals relate to broader patterns of intergroup relations. Because typically such patterns include quite negative forms, including domination, discrimination, prejudice, and exclusion, much of social psychology's attention has focused on ways to ameliorate these problems. More recently, social psychologists have also attended to positive forms of intergroup relations, such as intergroup cooperation and organizational diversity initiatives. Nevertheless, the field's dominant tenor has been that intergroup relations are fundamentally problematic. It is in this context that social psychologists have considered the implications and effects of affirmative action (AA), or more generally, societal and organizational policies designed to proactively reduce or eliminate unfair group-based historical disadvantages.

AA policies have been the object of much contention. In this chapter, we delineate the social psychological issues involved in the controversies over AA in the United States and review both theory and empirical research regarding reactions to AA policies. First placing AA in the context of historical patterns of discrimination, we go on to describe what AA is and why it is needed. We then review evidence regarding reactions to AA by both direct beneficiaries and members of privileged groups. Finally, we provide perspectives for enhancing future theory and research on AA.

The authors are grateful to Carol Bronson, Alice Eagly, David Kravitz, and the editors of this volume for carefully and thoughtfully commenting on earlier versions of this chapter.

Intergroup Discrimination and Exclusion

AA policies and programs exist in the context of and in response to long societal histories of systematic and institutionalized exclusion and discrimination. For example, in the United States, women have long been denied entry to the full range of educational and professional opportunities. Before the 1964 Civil Rights Act, legal segregation and discrimination by race were widespread. Past prejudice and discrimination have had persistent effects. Currently in the United States, racism and sexism mean that despite civil rights and other legislation designed to create equality, the experience and opportunities available to individuals are shaped by the relationships of their group to other groups (Benokraitis, 1997; Dovidio & Gaertner, 1998; Jones, 1997; Operario & Fiske, 1998).

While affirmative action policy is designed to overcome a long-term legacy of invidious intergroup discrimination, AA is not a perfect policy. Nor is it always perfectly implemented. This makes AA a particularly rich and challenging subject for psychologists. It is also a topic on which psychologists must be self-reflective. Although many psychologists attempt to portray their approach as objective and racially unbiased, the legacy of the field has been otherwise (Morawski, 1997) and one cannot really remain neutral on the topic. Views of affirmative action – pro and con – link to views about the proper relations among various groups (e.g., women and men) and between individuals within groups.

How investigators approach their research reveals a great deal about their assumptions regarding the phenomena of interest. In the case of AA, some researchers (e.g., Heilman, 1996; Nacoste, 1994) have made pronouncements about AA's potentially deleterious effects on the basis of results from experiments in which participants reacted to either merit-based or category-based selections of people for tasks and rewards. The persistent juxtaposition of merit-based versus category-based selection is based on the assumption that one cannot simultaneously pay attention to both merit and group membership. Yet most identity-conscious AA programs do exactly that. Some experimental designs assume, in other words, that selecting individuals for positions in a group-conscious fashion necessarily means that merit cannot be considered. But as Konrad and Linnehan (1999) point out, research designs that ask participants to consider both qualifications and group membership would more closely parallel actual AA practices. If they are to avoid bias, researchers must not expect their participants to assume that anyone selected for a job will be qualified except for persons from under-represented groups, such as men and women of color, or White women. The term "qualified minority" or "qualified woman" carries many associations, including the implication that these associations are not commonly expected. In the United States, however, we do not usually see – in the context of selection for jobs – the term "qualified majority group member."

Affirmative Action: What is it and Why is it Needed?

Affirmative action is a term that often appears in the media but that rarely is defined. In the broadest sense, AA occurs whenever an organization expends energy to make sure that equal opportunity exists. AA policies exist in a number of countries, including Australia (Kramer, 1994), Belgium, France, the Netherlands (Chalude, De Jong, & Laufer, 1994; De Vries & Pettigrew, 1994), Canada (Leck & Saunders, 1992), Malaysia (Abdullah, 1997), and Pakistan (Waseem, 1997). It is in the United States that AA has the longest – and possibly the most complicated – history.

In employment, AA has been the law in the United States since 1965, when President Johnson signed Executive Order 11246. At that time "classical affirmative action" (American Psychological Association, 1996) began. Classical AA essentially involves two steps. First, using well-established guidelines, an organization monitors its own practices to make sure it employs qualified people in designated groups in proportion to their availability. Second, if imbalances between availability and utilization are discovered, corrective measures are taken. Clearly, the monitoring processes require an organization to be aware of people's group memberships to make sure that it utilizes qualified people from the targeted groups (e.g., White women; African American, Hispanic, Native American, and Asian American men and women) in proportion to their availability. Since 1965, practices such as "set-asides" (reserving a specific proportion of jobs or contracts for members of a given set of groups) and "quotas" (requiring the hiring of specific numbers in targeted groups) were instituted by some organizations. Such practices rarely withstand legal challenge. President Clinton's administration has sought to eradicate practices that do not conform to the classical defini-tion of AA (Stephanopoulos & Edley, 1995).

In education, as in employment, the thrust of AA is to rid the system of hidden pockets of previously unacknowledged privilege and to open institutions to people from all backgrounds. Consider the University of California where the Regents have forbidden officials to notice ethnicity or gender in admissions. Administrators there support vigorous outreach programs to high schools and even to elementary schools. In addition, leaders like Chancellor Berdahl at Berkeley have urged reform of the admissions formula. Currently, extra points are awarded to Advanced Placement (AP) courses. Thus a B in an AP course receives four points – just the same number as an A in a "regular" course. Admissions to the university are determined in large part by a student's high school grade point average. Because wealthy school districts can afford to offer AP courses while poor ones cannot, the system unfairly advantaged wealthy people, who are disproportionately White. Now that vigilance has revealed the problem, thoughtful minds can work on solutions.

AA has had a critical role in reducing discrimination in the United States. A number of studies by economists have documented that both gender and ethnic disparities in pay are less pronounced among AA employers than among other employers (Tomasson, Crosby, & Herzberger, 1996). Recent scholarship has also shown that AA employers are more profitable than other employers (Reskin, 1998). AA has apparently fostered selection procedures that are more fair and valid than previous procedures (Konrad & Linnehan, 1999), perhaps especially by opening the doors to highly qualified applicants of all backgrounds.

What accounts for the superior economic effectiveness of affirmative action relative to passive equal opportunity? The superior effectiveness derives at least in part from the way that AA minimizes the consequences of a set of psychological processes that have been the object of intense study in the last decade. In 1982 Crosby first described what she has called "the denial of personal disadvantage." Over a dozen investigations have now replicated

Crosby's essential finding that individuals from disadvantaged groups tend to imagine that they personally are exempt from the problems that they know affect their group. It seems that people only notice the personal relevance of societal discrimination when the injustices are flagrant. In addition, a set of laboratory studies has demonstrated how even very intelligent and highly educated decision makers have difficulty detecting small inequities unless the data are presented in aggregated form (Clayton & Crosby, 1992). Because AA does not rely on aggrieved individuals to come forward on their own behalf, it helps organizations avoid allowing small injustices accumulate to the boiling point. Because classical AA operates by aggregating information, furthermore, it allows administrators to head off problems before they erupt into explosive situations. Research by Konrad and Linnehan (1995a) showed that identity-conscious strategies adopted because of AA were more likely to have a positive impact on the employment status of White women and men and women of color, while identity-blind structures did not lead to improved outcomes for members of these groups.

Reactions to Affirmative Action Programs

AA policy and AA programs (AAPs) are highly controversial. Why does one person endorse AA and another resist or disfavor it? While some polemicists (e.g., Steele, 1991) explain people's reactions in simplistic terms, most scholars (e.g., Bergmann, 1996; Bobo & Kluegel, 1993; Kravitz et al., 1997; Reskin, 1998; Tomasson et al., 1996; Turner & Pratkanis, 1994) acknowledge that a number of factors contribute to the range of reactions among White men, White women, and men and women of color in the United States.

Conceptualizing the factors

Some researchers focus on self-interest (including interested reactions on behalf of one's group) as one influence on people's reactions both to the policy and the practice of AA (Esses & Seligman, 1996). With few exceptions (Murrell, Dietz-Uhler, Dovidio, Gaertner, & Drout, 1994) women favor AA more than men do (Dovidio, Mann, & Gaertner, 1989; Golden, Hinkle, & Crosby, 1998; Goldsmith, Cordova, Dwyer, Langlois, & Crosby, 1989; Kravitz & Platania, 1993; Little, Murray, & Wimbush, 1998; Ozawa, Crosby, & Crosby, 1996; Tickamyer, Scollay, Bokemeier, & Wood, 1989). Endorsement of AA is greater among people of color than among Whites (Bobo & Kluegel, 1993; Bobo & Smith, 1994; Fine, 1992a; Golden et al., 1998; Kinder & Sanders, 1990; Konrad & Linnehan, 1995b; Kravitz, Klineberg, Avery, Nguyen, Lund, & Fu, in press; Little et al., 1998; Sigelman & Welch, 1991; Tomasson et al., 1996). Sometimes (Klineberg & Kravitz, 1999; Kravitz & Platania, 1993) but not always (Vargas-Machuca & Kottke, 1999) the reactions of Latinos fall somewhere between those of Whites and Blacks.

Given the vehement opposition to AA on the part of some Black men (e.g., Carter, 1991; Sowell, 1994; Steele, 1991) and some White women (e.g., Heilman, 1996), it seems unlikely that narrow self-interest is the only determinant of people's reactions to AA. Similarly, the resolute endorsement of AA specifically and of diversity initiatives generally by many White men shows that opinions about affirmative action are not simply dictated by personal self-interest (see e.g., Bowen & Bok, 1998; Ferdman & Brody, 1995; Wu & Taylor, 1996), Other factors must be at play.

Another important factor is fairness. For many people, AA is equated with unjustified preferential treatment (Belkin, 1998; Crosby & Cordova, 1996; Fine, 1992a), which violates basic principles of procedural or distributive justice (Clayton & Tangri, 1989; Opotow, 1997; Tyler, 2001). Unlike "equal opportunity" policies, AA may appear to some to penalize White males (Crosby, 1994; Heilman, 1996). Members of both dominant and nondominant groups react most favorably to outreach and other "soft" AAPs and least favorably to programs which are construed as giving preferential treatment to specific target groups (Kravitz, 1995; Kravitz & Platania, 1993; Nacoste, 1985).

Yet considerations of fairness may not be as straightforward as they first appear. Whether one sees AA as a fair or unfair policy may itself be an indicator of one's commitment to the dominant ideology in the United States. According to Kluegel and Smith (1986), three cognitions combine in the dominant meritocratic ideology. These cognitions are: (1) that everyone has an opportunity to succeed economically; (2) that success and failure are caused by individual factors instead of structural factors; and (3) that unequal outcomes are appropriate because they reflect the inequality of contributions. Those who are skeptical about the dominant ideology or distrust how the meritocratic ideal works in reality may see AA as a means to achieve real fairness (Crosby & Cordova, 1996; Haney & Hurtado, 1994), while those who subscribe to the dominant ideology and trust the operation of the meritocratic ideal may dislike AA (Crosby, 1994). The group-based systemic approach of AA, furthermore, may be uncongenial to individualistically oriented Americans, even when those Americans perceive that a problem exists (Ozawa et al., 1996). Deep ideological rifts may thus explain how opponents of AA can genuinely bristle at what they see as the injustice of the policy while proponents can, with equal sincerity, be dismayed at the hidden injustices of so-called "equal opportunity" which they envision as being exposed and corrected by AA.

When opposition to AA derives from a reluctance to acknowledge (let alone dismantle) the privileges of those at the top of the social hierarchy, then opposition may also be linked to racism and sexism. The unthinking equation of diversity with a lowering of standards is certainly racist and sexist. Racial prejudice is the belief that racial differences are tantamount to inherent superiority of a particular race. In their theory of aversive racism, Gaertner and Dovidio (1986) propose that White people are able to adopt egalitarian values while still possessing negative perceptions of Black people. McConahay (1986) argues that although modern racists shun traditionally racist beliefs, they have not entirely discarded their negative attitudes toward Black people. Based on these theories, it seems likely that there will be a relationship between attitudes toward AA and prejudice. If racism were dead in the United States, how could we explain that White people endorse programs designated to help (White) women overcome discrimination more than they endorse programs designated to help Black people overcome discrimination (Tomasson et al., 1996)? The finding that White students who think they are judging journalists' essays evaluate anti-AA editorials more positively than pro-AA editorials, especially when a Black writer is supposed to have written the editorial against AA (Sheppard & Bodenhausen, 1992) supports the proposition that racism helps fuel anti-AA sentiment. Similarly, sexist attitudes have been shown to affect not only men's general evaluations of various AA plans but also how just they perceive the plans to be (Tougas, Crosby, Joly, & Pelchat, 1995).

Of course, people's reactions to AA must be analyzed in terms of their understanding of the term. Many people openly admit that they are unsure about what AA really is and how it operates (Winkelman & Crosby, 1994). Political rhetoric muddies the waters considerably (Crosby, 1998). At least one survey has shown that people's definitions of AA influence their attitudes toward AA, even after taking into account gender, ethnicity, social class, and political orientation (Golden et al., 1998). Those who understand AA to be a system whereby organizations monitor themselves to make sure that utilization matches availability endorse the policy, but those who conceive of AA as a quota system do not. Researchers have demonstrated that they can affect people's assessment of AA by how they frame the issues (Kinder & Sanders, 1990).

Empirical evidence: Attitudes of the direct beneficiaries

Predictors of endorsement for affirmative action among direct beneficiaries. What factors are associated with endorsement for or opposition to AA among those who are not part of society's dominant group and who are members of groups typically targeted by AA programs? The data are not copious, but several studies are available.

Fairness is one factor determining how men of color and women react to AA. Vargas-Machuca and Kottke (1999) surveyed 126 Latino and 105 White women college students and employees about gender-based AA plans. The most powerful predictor of attitudes was perceived fairness: Women who thought AA was fair endorsed it. Perceptions of discrimination and acculturation did not predict attitudes toward the AAP, and self-interest and ethnic identity did, but much less strongly than fairness. Similarly, in a telephone survey of Hispanic immigrants and native-born Whites, Blacks, and Hispanics, Klineberg and Kravitz (1999) found that, overall, the key predictors of opposition to the typical AAP were the beliefs that AA gives unfair advantages to women and minorities and that the typical AAP involves strong preferential treatment. The belief that AA involves strong preferential treatment was not a significant predictor in the Hispanic groups, however.

Ideology has also been shown to be important. In a secondary analysis of election studies, Fine (1992b) looked at how age, education, income, gender, partisan affiliation, and core values (e.g., belief in hard work) statistically influenced opinions about governmental programs such as AA. Only 13% of the respondents disliked AA, while 26% endorsed it moderately and 61% endorsed it strongly. Those who believed in hard work were more likely to favor AA.

Self-interest matters too. Kravitz (1994) reported the results of five studies, including a telephone survey of 60 adults (13 White, 23 Black, and 24 Hispanic) employed in the Miami area. The survey assessed attitudes toward AAPs targeted at Blacks or Hispanics. Respondents' attitudes were more positive when the AAP was targeted toward their own ethnic group.

It is unclear whether knowledge (either first hand or theoretical) about AA is a strong predictor of attitudes among its direct beneficiaries. In an early case study by Goldsmith et al. (1989), a random sample of women and men employees and women students at Smith College spoke with an interviewer about AA and also rated the extent of their knowledge of AA. Trained coders also transcribed and coded the interviews for degree of knowledge about the law and its operation. Neither self-rated nor coder-rated knowledge predicted attitudes toward AA among the women employees or students. More recently, in a much larger-scale interview of randomly sampled Chicago area residents, Golden et al. (1998) found self-rated knowledge to predict endorsement of AA among women but not men and among ethnic minorities but not White people in the sample. Golden et al. also found that those with higher self-rated knowledge (and with more education) were more likely to characterize AA as a monitoring system whereas those with lower self-rated knowledge (and less education) were more likely to characterize AA as a quota system. Taylor-Carter, Doverspike, and Alexander (1995) presented a gender-based AA plan to respondents, accompanied by a strong argument in favor or against the fairness of the plan. They found a clear effect for the persuasive communication and no clear effect for raters' involvement or experience with AA.

Also unclear are the effects of first-hand experiences with racism and sexism. Vargas-Machuca and Kottke (1999) found that their participants' attitudes did not vary as a function of experiences with racism and sexism or of acculturation. On the other hand, in a series of studies, Matheson, Echenberg, Taylor, Rivers, and Chow (1994) found large differences between women in college and women working in the trades. The latter group, who had had more opportunities to experience sexism first-hand, supported AA much more strongly than the former.

Affirmative action and self-doubt.   Shelby Steele (1991) and others (Carter, 1991; Heilman, 1996) have proposed that AA can stigmatize its intended beneficiaries. Steele has voiced the related idea that the Black people who endorse and rely on AA are those with damaged pride. Similar ideas are often repeated in the media (e.g., Connerly, 1995). Meanwhile, other scholars (e.g., Branscombe & Ellemers, 1998) have proposed that opposition to AA among members of disadvantaged groups may indicate that the target has internalized society's stigma so that he or she can only bolster self-esteem and personal status by alienation from the ingroup.

What does the empirical evidence show? Although not voluminous, it shows that most women and most men of color do not feel diminished by AA policies. A 1995 Gallup poll asked 708 White women and minority group members the question, "Have you ever felt that your colleagues at work or school privately questioned your abilities or qualifications because of affirmative action or have you never felt this way?" (Gallup Short Subjects, 1995). Results showed that only 8% of White women, 19% of African American women, and 29% of African American men answered yes.

While most disadvantaged people feel undermined when told that they received benefit through special privilege instead of merit (Arthur, Doverspike, & Fuentes, 1992; Heilman, 1994, 1996; Nacoste, 1994; for a review, see Kravitz et al., 1997), only a minority of society's disadvantaged confuse AA with special privilege. In an early study (Ayers, 1992), a small sample of women of color reported on their reactions to being selected through AA for honors, awards, or jobs. One young woman was angered to have been chosen as the "best Black" student, but the older women expressed gratitude for being given an opportunity to show their value. A very senior administrator articulated the opinion that White people's distrust of an AA candidate is simply White people's contemporary "acceptable" form of racism, a form that is less detrimental than previous forms. A recent in-depth study of 800 women of color in U.S. corporations conducted by Catalyst (1998) echoes the results of Ayers's study: Most women of color see AA as a set of practices which enhance, and do not displace, the true reward of merit.

The positive effect is not limited to women. Taylor (1994) studied the responses of 319 White women, 40 Black women, and 32 Black men who were employed by companies that either did or did not have an AAP in place. Taylor found no evidence of AA's supposed deleterious effects. Instead, she found strong positive effects for workplace AAPs. For example, Black men employed by firms that utilized AA reported more occupational ambition and less cynicism than those who worked for companies without AAPs. One might wonder how (tiny) self-doubt that may arise from participating in an affirmative action program compares to the (enormous) self-doubt that arises from unemployment.

Nor do students appear undermined in their self-esteem by AA policies. In one survey (Truax, Cordova, Wood, Wright, & Crosby, 1998), 351 undergraduate students were asked their reactions to AA and also whether they wondered if their peers and professors thought that they had been admitted to college because of their ethnicity and not their intellectual abilities. Few of the White and Asian American students but a great majority of the African American, Hispanic, and Native American students felt that others doubted their ability in this way. These students also felt that their academic abilities were judged on the basis of ethnic stereotypes. Yet they overwhelmingly endorsed AA. Support for affirmative action and worry about the perceptions of Whites were positively although marginally correlated.

Schmermund, Sellers, Mueller and Crosby (1998) extended Truax et al.'s work by administering surveys to 181 Black students at five institutions in Western Massachusetts. Although Truax et al. could infer from the pattern of their data that students of color had not internalized what Major, Feinstein, and Crocker (1994) call "suspicion of inferiority," they had no direct evidence of students' academic self-esteem. The students in Schmermund et al.'s study also strongly endorsed AA and often claimed that their fellow students and professors viewed them with suspicion. While approximately 60% of the students thought other students doubted their competence and 50% thought professors did, less than one-third of the sample admitted that they sometimes doubted their own academic merit. Interestingly, there was a marginally significant negative association between self-doubt and endorsement for AA: Students who disliked AA felt more academically insecure than those who liked the policy. This relationship is the opposite of what Shelby Steele (1991) or some others (e.g., Heilman, 1996) would predict.

Data exist for samples even younger than college students. Miller and Clark (1997) asked 161 U.S. high school students about their faith in the American dream. The students endorsed the dream, but Black students agreed less than Hispanic, Asian, or White students with the concept that the United States provides equal opportunities for all races and classes. For these students, concluded Miller and Clark, outreach programs and other forms of AA were essential for the preservation of hope.

Empirical evidence: Attitudes among members of privileged groups

The great majority of studies have been done in the last decade among White males and others whom the researchers do not envision as the direct beneficiaries of AA. Many, but not all, of the studies include college students as the participants. Most, but not all, assess a number of different attitudes to see which of the attitudes alone and in concert statistically predict opinions about AA. To date there is no standard scale measuring attitudes toward AA, so some of the variability across studies may be due to differences in question wording.

Taken as a whole the available studies do warrant some conclusions in spite of variations. First, resistance to AA is often associated with prejudice. Second, opposition to AA among privileged people cannot be understood wholly in terms of prejudice or other undesirable traits such as base self-interest. Third, the association between prejudice and negative attitudes toward AA has remained fairly stable throughout the 1990s. All three conclusions are visible in Table 9.1, which like the text, presents the studies in chronological order to underscore the third point.

In chronological order, the first study published in the 1990s was a quasi-experiment conducted by Kravitz and Platania (1993). They asked 349 undergraduates – diverse in gender and ethnicity – to define AA and then to evaluate 24 practices (e.g., hiring to meet quotas, giving special training) as to how likely they were to be part of an affirmative plan and as to how good they were. For one-third of the participants, AA was framed in terms of women; for another third, it was framed in terms of minorities; and for the last third it was framed in terms of the "handicapped." Participants supported AA measures involving quotas less than other measures, and they supported AA for those with disabilities more than for women or ethnic minorities. Although, as we have already noted, women and ethnic minorities supported AA more strongly than men and White participants, there were no interactions involving gender or ethnicity of participants and of target groups.

Another study that found participants more set against AA programs for ethnic minorities than for others was conducted by Murrell et al. (1994). These researchers asked White students to evaluate AAPs that differed in terms of the target group (elderly, physically handicapped, or Black) and that were or were not justified by an explanation of their necessity. Reactions toward policies presented with justification were more positive than to those presented without justification. Programs said to benefit Blacks were evaluated much less favorably than programs said to benefit the elderly or the handicapped, especially when the programs were not justified in terms of diversity goals or past injustices.

The influences both of prejudice and of fairness considerations were demonstrated again – in nonstudent samples – in two quasi-experiments by Tougas et al. (1995). A neo-sexism scale was used to divide samples of male managers and professionals into those high or low in sexism. Participants were randomly assigned to read about programs in which merit was or was not emphasized and were then asked to evaluate the worthiness and fairness of the programs. Neo-sexism predicted low support for the programs in both studies, and explanations stressing merit predicted high ratings of fairness.

To test the hypothesis that attitudes toward AA are derived from perceptions of fairness, Kravitz (1995) used a questionnaire to assess attitudes of White and Hispanic university students toward eight different AA plans directed at Blacks. He found that attitudes toward specific AAPs were completely mediated by perceptions of fairness and not by evaluations of personal or collective self-interest. Attitudes toward AA as a policy varied as functions of self-interest and racism.

Nosworthy, Lea, and Lindsay (1995) used a similar methodology. In a study of Canadian undergraduates, they found that support depended on the nature of the AA program described to respondents. They also found that racial prejudice and adherence to justice norms contributed – both separately and in conjunction – to the students' feelings about the "soft" programs such as outreach. While all students were opposed to the use of quotas or to "hard" AA programs, only those who were racist or had a strong belief in the just world took issue with mild forms of AA such as an advertising campaign.

Clayton (1996), in two studies designed to evaluate college students' opinions about categorizing people on the basis of group membership, manipulated both the type of social group involved and the purpose of the categorization. Participants objected most to categorizing people on the basis of race, religion, or sexual orientation.

Sidanius, Pratto, and Bobo (1996) analyzed three extensive data sets. In a large random sample of White students at the University of Texas, they found that opposition to AA increased as a function of racism and also of conservatism. They replicated these findings in a random sample of White residents of Los Angeles County, among whom they also found that anti-Black hostility had little predictive value and that opposition to AA was greatest among those who believed that society ought to be hierarchically ordered. This was especially true among college graduates. The third sample of White students came from UCLA. Again, attitudes toward AA were most positive among nonracist liberals who desired an egalitarian rather than a hierarchical society.

Dietz-Uhler and Murrell (1998) asked 79 university students to evaluate a woman applying for admission to either their own university (ingroup, condition) or another university (outgroup condition) where the institution used standard or "affirmative action" (undefined) admissions programs. The standard admissions policy was seen as more just than the AA policy and highly qualified applicants received more favorable evaluations than applicants with weaker qualifications. Evaluations of the ingroup applicant were affected by the perceived fairness of the AA policy, but evaluations of the outgroup member were not.

Bobocel, Song Hing, Davey, Stanley, and Zanna (1998) conducted three studies to investigate whether people oppose AA because they perceive it to be unfair or because they are prejudiced. They found that, independent of prejudice level, opposition to AAPs was correlated with perceived violation of distributive and procedural justice norms. However, when participants were asked to evaluate AAPs that did not explicitly violate justice norms, opposition was positively associated with prejudice level. The authors concluded that prejudice and concern for justice are distinct sources of opposition to AA.

In a survey of Chicago area residents, Golden et al. (1998) found that people's definitions of AA significantly predicted their evaluations of the policy – even after controlling for ethnicity, gender, and political orientation. People who equated AA with a monitoring system endorsed the policy significantly more strongly than those who equated AA with quotas. Only 16% of the sample strongly opposed AA.

Little et al. (1998) surveyed university students (60% female, 21% non-White) about to enter the workforce regarding their opinions on equal opportunity employment and AA. Participants with lower levels of self-esteem were more likely to think that AAPs in the workplace would impair their future self-interests. A relationship between respondents' negative perceptions of AAPs and conviction that women and minorities were being given unfair advantages in society was also found.

Kravitz and Klineberg (1999) used data from an annual public opinion telephone survey of 424 U.S.-born Whites. Reactions to a tiebreak procedure (i.e., a statement explaining that a company would choose a Black candidate over a White candidate when they both had identical qualifications and Blacks were underrepresented in the company) were contrasted with reactions to a typical AAP. White respondents preferred the tiebreak procedure to other procedures, and the preference was strongest among the politically conservative.

Swim and Miller (1999) also reported multiple studies with college and noncollege populations. They examined the relationships among prejudice, White guilt, and attitudes toward a type of AA which some (e.g., Clayton & Tangri, 1989) would call "retributive affirmative action" in four different samples. Racial prejudice and White guilt were inversely related. Multiple regression analyses showed that prejudiced and guiltless Whites were more likely to dislike retributive AA.

Kravitz et al. (in press) conducted two studies designed to assess attitudes toward AA in the workplace. It was found that positive attitudes toward AA are related to the belief that the target group needs help and that AA will not impair organizational performance, but that White respondents whose AA schemata featured Black and Hispanic targets harbored negative attitudes toward AA.

In sum. Table 9.1 presents a summary. Nine of the surveys published in the 1990s assessing attitudes toward AA among the privileged members of society showed a link between prejudice and opposition to AA. Meanwhile, from seven of the studies one could infer that considerations of fairness were also influential.

Of course, we would be naive to assume that people's perceptions of fairness are unrelated to their preconceptions or prejudices. Consider in this regard the study by Kravitz and Klineberg (1999) where Whites endorsed a tiebreak procedure. It should be noted that other evidence, summarized by Dovidio and Gaertner (1998), suggests that it is highly unlikely that White judges would evaluate the same qualifications equally when held by Blacks and by Whites. Thus, a prejudiced person who values impartiality may see himself or herself as being impartial even when he or she is not (see also Brief et al., 1997).

Unlike the literature on attitudes among the direct beneficiaries reviewed above, only one survey of White people (Swim & Miller, 1999) linked attitudes toward AA with attitudes towards the ingroup. The lack of parallel is interesting. Why do so few researchers look at how attitudes toward affirmative action relate to identity issues among White people? Perhaps researchers are right to think that affirmative action poses no threat to the self-concept of Whites. Or maybe the researchers are just assuming that Whites are relatively invulnerable because American scholarship presumes that White people are the standard against which all other groups must be compared.

Table 9.1 Studies of the Bases of Reactions to Affirmative Action among the Privileged

Date	Researcher(s)	Population	Basis of Reactions			
			Fairness	*Prejudice*	*Self-interest*	*Other*
1993	Kravitz & Platania	Undergraduate students	X			
1994	Murrell et al.	White students	X	X		
1995	Tougas et al.	Male managers	X	X		
1995	Kravitz	Students rating AA policy	X	X		
		Students rating AA plans	X		No	
1995	Nosworthy et al.	Canadian students			X	
1996	Clayton	Students				X
		White students in Texas		X		
1996	Sidanius et al.	White people in Los Angeles		X		X
		White students at UCLA		X		X
1998	Dietz-Uhler & Murrell	Students	X			
1998	Bobocel et al.	3 samples	X	X		
1998	Golden et al.	Chicago residents			X	X
1998	Little et al.	University students				X
1999	Kravitz & Klineberg	Telephoned sample of Whites				X
1999	Swim & Miller	Various samples		X		
In press	Kravitz et al.	Whites		X	X	

Expanding the Conversation

Even people who agree that equality is desirable and that discrimination should be both avoided and redressed disagree on how best to achieve the desired results. The debate often can be reduced to the issue of whether group-conscious or identity-blind approaches are preferable (Ferdman, 1997). Group-conscious approaches to making choices about individuals take into consideration their identities and the group contexts that have shaped them. Identity-blind approaches seek to apply general principles to all individuals, regardless of group memberships (or at least those group memberships assumed to be irrelevant to the decision at hand). Affirmative action is a group-conscious approach for addressing discrimination; it seeks to proactively identify, assist, and include members of targeted groups that have been hurt by current or historical patterns of exclusion.

Both in the workplace and in education, much of the controversy over AA has to do with whether one sees people as members of a group or as isolated individuals. Many people, especially in Western cultures, react negatively when asked to think about themselves and others in terms of their ethnic group memberships (Ferdman, 1995; Markus & Kitayama, 1994; Sampson, 1989) because they believe that doing so is unfair. From an *individualistic perspective*, the ideal of justice is based on the notion that group memberships should not determine what happens to individuals (Ferdman, 1997; Gottfredson, 1988; Kluegel & Smith, 1986). Those taking a *group perspective* see rampant individualism as a way to obscure the disparate treatment and differential power that have characterized the history of race and ethnic relations in the United States (see e.g., Alderfer & Thomas, 1988; Gaines & Reed, 1995; Glasser, 1988; Jones, 1997; McIntosh, 1988; Nemetz & Christensen, 1995; Palmer, 1994). Indeed, a number of scholars (e.g., Haney & Hurtado, 1994; Ibarra, 1995; Pettigrew & Martin, 1987; Schofield, 1986) have shown how meritocratic policies in the United States, under the guise of being race-blind, have actually served to maintain and even enhance privilege for Whites. For example, most people find their jobs through someone they know. Because social networks are quite divided by race (Sincharoen & Hu, 1999), predominantly White organizations are more likely to find White applicants for job openings, unless proactive steps are taken to advertise among people of color. Also, the criteria used to define "merit" in most organizations are based on majority-culture norms. Ignoring group memberships will simply serve to perpetuate those norms and therefore give preferences to members of the dominant culture (Ferdman, 1997). Similarly, not paying attention to gender can be a way of reinforcing organizational cultures that give preference to traditionally masculine styles and characteristics (Jacques, 1997; Maier, 1999).

Not all subordinate groups in the United States share the same relation to dominant groups. The current and historical patterns of power relations between the groups, and the specific nature of contact and/or conflict between the groups are all variables that can impact and interact with AA policies. Thus, implementation of an outreach program for women that ends up targeting primarily White women may be seen quite differently by the mostly White men in a law firm than a selection system targeted at African American men and women. The latter may be seen, for example, as more different, less likely to assimilate, and as greater threats to the intergroup hierarchy (Sidanius & Pratto, 1999). Programs geared at Latinos in general have often not resulted in increased representation of Chicanos and Puerto Ricans, relative to the increase in other Latino subgroups, even though these are the two Latino groups that have been most discriminated against historically. This could be, in part, because the patterns of intergroup relations between Anglo Whites on the one hand and South Americans and Cubans on the other are quite different and generally less conflictual than those between Anglo Whites and Chicanos or Puerto Ricans.

Affirmative action practices share two goals, but not always in equal measure. First, AA exists to enhance diversity in specified groups such as undergraduate students or corporate managers. Second, AA exists to achieve fairness for all. AA's road to fairness rests on two underlying assumptions. The first is that fairness requires an explicit effort, especially given the unfair discrimination and oppression of yesterday and, oftentimes, of today. The second assumption is that fairness to individuals within categories is aided by taking cognizance of those categories. Thus, for example, if we are to assure the fair treatment of women and men, we must first notice who is male and female and note the treatment of people in each category. In this view, justice involves treating the whole group equally, not only selected individuals (Ferdman, 1997).

The importance of noting categorical information is probably greatest when previously monolithic groups embark on the quest for diversity (Dass & Parker, 1999; Ferdman & Brody, 1996; R. Thomas, 1990). But as organizations, and indeed society as a whole, come to embrace diversity, number counts will need to give way to more sophisticated analyses. Assessment of group representation purely in terms of numbers often tends to be framed from an assimilationist perspective (see Ferdman, 1997; Jones, 1998; Miller & Katz, 1995). When psychologists come to value truly diverse ways of thinking and acting, and when even the privileged White people see diversity as being in their own self-interest (Potts, 1994; Wheeler, 1994, 1995), we can help assure that AA goes beyond addressing and redressing discrimination toward diversity and inclusion. If we are thoughtful about affirmative action, we may come to consider not only the problems but also the opportunities created by intergroup distinctions.

REFERENCES

Abdullah, F. H. (1997). Affirmative action policy in Malaysia: To restructure society, to eradicate poverty. *Ethnic Studies Report, 15*, 189–221.

Alderfer, C. P., & Thomas, D. A. (1988). The significance of race and ethnicity for understanding organizational behavior. In C. L. Cooper & I. T Robertson (Eds.), *International review of industrial and organizational psychology* (pp. 1–41). Chichester, UK: Wiley.

American Psychological Association (1996). *Affirmative action: Who benefits?* Washington, DC.

Arthur, W., Jr., Doverspike, D., & Fuentes, R. (1992). Recipients' affective responses to affirmative action interventions: A cross-cultural perspective. *Behavioral Sciences and the Law, 10*, 229–243.

Ayers, L. R. (1992). Perceptions of affirmative action among its beneficiaries. *Social Justice Research, 5*, 223–238.

Belkin, L. (1998, November). She says she was rejected by a college for being White. Is she paranoid, racist, or right? *Glamour, 96*, 278.

Benokraitis, N. V. (Ed.) (1997). *Subtle sexism: Current practice and prospects for change*. Thousand Oaks, CA: Sage.

Bergmann, B. R. (1996). *In defense of affirmative action*. New York: Basic Books.

Bobo, L., & Kluegel, J. R. (1993). Opposition to race-targeting: Self-interest, stratification ideology, or racial attitudes? *American Sociological Review, 58*, 443–464.

Bobo, L., & Smith, R. A. (1994). Antipoverty policies, affirmative action, and racial attitudes. In S. H. Danziger, G. D. Sandefur, & D. H. Weinberg (Eds.), *Confronting poverty: Prescriptions for change* (pp. 365–395). Cambridge, MA: Harvard University Press.

Bobocel, D. R., Son Hing, L. S., Davey, L. M., Stanley, D. J., & Zanna, M. P. (1998). Justice-based opposition to social policies: Is it genuine? *Journal of Personality and Social Psychology, 75*, 653–669.

Bowen, W. G., & Bok, D. (1998). *The shape of the river: Long-term consequences of considering race in college and university admissions*. Princeton, NJ: Princeton University Press.

Branscombe, N. R., & Ellemers, N. (1998). Coping with group-based discrimination: Individualistic versus group-level strategies. In J. K. Swim & C. Stangor (Eds.), *Prejudice: The target's perspective* (pp. 37–60). San Diego, CA: Academic Press.

Brief, A. P., Buttram, R. T., Reizenstein, R. M., Pugh, S. D., Callahan, J. D., McCline, R. L., & Vaslow, J. B. (1997). Beyond good intentions: The next steps toward racial equality in the American workplace. *Academy of Management Executive, 11*(4), 59–72.

Carter, S. J. (1991). *Reflections of an affirmative action baby.* New York: Basic Books.

Catalyst (1998). *Women of color in corporate management: Dynamics of career advancement.* New York: Catalyst Inc.

Chalude, M., De Jong, A., & Laufer, J. (1994). Implementing equal opportunity and affirmative action programmes in Belgium, France, and The Netherlands. In M. J. Davidson & R. J. Burke (Eds.), *Women in management: Current research issues* (pp. 289–303). London: Paul Chapman.

Clayton, S. (1996). Reactions to social categorization: Evaluating one argument against affirmative action. *Journal of Applied Social Psychology, 26,* 1472–1493.

Clayton, S., & Crosby, F. J. (1992). *Justice, gender, and affirmative action.* Ann Arbor, MI: University of Michigan Press.

Clayton, S. D., & Tangri, S. S. (1989). The justice of affirmative action. In F. A. Blanchard & F. J. Crosby (Eds.), *Affirmative action in perspective* (pp. 177–192). New York: Springer-Verlag.

Connerly, W. (1995, May 3). UC must end affirmative action. *San Francisco Chronicle.*

Crosby, F. J. (1982). *Relative deprivation and working women.* New York: Oxford University Press.

Crosby, F. J. (1994). Understanding affirmative action. *Basic and Applied Social Psychology, 15,* 13–41.

Crosby, F. J. (1998). What is affirmative action? *Burkenroad Symposium.* A. B. Freeman School of Business. Tulane University.

Crosby, F. J., & Cordova, D. I. (1996). Words worth of wisdom: Toward an understanding of affirmative action. *Journal of Social Issues, 52,* 33–49.

Dass, P., & Parker, B. (1999). Strategies for managing human resource diversity: From resistance to learning. *Academy of Management Executive, 13*(2), 68–80.

Dietz-Uhler, B., & Murrell, A. J. (1998). Evaluations of affirmation action applicants: Perceived fairness, human capital, or social identity. *Sex Roles, 38,* 933–951.

Dovidio, J. F., & Gaertner, S. L. (1998). On the nature of contemporary prejudice. In J. L. Eberhardt & S. T Fiske (Eds.), *Confronting racism: The problem and the response* (pp. 3–32). Thousand Oaks, CA: Sage.

Dovidio, J. F., Mann, J., & Gaertner, S. L. (1989). Resistance to affirmative action: The implications of aversive racism. In F. A. Blanchard & F. J. Crosby (Eds.), *Affirmative action in perspective* (pp. 83–102). New York: Springer-Verlag.

Esses, V. M., & Seligman, C. (1996). The individual-group distinction in assessment of strategies to reduce prejudice and discrimination: The case of affirmative action. In R. M. Sorrentino & E. T. Higgins (Eds.), *Handbook of motivation and cognition: The interpersonal context* (Vol. 3, pp. 570–590). New York: Guilford Press.

Ferdman, B. M. (1995). Cultural identity and diversity in organizations: Bridging the gap between group differences and individual uniqueness. In M. Chemers, S. Oskamp, & M. A. Costanzo (Eds.), *Diversity in organizations: New perspectives for a changing workplace* (pp. 37–61). Thousand Oaks, CA: Sage.

Ferdman, B. M. (1997). Values about fairness in the ethnically diverse workplace. *Business and the Contemporary World, 9,* 191–208.

Ferdman, B. M., & Brody, S. E. (1996). Models of diversity training. In D. Landis & R. Bhagat (Eds.), *Handbook of intercultural training* (2nd ed., pp. 282–303). Thousand Oaks, CA: Sage.

Fine, T. S. (1992a). The impact of issue framing on public opinion toward affirmative action programs. *Social Science Journal, 29,* 323–334.

Fine, T. S. (1992b). Public opinion toward equal opportunity issues: The role of attitudinal and demographic forces among African Americans. *Sociological Perspectives, 35,* 705–720.

Gaertner, S. L., & Dovidio, J. F. (1986). The aversive form of racism. In J. F. Dovidio & S. L. Gaertner (Eds.), *Prejudice, discrimination, and racism* (pp. 61–89). Orlando, FL: Academic Press.

Gaines, S. O., & Reed, E. S. (1995). Prejudice: From Allport to Du Bois. *American Psychologist, 50*, 96–103.

Gallup Short Subjects (July, 1995). *Gallup Poll Monthly, 358*, 34–61.

Glasser, I. (1988). Affirmative action and the legacy of racial injustice. In P. A. Katz & D. Taylor (Eds.), *Toward the elimination of racism: Profiles in controversy* (pp. 341–357). New York: Plenum Press.

Golden, H., Hinkle, S., & Crosby, F. J. (1998). Reactions to affirmative action: Substance and semantics. *Institute for Research on Women and Gender Working Paper*. Ann Arbor, MI: University of Michigan, IRWAG.

Goldsmith, N., Cordova, D., Dwyer, K., Langlois, B., & Crosby, F. J. (1989). Reactions to affirmative action: A case study. In F. A. Blanchard & F. J. Crosby (Eds.), *Affirmative action in perspective* (pp. 139–146). New York: Springer Verlag.

Gottfredson, L. S. (1988). Reconsidering fairness: A matter of social and ethical priorities. *Journal of Vocational Behavior, 33*, 293–319.

Haney, D., & Hurtado, A. (1994). The jurisprudence of race and meritocracy: Standardized testing and "race neutral" racism in the workplace. *Law and Human Behavior, 18*, 223–248.

Heilman, M. E. (1994). Affirmative action: Some unintended consequences for working women. *Research in Organizational Behavior, 16*, 125–169.

Heilman, M. E. (1996). Affirmative action's contradictory consequences. *Journal of Social Issues, 52*, 105–109.

Ibarra, H. (1995). Race, opportunity, and diversity of social circles in managerial networks. *Academy of Management Journal, 38*, 673–703.

Jacques, R. (1997). The unbearable whiteness of being: Reflections of a pale, stale male. In P. Prasad, A. J. Mills, M. Elmes, & A. Prasad (Eds.), *Managing the organizational melting pot: Dilemmas of workplace diversity* (pp. 80–106). Thousand Oaks, CA: Sage.

Jones, J. M. (1997). *Prejudice and racism* (2nd ed.). New York: McGraw-Hill.

Jones, J. M. (1998). Psychological knowledge and the new American dilemma of race. *Journal of Social Issues, 54*, 641–662.

Kinder, D. R., & Sanders, L. M. (1990). Mimicking political debate with survey questions: The case of White opinion on affirmative action for Blacks. *Social Cognition, 8*, 73–103.

Klineberg, S. L., & Kravitz, D. A. (1999, April). *Ethnic differences in support for a "typical" affirmative action plan*. Paper presented at the Society for Industrial and Organizational Psychology meetings, Atlanta.

Kluegel, J. R., & Smith, E. R. (1986). *Beliefs about inequality: Americans' views of what is and what ought to be*. New York: Aldine de Gruyter.

Konrad, A. M., & Linnehan, F. (1995a). Formalized HRM structures: Coordinating equal employment opportunity or concealing organizational practices? *Academy of Management Journal, 38*, 787–820.

Konrad, A. M., & Linnehan, F. (1995b). Race and sex differences in line managers' reactions to equal employment opportunity and affirmative action interventions. *Group and Organization Management, 20*, 409–439.

Konrad, A. M., & Linnehan, F. (1999). Affirmative action: History, effects, and attitudes. In G. N. Powell (Ed.), *Handbook of gender and work* (pp. 429–452). Thousand Oaks, CA: Sage.

Kramer, R. (1994). Affirmative action in Australian organizations. In M. J. Davidson & R. J. Burke (Eds.), *Women in management: Current research issues* (pp. 277–288). London: Paul Chapman.

Kravitz, D. A. (1994, April). Public perceptions of affirmative action. In D. A. Kravitz (Chair), *Affirmative action: Psychological research and practitioner reactions*. Symposium conducted at the Society for Industrial and Organizational Psychology meetings, Nashville.

Kravitz, D. A. (1995). Attitudes toward affirmative action plans directed at Blacks: Effects of plan and individual differences. *Journal of Applied Social Psychology, 25,* 2192–2220.

Kravitz, D. A., Harrison, D. A., Turner, M. E., Levine, E. L., Chaves, W., Brannick, M. T., Denning, D. L., Russell, C. J., & Conrad, M. A. (1997). *Affirmative action: A review of psychological and behavioral research.* Bowling Green, OH: Society for Industrial and Organizational Psychology.

Kravitz, D. A., & Klineberg, S. L. (1999, April). *Predicting Whites' attitudes toward two affirmative action plans (AAPs).* Paper presented at Society for Industrial and Organizational Psychology meetings, Atlanta.

Kravitz, D. A., Klineberg, S. L., Avery, D. R., Nguyen, C. L., Lund, C., & Fu, E. J. (in press). Attitudes toward affirmative action: Correlations with demographic variables and with beliefs about targets, actions, and economic effects. *Journal of Applied Social Psychology.*

Kravitz, D. A., & Platania, J. (1993). Attitudes and beliefs about affirmative action: Effects of target and of respondent sex and ethnicity. *Journal of Applied Psychology, 78,* 928–938.

Leck, J. D., & Saunders, D. M. (1992). Canada's Employment Equity Act: Effects on employee selection. *Population Research and Policy Review, 11,* 21–49.

Little, B. L., Murray, W. D., & Wimbush, J. C. (1998). Perceptions of workplace affirmative action plans. *Group & Organization Management, 23,* 27–47.

Maier, M. (1999). On the gendered substructure of organization: Dimensions and dilemmas of corporate masculinity. In G. N. Powell (Ed.), *Handbook of gender and work* (pp. 69–93). Thousand Oaks, CA: Sage.

Major, B., Feinstein, J., & Crocker, J. (1994). Attributional ambiguity of affirmative action. *Basic and Applied Social Psychology, 15,* 113–141.

Markus, H. R., & Kitayama, S. (1994). A collective fear of the collective: Implications for selves and theories of selves. *Personality and Social Psychology Bulletin, 20,* 568–579.

Matheson, K., Echenberg, A., Taylor, D. M., Rivers, D., & Chow, I. (1994). Women's attitudes toward affirmative action: Putting action in context. *Journal of Applied Social Psychology, 24,* 2075–2096.

McConahay, J. B. (1986). Modern racism, ambivalence, and the Modern Racism Scale. In J. F. Dovidio & S. L. Gaertner (Eds.), *Prejudice, discrimination, and racism* (pp. 91–125). Orlando, FL: Academic Press.

McIntosh, P. (1988). *White privilege and male privilege: A personal account of coming to see correspondences through work in women's studies.* Working Paper No. 189. Center for Research on Women, Wellesley College, Wellesley, MA.

Miller, F., & Clark, M. A. (1997). Looking toward the future: Young people's attitudes about affirmative action and the American dream. *American Behavioral Scientist, 41,* 262–271.

Miller, F. A., & Katz, J. H. (1995). Cultural diversity as a developmental process: The path from monocultural club to inclusive organization. In J. W. Pfeiffer (Ed.), *The 1995 Annual: Volume 2, Consulting* (pp. 267–281). San Diego, CA: Pfeiffer.

Morawski, J. G. (1997). White experimenters, White blood, and other White conditions: Locating the psychologist's race. In M. Fine, L. Weis, L. C. Powell, & L. Mun Wong (Eds.), *Off White: Readings on race, power, and society* (pp. 13–28). New York: Routledge.

Murrell, A. J., Dietz-Uhler, B., Dovidio, J., Gaertner, S., & Drout, C. (1994). Aversive racism and resistance to affirmative action: Perceptions of justice are not necessarily color blind. *Basic and Applied Social Psychology, 15,* 71–86.

Nacoste, R. B. (1994). If empowerment is the goal . . . : Affirmative action and social interaction. *Basic and Applied Social Psychology, 15,* 87–112.

Nacoste, R. W. (1985). Selection procedure and responses to affirmative action: The case of favorable treatment. *Law and Human Behavior, 9,* 225–242.

Nemetz, P. L., & Christensen, S. L. (1995). The challenge of cultural diversity: Harnessing a diversity of views to understand multiculturalism. *Academy of Management Review*, *21*, 434–462.

Nosworthy, G. J., Lea, J. A., & Lindsay, R. C. (1995). Opposition to affirmative action: Racial affect and traditional value predictors across four programs. *Journal of Applied Social Psychology*, *25*, 314–337.

Operario, D., & Fiske, S. T. (1998). Racism equals power plus prejudice: A social psychological equation for racial oppression. In J. L. Eberhardt & S. T. Fiske (Eds.), *Confronting racism: The problem and the response* (pp. 33–53). Thousand Oaks, CA: Sage.

Opotow, S. (1997). What's fair? Justice issues in the affirmative action debate. *American Behavioral Scientist*, *41*, 232–245.

Ozawa, K., Crosby, M., & Crosby, F. (1996). Individualism and resistance to affirmative action: A comparison of Japanese and American samples. *Journal of Applied Social Psychology*, *26*, 1138–1152.

Palmer, J. (1994). Diversity: Three paradigms. In E. Y. Cross, J. H. Katz, F. A. Miller, & E. W. Seashore (Eds.), *The promise of diversity: Over 40 voices discuss strategies for eliminating discrimination in organizations* (pp. 252–258). Burr Ridge, IL: Irwin.

Pettigrew, T. F., & Martin, J. (1987). Shaping the organizational context for Black American inclusion. *Journal of Social Issues*, *43*, 41–78.

Potts, J. (1994). White men can help – but it's hard. In E. Y. Cross, J. H. Katz, F. A., Miller, & E. W. Seashore (Eds.), *The promise of diversity: Over 40 voices discuss strategies for eliminating discrimination in organizations* (pp. 165–169). Burr Ridge, IL: Irwin.

Reskin, B. (1998). *The realities of affirmative action in employment*. Washington, DC: American Sociological Review.

Sampson, E. E. (1989). The challenge of social change for psychology: Globalization and psychology's theory of the person. *American Psychologist*, *44*, 914–921.

Schmermund, A., Sellers, R., Mueller, B., & Crosby, F. (1998). *Attitudes toward affirmative action as a function of racial identity among Black college students*. Unpublished manuscript.

Schofield, J. W. (1986). Causes and consequences of the colorblind perspective. In J. F. Dovidio & S. L. Gaertner (Eds.), *Prejudice, discrimination, and racism* (pp. 231–253). Orlando, FL: Academic Press.

Sheppard, L. A., & Bodenhausen, G. (1992, August). *Prejudice and the persuasion process: Perceptions of affirmative action opponents and proponents*. Paper presented at the American Psychological Association Annual Convention, Washington, DC.

Sidanius, J., & Pratto, F. (1999). *Social dominance: An intergroup theory of social hierarchy and oppression*. Cambridge, UK: Cambridge University Press.

Sidanius, J., Pratto, F., & Bobo, L. (1996). Racism, conservatism, affirmative action, and intellectual sophistication: A matter of principled conservatism or group dominance? *Journal of Personality and Social Psychology*, *70*, 476–490.

Sincharoen, S., & Hu, L-T. (July, 1999). *Background characteristics and ethnic identity among African Americans*. Paper presented at the International Society for Political Psychology, Amsterdam, The Netherlands.

Sigelman, L., & Welch, F. (1991). *Black Americans' views of racial inequality: The dream deferred*. Cambridge, UK: Cambridge University Press.

Sowell, T. (1994). *Race and culture: A world view*. New York: Basic Books.

Steele, S. (1991). *The content of our character: A new vision of race in America*. New York: Morrow.

Stephanopoulos, G., & Edley, C., Jr. (1995, July 19). Affirmative action review. *Report to the President*. Washington, DC: Government Printing Office.

Swim, J. K., & Miller, D. L. (1999). White guilt: Its antecedents and consequences for attitudes toward affirmative action. *Personality and Social Psychology Bulletin*, *4*, 500–514.

Taylor-Carter, M. A., Doverspike, D., & Alexander, R. (1995). Message effects on the perceptions of the fairness of gender-based affirmative action: A cognitive response theory-based analysis. *Social Justice Research, 8,* 285–303.

Taylor, M. C. (1994). Impact of affirmative action on beneficiary groups: Evidence from the 1990 General Social Survey. *Basic and Applied Social Psychology, 15,* 143–178.

Thomas, R. R. (1990). From affirmative action to affirming diversity. *Harvard Business Review, 68*(2), 107–117.

Tickamyer, A., Scollay, S., Bokemeier, J., & Wood, T. (1989). Administrators' perceptions of affirmative action in higher education. In F. A. Blanchard & F. J. Crosby (Eds.), *Affirmative action in perspective* (pp. 125–138). New York: Springer-Verlag.

Tomasson, R., Crosby, F. J., & Herzberger, S. (1996). *Affirmative action: The pros and cons of policy and practice.* Washington DC: American University Press.

Tougas, F., Crosby, F., Joly, S., & Pelchat, D. (1995). Men's attitudes toward affirmative action: Justice and intergroup relations at the crossroads. *Social Justice Research, 8,* 57–71.

Truax, K., Cordova, D. I., Wood, A., Wright, E., & Crosby, F. (1998). Undermined? Affirmative action from the targets' point of view. In J. Swim & C. Stangor (Eds.), *Prejudice: The target's perspective* (pp. 171–187). New York: Academic Press.

Turner, M. E., & Pratkanis, A. R. (1994). Affirmative action as help: A review of recipient reactions to preferential selection and affirmative action. *Basic and Applied Social Psychology, 15,* 43–69.

Tyler, T. R. (2001). Social justice. In R. Brown & S. Gaertner (Eds.), *Blackwell handbook of social psychology: Intergroup processes* (pp. 344–364). Oxford: Blackwell Publishing.

Vargas-Machuca, I., & Kottke, J. L. (1999, April). *Latinos and affirmative action: Self-interest, fairness, past discrimination, and acculturation.* Poster presented at the Society for Industrial Organizational Psychology meetings, Atlanta.

De Vries, S., & Pettigrew, T. F. (1994). A comparative perspective on affirmative action: *Positieve aktie* in the Netherlands. *Basic and Applied Social Psychology, 15,* 179–199.

Waseem, M. (1997). Affirmative action policies in Pakistan. *Ethnic Studies Report, 15,* 223–244.

Wheeler, M. L. (1994). *Diversity training: A research report.* Report R-1083, The Conference Board, 845 Third Avenue, New York, NY 10022.

Wheeler, M. L. (1995). *Diversity: Business rationale and strategies: A research report.* Report 1130-95-RR, The Conference Board, 845 Third Avenue, New York, NY 10022.

Winkelman, C., & Crosby, F. J. (1994). Affirmative action: Setting the record straight. *Social Justice Research, 7,* 309–328.

Wu, C. M., & Taylor, W. L. (1996). *The resource: An affirmative action guide.* Washington DC: The Citizen's Commission on Civil Rights.

CHAPTER TEN

Intergroup Relations and National and International Relations

Thomas F. Pettigrew

Social psychology has long aspired to contribute to humane and rational public policy. This aspiration has been especially strong among those who focus on intergroup relations. Kurt Lewin, for example, established two research centers late in his life – one for basic group research at the Massachusetts Institute of Technology, the other for applied group research 200 miles away in New York City. He hoped to achieve "full-cycle" social psychology with basic and applied work mutually enhancing each other (Cialdini, 1995).

The discipline's ambitious policy aspirations have been only partially fulfilled. Yet there are many instances from around the world where social psychology has played an important role in shaping intergroup policy. A few examples of this influence are broad, dramatic, and well known. Most examples, however, are more circumscribed, out of view, and often achieved in concert with other social sciences. This chapter samples both types to provide an overview of the discipline's impact on policy. These varied cases then suggest critical issues that arise when social psychology ventures into the "real world" of intergroup relations.

Six Examples of Major Policy Influence

The racial desegregation of American schools

The first significant involvement of social psychology in dramatic social change remains the best-known instance of the discipline's influence. Kenneth Clark, working with the legal staff of the National Association for the Advancement of Colored People, rallied his social psychological colleagues to the cause of ending the racial segregation of the public schools in the United States. The list of those who testified as expert witnesses in federal district courts about the harmful effects of such segregation on African American children reads like a who's who of American social psychology at the time: Jerome Bruner, Kenneth Clark, Isadore Chein, Stuart Cook, Otto Klineberg, David Kretch, and Brewster Smith (Kluger, 1987).

Once the school cases were consolidated and reached the U.S. Supreme Court, Clark, Chein, and Cook prepared a social science appendix to the plaintiff's brief. Thirty-two experts signed this review of the evidence, with social psychologists joined by anthropologists, psychiatrists, and sociologists. In an unusual action, the High Court cited social science evidence in its historic opinion in the famous footnote 11 (U.S. Supreme Court, 1954). Having stated flatly that the "segregation of white and colored children in public schools has a detrimental effect upon the colored children," the Supreme Court found this finding to be "amply supported by modern authority." This social science authority, as listed in the footnote, cited specific papers by Clark and Chein on how racial segregation harmed the personality development of African American children. The Court also cited sociological evidence of the structural damage wrought by segregation as developed by Franklin Frazier and Gunnar Myrdal.

Later social psychologists again served as expert witnesses in shaping the implementation orders of lower courts in specific school districts. Here the distinction between merely desegregated and genuinely integrated schools became important. The distinction relied on Allport's (1954) intergroup contact hypothesis and the relevant contact research (Pettigrew, 1975). For further details, see Schofield and Eurich-Fulcer's chapter on school integration in this volume.

Worker participation in group decisions

Group dynamics were introduced into Japan after World War II by American occupation authorities and encouraged directly by Kurt Lewin (Sugiman, 1998). Japanese social psychologists soon replicated the classic Lewinian finding of the superiority of group decisions in behavior change (Lewin, 1952).

Japanese industry applied this extensive research to such programs as quality control circles and self-managed group activities. These programs altered the nature of employer–employee relations by providing workers' input into the decisions that directly affected the work process. Widely credited as a key factor in Japan becoming a low-cost producer of high quality goods, these worker participation programs became famous as an integral part of the nation's industrial efficiency. The irony is that this Western idea got recycled back to its origins as part of the widespread industrial adoption of "Japanese" methods (Sugiman, 1998). Japanese firms embraced this social psychological contribution to industrial policy while Western manufacturing resisted it until it saw Japan's success.

Second-language learning

Changing public perceptions on a crucial issue is difficult. But, if achieved, this new perspective can have major policy consequences. Wallace Lambert (1992) and his McGill University colleagues provide a striking example. In an extended project, McGill's social psychologists have addressed the intergroup language conflict in Canada's Quebec Province.

Their effort centered on developing bilingualism among children of English-speaking parents. Conventional wisdom and earlier research held bilingualism to be a serious handicap for school achievement, measured intelligence, and even adjustment. Lambert found this research literature extremely weak. No controls for social class, testing conducted only in the monolinguals' language, and other inadequacies characterized previous work. His research produced sharply different results. Bilingual children scored higher than monolingual children on a variety of tests of linguistic flexibility and on some cognitive tests as well. Nor were these results limited to Canada. Similar research showing advantages for bilinguals has been reported in Israel, Singapore, South Africa, Switzerland, and the United States with a variety of languages (Balken, 1970; Ben-Zeev, 1972; Ianco-Worrall, 1972; Torrence, Gowan, Wu, & Alioti, 1970).

Encouraged by such findings, Lambert set up "immersion education." English-speaking children spent their first three years of school almost exclusively surrounded by French with monolingual French teachers. The success of this effort has been widely recognized and emulated. In a reversal of traditional methods, second-language learning now employs immersion techniques in Canada and throughout the world. Despite some critical controversy, Lambert's research has substantially altered public perceptions about bilingualism and how it should be taught.

A bilingual compromise

While Lambert focused on the English speaking side of Quebec's bilingual issue, Richard Bourhis brought social psychological insights to the French-speaking side. As a cultural and linguistic minority within Canada, Francophones view Quebec as the last enclave in North America of a distinctive French society. Until the 1960s, English was the language of work and prestige in Quebec even though Francophones comprised most of the population. But then the Quebec government enacted a series of language laws designed to enhance the status of the French language. Anglophones resisted these new acts, and tensions between the groups heightened (Bourhis, 1994a, 1994b).

The controversy came to a boil in 1977 when the provincial government passed Bill 101. It banned the use of all languages other than French on all commercial and many road signs. Following a ruling by the Canadian Supreme Court on freedom of expression, the Quebec government had to consider a compromise. Militant Quebec nationalists wanted to retain only French on public signs, while Anglophones wanted a return to freedom of language choice.

At this point, Bourhis was called in by the Quebec government. He conducted research for the *Conseil de la Langue Française* that had a major influence in shaping a compromise. He proposed that bilingual signs again be allowed with the provision that French had to be twice as prominent as other languages.

Why the two-to-one split in favor of the French language? Bourhis based the ratio on research with the minimal group paradigm (Sachdev & Bourhis, 1991). By manipulating power differentials between ad hoc ingroup and outgroup members, these studies showed that respondents preferred membership in a dominant group whose share of power was not absolute (100%) but twice as much as that of the outgroup (Bourhis, 1994c). Then he tested his laboratory finding in the field with a probability survey of the Quebec population. The survey's results showed that relative to freedom of choice or French only, the majority of Francophones and Anglophones gave their preference for the 67–33% split. In 1993, the Quebec government allowed bilingual commercial signs with the two-thirds French requirement. Three years later, the compromise was even defended by the separatist *Parti Quebecois* minister who had originally crafted Bill 101.

Sex stereotypes and discrimination

The first U.S. Supreme Court recognition of social psychology's understanding of stereotyping came in 1989. Susan Fiske testified as an expert witness in *Hopkins* v. *Price Waterhouse*, a precedent-setting case involving sex discrimination.

Ann Hopkins, a competent professional at the accounting firm, was denied partnership in part because the firm evaluated her as "macho" and in need of becoming "more feminine" (Fiske, Bersoff, Borgida, Deaux, & Heilman, 1991, p. 1050). Fiske testified on her behalf. A major contributor to this literature, she focused on the discipline's research on stereotyping – the conditions that furthered it, indicators that reveal it, consequences of it, and remedies for it. On all counts, Fiske found that the firm had fashioned a situation where stereotypes can shape discriminatory treatment. Hopkins' solo situation encouraged stereotypes and did nothing to limit them.

In this and later cases, Fiske's testimony followed the outline she used in her writings on the subject (Fiske, 1998). Biases have automatic features; and in some ways such biases are socially pragmatic – people act on them or not according to the situation. Furthermore, if they are motivated, people can control their biases. And organizations and other social structures have the demonstrated power to motivate people to hold their biases in check. Each of these four steps in Fiske's testimony is supported by the discipline's available evidence (Fiske, 1998).

Increasing the importance of the case for psychology, the American Psychological Association (1991) filed an *amicus curiae* brief. It challenged the defendant's argument that Fiske's testimony was "intuitively divined" by providing a review of the evidence. Hopkins eventually won her discrimination suit, with the social psychological evidence on stereotyping playing a significant role throughout the seven-year litigation.

Peace in the Middle East

Many of the Palestinian and Israeli negotiators who engaged in the discussions that led to the Oslo Peace agreement in 1993 had worked together before. They shared a common vision that they could shape a win–win solution to achieve peace. Considering the long hostilities between the two opponents, how was this remarkable situation possible?

In part, it was achieved through the tireless efforts of Herbert Kelman. For more than two decades, Kelman (1997; Rouhana & Kelman, 1994) has applied his social psychological approach to Arabs and Israelis. His conflict resolution efforts use workshops that stress interactive problem solving. Numbering between 8 and 16 people, these small groups include social science facilitators. Politically influential people from both sides meet for unofficial and confidential interaction. Part of Kelman's skill is selecting the participants. They must be people who seriously entertain the notion of a peaceful solution to the conflict.

These workshops have a dual purpose (Kelman, 1997). One intention is to induce changes in the participants themselves as they develop a more differentiated view of their opponents. The workshops also increase the likelihood that the insights and proposals developed in the problem-solving interaction feed back into each community's political debate. The groups serve as a setting for direct interaction and have the potential of initiating coalitions of peace-minded participants across conflict lines. And the workshops present a model for a new relationship between the parties.

Amidst the varied influences operating in the Middle Eastern search for peace, one cannot isolate the full effects of Kelman's efforts. At the least his many workshops have developed cadres of Israelis and Palestinians who can conduct productive negotiations. And many have served in high-ranking positions in both communities.

Areas of Policy Influence

Beyond these dramatic cases, social psychology has influenced intergroup policy by applying its perspective to a host of specific issues. Intergroup issues often are directly raised when such factors as race and gender are involved. But intergroup concerns also are relevant in more subtle ways. "We" and "they" differentiations are readily triggered when ordinary citizens encounter specialized professionals in such central institutions as the law, education, medicine, and governmental bureaucracies.

Influence on the law

It is hardly coincidental that two of the cited examples involve the courts. There are numerous instances of social psychological influence on precedent setting litigation. Two focal areas have received major attention: eyewitness identification and testimony; and jury selection, size, voting rules, and decision making. Some social psychologists, such as Elizabeth Loftus (1986), routinely serve as expert witnesses and consultants in major trials. Two cases under different legal systems provide a glimpse into these contributions.

South African courts now accept social psychological phenomena as extenuating factors in murder trials involving mob violence. Colman (1991) presented to the courts an array of such established processes as obedience to authority, deindividuation, bystander apathy, and the fundamental attribution error. And this testimony helped spare the lives of numerous African defendants.

In Canada, Neil Vidmar (1996) influenced Canada's Supreme Court to broaden "probable cause" for challenging potential jurors. The Court cited Vidmar in finding that racial prejudice may be detrimental to a minority defendant in many ways – especially if there is "a perceived link' between race and the alleged crime. Accordingly, the Court held that widespread community bias raised "a realistic potential of partiality" and overturned a robbery conviction of an Aboriginal (*Regina* v. *Williams*).

There also are glaring instances when the discipline's findings go unheeded. Eyewitness identification made in court testimony remains highly influential in determining criminal trial outcomes. Yet the predominant conclusion of relevant research is the untrustworthiness of such testimony under a wide array of conditions (Tollestrup, Turtle, & Yuille, 1994). Cross-racial identification is especially problematic (Brigham & Barkowitz, 1978).

Similarly, decades of research have established the biasing effects of selecting only jurors who can conscientiously vote for the death penalty. Such "death-qualified jurors" are more likely than others to return guilty verdicts. Yet the U.S. Supreme Court in 1986 ruled this evidence constitutionally irrelevant and that such juries did not violate a defendant's right to a fair trial (Bersoff, 1987). Ellsworth (1988) relates a similar story of how the same court has disregarded research evidence in upholding capital punishment. Indeed, capital punishment remains in American law even though its disproportionate use against African Americans is a matter of record.

Influence on education

The classroom is a prime example of a social psychological specialty – situational dynamics. Not surprisingly, then, the discipline has devoted considerable attention to education – particularly to cooperative learning involving diverse groups. For instance, Elliot Aronson's ingenious jigsaw classroom substitutes intragroup cooperation for individual competition (Aronson & Patnoe, 1997). Inspired by the earlier work by Morton Deutsch (1949) and Muzifer Sherif (Sherif, Harvey, White, Hood, & Sherif, 1961), this technique has led to positive results for a variety of children around the globe: Australians (Walker & Crogan, 1998), Germans (Eppler & Huber, 1990), Israelis (Hertz-Lazarowitz, Sharan, & Steinberg, 1980), Japanese (Araragi, 1983), and Mexican Americans (Aronson & Gonzalez, 1988). The jigsaw approach has proven especially useful for schools with both majority-group and minority-group students.

Other cooperative techniques also have been developed, tested, and widely adopted in schools. Robert Slavin's (1986) extensive work has been particularly influential in changing educational policy. From his Center for Research on Effective Schooling for Disadvantaged Students at Johns Hopkins University, Slavin has demonstrated advantages for cooperative learning for a range of groups at risk in American schools – racial, cultural, and handicapped. These advantages include enhanced achievement, intergroup friendships, and intergroup relations generally.

With education's growing interest in classrooms with diverse students, intergroup contact theory (Allport, 1954; Pettigrew, 1998a) has proven particularly influential. Social psychologists have used the theory largely for improving relations between racial and ethnic groups. But educational specialists have used it to shape research and policy for a variety of groups. Extensive research literatures now exist on the contact effects of having children with physical and learning disabilities attend classes with nondisabled children. Meta-analyses of contact research reveals that these studies show an average reduction in prejudice toward the handicapped that is nearly comparable to that of racial and ethnic contact (Pettigrew & Tropp, 2000). Such results have played a major role in advancing the "mainstreaming" of handicapped children in regular classrooms.

Influence on medicine

Public health has served as an institutional bridge for social psychology to apply its perspective to medicine. In coordination with other social science disciplines and medical specialties, the discipline has influenced a great variety of health programs (Taylor, 1995). Social psychological work has been especially influential in efforts to combat AIDS (Weiss, Nesselhof-Kendall, Feck-Kandath, & Baum, 1990; Fisher & Misovich, 1990) and reduce tobacco use (Evans & Raines, 1990). It also has played a role in large-scale community health promotion programs (Loken, Swim, & Mittelmark, 1990). These efforts have intergroup implications, because stigmatized groups generally are medically underserved while being at greater risk.

Often social psychology takes the perspective of the less powerful and suggests changes in the behavior of the powerful. This micro-level tactic has the potential for macro-level alterations, since it is the powerful who control institutional settings. This recurrent theme often occurs in attempts to influence medical practice. For example, medical doctors are urged to change the way they interact with their patients to increase the likelihood that treatment recommendations are followed (Greenfield, Kaplan, Wary, Yano, & Frank, 1988). These changes are especially needed when the patients are from lower-status groups. Yet resistance is likely when change in the procedures of the powerful are recommended. Doctors typically oppose changing their routine ways of behaving when they view their patients as the cause of treatment recommendations not being followed.

Influence on service organizations

This theme of recommending institutional changes based on clients' perspectives characterizes the discipline's influence in numerous service organizations beyond medicine. Valerie Braithwaite provides an illustration involving the Australian Tax Office. As a member of a government task force, she persuaded the taxation officials to alter how they treat taxpayers so as to increase both trust and compliance.

Braithwaite's compliance model drew on theories of procedural justice, social identity, and cognitive consistency. Initial encounters with the Tax Office regarding noncompliance are framed by showing respect for the individual as a valued member of the community and by discourse that emphasizes citizenship, fairness, and strong and effective government. Harmony and security values are emphasized to anchor tax payment within the context of shared values. Research had repeatedly shown these values to be stable and widely supported by Australians (Braithwaite, 1997, 1998). Using values as a consensual base, the identity as a citizen is strengthened, and noncompliance is approached in a cooperative rather than adversarial fashion.

Braithwaite's model does not exclude the rewards and punishments that are fundamental to legal and economic responses to noncompliance. These levers for eliciting tax compliance remain, but they are not triggered until cooperative problem solving has failed. As with many social psychological applications, this institutional effort to preserve clients' sense of worth and dignity is given a place alongside traditional legal and economic theories of compliance.

Nine Difficult Issues Inherent in Influencing Policy

The translation of social psychological theory and research into policy is neither easy nor simple (Archer, Aronson, & Pettigrew, 1993; Pallak, 1990). This complexity applies with special force to intergroup applications. Nine difficult issues arise. Some issues are internal to the discipline; others involve the political context within which the applications occur.

Intradisciplinary issues

1. Social psychology is largely an inductive, empirically driven science. As such, it is less ready to apply its perspective to specific public problems. By contrast, economics, as a more deductive, theory-driven field, more easily shapes its existing models to provide timely guidance to policy makers. Social psychology is, however, slowly developing bold theory. In intergroup relations, social identity theory offers a promising example, but it remains an exception. As broader models emerge in social psychology, however, this barrier to rapid, custom-designed applications to critical policy decisions should diminish.

2. Social psychology's inexperience with implementing applications and influencing policy makers. Compared with other social scientists, social psychologists until recently have had little opportunity to implement their findings and shape public policy. In many countries, social science rose to prominence in social policy during the 1950s and 1960s. But during these years social psychologists focused on basic laboratory research to gain acceptance within psychology departments dominated by skeptical experimentalists. So, unlike other social sciences, the discipline generally failed to develop networks with policy makers and an understanding of how to gain acceptance of its applications.

Being "out of the policy loop" restricts the discipline's influence in many ways. For instance, it makes it less likely that a decision-making agency will directly sponsor social psychological research. And this lack of sponsorship limits policy influence as well as financial support. Caplan, Morrison, and Stambaugh (1975) found that 86% of the cases in which American government decision makers used social science knowledge involved research funded by the users' own agencies.

But times are changing. Increasingly, social psychologists specialize in these policy realms. They are in law, business, medical, and public health schools, in the mass media or directly in government. They "know the ropes," and can help their academic colleagues in the policy process. And new institutional bridges have emerged. At the Australian National University, for instance, the policy-oriented Research School of Social Sciences includes social psychologists on its interdisciplinary staff of social scientists.

3. The laboratory versus the "real world" issue. A popular explanation for social psychology's failure to make more of a policy difference concerns the external validity of laboratory research. The weak form of this view has merit. Decision makers frequently question the relevance of laboratory findings. The strong form of this contention, however, can be challenged. In many areas, laboratory results *have* proven robust in the field. Critics make too much of mundane realism (Aronson, Brewer, & Carlsmith, 1985; Berkowitz and Donnerstein, 1982). The generalizability of laboratory results is an empirical question, and the use of multiple methods strengthens the case.

Tetlock (1998, p. 773) cites three examples in world politics. (1) Laboratory research has shown how simpler modes of cognitive processing arise when time pressure, information load, and threat surpass optimal levels. (2) It has also shown the relative effectiveness of a tit-for-tat strategy in bargaining, and (3) an array of judgment biases. Archival and qualitative studies document all these phenomena on the world stage. Other examples of reasonably good fits between the laboratory and the field have been noted in aggression and organizational research (Anderson & Bushman, 1997; Locke, 1986).

Of course, field methods will not necessarily support all laboratory findings. But social psychologists who wish to influence public policy should seek – and are likely to find – confirmation of their findings with a variety of methods. Bold theories supported by a variety of research methods are the basis of effective applications to specific "real-world" intergroup problems.

4. Can policy applications be consistent across cultures and societies?   We noted how Lambert's work on second-language learning by immersion and Aronson's work on the jigsaw classroom have generalized widely across cultures and societies. Such generalization is not unusual for social psychological applications. Yet cultural and structural factors impinge strongly on social psychological processes (Moghaddam, Taylor, & Wright, 1993; Triandis, 1994). Is there a paradox here?

Sharp cultural and structural differences across societies that relate to social psychological processes are common. It does *not* follow, however, that basic social psychological principles will therefore operate inconsistently across societies. Consider overcrowding. The principal conclusions of the crowding research in North America are still valid given the cultural and structural conditions under which these studies were conducted. With differences in such macro-conditions, crowding may not have the same detrimental effects in such dense countries as India. Yet such mediators of crowding effects as perceived control operate in India as they do in North America (Ruback & Pandey, 1991). Further work on crowding in dense nations could expand our understanding of the phenomenon. This expansion would entail carefully specifying the mediating links between the macro-societal, meso-situational, and micro-individual levels of analysis. Such specification requires diverse sampling of structural contexts.

One such effort tested the basic social psychological processes underlying intergroup prejudice in France, Germany, Great Britain, and the Netherlands (Pettigrew et al., 1998). These nations have sharply different intergroup situations, histories, and levels of prejudice; and their outgroups range from Turks to West Indians. Yet the same correlates and processes operate in similar ways across them. To be sure, distinctive features characterize each nation and target group. But the thrust of these findings highlights the comparable operation of such processes as social identification and group relative deprivation acting as proximal causes of prejudice and mediators for social factors acting as distal causes.

These results suggest two interlocking hypotheses (Pettigrew et al., 1998). *The universality hypothesis* predicts that social psychological processes operate in similar ways across cultures

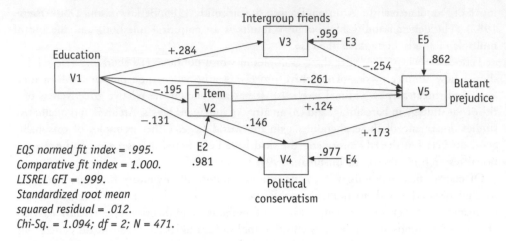

Figure 10.1A   British blatant prejudice against West Indians.

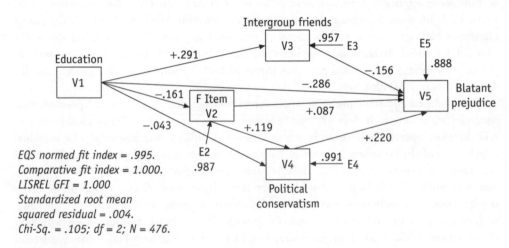

Figure 10.1B   Dutch blatant prejudice against Turks.

and societies although the macro-contexts vary widely. *The mediation hypothesis* holds that key social psychological predictors serve as critical mediators of the effects of social factors on dependent variables at the level of individuals. Hence, given divergent distal social factors, the same social psychological processes can lead to distinctly different outcomes in diverse settings.

Figures 10.1A and 10.1B illustrate these hypotheses (taken from Pettigrew, 1998b). The diagrams fit the same nearly saturated path model to data from two contrasting national samples concerning different minority targets. The model employs four predictors of blatant prejudice. Education is a consistently negative distal predictor of prejudice, and three proximal variables mediate its effects.

Sharpening the test, the two samples differ on four of the model's variables. The Dutch are better educated ($p < .0001$) and more authoritarian ($p < .0005$), the British more conservative ($p < .0001$) and prejudiced ($p < .0001$). Yet the models fit both situations. As predicted by the universality and mediation hypotheses, the proximal predictors mediate education's effects in highly similar ways in the contrasting samples. For both the British and Dutch, the well educated express less prejudice partly because they are less authoritarian and conservative and especially because they have more intergroup friends.

These data cover only Western countries; comparable work in non-Western nations is badly needed. This is what makes the Brewer and Campbell (1976) volume on intergroup attitudes in East Africa so valuable. Indeed, applications of social psychology in non-Western countries are sparse in general. This lacuna represents the most serious weakness in establishing the international utility of social psychology.

5. Missed opportunities.   Social psychologists have neglected some issues of critical societal importance. For example, Pruitt (1998) notes that, while two-party negotiation is well studied, the more policy-relevant forms of multiparty and intergroup negotiation have been slighted. And, while the discipline understands the propaganda side of persuasion, it has developed few policy guidelines for how to promote deliberative persuasion (Pratkanis & Aronson, 1992).

The discipline has neglected policy-relevant issues even in areas of special strength. Thus, social psychologists in both Europe and the United States have paid scant attention to the prejudice and discrimination directed against new immigrant minorities. For instance, the vast social identity literature has rarely examined minority relations in Europe. From 1986 to 1996, the 12 leading English-language journals of the discipline published only 18 such papers – 10 from the Netherlands alone (Ulrich Wagner's analysis in Pettigrew et al., 1998).

6. Connecting with the macro-level of analysis.   We noted how such bridge institutions as public health have furthered social psychological contributions to social policy. Effective influence on the law has occurred within the courtroom where legal rules and the adversarial system operate. And most social psychological policy offerings have been advanced as part of a broader social science intervention where the macro-fields supplied a structural context. Useful social psychological policy contributions, then, have typically been structurally grounded.

Yet social psychology often broaches its findings and theory in a societal and institutional vacuum. Social policy, however, is embedded in societal and institutional contexts. Hence, the discipline's socially ungrounded models appear irrelevant to policy makers – even though untested social psychological assumptions permeate their decisions. Objections to the field's ungrounded models are often raised in terms of the lack of integrated or "bold" theory (Cartwright, 1978, 1979; Kelley, 1983; Pettigrew, 1991) or that the discipline's theories are not "social" enough (Cartwright, 1978, 1979; Steiner, 1974).

Of course, social psychology can supply only parts of the puzzle of any major policy issue. All such issues, from peace to poverty, involve factors at all major levels of analysis. This makes it essential that the field shapes its contributions to link with the macro-levels of culture and social structure. Social psychological insights will not be useful to macro-level policy makers unless social psychologists themselves provide these cross-level links.

None the less, policy makers need social psychological contributions. Kelman (1997, p. 217) notes that even for international conflict ". . . there are . . . processes central to conflict resolution – such as empathy or taking the perspective of the other . . . and creative problem solving – that . . . take place at the level of individuals and interactions between individuals."

Add to this the unique contribution that social psychology can make by specifying the situational processes that mediate between the structural and individual levels of analysis. Other disciplines consider situations, but only social psychology focuses on situational mediation systematically. In doing so, the discipline provides both distinctive variables and explanations that usually involve subjective interpretations of the social environment. It is this situational and subjective perspective that is the discipline's unique contribution and forms the core of its applications to social policy (Ross & Nisbett, 1991). Moreover, situations frequently offer the optimal level at which to intervene. They require neither the "trickle down" effects of macro-changes nor time-consuming individual therapy.

Issues involving the political context

7. The question of values.   Social psychologists rarely concern themselves with the problem of values in policy applications. This neglect reflects the fact that most members of the discipline, unlike other social sciences, are not particularly politically active and share a relatively narrow range of center-left to center political persuasions. This situation also is changing. Both the political left (Billig, 1977; Sampson, 1981) and right (Tetlock, 1994) have challenged the discipline's unspoken value consensus. Like it or not, policy applications invoke values, and the discipline has yet to address the problem. So, these writers perform a service by opening the discussion.

It is too simple, however, merely to call for a "socially committed social psychology" (Billig, 1977). Nor is it helpful to claim "objectivity" for one's position while castigating opponents for their political bias (Tetlock, 1994). Social psychologists are human beings with their own values who study human beings. So value assumptions in theory and research are unavoidable. And the role of values is enhanced further when there is an attempt to influence social policy.

Gunnar Myrdal (1944) held that values are inherent in social science. Be aware of your values, he maintained, struggle against their biasing effects, and alert your readers to them. Objectivity becomes, then, a sought-for goal that is never fully attainable. This does *not* exclude social commitment. But such commitment must be made clear to others and combined with an equally strong commitment to competent research. Science and values need not conflict. Campbell (1959) argued that strong motivation can lead to a greater investment in tracing an accurate map of reality. Goal commitment, then, can lead to good science. The problem comes when the desired ends distort the means. This travesty results not only in poor science but in poor support of one's values as well. It is here that the Myrdalian struggle against value bias is relevant.

8. Protecting against the political misuse of social psychological theory and research.   There is no ultimate defense against the political misuse of scientific contributions. Yet there are ways of limiting such misuse. Social psychologists can take care to avoid victim blaming and to disseminate their findings widely.

Consider the widespread tendency to blame the victims of social problems (Ryan, 1971). Since psychology centers on individuals, it constantly runs the danger of having its analyses appear as if the victims of social problems are fundamentally the cause of these problems (Caplan & Nelson, 1973). Thus, such valuable concepts as relative deprivation and learned helplessness can be easily twisted into victim blaming once they enter the political arena. This is not to deny that difficult human conditions can cause changes in their victims that in turn exacerbate social problems. But it is to assert that such victim characteristics are not the basic cause of social problems, nor are remedial attempts that ignore structural causes likely to prove helpful. Linking findings and recommendations to their macro-level bases helps to avoid victim blaming. Once we include culture and social structure in an analysis, holding individuals solely responsible becomes untenable.

Another issue concerns information for whom. Information is power, and it is a two-edged sword. So, for whom do we do research? Becker (1967) points out that information flows up the status hierarchy. It provides elites with a more complete view and greater capability. Therefore, those who would effectively and ethically apply social psychology must be careful to make their results known throughout the status hierarchy – not just to the elites who may have sponsored the research. Becker also notes that when social scientists give equal access to non-elites, critics often perceive them as politically biased to the left. This raises another issue.

9. It's hot in the kitchen.   Social psychologists rarely are prepared for how scalding hot it is in the social policy kitchen. Intervention to influence policy arouses resistance. One soon learns that different perspectives apply outside of academia. Expert witnesses in American racial school desegregation cases were surprised by how defense lawyers questioned their research (Pettigrew, 1979). Had anyone conducted the research *in their particular city*? Just because massive studies had sampled schools throughout the country, why, lawyers asked, would anyone expect the results to hold true for their area?

Tense conflicts produce strong emotions. Kelman (1983) published a report on two lengthy interviews he held with Yasser Arafat, chair of the Palestine Liberation Organization. The article and its author were immediately attacked. Critics viewed it as cavorting with the enemy; they sternly rejected taking Arafat's word seriously. We now can see that this controversial paper was prophetic. It held that Arafat "has the capacity and will to negotiate an agreement with Israel, based on mutual recognition and peaceful coexistence, if afforded necessary incentives and reassurances" (Kelman, 1983, p. 203). The Oslo agreement a decade later proved Kelman correct.

Frequently the heat is generated within the discipline. Full consensus in any research area is rare in science. Suedfeld and Tetlock (1992), in *Psychology and Social Policy*, managed to find someone somewhere to attack the discipline's dominant consensus in many policy areas. Often the same critics are the challengers on many fronts. Elliott (1989, 1991, 1993), for example, not only opposes affirmative action for women in psychology but challenges the consensus views about death-qualified jurors and eyewitness testimony described earlier.

Besides pointed political differences, the critics and activists disagree about the standard required before scientific evidence should be used to influence social policy. Critics favor a standard higher than that required for scientific audiences. Activists counter that social psychologists should "tell what we know" rather than "wait for Godot" (Ellsworth, 1991). Science is open ended and dynamic; final conclusions are never reached; *all* the evidence is never in. Besides, they maintain, the standard that will prevail if no social science evidence is introduced is hardly exacting; it will consist only of the conventional wisdom of decision makers (Langenberg, 1991).

A Final Word

Compared with other social sciences – especially economics – social psychology has not had the impact on public policy that its adherents desire. Although social psychological assumptions saturate public policies, policy makers often ignore the discipline's relevant work (Pettigrew, 1988, 1998b). This harsh conclusion is true even for intergroup relations despite the urgency of intergroup conflict around the globe.

Those applications to broad social issues that have been effective have employed an extensive array of social psychological ideas. Thus, when Abrams, Hinkle, and Tomlins (1999) studied in 1992 the attitudes and intentions of Hong Kong residents in the midst of massive social transition, they drew upon five different theories of the discipline. The major contentions of social identity, reasoned action, relative deprivation, locus of control, and subjective norms all proved helpful. Abrams and his colleagues illuminated their subjects' critical decision concerning whether to stay or leave following the transfer of the colony to China. Moreover, their analysis allowed informed speculations about the future – such as the later Asian economic crisis.

Often ideas for policy-oriented work derive from both within and without the discipline. Kelman's efforts in the Middle East have employed a wide assortment of ideas. Thus, he culls insights from Floyd Allport's (1933) overlooked classic on institutional behavior and work by Lewin (1952) and others on participation. He finds useful Uri Bronfenbrenner's (1961) and Ralph White's (1965) mirror imaging of opponents' conceptions of each other. He draws widely on the attitude change literature and the work on mechanisms for neutralizing disconfirming information (Ross & Ward, 1995). Most directly, Kelman's approach relates to conflict negotiation principles (Pruitt, 1998) and the human need theory of the international relations specialist, John Burton (1979, 1984, 1988).

These successful cases illustrate the feedback that policy applications can provide for basic theory – the seldom recognized other side of the full-cycle process envisioned by Lewin. By drawing on a wide range of thought, policy studies provide important leads as to how the discipline's array of seemingly disparate ideas can be melded into the bolder, more inclusive theory so badly needed by social psychology.

REFERENCES

Abrams, D., Hinkle, S., & Tomlins, M. (1999). Leaving Hong Kong? The roles of attitude, subjective norm, perceived control, social identity, and relative deprivation. *International Journal of Intercultural Relations, 23*, 319–338.

Allport, F. (1933). *Institutional behavior.* Chapel Hill, NC: University of North Carolina Press.

Allport, G. W. (1954). *The nature of prejudice.* Reading, MA: Addison-Wesley.

American Psychological Association. (1991). In the Supreme Court of the United States: *Price Waterhouse* v. *Ann B. Hopkins. American Psychologist, 46*, 1061–1070.

Anderson, C. A., & Bushman, B. J. (1997). External validity of "trivial" experiments: The case of laboratory aggression. *Review of General Psychology, 1*, 19–41.

Araragi, C. (1983). The effect of the jigsaw learning method on children's academic performance and learning attitude. *Japanese Journal of Educational Psychology, 31*, 102–112.

Archer, D., Aronson, E., & Pettigrew, T. F. (1993). Making research apply: High stakes public policy in a regulatory environment. *American Psychologist, 47*, 1233–1236.

Aronson, E., Brewer, M., & Carlsmith, J. M. (1985). Experimentation in social psychology. In G. Lindzey & E. Aronson (Eds.), *Handbook of social psychology* (Vol. I). New York: Random House.

Aronson, E., & Gonzalez, A. (1988). Desegregation, jigsaw, and the Mexican-American experience. In P. A. Katz & D. A. Taylor (Eds.), *Eliminating racism: Profiles in controversy.* New York: Plenum Press.

Aronson, E., & Patnoe, S. (1997). *The jigsaw classroom* (2nd ed.). New York: Longman.

Balkan, L. (1970). *Les effets du bilingualisme français-anglais sur les aptitudes intellectuelles* [The effects of French-English bilingualism on intellectual aptitudes]. Brussels: Aimav.

Becker, H. (1967). Whose side are we on? *Social Problems, 14*, 239–247.

Ben-Zeev, S. (1972). The influence of bilingualism on cognitive development and cognitive strategy. Unpublished doctoral dissertation, University of Chicago, IL.

Berkowitz, L., & Donnerstein, E. (1982). External validity is more than skin deep: Some answers to criticisms of laboratory experiments. *American Psychologist, 37*, 245–257.

Bersoff, D. N. (1987). Social science data and the Supreme Court: *Lockhart* as a case in point. *American Psychologist, 42*, 52–58.

Billig, M. (1977). The new social psychology and "fascism." *European Journal of Social Psychology, 7*, 393–432.

Bourhis, R. Y. (1994a). *Conflict and language planning in Quebec.* Clevedon, UK: Multilingual Matters.

Bourhis, R. Y. (1994b). Ethnic and language attitudes in Quebec. In J. W. Berry & J. Laponce (Eds.), *Ethnicity and culture in Canada: The research landscape.* Toronto: Toronto University Press.

Bourhis, R. Y. (1994c). Power, gender, and intergroup discrimination: Some minimal group experiments. In M. P. Zanna & J. M. Olson (Eds.), *The psychology of prejudice: The Ontario symposium* (Vol. 7). Hillsdale, NJ: Erlbaum.

Brewer, M. B., & Campbell, D. T. (1976). *Ethnocentrism and intergroup attitudes: East African evidence.* Beverly Hills, CA: Sage.

Braithwaite, V. (1997). Harmony and security value orientations in political evaluation. *Personality and Social Psychology Bulletin, 23*, 401–414.

Braithwaite, V. (1998). The value balance model of political evaluations. *British Journal of Psychology, 89*, 23–247.

Brigham, J. C., & Barkowitz, P. (1978). Do "They all look alike?" The effect of race, sex, experience, and attitudes on the ability to recognize faces. *Journal of Applied Social Psychology, 8*, 306–318.

Bronfenbrenner, U. (1961). The mirror image in Soviet–American relations: A social psychologist's report. *Journal of Social Issues, 17*(3), 45–56.

Burton, J. W. (1979). *Deviance, terrorism, and war.* New York: St. Martin's Press.

Burton, J. W. (1984). *Global conflict.* Brighton, UK: Wheatsheaf.

Burton, J. W. (1988). Conflict resolution as a function of human needs. In R. A. Coate & J. A. Rosati (Eds.), *The power of human needs in world society.* Boulder, CO and London: Lynne Rienner.

Campbell, D. T. (1959). *Systematic errors to be expected of the social scientist on the basis of a general psychology of cognitive bias.* Paper presented at the annual meeting of the American Psychological Association, Cincinnati, OH.

Caplan, N. A., Morrison, A., & Stambaugh, R. J. (1975). *The use of social science knowledge in policy decisions at the national level: A report to respondents.* Ann Arbor, MI: Institute for Social Research, University of Michigan.

Caplan, N. A., & Nelson, S. D. (1973). On being useful: The nature and consequences of psychological research on social problems. *American Psychologist, 28,* 199–211.

Cartwright, D. (1978). Theory and practice. *Journal of Social Issues, 34*(4), 168–180.

Cartwright, D. (1979). Contemporary social psychology in historical perspective. *Social Psychology Quarterly, 42,* 82–93.

Cialdini, R. B. (1995). A full-cycle approach to social psychology. In G. G. Brannigan & M. R. Merrens (Eds.), *The social psychologists: Research adventures.* New York: McGraw-Hill.

Colman, A. M. (1991). Social psychology in South African murder trials. *American Psychologist, 46,* 1071–1079.

Deutsch, M. (1949). A theory of cooperation and competition. *Human Relations, 2,* 129–152.

Elliott, R. (1989). Preferential hiring for women in psychology is unwarranted and unwise: Reply to Bronstein and Pfennig. *American Psychologist, 44,* 1549–1550.

Elliott, R. (1991). Social science data and the APA: The *Lockhart* brief as a case in point. *Law and Human Behavior, 15,* 59–76.

Elliott, R. (1993). Expert testimony about eyewitness identification: A critique. *Law and Human Behavior, 17,* 423–437.

Ellsworth, P. C. (1988). Unpleasant facts: The Supreme Court's response to empirical research on capital punishment. In K. Hass & J. Inciardi (Eds.), *Challenging capital punishment: Legal and social science approaches.* Beverly Hills, CA: Sage.

Ellsworth, P. C. (1991). To tell what we know or wait for Godot? *Law and Human Behavior, 15,* 77–90.

Eppler, R., & Huber, G. L. (1990). Wissenserwerb im Team: Empirische Untersuchung von Effekten des Gruppen-Puzzles. *Psychologie in Erziehung und Unterricht, 37,* 172–178.

Evans, R. I., & Raines, B. E. (1990). Applying a social psychological model across health promotion interventions: Cigarettes to smokeless tobacco. In E. Edwards, R. S. Tindale, L. Heath, & E. J. Posavac (Eds.), *Social influence processes and prevention.* New York: Plenum Press.

Fiske, S. T. (1998). Stereotyping, prejudice and discrimination. In D. T. Gilbert, S. T. Fiske, & G. Lindzey (Eds.), *The handbook of social psychology* (Vol. 2., 4th ed.). New York: McGraw-Hill.

Fiske, S. T., Bersoff, D. N., Borgida, E., Deaux, K., & Heilman, M. E. (1991). Social science research on trial: Use of sex stereotyping research in *Price Waterhouse* v. *Hopkins. American Psychologist, 46,* 1049–1060.

Fisher, J. D., & Misovich, S. J. (1990). Social influences and AIDS-preventive behavior. In E. Edwards, R. S. Tindale, L. Heath, & E. J. Posavac (Eds.), *Social influence processes and prevention.* New York: Plenum Press.

Greenfield, S., Kaplan, S. H., Wary, J. E., Yano, E. M., & Frank, H. J. L. (1988). Patients' participation in medical care: Effects on blood sugar control and quality of life in diabetes. *Journal of General Internal Medicine, 3*, 448–457.

Hertz-Lazarowitz, R., Sharan, S., & Steinberg, R. (1980). Classroom learning style and cooperative behavior of elementary school children. *Journal of Educational Psychology, 72*, 99–106.

Ianco-Worrall, A. D. (1972). Bilingualism and cognitive development. *Child Development, 43*, 1390–1400.

Kelley, H. H. (1983). The situational origins of human tendencies: A further reason for the formal analysis of structures. *Personality and Social Psychology Bulletin, 9*, 8–30.

Kelman, H. C. (1983). Conversations with Arafat: A social-psychological assessment of the prospects for Israeli–Palestinian peace. *American Psychologist, 38*, 203–216.

Kelman, H. C. (1997). Group processes in the resolution of international conflicts: Experiences from the Israeli–Palestinian case. *American Psychologist, 52*, 212–220.

Kluger, R. (1987). *Simple justice.* New York: Knopf.

Lambert, W. E. (1992). Challenging established views on social issues: The power and limitations of research. *American Psychologist, 47*, 533–542.

Langenberg, D. N. (1991). Science, slogans, and civic duty. *Science*, 361–364,

Lewin, K. (1952). Group decision and social change. In G. E. Swanson, T. M. Newcomb, & E. L. Hartley (Eds.), *Readings in social psychology.* New York: Holt.

Locke, E. A. (Ed.) (1986). *Generalizing from laboratory to field settings.* Lexington, MA: Lexington Books.

Loftus, E. M. (1986). Ten years in the life of an expert witness. *Law and Human Behavior, 10*, 241–263.

Loken, B., Swim, J., & Mittelmark, M. B. (1990). Heart health program: Applying social influence processes in a large-scale community health promotion program. In E. Edwards, R. S. Tindale, L. Heath, & E. J. Posavac (Eds.), *Social influence processes and prevention.* New York: Plenum Press.

Moghaddam, F. M., Taylor, D. M., & Wright, S. C. (1993). *Social psychology in cross-cultural perspective.* New York: Freeman.

Myrdal, G. (1944). *An American dilemma.* New York: Harper & Row.

Pallak, M. S. (1990). Public policy and applied social psychology. In E. Edwards, R. S. Tindale, L. Heath, & E. J. Posavac (Eds.), *Social influence processes and prevention.* New York: Plenum Press.

Pettigrew, T. F. (1975). The racial integration of the schools. In T. F. Pettigrew (Ed.), *Racial discrimination in the United States.* New York: Harper & Row.

Pettigrew, T. F. (1979). Tensions between the law and social science: An expert witness view. In *Schools and the courts. Desegregation* (Vol. I). Eugene, OR: ERIC Clearinghouse for Educational Management, University of Oregon.

Pettigrew, T. F. (1988). Influencing policy with social psychology. *Journal of Social Issues, 44*(2), 205–219.

Pettigrew, T. F. (1991). Toward unity and bold theory: Popperian suggestions for two persistent problems of social psychology. In C. Stephan, W. Stephan, & T. F. Pettigrew (Eds.), *The future of social psychology.* New York: Springer-Verlag.

Pettigrew, T. F. (1998a). Intergroup contact theory. *Annual Review of Psychology, 49*, 65–85.

Pettigrew, T. F. (1998b). Applying social psychology to international social issues. *Journal of Social Issues, 54*(4), 663–675.

Pettigrew, T. F., Jackson, J., Ben Brika, J., Lemaine, G., Meertens, R. W., Wagner, U., & Zick, A. (1998). Outgroup prejudice in Western Europe. *European review of social psychology, 8*, 241–273.

Pettigrew, T. F., & Tropp, L. (2000). Does intergroup contact reduce prejudice? Recent meta-analytic findings. In S. Oskamp (Ed.), *Reducing prejudice and discrimination: Social psychological perspectives.* Mahwan, NJ: Erlbaum.

Pratkanis, A. R., & Aronson, E. (1992). *Age of propaganda*. New York: Freeman.

Pruitt, D. G. (1998). Social conflict. In D. T. Gilbert, S. T. Fiske, & G. Lindzey (Eds.), *The handbook of social psychology* (Vol. II, 4th ed.). New York: McGraw-Hill.

Ross, L., & Nisbett, R. E. (1991). *The person and the situation: Perspectives of social psychology*. New York: McGraw-Hill.

Ross, L., & Ward, A. (1995). Psychological barriers to dispute resolution. In M. Zanna (Ed.), *Advances in experimental social psychology* (Vol. 27). New York: Academic Press.

Rouhana, N. N., & Kelman, H. C. (1994). Promoting joint thinking in international conflicts: An Israeli–Palestinian continuing workshop. *Journal of Social Issues, 50*(1), 157–178.

Ruback, R. B., & Pandey, J. (1991). Crowding, perceived control, and relative power: An analysis of households in India. *Journal of Applied Social Psychology, 21*, 315–344.

Ryan, W. (1971). *Blaming the victim*. New York: Pantheon Books.

Sachdev, I., & Bourhis, R. Y. (1991). Power and status differentials in minority and majority group relations. *European Journal of Social Psychology, 21*, 1–24.

Sampson, E. E. (1981). Cognitive psychology as ideology. *American Psychologist, 36*, 730–743.

Sherif, M., Harvey, O. J., White, D. J., Hood, W. R., & Sherif, C. F. (1961). *Intergroup conflict and cooperation: The Robbers Cave experiment*. Norman, OK: University of Oklahoma Book Exchange.

Slavin, R. E. (1986). Cooperative learning: Engineering social psychology in the classroom. In R. S. Feldman (Ed.), *The social psychology of education: Current research and theory*. New York: Cambridge University Press.

Steiner, I. D. (1974). Whatever happened to the group in social psychology? *Journal of Experimental Social Psychology, 10*, 94–108.

Suedfeld, P., & Tetlock, P. E. (Eds.), *Psychology and social policy*. New York: Hemisphere.

Sugiman, T. (1998). Group dynamics in Japan. *Asian Journal of Social Psychology, 1*, 51–74.

Taylor, S. E. (1995). *Health psychology* (3rd ed.). New York: McGraw-Hill.

Tetlock, P. E. (1994). Political or politicized psychology: Is the road to scientific hell paved with good moral intentions? *Political Psychology, 15*, 509–530.

Tetlock, P. E. (1998). Social psychology and world politics. In D. T. Gilbert, S. T. Fiske, & G. Lindzey (Eds.), *The handbook of social psychology* (Vol. II, 4th ed.). New York: McGraw-Hill.

Tollestrup, P. A., Turtle, J., & Yuille, J. (1994). Actual victims and witnesses to robbery and fraud: An archival analysis. In D. Ross, J. Reed, & M. Toglia (Eds.), *Adult eyewitness testimony: Current trends and developments*. New York: Cambridge University Press.

Torrence, E. P., Gowan, J. C., Wu, J. M., & Alioti, N. C. (1970). *Journal of Educational Psychology, 61*, 72–75.

Triandis, H. C. (1994). *Culture and social behavior*. New York: McGraw-Hill.

U.S. Supreme Court (1954). *Brown v. Board of Education – I*. 347 U.S. 483.

Vidmar, N. (1996). Pretrial prejudice in Canada: A comparative perspective on the criminal jury. *Judicature, 79*, 249–255.

Walker, I., & Crogan, M. (1998). Academic performance, prejudice, and the jigsaw classroom: New pieces to the puzzle. *Journal of Community and Applied Social Psychology, 8*, 381–393.

Weisse, C. S., Nesselhof-Kendall, S. E. A., Feck-Kandath, C., & Baum, A. (1990). Psychosocial aspects of AIDS prevention among heterosexuals. In E. Edwards, R. S. Tindale, L. Heath, & E. J. Posavac (Eds.), *Social influence processes and prevention*. New York: Plenum Press.

White, R. K. (1965). Images in the context of international conflict: Soviet perceptions of the US and USSR. In H. C. Kelman (Ed.), *International behavior: A social psychological analysis*. New York: Holt, Rinehart, & Winston.

PART III

Business and Organizational Behavior

CHAPTER ELEVEN

Consumer Behavior

Sharon Shavitt and Michaela Wänke

The Consumer Domain: An Introduction

The broad field of consumer behavior spans many of the topics of interest to social psychologists – from micro-level events (e.g. psychophysiological responding to advertisements) to macro-level processes (e.g. family decision making; organizational buying behavior). Indeed, the breadth and volume of work in consumer behavior easily fills an entire handbook (e.g. Robertson & Kassarjian, 1991). This chapter is not intended to cover that field comprehensively. Instead, we focus on highlighting selected principles of consumer information processing (CIP) relevant to intraindividual, social psychological theories. The articles cited are not intended to be comprehensive either, and for some topics we cite review papers or a small subset of research articles for the sake of brevity.

Consumer research has been greatly influenced by social psychology. A citation analysis of the field's leading journal, *Journal of Consumer Research*, revealed that, when comparing individual disciplines, social psychology has had a greater impact than even marketing or economics (Leong, 1989). With a growing interest in CIP, research in social cognition has become a primary source of influence. In the first section of this chapter we give a brief overview of the encoding, inference, and memory processes that relate to consumer judgments and decisions. It will become clear that, regarding the underlying cognitive processes, consumer judgment does not differ much from social judgment.

Naturally, however, research on consumer cognition has focused on some themes central to consumer behavior. Below, we select some of these topics to give more detailed insight. The selection of topics is meant to illustrate the relevance of social cognition to the consumer domain.

Having pointed out the many parallels between the consumer literature and the social cognition literature, in the second section we turn to the differences. In particular, we are concerned with what social cognition can learn from the consumer domain. We will point to some areas where consumer research could inspire a more complete understanding of human information processing and, thus, balance the overwhelmingly one-sided interdisciplinary exchange more equally.

1   How Consumers Make Product Judgments

Consumers are daily exposed to a host of product-relevant information. Depending on their involvement and cognitive resources they attend to it, encode it, make inferences from it, and may use the results of their processing for a product evaluation or even decision. Because product choices and judgments are at least partially memory based (Alba, Hutchinson, & Lynch, 1991) they are then dependent on which brands and which brand-beliefs and brand-related affective responses were stored and are retrieved from long-term memory at the time of judgment. Even when external information is available, memory may play a role. For example, when consumers are exposed to a range of brands and packaging claims in the supermarket, they may nevertheless recall past product experiences, TV commercials, or reviews from consumer organizations, or they may attend more to the brands that they recognize. Thus, consumer choices and judgments often depend to a large extent on the accessibility of relevant information (e.g. Baker & Lutz, 1988; Feldman & Lynch, 1988) and how the activated information is used. However, as distinct from social cognition research, CIP research tends to focus on trying to understand the effects of a specific marketing-relevant variable, for example advertising execution or brand familiarity, on the product judgment, rather than understanding the cognitive processes *per se*. The following overview reflects this orientation to some extent.

Encoding

Independent of whether the judgment is stimulus based or memory based, in order to be considered for a product decision the information must have been perceived. Moreover, the more processing capacity is devoted to a stimulus for comprehension and elaboration, the greater is its later accessibility. Consequently, much of traditional theorizing in advertising postulated that grabbing consumers' attention is the key to effective advertising (e.g. Lewis, 1898; Rossiter & Percy, 1987) and researchers often focused on factors that capture consumers' attention (see O'Guinn & Faber, 1991).

A few caveats should be noted, however. First, our review will show that, although selectivity and intensity of attention are often positively correlated, the opposite is also true. Whereas some factors of a stimulus may catch consumers' attention, they may be detrimental to more intense processing and elaboration. Ads using sexual stimuli are a good example (Severn, Belch, & Belch, 1990). Second, some attention-grabbing executions may create negative affect. Recent Bennetton campaigns, which have featured war casualties and AIDS victims, are an example. Indeed, a growing body of research suggests that consumers resent attention-grabbing advertising (e.g. Campbell, 1995; see also section 2, below). Third, and perhaps most importantly, focal attention may not be necessary for information to be perceived and be influential at a later time, as will be discussed later.

What elicits attention and elaboration?

Whether a brand, an ad, a package, or any product information catches consumers' attention depends on where (when) it is placed, the goals, involvement, and cognitive resources of the consumer, and the characteristics of the stimulus. Placement is one of the most basic factors, and consequently consumer researchers were interested early on in placement effects (for a review see Wilkie, 1994, ch. 8). In magazines the most prominent spot is the back cover, in TV it is the first commercial in the commercial break. In cultures that read from left to right and from top to bottom, information presented in the upper-left corner receives greatest attention compared to other positions. In supermarkets, brands have a better chance of being chosen when placed at eye-level than on a lower shelf, presumably because they attract more attention at eye-level.

This example, however, also illustrates that much depends on the search strategies of the consumer. A consumer highly motivated to find the least expensive brand may also search the less prominent shelves. Models of consumers' external information search have identified four main factors: motivation, ability, perceived costs, and perceived benefits (Moorthy, Ratchford, & Talukdar, 1997; Schmidt & Spreng, 1996). Consumers engage in more search processes when the costs of making a suboptimal decision are high and the benefits of extended search are high. For inexpensive, or repeatedly purchased products, or when the market is perceived as homogeneous so that more search will not detect decisively better alternatives, search is low. External search processes also depend on a consumer's product or market knowledge. Moderately knowledgeable consumers will engage most in external search processes. Consumers with low knowledge lack the necessary representations to make use of the acquired information. Consumers with high knowledge, on the other hand, tend to rely more on their stored knowledge. Finally, spontaneous attention is also influenced by the consumer's current goals. A hungry consumer will be more likely to notice a restaurant than a consumer not looking for a bite to eat.

Certainly, characteristics of the presented information play an important role in capturing attention, and this may be what many view as advertising's prime objective: creating eye-catching executions. Not surprisingly, vivid information is more likely to be noticed than pallid information, and indeed, in advertising, a picture may be worth a thousand words, at least in terms of creating attention, eliciting recall, triggering inferences, and influencing judgments (e.g. Childers & Houston, 1984; Mitchell, 1986; Smith, 1991). When it comes to drawing attention, salience may actually be more important than vividness. In general, ads that are unusual, surprising, novel, or incongruent with expectations will capture attention, but such effects of novelty wear off with repetition (e.g. Calder & Sternthal, 1980).

Whereas vivid and salient information certainly attracts more selective attention, some research suggests that the advantage of vivid and salient executions is due to the greater elaboration that they elicit (e.g. Unnava & Burnkrant, 1991; Goodstein, 1993). On the other hand, catching attention may also be at the cost of comprehension and elaboration. For example, Houston, Childers, & Heckler (1987) found better recall for ad information when the picture and verbal information were discrepant, but only when ad recipients had plenty of time to process the ad and not if presentation time was short. This example demonstrates that whether elaboration occurs, and thus how an advertisement's execution affects judgment, both depend on consumers' cognitive resources (e.g. Keller & Block, 1997) and, of course, personal involvement (Greenwald & Leavitt, 1984).

Retrieval

We mentioned above that product choices often do not occur at the time that brand-related information is presented. Thus, most choices rely on the information recalled at the time of judgment, which is why retrieval processes are of prime interest in consumer research (for a review see Mitchell, 1993). Note, however, that recent literature also attests to the influence of information that is not explicitly recalled, as will be discussed later.

When consumers form a judgment at the time of information encoding, they may later simply retrieve the stored judgment rather than construct it anew by retrieving product attributes (Srull, 1989). However, although consumers may be able to retrieve a previous judgment, they may conclude that it is not adequate for the present situation (e.g. their current goals or alternatives) and may try to retrieve or acquire information that allows for a new judgment or adjust the previous one (Lynch, Marmorstein, & Weigold, 1988). As with external search processes, the extent of internal (memory) search increases with involvement and with cognitive resources, as described earlier.

Certainly, a prime factor in information retrieval is the accessibility of the information. We have already mentioned some variables that affect the accessibility of product-related information by way of attention and elaboration. Accessibility of brand-related information also depends on how it is organized in memory. Biehal & Chakravarti (1983) distinguish between brand based structures, which facilitate brand comparisons, and attribute based structures, which facilitate attribute based comparisons. The manner in which information is stored in memory depends on the goals present at encoding. In addition, prototypical brands within a product category (e.g. Ward & Loken, 1986) and recently or frequently activated brands or brand information (attributes or judgments) also enjoy an accessibility advantage (e.g. Berger & Mitchell, 1989; Nedungadi, 1990). Frequent or recent activation of a brand in a particular usage situation increases the association of brand and usage situation, so that activation of the latter may activate the brand (Ratneshwar & Shocker, 1991). Recency and frequency are of particular relevance because both can be manipulated through amount of advertising.

But not all information accessible in the judgment situation is the result of marketing efforts. Consumers may also recall past experiences. In particular, they may be likely to recall negative product experiences (Schul & Schiff, 1993) given that such experiences are usually unexpected and may be more extreme.

In general, the theories and models popular in CIP postulate a positive relationship between the accessibility of diagnostic information and its impact on judgment (Baker & Lutz, 1988; Feldman & Lynch, 1988; Kisielus & Sternthal, 1984). If a piece of information comes to mind, its evaluative implications will affect the judgment in the respective direction. However, in line with social cognition findings that the retrieval of information does not necessarily predict how the information is used for the judgment (see Martin, Strack, & Stapel, 2001), recent research in the consumer domain also challenged this assumption. As we will illustrate below, accessible information may also elicit contrast effects in product evaluation (Meyers-Levy & Tybout, 1997; Wänke, Bless, & Schwarz, 1998, in press-a, in press-b). Moreover, the impact of information depends not only on whether it comes to mind but also how it comes to mind. Evaluations of brands, products, and services were more in line with the implications of retrieved information when consumers experienced the retrieval as easy compared to when the retrieval felt difficult (Wänke & Bless, in press; Wänke, Bless, & Biller, 1996; Wänke, Bohner, & Jurkowitsch, 1997). When retrieval is experienced or merely anticipated as difficult, the impact of the evaluative implications may even reverse.

Consumer interpretations and inferences

Consumers are active information processors in that they interpret information, categorize it, generate counterarguments and draw inferences from it (for a review, see Kardes, 1993). Whether and how consumers make inferences about missing information is a particularly well-researched topic (see Kardes, 1993). Not surprisingly, only rather knowledgeable consumers notice when relevant product information is missing, whereas less knowledgeable consumers do so only when prompted, for example when competitor brands carry the respective information. Once consumers detect that relevant information is missing, they may use the available information to make specific inferences, as described below. If, however, the available information does not lend itself to specific inferences or consumers are not able or willing to make those inferences, they may form cautious and moderate judgments that are held with low confidence.

Several strategies for how consumers may spontaneously or intentionally go beyond the information given have been investigated (see also Alba & Hutchinson, 1987). Most simply, consumers may assume that the brand possesses a particular attribute at the same (average) level as other brands, provided the variance among these other brands is low. Equally basic, consumers may infer an attribute level from the overall product evaluation, as a sort of halo effect. Subjective theories, for example that high price signals high quality, are another source of inferences. Consumers may also draw inferences from category membership. A large CIP literature, for example, has looked at how consumers' product evaluations are influenced by the fact that the product carries a brand name about which they already have well-formed expectations (see below).

Of course, consumers are not infallible when relying on heuristics or even systematic strategies when evaluating brands (for a review of potential biases see Kardes, 1993). One interesting and obviously misleading heuristic was documented by Carpenter, Glazer, & Nakamoto (1994). In their study, nondiagnostic but differentiating brand attributes increased brand evaluation, especially under high price. Apparently, consumers inferred that if an attribute is advertised it must be valuable.

If consumers can be prompted to generate inferences themselves, this can bring a number of benefits to the marketer. Consumer inferences may be more memorable (Moore, Reardon,

& Durso, 1986) and less subject to counterarguing and reactance than explicitly stated information. Indeed, self-generated arguments and inferences are more persuasive and enduring (Sawyer & Howard, 1991; Shavitt & Brock, 1990), and attitudinal judgments based on self-generated inferences are more accessible than judgments involving less cognitive effort (for a review see Kardes, 1993). Accordingly, advertisements often leave claims open to inference.

However, relying on consumers' inferences is risky to the extent that consumers need sufficient knowledge, involvement, and cognitive resources to make spontaneous inferences (e.g. Johar, 1995; Sawyer & Howard, 1991). Moreover, the ease with which consumers make a particular inference may also play a role. Self-generated product benefits are only more persuasive than presented benefits when this generation is experienced or anticipated as easy (Wänke, Bless, & Biller, 1996; Wänke, Bohner, & Jurkowitsch, 1997), whereas difficult benefit generation backfires. Not surprisingly, prompting self-generated responses also backfires when those responses are unfavorable to the brand (Shavitt & Brock, 1986).

Choice

Consumer research is at least as interested in choice as in product judgment. This concerns not only how judgments affect actual behavior, but how information processing feeds into selections among multiple alternatives. One might assume that consumers form or retrieve a judgment about each alternative and subsequently choose the best brand. However, the range of alternatives may influence which attributes are attended to and how they are weighted. In addition, comparison processes introduce their own dynamics (e.g. Dhar & Simonson, 1992; Wänke, Schwarz, & Noelle-Neumann, 1995). Consequently a large literature in consumer research builds on research in behavioral decision making (for a review see Bettmann, Johnson, & Payne, 1991), which to a large extent is guided by exploring violations of presumably rational principles.

For example, although, logically, the relative choice between A and B should not be affected by adding C to the range of options, the likelihood of choosing product A increases versus product B when a product C is added that is (at least partly) inferior to A and makes A look good by comparison (Huber, Payne, & Puto, 1982; Tversky & Simonson, 1993). Choices also should not depend on how the alternatives are presented (framing effects), but they do. Consumers gladly accept a discount for paying cash instead of using their credit card (framing as a gain) but resent paying an extra fee for charging goods to their credit card (framing as a loss).

Recent research in consumer choice has begun to pay more attention to affective factors in decision making, in particular, research investigating predictions about future reactions and choices (e.g. Kahneman & Snell, 1992) and research involving hedonic choices (e.g. Dhar & Wertenbroch, 1997). One general finding is that people are surprisingly poor at predicting their own future hedonic reactions to products or experiences. Obviously, this deficit greatly affects the quality of consumer decisions as far as future outcomes are concerned, and it suggests that marketing strategies should be sensitive to the time lag between the purchase decision and actual consumption.

Highlighted Topics in Consumer Information Processing

Brand extensions

The overwhelming majority of new products are launched under an already-established brand name. This way marketers avoid the forbidding costs of creating a new brand image, exploiting instead an existing brand image in the hope that consumers will transfer existing brand beliefs to the new launch (for a review see Shocker, Srivastava, & Ruekert, 1994). In investigating the conditions for successful extensions, consumer research has built upon the assumption that consumers need to categorize the extension as a brand member in order to derive affect or beliefs from the brand membership. Consequently, research has focused on the antecedents of brand categorization.

Whether a new product is categorized as belonging to an existing brand was initially assumed to depend on the characteristics of product and brand, and how both contributed to category fit. This fit was assumed to facilitate the transfer of brand liking and/or the transfer of more specific brand beliefs. Most research looked at fit in terms of the product category (e.g. canned soup fits better as an extension of a food brand than a floor wax; Boush & Loken, 1991), the brand image (e.g. bracelets fit better with Rolex, which is associated with status products, than with Timex; Park, Milberg, & Lawson, 1991), or other kinds of relatedness (technology, manufacturing processes, etc.; Herr, Farquahar, & Fazio, 1996).

Other research showed that product categorization was not necessarily a function of the nature of the brand or product and inherent in their features but could also be manipulated by external factors, such as supplying consumers with specific category labels for grouping products together (Wänke, Bless, & Schwarz, in press-a). Moreover, whether a particular model was included or excluded from the brand representation could be influenced by marketing strategies (Wänke, Bless, & Schwarz, 1998).

Until recently, the focus on the antecedents of brand categorization came with a neglect of the consequences. The literature generally assumed that high fit resulted in high acceptance of the extension. But Broniarczyk & Alba (1994) demonstrated that even if brand beliefs are transferred to the extension, these attributes may not necessarily be desirable for the extension. Consumers may want different attributes in a compact car than in a sportscar. Other research challenged the previously held assumption that a failure to categorize the extension as a brand exemplar would merely decrease the transfer of brand beliefs. Wänke, Bless, & Schwarz (1998) found contrast effects; the brand extension was evaluated lower on brand beliefs when its inclusion in the brand was undermined as compared to when no information about its parent brand was given. It is argued that the brand and its previous models can serve as a standard of comparison against which the new model is measured. These results imply that an unsuccessful extension strategy may not only fail to exploit the brand image but may actually backfire. On the other hand, beliefs in opposition to the existing brand image may be useful for different positioning goals.

The reverse influence – how the brand extension affects perceptions of the parent brand – has mainly been studied from the perspective of diluting brand image (e.g. Loken & Roedder-John, 1993; Park, McCarthy, & Milberg, 1993). Again, the literature has focused on the category fit, and again one may assume that other influences may affect categorization processes. Moreover, categorization models suggest that including an extension into an existing brand category will result in assimilation of the parent brand to the evaluation of the extension, but exclusion from the existing brand category may result in contrast (e.g. Wänke, Bless, & Schwarz, in press-b).

Research on brand extensions parallels stereotype research in social psychology as far as the dynamics of categorization are concerned. In fact, market research often treats brands as personalities, rendering the parallels rather appealing. The parallels make brand extensions an excellent domain for the study of social psychological categorization models.

Mood effects on consumer judgments

Affect plays a role in many consumer topics, particularly in advertising, both as a dependent variable and an independent variable (for a review see Agres, Edell, & Dubitsky, 1990). A prime question in applied research is how affective states influence purchase behavior. Because purchase behavior is the complex end result of different factors, there is no clear answer to this question and it may depend very much on the product category.

For example, on the one hand the popular saying "when the going gets tough, the tough go shopping" suggests that bad mood states may increase purchase behavior overall. This belief is supported by studies that find increased consumption of what Gardner (1994) calls "mood-ameliorating" products, such as cigarettes and cookies, or at least more favorable attitudes towards such products (for a review see Gardner, 1994). On the other hand, the literature also suggests that consumers judge products more favorably when happy (Isen, Shalker, Clark, & Karp, 1978) and more negatively when sad (Axelrod, 1963). Products presented with stimuli inducing a happy mood are liked better than products associated with an unhappy mood, unless consumers are aware of the source of their mood (Gorn, Goldberg, & Basu, 1993). Moreover, happy mood may also induce less systematic processing of advertising (e.g. Batra & Stayman, 1990) and consequently a less critical product evaluation (for a general review of mood and information processing see Bless, 2001). In combination, this would suggest that the increased desire for some products following bad mood may be countered by the tendency toward more critical product attitudes.

One of the topics that has raised the most interest is the effect of moods induced by a TV program on the processing of commercials shown in the program. In other words, is advertising more effective when placed in a sitcom, a drama, or a documentary? A recent meta-analysis of relevant studies (Mattenklott, 1998) reveals ambiguous results for the effect of program induced mood on ad recall. Happy and funny programs seemed to be superior to extremely sad and depressing programs (e.g. about the Nuremberg trials) but inferior to neutral programs. It is argued that sad material is more involving than happy material and consequently distracts more from processing the ads that interrupt it. The programs that are affectively more neutral may increase the degree to which the commercials stand out, and thus the commercials are better recalled later (if one can assume that viewers stay tuned to the program – see below). As this illustrates, mood effects as elicited by TV programs are hard to distinguish from effects of arousal elicited by these programs. A study that separated arousal from valence (Pavelchak, Antil, & Munch, 1988) measured recall for ads shown during the Superbowl in the winning, losing, and a neutral city and found that recall remained unaffected by the valence of the emotion but was negatively related to the intensity of the emotion (i.e. arousal and extremity of emotion).

With regard to program effects on judgment, sad mood seems to decrease the liking for an advertised product (Axelrod, 1963; Yi, 1990). Interestingly, one study (Kamins, Marks, & Skinner, 1991) also looked at the affective tone of the commercial and found that the positive effect of happy programming only emerged for a happy commercial. A sad commercial, an appeal to drug abusers to seek professional help, was liked better when placed in a sad than in a happy program. In line with findings by Martin, Abend, Sedikides, & Green (1997), one may argue that consumers found the appeal more moving when in a sad rather than happy mood and consequently evaluated it more favorably.

Cross-cultural differences in advertising

As new global markets emerge, and existing markets become increasingly segmented along ethnic or subcultural lines, the need to communicate effectively with consumers who have different cultural values has never been more acute. Thus, it is no surprise that cultural differences are gaining increased attention in consumer research, as they are in social psychology.

Comparisons between individualistic cultures (e.g. North American and Western European countries) and collectivistic cultures (e.g. Asian, Latin American, and African countries; see Miller, 2001, for a general discussion of these concepts) have yielded sharp distinctions between these cultural types in the advertising appeals that tend to be used, as well as in the processing and persuasiveness of those appeals. For instance, American advertisers are often exhorted to focus on the brand's attributes and advantages (e.g. Ogilvy, 1985), based on the assumption that consumer learning about the brand precedes liking and buying the brand (e.g. Lavidge & Steiner, 1961).

In contrast, as Miracle (1987) has suggested, the typical goal of advertisements in Japan appears very different. There, ads tend to focus on "making friends" with the audience and showing that the company understands their feelings. The assumption is that consumers will buy once they feel familiar with and trust the company. Because Japan and other Pacific Rim countries are "high context" cultures that tend toward implicit and indirect communication practices (Hall, 1976), Miracle suggested that the mood and tone of commercials in these countries will be particularly important in establishing trust. Indeed, studies have shown that ads in Japan rely more on symbolism, mood, and aesthetics and less on direct brand comparisons than do ads in the US (e.g. Hong, Muderrisoglu, & Zinkhan, 1987).

This is not to suggest that advertisements in collectivist societies use a "soft sell" approach in contrast to a "hard sell," information-driven approach in the West. Information content in the ads of collectivist cultures can be very high, sometimes higher than in the US (for a review see Taylor, Miracle, & Wilson, 1997). It is more an issue of the type of appeal that the information is supporting.

For instance, a content analysis revealed that in Korea, compared to the US, magazine ads are more focused on family well-being, interdependence, and harmony, and are less focused on self-improvement, independence, and individuality (Han & Shavitt, 1994). How-ever, as one might expect, the nature of the advertised product moderates these effects. Cultural differences emerge strongly for products that tend to be purchased and used with other persons (e.g. groceries, cars). Products that do not tend to be shared (e.g. health and beauty aids, clothing) are promoted more in terms of personal, individualistic benefits in both countries.

The persuasiveness of appeals appears to mirror cultural differences in their prevalence. An experiment by Han & Shavitt (1994) showed that appeals to individualistic values (e.g. "Solo cleans with a softness that you will love") are more persuasive in the US and appeals to collectivistic values (e.g. "Solo cleans with a softness that your family will love") are more persuasive in Korea. Again, however, this effect was much more evident for products that are shared (laundry detergent, clothes iron) than for those that are not (chewing gum, running shoes). Zhang & Gelb (1996) in an experiment in the US and China found a similar pattern in the persuasiveness of individualistic versus collectivistic appeals. Moreover, this effect was moderated by whether the advertised product is socially visible (camera) versus privately used (toothbrush).

As to the role of culture in the processing of ad information, research is in its infancy. What is known suggests that general models of cognitive processing and cognitive respond-ing are useful frameworks across cultures (e.g. Aaker & Maheswaran, 1997; Shavitt, Nelson, & Yuan, 1997). However, cultural differences emerge in the diagnosticity of certain types of information. For instance, Aaker & Maheswaran (1997) showed that consensus information regarding other consumers' opinions is not treated as a heuristic cue by Hong Kong Chinese (as it is in the US; Maheswaran & Chaiken, 1991), but is instead perceived and processed as diagnostic information. Thus, collectivists resolve inconsistency in favor of consensus information, not brand attributes. This would be expected in a culture that stresses conform-ity and responsiveness to others' views. Yet cues whose (low) diagnosticity does not vary cross-culturally (e.g. number of attributes presented) elicit similar heuristic processing in the US and Hong Kong.

2   What Distinguishes the Consumer Domain from Other Social Domains?

In this section, we discuss some of the important and often unrecognized differences between the consumer domain and other social domains, and why those unique aspects may invite some expansion of social cognitive theories.

Distinction 1: Marketing Messages Have Important Implicit Effects

Marketing communications often influence consumers via mechanisms that are implicit and unconscious. In psychology, interest in implicit social cognition is rapidly increasing (see Banaji, Lemm, & Carpenter, 2001). Nevertheless, although there are exceptions, most studies of communication and persuasion focus on conscious and explicit processes of message evaluation. Explicit processes are relevant in cases where focal attention is directed to the message. Indeed, in laboratory persuasion experiments, participants often have little choice but to so direct their attention. However, in the real world, hundreds of messages compete daily for our attention. Most of them are hardly noticed, yet they may well influence later judgments. Interest in implicit processes in the consumer domain predated much of the social cognition research on the topic. In a classic paper, Herbert Krugman (1965) hypothesized that consumer judgments and purchase decisions may often be influenced by incidental learning of advertising information (see also Greenwald & Leavitt, 1984). Moreover, a repetitive TV ad campaign may not only effect the "overlearning" of unattended product information, it may also change the *structure* of product perceptions. Thus, repeated exposure to an ad for, say, a soft drink may gradually shift the attributes that are salient in evaluating the beverage from "refreshing taste" to "youthful" or "modern." These shifts may not be detected by standard attitude measures. Indeed, they may not even be noticeable prior to a behavioral decision. As Krugman suggested, "the purchase situation is the catalyst that reassembles or brings out all the potentials for shifts in salience that have accumulated up to that point. The product or package is then suddenly seen in a new, "'somehow different' light although nothing verbalizable may have changed *up to that point*." To assess such effects, "one might look for gradual shifts in perceptual structure, aided by repetition, activated by behavioral-choice situations, and *followed* at some time by attitude change" (Krugman, 1965, pp. 354–355; italics in original).

Recent research has yielded robust evidence that incidental exposure to information may affect consumer judgments and that it is not necessary that the consumer recollect the initial exposure or material (e.g. Janiszewski, 1993; Shapiro, MacInnis, & Heckler, 1997). In a typical study, consumers are exposed to advertisements, brand names, or packaging stimuli while their focal attention is directed elsewhere. In line with prior research on mere exposure effects (see Bornstein, 1989), these preattentive exposures elicit greater subsequent liking for the ad or brand, and even an increased likelihood of including the advertised product in a consideration set for a hypothetical purchase (Shapiro, MacInnis, & Heckler, 1997). Moreover, although behavioral effects of unattended ad exposure have not yet been demonstrated, recent findings in social cognition have shown that direct behavioral effects of incidentally encountered stimuli are possible when those stimuli prime existing stereotypes (e.g. Bargh, Chen, & Burrows, 1996). Thus, it seems likely that preattentively processed marketing messages could elicit behavioral effects when they activate existing product-user stereotypes or usage-related concepts in memory.

At a somewhat higher level of processing involvement, in which focal attention is directed at comprehending but not evaluating brand claims, simple repetition of ad claims heightens their perceived validity (e.g. Hawkins & Hoch, 1992; see also Hasher, Goldstein, & Toppino, 1977). Thus, existing research provides substantial support for Krugman's (1965) theorizing, at least in terms of the repetition-induced "overlearning" of information that receives little or no focal processing. The evidence is all the more impressive given that these studies typically rely upon explicit attitudinal measures.

Because a large proportion of the consumer information to which we are exposed is not elaborated or even perceived consciously, the consumer domain provides a prime field for further research on preattentive processes. In particular, studies are needed to examine the processes by which unattended messages can alter the structure of product or topic perceptions. Can repeated, preattentive exposures to an ad campaign influence not only whether a brand is liked but also whether the characteristics claimed in the ad (e.g. "youthful") become more salient and drive that evaluation? If the salience of advertised characteristics does indeed increase as a function of preattentive ad exposure, does it influence the basis on which one compares and selects (e.g. choosing the brand that is perceived to be "most youthful")? At what point, if ever, are these effects recognized by the consumer? In line with Krugman (1965), we suggest that research in this area will yield the strongest evidence to the extent that it relies on implicit measures of attribute salience, the behavioral choices that reflect relative salience, and other indirect measures.

Distinction 2: Marketing Messages Communicate via Non-verbal Channels

Social psychological research on message processing and persuasion has focused mainly on the processing of verbal information to the relative neglect of other modes of communication. But marketers use pictures, fonts, logos, colors, layouts, and other visual elements to draw attention, evoke associations, and convey meanings. The same is true for the use of music, jingles, sounds effects, and other auditory stimuli, as well as for fragrances and textures (e.g. "smooth as silk"; see Solomon, 1992). All of these non-verbal modalities may affect judgments directly. They may affect the processing of verbal information by distracting from, facilitating, or biasing it. They may serve as recall or recognition cues for brand information. But most importantly they may carry meaning in their own right.

Many CIP studies of non-verbal inputs have been inspired by psychological constructs and theories. For example, the role of attractive photographs or pleasing music in influencing brand attitudes via classical-conditioning or mood-eliciting processes has been explored (e.g. Gorn, Goldberg, & Basu, 1993; Stuart, Shimp, & Engle, 1987), as has the role of visual inputs as cues that can provide product information in simplified form (e.g. Mitchell & Olson, 1981; Petty, Cacioppo, & Schumann, 1983). Other work has paid greater attention to the unique qualities of these modalities and the ways in which they influence processing (e.g. Kellaris, Cox, & Cox, 1993; MacInnis & Park, 1991), as well as convey meaning (Phillips, 1997; Scott, 1990, 1994). It is on these latter effects of non-verbal inputs that we focus. We review a sampling of this large literature below, focusing primarily on the role of visual elements.

Visual elements are critical in virtually all forms of marketing communications and influence consumer perceptions in multiple ways. For instance, the colors used on packaging and in ads can directly influence product perceptions through their symbolic meanings and cultural associations. Gold lettering on a wine bottle conveys wealth and elegance, whereas yellow packaging for snack food connotes "fun" (for a review see Solomon, 1992).

CIP researchers have also shown that the effects of visuals on judgment and recall depend on the match between the degree or nature of the visual presentation and several other factors, such as the consumer's decision-making style (Meyers-Levy & Peracchio, 1996) and the level of visual imagery associated with the product information (Unnava & Burnkrant,

1991). The effects of ad visuals also depend on the congruity or consistency between the verbal and visual elements in the ad (e.g. Smith, 1991; see Kellaris, Cox, & Cox, 1993, for similar conclusions regarding the congruity of verbal and musical elements). The function of the product attitude may also influence the way certain visual depictions are processed. Shavitt, Swan, Lowrey, and Wänke (1994) showed that pictures of spokespersons convey social-image information that may be centrally processed when the product evaluation serves a social-identity function.

In a number of studies, researchers have investigated the effects of visual elements such as the camera angle of ad photos, the use of color in ads, and ad layout characteristics (e.g. Meyers-Levy & Peracchio, 1995, 1996). Under low motivation to process the ad, consistent with dual process models of persuasion, the general finding is that visual elements can act as peripheral cues. However, under higher motivation to process, the effects are more complex because visual elements can either enhance or impede attempts to evaluate the product. For instance, full color ads may outperform black-and-white ads when processed peripherally, but may swamp the available cognitive resources needed to scrutinize ad claims when processing more elaborately (see MacInnis & Park, 1991, for similar conclusions regarding the effects of musical elements on information processing).

Clearly, then, visuals are more than mere affect or simple cues that are easily processed. Researchers who analyze the meaning that pictures convey from a rhetorical standpoint have offered a distinct viewpoint on the processing and interpretation of visuals. For instance, Scott (1994) suggests that some psychological research on the effects of visuals has tended to view visuals as simple reflections of reality that require little interpretive activity. However, as she points out, viewers actively interpret visual material based on extensive past experience with pictorial stimuli. These experiences render visuals a shared symbol system, like language, that communicates not through resemblance to reality but through pictorial *conventions*. Viewers' interpretations are sensitive to context and to stylistic mannerisms in the visual depiction. Thus, for instance, a picture of a fluffy, black kitten paired with a package of toilet paper would elicit a metaphorical interpretation ("soft as a kitten"; Mitchell & Olson, 1981), but paired with an allergy medicine would elicit very different inferences, and rendered in Halloween style would trigger still other associations (see Scott, 1990, for similar conclusions regarding the rhetorical role of music in advertising).

We suggest that psychological understanding of information processing and persuasion would be enhanced by a greater focus on non-verbal elements, particularly by taking into account the rhetorical richness of those elements.

Distinction 3: Product Evaluation is Not the Only Goal of Consumers

Social psychological research on information processing focuses principally on the goal of forming valid attitudes or judgments toward objects or message topics. The result is that the knowledge derived from this voluminous literature consists largely of principles about how messages influence recipients' attitudes toward advocated positions. This is a very important body of knowledge, and earlier we discussed the profound influence it has had upon consumer research in general.

However, the assumption that the goal of topic-attitude validity drives message processing implies that people typically approach marketing communications with the goal of extracting brand information. Actually, their goals may be much broader, including the hedonic motives served by ad exposure. The notion that people can enjoy ad exposure may seem odd to psychologists, who typically study and view ads as (often unwelcome) carriers of product information. However, in a recent national survey, most respondents reported that they like to look at the advertisements to which they are exposed (Shavitt, Lowrey, & Haefner, 1998). Indeed, data on the structure of advertising attitudes have repeatedly shown that the hedonic experience associated with ad exposure contributes greatly to driving public attitudes toward advertising, sometimes more so than do perceptions of the usefulness or trustworthiness of ad information (see Shavitt, Lowrey, & Haefner, 1998).

Recognizing that enjoyment is a primary basis for evaluating advertising can draw attention to other CIP facets than those that assume argument based discourse. As Wells (1988) points out, many ads are not lectures but dramas. Ads with dramatic elements appear to be processed differently than argument based ads, eliciting persuasion via empathy rather than argument evaluation (Deighton, Romer, & McQueen, 1989). Dramatic appeals are effective to the extent that they generate feeling responses and a sense of verisimilitude to their stories.

The use of storytelling and entertainment as persuasive strategies is neither new nor limited to commercial appeals. Further social psychological research on these processes would illuminate our understanding of the persuasive effects of narratives in editorials, political speeches, charity appeals, as well as ads.

Distinction 4: The Message Itself is a Target of Judgment

As already noted, consumer researchers have recognized that consumers have other goals pertaining to persuasion events besides the formation of valid topic attitudes. Among these goals are the evaluation of the message itself and those responsible for it. Therefore, consumer research has emphasized recipients' reactions to the *enterprise* of advertising persuasion – focusing upon advertisements and the practice of advertising as attitude objects.

Attitude toward the ad

In a recent commercial for Kellogg's Special K cereal, a series of middle-aged men appear on screen, each bemoaning some aspect of his physical build. The ad gently parodies women's obsession with their weight by having the men speak in feminine clichés (e.g. "I have my mother's thighs. I just have to accept that."). The intended audience, health- and weight-conscious women, is likely to find the ad hilarious, if somewhat mocking. Yet, although the emphasis on weight-control is consistent with Special K's established positioning strategy in the highly competitive breakfast-cereal market, virtually no information about the cereal itself is presented in the commercial. How, then, can we conceptualize the likely persuasive impact of this campaign?

One might view the effects of this campaign as illustrating simple affect transfer or classical conditioning. One might consider the humorous nature of the ad as constituting a peripheral cue to product evaluation, although what would be cued by the humor is not clear. Or one might consider that ad viewers are processing this ad more thoughtfully, drawing inferences about the company based on the rhetorical strategy it has chosen. All of these inferences, perceptions, affective reactions, and the resultant *attitudes toward the ad* may ultimately influence perceptions of the advertised brand in a variety of ways.

The attitude-toward-the-ad construct (A_{ad}) has been extensively researched in CIP. A_{ad} has been conceptualized in ways that parallel other attitude definitions (for a review see Cohen & Areni, 1991). Thus, A_{ad} can be formed either via the central or the peripheral route and can be based on affective or cognitive factors. The key assumption is that the consumer's A_{ad} is distinct from her attitude toward the brand (A_{brand}), and that A_{ad} mediates the effect of an ad on A_{brand} under certain conditions (Mitchell & Olson, 1981). A number of mediational models have been proposed, and research has yielded evidence for different mechanisms by which A_{ad} might mediate advertising effects on A_{brand} (see Cohen & Areni, 1991).

A variety of factors are thought to influence A_{ad}. Pictures, music, and other non-verbal elements influence A_{ad}, and some of the studies of non-verbal elements cited earlier have conceptualized these elements as influencing A_{brand} via their impact on A_{ad} (e.g. MacInnis & Park, 1991; Mitchell & Olson, 1981). In addition to executional factors, Lutz (1985) hypothesized a variety of other antecedents of A_{ad}, including the ad's credibility, attitude toward the advertiser and toward advertising, and the recipient's mood state. Recent evidence has supported the impact of some of these factors on A_{ad} (e.g. Obermiller & Spangenberg, 1998).

Ad skepticism

Research on ad skepticism has included studies of public opinion toward ad trustworthiness and believability of ads as well as research on the factors that elicit skeptical responses. Public opinion toward advertising has long been a focus of survey research (for a review see Calfee & Ringold, 1994). Many of these surveys point to widespread and enduring skepticism about advertising, coexisting with a belief in the utility of advertising information. Indeed, when focused upon their own experiences and personally relevant decisions, survey respondents view advertising as more reliable and express greater confidence in it than when rating the trustworthiness of advertising in general terms (Shavitt, Lowrey, & Haefner, 1998).

A number of factors affect the skepticism with which a message is received. For instance, certain attention-getting tactics in advertisements (e.g. the delayed identification of the product being advertised) may tend to invite consumer skepticism (Campbell, 1995). The effects of these tactics on persuasion appear to be mediated by inferences that the ad is attempting to manipulate, or unfairly persuade, the recipient. Once those inferences are triggered by structural features of the ad, resistance to persuasion may result.

Also, some people are more likely than others to respond skeptically to advertisements. Obermiller & Spangenberg (1998) showed that reliable individual differences in ad skepticism exist, and that one's degree of ad skepticism predicts the degree to which one responds unfavorably to ads. Ad skepticism is not unrelated to the more general social psychological construct of influenceability (see Rhodes & Wood, 1992). Indeed, as with individual differences in influenceability, individuals higher in ad skepticism tend to be higher in self-esteem. However, Obermiller and Spangenberg showed that ad skepticism does not reflect a general tendency to disbelieve communications. It appears instead to be associated with consumers' implicit theories about the marketplace.

Persuasion knowledge

The above research examples demonstrate the value of considering that advertising is a shared sociocultural experience with which consumers have extensive experience and about which consumers develop extensive folk knowledge (Friestad & Wright, 1994). They recognize that advertisements are designed to persuade, and that the visuals, music, and copy all are crafted with particular rhetorical intentions.

Thus, consumers likely approach advertisements with the goal of "sizing up" the qualities of the message and the agent behind it. Indeed, drawing such inferences can be important to making effective marketplace decisions. The Persuasion Knowledge Model (PKM: Friestad & Wright, 1994) focuses on these processes. According to the PKM, consumers over time develop personal knowledge about the tactics that persuasion practitioners use. In any persuasion episode, the consumer deploys her available knowledge about the topic, the agents, and about persuasive tactics in general in order to evaluate the situation and guide her responses to it. The model has some relevance to the social psychological literature on forewarning of persuasive intent (e.g. Haas & Grady, 1975) and on attribution-theory accounts of persuasion (e.g. Eagly, Wood, & Chaiken, 1978), but focuses in greater detail on lay knowledge about persuasion processes in general, as well as on the accumulation and impact of that knowledge.

Friestad and Wright theorize that persuasion knowledge may interact with and qualify the effects of other variables on persuasion. For instance, individual differences in persuasion knowledge may moderate the effectiveness of particular persuasive tactics. Also, the awareness or labeling of an agent's action as a "persuasion tactic" may prompt changes in the processing and effectiveness of the message, as well as in a consumer's construal of persuasion attempts in general. A number of studies have yielded data congenial to the PKM. For instance, extensive research has indicated that consumers draw specific, predictable conclusions about marketers and their products from particular ad campaign elements (conclusions that are unstated and possibly unintended by the advertiser). Kirmani (1997) demonstrated that the number of times an ad is repeated serves as a signal to the quality of an unfamiliar brand. However, at very high levels of repetition, consumers perceive the expenditure as excessive and infer that "something must be wrong" with the brand. This relationship between repetition and quality perceptions is mediated not by irritation and boredom (as implied by information-processing views of repetition; e.g. Batra & Ray, 1986; Cacioppo & Petty, 1979) but by perceptions about the manufacturer's confidence in the brand.

These findings point to the importance of recognizing that the consumer's task in responding to an ad campaign is much more complex than the evaluation of specific message arguments.

The consumer responds to a broader set of message factors whose implications for judgment are often inferred through the use of extensive folk knowledge about the persuasion enterprise.

Conclusion

Clearly, social-cognition principles have translated very well into the consumer domain. Above, we have reviewed the substantial evidence for some of these principles in the consumer context. However, despite overlap in these domains, it should be stressed that consumer research is not simply social psychology applied to products instead of persons. Each field focuses on questions specific to its domain. That is, social-cognitive models have generally been designed to illuminate processes in the perception of persons, social groups, or social/political issues. CIP models have attempted to address issues that are salient in the marketplace of products and messages.

So far, the interdisciplinary exchange has been rather one-sided, but above we have pointed out a number of arenas where opportunities exist for more balanced exchange. Being cognizant of the unique features of the consumer domain will serve both to enhance knowledge about consumer behavior and to stimulate expansion of basic social-cognitive models.

REFERENCES

Aaker, J. L., & Maheswaran, D. (1997). The effect of cultural orientation on persuasion. *Journal of Consumer Research*, *24*(3), 315–328.

Agres, S. J., Edell, J. A., & Dubitsky, T. M. (1990). *Emotion in advertising: Theoretical and practical explorations*. New York: Quorum Books.

Alba, J. W., & Hutchinson, J. W. (1987). Dimensions of consumer expertise. *Journal of Consumer Research*, *13*, 411–454.

Alba, J. W., Hutchinson, J. W., & Lynch, J. G. (1991). Memory and decision making. In T. S. Robertson & H. H. Kassarjian (Eds.), *Handbook of consumer behavior* (pp. 1–49). Englewood Cliffs, NJ: Prentice-Hall.

Axelrod, J. (1963). Induced moods and attitudes toward products. *Journal of Advertising Research*, *3*, 19–24.

Baker, W. E., & Lutz, R. J. (1988). The relevance-accessibility model of advertising effectiveness. In S. Hecker & D. M. Stewart (Eds.), *Nonverbal communications in advertising* (pp. 59–84). Lexington, MA: Lexington.

Banaji, M. R., Lemm, K. M., & Carpenter, S. J. (2001). The social unconscious. In A. Tesser & N. Schwarz (Eds.), *Blackwell handbook of social psychology: Intraindividual processes* (pp. 134–158). Oxford: Blackwell Publishing.

Bargh, J. A., Chen, M., & Burrows, L. (1996). Automaticity of social behavior: Direct effects of trait construct and stereotype activation on action. *Journal of Personality and Social Psychology*, *71*(2), 230–244.

Batra, R., & Ray, M. L. (1986). Situational effects of advertising repetition: The moderating influence of motivation, ability, and opportunity to respond. *Journal of Consumer Research*, *12* (March), 432–445.

Batra, R., & Stayman, D. M. (1990). The role of mood in advertising effectiveness. *Journal of Consumer Research*, *17*, 203–214.

Berger, I. E., & Mitchell, A. A. (1989). The effect of advertising on attitude accessibility, attitude confidence, and the attitude-behavior relationship. *Journal of Consumer Research, 16,* 269–279.

Bettmann, J. R., Johnson, E. J., & Payne, J. W. (1991). Consumer decision making. In T. S. Robertson & H. H. Kassarjian (Eds.), *Handbook of consumer behavior* (pp. 50–84). Englewood Cliffs, NJ: Prentice-Hall.

Biehal, G. J., & Chakravarti, D. (1983). Information accessibility as a moderator of consumer choice. *Journal of Consumer Research, 10,* 1–14.

Bless, H. (2001). The consequences of mood on the processing of social information. In A. Tesser & N. Schwarz (Eds.), *Blackwell handbook of social psychology: Intraindividual processes* (pp. 391–412). Oxford: Blackwell Publishing.

Bornstein, R. F. (1989). Exposure and affect: Overview and meta-analysis of research, 1968–1987. *Psychological Bulletin, 106* (September), 265–289.

Boush, D., & Loken, B. (1991). A process tracing study of brand extension evaluations. *Journal of Marketing Research, 19,* 16–28.

Broniarczyk, S. M., & Alba, J. W. (1994). The importance of the brand in brand extension. *Journal of Marketing Research, 31,* 214–228.

Cacioppo, J. T., & Petty, R. E. (1979). Effects of message repetition and position on cognitive response, recall, and persuasion. *Journal of Personality and Social Psychology, 37* (January), 97–109.

Calder, B. J., & Sternthal, B. (1980). Television commercial wearout: An information processing view. *Journal of Marketing Research, 17,* 173–186.

Calfee, J. E., & Ringold, D. J. (1994). The seventy-percent majority: Enduring consumer beliefs about advertising. *Journal of Public Policy and Marketing, 13,* 228–238.

Campbell, M. (1995). When attention-getting advertising tactics elicit consumer inferences of manipulative intent: The importance of balancing benefits and investments. *Journal of Consumer Psychology, 4,* 225–254.

Carpenter, G. S., Glazer, R., & Nakamoto, K. (1994). Meaningful brands from meaningless differentiation: The dependence on irrelevant attributes. *Journal of Marketing Research, 31,* 339–350.

Childers, T. L., & Houston, M. J. (1984). Conditions for a picture-superiority effect on consumer theory. *Journal of Consumer Research, 15,* 643–654.

Cohen, J. B., & Areni, C. S. (1991). Affect and consumer behavior. In T. S. Robertson & H. H. Kassarjian (Eds.), *Handbook of consumer behavior* (pp. 188–240). Englewood Cliffs, NJ: Prentice-Hall.

Deighton, J., Romer, D., & McQueen, J. (1989). Using drama to persuade. *Journal of Consumer Research, 16*(3), 335–343.

Dhar, R., & Simonson, I. (1992). The effects of the focus of comparison on consumer preferences. *Journal of Marketing Research, 29,* 430–440.

Dhar, R., & Wertenbroch, K. (1997). Consumer choice between hedonic and utilitarian goods. Unpublished manuscript. New Haven, CT: Yale University.

Eagly, A. H., Wood, W., & Chaiken, S. (1978). Causal inferences about communicators and their effect on opinion change. *Journal of Personality and Social Psychology, 36,* 424–435.

Feldman, J. M., & Lynch, J. G. (1988). Self-generated validity and other effects of measurement on belief, attitude, intention, and behavior. *Journal of Applied Psychology, 73,* 421–435.

Friestad, M., & Wright, P. (1994). The persuasion knowledge model: How people cope with persuasion attempts. *Journal of Consumer Research, 21*(1), 1–31.

Gardner, M. P. (1994). Responses to emotional and informational appeals: The moderating role of context-induced mood states. In E. M. Clark & T. C. Brock (Eds.), *Attention, attitude, and affect in response to advertising* (pp. 207–221). Hillsdale, NJ: Lawrence Erlbaum Associates.

Goodstein, R. C. (1993). Category-based applications and extensions in advertising: Motivating more extensive ad processing. *Journal of Consumer Research, 20*, 87–99.

Gorn, G. J., Goldberg, M. E., & Basu, K. (1993). Mood, awareness, and product evaluation. *Journal of Consumer Research, 2*, 237–256.

Greenwald, A. G., & Leavitt, C. (1984). Audience involvement in advertising: Four levels. *Journal of Consumer Research, 11* (June), 581–592.

Haas, R. G., & Grady, K. (1975). Temporal delay, type of forewarning, and resistance to influence. *Journal of Experimental Social Psychology, 11* (September), 459–469.

Hall, E. T. (1976). *Beyond culture*. Garden City, NJ: Anchor Press/Doubleday.

Han, S., & Shavitt, S. (1994). Persuasion and culture: Advertising appeals in individualistic and collectivistic societies. *Journal of Experimental Social Psychology, 30*, 326–350.

Hasher, L., Goldstein, D., & Toppino, T. (1977). Frequency and the conference of referential validity. *Journal of Verbal Learning and Verbal Behavior, 16*(1), 107–112.

Hawkins, S. A., & Hoch, S. J. (1992). Low-involvement learning: Memory without evaluation. *Journal of Consumer Research, 19*(2), 212–225.

Herr, P. M., Farquahar, P. H., & Fazio, R. H. (1996). Impact of dominance and relatedness on brand extensions. *Journal of Consumer Psychology*, 135–160.

Hong, J. W., Muderrisoglu, A., & Zinkhan, G. M. (1987). Cultural differences in advertising expression: A comparative content analysis of Japanese and US magazine advertising. *Journal of Advertising, 16*(1), 55–62.

Houston, M. J., Childers, T. L., & Heckler, S. E. (1987). Picture-word consistency and the elaborative processing of advertisements. *Journal of Marketing Research, 24*, 359–370.

Huber, J., Payne, J. W., & Puto, C. (1982). Adding asymmetrically dominated alternatives: Violations of regularity and the similarity heuristic. *Journal of Consumer Research, 9*, 90–98.

Isen, A. M., Shalker, T. E., Clark, M., & Karp, L. (1978). Affect, accessibility of material in memory, and behavior: A cognitive loop? *Journal of Personality and Social Psychology, 36*, 1–12.

Janiszewski, C. (1993). Preattentive mere exposure effects. *Journal of Consumer Research, 20*(3), 376–392.

Johar, G. V. (1995). Consumer involvement and deception from implied advertising claims. *Journal of Marketing Research, 32*, 267–279.

Kahneman, D., & Snell, J. S. (1992). Predicting a changing taste: Do people know what they will like? *Journal of Behavioral Decision Making, 5*, 187–200.

Kamins, M. A., Marks, L. J., & Skinner, D. (1991). Television commercial evaluation in the context of program induced mood: Congruency versus consistency effects. *Journal of Advertising, 20*, 1–14.

Kardes, F. R. (1993). Consumer inference: Determinants, consequences, and implications for advertising. In A. A. Mitchell (Ed.), *Advertising exposure, memory and choice* (pp. 163–191). Hillsdale, NJ: Lawrence Erlbaum Associates.

Kellaris, J. J., Cox, A. D., & Cox, D. (1993). The effect of background music on ad processing: A contingency explanation. *Journal of Marketing, 57*(4), 114–125.

Keller, P. A., & Block, L. (1997). Vividness effects: A resource-matching perspective. *Journal of Consumer Research, 24*, 295–304.

Kirmani, A. (1997). Advertising repetition as a signal of quality: If it's advertised so much, something must be wrong. *Journal of Advertising, 26*(3), 77–86.

Kisielius, J., & Sternthal, B. (1984). Detecting and explaining vividness effects in attitudinal judgments. *Journal of Marketing Research, 21*, 54–64.

Krugman, H. E. (1965). The impact of television advertising: Learning without involvement. *Public Opinion Quarterly, 29*(3), 349–356.

Lavidge, R. C., & Steiner, G. A. (1961). A model for predictive measurements of advertising effectiveness. *Journal of Marketing*, *25*(4), 59–62.

Leong, S. M. (1989). A citation analysis of the Journal of Consumer Research. *Journal of Consumer Research*, *15*, 492–497.

Lewis, E. S. E. (1898). Die AIDA-Regel. Cited from H. Jacobi (1963). *Werbepsychologie*. Wiesbaden: Gabler.

Loken, B., & Roedder-John, D. (1993). Diluting brand beliefs: When do brand extensions have a negative impact? *Journal of Marketing*, *57*, 71–84.

Lutz, R. J. (1985). Affective and cognitive antecedents of attitude toward the ad: A conceptual framework. In L. F. Alwitt & A. A. Mitchell (Eds.), *Psychological processes and advertising effects: Theory, research and applications* (pp. 45–63). Hillsdale, NJ: Erlbaum.

Lynch, J. G., Marmorstein, H., & Weigold, M. F. (1988). Choices from sets including remembered brands: Use of recalled attributes and prior overall evaluations. *Journal of Consumer Research*, *15*(2), 169–184.

MacInnis, D. J., & Park, C. W. (1991). The differential role of characteristics of music on high- and low-involvement consumers' processing of ads. *Journal of Consumer Research*, *18*(2), 161–173.

Maheswaran, D., & Chaiken, S. (1991). Promoting systematic processing in low-motivation settings: Effect of incongruent information on processing and judgment. *Journal of Personality and Social Psychology 61* (July), 13–25.

Martin, L. L., Abend, T., Sedikides, C., & Green, J. D. (1997). How would it feel if . . . ? Mood as input to a role fulfillment evaluation process. *Journal of Personality and Social Psychology*, *73*, 242–253.

Martin, L. L., Strack, F., & Stapel, D. A. (2001). How the mind moves: Knowledge accessibility and the fine tuning of the cognitive system. In A. Tesser & N. Schwarz (Eds.), *Blackwell handbook of social psychology: Intraindividual processes* (pp. 236–256). Oxford: Blackwell Publishing.

Mattenklott, A. (1998). Werbewirkung im Umfeld von Fernsehprogrammen: Programmvermittelte Aktivierung und Stimmung. *Zeitschrift für Sozialpsychologie*, *29*, 175–193.

Meyers-Levy, J., & Peracchio, L. A. (1995). Understanding the effects of color: How the correspondence between available and required resources affects attitudes. *Journal of Consumer Research*, *22*, 121–138.

Meyers-Levy, J., & Peracchio, L. A. (1996). Moderators of the impact of self-reference or persuasion. *Journal of Consumer Research*, *22*, 408–423.

Meyers-Levy, J., & Tybout, A. M. (1997). Context effects at encoding and judgment in consumption settings: The role of cognitive resources. *Journal of Consumer Research*, *24*(1), 1–14.

Miller, J. G. (2001). The cultural grounding of social psychology theory. In A. Tesser & N. Schwarz (Eds.), *Blackwell handbook of social psychology: Intraindividual processes* (pp. 22–43). Oxford: Blackwell Publishing.

Miracle, G. E. (1987). Feel-do-learn: An alternative sequence underlying Japanese consumer response to television commercials. In F. G. Feasley (Ed.), *The proceedings of the 1987 conference of the American Academy of Advertising* (pp. R73–R78). Columbia, SC: University of South Carolina.

Mitchell, A. A. (1986). The effects of verbal and visual components of advertisements on brand attitudes and attitude toward the advertisement. *Journal of Consumer Research*, *13*, 12–24.

Mitchell, A. A. (Ed.) (1993). *Advertising exposure, memory, and choice*. Hillsdale, NJ: Lawrence Erlbaum Associates.

Mitchell, A. A., & Olson, J. C. (1981). Are product attribute beliefs the only mediator of advertising effects on brand attitude? *Journal of Marketing Research*, *18*, 318–332.

Moore, D. J., Reardon, R., & Durso, F. T. (1986). The generation effect in advertising appeals. *Advances in Consumer Research*, *13*, 117–120.

Moorthy, S., Ratchford, B. T., & Talukdar, D. (1997). Consumer information search revisited: Theory and empirical analysis. *Journal of Consumer Research, 23*, 263–277.

Nedungadi, P. (1990). Recall and consumer consideration sets: Influencing choice without altering brand evaluations. *Journal of Consumer Research, 17*, 263–276.

Obermiller, C., & Spangenberg, E. R. (1998). Development of a scale to measure consumer skepticism toward advertising. *Journal of Consumer Psychology, 7*(2), 159–186.

Ogilvy, D. (1985). *Ogilvy on advertising.* New York: Vintage Books.

O'Guinn, T. C., & Faber, R. J. (1991). Mass communication and consumer behavior. In T. S. Robertson & H. H. Kassarjian (Eds.), *Handbook of consumer behavior* (pp. 349–400). Englewood Cliffs, NJ: Prentice-Hall.

Park, C. W., McCarthy, M. S., & Milberg, S. J. (1993). The effects associated with direct and associative brand extension strategies on consumer response to brand extensions. *Advances in Consumer Research, 20,* 28–33.

Park, C. W., Milberg, S., & Lawson, R. (1991). Evaluation of brand extensions: The role of product feature similarity and brand concept consistency. *Journal of Consumer Research, 18*, 185–193.

Pavelchak, M. A., Antil, J. H., & Munch, J. M. (1988). The Super Bowl: An investigation into the relationship among program context, emotional experience, and ad recall. *Journal of Consumer Research, 15*, 360–367.

Petty, R. E., Cacioppo, J. T., & Schumann, D. (1983). Central and peripheral routes to advertising effectiveness: The moderating role of involvement. *Journal of Consumer Research, 10*(2), 135–146.

Phillips, B. J. (1997). Thinking into it: Consumer interpretation of complex advertising images. *Journal of Advertising, 26*(2) 77–87.

Ratneshwar, S., & Shocker, A. D. (1991). Substitution in use and the role of usage context in product category structures. *Journal of Marketing Research, 28*, 281–295.

Rhodes, N., & Wood, W. (1992). Self-esteem and intelligence affect influenceability: The mediation role of message reception. *Psychological Bulletin, 111*, 156–171.

Robertson, T. S., & Kassarjian, H. H. (Eds.) (1991). *Handbook of consumer behavior.* Englewood Cliffs, NJ: Prentice-Hall.

Rossiter, J. R., & Percy, L. (1987). *Advertising and promotion management.* New York: McGraw-Hill.

Sawyer, A. G., & Howard, D. J. (1991). Effects of omitting conclusions in advertisements to involved and uninvolved audiences. *Journal of Marketing Research, 28*, 467–474.

Schmidt, J. B., & Spreng, R. A. (1996). A proposed model of external consumer information search. *Journal of the Academy of Marketing Science, 24*, 246–256.

Schul, Y., & Schiff, M. (1993). Measuring satisfaction with organizations. *Public Opinion Quarterly, 57*, 536–551.

Scott, L. M. (1990). Understanding jingles and needledrop: A rhetorical approach to music in advertising. *Journal of Consumer Research, 17* (September), 223–237.

Scott, L. M. (1994). Images in advertising: The need for a theory of visual rhetoric. *Journal of Consumer Research, 21*(2), 252–273.

Severn, J., Belch, G. E., & Belch, M. A. (1990). The effects of sexual and non-sexual advertising appeals and information level on cognitive processing and communication effectiveness. *Journal of Advertising, 19*, 14–22.

Shapiro, S., MacInnis, D. J., & Heckler, S. E. (1997). The effects of incidental ad exposure on the formation of consideration sets. *Journal of Consumer Research, 24*(1), 94–104.

Shavitt, S., & Brock, T. C. (1986). Self-relevant responses in commercial persuasion: Field and experimental tests. In J. Olson & K. Sentis (Eds.), *Advertising and consumer psychology*, Vol. 3 (pp. 149–171). New York: Praeger Publishers.

Shavitt, S., & Brock, T. C. (1990). Delayed recall of copytest responses: The temporal stability of listed thoughts. *Journal of Advertising, 19*(4), 6–17.

Shavitt, S., Lowrey, P., & Haefner, J. (1998). Public attitudes toward advertising: More favorable than you might think. *Journal of Advertising Research, 38*(4), 7–22.

Shavitt, S., Nelson, M. R., & Yuan, R. M. L. (1997). Exploring cross-cultural differences in cognitive responding to ads. In M. Brucks & D. J. MacInnis (Eds.), *Advances in consumer research*, Vol. 24 (pp. 245–250). Provo, UT: Association for Consumer Research.

Shavitt, S., Swan, S., Lowrey, T. M., & Wänke, M. (1994). The interaction of endorser attractiveness and involvement in persuasion depends on the goal that guides message processing. *Journal of Consumer Psychology, 3*(2), 137–162.

Shocker, A. D., Srivastava, R. K., & Ruekert, R. W. (1994). Challenges and opportunities facing brand management: An introduction to the special issue. *Journal of Marketing Research, 31*, 149–158.

Smith, R. A. (1991). The effects of visual and verbal advertising information on consumers' inferences. *Journal of Advertising, 20*, 13–23.

Solomon, M. R. (1992). *Consumer behavior: Buying, having, and being.* Needham Heights, MA: Allyn and Bacon.

Srull, T. K. (1989). Advertising and product evaluation: The relation between consumer memory and judgment. In P. Cafferata & A. M. Tybout (Eds.), *Cognitive and affective responses to advertising* (pp. 121–134). Lexington, MA: Lexington Books/D. C. Heath.

Stuart, E. W., Shimp, T. A., & Engle, R. W. (1987). Classical conditioning of consumer attitudes: Four experiments in an advertising context. *Journal of Consumer Research, 14*, 334–349.

Sujan, M. (1985). Consumer knowledge: Effects on evaluation strategies mediating consumer judgments. *Journal of Consumer Research, 12*, 31–46.

Taylor, C. R., Miracle, G. E., & Wilson, R. D. (1997). The impact of information level on the effectiveness of US & Korean television commercials. *Journal of Advertising, 26*(1), 1–18.

Tversky, A., & Simonson, I. (1993). Context dependent preferences. *Management Science, 39*, 1179–1189.

Unnava, H. R., & Burnkrant, R. E. (1991). An imagery-processing view of the role of pictures in print advertisements. *Journal of Marketing Research, 28*, 226–231.

Wänke, M., & Bless, H. (in press). Possible mediators of ease of retrieval effects in attitudinal judgments. In H. Bless & J. Forgas (Eds.), *The role of subjective states in social cognition and behavior.* Psychology Press.

Wänke, M., & Bless, H. (in press). The effects of subjective ease of retrieval on attitudinal judgments: The moderating role of processing motivation. In H. Bless & J. P. Forgas (Eds.), *The message within: The role of subjective experience in social cognition and behavior.* Philadelphia: Psychology Press.

Wänke, M., Bless, H., & Biller, B. (1996). Subjective experience versus content of information in the construction of attitude judgments. *Personality and Social Psychology Bulletin, 22*, 1105–1113.

Wänke, M., Bless, H., & Schwarz, N. (1998). Context effects in product line extensions: Context is not destiny. *Journal of Consumer Psychology, 7*, 299–322.

Wänke, M., Bless, H., & Schwarz, N. (in press-a). Lobster, wine, and cigarettes: Ad hoc categorizations and the emergence of context effects. *Marketing Bulletin.*

Wänke, M., Bless, H., & Schwarz, N. (in press-b). Assimilation and contrast in brand and product evaluations: Implications for marketing. *Advances in Consumer Research.*

Wänke, M., Bohner, G., & Jurkowitsch, A. (1997). There are many reasons to drive a BMW: Does imagined ease of argument generation influence attitudes? *Journal of Consumer Research, 24*(2), 170–177.

Wänke, M., Schwarz, N., & Noelle-Neumann, E. (1995). Question wording in comparative judgments: Understanding and manipulating the dynamics of the direction of comparison. *Public Opinion Quarterly, 59,* 347–372.

Ward, J., & Loken, B. (1986). The quintessential snack food: Measurement of product prototypes. In R. J. Lutz (Ed.), *Advances in consumer research,* Vol. 13 (pp. 126–131). Provo, UT: Association for Consumer Research.

Wells, W. D. (1988). Lectures and dramas. In P. Cafferata & A. M. Tybout (Eds.), *Cognitive and affective responses to advertising.* Lexington, MA: Lexington Books/D. C. Heath.

Wilkie, W. L. (1994). *Consumer behavior.* New York: Wiley.

Yi, Y. (1990). The effects of contextual priming in print advertisements. *Journal of Consumer Research, 17*(2), 215–222.

Zhang, Y. & Gelb, B. D. (1996). Matching advertising appeals to culture: The influence of products' use conditions. *Journal of Advertising, 25*(3), 29–46.

CHAPTER TWELVE

The Death and Rebirth of the Social Psychology of Negotiation

Max H. Bazerman, Jared R. Curhan,
and Don A. Moore

Introduction

In the 1970s, social psychology was one of the best-represented disciplines in negotiation research (Druckman, 1977; Pruitt, 1981; Rubin & Brown, 1975). Yet, as the social cognitive movement took hold within psychology during the 1980s, the study of negotiations did not fit readily into the changing field and largely disappeared from social psychology. In business schools, by contrast, negotiation was perhaps the fastest growing topic of research in that decade. However, the dominant research perspective of negotiation that emerged during the 1980s was grounded in behavioral decision research and emphasized the systematic and predictable mistakes that negotiators make (i.e., departures from rationality). It left the social variables in negotiations largely unexamined. At the beginning of the twenty-first century, we see the reemergence of the social psychological study of negotiation. This reemergence has been affected profoundly by the behavioral decision theory perspective of the 1980s and 1990s. Yet it also highlights social phenomena that were ignored by investigators with a more cognitive orientation.

In this chapter, we present a brief history of the life and death of negotiation research in social psychology during the 1970s and 1980s as well as the behavioral decision theory perspective that prevailed in business schools during the 1980s and the early 1990s. The chapter also reviews current research heralding the rebirth of the social psychology of negotiations and highlighting important new directions in this area of study.

The authors received support for this research from the Dispute Resolution Research Center at Northwestern University, the Dean's office of the J. L. Kellogg Graduate School of Management at Northwestern University, and Faculty Research Support from Harvard Business School. The second author was supported by a National Science Foundation Graduate Research Fellowship. The third author held a visiting position at the Harvard Business School for much of the time spent writing this paper. The paper benefited from excellent feedback obtained from Margaret Clark, Margaret Neale, Susan Rees, Hannah Riley, Rob Robinson, Lee Ross, Katie Shonk, and Leigh Thompson.

Negotiations research before 1980

Throughout the 1960s and 1970s, the study of negotiations in social psychology consisted of two main streams of research – the study of individual differences among negotiators and the study of situational factors that facilitate or impede the negotiation process. The dominant psychological research on negotiations emphasized individual difference variables (Rubin & Brown, 1975), including both demographic characteristics (such as gender) and personality variables (such as risk-taking tendencies). Gender, race, age, risk-taking tendencies, locus-of-control, cognitive complexity, tolerance for ambiguity, self-esteem, authoritarianism, and Machiavellianism were all research topics in the 1960s negotiation literature (Lewicki, Weiss, & Lewin, 1988; Neale & Bayerman, 1992; Rubin & Brown, 1975).

Since bargaining is clearly an interpersonal activity, it seems logical that the participants' dispositions should exert significant influence on the process and outcomes of negotiations. However, despite hundreds of studies on individual differences such as those mentioned above, such factors typically do not explain much variance in negotiator behavior (Thompson, 1990). Furthermore, and consistent with findings from the broader field of social psychology (Ross & Nisbett, 1991), slight changes in situational or contextual features often swamp any individual difference effects.

Research on gender differences in negotiation provides a good example of a failed attempt to find individual differences in negotiator behavior. Across hundreds of studies, there has been no consistent evidence to support a main effect for gender differences in negotiator performance (Lewicki, Litterer, Minton, & Saunders, 1999). Thompson (1990) argued that the findings that do support gender effects must be viewed skeptically. She asserted that studies have reported gender differences inconsistently, often as a secondary analysis. The implication is that there may be an even larger number of studies that have never reported findings on gender differences because of the lack of a statistically demonstrable effect. Walters, Stuhlmacher, and Meyer (1998), in their meta-analysis of 62 studies of gender and negotiator competitiveness, concluded that gender differences account for less than 1 percent of the variance in competitiveness. Furthermore, based on a review of 34 research studies conducted since 1975, Watson (1994) asserted that situational factors, such as situational power, are better predictors of negotiation behavior and outcomes than is gender. Walters et al. (1998) concluded: "It appears that even small variations in experimental conditions can eliminate these differences entirely, or more surprisingly, cause them to change direction. Considering all of the factors that shape our decision to be competitive or cooperative in interpersonal bargaining, our gender accounts for but a small fraction" (p. 23).

Although the debate continues (Barry & Friedman, 1998), a number of authors have reached the conclusion that individual differences offer little insight into predicting negotiator behavior and negotiation outcomes (Lewicki et al., 1999; Pruitt & Carnevale, 1993). Lewicki et al. concluded that ". . . there are few significant relationships between personality and negotiation outcomes." Similarly, Hermann and Kogan (1977) argued: "From what is known now, it does not appear that there is any single personality type or characteristic that is directly and clearly linked to success in negotiation." While to have searched and largely not found predictive value in individual difference variables might be considered a discovery unto itself, it is not a particularly rewarding one.

In addition to the lack of predictability of individual difference findings, the individual difference literature also has been criticized for its lack of relevance to practice. Bazerman and Carroll (1987) argued that individual differences are of limited value because of their fixed nature – i.e., they are not under the control of the negotiator. Of course, one could argue that knowing both the personal characteristics of one's counterpart and the effects of those characteristics might have practical implications. However, individuals, even so-called experts, are known to be poor at making clinical assessments about another person's personality in order to accurately formulate an opposing strategy (Bazerman, 1998; Morris, Larrick, & Su, 1998; Morris, Leung, & Sethi, 1998). Cultural differences in negotiation may be an exception to this generalization in that an understanding of such differences might help negotiators formulate strategies (Bazerman, Curhan, Moore, & Valley, 2000).

The second stream of research on negotiation in social psychology during the 1960s and 1970s was the study of situational variables, or relatively fixed, contextual components that define a negotiation. In the language of game theory, situational characteristics define the game. Situational factors include the presence or absence of a constituency (Druckman, 1967), the form of communication between negotiators (Wichman, 1970), the outcome payoffs available to the negotiators (Axelrod & May, 1968), the relative power of the parties (Marwell, Ratcliff, & Schmitt, 1969), deadlines (Pruitt & Drews, 1969), the number of people representing each side (Marwell & Schmitt, 1972), and the effects of third parties (Pruitt & Johnson, 1972). Research on situational variables has contributed to our understanding of the negotiation process and has directed both practitioners and academics to consider important structural components of negotiations. For example, the presence of observers has been shown to produce greater advocacy on behalf of previously announced positions (Lamm & Kogan, 1970) and to foster a more competitive bargaining atmosphere (Vidmar, 1971).

However, from an applied perspective, research on situational factors shares a critical shortcoming with research on individual differences. Situational factors represent aspects of the negotiation that are usually beyond the control of an individual negotiator. Drawing upon the example above, politicians cannot wish away the presence of their constituents. In organizational settings, participants' control over third-party intervention is limited by their willingness to make the dispute publicly visible. If and when the participants do make their disputes public, their managers typically are the ones who determine how and when to intervene (Murnighan, 1986; Pinkley, Brittain, Neale, & Northcraft, 1995). This lack of control applies to other situational factors as well, such as the relative power of the negotiators and prevailing deadlines. While negotiators can be advised to identify ways in which to manipulate their perceived power, obvious power disparities that result from resource munificence, hierarchical legitimacy, or expertise are less malleable. Negotiators are often best served by developing strategies for addressing these power differentials instead of trying to change them.

Our view is that negotiation is most usefully studied from an interpretive perspective. Consistent with social psychology's principle of construal (Nisbett & Ross, 1980; Ross & Nisbett, 1991), we believe that the effects of objective, external aspects of a situation depend on the way the negotiator perceives these features and uses those perceptions to interpret and screen information. This view follows directly from the work of Kelley and Thibaut (1978), who suggested that negotiators psychologically transform the structure of the negotiation to create the "effective" game that is to be played. The 1960s and1970s situational research in the negotiation literature suffered from a prescriptive void because it failed to consider this interpretive process.

In summary, the dominant social psychological approaches of the 1960s and 1970s research suffered from critical shortcomings. The individual difference literature from hundreds of studies yielded few consistent findings and thus failed to produce a compelling theory of negotiator behavior that could move the field ahead. The situational literature did not consider the importance of the negotiator's construal in interpreting the negotiation situation. Both literatures were limited in their practical usefulness by a prescriptive silence because they focused on aspects of the process that are beyond the negotiator's control. Moreover, these characteristics of the negotiation field proved inconsistent with the social cognitive movement in social psychology. Thus, in the 1980s and early 1990s, the study of negotiation lost its social psychological focus.

The behavioral decision theory perspective

During the 1980s, scholars in business schools, perhaps influenced by the social cognitive movement, began to recognize ways in which the expanding body of research on decision making might inform negotiation theory. If the typical negotiator is confronted with a situation and an opponent, and has relatively little power to change either one, then the only important feature of the negotiation situation that is routinely within the negotiator's control is how he or she makes decisions. The marriage of negotiation and decision-making research meant that individual axioms of decision making could be applied to negotiation research, lending theoretical rigor to the study of negotiation. Thus, the dominant perspective practiced by negotiation researchers became behavioral decision theory.

Decision researchers from various disciplines have offered a variety of theoretical perspectives on how to improve decision making (Bell, Raiffa, & Tversky, 1989). One aspect that differentiates these perspectives is the descriptive/prescriptive distinction. Behavioral researchers (e.g., psychologists, sociologists, and organizational behaviorists) tend to focus on describing how people *actually* make decisions, while more analytic fields (e.g., economics and decision analysis) typically prescribe how people *ought* to make decisions. Unfortunately, too little interaction has occurred between the descriptive and prescriptive camps.

A central premise of our perspective is that the most useful model of negotiation, and the individual decision making that occurs within it, will include both description and prescription (Lax & Sebenius, 1986). Raiffa made an important theoretical connection between these two camps when he advocated an "asymmetrically prescriptive/descriptive" approach (1982). This approach describes how decision analysis can be used to help individual negotiators ("asymmetric") predict the behavior of their counterparts ("descriptive") and then develop appropriate strategies to deal with those behaviors ("prescriptive").

Raiffa's work represents a turning point in negotiation research for a number of reasons. First, in the context of a prescriptive model, he explicitly acknowledged the importance of developing accurate descriptions of the opponent, rather than assuming the opponent to be fully rational. Second, his realization that negotiators need advice implicitly acknowledges that negotiators themselves do not intuitively follow purely rational strategies. Most importantly, Raiffa initiated the groundwork for dialogue between prescriptive and descriptive researchers. The focal negotiator must use descriptive models to anticipate the likely behavior of the opponent but must also rely on prescriptive advice to overcome his or her own decision biases.

Recently, Bazerman and Neale (1992; Bazerman, 1998; Neale & Bazerman, 1991) and Thompson (1990, 1998) introduced a body of research that addresses some of the questions that Raiffa's work left unexamined. For example, if the negotiator and his or her opponent do not act rationally, what systematic departures from rationality can be predicted? Building on work in behavioral decision theory, a number of deviations from rationality that can be expected in negotiations have been identified. Specifically, research on two-party negotiations suggests that negotiators tend to: (1) be inappropriately affected by the positive or negative frame in which risks are viewed (Bazerman, Magliozzi, & Neale, 1985); (2) anchor their number estimates in negotiations on irrelevant information (Northcraft & Neale, 1987; Tversky & Kahneman, 1974); (3) rely too heavily on readily available information (Neale, 1984); (4) be overconfident about the likelihood of attaining outcomes that favor themselves (Bazerman & Neale, 1982); (5) assume that negotiation tasks are necessarily fixed-sum and thereby miss opportunities for mutually beneficial trade-offs between the parties (Bazerman et al., 1985); (6) escalate commitment to a previously selected course of action when it is no longer the best alternative (Bazerman & Neale, 1983; Diekmann, Tenbrunsel, Shah, Schroth, & Bazerman, 1996); (7) overlook the valuable information that can be obtained by considering the opponent's cognitive perspective (Bazerman & Carroll, 1987; Samuelson & Bazerman, 1985); and (8) reactively devalue any concession that is made by the opponent (Ross & Stillinger, 1991).

The primary contribution that prescriptive models make to descriptive research is to provide a benchmark of optimality. Indeed, the growth and expansion of behavioral decision research has been fueled by the usefulness of performance standards based on perfect rationality, against which actual performance can be compared (Kahneman, Slovic, & Tversky, 1982) and improved (Bazerman, 1998).

In sum, the negotiation research of the 1980s and early 1990s was largely influenced by a behavioral decision theory perspective. This new perspective, informed by Raiffa's "asymmetrically prescriptive/descriptive" approach (1982), prompted a large body of research that outlines systematic departures from rationality in negotiator cognition. Thus, recent descriptive research informs a prescriptive approach by providing necessary information on the impediments to individual rationality.

The rebirth of negotiations research in social psychology

While the behavioral decision perspective has had a significant influence on the scholarship and practice of negotiation, it missed several key social components that are critical to the practical task of negotiating more effectively. In recent years, research has incorporated these missing social factors within the behavioral decision perspective. In the remainder of this chapter we review this set of previously underrepresented topics in the social psychological study of negotiation. Specifically, we focus on work dealing with social relationships, egocentrism, attribution and construal processes, motivated illusions, and emotion. Importantly, we examine this research within the context of a descriptive/prescriptive, decision perspective, highlighting how social factors can create shortcomings that need to be managed.

Social Relationships in Negotiation

Although the importance of relationships in negotiation has been cited repeatedly throughout the history of the negotiation field (e.g., Rubin & Brown, 1975; Rubin, Pruitt, & Kim, 1994; Walton & McKersie, 1965), the late 1980s and early 1990s, in particular, have witnessed a proliferation of studies on the topic (for reviews, see Greenhalgh & Chapman, 1996; Valley, Neale, & Mannix, 1995). The majority of these studies are influenced by the prescriptively descriptive focus of the behavioral decision theory perspective.

For the most part, the study of relationships and negotiation has occurred within three basic domains – the individual, the dyad, and the network. The first domain includes studies of how the judgments and preferences of individual negotiators are influenced by their social context (e.g., Clark, Mills, & Corcoran, 1989; Messick & Sentis, 1985; Morgan & Sawyer, 1967; Polzer, Neale, & Glenn, 1993; Thompson, Valley, & Kramer, 1995; for a review, see Clark & Chrisman, 1994). The second domain explores how social relationships within dyads can influence negotiation processes and outcomes (e.g., Greenhalgh & Chapman, 1996; Halpern, 1992, 1994, 1997a, 1997b; Schoeninger & Wood, 1969; Thompson & DeHarpport, 1990, 1998; for a review, see Valley et al., 1995). Finally, the third domain is concerned with the influence of relationships on the functioning of organizational networks (e.g., Baker, 1984, 1990; Halpern, 1996; Shah & Jehn, 1993; Sondak & Bazerman, 1989; Valley, 1992). Each of these domains is further described below, with a particular focus on the ways in which social relationships help or hinder the negotiation process.

Influence of relationships on the judgment and preferences of individual negotiators

There is evidence to support the argument that individual negotiators evaluate their own outcomes relative to outcomes obtained by their counterparts (Loewenstein, Thompson, & Bazerman, 1989; Thompson et al., 1995). For example, Loewenstein et al. found that disputants' preferences for hypothetical monetary payoffs are greatly influenced by payoffs to their hypothetical counterparts. Disputants generally were found to prefer equal payoffs to unequal payoffs, even when unequal payoffs slightly favored themselves. Such a socially influenced preference structure has been called "social utility" (Loewenstein et al., 1989; Messick & Sentis, 1979). However, when participants were instructed to imagine a negative relationship with their counterparts, they prefered inequality that favored themselves. This result suggests that the impact of social utility on negotiator preferences depends on the relationships among negotiators.

There has been some controversy over which distribution rule, in general, governs inter-actions that occur in close relationships (Clark & Chrisman, 1994). The controversy has centered on three rules in particular: equity, equality, and need (Deutsch, 1975). The question not only concerns which rule is followed, but also which rule tends to be preferred by individuals in close relationships.

Studies using self-reports from intimate couples have found that serious marital relationships tend to be characterized by equity (i.e. proportionality between contributions and benefits) rather than equality (i.e. absolute equality of benefits) (Sabatelli & Cecil-Pigo, 1985; Utne, Hatfield, Traupmann, & Greenberger, 1984). However, a number of laboratory studies (e.g., Austin, 1980; Greenberg, 1983a; Morgan & Sawyer, 1967; Polzer et al., 1993; Thompson et al., 1995) have found the opposite result: namely that equality is preferred over equity in close relationships. For example, Austin (1980) had participants allocate $5 between them-selves and a stranger or a roommate (presumably representing a close personal tie) after receiving false feedback on a word-find task. Strangers were guided primarily by self-interest, allocating the money equally when they believed they had done poorly on the task and equitably when they believed they had done well on the task. Roommates, on the other hand, almost always divided the money equally regardless of differences in task performance.

Clark and Chrisman (1994) argue that these two seemingly contradictory perspectives – equity and equality – can be reconciled through the principle of need (i.e. proportionality between exigency and benefits). The studies supporting the use of an equity allocation rule are based on correlation between self-reported measures, making them subject to a great number of alternative explanations. Studies that have found support for the equality rule typically do not provide participants with information about needs, leaving participants to apply the equality rule as a reasonable substitute for need (Clark & Chrisman, 1994).

A study by Sondak, Pinkley, and Neale (1994) supports Clark and Chrisman's (1994) assertion. Sondak et al. manipulated the scarcity of a jointly held resource and found that, while strangers often use an equity rule in their negotiations, roommates allocate according to equality when resources are available but according to need when resources are scarce. There-fore, an equality rule seems to be used by roommates only in the absence of information about needs. Whenever roommates' needs are made salient, they allocate according to need.

When compared against a standard of rationality, allocation according to need may appear to demand undue concessions on the part of less needy parties. However, this conclusion ignores the inter-temporal nature of a long-term relationship and the possibility of integrat-ive trade-offs over time (Mannix, Tinsley, & Bazerman, 1995). For example, Clark and Chrisman described need-based allocation in the context of an ongoing intimate relation-ship: "Each person should benefit the other in response to that other's needs without expect-ing specific repayments but reasonably expecting the other to be responsive to his/her needs if and when those needs arise and if the other has the ability to do so" (1994, p. 75).

Influence of relationships on negotiation processes and outcomes within dyads

In the previous section, we described research on how individuals evaluate and apply distribu-tion rules within social relationships. Inherent in this approach is the assumption that the preferences and actions of individuals, at least to some degree, influence negotiations. However, Bazerman, Gibbons, Thompson, and Valley (1998) argued that certain behaviors that appear irrational from the individual perspective may be rational from the perspective of the dyad. For example, given the opportunity to communicate freely, negotiators often appear irrational in their individual decision making yet reach dyadic outcomes that *outperform* game theoretic models (Valley, Moag, & Bazerman, 1998; Bazerman et al., 1998). That is, individuals negotiating face-to-face routinely divulge more high-quality information than a prescriptive analysis would say they should (i.e., individuals do not fully exploit each other), however, because of the nature of the simulation (cf., Akerlof, 1970), such revelation makes profitable agreement possible for both parties where it would not otherwise be. Consequently, an alternative approach to the study of relationships and negotiation is to view the *dyad* and its relationship as the critical unit of analysis (Greenhalgh & Chapman, 1995). In this tradition, researchers have asked how the relationship within a dyad influences that dyad's joint process and outcome.

A substantial number of studies have examined whether close relationships (social, collegial, or romantic) help or hinder dyadic negotiations. Although one might expect that close relationships would *improve* the overall quality of negotiations, the results of studies suggest that effects of relationships on negotiations are quite complex (Valley et al., 1995). In terms of negotiation process, close relationships are associated with more information sharing (Fry, Firestone, & Williams, 1983; Greenhalgh & Chapman, 1996), less coercive behavior (Fry et al., 1983; Greenhalgh & Chapman, 1996), less demanding initial offers (Halpern, 1992, 1994, 1997a, 1997b; Schoeninger & Wood, 1969; Thompson & DeHarpport, 1998), and faster completion of agreements (Schoeninger & Wood, 1969). However, most studies indicate that close dyadic relationships do *not* directly improve joint outcomes (Greenhalgh & Chapman, 1996; Thompson & DeHarpport, 1990, 1998).

In fact, in some cases, close relationships may contribute to a *reduction* in joint outcomes (Fry et al., 1983; Schoeninger & Wood, 1969). For example, Fry et al. compared the performance results of 74 dating couples with 32 mixed-sex stranger dyads on a three-issue negotiation simulation with integrative potential. Although dating couples exchange more truthful information and engage in less contentious behavior, they reach less integrative final agreements (i.e., lower joint profit; Pruitt, 1983). This effect is strongest for couples who rate themselves as highest on Rubin's love scale (1970) – i.e., couples who are defensive or possessive in their orientation toward one another.

Data from studies on the impact of close relationships on negotiation among dyads seems inconsistent until one considers that relationships are defined differently across studies – some studies used participants who were friends or colleagues while other studies used romantic partners. In their 1995 review of the relationships and negotiation literature, Valley, Neale, and Mannix noted that the few studies finding a reduction in integrativeness among close dyads (Fry et al., 1983; Schoenmger & Wood, 1969) used *lovers*, rather than friends, as participants. Therefore, Valley et al. (1995) proposed a curvilinear model to describe the association between relationship closeness and outcome integrativeness, suggesting that strangers and lovers fare worse than friends and colleagues. However, no study has demonstrated that friends and colleagues reach better joint outcomes than do strangers. The reason for this may lie in the nature of the outcomes measurable by conventional negotiation simulations. As Valley et al. explain: "Two friends coming to a laboratory to negotiate an artificial scenario cannot be expected to find the issues in the negotiation as important as maintaining their actual relationship" (1995, p. 87).

This explanation for the lack of association between relationship closeness and integrativeness is supported by research on the moderating effects of pressures to reach a *good* agreement. Ben-Yoav and Pruitt (1984) found that when participants are encouraged to have high aspirations, those who are led to expect cooperative future interaction achieve more integrative outcomes than do those who are not. Conversely, when participants are not encouraged to have high aspirations, expectations of future interaction are associated with less integrative outcomes. To the extent that anticipation of presumably cooperative future interaction is a feature of close relationships (Greenhalgh & Chapman, 1996; Greenhalgh & Gilkey, 1993), these findings suggest that high aspirations might be the key to realizing the benefits of friendly and collegial relationships. If supported by future research, this notion qualifies Valley et al.'s (1995) theory of the curvilinear relationship between closeness and integrativeness.

Influence of relationships on the functioning of organizational networks

Many contexts involve the availability of multiple potential negotiation partners. Therefore, a substantial body of research has addressed the question of how relationships influence negotiations in networks. For example, social networks have been found to predict stock market trading patterns (Baker, 1990), market ties between corporations (Baker, 1984), organizational allocations within a newspaper newsroom (Valley, 1992), and business relationships among senior real estate agents (Halpern, 1996).

While the existence of friendships within pre-existing small groups has been found to produce efficient decision-making and motor skills (Shah & Jehn, 1993), larger groups tend to be less efficient (Roth, 1982; Sondak & Bazerman, 1989, 1991), particularly when their member-to-member matching patterns are influenced by social relationships (Tenbrunsel, Wade-Benzoni, Moag, & Bazerman, 1998). Just as negotiator dyads in especially close relationships might choose to preserve their long-term relationships by making concessions rather than painstakingly searching for the most fully integrative outcomes, so too do individuals "satisfice" (March & Simon, 1958) by making deals with people they already know rather than seeking out new partners (Tenbrunsel et al., 1998).

Tenbrunsel et al. simulated a real estate market and examined the influence of pre-existing relationships. The results of their experiment demonstrate not only the clear sub-optimality of negotiators' partner selection (or "matching") process, but also how this sub-optimality is greatest when social relationships guide negotiator partner selection. In a follow-up study involving a more qualitative analysis, Tenbrunsel et al. determined a number of reasons why negotiators are influenced by social relationships, even though their doing so leads to sub-optimality. First, participants unwittingly abbreviate their partner-search activity in favor of matching with a person with whom they have a close personal tie. As in the dyad studies, negotiators place a value on non-scored factors such as fairness, trust, exchange of information, and ease of transaction. However, giving weight to these criteria does not pay off monetarily in terms of the actual negotiations. Instead, negotiators who deal with persons with whom they have close ties are more modest in their reservation prices and aspiration levels. In other words, in an attempt to enhance non-monetary payoffs such as friendship or ease of transaction, negotiators often search for negotiation partners with whom they share personal relationships, even when such partnering preferences reduce their expected monetary payoff.

Summary

Taken together, these three domains of research provide converging evidence of the potential positive *and* negative impact of relationships on negotiations. The literature on networks suggests that negotiators place value on the non-monetary benefits of relationships, leading to sub-optimal matching from a standpoint of monetary concerns and point payoffs (Tenbrunsel et al., 1998). However, research on dyadic interaction provides a potential alternative explanation for this apparent lack of rationality. That is, especially when pressures to reach good outcomes are weak (Ben-Yoav & Pruitt, 1984), dyads in laboratory studies are likely to prioritize maintaining or improving their real relationships over the substance of hypothetical role-play situations (Valley et al., 1995). Moreover, the tendency for dyads to achieve low joint outcomes could be a result of their reliance on the need rule (Sondak et al., 1994). Such use of the need rule, while seemingly irrational in one-shot negotiations, mighprove to facilitate inter-temporal logrolling or integrativeness *across* negotiations (Mannix et al., 1995).

Egocentrism in Negotiation

Whether or not they have close relationships with their negotiating partners, negotiators care about fairness. Indeed, fairness arguments play powerful roles in negotiation (Loewenstein et al., 1989; Messick & Sentis, 1979, 1985; Roth & Murnighan, 1982), even when enforcing standards of fairness results in a reduction of material payoffs to the individual (Loewenstein, Babcock, Issacharoff, & Camerer, 1993). However, as we shall see below, ambiguities in determining what is fair make room for egocentric or self-serving interpretations of fairness.

Evidence on egocentrism in negotiation

Walster, Walster, and Berscheid (1978) proposed that parties' interest in fairness is not purely objective, but that people may tend to overweigh the interpretations or fairness rules that favor themselves (see Diekmann, Samuels, Ross, & Bazerman, 1997). The result is that even though people display a preference for fairness, the desire for fairness in negotiated outcomes is easily biased in their own favor (for recent reviews, see Babcock & Loewenstein, 1997; Wade-Benzoni, Tenbrunsel, & Bazerman, 1997). This self-serving bias in assessment or interpretation has been referred to in the literature as egocentrism.

Thompson and Loewenstein (1992) found evidence of egocentrism in reports of fairness, and that egocentrism reduced negotiators' ability to come to agreement. In their first experiment, a negotiation over wages, participants played the role of either management or union. Participants in both roles prepared with the same case information. Before the negotiation, but after receiving their role assignments, parties were asked what they believed a fair outcome to be. These estimates were egocentrically biased: representatives of the union tended to believe that a higher wage was fairer, whereas representatives of management tended to report that a lower wage was fairer. Parties then proceeded to trade bids until they converged on an agreement. Delay was costly to both parties because it meant that the union would go on strike. Thompson and Loewenstein found that the amount of egocentric bias displayed in these pre-negotiation assessments of fairness predicted the length of time it would take parties to reach agreement. The greater egocentricity seen in the partie's *ex ante* perceptions of fairness, the longer strikes tended to last. (See also replications by Babcock, Loewenstein, Issacharoff, & Camerer, 1995; Camerer & Loewenstein, 1993; Loewenstein et al., 1993.)

In their second experiment, Thompson and Loewenstein varied the amount of information provided to participants. Some participants received only the bare facts about the case, whereas others received detailed background information that had been rated as "neutral" in pre-testing. It might be expected that more information should reduce uncertainty and facilitate agreement (Priest & Klein, 1984). However, Thompson and Loewenstein found that more information is associated with greater egocentrism. Those participants who received the background information tended to make more extreme self-serving estimates of a fair outcome (see also Camerer & Loewenstein, 1993). Furthermore, when participants were later tested for recall of the background information, they showed a self-serving recall bias in their tendency to best remember those facts that favored themselves. This self-serving recall effect has been replicated elsewhere (Camerer & Loewenstein, 1993; Loewenstein et al., 1993), and suggests that memory biases contribute to egocentrism during either encoding or retrieval.

Babcock et al. (1995) provided a clever demonstration of the biasing effect of self-interest on the encoding of information. The investigators varied the point at which the participants in the experiment learned which negotiation role they were to play. In particular, all participants received the same case background information, but some read it knowing their roles while others read it without knowing their roles. The results of this subtle manipulation were dramatic. Parties who know their roles before they read the case materials are four times as likely to reach impasse as are dyads who do not know their roles when they read that information. Those who know their roles from the outset also are significantly more egocentric both in their estimations of a fair solution and in their predictions of what a judge will determine to be the just outcome.

Participants in the studies cited here did not make their fairness judgments public. As such, these judgments could not be expected by the parties to influence the other participants' negotiation behavior and thus were unlikely to be "strategic misrepresentations." However, two studies (Babcock et al., 1995; Loewenstein et al., 1993) offered a specific incentive for participants to be accurate in these private fairness judgments. Participants were told that the individual whose fairness assessments came closest to the determinations of an objective third party would be given an extra cash award. This incentive did not eliminate egocentrism in participants' interpretations of fairness, suggesting that their fairness reports reflect actual beliefs.

Wade-Benzoni, Tenbrunsel, and Bazerman (1996) extended this work on egocentrism to a four-party social dilemma. All participants in their experiment were given identical information to prepare for the negotiation and were asked to report, both before and after negotiation, what they believed to be a fair allocation of limited resources among the four parties. The investigators report two important findings. First, communication reduces egocentrism, a result that replicates Thompson and Loewenstein's (1992) finding that disputants' interpretations of fairness are significantly closer after negotiation than before. Second, asymmetry in available payoffs increases egocentrism. When the four parties face identical payoffs, they tend to share common perceptions of fairness; when payoffs are varied among the four parties, perceptions of fairness are divergent. This finding replicates the highly consistent pattern observed elsewhere (Babcock & Olson, 1992; Camerer & Loewenstein, 1993; Diekmann, 1997; Diekmann et al., 1997; Messick & Sentis, 1983) that ambiguity in problem solving creates an opening in the decision-making process in which egocentrism can develop via differential interpretation of the facts and application of the relevant fairness rules.

Consequences of egocentrism in negotiation

A number of researchers have used egocentric interpretations of fairness to explain the vexing problem of impasse in negotiation (Babcock & Loewenstein, 1997; Babcock et al., 1995; Babcock & Olson, 1992; de Dreu, Nauta, & van de Vliert, 1995; Thompson & Loewenstein, 1992). Evidence on egocentrism can help account for why disputants pay the high costs of strikes, litigation, delay, stalemate, and deadlock, despite strong incentives to reach agreement. If both parties seek a fair outcome, yet their self-serving interpretations of fairness are incommensurable, the ironic result is that negotiators may impasse despite a positive bargaining zone and motivation to be fair (Babcock & Loewenstein, 1997; Drolet, Larrick, & Morris, 1998; Thompson & Loewenstein, 1992).

There are two ways to understand how this clash could result in impasse. First, self-serving interpretations of fairness may result in an equitable agreement being perceived as unfair and exploitative. Perceptions of exploitation by another party may give rise to a desire for vengeance. The resulting motivation to punish the opponent for unfair behavior can lead to rejection of otherwise profitable agreements. This motive can be seen most clearly in ultimatum bargaining experiments where recipients reject profitable offers they perceive to be unfair (Ochs & Roth, 1989; Pillutla & Murnighan, 1996). Blount (1995) has shown that uneven allocations are more likely to be accepted when they are simply uneven (generated by a random device) than when they are unfair (generated by a person who benefits from the unevenness).

A second, simpler way to understand how egocentrism leads to impasse is to assume that negotiators have a utility for fairness — that they would prefer a moderately profitable, but equal, alternative to a highly profitable alternative involving inequality that favors the other side. Data supporting this point of view come from work on social utility (Loewenstein et al., 1989; Messick & Sentis, 1985) — people care very much about how their outcomes compare with others' and they display a powerful disutility for disadvantageous inequality (Neale & Bazerman, 1991). In negotiation, social utility may be magnified because negotiator aspirations tend to mirror their fairness judgments (Drolet et al., 1998). In this way, egocentric interpretations of fairness can lead to unrealistic aspirations, which in turn are likely to increase contentious behavior and delay settlement. De Dreu, Nauta, and van de Vliert (1995) offered correlational evidence from actual negotiations, suggesting that egocentric evaluations are associated with escalation of conflict. The cumulative result of these effects is that impasses exact high costs from individuals, businesses, and societies (Pruitt, Rubin, & Kim, 1994).

The practical question is, how can egocentrism be reduced? Bazerman and Neale (1982) were able to successfully debias negotiators by providing them with facts about overconfidence and egocentrism in negotiation. Thus, negotiators may inoculate themselves against egocentric biases by learning about their dangers. While some have argued that egocentrism may help negotiators claim value, we advise negotiators to strive to obtain the most accurate perceptions possible. One may certainly choose a contentious strategy or an extreme bargaining position, but negotiators are best prepared when they have the best information. Critics of research on egocentrism have argued that these effects are likely to be exaggerated in a laboratory situation with minimal context and naïve negotiators. However, others have found the familiar pattern of self-serving biases and egocentrism in real conflicts involving experienced professionals (Babcock & Olson, 1992; Babcock, Wang, & Loewenstein, 1996), including professional negotiators (de Dreu, Nauta, & van de Vliert 1995). Indeed, evidence suggests that the more a partisan is involved in and cares about a dispute, the more biased he or she is likely to be (Thompson, 1995).

Motivational forces

Although some have argued that egocentrism can arise through unbiased psychological processes (Ross & Sicoly, 1979), the data presented here clearly suggest motivated processing. The general pattern of motivational forces that emerges from studies of fairness in negotiation is that individuals behave as if they are attempting to maximize a complex function made up of three variables of concern. First, people obviously care about their own outcomes. Diekmann (1997) argued that self-interest is a ubiquitous motivation, and that it will tend to bias all judgments in which the decision maker holds a stake. Messick and Sentis (1983) proposed that preferences are basic and immediate, but that we must determine through reflection what is fair, and that this process is vulnerable to bias. When the situation becomes more complex, fairness becomes ambiguous (Messick & Sentis, 1983), and parties in a dispute tend to interpret fairness and invoke fairness rules in ways that favor themselves (de Dreu, 1996; Diekmann et al., 1997; Messick & Sentis, 1979).

Second, people work to manage the way they are perceived by others. It is desirable to be perceived as fair by others (Greenberg, 1990). Diekmann (1997) found that people tend to reach egocentric fairness judgments and allocate accordingly when they are allocating in private. Egocentrism is eliminated, however, in public allocations to the self.

Third, people work to manage their own self-perceptions. People prefer to imagine themselves to be fair, even generous (Greenberg, 1990; Messick, Bloom, Boldizar, & Samuelson, 1985). By having some of his participants make allocation decisions in a room filled with mirrors, Greenberg (1983b) heightened self-awareness and demonstrated the importance of self perception in egocentrism. While participants assigned to the no-mirror control group evaluate disadvantageous inequality as more unfair than the same inequality when it favors them, those participants who are made self-aware by being in a room filled with mirrors do not exhibit this egocentric bias in their fairness judgments.

Summary

While fairness concerns play an important role in negotiation, partisans tend to offer egocentric assessments of fairness, even when the assessments are private and therefore not motivated by any conscious strategic intent (Loewenstein et al., 1993). Ambiguity and information richness make room for biased interpretations of fairness (Thompson & Loewenstein, 1992), which can occur through differential weighting of available information (Diekmann et al., 1997) or selective encoding and retrieval (Babcock et al., 1995). Egocentrism grows from individuals' tendency to be self-interested (Messick & Sentis, 1983), but it is moderated by the desire to appear fair both to themselves (Greenberg, 1983b) and to others (Diekmann, 1997).

Attributions and Construal in Negotiation

Two reasons why negotiation outcomes deviate from the predictions of classical game theory are the attributions negotiators make about their counterparts and the construals negotiators form about their situations. While the literature on attributions in negotiation is quite broad, in this section we review only literature that relates directly to the behavioral decision perspective outlined earlier. As a result, we omit a number of significant contributions that do not meet this criterion (e.g., Baron, 1985, 1988, 1990a; Betancourt & Blair, 1992; Bies, Shapiro, & Cummings, 1988; Bradbury & Fincham, 1990; de Dreu, Carnevale, Emans, & van de Vliert, 1994, 1995; Forgas, 1994; Friedland, 1990; Johnson & Rule, 1986; Kette, 1986; Lord & Smith, 1983).

Attributions negotiators make about their counterparts

Work by Robinson and colleagues has shown that partisans to conflict tend to exhibit a false polarization effect. That is, they exaggerate the distance between opposing groups in a conflict. Robinson, Keltner, Ward, and Ross (1995) demonstrated this false polarization effect on a variety of social and political issues (Keltner & Robinson, 1996; Robinson et al., 1995; Robinson & Keltner, 1996). For example, participants, who had identified themselves as either pro-life or pro-choice, responded to a variety of questions surveying their own attitudes about abortion, as well as the attitudes they believed to be held by the average pro-life or pro-choice advocate. The results clearly demonstrate that participants overestimate the degree of ideological difference between themselves and their opponents and caricature their ideological opponents as being more extreme than they actually are. Participants even perceive their *own* group as being more extreme than it actually is. Moreover, this effect is exacerbated for groups that represent the more powerful status quo position (Robinson & Keltner, 1997).

In a similar vein, Kramer (1994) found participants remarkably ready to attribute sinister motivations to others when the basis for their behavior is ambiguous. Kelley (1972) has argued that disputants readily attribute the causes of others' behavior to malevolent ulterior motives where such explanations are plausible. Benign explanations for behavior that are provided by the opponent will be discounted to the extent that more sinister explanations are plausible (Robinson & Friedman, 1995). If parties attribute to their opponents more extreme positions than their opponents actually hold, conflict resolution becomes more difficult (Robinson et al., 1995). Both Kramer's sinister attribution error and Robinson and Keltner's false polarization increase the likelihood that disputants will assume that their interests are opposed, even when they are not (Thompson & Hrebec, 1996). Such attributions are likely to engender blame and hostility that make agreement difficult (Keltner & Robinson, 1993).

What prescriptions can be offered to the negotiator? Rubin et al. (1994) expressed pessimism about the ability of negotiators to counteract the effects of attributional conflict. They argued that selective perceptions will limit the opportunities for parties to correct sinister and fanatical attributions of opponents in three ways. First, partisans tend to be biased in their evaluation of behaviors by the disputants (Hastorf & Cantril, 1954; Oskamp, 1965). Second, confirmation biases in the search for information about other parties magnifies the likelihood that disputants will only reconfirm their prior suspicions (Snyder & Swann, 1978). Third, evidence on attributional distortion has shown that, consistent with the fundamental attribution error (Ross, 1977), people are more likely to attribute opponents' behavior to stable aspects of their personalities than to situational pressures (Morris, Larrick, & Su, 1998), especially when behavioral evidence confirms prior beliefs about the disposition of the opponent. Disconfirming behavioral evidence is more likely to be attributed to situational pressures (Hayden & Mischel, 1976; Regan, Straus, & Fazio, 1974).

Consistent with this logic, Kramer found that careful reflection did not ameliorate the tendency to commit the sinister attribution error. On the contrary, Kramer found that both self consciousness and rumination *increase* the tendency to ascribe malevolent motivations to others (Kramer, 1994). Fortunately, the data on attenuating false polarization offer more hope. Keltner and Robinson (1993) found that when both negotiators disclose their ideological views in a non-contentious way prior to negotiation, outcomes are more complete and more integrative. Qualifying these results, subsequent research by Puccio and Ross (1998) found that disclosure of one's own views is less effective at reducing false polarization than describing the "most legitimate and convincing" arguments on the other side.

Negotiators' construals of their situations

Just as negotiators make attributions about their counterparts, so do they form interpretations or construals about their situations. The principle of situationism in social psychology (Lewin, 1935) asserts that seemingly insignificant aspects of situations can represent potent forces in determining individual behavior. Negotiators not only see and act in biased ways, they misattribute the source of this bias to the malevolence or extremism of the other side rather than the more mundane tendency for people to construe the world in light of their expectations and self-interest (Ross & Ward, 1996). However, as stated earlier, the 1960s and 1970s negotiation literature failed to consider the negotiator's interpretive construal process (Kelley & Thibaut, 1978; Nisbett & Ross, 1980; Ross & Nisbett, 1991). A negotiator responds not only to objective features of his or her situation, but also to his or her *construal* of those features.

One way to study negotiators' construal processes is to examine their pre-existing modes of viewing conflict situations. For example, Pinkley and Northcraft (1994) studied the degree to which individual conflict frames, measured prior to negotiation (Pinkley, 1990), predicted negotiation behavior. Both task orientation (i.e., lack of concern for relationship) and cooperative frame (i.e., lack of competitiveness) are associated with higher individual and joint profit. Although certainly intriguing, the results of this study are correlational, and therefore subject to a number of alternative explanations.

Other studies have mitigated such alternative explanations by *manipulating*, rather than measuring, conflict frame. Ross and Samuels (1993) found that the behavior of participants in a prisoner's dilemma game could be drastically influenced by the name assigned to that game. Participants who played "The Community Game," cooperated approximately twice as frequently as participants who played the identical game entitled "The Wall Street Game" (Ross & Ward, 1995). A similar study by Larrick and Blount (1997) found that manipulating the presentation of an ultimatum game influences the behavior of participants. When the identically structured game is described as a social dilemma (mutual "claiming" of a shared resource) rather than an ultimatum game (a "proposed division" followed by "accepting" or "rejecting"), those who propose the division ("first movers") are more generous in their allocations and those who "accept" or "reject" the division ("second movers") are more tolerant of inequalities that favor the other player. In fact, second movers are approximately three times more likely to accept allocations of zero for themselves when the game is described as a social dilemma ("claiming") rather than an ultimatum game ("rejecting"/ "accepting") (Larrick & Blount, 1997).

Still other studies have examined whether these patterns generalize from decision games like the prisoner's dilemma game and the ultimatum game to negotiations (Bottom & Paese, 1997; O'Connor & Adams, 1998; Thompson & DeHarpport, 1998). The results seem to depend on specific features of the manipulations. For example, those for whom a negotiation task is framed as problem solving ("two people face a common problem") rather than as bargaining ("each person is trying to get what he or she wants") are found to expect higher individual profit, more cooperation, and a more collaborative process yielding a fairer outcome. However, the problem-solving task frame does not correlate with actual outcomes (Thompson & DeHarpport, 1998).

In contrast, O'Connor and Adams (1998) found that framing the negotiation task as a joint search for the one and only solution to a problem, or framing it as a negotiation situation in which both parties are trying to reach agreement, influences both pre-negotiation expectations and joint profit. Furthermore, those who are instructed to view the conflict as a joint search for one solution have a more accurate assessment of their counterparts' interest and reach more integrative outcomes.

Although more research is necessary to clarify the specific situational attributions that lead to differences in negotiation behavior, the existing research demonstrates that negotiators' responses to situations do depend on their interpretations or construals of those situations. As noted earlier, situations represent relatively fixed aspects of negotiations unlikely to be under the control of the individual negotiator (Murnighan, 1986; Pinkley et al., 1995). However, the implication of the studies just described is that negotiators may be able to influence their own or their counterparts' construals of those situations and, in doing so, affect negotiation outcomes. More research is necessary to test this assertion.

Summary

The assumptions negotiators make about their counterparts and the ways they construe their situations are important predictors of negotiator attitudes and outcomes. Such attributions can reduce or magnify conflict between parties. For example, although partisans tend to assume that their opponents are more fanatical and extreme than they actually are, certain types of mutual disclosure seem to mitigate harmful attributions about one's counterpart. Although comparatively less researched, strategic re-framing of otherwise fixed conflict situations by individual negotiators may influence negotiator attitudes and outcomes. We consider a negotiator's management of these attributional and construal processes, through these and other means, to be a critical factor in the resolution of conflict.

Motivated Illusions and Negotiation

Beginning in the mid-1980s, a new set of biases entered the social psychology arena: positive illusions (Messick et al., 1985). Evidence on positive illusions suggests that most people view themselves, the world, and the future in a considerably more positive light than reality can sustain (Taylor, 1989). Taylor and Brown (1988) argued that these illusions can enhance and protect self-esteem, increase personal contentment, encourage individuals to persist at difficult tasks, and help people cope with aversive and uncontrollable events. Taylor (1989) even argued that positive illusions are beneficial to physical and mental health. This research is related to the self-serving nature of the egocentric interpretations described earlier. However, while egocentrism tends to be specifically related to judgments of fairness, positive illusions have a broader effect. We highlight four types of motivated illusions of particular relevance to negotiation: (1) unrealistically positive views of the self, (2) unrealistic optimism, (3) the illusion of control, and (4) self-serving attributions. We review each of these motivated illusions and discuss their impact on negotiation.

Unrealistically positive views of the self

We tend to perceive ourselves as being better than others on desirable attributes (Brown, 1986; Messick et al., 1985), causing us to have unrealistically positive self-evaluations (Brown, 1986). For example, people perceive themselves as being better than others across a number of traits, including honesty, cooperativeness, rationality, driving skill, health, and intelligence (Kramer, 1994).

Unrealistic optimism

Unrealistic optimism refers to a tendency to believe that our futures will be better than those of other people (Kramer, 1994; Taylor, 1989). Taylor provided evidence that students expect that they are far more likely to graduate at the top of the class, to get a good job with a high salary, to enjoy their first job, to get written up in the newspaper, and to give birth to a gifted child than reality suggests. Similar results have emerged for groups other than students. Taylor pointed out that we persist in expecting that we can achieve more in a given day than is possible, and that we are immune to the continued feedback that the world provides on our limitations. More directly relevant to negotiation, Kramer (1991) found that 68 percent of the MBA students in a negotiation class predicted that their bargaining outcomes would fall in the upper 25 percent of the class. These students also expected that they would learn more than their classmates would learn, with more unique results, and that they would contribute more to the class experience.

The illusion of control

We also falsely believe that we can control uncontrollable events (Crocker, 1982) and overestimate the extent to which our actions can guarantee a certain outcome (Miller and Ross, 1975). Gamblers believe that "soft" throws of dice are more likely to result in lower numbers being rolled (Taylor, 1989). These gamblers also believe that silence by observers is relevant to their success. Langer (1975) found that people have a strong preference for choosing their own lottery card or numbers, even when this has no effect on improving the likelihood of winning. Many superstitious behaviors are the result of an illusion of control. Kramer (1994) and Bazerman (1998) suggest that negotiators are likely to falsely believe that they have greater control of the behavior of adversaries, the timing of negotiation, and the broader context of their negotiations than is true in reality.

Shafir and Tversky (1992), and Morris, Sim, and Girotto (1998) provided evidence that parties in a prisoner's dilemma act as if their decision will control the decision of the other party, even when doing so is logically impossible. Essentially, this work suggests that one reason that parties cooperate in one-shot prisoner dilemma games is the illusion that their cooperation will create cooperation in the other party. Shafir and Tversky had participants make decisions about whether to cooperate or defect in a prisoner's dilemma game: (1) when the decision of the other party was unknown, (2) when it was known that the other party had cooperated, and (3) when it was known that the other party had defected. Interestingly, many participants cooperate under the first of these conditions, but defect under the latter two.

Shafir and Tversky (1992) argue that this behavior violates Savage's (1954) "sure thing" principle, which states that if you would defect regardless of the decision of the other party, it logically follows that you should defect if you do not know their decision; Morris, Sim, and Girotto (1998) developed this one step further by noting that this result is only common when the other party has not yet made their decision. If the other party has made their decision, participants are much more likely to defect in the unknown condition. Morris, Sim, and Girotto concluded that the illusion of control explains this pattern. When the decision of the other party has already been made, it is no longer intuitively plausible that the participant can control the decision of the other party.

Self-serving attributions

Finally, returning to the theme of attributions developed earlier, people are biased in how they explain the causes of events. We tend to take a disproportionately large share of the credit for collective successes and to accept too little responsibility for collective failures (Kramer, 1994). John F. Kennedy understood this when he said: "Victory has a thousand fathers, but defeat is an orphan." Similarly, when negotiators are asked why they are so successful, they tend to give internal attributions – reasons related to the decisions they made. However, when asked about a failure, they tend to give external attributions – they explain the failure as the result of the unfortunate situation in which they found themselves (Bazerman, 1998). Self-serving biases also play a role in the assignment of blame for a variety of problems. Consider an environmental dispute: What is the cause of global warming? The US blames emerging economies for burning the rain forests and for overpopulation. Emerging nations blame the West for pollution caused by industrialization and excessive consumption. The problem is that in the process of attributing the blame to others, parties reduce their motivation to change their own behaviors so as to contribute to a solution (Wade-Benzoni, Tenbrunsel, and Bazerman, 1997).

We also see the reverse of positive illusions in the context of judgments about opponents. Salovey and Rodin (1984) found that individuals tend to denigrate others who are more successful than they are. Kramer (1994) shows that less-successful MBA students downgrade the performance of more-successful students in negotiation simulations. These MBA students are more likely to attribute the success of other students to uncooperative and unethical bargaining tactics, to ascribe more negative motivations to successful negotiators, and to rate these other students as excessively competitive and self-interested. Both Diekmann (1997) and Tenbrunsel (1995) have found that while students rate themselves above the mean of their class on a variety of positive attributes, they rate their specific negotiation opponent below the mean on these attributes. Kramer (1994), basing his argument partially on Janis's (1962) analysis of political events, tied this pattern of behaviors to tragic mistakes made in politics. Kramer (1994) argued that the mismanagement of the Watergate embarrassment by the Nixon administration was partially the result of denigrating the competence and motivation of their opponents.

The dysfunctional consequences of motivated illusions in negotiation

The self-serving illusions we have reviewed have obvious implications for the negotiation process. For example, Kramer, Newton, and Pommerenke (1993) pointed out that opponent denigration has important negative implications for the process of negotiation. The authors maintained that negotiators' willingness to reveal information about their own interests may be contingent upon their expectation that the other party will reciprocate such disclosures. Individuals' judgments regarding such attributes as the other party's cooperativeness, fairness, and trustworthiness might be expected to play an important role in their negotiations. With the combined effects of self-enhancement and the denigration of opponents, negotiators who see themselves as better than others may undermine their ability to appreciate or fully empathize with the perspective of the other party. This may help explain why negotiators are not very good at understanding the cognitions of the other party (Bazerman & Carroll, 1987). Both parties to a negotiation may feel that they tried harder to reach agreement and offered more substantial concessions than the other party, and that it was only the recalcitrance of the other that forestalled agreement. In a group decision-making study, Polzer, Kramer, and Neale (1997) found that positive illusions about individual performance in a group are positively correlated with the level of conflict in that group

Motivated illusions also may lead to dysfunctional behaviors for the broader society. Specifically, motivated illusions are argued to lead to defection in large-scale social dilemma problems (Wade-Benzoni, Thompson, & Bazerman, 1998). Positive illusions may lead people to think that, in comparison to others, their behaviors and attitudes are environmentally sensitive, and that they are doing their fair share of sacrificing and working toward the resolution of environmental problems, even though their self-assessments may, in reality, be inflated (Wade-Benzoni et al., 1998). Consistent with Allison, Messick, and Goethals (1989), Wade-Benzoni et al. found self-assessment of environmental sensitivity to depend on how much ambiguity surrounds the self-assessment. Specifically, individuals maintain unrealistically positive beliefs about their degree of environmental sensitivity when their self-evaluation is difficult to disconfirm, but possess more realistic assessments of themselves when they are constrained by the objectivity of the evaluation (cf. Kunda, 1990). For example, assessments of general beliefs such as one's awareness of, concern for, understanding of, and interest in environmental issues and problems are difficult to confirm or disconfirm. However, beliefs about how well one performs on specific activities such as recycling, donating money to environmental organizations, and using energy-saving light bulbs can be checked against objective measures. If individuals define their environmental sensitivity in terms of general (not easily confirmable) behaviors instead of specific (objectively measurable) behaviors, their self-evaluations are likely to be inflated.

Taylor (1989) argued that positive illusions are adaptive. These illusions are said to contribute to psychological well-being by protecting an individual's positive sense of self (Taylor & Brown, 1988). In addition, Taylor and Brown argued that positive illusions increase personal commitment, help individuals persist at difficult tasks, and facilitate coping with aversive and uncontrollable events. Certainly, it is reasonable to argue that positive illusions help create entrepreneurs who are willing to discount risks. Positive illusions help people maintain cognitive consistency, belief in a just world, and perceived control (Greenwald, 1980). Seligman (1991) advocated the selection of salespeople based on the magnitude of their positive illusion – what he calls "learned optimism." He argued that unrealistically high levels of optimism are useful for maintaining persistence in a sales force.

We believe that each of these findings is true and that, in some specific situations (e.g., severe health conditions), positive illusions may prove beneficial. In addition, positive illusions may be useful for coping with tragic events, particularly when the individual has no other alternatives and is not facing any major decisions. However, we also believe that this evidence leads to an incomplete and dangerous story in most decision-making and negotiation environments. Countries go to war because of their positive illusions about the strength of their side. The opportunity to reach agreement with significant others, business partners, and negotiation opponents is lost because of these illusions. We believe that one cannot maintain positive illusions without reducing the quality of decisions that one makes.

In the context of negotiation, the logic of the impact of positive illusions on negotiation success is clearly affected by the choice of the dependent variable. Positive illusions increase the quality of agreements for the party possessing the bias, if an agreement is reached (Loewenstein et al., 1993; Riley, 1999; Riley and Robinson, 1998). However, positive illusions also increase the likelihood of impasse – even when a positive bargaining zone exists (Bazerman, 1998; Bazerman and Neale, 1982; Thompson and Loewenstein, 1992). On balance, we clearly recommend against the acceptance of positive illusions as a positive influence on negotiators. We want a more reasoned trade-off between the claiming of value and the risk of impasse than is possible under the effect of positive illusions.

Our negative reaction to positive illusions in negotiation is shared by a growing number of scholars. These scholars argue that positive illusions are likely to have a negative impact on learning, the quality of decision making, personnel decisions, and responses to organizational crises ("the oil in the water isn't really that big a problem"). Positive illusions can also contribute to conflict and discontent (Brodt, 1990; Kramer, 1994; Kramer et al., 1991; Tyler & Hastie, 1991).

Summary

Substantial evidence demonstrates that many errors made in negotiation result from motivational biases. In contrast to the cognitive biases that dominated the earlier negotiation literature, recent research has highlighted the importance of biases that stem from the desire to see oneself or one's world in a positive light. Although such biases serve a psychological function, we believe that resulting decisions lower the overall benefit to the decision maker and are inconsistent with what the individual would prefer for him- or herself when acting more reflectively.

Out-of-control Behavior and Emotion in Negotiation

The final aspects of social behavior that we seek to integrate into a decision theoretic perspective of negotiation are emotions and out-of-control behavior. Most of us know intuitively that emotions are critical to negotiator behavior, and researchers have a growing sense that emotions in negotiation have been underexplored (Barry & Oliver, 1996; Keltner, 1994; Thompson, Nadler, & Kim, 1999). However, the negotiation literature is not very informative about how emotion affects negotiator performance. Thompson et al. (1999) attributed this void to the cognitive revolution in general, and more specifically to the cognitive tilt of the decision analytic perspective to negotiation. Davidson and Greenhalgh (1999; Greenhalgh & Okun, 1998) argued more strongly that the laboratory/cognitive approach that has dominated negotiation research in the 1980s and 1990s excludes the most important variables for the convenience of the laboratory experimentalist.

Much of the prescriptive writings on negotiation imply that emotions should be controlled (Fisher & Ury, 1981). Emotions generally are viewed as forces that lead negotiators to act against their long-term self-interest (Bazerman, Tenbrunsel, & Wade-Benzoni, 1998). In contrast, Keltner and Kring (1998) described a functional view of emotions. They argued that emotions perform an informative function by signaling information about feelings and intentions. In addition, they argued that emotions serve an incentive function by rewarding or punishing the behavior of the other side. Barry (1999) and Thompson et al. (1999) described how emotions can be used by negotiators for tactical and strategic advantage. Thompson et al. (1999) argue that negotiators learn to maintain what they perceive to be a happy mood in others, and change what they perceive to be a negative mood. They also argue that when people anticipate a negative reaction, they attempt to reduce the negativity by adjusting their own emotional expression.

Emotion in negotiation

There have been a small number of studies directly examining the role of mood on negotiation outcomes. Carnevale and Isen (1986) showed that negotiators in positive moods were less likely to adopt contentious behaviors and more likely to obtain integrative outcomes. Similarly, Baron (1990b) showed that negotiators in good moods make more concessions and are less likely to engage in dysfunctional, competitive behaviors. Kramer et al. (1993) also found that positive moods lead negotiators to believe that they perform better than their opponents and better than other negotiators playing the same role. Forgas (1998) found that good mood enhances, and bad mood reduces, the tendency to select a cooperative strategy in negotiation. Furthermore, Forgas argued that negotiators in a positive mood negotiating against negotiators in a negative mood get more than half of the pie of available resources. Forgas interprets this as resulting from the tendency of a good mood to lead to positive expectations, which as noted earlier, increases the distributive success of the negotiator.

There is less evidence about the effect of negative moods on negotiator performance. This is partly a result of the complexity and ethical concerns of inducing negative moods in controlled experimentation. However, Allred, Mallozi, Matsui, and Raia (1997) did find that angry negotiators are less accurate in judging the interests of opponent negotiators and achieve lower joint gains. Loewenstein et al. (1989) found that negative emotions arising from a negative relationship make negotiators more self-centered in their preferences about the allocation of scarce resources. Loewenstein et al. found that, while those in neutral or positive moods are willing to pay a personal price for equality, those in a negative mood are far less concerned with the outcomes of another party. Pillutla and Murnighan (1996) showed that anger is a key explanatory factor in the rejection of ultimatums in the ultimatum game. That is, when an ultimatum makes people angry, they are likely to reject that ultimatum even when rejection leads to a worse outcome than acceptance.

The good news for these researchers was that, throughout this research, fairly mild manipulations were able to create moderately strong effects. The bad news is that the nature of the emotion/affect manipulations was too "cold" (Janis, 1982) to capture the essence of why people find the role of emotion in negotiation so compelling. When we think about emotion in negotiation, we think of the out-of-control marital argument or the angry customer, instead of the more muted emotions associated with receiving a trivial gift in advance of a negotiation. Thus, ease of experimentation has biased research toward exploring positive and "cold" emotions, rather than the negative, "hot" emotions that we intuitively believe to be the most prevalent emotions in negotiation. Despite the lack of direct evidence, the rest of this section explores the role of "hot" emotions, or out-of-control behaviors, on negotiation.

Out-of-control behavior in conflict situations

Following work on multiple selves by Schelling (1984) and Thaler and Shefrin (1981), Bazerman, Tenbrunsel, and Wade-Benzoni (1998) see emotion as playing a critical role in negotiation. Emotion can create a divide between what people think that they *should* do (cognitive) versus what they *want* to do (emotion). According to this view, people involved in conflicts deal with internal inconsistencies between transient concerns and long-term self-interest. They want to tell their boss what they really think of the recent budget allocation decisions but think that they should keep these insights to themselves. This conflict between cognition and emotion is broadly consistent with Loewenstein's (1996) perspective of visceral responses (emotion) overpowering self-interest (cognition). Loewenstein pointed out that success in many professions is achieved with the skill of manipulating emotions in other people. Salespeople and real estate agents try to close deals by targeting the customer's emotional desire for a commodity, while encouraging them to ignore other options and long-term financial issues. Con men capitalize on the greed of their potential victims. To defend people against their own emotions, many states try to protect consumers from impulses brought on by transient concerns by legislating periods of revocability for high-priced items, such as condominium share purchases (Loewenstein, 1996).

In a study that asked participants to think of a real world episode where they experienced internal conflict between what they wanted versus what they thought that they should do, O'Connor, de Dreu, Schroth, Barry, Liturgy, & Bazerman (1999) found that actual behavior is more closely related to their emotional response (want response) than to their cognitive assessment (should response). Consistent with Loewenstein (1996), this research also showed that study participants are more emotional at the moment of decision than when they are either looking back on the conflict or looking ahead to a future conflict. We posit that these differences in preferences occur because the cognitive self dominates when decision makers are looking toward the future but that emotions, triggered by the immediacy of rewards, often dominate at the point of the decision.

Summary

What research there is on emotion in negotiation has been limited by the practical and ethical difficulties associated with inducing the sorts of powerful emotions that are important in many actual negotiations. It appears that mild positive moods increase cooperative behavior and decrease competitive behavior, improve negotiators' perceptions of their own perform-ance, and actually may improve negotiators' abilities to obtain integrative joint outcomes. Mild negative moods, on the other hand, seem to reduce insight into one's opponents' interests, reduce concern with one's opponents' outcomes, and are associated with the rejec-tion of offers. The "multiple selves" problem explores emotional behavior that is beyond the control of the more deliberative part of the self. Impulsiveness appears to be strongest in the heat of conflict.

Conclusions

The negotiation literature of the 1980s was dominated by a strong cognitive tilt, leaving many important social psychological issues underexplored. This situation was in part due to the failure of the social psychology literature of the 1960s and 1970s to answer prescriptive questions of great importance to negotiators. Behavioral decision research in negotiation of the 1980s and early 1990s emphasized a prescriptive approach to negotiation. In particular, it provided guidance to negotiators about how their own behavior and the behavior of their negotiation opponents might deviate from a rational model. However, this research stream has ignored several key social variables.

This paper has charted the rebirth of the social psychology of negotiations. Relationships between negotiators, concerns for fairness, attribution and construal processes, motivated illusions, and emotions are among the most critical social-psychological variables in this re-emerging literature. We have selectively reviewed each of these variables with a particular focus on their relevance to negotiators.

Negotiation research, especially over the past three decades, has been fueled by concerns of practical relevance. As a result, more negotiation research has taken place in professional schools than in psychology departments. We have attempted to position the new social psychology of negotiation in a way that will preserve this practical relevance by helping us understand, predict, and give advice to a focal negotiator, including advice on how to anticipate the behavior of others. In addition to its practical value, however, the rebirth of the social psychology of negotiation is important because of its theoretical significance. Negotiation – the interpersonal process of conflict resolution – is one of the most basic and most important forms of social interaction. Research on negotiation is an essential step in the process of building a complete understanding of social and organizational behavior.

The beginning of the twenty-first century should be an important period in the develop-ment of the social psychology of negotiation. The demand for more social-psychological insights is strong, and many fruitful research directions have begun. We believe a critical determinant of the success of future social psychological research will be the degree to which it provides insights that make negotiators wiser. This value was deficient in early research on the social psychology of negotiations, but has been incorporated in its rebirth. We hope this pattern continues into the next decade and beyond.

REFERENCES

Akerlof, G. (1970). The market for lemons: Qualitative uncertainty and the market mechanism. *Quarterly Journal of Economics, 89,* 488–500.

Allison, S. T., Messick, D. M., & Goethals, G. R. (1989). On being better but not smarter than others: The Mohammad Ali effect. *Social Cognition, 7,* 275–296.

Allred, K., Mallozi, J. S., Matsui, F., & Raia, C. P. (1997). The influence of anger and compassion on negotiation performance. *Organizational Behavior and Human Decision Processes, 70,* 175–187.

Austin, W. (1980). Friendship and fairness: Effects of type of relationship and task performance on choice of distribution rules. *Personality and Social Psychology Bulletin, 6,* 402–408.

Axelrod, S., & May, J. G. (1968). Effect of increased reward on the two-person non-zero-sum game. *Psychological Reports, 23,* 675–678.

Babcock, L., & Loewenstein, G. (1997). Explaining bargaining impasse: The role of self-serving biases. *Journal of Economic Perspectives, 11,* 109–126.

Babcock, L., Loewenstein, G., Issacharoff, S., & Camerer, C. (1995). Biased judgments of fairness in bargaining. *American Economic Review, 85,* 1337–1343.

Babcock, L., & Olson, C. (1992). The causes of impasses in labor disputes. *Industrial Relations, 31,* 348–360.

Babcock, L., Wang, X. H., & Loewenstein, G. (1996). Choosing the wrong pond: Social comparisons in negotiations that reflect a self-serving bias. *Quarterly Journal of Economics, 111,* 1–19.

Baker, W. E. (1984). The social structure of a national securities market. *American Journal of Sociology, 89,* 775–811.

Baker, W. E. (1990). Market networks and corporate behavior. *American Journal of Sociology, 96,* 589–625.

Baron, R. A. (1985). Reducing organizational conflict: The role of attributions. *Journal of Applied Psychology, 70,* 434–441.

Baron, R. A. (1988). Attributions and organizational conflict: The mediating role of apparent sincerity. *Organizational Behavior and Human Decision Processes, 41,* 111–127.

Baron, R. A. (1990a). Countering the effects of destructive criticism: The relative efficacy of four interventions. *Journal of Applied Psychology, 75,* 235–245.

Baron, R. A. (1990b). Environmentally induced positive affect: Its impact on self-efficacy, task performance, negotiation, and conflict. *Journal of Applied Social Psychology, 20,* 368–384.

Barry, B. (1999). The tactical use of emotion in negotiation. In R. J. Lewicki, R. J. Bies, & B. H. Sheppard (Eds.), *Research on negotiation in organizations* (Vol. 7). Greenwich, CT: JAI Press.

Barry, B., & Friedman, R. A. (1998). Bargainer characteristics in distributive and integrative negotiation. *Journal of Personality and Social Psychology, 74,* 345–359.

Barry, B., & Oliver, R. L. (1996). Affect in dyadic negotiation: A model and propositions. *Organizational Behavior and Human Decision Processes, 67,* 127–143.

Bazerman, M. (1998). *Judgment in managerial decision making.* New York: Wiley.

Bazerman, M. H., & Carroll, J. S. (1987). Negotiator cognition. *Research in Organizational Behavior, 9,* 247–288.

Bazerman, M. H., Curhan, J. R., Moore, D. A., & Valley, K. L. (2000). Negotiation. *Annual Review of Psychology, 51,* 279–314.

Bazerman, M. H., Gibbons, R., Thompson, L., & Valley, K. L. (1998). Can negotiators outperform game theory? In J. J. Halpern & R. N. Stern (Eds.), *Debating rationally: Nonrational aspects in organizational decision making*. Ithaca, NY: ILR Press.

Bazerman, M. H., Magliozi, T., & Neale, M. A. (1985). The acquisition of an integrative response in a competitive market. *Organizational Behavior and Human Performance, 34*, 294–313.

Bazerman, M. H., & Neale, M. A. (1982). Improving negotiation effectiveness under final offer arbitration: The role of selection and training. *Journal of Applied Psychology, 67*, 543–548.

Bazerman, M. H., & Neale, M. A. (1983). Heuristics in negotiation: Limitations to dispute resolution effectiveness. In M. H. Bazerman & R. J. Lewicki (Eds.), *Negotiating in organizations*. Beverly Hills, CA: Sage.

Bazerman, M. H., & Neale, M. A. (1992). *Negotiating rationally*. New York: Free Press.

Bazerman, M. H., Tenbrunsel, A. E., & Wade-Benzoni, K. A. (1998). Negotiating with yourself and losing: Understanding and managing conflicting internal preferences. *Academy of Management Review, 23*, 225–241.

Bell, D. E., Raiffa, H., & Tversky, A. (1989). *Decision making: Descriptive, normative and prescriptive interactions*. Cambridge, England: Cambridge University Press.

Ben-Yoav, O., & Pruitt, D. G. (1984). Resistance to yielding and the expectation of cooperative future interaction in negotiation. *Journal of Experimental Social Psychology, 20*, 323–335.

Betancourt, H., & Blair, I. (1992). A cognition (attribution)-emotion model of violence in conflict situations. *Personality and Social Psychology Bulletin, 18*, 343–350.

Bies, R. J., Shapiro, D. L., & Cummings, L. L. (1988). Causal accounts and managing organizational conflict: Is it enough to say it's not my fault? *Communication Research, 5*, 381–399.

Blount, S. (1995). When social outcomes aren't fair – the effect of causal attributions on preferences. *Organizational Behavior and Human Decision Processes, 63*, 131–144.

Bottom, W. P., & Paese, P. W. (1997). False consensus, stereotypic cues, and the perception of integrative potential in negotiation. *Journal of Applied Social Psychology, 27*, 1919–1940.

Bradbury, T. N., & Fincham, F. D. (1990). Attributions in marriage: Review and critique. *Psychological Bulletin, 107*, 3–33.

Brodt, S. E. (1990). Cognitive illusions and personnel management decisions. In C. L. Cooper & I. T. Robertson (Eds.), *International Review of Industrial and Organizational Psychology* (Vol. 5, pp. 229–279). New York: Wiley.

Brown, J. D. (1986). Evaluations of self and others: Self-enhancement biases in social judgments. *Social Cognition, 4*, 353–376.

Camerer, C., & Loewenstein, G. (1993). Information, fairness, and efficiency in bargaining. In B. A. Mellers & J. Baron (Eds.), *Psychological perspectives on justice* (pp. 155–181). Boston: Cambridge University Press.

Carnevale, P. J., & Isen, A. M. (1986). The influence of positive affect and visual access on the discovery of integrative solutions in bilateral negotiations. *Organizational Behavior and Human Decision Processes, 37*, 1–13.

Clark, M. S., & Chrisman, K. (1994). Resource allocation in intimate relationships: Trying to make sense of a confusing literature. In M. J. Lerner & G. Mikula (Eds.), *Entitlement and the affectional bond*. New York: Plenum.

Clark, M. S., Mills, J., & Corcoran, D. (1989). Keeping track of needs and inputs of friends and strangers. *Personality and Social Psychology Bulletin, 15*, 533–542.

Crocker, J. (1982). Biased questions in judgment of covariation studies. *Personality and Social Psychology Bulletin, 8*, 214–220.

Davidson, M. N., & Greenhalgh, L. (1999). *The role of emotion in negotiation: The impact of anger and race*. Unpublished manuscript.

de Dreu, C. K. W. (1996). Gain-loss frame in outcome-interdependence: Does it influence equality or equity considerations? *European Journal of Social Psychology, 26*, 315–324.

de Dreu, C. K. W., Carnevale, P. J. D., Emans, B. J. M., & van de Vliert, E. (1994). Effects of gain-loss frames in negotiation: Loss aversion, mismatching, and frame adoption. *Organizational Behavior and Human Decision Processes, 60*, 90–107.

de Dreu, C. K. W., Carnevale, P. J. D., Emans, B. J. M., & van de Vliert, E. (1995). Outcome frames in bilateral negotiation: Resistance to concession making and frame adoption. In W. Stroebe & M. Hewstone (Eds.), *European review of social psychology, 6*, 97–125.

de Dreu, C. K. W., Nauta, A., & van de Vliert, E. (1995). Self-serving evaluations of conflict behavior and escalation of the dispute. *Journal of Applied Social Psychology, 25*, 2049–2066.

Deutsch, M. (1975). Equity, equality, and need: What determines which value will be used for distributive justice? *Journal of Social Issues, 31*, 137–150.

Diekmann, K. A. (1997). "Implicit justifications" and self-serving group allocations. *Journal of Organizational Behavior, 18*, 3–16.

Diekmann, K. A., Samuels, S. M., Ross, L., & Bazerman, M. H. (1997). Self-interest and fairness in problems of resource allocation: Allocators versus recipients. *Journal of Personality and Social Psychology, 72*, 1061–1074.

Diekmann, K. A., Tenbrunsel, A. E., Shah, P. P., Schroth, H. A., & Bazerman, M. H. (1996). The descriptive and prescriptive use of previous purchase price in negotiations. *Organizational Behavior and Human Decision Processes, 66*, 179–191.

Drolet, A., Larrick, R., & Morris, M. W. (1998). Thinking of others: How perspective taking changes negotiators' aspirations and fairness perceptions as a function of negotiator relationships. *Basic and Applied Social Psychology, 20*, 23–31.

Druckman, D. (1967). Dogmatism, prenegotiation experience, and simulated group representation as determinants of dyadic behavior in a bargaining situation. *Journal of Personality and Social Psychology, 6*, 279–290.

Druckman, D. (Ed.). (1977). *Negotiations: Social-psychological perspectives*. Beverly Hills, CA: Sage.

Fisher, R., & Ury, W. (1981). *Getting to YES: Negotiating agreement without giving in*. New York: Houghton Mifflin.

Forgas, J. P. (1994). Sad and guilty? Affective influences on the explanation of conflict in close relationships. *Journal of Personality and Social Psychology, 66*, 56–68.

Forgas, J. P. (1998). On feeling good and getting your way: Mood effects on negotiator cognition and bargaining strategies. *Journal of Personality and Social Psychology, 74*, 565–577.

Friedland, N. (1990). Attribution of control as a determinant of cooperation in exchange interactions. *Journal of Applied Social Psychology, 20*, 303–320.

Fry, W. R., Firestone, I. J., & Williams, D. L. (1983). Negotiation process and outcome of stranger dyads and dating couples: Do lovers lose? *Basic and Applied Social Psychology, 4*, 1–16.

Greenberg, J. (1983a). Equity and equality as clues to the relationship between exchange participants. *European Journal of Social Psychology, 13*, 195–196.

Greenberg, J. (1983b). Overcoming egocentric bias in perceived fairness through self-awareness. *Social Psychology Quarterly, 46*, 152–156.

Greenberg, J. (1990). Looking fair versus being fair: Managing impressions of organizational justice. In B. M. Staw & L. L. Cummings (Eds.), *Research in Organizational Behavior* (Vol. 12). Greenwich, CT: JAI Press.

Greenhalgh, L., & Chapman, D. I. (1995). Joint decision making: The inseparability of relationships and negotiation. In R. M. Kramer & D. M. Messick (Eds.), *Negotiation as a social process* (pp. 166–185). Thousand Oaks, CA: Sage.

Greenhalgh, L., & Chapman, D. I. (1996). *Negotiator relationships: Construct measurement and demonstration of their impact on the process and outcomes of negotiations.* Unpublished manuscript, Dartmouth College.

Greenhalgh, L., & Gilkey, R. W. (1993). The effect of relationship orientation on negotiators' cognitions and tactics. *Special Issue: Relationships in group decision and negotiation. Group Decision & Negotiation, 2,* 167–183.

Greenhalgh, L., & Okun (1998). Negotiation and conflict resolution. In H. S. Friedman (Ed.), *Encyclopedia of mental health.* San Diego, CA: Academic Press.

Greenwald, A. G. (1980). The totalitarian ego: Fabrication and revision of personal history. *American Psychologist, 35,* 603–618.

Halpern, J. J. (1992). The effect of friendship on bargaining: Experimental studies of personal business transactions. In J. L. Wall and L. R. Jauch (Eds.), *Best paper proceedings* (pp. 64–68), Las Vegas, NV: Academy of Management.

Halpern, J. J. (1994). The effect of friendship on personal business transactions. *Journal of Conflict Resolution, 38,* 647–664.

Halpern, J. J. (1996). The effect of friendship on decisions: Field studies of real estate transactions. *Human Relations, 49,* 1519–1547.

Halpern, J. J. (1997a). Elements of a script for friendship in transactions. *Journal of Conflict Resolution, 41,* 835–868.

Halpern, J. J. (1997b). The transaction index: A method for standardizing comparisons of transaction characteristics across different contexts. *Group Decision and Negotiation, 6,* 557–572.

Hastorf, A. H., & Cantril, H. (1954). They saw a game: A case study. *Journal of Abnormal and Social Psychology, 49,* 129–134.

Hayden, T., & Mischel, W. (1976). Maintaining trait consistency in the resolution of behavioral inconsistency: The wolf in sheep's clothing? *Journal of Personality, 44,* 109–132.

Hermann, M. G., & Kogan, N. (1977). Effects of negotiators' personalities on negotiating behavior. In D. Druckman (Ed.), *Negotiation: Social psychological perspectives.* Beverly Hills, CA: Sage.

Janis, I. (1962). Psychological effects of warnings. In G. W. Baker & D. W. Chapman (Eds.), *Man and society in disaster.* New York: Basic Books.

Janis, I. L. (1982). *Groupthink: Psychological studies of policy decisions and fiascoes.* Boston: Houghton Mifflin.

Johnson, T. E., & Rule, B. G. (1986). Mitigating circumstance information, censure, and aggression. *Journal of Personality and Social Psychology, 50,* 537–542.

Kahneman, D., Slovic, P., & Tversky, A. (1982). *Judgment under uncertainty: Heuristics and biases.* New York: Cambridge University Press.

Kelley, H. (1972). Attribution in social interaction. In E. E. Jones, D. E. Kanouse, H. H. Kelley, et. al. (Eds.), *Attribution: Perceiving the causes of behavior* (pp. 1–26). Morristown, NJ: General Learning Press.

Kelley, H. H., & Thibaut, J. W. (1978). *Interpersonal relations: A theory of interdependence.* New York: Wiley.

Keltner, D. (1994). *Emotion, nonverbal behavior, and social conflict.* Paper presented to the Harvard Project on Negotiation.

Keltner, D., & Kring, A. M. (1998). Emotion, social function, and psychopathology. *Review of General Psychology, 2,* 320–342.

Keltner, D., & Robinson, R. J. (1993). Imagined ideological differences in conflict escalation and resolution. *International Journal of Conflict Management, 4,* 249–262.

Keltner, D., & Robinson, R. J. (1996). Extremism, power, and the imagined basis of social conflict. *Current Directions in Psychological Science, 5,* 101–105.

Kette, G. (1986). Attributions restore consistency in bargaining with liked/disliked partners. *European Journal of Social Psychology, 16,* 257–277.

Kramer, R. M. (1991). Intergroup relations and organizational dilemmas: the role of categorization processes. *Research in Organizational Behavior, 13,* 191–228.

Kramer, R. M. (1994). The sinister attribution error: Paranoid cognition and collective distrust in organizations. *Motivation and Emotion, 18,* 199–230.

Kramer, R. M., Newton, E., & Pommerenke, P. L. (1993). Self-enhancement biases and negotiator judgment: Effects of self-esteem and mood. *Organizational Behavior and Human Decision Processes, 56,* 110–133.

Kunda, Z. (1990). The case for motivated reasoning. *Psychological Bulletin, 108*(3), 480–498.

Lamm, H., & Kogan, N. (1970). Risk taking in the context of intergroup negotiations. *Journal of Experimental Social Psychology, 6,* 351–363.

Langer, E. (1975). The illusion of control. *Journal of Personality and Social Psychology, 32,* 311–328.

Larrick, R. P., & Blount, S. (1997). The claiming effect: Why players are more generous in social dilemmas than in ultimatum games. *Journal of Personality and Social Psychology, 72,* 810–825.

Lax, D. A., & Sebenius, J. K. (1986). *The manager as negotiator.* New York: Free Press.

Lewicki, R. J., Litterer, J. A., Minton, J. W., & Saunders, D. W. (1999). Negotiation (3rd ed.). Burr Ridge, IL: Irwin.

Lewicki, R. J., Weiss, S., & Lewin, D. (1988). *Models of conflict, negotiation, and third party intervention: A review and synthesis.* Working Paper Series (WPS 88–33). College of Business, Ohio State University.

Lewin, K. (1935). *Dynamic theory of personality.* New York: McGraw-Hill.

Loewenstein, G. (1996). Out of control: Visceral influences on behavior. *Organizational Behavior and Human Decision Processes, 65,* 272–292.

Loewenstein, G., Babcock, L., Issacharoff, S., & Camerer, C., (1993). Self-serving assessments of fairness and pretrial bargaining. *Journal of Legal Studies, 22,* 135–159.

Loewenstein, G., Thompson, L., & Bazerman, M. H. (1989). Social utility and decision making in interpersonal contexts. *Journal of Personality and Social Psychology, 57,* 426–441.

Lord, R. G., & Smith, J. E. (1983). Theoretical, information processing, and situational factors affecting attribution theory models of organizational behavior. *Academy of Management Review, 8,* 50–60.

Mannix, E. A., Tinsley, C. H., & Bazerman, M. H. (1995). Negotiation over time: Impediments to integrative solutions. *Organizational Behavior and Human Decision Processes, 62,* 241–251.

March, J. G., & Simon, H. A. (1958). *Organizations.* New York: Wiley.

Marwell, G., Ratcliff, K., & Schmitt, D. R. (1969). Minimizing differences in a maximizing difference game. *Journal of Personality and Social Psychology, 12,* 158–163.

Marwell, G., & Schmitt, D. R. (1972). Cooperation in a three-person prisoner's dilemma. *Journal of Personality and Social Psychology, 21,* 376–383.

Messick, D. M., Bloom, S., Boldizar, J. P., & Samuelson, C. D. (1985). Why we are fairer than others. *Journal of Experimental Social Psychology, 21,* 480–500.

Messick, D. M., & Sentis, K. P. (1979). Fairness and preference. *Journal of Experimental Social Psychology, 15,* 418–434.

Messick, D. M., & Sentis, K. P. (1983). Fairness, preference, and fairness biases. In D. M. Messick & K. S. Cook (Eds.), *Equity theory: Psychological and sociological perspectives.* New York: Praeger.

Messick, D. M., & Sentis, K. P. (1985). Estimating social and nonsocial utility functions from ordinal data. *European Journal of Social Psychology, 15,* 389–399.

Miller, D. T., and Ross, M. (1975). Self-serving biases in attribution of causality: Fact or fiction? *Psychological Bulletin, 82,* 213–225.

Morgan, W., & Sawyer, J. (1967). Bargaining expectations and the preference for equality over equity. *Journal of Personality and Social Psychology, 6*, 139–149.

Morris, M. W., Larrick, R. P., & Su, S. K. (1998). *Misperceiving negotiation counterparts: When situationally determined bargaining behaviors are attributed to personality traits.* Unpublished manuscript.

Morris M. W., Leung, K., & Sethi, S. (1998). *Person perception in the heat of conflict: Perceptions of opponents' traits and conflict resolution choices in two cultures.* Unpublished manuscript.

Morris, M. W., Sim, D. L. H., & Girotto, V. (1998). *Distinguishing sources of cooperation in the one-round prisoner's dilemma: Evidence for cooperative decisions based on illusion of control.* Unpublished manuscript.

Murnighan, J. K. (1986). The structure of mediation and intravention: Comments on Carnevale's strategic choice model. *Negotiation Journal, 4*, 351–356.

Neale, M. A. (1984). The effect of negotiation and arbitration cost salience on bargainer behavior: The role of arbitrator and constituency in negotiator judgment. *Organizational Behavior and Human Performance, 34*, 97–111.

Neale, M. A., & Bazerman, M. H. (1991). *Cognition and rationality in negotiation.* New York: Free Press.

Neale, M. A., & Bazerman, M. H. (1992). Negotiator cognition and rationality: A behavioral decision theory perspective. *Organizational Behavior and Human Decision Processes, 51*, 157–175.

Nisbett, R., & Ross, L. (1980). *Human inference: Strategies and shortcomings of social judgement.* Englewood Cliffs, NJ: Prentice Hall.

Northcraft, G. B., & Neale, M. A. (1987). Expert, amateurs, and real estate: An anchoring-and-adjustment perspective on property pricing decisions. *Organizational Behavior and Human Decision Processes, 39*, 228–241.

Ochs, J., & Roth, A. E. (1989). An experimental study of sequential bargaining. *American Economic Review, 79*, 335–385.

O'Connor, K. M., & Adams, A. A. (1998). *Debiasing negotiators' cognitions: The impact of task construal on negotiators' perceptions, motives, and outcomes.* Working paper, Johnson Graduate School of Management, Cornell University.

O'Connor, K., de Dreu, C., Schroth, H., Barry, B., Liturgy, T., & Bazerman, M. H. (1999). *Intrapersonal conflict across time.* Manuscript submitted for publication.

Oskamp, S. (1965). Attitudes towards U.S. and Russian actions: A double standard. *Psychological Reports, 16*, 43–46.

Pillutla, M. M., & Murnighan, J. K. (1996). Unfairness, anger, and spite: Emotional rejections of ultimatum offers. *Organizational Behavior and Human Decision Processes, 68*, 208–224.

Pinkley, R. L. (1990). Dimensions of conflict frame: Disputant interpretations of conflict. *Journal of Applied Psychology, 75*, 117–126.

Pinkley, R. L., Brittain, J. W., Neale, M. A., & Northcraft, G. B. (1995). Managerial third party dispute intervention: An inductive analysis of intervenor strategy selection. *Journal of Applied Psychology, 80*, 386–402.

Pinkley, R. L., & Northcraft, G. B. (1994). Conflict frames of reference: Implications for dispute processes and outcomes. *Academy of Management, 37*, 193–205.

Polzer, J. T., Kramer, R. M., & Neale, M. A. (1997). Positive illusions about oneself and one's group. *Small Group Research, 28*, 243–266.

Polzer, J. T., Neale, M. A., & Glenn, P. O. (1993). The effects of relationships and justification in an interdependent allocation task. *Special Issue: Relationships in group decision and negotiation. Group Decision & Negotiation, 2*, 135–148.

Priest, G., & Klein, B. (1984). The selection of disputes for litigation. *Journal of Legal Studies, 13*, 1–55.

Pruitt, D. G. (1981). *Negotiation Behavior*. New York: Academic Press.

Pruitt, D. G. (1983). Achieving integrative agreements. In M. H. Bazerman & R. J. Lewicki (Eds.), *Negotiating in organizations*. Beverly Hills, CA: Sage.

Pruitt, D. G., & Carnevale, P. J. (1993). *Negotiation in social conflict*. Pacific Grove, CA: Brooks-Cole.

Pruitt, D. G., & Drews, J. L. (1969). The effect of time pressure, time elapsed, and the opponent's concession rate on behavior in negotiation. *Journal of Experimental Social Psychology*, 5, 43–69.

Pruiu, D. G., & Johnson, D. F. (1972). Mediation as an aid to face saving in negotiation. *Journal of Personality and Social Psychology*, 14, 239–246.

Pruitt, D. G., Rubin, J. Z., & Kim, S. H. (1994). *Social conflict: Escalation, stalemate, and settlement*, 2nd edn. New York: McGraw-Hill.

Puccio, C., & Ross, L. (1998). *Attenuating false polarization: Debiasing the social presentation of partisans*. Working paper, Stanford University.

Raiffa, H. (1982). *The art and science of negotiation*. Cambridge, MA: Belknap.

Regan, D. T., Straus, E., & Fazio, R. H. (1974). Liking and the attribution process. *Journal of Experimental Social Psychology*, 10, 385–397.

Riley, H. C. (1999). *Optimism and performance in negative-sum negotiation*. Working paper, Harvard Business School.

Riley, H. C., & Robinson, R. J. (1998). *How high can you go? Preliminary findings on the peril and benefits of negotiator confidence in distributive bargaining*. Working paper. Harvard Business School.

Robinson, R. J., & Friedman, R. A. (1995). Mistrust and misconstrual in union–management relationships: Causal accounts in adversarial contexts. *International Journal of Conflict Management*, 6, 312–327.

Robinson, R. J., & Keltner, D. (1996). Much ado about nothing? Revisionists and traditionalists choose an introductory English syllabus. *Psychological Science*, 7, 18–24.

Robinson, R. J., & Keltner, D. (1997). Defending the status quo: Power and bias in social conflict. *Personality and Social Psychology Bulletin*, 23, 1066–1077.

Robinson, R. J., Keltner, D., Ward, A., & Ross, L. (1995). Actual versus assumed differences in construal: Naïve Realism in intergroup perception and conflict. *Journal of Personality and Social Psychology*, 68, 404–417.

Ross, L. (1977). The intuitive psychologist and his shortcomings: Distortions in the attribution process. In L. Berkowitz (Ed.), *Advances in experimental social psychology*, 10, 173–220. New York: Academic Press.

Ross, L., & Nisbett, R. E. (1991). *The person and the situation: Perspectives of social psychology*. New York: McGraw-Hill.

Ross, L., & Samuels, S. M. (1993). *The predictive power of personal reputation vs. labels and construal in the Prisoner's Dilemma game*. Unpublished manuscript, Stanford University, Palo Alto, CA.

Ross, I.., & Sicoly, F. (1979). Egocentric biases in availability and attribution. *Journal of Personality and Social Psychology*, 37, 322–336.

Ross, L., & Stillinger, C. (1991). Barriers to conflict resolution. *Negotiation Journal*, 7, 389–404.

Ross, L., & Ward, A. (1995). Psychological barriers to dispute resolution. *Advances in Experimental Social Psychology*, 27, 255–303.

Ross, L., & Ward, A. (1996). Naïve realism in everyday life: Implications for social conflict and misunderstanding. In T. Brown, E. Reed, & E. Turiel (Eds.), Values and knowledge (pp. 103–135). Hillsdale, NJ: Erlbaum.

Roth, A. E. (1982). The economics of matching: Stability and incentives. *Mathematics of Operations Research*, 7, 617–628.

Roth, A. E., & Murnighan, J. K. (1982). The role of information in bargaining: An experimental study. *Econometrica*, 50, 1123–1142.

Rubin, J. Z., & Brown, B. R. (1975). *The social psychology of bargaining and negotiation.* New York: Academic Press.

Rubin, J. Z., Pruitt, D. G., & Kim, S. H. (1994). *Social conflict: Escalation, stalemate, and settlement.* New York: McGraw-Hill.

Rubin, Z. (1970). Measurement of romantic love. *Journal of Personality and Social Psychology, 16,* 265–273.

Sabatelli, R. M., & Cecil-Pigo, E. F. (1985). Relational interdependence and commitment in marriage. *Journal of Marriage and the Family, 47,* 931–937.

Salovey, P., & Rodin, J. (1984). Some antecedents and consequences of social comparison jealousy. *Journal of Personality and Social Psychology, 47,* 780–792.

Samuelson, W. F., & Bazerman, M. H. (1985). The winner's curse in bilateral negotiations. In V. Smith (Ed.), *Research in Experimental Economics, 3* (pp. 105–137). Greenwich, CT: JAI Press.

Savage, L. J. (1954). *The foundations of statistics.* New York: Wiley.

Schelling, T. C. (1984). *Choice and consequence: Perspectives of an errant economist.* Cambridge, MA: Harvard University Press.

Schoeninger, D., & Wood, W. (1969). Comparison of married and ad hoc mixed-sex dyads negotiating the division of a reward. *Journal of Experimental Social Psychology, 5,* 483–499.

Seligman, M. E. P. (1991). *Learned optimism.* New York: Pocket Books.

Shafir, E., & Tversky, A. (1992). Thinking through uncertainty: Nonconsequential reasoning and choice. *Cognitive Psychology, 24,* 449–474.

Shah, P. P., & Jehn, K. A. (1993). Do friends perform better than acquaintances? The interaction of friendship, conflict, and task. *Special Issue: Relationships in group decision and negotiation. Group Decision & Negotiation, 2,* 149–165.

Snyder, M., & Swann, W. B., Jr. (1978). Behavioral confirmation in social interaction: From social perception to social reality. *Journal of Experimental Social Psychology, 14,* 148–162.

Sondak, H., & Bazerman, M. H. (1989). Matching and negotiation processes in quasi-markets. *Organizational Behavior and Human Decision Processes, 44,* 261–280.

Sondak, H., & Bazerman, M. H. (1991). Power balance and the rationality of outcomes in matching markets. *Organizational Behavior and Human Decision Processes, 50,* 1–23.

Sondak, H., Pinkley, R., & Neale, M. (1994). *Relationship, input, and resource constraints: Determinants of individual preferences and negotiated outcomes in resource allocation decisions.* Working paper, Duke University.

Taylor, S. E. (1989). *Positive Illusions.* New York: Basic Books.

Taylor, S. E., & Brown, J. D. (1988). Illusion and well-being: a social psychological perspective on mental health. *Psychological Bulletin, 103,* 193–210.

Tenbrunsel, A. E. (1995). *Justifying unethical behavior: The role of expectations of others' behavior and uncertainty.* Unpublished doctoral dissertation. Northwestern University.

Tenbrunsel, A. E., Wade-Benzoni, K. A., Moag, J., & Bazerman, M. H. (1998). *The social aspect of the matching process: Relationships and partner selection.* Unpublished manuscript.

Thaler, R., & Shefrin, H. M. (1981). An economic theory of self control. *Journal of Political Economy, 89,* 392–406.

Thompson, L. (1990). Negotiation behavior and outcomes: Empirical evidence and theoretical issues. *Psychological Bulletin, 108,* 515–532.

Thompson, L. (1995). "They saw a negotiation": Partisanship and involvement. *Journal of Personality and Social Psychology, 68,* 839–853.

Thompson, L. (1998). *The mind and heart of the negotiator.* Upper Saddle River, NJ: Prentice Hall.

Thompson, L. L., & DeHarpport, T. (1990). Negotiation in long-term relationships. Paper presented at the International Association for Conflict Management, Vancouver, Canada.

Thompson, L., & DeHarpport, T. (1998). Relationships, goal incompatibility, and communal orientation in negotiations. *Basic and Applied Social Psychology, 20*, 33–44.

Thompson, L., & Hrebec, D. (1996). Lose-lose agreements in interdependent decision making. *Psychological Bulletin, 120*, 396–409.

Thompson, L., & Loewenstein, G. (1992). Egocentric interpretations of fairness and interpersonal conflict. *Organizational Behavior and Human Decision Processes, 51*, 176–197.

Thompson, L., Nadler, J., & Kim, P. H. (1999). Some like it hot: The case for the emotional negotiator. In L. Thompson, J. Levine, & D. Messick (Eds.), *Shared cognition in organizations: The management of knowledge* (pp. 139–161). Hillsdale, NJ: Erlbaum.

Thompson, L., Valley, K. L., & Kramer, R. M. (1995). The bittersweet feeling of success: An examination of social perception in negotiation. *Journal of Experimental Social Psychology, 31*, 467–492.

Tversky, A., & Kahneman, D. (1974). Judgment under uncertainty: Heuristics and biases. *Science, 185*, 1124–1131.

Tyler, T., & Hastie, R. (1991). The social consequences of cognitive illusions. In M. H. Bazerman, R. J. Lewicki, & B. Sheppard (Eds.), *Handbook of negotiation research: Research on negotiation in organizations* (Vol. 3). Greenwich, CT: JAI Press.

Utne, M. K., Hatfield, E., Traupmann, J., & Greenberger, D. (1984). Equity, marital satisfaction, and stability. *Journal of Social and Personal Relationships, 1*, 323–332.

Valley, K. L. (1992). *Relationships and resources: A network exploration of allocation decision*. Unpublished dissertation, Northwestern University.

Valley, K. L., Moag, J., & Bazerman, M. H. (1998). "A matter of trust": Effects of communication on the efficiency and distribution of outcomes. *Journal of Economic Behavior & Organization, 34*, 211–238.

Valley, K. L., Neale, M. A., & Mannix, E. (1995). Friends, lovers, colleagues, strangers: The effects of relationships on the process and outcomes of dyadic negotiations. *Research on Negotiation in Organizations, 5*, 65–93.

Vidmar, N. (1971). Effects of representational roles and mediators on negotiator effectiveness. *Journal of Personality and Social Psychology, 17*, 48–58.

Wade-Benzoni, K. A., Tenbrunsel, A. E., & Bazerman, M. H. (1996). Egocentric interpretations of fairness in asymmetric, environmental social dilemmas: Explaining harvesting behavior and the role of communication. *Organizational Behavior and Human Decision Processes, 67*, 111–126.

Wade-Benzoni, K. A., Tenbrunsel, A. E., & Bazerman, M. H. (1997). Egocentric interpretations of fairness as an obstacle to just resolution of environmental conflict. In R. J. Lewicki, R. J. Bies, & B. H. Sheppard (Eds.), *Research on Negotiation in Organization* (Vol. 6). Greenwich, CT: JAI Press.

Wade-Benzoni, K. A., Thompson, L. L., & Bazerman, M. H. (1998). *The malleability of environmentalism*. Working paper.

Walster, E., Walster, G. W., & Berscheid, E. (1978). *Equity: Theory and research*. Boston: Allyn & Bacon.

Walters, A. E., Stuhlmacher, A. F., Meyer, L. L. (1998). Gender and negotiator competitiveness: A meta-analysis. *Organizational Behavior and Human Decision Processes, 76*, 1–29.

Walton, R. E., & McKersie, R. B. (1965). *A behavioral theory of labor negotiation*. New York: McGraw-Hill.

Watson, C. (1994). Gender versus power as a predictor of negotiation behavior and outcomes. *Negotiation Journal, 10*, 117–127.

Wichman, H. (1970). Effects of isolation and communication on cooperation in a two-person game. *Journal of Personality and Social Psychology, 16*, 114–120.

CHAPTER THIRTEEN

Communication Technologies, the Internet, and Group Research

Andrea B. Hollingshead

Communication technologies and the Internet have transformed groups in the workplace and in our communities. Members of groups no longer need to be co-present: to be together in time and place to collaborate, to share information, or to socialize. As a result, new group forms have emerged in organizations and on the Internet. Two examples of these new group forms are virtual teams in organizations and social support groups on the Internet.

Fast communication systems, more powerful processors, and new software enable organizations to form virtual teams of members who are separated temporally and spatially. For example, British Petroleum Co. has developed a virtual team network that allows people to work cooperatively and share knowledge quickly regardless of time, distance, and organizational boundaries (*Harvard Business Review*, 1997). The network gives users access to communication technologies, such as videoconferencing, electronic blackboards, scanners, faxes, and information databases. British Petroleum also has an in-house intranet that contains a growing number of home pages where experts in different technical areas describe their expertise and provide information for fellow employees. The company has reported benefits of the virtual team network such as: improved interactions between land-based drilling engineers and offshore rig crews, the avoidance of a refinery shutdown because technical experts at another location could examine a corrosion problem remotely, and a reduction in reworking during construction projects because designers, fabricators, construction workers, and operations people could collaborate more effectively. According to the company's estimates, the virtual team network saved at least $30 million in its first year alone (*Harvard Business Review*, 1997).

Thousands of support groups have been established on the Internet (Alexander, Wille, & Hollingshead, in press). In the last few decades, Americans have turned increasingly to support groups for aid in coping with physical illnesses, addictions, and mental health problems. Members of support groups have common goals that are to share information, to offer and to receive emotional support, and to release built-up stress (Ballinger & Yalom, 1995). Internet support groups exist for a large number of afflictions ranging from cancer, AIDS, rape, incest, fat acceptance, shyness, addiction, suicide, and even rare illnesses like male breast cancer. Many traditional face-to-face support groups such as Alcoholics Anonymous and Parents without Partners have established groups on the Internet. Unlike face-to-face support groups, Internet support groups have no specific meeting places or times and are accessible 24 hours a day, seven days a week. Internet support groups allow individuals who live in remote areas, who are too sick to leave their homes, or who want anonymity when discussing their problems, an opportunity to participate. It is estimated that more than 10 million Americans belong to support groups that meet regularly face to face (Katz, 1993), but it is unknown how many Americans belong to Internet support groups.

As indicated in the above examples, technologies that support group communication and collaboration provide many benefits to groups by linking people who have common goals and interests but are separated in time and space. They enable organizations to develop effective teams from workers who are geographically distributed; they improve the group's access to databases inside and outside the organization; and they enable the organization to hire and retain the best people, regardless of location (Townsend, DeMarie, & Hendrickson, 1996). They also allow individuals who want to participate in a support group, but not in a face-to-face setting due to logistical or personal reasons, to connect with similar others in a more anonymous setting (McKenna & Barge, 1998). But these technologies can also present challenges to the groups that use them (Hollingshead, in press). Virtual teams can lack the camaraderie and the development of close personal relationships of their face-to-face counterparts (Melymuka, 1997). And in Internet support groups, cases have been documented of participants feigning illness and suffering either for fun or for receiving the attention and sympathy that they have been unable to get in appropriate ways (Grady, 1998). In these cases, other participants expressed feelings of suspicion, anger, and betrayal.

The study of technology and groups is important for several reasons. As communication technologies become a larger part of our work and social lives, it is important to understand their short-term and long-term effects on group processes and group outcomes. Communication technologies also represent an important means for experimentally controlling group interaction processes, and thereby provide a useful tool for the study of group communication and decision. Researchers can use computer-mediated communication to separate and isolate components of group interaction processes to further understand how complex communication processes impact group decisions in face-to-face as well as in computer-mediated settings.

This chapter discusses research on the social psychological effects of communication technologies on the behavior of groups and of their members. It begins with a classification system and description of group communication technologies. It continues with a discussion of the role of communication technologies in group research, and with a presentation of important empirical findings. The chapter concludes with a discussion of how communication technologies will transform the ways that group researchers conduct their studies and with some directions for future research.

A Classification of Technologies that Support Groups

McGrath and Hollingshead (1993, 1994) classified technologies into four major categories based on the functional role that the technology plays in the work of the group: (1) providing or modifying within-group communication (i.e., Group Communication Support Systems or GCSS); (2) supplementing information available to the group or its members by information drawn from databases (i.c., Group Information Support Systems or GISS); (3) providing or modifying external communication with those outside the group (i.e., Group eXternal Support Systems or GXSS); and (4) channeling or modifying the group's task performance processes and task products (i.e., Group Performance Support Systems or GPSS). That classification system was developed in the early 1990s when the World Wide Web was in its infancy. This updated version includes a brief description of some collaboration technologies available via the Internet. As in the original classification system, any given technology may serve more than one of these four functions. This chapter will focus primarily on research that deals with those technologies that serve the first function: providing or modifying within-group communication.

GCSS: Technologies that provide or modify
within-group communication

In contrast to face-to-face communication, all GCSS permit, but do not require, group members to be spatially separated from each other – in different buildings, different cities, different countries, or merely in different rooms – while they are communicating. Some GCSS support asynchronous communication for group members acting in different time periods; some require that group members interact synchronously.

GCSS also vary in the channels that are available to group members: visual, auditory, text and graphics. For example, telephone conferencing does not allow for nonverbal communication exchange. The importance of that reduction of modalities depends on the particular task(s) and activities in which the group is engaged, the experience of the group with the technology, and the degree to which group members have a shared conceptualization of relative expertise (Hollingshead, 1998a, 1998b; Hollingshead, McGrath, & O'Connor, 1993).

GCSS often alter communication times, as well as the sequence and synchrony of messages (McGrath & Hollingshead, 1994). For electronic communication systems, the flow of a given communication cycle entails a finite (though relatively short) transmission time, a fairly substantial composition time (because typing is slower than talking), and perhaps an extensive editing time. In asynchronous computer communication systems, there may be no automatic feedback about the reception of a message, and there may be no unambiguous cues regarding acknowledgment and feedback – such cues are usually available for face-to-face or for synchronous computer, video, and telephone communication. Hence, there is no direct means for a sender to know that his or her message has been received by any particular potential receiver.

GCSS differ in the size, nature, and ambiguity of the set of interactive partners. In face-to-face groups, the set of interactive partners is likely to be relatively small and that set is by definition a closed set. It is much more difficult for researchers to identify who is and who is not a member in Internet groups. For example, in many news groups, such as Internet cancer support groups, there are literally hundreds of people who post at least one message to the

Table 13.1 A Typology of Group Communication Support Systems

Modalities available	Synchronous	Asynchronous
Visual	Video conference	Videocassette exchange
Audio	Phone conference	Voice mail Audiotape exchange
Text, graphics	Computer conference	E-mail FAX
Internet	News groups Chat rooms	Home pages, Web sites

news group. Some individuals post messages often, daily or weekly; some post infrequently, biweekly or monthly, and some members post only once (Alexander et al., in press). A large percentage of individuals who subscribe to news groups regularly read messages by other members, but never post messages themselves. These individuals are typically referred to as lurkers (Wellman & Gulia, 1998). Lurkers rarely participate in surveys of news groups, so little is known about who they are and about their motivation to read the messages of the news groups. Although lurkers are subscribers, it is debatable whether these individuals can be considered group members (McLaughlin, Osborn, & Smith, 1995).

Table 13.1 provides examples of GCSS organized by the modalities provided by the technology (video, audio, text/graphics), and the temporal distribution of members, that is, whether they are communicating synchronously or asynchronously. All of these technologies can support communication between members who are co-present or are geographically distributed. The organizing scheme also includes categories for Internet technologies, although World Wide Web browsers such as Netscape and Internet Explorer can support videoconferencing, audio conferencing, and document sharing via the Internet. See McGrath and Hollingshead (1994) for more detail about many of these technologies.

GISS: Supplementing information available to the group

All individuals have access to many bodies of information or knowledge from sources other than "online" communication with group members. These sources include quantitative databases, such as sales records and production and cost data, and qualitative databases or archives, such as information stored in libraries and newspaper files.

Intranets are technologies that support knowledge distribution among networks of teams within organizations. The types of knowledge that are available to group members on intranets can include: (i) human resources; (ii) sales and marketing activities; (iii) financial information; and (iv) design and manufacturing specifications and innovations (Bar, Borrus, & Hanson, 1998). Another example of GISS is information management programs that organize schedules, files, contacts, and other information on desktops to facilitate information exchange with other members. Microsoft Outlook, which comes pre-loaded on many PC-compatible computers, is one such information management program.

GXSS: Supporting external communication

This function is a special case of both the GCSS function and the GISS function, already discussed. In general, the types of support systems already described under GCSS are applicable to GXSS as well. That is, communication between the group (or its members) and key agents external to it can be done with systems using any of the three combinations of modalities (video, audio, text/graphics), and patterns of temporal distribution described for GCSS systems. Consequently, much of what has already been said about the types of GCSS applies, as well, to the group's external communication system.

At the same time, one can consider interaction with individuals outside the group as accessing another kind of information database, thus a special case of GISS. Organizations are increasingly able to interconnect seamlessly their intranets with those of their clients, partners, suppliers or subcontractors, via secure "extranets" (Barr, Borrus, & Hanson, 1998). For example, a provider of software has established extranets that allow established customers to obtain upgrades and provide feedback to the software designers. Other extranets link companies with consulting firms that advise end-users on the application of its products. Extranets create knowledge management networks that reach beyond traditional organizational boundaries.

GPSS: Modifying the group's task performance

Since before 1950, practitioners have devised ways to improve group effectiveness, and specifically to help groups avoid what Steiner (1972) subsequently called "process losses" by modifying how the group approaches its task. All of the systems used in earlier decades did not involve use of electronic or other "hi-tech" devices. Computer-based group performance support systems, also called GDSS or group decision support systems, are relatively recent developments (see Jessup & Valacich, 1993, for discussion). Group performance support systems vary on the type of task support provided to groups, the size of groups that can use the system, and whether a trained facilitator is necessary (McGrath & Hollingshead, 1994).

Electronic systems that provide direct task support for groups usually incorporate an array of "modules," each of which structures a different subset of a group's tasks or different portions of the group process on a given project. For example, a GPSS might include tools or modules for electronic brainstorming; for structuring various forms of evaluation and voting (rating, ranking, weighing, pick one, pick any, etc.); for identifying stakeholders and bringing their assumptions to the surface; for exchanging anonymous or identified comments on any or all topics. In the late 1980s and early 1990s, most of these GPSS were in the form of "decision rooms," especially equipped computer labs supporting synchronous groups with co-located members. Most groups used these systems to augment their face-to-face decisions. Efforts are underway to develop these systems to support asynchronous and synchronous groups via the Internet.

Social Psychological Effects of Technology on Groups

Several scholars have presented literature reviews that examine the impacts of technologies on groups (e.g., Hollingshead & McGrath, 1995; Kiesler & Sproull, 1992; McLeod, 1992, 1996). Most of these reviews have compared the interaction processes and outcomes of computer-mediated groups to those of face-to-face groups. Several of those reviews have reached the same conclusions about the state of knowledge in this area. Namely, that much of the empirical research is fragmented, and that more theory-guided and programmatic research is needed (e.g., Hollingshead & McGrath, 1995; McLeod, 1992). Rather than reiterate the general findings and conclusions made in those reviews in this chapter, this discussion will focus on studies that support some general findings that are particularly important and relevant to the study of groups in social and organizational settings. These studies also demonstrate how researchers can use communication technologies to learn more about group interaction in face-to-face as well as in computer-mediated settings. Those findings are:

1 Nonverbal communication and paralanguage play an important role in the exchange of information, particularly for people who know each other well.
2 Computer-mediated communication can lead to information suppression: a reduction in the amount of information that computer-supported groups discuss and use in their decisions relative to face-to-face groups.
3 Status differences among members affect patterns of participation, influence, and group outcomes in similar ways in both face-to-face and computer-mediated groups.
4 Groups adapt to their communication medium quickly, so many of the observed effects in comparisons between face-to-face and computer-mediated groups may disappear over time.

1 Importance of nonverbal and paralinguistic cues in information exchange

Nonverbal communication conveys information outside spoken language in the form of facial expressions, kinesics, visual behavior, and proxemics (Harper, Wiens, & Matarazzo, 1998). Paralanguage or paraverbal communication involves how something is said and not the actual meaning of the spoken words. Some examples of paralanguage are the cadence, tone, and number of pauses in a spoken message (Harper, Wiens, & Matarazzo, 1978). Nonverbal communication and paralanguage help to regulate the flow of communication (e.g., the timing of turn taking) and aid in the expression of emotion (McGrath & Hollingshead, 1994).

Many individual differences exist in how speakers and listeners use nonverbal and paralinguistic communication (Scherer & Ekman, 1982). For example, depending on the person and the situation, prolonged eye contact may signal attention, understanding, confusion, agreement, conflict, confidence, disbelief, or nothing. In addition, eye contact can serve as a sign to others to participate in a collaborative search for information when speakers have trouble retrieving information (M. Goodwin & C. Goodwin, 1986). For people in close personal or work relationships, nonverbal and paralinguistic cues may have more information value than for strangers. Members learn how to interpret the meaning of others' nonverbal and paralinguistic communication through their conversations and shared experiences over time. People in close relationships rely more on nonverbal and paralinguistic cues to retrieve, communicate, and evaluate information than strangers, and are negatively affected when they do not have access to either nonverbal or paralinguistic communication when they make decisions. This was demonstrated empirically in two experiments presented by Hollingshead (1998a).

In Experiment 1, dating couples and strangers worked together on a general knowledge test that assessed knowledge in five different domains in one of two communication environments: face to face, or via a synchronous computer conferencing system that supported text-based communication and that prevented the exchange of paralinguistic and nonverbal communication cues. The results showed that face-to-face dating couples scored significantly better on the task than computer-mediated dating couples, and better than pairs of strangers in either communication media conditions. (There were no significant differences between conditions for individual-level knowledge.) Further analyses indicated that face-to-face dating couples did better because they were better able than dyads in the other conditions to determine which partner knew the correct answer on questions where only one member was correct prior to discussion. In these situations, dating couples tended to look at one another more and worked together more to remember information than strangers, and this was positively associated with performance.

Experiment 2 took a closer look at the respective roles of paralinguistic and nonverbal communication in transactive memory systems by investigating three additional communication conditions: (1) note passing with visual access; (2) talking without visual access; and (3) note passing without visual access. The computer-mediated conferencing system used in Experiment 1 was much like note passing without visual access. Dating couples worked on the same knowledge task as in Experiment 1 in one of the three communication conditions. The results showed that dating couples pooled knowledge more effectively in the note passing with visual access and in the talking without visual access conditions than in the note passing without visual access condition. In other words, the dating couples did better when they had access to either nonverbal or paralinguistic communication than when they had access to neither. This finding is consistent with previous research indicating that nonverbal communication and the associated paralinguistic communication are highly redundant (Williams, 1977). For example, confidence can be communicated through tone of voice or prolonged eye contact. When people in close relationships use a communication medium that precludes access to nonverbal cues, they can adjust their communication effectively when they have access to paralinguistic cues and vice versa.

It is likely that face to face was the primary mode of communication in everyday life for the couples who participated in these experiments. However, e-mail may be the primary mode of communication for people in some work relationships, for example, colleagues at different universities who are collaborating on a project. In such collaborations, nonverbal and paralinguistic communication cues may not be as important for effective communication. The functions of paralanguage cues in group interaction can be partly replaced in text-based form using a variety of techniques. Punctuation and capitalization can be used to communicate emphasis or confidence (Hollingshead, 1998b). For example, "YES!!!!" clearly indicates strong agreement.

Computer-supported groups can replace the expressive function of nonverbal cues by use of special text-based symbols and conventions. Emotions and sentiments can be created by putting together keyboard symbols to represent facial expressions. For example, ";-)" signifies a wink. These text-based facial expressions are often referred to as "emoticons." More research is needed to examine how naturally occurring groups that interact primarily via e-mail, such as virtual teams in organizations, embed emotion, and communicate subtle meanings, emphasis, understanding, and agreement through text.

2   Information suppression in computer-mediated groups

A number of studies have found that computer-mediated groups exchange less information than face-to-face groups. In some cases, this reduction can lead to poorer outcomes.

Straus and McGrath (1994) examined the quality and quantity of group performance on three different tasks with and without computer-mediated communication. The three tasks were brainstorming, solving a problem with a correct answer, and making a decision that did not have a correct answer. In general, face-to-face groups were more productive than computer-mediated groups, that is, they generated more discussion and possible solutions on all three tasks. However, the two media did not differ in the average quality of task per-formance. For features of the group's interaction patterns, and for members' reactions to their experience, there was an interaction between medium and task type. For brainstorming tasks where group members only generated ideas, computer-mediated and face-to-face groups did not differ on these variables. For problem-solving and decision-making tasks, face-to-face groups differed from computer-mediated groups on affect and cohesion.

Hollingshead (1996b) examined the impact of procedural factors on information sharing and group decision quality. Groups worked on an investment decision that was structured as a hidden-profile task where critical information was distributed unevenly among members prior to group discussion (cf. Stasser & Stewart, 1992). Groups instructed to rank order the alternatives, compared to groups instructed to choose the best alternative, were more likely to fully consider all of the alternatives, exchange information about unpopular alternatives, and make the best decision. But these effects occurred only in face-to-face groups. In computer-mediated groups, there was general information suppression (i.e., members exchanged little information about decision alternatives) and no effect of group decision procedure. Groups expressed more difficulty communicating and reaching consensus in the computer-mediated conditions. Taken together, these data suggest that procedural aspects of group discussion which improve information exchange and group decisions in face-to-face settings may not have the same effect in computer-mediated settings.

The information suppression effect of computer-mediated communication was also found in Hollingshead (1996a) and in McLeod, Baron, Marti, and Kuh (1997). These two studies will be discussed in more detail in the next section. Future research needs to address whether this information suppression effect is stable over time with established groups that commun-icate primarily via e-mail.

3 Status, anonymity, and participation in computer-mediated groups

Status is "a characteristic around which differences in cognitions and evaluations of individuals or social types come to be organized" (Berger & Zelditch, 1977, p. 5; also see Ridgeway, 2001). In other words, status embodies those characteristics that lead groups to think about members in terms of their personal characteristics and what contributions they can make to the task at hand. Such characteristics include but are not limited to expertise, tenure, gender, age, and ethnicity.

Low-status members in face-to-face groups participate less and exert less influence on group decisions than high-status members (see Bonito & Hollingshead, 1997, for a review). Low-status members tend to yield more in decision making than high-status members (Schneider & Cook, 1995). In addition, low-status members care more about acceptance by high-status members, and may conform more to their views (Humphreys & Berger, 1981). These findings suggest that when a low-status member of a face-to-face group has information that is critical for a group decision, he or she may be reluctant to contribute that information to the group, and that high-status group members may be less likely to attend to it even if the low-status member decides to contribute it. This situation can lead to negative outcomes for the group.

One possible solution to the problem of inhibited participation of low-status group members, suggested in previous research, is to change the group's medium of communication from face to face to a computer network. Many studies have revealed that groups interacting via computers have more equal participation among members than groups interacting face to face (e.g., Clapper, McLean, & Watson, 1991; Daly, 1993; Dubrovsky, Kiesler, & Sethna, 1991; George, Easton, Nunamaker, & Northcraft, 1990; Hiltz, Johnson, & Turoff, 1986; McLeod, 1992; Rice, 1984; Siegel, Dubrovsky, Kiesler, & McGuire, 1986; Straus, 1996; Straus & McGrath, 1994; Zigurs, Poole, & DeSanctis, 1988). This general finding has been labeled the "participation equalization effect." The general explanation for the effect is that people feel less inhibited when interacting through a computer network as a result of the reduction in social cues that provide information regarding one's status in the group. Because people communicating electronically are less aware of social differences, they feel a greater sense of anonymity and detect less individuality in others (Sproull & Kiesler, 1991). It is important to note some common elements across this set of studies. These studies were conducted during one experimental session with ad hoc groups consisting of students in a laboratory setting. It is also important to note that this finding was observed across a variety of communication technologies.

Several studies showed no evidence of the participation equalization effect in computer-mediated groups (Berdahl & Craig, 1996; Hollingshead, 1996b; Lea & Spears, 1991; McLeod & Liker, 1992; Spears & Lea, 1992; Watson, DeSanctis, & Poole, 1988; Weisband, 1992; Weisband, Schneider, & Connolly, 1995). What explains these seemingly contradictory findings? One possible explanation is that status differences among members within the groups may have been differentially salient across studies. Some studies experimentally controlled the status of participants within the group with mixed results. Dubrovsky et al. (1991) showed that when groups made controversial decisions through a synchronous computer conferencing system, patterns of participation and influence among members in mixed-status groups were more nearly equal in the computer-supported than in the face-to-face condition. They concluded that the reduction of status cues led low-status members in the computer condition to feel less inhibited and to participate relatively more in the discussion. However, Spears and Lea (1992) observed that when member identities were known or were visually available, status differences persisted even in a computer-mediated setting. Scott and Easton (1996) found that influence patterns among members who had high or low influence in their face-to-face groups were maintained in a computer-mediated setting. Saunders, Robey, and Vaverek (1994) also provided evidence that status differences are maintained in computer-mediated contexts: physicians and hospital administrators were afforded higher status in an asynchronous computer conference than were nurses.

Hollingshead (1996a) investigated the problem of inhibited participation of low-status group members more directly. The most important information for solving a problem was given to just one group member in a three-person group. The groups were composed such that the critical information required to make the best decision was held only by the low-status member in mixed-status groups, and randomly given to one member in equal-status groups. (Status was controlled and was defined in this study by age and experience.) The results indicated that mixed-status groups made poorer decisions than equal-status groups, in part because low-status members were less likely to share their critical information in the group discussion. The effects of status did not interact with communication media for quality of group decision, indicating that the effects of status persisted in computer-mediated interaction. However, status and communication media did interact on measures of information and perceived influence: computer communication attenuated the impact of status on these measures, primarily by suppressing information exchange and the perceived influence of all members.

McLeod et al. (1997) reported similar findings in an experiment comparing face-to-face groups with anonymous and identified computer-supported groups. Minority opinion holders expressed their arguments most frequently under anonymous computer communication, but the influence of the minority arguments on private opinions and on group decisions was highest under face-to-face communication. These results suggest that the conditions that facilitate the expression of minority arguments may also diminish the influence of those arguments.

Weisband, Schneider, and Connolly (1995) examined the extent to which mixed-status groups label individuals according to social status. In a set of three experiments, they uncovered no evidence of the participation equalization effect when the group members were clearly identified in unequal status groups. High-status members talked more and were perceived as contributing more to the final decision than low-status members. When status labels were hidden and low-status members were in the majority, status differences in participation were slightly reduced, though not eliminated, but status differences in influence virtually disappeared. The investigators concluded that status labels and the impressions formed from those labels have a larger impact on participation and influence than communication media.

The question has arisen of whether the participation equalization effect was an artifact of the pragmatic and technical demands of that communication medium and of the experimental studies that have been reported (Spears & Lea, 1994; Weisband et al., 1995). The participation equalization effect observed in computer-mediated groups may be an indication of how the medium reduces the baseline of each member's participation rather than how the medium leads to increased participation of low-status members during the group discussion (McGrath & Hollingshead, 1994; Spears & Lea, 1994). It takes more time to type a message on a computer network than it does to say that same message verbally. In the experiments cited above, the computer sessions were at least as long as those face-to-face group meetings; however, the amount and the rate of communication in the computer-mediated setting were much less. Another possible technological explanation for greater egalitarian participation patterns in computer-mediated settings is that electronic group members have the ability to participate without interruption, since turn taking is not a norm in a computer-mediated environment (Weisband et al., 1995).

Even though status differences were controlled in several studies described above, the experimental status manipulations were relatively minor and may not apply in organizations in which status differences are much larger and have organizational consequences (Spears & Lea, 1994). Status labels are expressed in various ways in computer-mediated groups in natural settings. An e-mail address provides information that can serve as a status label and often includes clues about the name, the occupation, and the nationality of the sender. For example, for locations in the United States, the address suffix indicates whether the sender works for an institution of higher education (.edu), the government (.gov), a non-profit (.org) or for-profit organization (.com). Members of online groups can identify themselves in their messages by using either their given names, a pseudonym, or no name to maintain a sense of anonymity. Members also express and develop identities through signature files. Signature files appear at the end of messages and might consist of professional titles, quotes, pictures, or other information. For example, a doctor who posts messages to one of the Internet cancer support groups includes a disclaimer as a signature file indicating that the contents of his messages are not generated as part of a professional evaluation. Even though this file is probably meant to protect him from malpractice, it reminds participants that he is a doctor, and therefore solidifies his role as a medical authority (Alexander et al., in press).

4   Diminished effects of computer-mediated communication on groups over time

Longitudinal research comparing the impact of computer-mediated and face-to-face communication over time has brought into question findings of previous studies that have found significant differences in performance between face-to-face and computer-mediated groups. That research has shown that computer-mediated communication hinders the interaction process and performance of groups initially, but over time, groups can adjust successfully to their mode of communication (see McGrath, Arrow, Gruenfeld, Hollingshead, & O'Connor, 1993 and Arrow et al., 1996 for overviews).

Hollingshead, McGrath, & O'Connor (1993) examined the task performance effects of computer-mediated and face-to-face groups over time. As a requirement of an advanced undergraduate psychology class, students were randomly assigned into groups and took part in a weekly 2-hour lab session for 13 weeks. In those sessions, groups worked on tasks that were cognitive in nature and fit into one of these four categories of the task circumplex (McGrath, 1984): idea generation, intellective, decision making, or negotiation. Each group was randomly assigned to a communication medium (either face to face or synchronous computer conferencing system that supported only text-based communication).

The results showed that computer-mediated groups had poorer task performance than face-to-face groups initially, but after three weeks there were no task performance differences. When face-to-face groups were shifted to the computer-mediated communication condition for two weeks midway through the study, they experienced a similar decrement in performance. This finding suggested that inexperience with the technology rather than inexperience with group members explained the initial performance difference. This research is important because it suggests that static findings – even those that are apparently robust over studies – may not be robust over time and with increased experience with the communication technology. Arrow (1997) examined the change in group structure over the 13 weekly work sessions, and found that computer-mediated groups showed patterns supporting a robust equilibrium model: fluctuation in early time periods, then stability later. Arrow et al. (1996) using a similar methodology, replicated many of the findings described in Hollingshead et al. (1993) and in McGrath et al. (1993).

Walther's work on the interpersonal and relationship aspects of computer-mediated communication over time complements the findings of Hollingshead et al. (1993). Prior research on the relational aspects of computer-mediated communication has suggested strong depersonalizing effects of computer-mediated communication due to the absence of nonverbal cues (Kiesler, Siegel, & McGuire, 1984). Walther and Burgoon (1992) studied the effects of time and communication channel (asynchronous computer conferencing vs. face-to-face meetings) on relational communication in groups composed of three undergraduate students. The groups completed three tasks over several weeks' time. The results indicated that members of computer-mediated groups felt less connected to one another initially. Over time, members of computer-mediated groups expressed more positive feelings about one another that approximated those expressed by members of face-to-face groups. Walther (1996) illustrated a new perspective on hyperpersonal communication, subprocesses pertaining to receivers, senders, channels, and feedback elements in computer-mediated communication that enhance interpersonal impressions and relations relative to face-to-face communication.

Current Research Trends

Recently, researchers have begun to examine more closely the interpersonal and social aspects of online communication and the Internet, focusing primarily on community and culture. A number of edited books (e.g., Gackenbach, 1999; Jones, 1995, 1997, 1998; Kiesler, 1997; Kollock & Smith, 1998) and empirical studies have been published on this topic. The bottom line is that even though members of online groups are physically isolated from one another and have some degree of anonymity, the experience of belonging to an online group can be very real. Online groups can have a strong group identity (Bouas & Arrow, 1996; McKenna & Barge, 1998). Members can build close personal relationships (Alexander et al., in press). Subcultures and minority factions can develop (Latané & Bourgeois, 1996; Latané & L'Herrou, 1996). Online groups can influence member behavior off line, and can have important real-life consequences for their members (McKenna & Barge, 1998).

Conclusions and Future Research Directions

Face-to-face interaction is no longer a prerequisite for classifying a collection of individuals as a group. Understanding the impacts of technologies on groups over time will become more important in the 21st century, as technologies become more sophisticated and support communication of an increased bandwidth. It is possible that current text-supported communication technologies on the Internet such as e-mail, news groups, and chat rooms will become v-mail (video mail), video groups, and virtual coffeehouses. But it is also possible that those text-based communication technologies will persist and will continue to be used by groups in the future. When does visual access to other group members improve interactions and lead to positive individual, group, social and organizational outcomes and when does it hinder interaction and lead to negative outcomes? Previous research has begun to answer that question. Future research on the social psychological effects of technologies will help us to predict what types of group communication technologies will emerge (or won't emerge) in the future and will help us to explain the social and psychological impacts of these technologies on groups and their members.

Communication technologies present important advantages to group researchers from a methodological standpoint as well. As the studies described in this chapter indicate, they give researchers an opportunity to isolate and control aspects of face-to-face interaction such as anonymity, physical distance, nonverbal communication and paralanguage in order to learn more about their specific impacts on group interaction and performance. In some cases, they can allow researchers to test theory that for practical reasons is difficult to test in a face-to-face setting (e.g., Latané & L'Herrou, 1996).

Davis and Stasson (1988) reported the difficulties inherent in conducting group research. These included the large number of participants needed to conduct group studies, adequate lab space, and the time and effort to code interaction. Communication technologies and the Internet can alleviate these difficulties. Virtual group research laboratories can be created and used on the World Wide Web to recruit participants, to conduct experiments, to administer surveys, and to code group interaction data. This will reduce group researchers' reliance on subject pools and lab space in their departments. Group research in social psychology should flourish in the future due to the growing interest and importance of communication technologies in our social and organizational lives, and to the opportunities afforded by communication technologies and the Internet that make it feasible to conduct group research.

REFERENCES

Alexander, S. C., Wille, J., & Hollingshead, A. B. (in press). Support at your keyboard: A study of on-line support groups. In L. Frey (Ed.), *Group communication in context* (Vol. 2), Hillsdale, NJ: Erlbaum.

Arrow, H. (1997). Stability, bistability, and instability in small group influence patterns. *Journal of Personality and Social Psychology, 72*, 75–85.

Arrow, H., Berdahl, J. L., Bouas, K. S., Craig, K. M., Cummings, A., Lebie, L., McGrath, J. E., O'Connor, K. M., Rhoades, J. A., & Schlosser, A. (1996). Time, technology, and groups: An integration. *Computer Supported Cooperative Work, 4*, 253–261.

Ballinger, B., & Yalom, I. (1995). Group therapy in practice. In B. M. Bongar & L. E. Beutler (Eds.), *Comprehensive textbook of psychotherapy: Theory and practice* (pp. 189–204). New York: Oxford University Press.

Bar, F., Borrus, M., & Hanson, W. (1998). *Web portfolios: Leveraging intranets, extranets, and the Internet for strategic gain*. Stanford University working paper.

Berdahl, J. L., & Craig, K. L. (1996). Equality of participation and influence in groups: The effects of communication medium and sex composition. *Computer Supported Cooperative Work, 4*, 179–202.

Berger, J., & Zelditch, Jr., M. (1977). Status characteristics and social interaction: The status-organizing process. In J. Berger, M. H. Fisek, R. Z. Norman, & M. Zelditch, Jr. (Eds.), *Status characteristics and social interaction: An expectation-states approach* (pp. 3–87). New York: Elsevier.

Bonito, J. A., & Hollingshead, A. B. (1997). Participation in small groups. *Communication Yearbook, 20*, 227–261.

Bouas, K. S., & Arrow, H. (1996). The development of group identity in face-to-face and computer-mediated groups with membership change. *Computer Supported Cooperative Work, 4*, 153–178.

Clapper, D. L., McLean, E. R., & Watson, R. T. (1991). An experimental investigation of the effect of group decision support on normative influence in small groups. In J. I. De Gross, I. Benbasat, G. DeSanctis, & C. M. Beath (Eds.), *Proceedings of the twelfth international conference on information systems* (pp. 273–282), New York.

Daly, B. (1993). The influence of face-to-face versus computer-mediated communication channels on collective induction. *Accounting, Management & Information Technology, 3*(1), 1–22.

Davis, J. H., & Stasson, M. F. (1988). Small group performance: Past and present research trends. *Advances in Group Processes, 5*, 245–277.

Dubrovsky, V. J., Kiesler, S., & Sethna, B. N. (1991). The equalization phenomenon: Status effects in computer-mediated and face-to-face decision making groups. *Human-Computer Interaction, 6*, 119–146.

Gackenbach, J. (Ed.) (1999). *Psychology and the Internet: Intrapersonal, interpersonal, and transpersonal implications*. San Diego, CA: Academic Press.

George, J., Easton, G., Nunamaker, J., & Northcraft, G. (1990). A study of collaborative group work with and without computer-based support. *Information Systems Research, 1*(4), 394–415.

Goodwin, M. H., & Goodwin, C. (1986). Gesture and coparticipation in the activity of searching for a word. *Semiotica, 62*, 51–75.

Grady, D. (1998). Faking pain and suffering in Internet support groups. *New York Times*, April 23, 1998 (D1).

Harvard Business Review (1997). Sharing knowledge through Bp's virtual team network, *75*, 152–153.

Harper, R. G., Wiens, A. N., & Matarazzo, J. D. (1978). *Nonverbal communication: The state of the art*. New York: Wiley.

Hiltz, S. R., Johnson, K., & Turoff, M. (1986). Experiments in group decision making, 1: Communications process and outcome in face-to-face vs. computerized conferences. *Human Communication Research, 13*, 225–252.

Hollingshead, A. B. (1996a). Information suppression and status persistence in group decision making: The effects of communication media. *Human Communication Research, 23*, 193–219.

Hollingshead, A. B. (1996b). The rank order effect: Decision procedure, communication technology and group decisions. *Organizational Behavior and Human Decision Processes, 68*(3), 1–13.

Hollingshead, A. B. (1998a). Retrieval processes in transactive memory systems. *Journal of Personality and Social Psychology, 74,* 659–671.

Hollingshead, A. B. (1998b). Distributed knowledge and transactive processes in groups. In M. A. Neale, E. A. Mannix, & D. H. Gruenfeld (Eds.), *Research on managing groups and teams* (Vol. 1, pp. 103–123). Greenwich, CT: JAI Press.

Hollingshead, A. B. (in press). Truth and deception in computer-mediated groups. To appear in M. A. Neale, E. A. Mannix, & T. Griffith (Eds.), *Research in managing groups and teams* (Vol. 3: Technology and teams) Greenwich, CT: JAI Press.

Hollingshead, A. B., & McGrath, J. E. (1995). Computer-assisted groups: A critical review of the empirical research. In R. A. Guzzo & E. Salas (Eds.), *Team effectiveness and decision making in organizations* (pp. 46–78). San Francisco, CA: Jossey-Bass.

Hollingshead, A. B., McGrath, J. E., & O'Connor, K. M. (1993). Group task performance and communication technology: A longitudinal study of computer-mediated versus face-to-face work groups. *Small Group Research, 24,* 307–333.

Humphreys, P., & Berger, J. (1981). Theoretical consequences of the status characteristics formulation. *American Journal of Sociology, 86,* 953–983.

Jessup, L. M., & Valacich, J. E. (Eds.) (1993). *Group support systems: New perspectives.* New York: Macmillan.

Jones, S. G. (Ed.) (1995). *Cybersociety: Computer-mediated communication and community.* Thousand Oaks, CA: Sage.

Jones, S. G. (Ed.) (1997). *Virtual culture: Identity and communication in cybersociety.* London: Sage.

Jones, S. G. (Ed.) (1998). *Cybersociety 2.0: Revisiting computer-mediated communication and community.* Thousand Oaks, CA: Sage.

Katz, A. (1993). *Self-help in America: A social movement perspective.* New York: Twayne.

Kiesler, S. (Ed.) (1997). *Culture of the Internet.* Mahwah, NJ: Erlbaum.

Kiesler, S., & Sproull, L. (1992). Group decision making and technology. *Organizational Behavior and Human Decision Processes, 52,* 96–123.

Kiesler, S., Siegel, J., & McGuire, T. W. (1984). Social psychological aspects of computer-mediated communication. *American Psychologist, 39,* 1123–1134.

Kollock, P., & Smith, M. (Eds.) (1998). *Communities in cyberspace.* London: Routledge.

Latané, B., & Bourgeois, M. J. (1996). Experimental evidence for dynamic social impact: The emergence of subcultures in electronic groups. *Journal of Communication, 46,* 35–47.

Latané, B., & L'Herrou, T. (1996). Spatial clustering in the conformity game: Dynamic social impact in electronic groups. *Journal of Personality and Social Psychology, 70,* 1218–1230.

Lea, M., & Spears, R. (1991). Computer-mediated communication, de-individuation, and group decision making. *International Journal of Man-Machine Studies, 34,* 283–301.

McGrath, J. E. (1984). *Groups, interaction, and performance.* Englewood Cliffs, NJ: Prentice Hall.

McGrath, J. E., Arrow, H., Gruenfeld, D. H., Hollingshead, A. B., & O'Connor, K. M. (1993). Groups, tasks, technology, and time: An integration. *Small Group Research, 24,* 406–420.

McGrath, J. E., & Hollingshead, A. B. (1993). Putting the "G" Back in GSS: Some theoretical issues about dynamic processes in groups with technological enhancements. In L. M. Jessup & J. E. Valacich (Eds.), *Group support systems: New perspectives.* New York: Macmillan.

McGrath, J. E., & Hollingshead, A. B. (1994). *Groups interacting with technology.* Newbury Park, CA: Sage.

McKenna, K. Y., & Bargh, J. A. (1998). Coming out in the age of the Internet: Identity "demarginalization" through virtual group participation. *Journal of Personality & Social Psychology, 75,* 681–694.

McLaughlin, M. L., Osborn, K. K., & Smith, C. B. (1995). Standards of conduct on usenet. In S. E. Jones (Ed.), *CyberSociety: Computer-mediated communication and community* (pp. 90–111). Thousand Oaks, CA: Sage.

McLeod, P. L. (1992). An assessment of the experimental literature on the electronic support of group work: Results of a meta-analysis. *Human Computer Interaction, 7*(3), 257–280.

McLeod, P. L. (1996). New communication technologies for group research: Toward an integrative framework. In R. Hirokawa & M. S. Poole (Eds.), *Communication and group decision making* (2nd Ed., pp. 426–462). Thousand Oaks, CA: Sage.

McLeod, P. L., Baron, R. S., Marti, M. W., & Kuh, Y. (1997). The eyes have it: Minority influence in face-to-face and computer-mediated group discussion. *Journal of Applied Psychology, 82*(5), 706–718.

McLeod, P. L., & Liker, J. K. (1992). Electronic meeting systems: Evidence from a low structure environment. *Information Systems Research, 3*, 195–223.

Melymuka, K. (1997). Virtual realities (virtual teams at ARCO Alaska). *Computerworld, 31*(Apr), 70–72.

Rice, R. E. (1984). Mediated group communication. In R. E. Rice & Associates (Eds.), *The new media: Communication, research, and technology* (pp. 129–154). Beverly Hills, CA: Sage.

Ridgeway, C. L. (2001). Social status and group structure. In M. A. Hogg & S. Tindale (Eds.), *Blackwell handbook of social psychology: Group processes* (pp. 357–375). Oxford: Blackwell Publishing.

Saunders, C., Robey, D., & Vaverek, K. (1994). The persistence of status differentials in computer conferencing. *Human Communication Research, 20*, 443–472.

Scherer, K. R., & Ekman, P. (1982). Methodological issues in studying nonverbal behavior. In K. R. Scherer & P. Ekman (Eds.), *Handbook of methods in nonverbal behavior research* (pp. 1–40). Cambridge, UK: Cambridge University Press.

Schneider, J., & Cook, K. (1995). Status inconsistency and gender: combining revisited. *Small Group Research, 26*, 372–399.

Scott, C. R., & Easton, A. C. (1996). Examining equality of influence in group decision support system interaction. *Small Group Research, 27*, 360–382.

Siegel, J., Dubrovsky, V., Kiesler, S., & McGuire, T. W. (1986). Group processes in computer-mediated communication. *Organizational Behavior & Human Decision Processes, 37*, 157–187.

Spears, R., & Lea, M. (1992). Social influence and the influence of the "social" in computer-mediated communication. In M. Lea (Ed.), *Contexts of computer-mediated communication* (pp. 30–65). London: Harvester-Wheatsheaf.

Spears, R., & Lea, M. (1994). Panacea or panopticon? The hidden power in computer-mediated communication. *Communication Research, 21*, 427–459.

Sproull, L. S., & Kiesler, S. (1991). *Connections: New ways of working in the networked organization.* Cambridge, MA: MIT Press.

Stasser, G., & Stewart, D. (1992). The discovery of hidden profiles by decision-making groups: Solving a problem versus making a judgment. *Journal of Personality and Social Psychology, 63*, 426–434.

Steiner, I. D. (1972). *Group process and productivity.* New York and London: Academic Press.

Straus, S. (1996). Getting a clue: The effects of communication media and information distribution on participation and performance in computer-mediated and face-to-face groups. *Small Group Research, 27*, 115–142.

Straus, S., & McGrath, J. E. (1994). Does the medium matter? The interaction of task type and technology on group performance and member reactions. *Journal of Applied Psychology, 79*, 87–97.

Townsend, A. M., DeMarie, S. M., & Hendrickson, A. R. (1996). Are you ready for virtual teams? *HRMagazine, 41*, 122–126.

Walther, J. B. (1996). Computer-mediated communication: Impersonal, interpersonal, and hyperpersonal interaction. *Communication Research, 3–43.*

Walther, J. B., & Burgoon, J. K. (1992). Relational communication in computer-mediated interaction. *Human Communication Research, 19*, 50–88.

Watson, R., DeSanctis, G., & Poole, M. S. (1988). Using a GDSS to facilitate group consensus: Some intended and unintended consequences. *MIS Quarterly, 12*, 463–478.

Weisband, S. P. (1992). Group discussion and first advocacy effects in computer-mediated and face-to-face decision making groups. *Organizational Behavior and Human Decision Processes, 53*, 352–380.

Weisband, S. P., Schneider, S. K., & Connolly, T. (1995). Electronic communication and social information: Status salience and status differences. *Academy of Management Journal, 38*, 1124–1151.

Wellman, B., & Gulia, M. (1998). Netsurfers don't ride alone: Virtual communities as communities. In P. Kollock & M. Smith (Eds.), *Communities in cyberspace* (pp. 163–170). London: Routledge.

Williams, E. (1977). Experimental comparisons of face-to-face and mediated communication: A review. *Psychological Bulletin, 84*(5), 963–976,

Zigurs, I., Poole, M. S., & DeSanctis, G. (1988). A study of influence in computer-mediated group decision making. *MIS Quarterly, 12*, 625–644.

CHAPTER FOURTEEN

Group Processes in Organizational Contexts

Joseph E. McGrath and Linda Argote

This chapter is about an interrelated set of processes that take place within, and constitute the action of, groups in organizations. Six years ago we wrote a chapter on group processes in organizations (Argote & McGrath, 1993), in which we considered four CORE processes (construction, operation, reconstruction, and external relations). In that chapter, we stressed three themes:

1 that groups need to be studied as intact complex systems;
2 that groups are adaptive systems that are in continuous interchange with their embedding contexts and their embedded members, and therefore that the focus of study needs to be not just on the group as a system, but also on the interchanges between that group and its embedding contexts and embedded members; and
3 that groups are dynamic systems that need to be studied over time.

Those three points can be summarized by asserting that groups are *complex, adaptive, dynamic systems.*

Since then we have come to stress those three themes even more highly than we did in that earlier chapter. They are central to our other research activities in the interim. For example, those three themes are at the heart of a theoretical formulation by McGrath and colleagues (Arrow, McGrath, & Berdahl, 2000; McGrath, Arrow, & Berdahl, in press) in which they draw on concepts from general systems theory, dynamical systems theory, and complexity theory to construct a general theory of groups. Similarly, Argote and colleagues have emphasized those same themes of complexity, adaptation, and dynamics in their studies of knowledge transfer in franchises (Darr, Argote, & Epple, 1995) and new product development teams (Olivera & Argote, 1999).

In this chapter, we will draw on our earlier chapter, and on the bodies of related work that each of us has done in the interim, to once again examine group processes in work organizations with an emphasis on those three themes. We will blend the ideas embedded in the CORE processes with the ideas embedded in the Arrow, McGrath, and Berdahl (2000) theory of groups as complex systems, in the following way. First, we will sketch out some key features of the Arrow, McGrath, and Berdahl formulation – about the nature of groups, group functions, attributes of members, levels of causal dynamics in groups, and modes of group life. The rest of the chapter will deal extensively with two of the modes formulated by Arrow et al. (2000) – Formation and Operations – but not with their third "Metamorphosis" mode. Within the formation mode, we will discuss the forces that can be at play when a group forms, and variations in the kinds of groups that can thereby be created. In the operations mode, we will consider three major sets of processes that operate continuously and simultaneously in groups: (a) Coordination processes, by which the group establishes, enacts, monitors, and modifies the pattern of member–task–tool relations through which the group pursues its purposes; (b) Adaptation processes, by which the group carries out its two-way interchanges with its embedding contexts and its embedded members; and (c) Learning processes, by which the results of both coordination and adaptation processes affect the development and modification of the group itself. We will close the chapter with a brief discussion of issues that arise because groups are dynamic systems, operating within temporal and organizational contexts that show complex temporal patterns over time.

Before presenting that reformulated view of groups, however, we will make a few comments about the history of the study of groups in organizations, and about the current state of that field.

Research on Groups in Organizations

Past research on groups

There is a rich tradition of research on groups in the social sciences. The study of groups as a separate field, "group dynamics," emerged in the United States in the 1930s under the leadership of Kurt Lewin (Cartwight & Zander, 1968). Early definitions of the field of group dynamics share much in common with the dimensions of groups we emphasize here. For example, Cartwright and Zander (1968) offered the following definition of the field of group dynamics: "a field of inquiry dedicated to achieving knowledge about the nature of groups, the laws of their development, and their interrelationships with individuals, other groups, and larger institutions" (p. 4). Cartwright and Zander (1968) further noted that characteristics that distinguish group dynamics from related fields are: its emphasis on theoretically significant empirical research; its focus on dynamics and interdependence of phenomena; its interdisciplinary orientation; and the potential applicability of its findings to practical problems. Thus, early approaches to group dynamics emphasized the interdependent and dynamic nature of groups and their embeddedness in larger social contexts.

Early empirical research reflected these important underlying dimensions of groups. For example, Lewin, Lippitt, and White (1939) examined how leadership styles affected the attitude and behavior of groups. Groups of ten- and eleven-year-olds met regularly over several weeks under the leadership of an adult who adopted an autocratic, democratic, or laissez faire leadership style. The study examined the development of attitudes and performance over time and thereby focused on the dynamics of the groups. Interdependence of phenomena was acknowledged: the effect of one factor (e.g., leadership style) was analyzed in conjunction with the effect of others (e.g., social climate). Although the relationships among groups was not focused on explicitly in the study, it was implicitly included by examining interactions between groups meeting in the same room at the same time. A classic study by Sherif, Harvey, White, Hood, and Sherif (1961) explicitly focused on intergroup relations and the embedded nature of group life.

Although early work on groups reflected the properties of groups we emphasize here, much subsequent work neglected the dynamic, interdependent, and embedded nature of groups. In an analysis of research reported in the leading social psychological journals between 1975 and 1993, Moreland, Hogg, and Hains (1994) found that over three-fourths of the studies on groups published during this period were laboratory experiments. In the prototypical experiment, a group of strangers is brought together for a short period of time to perform a task or form a judgment in the laboratory. These groups do not have a history or expect a future. They do not exist in an embedding context where the management of relationships with other groups matters. These laboratory studies typically manipulate one (or a small number of) variables. Thus, the studies are not well suited for capturing the interdependence of group phenomena, or the complex, adaptive, dynamic nature of groups.

The prevalence of the laboratory method in social psychological studies during this period is consistent with Steiner's (1986) characterization of "paradigmatic preferences" among social psychologists. Steiner (1986) noted that several preferences characterize the work of social psychologists: focusing on the individual rather than the group as the level of analysis; manipulating behavior in the laboratory rather than studying it in more naturalistic contexts; and building theories around single rather than multiple causal factors.

In general, Moreland, Hogg, and Hains (1994) found that research on groups in social psychology decreased in the 1970s and for much of the 1980s, then increased in the late 1980s and early 1990s. Examining the popularity of specific topics over time, Moreland, Hogg, and Hains (1994) found a dramatic increase in research on stereotyping and biases associated with intergroup relations. By contrast, research on intragroup phenomena such as group composition, conflict within groups, and group performance appeared less often in social psychology journals during this period.

In a complementary analysis of work published in organizational psychology journals from 1975 to 1994, Sanna and Parks (1997) found that intragroup research on the internal processes and performance of groups had been taken up by organizational (rather than by social) psychologists (see also Levine & Moreland, 1990): 98% of group research articles published in leading organizational psychology journals during this period focused on internal processes and performance. A smaller percentage of organizational psychology articles (50%) relied on laboratory methods compared to social psychology articles employing laboratory methods (76%). The same general nonmonotonic pattern was found over time for the popularity of articles about groups in the organizational psychology journals as was described previously for the social psychology journals: research on groups within organizational psychology decreased from the mid-1970s to the mid-1980s and then increased in the late 1980s and early 1990s.

These reviews indicate that research on groups is increasing – in both social and organizational psychology. Research that examines interpersonal relations such as stereotyping and prejudice appears primarily in social psychology journals whereas research on intragroup processes and performance is published primarily in organizational psychology journals (Sanna & Parks, 1997). Research on groups is also on the increase in management journals (Cohen & Bailey, 1997).

The current state of the field

What accounts for the increased interest in research on groups in the late 1980s and 1990s? We believe several important factors contribute, including theoretical developments, methodological developments, prevailing practical concerns, and the institutional home of the researcher.

On the theoretical side, Moreland, Hogg, and Hains (1994) presented evidence that much of the resurgence of interest in groups on the part of social psychologists, especially the increased interest in intergroup relations, was due to the influence of European and social cognition approaches to studying groups. Much of that work focuses on intergroup, rather than on intragroup phenomena. By contrast, Sanna and Parks (1997) found that the European and social cognition approaches had little influence on research on groups published in the organizational psychology literature.

We believe that much of the resurgence of interest in research on groups, especially in organizational psychology and management, reflects the increasing use of groups as the basic building blocks of organizations during the 1980s. During this period, many organizations in the United States experienced large productivity problems (Minabe, 1986). Although firms in the United States had once been more productive than their counterparts in other industrial countries, the productivity of firms in other countries, especially Japan, caught up with or surpassed U.S. productivity in many sectors during this period (Krugman, 1991). Acknowledging the remarkable productivity advances of Japanese firms, the United States looked to Japan for effective models of management. Analyses of why Japanese firms, especially manufacturing firms, were so effective cited their heavy reliance on groups and teams as a key factor contributing to their productivity (Hayes & Wheelright, 1984; Womack, Jones, & Roos, 1990). The use of groups and teams as the basic units through which tasks are accomplished increased in the United States during the 1980s (Cohen & Bailey, 1997).

The increased use of teams stimulated more research on teams. Given the time it takes to complete research and publication lags, most of the research appearing in the late 1980s – the period when publications on groups increased – would have been started in the early or mid-1980s – the period when productivity problems were most pressing. Thus, we believe a significant component of the resurgence of interest in groups was stimulated by increased interest in groups as a unit for getting work done in organizations.

Group research is increasingly likely to be done by researchers in professional schools, especially management, rather than by researchers in psychology departments. In their study of organizational psychology journals, Sanna and Parks (1997) found that the last year in which a majority of first authors of papers published in these journals was affiliated with psychology departments was 1979. Being in management departments may expose group researchers to the practical problems practitioners grapple with as they manage their firms. For example, Paul Allaire, the Chief Executive Officer of Xerox, has argued that managing knowledge transfer across groups is a fundamental problem for firms (Allaire, 1997). Understanding knowledge transfer across groups requires a recognition of the embedded, dynamic, and interdependent nature of groups. More generally, responding to issues involved in the management of intact groups in organizational contexts requires an appreciation of the interdependent, dynamic, and embedded nature of group-level phenomena.

At the same time, new conceptual and methodological developments, arising from a variety of both basic and applied disciplines, have enabled group researchers to begin studying groups in a more systematic and rigorous way that better reflects the realities of ongoing, intact groups in organizational contexts. For example, more sophisticated statistical techniques enable researchers to examine the effects of multiple variables and their interactions on group-level phenomena. Developments in time series and process analysis let researchers begin to capture some of the dynamics of group processes and performance (see McGrath & Altermatt, 2001, for a review). These new advances are reflected in several aspects of recent group research. Some researchers have begun examining the dynamics of group phenomena by studying how group processes and performance change over time (e.g., Gersick, 1988; Gruenfeld & Hollingshead, 1993; McGrath & Kelly, 1986; Moreland & Levine, 1982; Weingart, 1997). Some research has begun to focus on the embedded character of groups by examining how groups manage relationships or share knowledge with other groups (Ancona & Caldwell, 1992; Darr, Argote, & Epple, 1995). Such new conceptual and methodological approaches enable group researchers to begin to capture the dynamic, interdependent, and embedded nature of groups. Thus, group research in the late 1980s and 1990s not only has increased in volume (compared to the 1970s and early 1980s), but also better reflects the realities of intact groups in organizational contexts.

A Reformulation: The Nature of Groups in Organizational Contexts

Definitions

Recent definitions of groups emphasize their complex and adaptive character. For example, Guzzo and Dickson (1996) defined a group as "made up of individuals who see themselves and who are seen by others as a social entity, who are interdependent because of the tasks they perform as members of a group, who are embedded in one or more larger social systems (e.g., an organization), and who perform tasks that affect others (such as customers or coworkers)" (pp. 308–309). Similarly, Cohen and Bailey (1997) defined a team in an organizational setting as a collection of individuals who are interdependent in their tasks, who see themselves and are seen by others as an intact social entity and who are embedded in a larger social system.

These definitions emphasize several characteristics of groups: task interdependence (what one member does affects and is affected by other group members); social-psychological awareness (members perceive themselves as a group and are perceived by others as a group); and social embeddedness (the group exists in a larger social system). These definitions agree with our emphasis on the interdependent and adaptive nature of groups. We also emphasize their dynamic nature: groups exist in a temporal context.

In our view, groups are complex and intact systems, made up of *people* who become the group's *membership* (a set of interrelated members), *intentions* that become the group's *projects* (a set of interrelated tasks), and *resources (both tangible and intangible)* that become a group's *technology* (a set of interconnected tools, both hardware and software, by which the group does its work). The elements of those sets are interrelated with one another, within and across sets, ultimately within an overall set of member–task–tool relations that we will refer to as the group's *coordination network*.

Criterion domains

Groups always have two main intrinsic functions: the accomplishment of group projects and the fulfillment of member needs. To pursue those functions effectively, a group must also undertake a third (instrumental) function: establishment and maintenance of the group as an integral system. These three functions (*group projects*, *member needs*, and *system integrity*) point to three inherent criterion domains for considering the success of any group. A group is successful to the extent that it accomplishes group purposes (projects), fulfills member needs, and maintains the integrity of the group as an ongoing system.

The group's activities, as it pursues those functions, can involve any of three main derivative functions:

- processing information;
- managing conflict and consensus; and
- coordinating member actions

The importance of these three functions differs among groups, depending on those groups' central projects, but all are involved to some degree in virtually all group projects. Hence, a group's effectiveness in carrying out these three instrumental functions represents three more criterion domains for considering the success of any group.

Elements of groups: Member attributes and needs; project and task requirements; technological affordances

Members come to the group with sets of attributes and needs. The attributes constitute potential bases for contributing to the fulfillment of group purposes; the needs represent potential bases for benefiting from group membership. Member attributes include various knowledge, skills, and abilities in regard to carrying out task, interpersonal and process (or procedural) activities; various values, beliefs and attitudes; and various personality, cognitive and behavioral styles. Members also come to the group with various personal and organizational demographic characteristics, which sometimes are used by others as proxies for estimating the attributes of the other three sets (that is, their abilities, values, and personalities). Member needs include needs for achievement, for affiliation, for power/control, and for material resources.

Group projects, and the tasks that make them up, vary widely in terms of the extent to which they entail requirements for processing information, managing conflict and consensus, and coordinating member activity, and in the extent to which they require task, procedural, and interpersonal activities. The tools of a group's technology also differ in terms of how effectively they support information processing, conflict and consensus management, and coordination of member activity, and in how effectively they support task, procedural, and interpersonal activities (see Hollingshead, this volume, chapter 13).

Levels of causal dynamics and modes of group life

In our earlier treatment of group processes in organizations (see Argote & McGrath, 1993), we viewed the course of group interaction in terms of four partially time-ordered but intertwined core processes (Construction, Operations, Reconstruction, and External Relations). Here, instead, we will view a group as a system with three basic modes of its life course, within which three levels of causal dynamics are simultaneously and continually operating. The three modes are: Formation (when people, intentions, and resources come together into an intact group-as-a-system); Operation (the main portion of the group's life during which it pursues group projects and member needs); and Metamorphosis (when the group ends or becomes transformed into a recognizably different system). Throughout the course of a group's existence, three levels of causal dynamics operate continuously and simultaneously: (a) local dynamics (the "rules" governing the occurrence and recurrence of patterns of member–task–tool relations and actions); (b) global dynamics (the emergent system level or global properties that subsequently shape local dynamics); and (c) contextual dynamics (the anticipation, occurrence, and consequences of actions and events that are external to but have impact upon the system, and the group's responses to those events).

While all three levels of dynamics operate continuously, they can be considered separately for analytic purposes. In the group's operations mode (the main period of its life during which it carries out its work), the basic operation of its local dynamics can be thought of as Coordination. Local dynamics lead to the emergence of global-level variables in what can be regarded as the process of group Development. Both local and global dynamics are affected by contextual dynamics, that is, the interaction of the group with its embedding contexts. That process can be regarded as Adaptation. Both the operation of the system itself (its coordination and group development over time), and the adaptive relation between the group and its embedding contexts, can lead to group Learning.

That is, coordination, group development, and adaptation all can lead to changes in the group-as-a-system that persist over time.

Formation Processes

Forces in group formation

Both external and internal forces operate in the formation of groups, and both "top-down" and "bottom-up" (or planning and emergent) forces operate as well. This suggests four prototypical forms of groups: *Concocted* groups are top-down or designed groups impelled by outside forces (e.g., a manager); *Founded* groups are top-down or designed groups impelled by inside forces (i.e., one or more people who themselves will be members of the new group); *Self-organized* groups are impelled by bottom-up or emergent forces and internal forces; *Circumstantial* groups are impelled by the situation, an external force, and the formation of a group is emergent or bottom-up.

All four kinds of group formation apply to work organizations but with different frequencies. Most work groups are concocted, that is, created by someone outside the group who has the power to reassign people and resources. Sometimes top management members found groups of which they will be (high-status) members. Sometimes "informal" groups arise as self-organized groups (e.g., those groups that plagued the Hawthorne plant's incentive plan). And probably circumstantial groups sometimes form within organizations, especially in the face of catastrophes or perceived threats.

Types of groups

For all of these forms of groups, we can think of "group types" in terms of two factors: (a) whether the group gives priority to group projects or to member needs; and (b) the importance given to, and the timing with which, different aspects of the group (members, tasks, tools) are selected and different sets of relations (member–task, member–tool, task–tool) are established. We can consider three types of group project-oriented groups (which Arrow, McGrath, & Berdahl, 2000, call *work groups*) and three types of member needs-oriented groups (which those authors call *clubs*).

The three types of work groups, that emphasize completion of group projects are:

1 *Teams*, in which the members and the member–tool relations are primary, and the sets of relations are expected to last for a long (or indefinite) time;
2 *Task Forces*, in which the project and the member–task relations are primary, and where the group is expected to continue only until that project is completed; and
3 *Crews*, in which the technology and the task–tool relations are primary, and the sets of relations are expected to continue only for a "shift" of relatively brief duration.

These different forms of groups (all of which are plentiful in work organizations) have major implications for how, and how effectively, groups can accomplish their purposes, and for how vulnerable the group is to changes in different aspects of the group. Task forces are very vulnerable to changes in the assigned project; teams to changes in members; and crews to changes in technology.

The three kinds of groups or clubs that focus on fulfillment of member needs are:

4 *Economic clubs* which focus on the material resources and power/control needs that members can fulfill from group membership;
5 *Social clubs* which focus on the affiliative needs that members can fulfill from group membership; and
6 *Activity clubs* which focus on the activity/achievement needs that members can fulfill from group membership.

From the point of view of management, only groups that focus on completion of group projects have legitimate status, although sometimes management is aware of the existence of member-oriented groups (as in the informal groups of the Hawthorne studies). From the point of view of an individual member, membership in an organization and in groups within that organization must always, to some degree, entail expectations of need fulfillment. Thus, any given member may be associated with one or more of these types of "clubs," as well as with one or another of the group project-oriented types of work groups listed above.

Of course, these types are prototypes or exemplars, not mutually exclusive categories. Any given group is likely to be a blend of all six types. But most groups are liable to be uneven mixes of these various aspects, hence more of some kinds than of others.

Coordination Processes

Coordination network

To pursue their functions effectively, groups must establish and enact a pattern of member–task–tool relations that we will call the coordination network. Note, however, that there are at least three meanings of coordination: (a) coordination of interests: alignment of intentions (hence of underlying values) among group members; (b) coordination of understandings: agreement about the meanings of information and events pertinent to the group; and (c) coordination of action: synchronization, in time, place, and content, of actions of group members. These three correspond, quite closely, to the three instrumental functions noted above: managing conflict and consensus, processing information, and motivation and regulation of member behavior.

The group as an operating system can be thought of as *the establishment, enactment, monitoring, and modification* of a pattern of relations among its constituent parts – its membership, projects, and technology. The overall pattern of member–task–tool relations (which Arrow, McGrath, & Berdahl call the coordination network) is composed of six subnetworks: the set of member–member relations (the member or social network); the set of task–task relations (the task network); the set of tool–tool relations (the tool network); the set of member–task relations (division of labor or labor network); the set of member–tool relations (the role network); and the set of task–tool relations (the job network).

The set of member–member relations is the social network that connects group members. The set of task–task relations (the task network) is the recurring sequences of tasks used to produce the group's product. For example, a team in a fast-food franchise might use a particular sequence of tasks for making each product. The tool–tool network is the interrelationships among the various tools or technologies used to produce the product. For example, a car manufacturer would use a set sequence of tools to assemble each product.

The set of member–task relations is the division of labor. The division of labor specifies which member does which tasks. The set of member–tool relations or the role network maps each member onto particular tools. For example, in an underground coal mine, a member with the role of the "shuttle car operator" operates the shuttle car that moves the coal that has been extracted from the coal face to the surface of the mine. Similarly, the member with the role of the "roof bolter" advances into the mine and uses a tool (the roof bolter) to prop up the roof and prevent its collapse. The set of task–tool relations maps each task onto particular tool(s). Returning to the coal mine example, the task of moving the coal is accomplished through the use of the shuttle car tool and the task of securing the roof is performed with the roof bolter tool.

Group performance is facilitated when each of these various subnetworks is internally compatible and compatible with the other networks. The task network should be a functional/instrumental set of relations by which the entire project can get done. At the same time, the member–task network should have all the tasks allocated to members with appropriate skills and tools (i.e., the member–task network should be compatible with the role network). The overall coordination network (the pattern of member–task–tool relations) should have tasks allocated to members who have appropriate skills and have access to appropriate tools. Groups vary in the extent to which they achieve compatibility of their networks. This variation contributes to differences in group performance outcomes.

Coordination as recurrent establish–enact–monitor–modify cycles

The coordination network gets partially established during group formation, then more fully articulated, enacted, monitored, and modified when the group is in its operations mode. For example, as the group gains experience, it learns who is good at what and how to assign tasks to take better advantage of each member's skills. That enacting–monitoring–modifying (feedback) cycle is crucial. Out of this recurrent establish–enact–monitor–modify cycle come emergent or global properties of the group – things like cohesiveness, efficacy, task performance routines, and so on. These emergent patterns (global dynamics) shape the subsequent operation and development of the group.

Adaptation Processes

We use the idea of adaptation to refer to (reciprocal) changes in the group as a system, and in parts of its embedding contexts, that arise subsequent to actions and events in the embedding systems that have implications for the group. It carries the implication of "response to change." It does not carry the implication of "effective response."

Embedding contexts vary in richness (potential resources) and volatility (rate and temporal patterning of change). Changes vary in terms of their predictability and controllability. If predictable and controllable, they can be prevented, or induced (if favorable) at the time and circumstances of the group's choosing. If they are unpredictable, and/or uncontrollable, they pose potential problems (or opportunities) for the group. There are many potential patterns of response to external events/actions, including accommodation; attempts to assimilate the change or attenuate its effects; and "doing nothing," which is sometimes both a deliberate and a wise strategy. Changes often lead to unintended consequences. Moreover, there is often a non-proportional relation between amount and type of change event and the size and direction of change in the group. Sometimes big events yield small changes or none at all; sometimes small events yield big changes.

We assume that groups operate in what systems theorists call a "fitness landscape." Some "locations" (i.e., states) of the group in relation to its external contexts are better for the group than others – they have better payoffs for the group and its members, and/or lower costs. For example, a group that is operating in a context in which its main output is scarce and highly valued is in a better "fitness" situation than is a group whose main product is plentiful and/or not much sought after. A group that depends on a particular resource is very vulnerable to variations in the environment that alter the availability of that resource. Such changes would be exemplified by a shift in the relation of the political regime that controls a resource such as crude oil, or adverse weather conditions that alter prospects for crop growth. Changes in the group's relation to its external contexts are sometimes advantageous to the group and sometimes detrimental.

Types of adaptation and change

Adaptation may be *directed* or *undirected*. Undirected adaptation, like species evolution, is a cycle of variation (in structure, in behavior, or in the environment), selection, and stabilization (retention). Directed change is a cycle of information processing (about the system, its environment, and their relations), planning, choice, and self-regulation. There are barriers to both kinds of adaptation, including a fluctuating and unpredictable environment, and situations in which what is good for individuals or parts of a system is not correspondent with what is good for the system as a whole. For example, a manufacturing department may increase its efficiency by minimizing product changeovers that require retooling equipment and thereby reduce the amount of time the production line is operating. Maximizing the efficiency of the production department, however, may cost the organization customers who take their business elsewhere because they are dissatisfied with the organization's responsiveness to their requests.

For undirected adaptation, barriers include conditions in which there is too little variation in the environment, or a too forgiving environment; conditions when selection is based on false association (superstitions, or spurious correlation); and conditions when it is difficult to maintain or stabilize a new "form."

For directed adaptation, barriers include errors in understanding or prediction of the environment (i.e., errors in the group's "mental model" of the fitness landscape); disagreement in the group regarding strategy or tactics (i.e., failure to achieve a coordination of interest, of understandings, and/or of action); inability to keep the group on track after setbacks; and "resistance" by entrenched routines or factions.

The latter suggests that internal factors also affect ability to adapt. Such internal factors include the state of the system at the time of the event (i.e., the group's current structure and functioning), the "legacy of the past" (its history, including its entrenched routines and its record of past actions and effects), and the type of group it is. Different types of groups (e.g., teams, task forces, etc.) are vulnerable to different types of changes.

Adaptation is also affected by different developmental or "change motors" that may be operating in the group, and by the "shadow of the future." Only certain types of groups (e.g., teams) fit the "life course" developmental change model that is the most prevalent one used in group research. Other types of groups such as crews, may fit a "crisis adaptation" model. Still others, such as task forces, may fit a "robust equilibrium" type model, or a "punctuated equilibrium" model as did Gersick's (1988, 1989) groups.

Change events may come in various forms. First of all, changes may come from inside or outside the referent system. Outside changes may come in the form of intrusive or non-intrusive changes; that is, they may simply change the environment with no direct impact on the group (they change the "fitness landscape" that the group is operating in), or they may directly impinge on the group itself. Change events also differ in magnitude, and in valence.

Change events have temporal properties as well. They vary in abruptness of onset, in rate and frequency, and in temporal patterning. In regard to the latter: If there is a series of changes all of the same kind and in the same direction, that is a trend. Alternatively, a set of changes, collectively, can constitute a cycle. Or, a set of changes can vary in an apparently random way, constituting "fluctuation" in no apparent pattern. Changes also vary in uncertainty, predictability, and controllability.

Time-shifting responses

Groups often "time shift" their response to a given change. Such time shifts may place the response in any of five "temporal zones" with respect to the event itself (McGrath & Beehr, 1990). For negative events, those five zones can be labeled as different temporal forms of coping with potential stressors, as follows:

1 actions taken long before the change event are Preventive coping;
2 actions taken before the event are Anticipatory coping;
3 actions taken during the event are Dynamic coping;
4 actions taken after the event are Reactive coping; and
5 actions taken long after the event are Residual coping.

Preventive coping may try to prevent the event, but more often it is an attempt to mitigate its consequences. The building of a levee along a river bank does not prevent some later rise in the level of the water in the river, but rather prevents or attenuates the negative consequences of that high water for land beside the river. While for negative events these are reasonably called "forms of coping," for positive events they reflect different timing in the pursuit of opportunities.

Forms of response to change events

From a systems-process point of view, there are four general forms of responses to such external system actions or events:

1 *Negative feedback loops.* These are system responses that attempt to attenuate or eliminate the impact of the change on the system. When done before the event, these would be "preemption." During the event, they could be characterized as "buffering." After the event they constitute "repair."

2 *Positive feedback loops.* These are system responses that magnify the impact of the change on the system. This can be in the form of: (a) switching (before, during, or after) to alternative structures or functions; (b) increased disorder beyond what is directly produced by the change event itself and, if the increased disorder is extreme enough; (c) either "creative innovation" or "collapse."

3 *No response.* The system may give no response to a given event: (a) because the group failed to note the event, or assumed it would not alter the group's "fitness landscape"; or (b) because of some feature of the group's history, its self-regulatory processes, and/or its routines that cannot be overcome. Alternatively, "no response" may be erroneously imputed to a system by an observer because the system's response to the event is a time-shifted response, already anticipated or delayed, so that the response occurs before or long after the observer "looks" at the group and concludes "no response."

4 *Co-evolution.* These are mutual reciprocal changes of the system and of its embedding contexts. But such co-evolution only applies for those parts of the environment that are interactive with the system, not the parts (such as climate or general economic conditions) that affect but are not affected by the system.

Concluding comments

Negative feedback dampens the impact of events. Positive feedback magnifies the impact. Time shifting obscures the impact. Hence, we should not expect to find the impact of events on the system to be isomorphic, in either valence or magnitude, with the valence and magnitude of the event.

Several "principles" of adaptation are implied in this discussion:

1 There is likely to be a non-proportionality of event and responses.
2 There often are unintended consequences.
3 Temporal displacement can obscure the fact and the nature of adaptive changes.

We should add a fourth, not particularly implied in the above but none the less likely:

4 There may be spontaneous innovation; that is, changes may occur that are not traceable to any particular event in the system's embedding contexts; they may sometimes be attributable to the intentionality of the system or its embedded members.

Learning Processes

Group learning is the process through which members acquire, share, and combine knowledge into a collective product through experience of working together (Argote, Gruenfeld, & Naquin, in press). Group learning manifests itself through changes in knowledge and/or in performance. For example, as groups gain, experience, they may acquire knowledge about the capabilities of group members, about how to sequence tasks, or about how to use tools. This knowledge may in turn improve their performance.

Learning implies the persistence of some change in the system or its behavior. To be a "persistent change," some information or knowledge regarding that change must somehow be "located" somewhere in that system. In our terms, that implies a persistent alteration of some aspect of the coordination network, which embodies the "group-as-a-system-in-action." As indicated earlier, the group's coordination network can be viewed as composed of a set of six partially redundant subnetworks. At one level of consideration, there are networks of relations among the component parts of each of the group's three kinds of constituent elements; that is, there are networks of relations among members, among tasks, and among tools. At another level, the coordination network involves subnetworks of relations among elements of different kinds; that is, a set of member–task relations or a division of labor, a set of member–tool relations or a role network, and a set of task–tool relations or a job network. For a change to be persistent (hence considered "learning"), the "new knowledge" that denotes that change must be embedded somewhere in one or more of those six subnetworks.

Repositories of knowledge

So we can view the knowledge that groups acquire as they gain experience as residing in various repositories or "retention bins' (Argote, 1999; Levitt & March, 1988; Walsh & Ungson, 1991). That knowledge can be embedded in individual group members, the group's tasks, its tools, the group's member–tool network, its member–task network, or its task-tool network. For example, as groups acquire experience, *individual members* may learn new skills and become more proficient at their particular tasks. This knowledge is embedded in individual group members. As groups gain experience, they may also modify the *tasks* that constitute the project. For example, they may discover better ways to sequence tasks or to layout the production process. Thus, some of the knowledge that groups acquire with experience is embedded in the task network. As groups gain experience, they may also modify their *tools* and how they use them, and thereby embed knowledge in the technology. For example, a car manufacturer may modify the software in its paint shop to achieve the desired colors on cars or a pizza maker may develop a tool for achieving an even distribution of cheese on pies.

As groups gain experience, the *member–task* and *member–tool* relations – the division of labor and role networks – also change. Groups acquire knowledge about who is good at what (Liang, Moreland, & Argote, 1995) and assign tasks to take advantage of each member's capabilities. This knowledge about who is good at what becomes embedded in the *member–task* network and/or in the *member–tool* network. The group acquires information about who is proficient at using which tools and assigns tasks and roles accordingly. Similarly, knowledge may be embedded in the *task–tool* relations or the job network. Groups acquire information about which tasks are best performed with which tools and how to structure the relationships between tools and tasks better, and embody that knowledge in their *task–tool* networks.

Of course, the three kinds of elements are quite different when viewed as potential "repositories of knowledge." The idea of members as repositories of knowledge is a familiar one, and such knowledge repositories are subject to an array of strengths and weaknesses of humans as cognitive and motivational systems – learning rate, forgetting, fatigue, positive and negative transfer, attention and motivational fluctuations, and so on. "Tools" as a location for the deposit of knowledge is a less familiar idea. Considering that "tools," as used here, includes both hardware and software, the embedding of new knowledge in tools includes both the idea of a change in hardware (such as modification of the design of a wrench) or in software (such as change in the software that runs the "paint shop" of a plant). The idea of tasks as a location for new knowledge is also somewhat novel. Since projects are the focused embodiment of intentions, and tasks are proper parts of projects, tasks are therefore "subintentions." Learning a new way to carry out a project often entails the "division" of the overall project into a new set of tasks – new either in that some of the tasks are different than those into which the project was divided before, or in the sense that some of the tasks are clustered or sequenced in new ways. If we think of the task network as a template for the activities needed to complete a project, then when there is a change either in the parts of that template or the patterning of those parts, that can be regarded as a "knowledge repository" of what has been learned.

Learning that involves the embedding of knowledge in these different subnetworks is subject to different strengths and vulnerabilities. Changes in the tool network and the task network by definition involve explicit knowledge, and are accessible to all members of the group. Changes in members, however, may involve either explicit or tacit knowledge, and may be available only to individual members.

The situation with regard to the three between-element networks is even more complicated. Embedding of knowledge regarding changes involving the member–task network (i.e., the division of labor) impacts both those members and those tasks. Similarly, embedding of knowledge regarding changes in the member–tool network impacts both members and tools, and embedding of knowledge regarding changes in the task–tool network impacts both tasks and tools. So knowledge that is embedded in any of these between-element subnetworks is liable to have the vulnerabilities and limitations of both kinds of elements. For example, any given piece of knowledge regarding the division of labor (member–task network) must be accessible to many or all members, not just to the one(s) directly involved in those tasks. Similarly, knowledge regarding changes in the role network must be accessible to both those in the relevant roles and those affected by that role performance.

Ultimately, of course, while tasks can "contain" or reflect new knowledge (new tasks to be done and/or new sequencing of tasks), and tools can "contain" or reflect new knowledge (new physical features and/or modified procedures), only individual humans – members – can "know" something in our usual meaning of that verb. But while "know" as a verb refers to a distinctly human characteristic, knowledge as a noun refers to "repositories," tangible or intangible, that are potentially accessible not just to a single individual but to many.

Consequences of where knowledge is embedded

Embedding group knowledge in these various repositories has implications for the persistence and accessibility of the knowledge over time, for the group's ability to transfer the knowledge to new tasks or settings, and for the performance of the group.

Individuals.   Embedding knowledge in individual members has both positive and negative consequences for group outcomes. On the positive side, individual members are particularly well suited for storing and transferring tacit knowledge, knowledge that is not easily articulated (Polanyi, 1966). Individuals can apply their tacit knowledge to a new task or setting without converting the tacit knowledge to explicit knowledge. The ability of individual members to transfer tacit knowledge was demonstrated in a series of experiments showing that individuals were able to transfer tacit knowledge acquired on one task to another, even though individuals were not able to articulate their knowledge or why their performance improved with experience (Berry & Broadbent, 1984, 1987). Alternatively, tacit knowledge can be converted to explicit knowledge (Nonaka, 1991). This conversion typically involves a period of apprenticeship in which another individual observes the group member with the tacit expertise and converts his or her tacit knowledge to explicit knowledge that others can access.

A potential negative performance consequence of embedding knowledge in individual members is the vulnerability of this knowledge to member turnover. When individual members leave, they take their knowledge with them. The turnover of individual members has been found to be particularly harmful to group performance when the departing members are high performers, the replacements are less experienced or less competent than departing members, the group lacks formal structure, opportunities for innovation are low, and the group has not had previous experience with turnover (see Argote, 1999, for a review).

Another challenge of embedding knowledge in individual members is that it may decay faster than knowledge embedded in other repositories. Research has found that knowledge embedded in groups (hence, in some subnetwork) is more stable than knowledge embedded in individual members, even when there is no member turnover. Weldon and Bellinger (1997) found that groups exhibited less forgetting and more consistency than individuals. Knowledge embedded in tools, as in redesigned hardware, also is available even if there is member turnover.

Another challenge associated with embedding knowledge in individual members is that individuals may not share their knowledge. This tendency is particularly pronounced when a group member is the sole possessor of a particular piece of task-relevant information. A substantial body of research suggests that group members do not share information they uniquely hold (see Wittembaum & Stasser, 1996, for a review). Several explanations have been offered for why groups focus on ideas that members already hold in common, rather than discuss unshared ideas that are uniquely held by individual members. One explanation focuses on the "sampling advantage" of shared information: since more members possess the shared information, it is more likely to be mentioned in group discussion (Stasser & Titus, 1985). Another explanation focuses on the influence of shared information on members' pre-discussion preferences rather than its effect on what is mentioned during group discussion (Gigone & Hastie, 1993). Other explanations have emphasized political concerns and noted that individual members may hoard knowledge they uniquely possess to protect the basis of their power and influence (Engeström, Brown, Engeström, & Korstinen, 1990).

Thus, individual members provide both a sensitive and a vulnerable medium for storing and transferring knowledge. Individuals are capable of capturing tacit knowledge and subtle understanding that other repositories may miss. Individuals can transfer their knowledge, including their tacit knowledge, to new tasks or settings and adapt it appropriately. On the other hand, knowledge embedded in individual members is particularly vulnerable to turnover and to decay (even when there is no turnover). Further, individuals who uniquely possess key information may not be motivated to share the information.

Tools.   Tools or technology are effective repositories for retaining explicit knowledge. Knowledge embedded in tools appears less subject to decay or depreciation than knowledge embedded in other repositories. High-technology organizations such as highly automated truck assembly plants have been found to exhibit less "forgetting" or knowledge decay than low technology organizations such as fast-food franchises (Argote, 1999). A significant component of the knowledge at these highly automated organizations is embedded in their tools and technology.

Knowledge embedded in tools or technology also transfers readily to other groups. A long line of literature on technology transfer indicates that embedding knowledge in tools or technology and transferring it to another group can result in substantial savings for the recipient group (Gallbraith, 1990). Similarly, a study of within-plant knowledge transfer across shifts in a manufacturing plant found that embedding knowledge in technology was an effective way to transfer knowledge from one shift to another (Epple, Argote, & Murphy, 1996).

Knowledge embedded in tools may be more resistant to change than knowledge embedded in other repositories. An example of the rigidity associated with embedding knowledge in tools or technology can be found in Ford's production of the Model T. According to Abernathy and Wayne (1974), Ford's almost exclusive embedding of knowledge in "hard" automation (i.e., tools and technology) made it more difficult for Ford to adapt to changing customer preferences and offer a more varied product line.

Thus, embedding knowledge in tools and technology has many advantages from the perspective of minimizing knowledge decay and facilitating knowledge transfer across groups. Knowledge embedded in tools decays less over time and transfers more readily to other units than knowledge embedded in other repositories. Knowledge embedded in technology, however, is more rigid than knowledge embedded in "softer" repositories and more difficult to change. Embedding knowledge almost exclusively in technology can hamper an organization's ability to adapt.

Tasks.   Knowledge can also be embedded in the task network – in the set of tasks and the sequencing or interrelations among them. The task network has been referred to by other writers as routines, programs, or repetitive patterns of tasks or activities (e.g., see Cyert & March, 1963; Gersick & Hackman, 1990; Nelson & Winter, 1982).

Groups embed a significant component of the knowledge they acquire with experience in their task network or system of routines. For example, an automobile manufacturing plant embedded a new method for painting two-tone trucks that required fewer steps and less material in a task network that all workers used (Argote, 1999). Similarly, a fast-food franchise embedded a new procedure for preparing a product that improved its quality in the network of tasks used by employees of the corporation at locations all over the world (Darr, Argote, & Epple, 1995).

Embedding knowledge in the task network has many of the same advantages and disadvantages of embedding knowledge in the tool network – but to a lesser extent. Embedding knowledge in the task network is an effective way to promote knowledge persistence and minimize knowledge decay. Cohen and Bacdayan (1994) found that interruptions did not slow down the performance of social systems that had evolved stable task networks. Embedding knowledge in task networks also makes it more resistant to employee turnover since the knowledge no longer depends on particular individuals but rather is codified in a task network that all individuals can use.

Embedding knowledge in a task network also facilitates knowledge transfer to other groups. A study of knowledge transfer in fast-food franchises found that knowledge embedded in task networks transferred readily outside the store of origin. By contrast, knowledge embedded in individual members remained at the store of origin (Argote & Darr, in press). In order to be embedded in a task network, knowledge must be codified. This codification makes it accessible to others and thereby facilitates knowledge transfer.

A disadvantage of relying on knowledge embedded in the task network is that a particular task network may be invoked inappropriately when it does not fit the situation. In order to realize the full potential of task networks, groups need to specify the conditions under which various task networks are appropriate and have mechanisms for switching from one task network to another or for generating new task networks when initially novel situations become recurrent (March & Simon, 1958).

In short, the task network is a mechanism for getting work done efficiently. It promotes knowledge persistence over time and facilitates knowledge transfer. If performance is to improve, however, the task network must be invoked thoughtfully to insure that it is appropriate to the situation.

Cross-element subnetworks.   Knowledge embedded in the labor, role, and job networks tend to blend the strengths and vulnerabilities of the two kinds of elements that comprise them. For example, the labor network has features that combine those of knowledge embedded in the individual members and knowledge embedded in tasks. As groups gain experience in production, an important source of the productivity gains they typically experience is learning who in the group is good at what and assigning tasks accordingly (Argote, 1999). This knowledge of who knows what is embedded in the member–task network and in the member–tool network. Studies have documented the benefits of groups knowing who knows what for subsequent group performance (Liang, Moreland, & Argote, 1995; Moreland & Myakovsky, 1998). This knowledge of who knows what has been termed a "transactive memory" system (Wegner, 1986). These memory systems have been found to facilitate coordination and group performance. But member–task and member–tool networks depend to some extent on individual members. Thus, the systems are vulnerable to member turnover (Moreland, Argote, & Krishnan, 1996). When key individuals depart, the member–task network may need to be realigned, if those individuals have idiosyncratic skills or knowledge not easily replaced.

Since individual members are involved in the labor and role networks, those repositories are more flexible and afford more opportunities to innovate than knowledge embedded solely in "hard" form in tasks or tools. Since the member–task and member–tool networks are tailored to take advantage of individual member skills, the networks are somewhat vulnerable to turnover.

The task–tool network is the most rigid of the various repositories. Knowledge embedded in the task–tool network exhibits the most persistence over time and the most transfer – at least to very similar situations. Knowledge embedded in the task–tool network is not affected by member turnover or members' choices about participation. Although knowledge embedded in the task–tool network is not subject to the vagaries of individual member participation, it suffers from the loss of flexibility and creativity that individual members can provide. Groups that embed large amounts of knowledge in task–tool networks are less adaptable than those relying more on knowledge repositories involving individual members.

Temporal and Contextual Issues

As we noted earlier, some of the major limitations of earlier work on groups, by scholars with both basic and applied interests, is that groups have been studied as relatively static entities and in isolation from the organizational contexts in which they are embedded. We want to reemphasize these issues by discussing them briefly in this concluding section.

Temporal issues

The one-hour "lifetimes" of laboratory groups in most experiments is in stark contrast to the extended, and often complicated, lifetimes of actual groups in actual work organizations. Similarly, the tendency of both laboratory and field studies to assess variables at one or a very few points in time, and to treat causal processes as one-shot occurrences seriously undervalues the dynamic nature of causal processes in groups. This neglect of temporal processes in groups has occurred at each of three levels of consideration, which are discussed below. That neglect, in turn, limits our ability to understand, much less to predict, the behavior of groups in organizations.

Dynamic processes. The first level of consideration has to do with the dynamic nature of processes within groups. All of the processes we have discussed thus far in the chapter – in formation, coordination, adaptation, and learning – take place more or less continuously over time. They cannot be assessed, appropriately, via "input–output" designs, for several reasons (some of which were suggested in earlier sections). First, there is often a disproportionality between the magnitude of "cause" and of "effect." Because system responses to change can be dampened by negative feedback loops, amplified by positive feedback loops, or show no (apparent) response, some strong causes yield weak effects, and vice versa. Moreover, in human systems in which intentionality, perception, and learning play a part, "effects" do not have to follow immediately after "causes." Sometimes systems react to anticipated events before the event occurs, sometimes reactions don't occur until much later. Furthermore, systems tend to reflect complex interdependencies among many variables – including recursive and nonmonotonic relations – rather than simple, univariate, directional ones.

Various system processes reflect different temporal "cadences" and forms; some are self-limiting cycles, some are nonlinear though monotonic, some have the potential for more than one pattern (as in "catastrophic bifurcations" of the type that are studied in "chaos theory"). All of these complexities make it very likely that any given group will show complex dynamic processes, even in relatively short periods of time, that are unlikely to be captured, much less clarified, in simple "input–output" designs.

Group development.   A second level of temporal consideration has to do with the relatively long-run dynamics of the group's own development. Even assuming a constant set of members, projects, and technology, the very nature of the group as an intact system evolves continuously over time. When a group has been in business for a year, even with "constant" constituent elements (i.e., members, projects, technology), its members are different – qua individuals, qua members, and qua relationships – than they were at the outset. They are older, probably wiser, have different capabilities, experience, and needs. The tasks and task network, and the tools and tool network, as well as the labor and role and job networks, also have evolved. Even though it has the same constituent parts nominally, it is not the "same" group. (The words of Heraclitus, the Greek philosopher – that you can't step in the "same" river twice – are apt here.)

Change over time.   At a third level of consideration, we must recognize that the elements of the group – its members, its projects, its technology – seldom do stay "constant" over long periods of the group's life. Members change, either voluntarily or otherwise. So do the group's projects (and, of course, the members' needs); and so do the total collection of tools, rules, and procedures with which the group can work. In fact, since many formally designated groups within work organizations (e.g., the U.S. Supreme Court, the New York Yankees team, the Board of Trustees of a university) exist beyond ordinary life-spans or career-spans, to some degree member change is inevitable. Moreover, there is likely to be substantial change in features of the group's embedding contexts – its organizational setting, that organization's markets and resources and alternatives, and so on – that impinge on the group in the mutual adaptation processes discussed earlier in this chapter. So temporal processes are reflected, as well, in the adaptation and change processes within which the group is embedded.

Contextual issues

Another major limitation of research on groups is its neglect of the context in which groups function. In the prototypical laboratory study, groups are created and studied in isolation. The majority of field studies also focus on the internal structure and processes of groups – their composition, communication, leadership, and so on – with little regard to the external processes of groups and their relationships with their embedding contexts.

Yet groups in organizations are intricately embedded in larger organizational and cultural contexts. These groups depend on the embedding organizational context for acquiring members, tasks, and technology. Further, groups acquire knowledge from the embedding context that may lead them to modify their members, tasks, or technology and the subnetworks of relations among them.

The neglect of the relations between groups and their embedding contexts limits our ability to understand and predict the behavior of groups in organizations. How groups manage their relationships with their embedding contexts, and share knowledge with components of the context, is critical to their success. For example, a study of knowledge transfer across fast-food stores found that the ability of a store to "learn" from or benefit from the experience of other stores contributed significantly to a focal store's performance (Darr, Argote, & Epple, 1995). Focusing only on the internal processes of each store would have neglected an important contribution to their performance – their ability to transfer knowledge from other stores in the embedding context.

Contextual effects on constituent elements of groups.   As was the case for temporal issues, as previously discussed, the neglect of contextual factors limits our understanding of groups on several levels. At one level of consideration, the elements of the group – its members, its tasks, its technology – are affected by the group's embedding organizational context. Members are affected by the training, socialization, reward practices, and so on of the parent organization and the broader social/political/economic context. The group's tasks are affected by the goals, plans, and purposes of the parent organization. Further, the group's technology may be circumscribed by the parent firm.

Contextual effects on core processes.   The second level of consideration of context has to do with the core processes themselves. Most of the processes we have discussed in this chapter – formation, coordination, adaptation, learning – are affected by the organization's context. Groups depend on the organizational context for acquiring members, tasks, or technology in their formation process. The interplay between the group and its embedding context is at the core of the adaptation process. Not only do groups learn from and modify themselves on the basis of their own direct experience, they also learn from the experience of other groups in their embedding context. For example, an innovation made by one group in an organization may transfer to another. Thus, the group's relationship with its embedding context affects its learning processes.

Effects of dynamic features of the organizational context.   At still another level, groups affect and are affected by dynamic features of the group's embedding contexts. Not only does the context have a direct effect on the elements and processes of groups, groups both anticipate and respond to events and actions external to the group that appear to have implications for it. As noted earlier in this chapter, in our discussion of adaptation, members anticipate events in the context and adjust to actual and anticipated external events in ways that affect both the group and the embedding context.

Concluding Comments

We have ended this chapter as we began it – emphasizing the importance of viewing groups as complex, adaptive, dynamic systems. Groups in work organizations reflect the effects of myriad temporal processes that operate: (a) in the short-term process dynamics of complex systems; (b) in the longer term developmental dynamics of such complex systems; and (c) in the dynamics of change and of the system's responses to it. Groups in work organizations also reflect effects of a variety of contextual processes that operate: (a) directly on their fundamental elements; (b) directly on their core processes; and (c) indirectly by altering their relations with embedding contexts. In our view, major advances in our understanding of groups in the future will require a much fuller appreciation of how temporal and contextual factors affect and are affected by the group's elements, core processes, developmental patterns, and the overall dynamics of the embedding contexts than our past research preferences have allowed. This, in turn, will require group researchers – from both basic and applied disciplines – to modify and expand the methodological and conceptual preferences and practices that have underpinned the work in this field for nearly a century. We hope the conceptual framework offered here can provide a useful template for concocting the "new look" in group theory that will be needed to launch the next century of scholarly efforts to understand groups in organizations.

REFERENCES

Abernathy, W. J., & Wayne, K. (1974). Limits of the learning curve. *Harvard Business Review, 52*(5), 109–119.

Allaire, P. (1997). *Managing for knowledge*. Paper presented at the Conference on Knowledge in International Corporations, Carnegie Bosch Institute, Rome, November, 1997.

Ancona, D. G., & Caldwell, D. F. (1992). Bridging the boundary: External activity and performance in organizational teams. *Administrative Science Quarterly, 37*, 634–665.

Argote, L. (1999). *Organizational learning: Creating, retaining and transferring knowledge*. Norwell, MA: Kluwer.

Argote, L., & Darr, E. D. (in press). Repositories of knowledge in franchise organizations: Individual, structural and technological. In G. Dosi, R. Nelson, & S. Winter (Eds.), *Nature and dynamics of organizational capabilities*.

Argote, L., Gruenfeld, D., & Naquin, C. (in press). Group learning in organizations. In M. E. Turner (Ed.), *Groups at work: Advances in theory and research*. Mahwah, NJ: Erlbaum.

Argote, L., & McGrath, J. E. (1993). Group processes in organizations: Continuity and change. *International Review of Industrial and Organizational Psychology, 8*, 333–389.

Arrow, H., McGrath, J. E., & Berdahl, J. L. (2000). *Small groups as complex systems: Formation, coordination, development and adaptation*. Thousand Oaks, CA: Sage.

Berry, D. C., & Broadbent, D. E. (1984). On the relationship between task performance and associated verbalizable knowledge. *Quarterly Journal of Experimental Psychology, 36A*, 209–231.

Berry, D. C., & Broadbent, D. E. (1987). The combination of explicit and implicit learning processes in task control. *Psychological Research, 49*, 7–15.

Cartwright, D., & Zander, A. (Eds.) (1968). *Group dynamics* (3rd Ed.). New York: Harper & Row.

Cohen, M. D., & Bacdayan, P. (1994). Organizational routines are stored as procedural memory: Evidence from a laboratory study. *Organization Science, 5*, 554–568.

Cohen, S. G., & Bailey, D. E. (1997). What makes teams work: Group effectiveness research from the shop floor to the executive suite. *Journal of Management, 23*, 239–290.

Cyert, R. M., & March, J. G. (1963). *A behavioral theory of the firm*. Englewood Cliffs, NJ: Prentice-Hall.

Darr, E., Argote, L., & Epple, D. (1995). The acquisition, transfer, and depreciation of knowledge in service organizations: Productivity in franchises. *Management Science*, *41*, 1750–1762.

Engeström, Y., Brown, K., Engeström, R., & Korstinen, K. (1990). Organizational forgetting: An activity theoretical perspective. In D. Middleton & D. Edwards (Eds.), *Collective remembering* (pp. 139–168). London: Sage.

Epple, D., Argote, L., & Murphy, K. (1996). An empirical investigation of the micro structure of knowledge acquisition and transfer through learning by doing. *Operations Research*, *44*, 77–86.

Galbraith, C. S. (1990). Transferring core manufacturing technologies in high technology firms. *California Management Review*, *32*(4), 56–70.

Gersick, C. (1988). Time and transition in work teams: Toward a new model of group development. *Academy of Management Journal*, *31*, 9–41.

Gersick, C. (1989). Marking time: Predictable transitions in task groups. *Academy of Management Journal*, *32*, 274–309.

Gersick, C., & Hackman, J. R. (1990). Habitual routines in task-performing groups. *Organizational Behavior and Human Decision Processes*, *47*, 65–97.

Gigone, D., & Hastie, R. (1993). The common knowledge effect: Information sharing and group judgment. *Journal of Personality and Social Psychology*, *65*, 959–974.

Gruenfeld, D. H., & Hollingshead, A. B. (1993). Sociocognition in work groups: The evolution of group integrative complexity and its relation to task performance. *Small Group Research*, *24*, 383–405.

Guzzo, R. A., & Dickson, M. W. (1996). Teams in organizations: Recent research on performance and effectiveness. *Annual Review of Psychology*, *47*, 307–338.

Hayes, B. H., & Wheelright, S. C. (1984). *Restoring our competitive edge: Competing through manufacturing*. New York: Wiley.

Levine, J. M., & Moreland, R. L. (1990). Progress in small group research. *Annual Review of Psychology*, *41*, 585–634.

Levitt, B., & March, J. G. (1988). Organizational learning. *Annual Review of Sociology*, *14*, 319–340.

Lewin, K., Lippitt, R., & White, R. (1939). Patterns of aggressive behavior in experimentally created "social climates." *Journal of Social Psychology*, *10*, 271–298.

Liang, D. W, Moreland, R., & Argote, L. (1995). Group versus individual training and group performance: The mediating role of transactive memory. *Personality and Social Psychology Bulletin*, *21*, 384–393.

Krugman, P. A. (1991, November 8). Myths and realities of U.S. competitiveness. *Science*, *254*, 811–815.

March, J. G., & Simon, H. A. (1958). *Organizations*. New York: Wiley.

McGrath, J. E., & Altermatt, T. W. (2001). Observation and analysis of group interaction over time – some methodological and strategic choices. In M. A. Hogg & S. Tindale (Eds.), *Blackwell handbook of social psychology: Group processes* (pp. 525–556). Oxford: Blackwell Publishing.

McGrath, J. E., Arrow, H., & Berdahl, J. L. (in press). Cooperation and conflict as manifestations of coordination in small groups. *Polish Psychological Bulletin*.

McGrath, J. E., & Beehr, T. A. (1990). Time and the stress process: Some temporal issues in the conceptualization and measurement of stress. *Stress Medicine*, *6*, 95–104.

McGrath, J. E., & Kelly, J. R. (1986). *Time and human interaction: Toward a social psychology of time*. New York: Guilford Press.

Minabe, S. (1986, July 18). Japanese competitiveness and Japanese management. *Science*, *233*, 301–304.

Moreland, R. E., & Levine, J. M. (1982). Socialization in small groups: Temporal changes in individual-group relations. In L. Berkowitz (Ed.), *Advances in experimental social psychology* (Vol. 15, pp. 137–192). New York: Academic Press.

Moreland, R. L., Argote, L., & Krishnan, R. (1996). Socially shared cognition at work: Transactive memory and group performance. In J. L. Nye & A. M. Brower (Eds.), *What's so social about social cognition? Social cognition research in small groups* (pp. 57–84). Thousand Oaks, CA: Sage.

Moreland, R. L., Hogg, M. A., & Hains, S. C. (1994). Back to the future: Social psychological research on groups. *Journal of Experimental Social Psychology, 30*, 527–555.

Moreland, R. L., & Myaskovsky, L. (1998). *Exploring the performance benefits of group training: Transactive memory or improved communication.* Paper presented at the Carnegie-Wisconsin Conference on Knowledge Transfer and Levels of Learning. Pittsburgh, June 1998.

Nelson, R. R., & Winter, S. G. (1982). *An evolutionary theory of economic change.* Boston, MA: Belkman Press.

Nonaka, I. (1991). The knowledge-creating company. *Harvard Business Review, 69*(6), 96–104.

Olivera, F., & Argote, L. (1999). Organizational learning and new product development: CORE processes. In L. Thompson, D. M. Messick, & J. M. Levine (Eds.), *Shared knowledge in organizations* (pp. 297–325). Mahwah, NJ: Erlbaum.

Polanyi, M. (1966). *The tacit dimension.* Garden City, NJ; Doubleday.

Sanna, L. J., & Parks, C. D. (1997). Group research trends in social and organizational psychology: Whatever happened to intragroup research? *Psychological Science, 8*, 261–267.

Sherif, M., Harvey, O. K., White, R. J., Hood, W. R., & Sherif, C. W. (1961). *Intergroup conflict and cooperation.* Norman, OK: Institute of Social Relations.

Stasser, G., & Titus, W. (1985). Pooling of unshared information in group decision making: Biased information sampling during discussion. *Journal of Personality and Social Psychology, 48*, 1467–1478.

Steiner, I. D. (1986). Paradigms and groups. In L. Berkowitz (Ed.), *Advances in experimental social psychology* (Vol. 19, pp. 251–289). Orlando, FL: Academic Press.

Walsh, J. P., & Ungson, G. R. (1991). Organizational memory. *Academy of Management Review, 16*, 57–91.

Wegner, D. M. (1986). Transactive memory: A contemporary analysis of the group mind. In B. Mullen & G. R. Goethals (Eds.), *Theories of group behavior* (pp. 185–205). New York: Springer-Verlag.

Weingart, L. E. (1997). How did they do that? The ways and means of studying group process. *Research in Organizational Behavior, 19*, 189–239.

Weldon, M. S., & Bellinger, K. D. (1997). Collective memory: Collaborative and individual processes in remembering. *Journal of Experimental Psychology: Learning, Memory and Cognition, 23*, 1160–1175.

Wittenbaum, G. M., & Stasser, G. (1996). Management of information in small groups. In J. L. Nye & A. M. Brower (Eds.), *What's social about social cognition? Research on socially shared cognition in small groups* (pp. 3–28). Thousand Oaks, CA: Sage.

Womack, J. P., Jones, D. T., & Roos, D. (1990). *The machine that changed the world.* New York: Rawson Associates.

Author Index

Subject Index